EIGHT CENTURIES
OF MILLING
IN
NORTH EAST YORKSHIRE

JOHN K HARRISON

THIS BOOK IS DEDICATED TO
ANNE, JOHN, JULIA AND LINDA

COVER: STONE FLOOR AT TOCKETTS MILL (PHOTOGRAPH, P W MORGAN)

Published by the North York Moors National Park Authority,
with financial assistance from the Yorkshire Archaeological Society.

The Cleveland Industrial Archaeology Society supported the publication of this book in
acknowledgement of the author's three decades of sterling service to the society.

First published 2001
This edition published 2008
© Copyright, J K Harrison 2008

ISBN 978-1-904622-17-8

Summary

Harrison J K, 2008,

EIGHT CENTURIES OF MILLING IN NORTH EAST YORKSHIRE,
North York Moors National Park, ISBN 978-1-904622-17-8

This book surveys sites, buildings and machinery concerned with grain milling in north east Yorkshire. The selected geographical area is centred on the North York Moors and bounded by the Derwent to the south, Cod Beck to the west, the Tees to the north, with additional cover of windmills on the north bank of the Tees.

The book contains

- measured drawings, photographs etc of about one hundred mills in the region
- a text which traces the geographical and economic background and the history of milling from 1086 to the end of the nineteenth century
- a gazetteer containing historical references for over one hundred and fifty water mill and seventy windmill sites and, where relevant, a description of surviving remains.

This second edition includes major revisons relating to 18th century developments, coastal trading windmills, and millwrights and milling equipment.

Résumé

Harrison J K, 2008,

HUIT SIÈCLES DE MEUNERIE DANS LE NORD-EST DU YORKSHIRE,
North York Moors National Park, ISBN 978-1-904622-17-8

Cet ouvrage étudie les sites, bâtiments et équipements associés à la meunerie dans le nord-est du Yorkshire. La région géographique choisie est concentrée sur les North York Moors et délimitée par le Derwent au sud, le Cod Beck à l'ouest et la Tees au nord. Quelques moulins situés sur la rive nord de la Tees sont également inclus.

L'ouvrage contient

- dessins à échelle, photographies, etc. sur environ cent moulins de la région
- un texte retraçant le contexte géographique et économique ainsi que l'histoire de la meunerie de 1086 à la fin du dix-neuvième siècle
- un index contenant des références historiques pour plus de cent cinquante sites de moulins à eau et soixante-dix moulins à vent avec, dans les cas appropriés, une description des ruines.

Cette deuxième édition contient des révisions importantes concernant les développements techniques datant du 18 ème siècle, le commerce des moulins à vent côtiers, les ingénieurs concevant les moulins et l'équipement pour mouliner.

Zusammenfassung

Harrison J K, 2008,

ACHT JAHRHUNDERTE DES MÜHLENBAUS IN NORDOST-YORKSHIRE,
North York Moors National Park, ISBN 978-1-904622-17-8

Dieses Buch enthält einen Überblick der Standorte, Gebäude und Maschinen für das Getreidemahlen in Nordost-Yorkshire. Der ausgewählte geographische Bereich konzentriert sich auf Nord-Yorkshire und wird im Süden vom Fluß Derwent, im Westen vom Cod Beck und im Norden vom Fluß Tees umgrenzt, mit zusätzlichen Windmühlen am nördlichen Tees-Ufer.

Das Buch enthält

- abgemessene Zeichnungen, Photographien usw. von zirka einhundert Mühlen in der Region
- einen Text, der den geographischen und wirtschaftlichen Hintergrund sowie die Geschichte des Mahlens und Mühlenbaus vom Jahre 1086 bis zum Ende des neunzehnten Jahrhunderts nachverfolgt
- ein Ortslexikon welches historische Querverweise für über hundertfünfzig Wassermühlen und siebzig Windmühlen enthält und, wo dies relevant ist, eine Beschreibung der überbleibenden Ruinen.

Diese 2. Auflage beinhaltet bedeutende Änderungen in Bezug auf die Entwicklungen im 18. Jahrhundert, gewerblich betriebene Windmühlen an der Küste, Mühlenbauer sowie Ausstattung der Mühlen.

ACKNOWLEDGEMENTS

Research and fieldwork started in 1965, since when many mill owners and occupants have given permission to record their mills.

Alan Stoyel stimulated my initial interest during his courses on the subject in the 1960s and has remained a staunch ally ever since. He has very kindly read the proof for the book. During the later years Graham Lee, North York Moors National Park Archaeologist, has never wavered in his support for the project and has guided the book through its production stages with patience and good humour. Rachel Smith and Gillian Sunley (North York Moors National Park) helped edit the text.

In the early years the late Raymond Hayes gave generously of his collected notes and photographs of mills. As an amateur I have particularly appreciated the support given by Philip Rahtz, former Professor of Archaeology at York University. Barry Harrison of the Leeds University School for Continuing Education made available course notes containing much historical detail and many leads, and he has very kindly read the medieval sections of the text. Blaise Vyner was supportive both during his time as Archaeologist for Cleveland County and again when he edited Moorland Monuments, CBA Research Report, no 101, in 1995. Michael Ashcroft and his staff at North Yorkshire County Record Office have been helpful over many years.

Students and staff of Eston Grammar School and later of South Park Sixth Form College (particularly Peter Morgan, Peter Oberon and the late Peter Verrill) were involved in field recording and, later, restoration work at Tocketts mill. Members of the Cleveland Industrial Archaeology Society and of the Friends of Tocketts Mill have been supportive throughout.

It would be impossible to itemise the contributions of all who have generously provided information on individual mills and topics but I would like to place on record the following: Dr J K Almond, Madge Allison, Mrs D V Arnold, Don Atkinson, Fred Banks, R Barker, Dr J Binns, the late A Bradley (Hauxwells of Yarm), Pamela Browarska, the late Arthur Champion, Carol Cook, Margaret Denham, the late Grace Dixon, Harold Dobson, Janet Dring, the late William Featherston, the late Ted Garbutt, J R Garbutt, Ruth George, David Glendinning, Ann Hadley, Jane Hatcher, Tom Hay, Jenny Hunt, George Jewitt, Roy Johnson (then of the National Rivers Authority), Peter Jopling, Paddy Lowndes, Valerie Martin, Isabel McLean, Miles Moorby, Mrs T M Nattrass, the late John Owen, Ian Pattison (RCHM), Jackie Quarmby, Rene Ridley, Peter Rowe (Tees Archaeology), Ann Screeton (York Excavation Group), Martin and Sue Watts, the late Frank Weatherill, Pat Wood, Dr Peter Wyon. Robert White (Yorkshire Dales National Park) commented on the final draft of the text.

The first edition was published by the North York Moors National Park Authority, with financial assistance from the Cleveland Buildings Preservation Trust, the Council for British Archaeology (North), the Yorkshire Archaeological Society and Tees Archaeology.

*　　*　　*

For this second edition I acknowledge new information provided by Dr J K Almond, Madge Allison, Judith Bell, John Bradley, Robin Clarke, Roy Gregory, Gareth Hughes, Dr Stafford Linsley, Tony Pacitto, Stewart Ramsdale, Peter Rowe, Nigel Wardell and Basil Wharton. In particular, I wish to thank Peter Morgan for his continued support and Enid Radcliffe for important new information on the windmills of Stockton. Graham Lee (Senior Archaeologist, North York Moors National Park) has, with patience and persistence, guided the second edition through its editing and production stages. Design is by Barbara Allen with additional graphic design by Gillian Sunley (North York Moors National Park).

I wish to acknowledge the tremendous support given by my family, in particular Anne who has helped unstintingly with fieldwork, checking scripts and with constructive criticism and encouragement at all stages; and also John, Julia and Linda.

FOREWORD

It was in 1966 that I first met John Harrison. Significantly, this occurred in a mill, Crathorne mill, which was then the only one in the area still grinding corn by waterpower. It was an impressive brick building and it is now no more than a memory. Through the years I have admired the quality of John's investigation and research and the standard of the scale drawings he produces. EIGHT CENTURIES OF MILLING IN NORTH EAST YORKSHIRE is the result of his work on the wind and water mills of this region carried out over a period of more than thirty years. It pulls together the evidence, not only of the architecture but also the working parts, the historical references and the archaeology in an analytical way that has broken new ground to produce a balanced, in-depth study. This is not a bland history. It is thought-provoking and, as a consequence, there are some views that are bound to be controversial.

It is too easy to concentrate on what has gone, rather than to appreciate and understand what still survives. This book demonstrates just how much of interest does survive. The buildings of the mills of north east Yorkshire, of beautifully-dressed stone or mellow brickwork, have a special charm. Most are in attractive surroundings and some of them still contain working parts of outstanding survival value. Since the beginnings of this study much has been lost, including precious examples such as the mills at Stokesley, Ingleby Greenhow and Scaling.

The water mills in particular are often on sites that, like the parish church, have endured for centuries. Like churches they show evolutionary phases. Mills are not merely buildings. They are basic functional elements that were vital to the economy of a settlement. With the civil engineering involved in harnessing the water and the daily need for transport of goods they became focal elements in the landscape. Usually, what survives is the last of a series of entrepreneurial phases whereby the mill site has been developed to a degree that was dictated by the availability of local resources and technology. History has brought this to life, and such contrasting and exciting examples as the mills at Arden and Sinnington can be better appreciated.

We are indebted to John for his scholarly work. This publication will help the owners and occupiers of the buildings to appreciate and care for them. It will assist planning and conservation officers to understand better those features that merit sympathetic preservation in any proposed alteration or redevelopment. It will enable archaeologists and molinologists to compare and contrast the mills of this area with those elsewhere. In addition, it will appeal to anyone interested in broadening his appreciation of a traditional occupation that has contributed so much to this area for more than eight centuries.

ALAN STOYEL, APRIL, 2000

FOREWORD TO THE SECOND EDITION

It is a privilege to update the Foreword to the 1st Edition of EIGHT CENTURIES OF MILLING IN NORTH EAST YORKSHIRE. With its wealth of scale drawings, photographs and historical notes the work has now been accepted as the definitive record of corn milling in the North York Moors National Park and surrounding region.

ALAN STOYEL, DECEMBER, 2006

CONVENTIONS

All maps are drawn with a northerly orientation. Scales of maps vary with the information to be relayed.

All architectural drawings were originally surveyed using a scale of one quarter of an inch to one foot (approximately 1:50) and are presented uniformly in the book to a scale of one sixteenth of an inch to one foot (approximately 1:200).

Changes in masonry and brickwork are shown in plans and sections by drawing the oldest structure in black and later additions by hatching.

Sums of money are given in £ s d. They can be translated into decimal currency by remembering that 12d was equal to 1s and 20s equal to £1. The mark, used in medieval times, was worth 13s 4d or two thirds of £1.

Weights are given in long tons, 20 hundredweights equalling one ton.

Volumes are given in quarters and bushels. A bushel is a dry measure of eight gallons. The weight of a bushel varied according to the grain, eg an average bushel of wheat weighed 60 pounds but a bushel of oats, which packs less densely, weighed only 40 pounds. 8 bushels equalled one quarter and, therefore, a quarter of wheat weighed 480 pounds. 4 pecks equalled one bushel. The terms peck and bushel were used at the mill while the quarter was used in trade and shipping.

CONTENTS

ILLUSTRATIONS

Please note that all mills covered by this survey are private property. Access is restricted and permission to visit is required.

INTRODUCTION

On 23 May 1740 Mr William Barker, a corn merchant of Stockton, recorded in his private letters that *"The mob have broke my windows, and will not suffer any wheat to be shipt; all the town is in the utmost fear"*. The full story was revealed in further notes over the next three weeks. On 8 June he wrote that *"... Last Friday I had a shocking day, for the mob seized my boat with seven lasts of wheat, on which I went on board and was glad to get on shore again, being stopped by them at landing and twice thrown down within a yard of the river, and I had certainly been put into the river had not two lusty fellows of the heads assisted me, and many of the women turned on my side, so that to save my life I had a majority; but all were against my property. They carried my boat to the quay, landed the wheat, and are still in possession. They put a broom to the mast-head, and put her up for sale, declaring her a legal prize ..."*, and on 13 June he added that *"... though I had two justices and eighty soldiers in arms I could not carry off my wheat they had seized. I have had a most terrible time of it, for I dare not lay in my own house; hundreds threaten to murder me, and God knows what will be my fate"* (Thomas Richmond, 1868, 63-4).

Barker's troubles arose from a severe winter and a consequent increase in the price of grain during the following spring. The starving poor of the town took action against him for continuing to ship wheat down the river. Who can doubt the importance of a daily supply of wheat flour or oat meal and the desperate situation which arises when it is interrupted?

I first became interested in the mills of this small and distinctive region in the mid-1960s. Sometimes, in the early days, I met retired millers who had followed a tradition going back thirty generations or more. Gradually the idea emerged of trying to collect as much as possible of the archaeological and historical evidence. It was clear from the outset that north east Yorkshire had rarely been in the forefront of the development of milling technology but, in fact, this was an advantage because the story could concentrate on what was typical rather than on what was exceptional. On the other hand, the geographical diversity of the region is interesting since the varying conditions of the moorland dales and the estuarine lowlands, for example, produced different responses to the problem of corn milling.

This book is concerned with corn milling. Textile, paper and other industrial mills are noted in passing, and are listed in the gazetteer. Essentially, however, this is the story of two major periods of expansion in corn milling, the first relating to the great, open fields of the early medieval grain growing economy and the second to the seventeenth to nineteenth century growth of towns and industry.

By the time of the Black Death (1349) almost all the present day settlements within the region had been established, the exceptions being fishing villages such as Staithes and Robin Hood's Bay and the alum workers' and ironstone miners' hamlets and villages of East Cleveland. The period from 1066 to 1349 had seen colonization and population growth on a grand scale. Because crop yields were low, very large fields were needed to support each community and the resulting pressure on the land meant that by the end of the period much of the moorland dales and the estuarine lowlands had been put to the plough. In 1086 there were very few mills in this region but by 1349 the majority of water driven corn mill steadings known today had been established. There were also windmills around the Tees estuary and along the east coast.

After the Black Death the mainly subsistence ploughing economy was replaced by a much more varied economy, increasingly based on industry. The diversification led eventually to the growth of capital and to the development of towns. By the seventeenth century there were large new lowland water mills at, for instance, Thornton-le-Street, Newburgh and Stokesley. In the eighteenth century the introduction of the 'Blue' or 'Cullin' stones for flour milling led to the introduction of gearing systems whereby two or three sets of mill stones could be driven from the same waterwheel. The pace of change quickened dramatically from the closing years of the eighteenth century as a result of explosive population growth in Newcastle and Sunderland to the north, London to the south and Leeds to the west, all of which were becoming accessible by coastwise shipping or by turnpike road. The growing demand for bread led

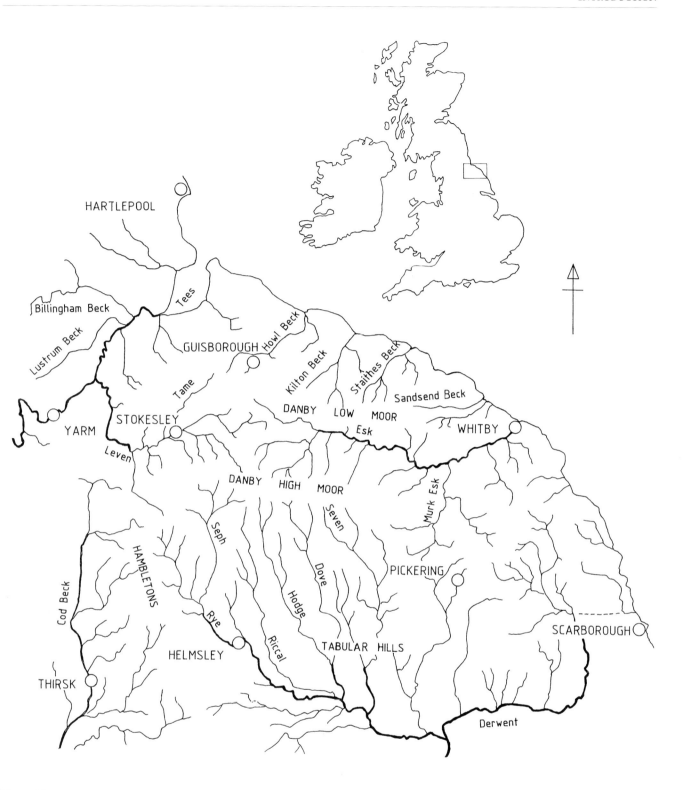

FIG 1. NORTH EAST YORKSHIRE.

not only to a new expansion in the amount of land under the plough but also to many developments in corn mills. Almost all of the older water mills were 'improved' at this time and large tower windmills were built along the Tees and the coast.

Traditional milling by water and wind power reached its peak production in the third quarter of the nineteenth century. After the mid 1880s rural flour milling was in sudden decline. R H Appleton's steam driven Cleveland Flour Mill at South Stockton had, by 1884, a capacity which was greater than that of all of the old water and windmills in the region. By the end of the century the tradition of water milling, which had flourished from the time of the Domesday Survey, was beginning to fade and windmills were already almost a thing of the past.

During these eight centuries the milling of flour and

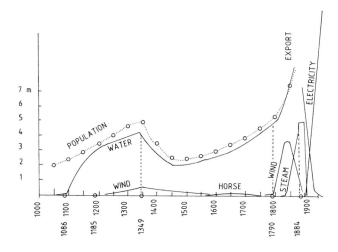

FIG 2. TYPES OF FLOUR MILL IN NORTH EAST YORKSHIRE PLOT-
TED AGAINST A POPULATION GRAPH OF ENGLAND (NOTIONAL).

meal has been of profound importance in the lives of the people of north east Yorkshire. Taking a broad view, the woes of poor Mr Barker, "corn merchant of Stockton", were merely a temporary upset. The core content of this book is a record of the relics of an activity which was both vital and well able to adapt to changing conditions.

Methodology

THE TITLE AND THE BOUNDARY The upland heart of north east Yorkshire is an area of special geographical characteristics and as such has been designated the North York Moors National Park. However, while the core is clearly defined, the boundaries for this study are not so readily drawn. Economically the moorland proper was always dependent on the surrounding lowlands and, therefore, the moorland edges cannot be seen as a sensible boundary. Somewhat arbitrarily, this study takes for its boundary the three major rivers surrounding the moors; the Tees to the north, the Derwent to the south and Cod Beck to the west. This choice has defined a distinctive moorland and lowland region. However, it has been useful to extend the boundary to the north of the Tees for an insight into the main coastal trading river and the windmills and steam mills that served it.

THE TEXT Although the old dialect has noticeably declined in the past 30 years I have still chosen to use some dialect words. For instance, "dale" is preferred to valley, "beck" is preferred to stream, "gill" for a steep sided valley, "rigg" for a ridge, "force" for a waterfall, "keld" for a spring and "wath" for a ford.

THE DRAWINGS The drawings result from fieldwork, the earliest dating from the mid-1960s at a time when many old mills stood derelict and with gaping doors. They were prepared to a scale of a quarter of an inch to one foot. There was the advantage that feet and inches were the dimensions used when the mills were built. With this relatively small scale it is necessary to do a certain amount of rounding up and vice versa. This was not important in recording masonry since an error of half an inch when recording a dry stone wall is neither here nor there but there was more of a problem when recording machinery. For instance, drawing gear teeth to scale presented a problem. Clearly, more data could have been obtained by recording to a larger scale but, in fact, a good deal of my work can be described as rescue recording; the alternatives were either something or nothing.

An obvious advantage of a drawing over a photograph is that visually disruptive modern features can be omitted. Corrugated iron sheets were not included and where windows had modern glazing bars then only the outer frames were drawn.

INTRODUCTION TO THE SECOND EDITION

Information that has come to light since 2001 has resulted in three major revisions. The first covers the significance of surviving remains in north east Yorkshire of blue millstones and two-stage gearing in eighteenth century watermills (J K Harrison, 2005, *The 'rise' of the white loaf; evidence from the North of England concerning the development of milling technique in the Eighteenth century, Rex Wailes Memorial Lecture SPAB*). The second arises from research by Eric Radcliffe into the windmills of Stockton, which throws new light on the introduction of tower windmills around the Tees estuary. The third extends the sections on Millwrights and on Milling Equipment.

MEDIEVAL WATER MILLS

The First Mills

The best estimate is that rather more than 6,000 mills were listed in the Domesday Survey of England (1086) excluding Northumbria and Cumbria (H C Darby, 1977, 272). It is unlikely that all of these had been built in the twenty years from the Conquest and the conclusion must be that water mills were well-established by late Anglo-Saxon times. However, there was a stark contrast between the large numbers of mills in most of the southern counties and the small number in Yorkshire. In Yorkshire, the biggest county in the country but with a population of about 30,000, there were only between 92 and 102 mills (H C Darby, 1986, 361). These included two *"new"* mills in York, which were recorded as having been destroyed to make way for the King's fish-pond, and 12 other mill sites where, presumably, the mills had either been destroyed or were being built. Also, within this general sparsity, the distribution of mills between the three former Ridings of Yorkshire was very uneven. There were some 30 mills and two sites in the East Riding and 40 mills in the West Riding, all well clear of the Pennines, while in the North Riding there were only 23 mills and one site. Even within the North Riding there was an uneven distribution. To the north west there was a separate group of seven, belonging to Count Alan of Richmond, on the River Swale and its tributaries. There was a small group near Thirsk and a third group in Ryedale and the Vale of Pickering. But in the high northern moors and the skirting lowlands there were only three; one at Whitby/Sneaton, one at Guisborough and one at Stokesley.

The record of the Domesday Survey for Yorkshire may not be complete but, nevertheless, from the sparsity of mills listed in north east Yorkshire it seems that most of the land of the North York Moors and the Tees estuary was not being worked by the plough in 1086. The proportion of land suitable for the plough in both the moorland dales and surrounding lowlands was less than in most of the rest of England since the flatlands bordering the Tees were un-drained at that time while, inland, much of the region is high, peat moorland with narrow dales between.

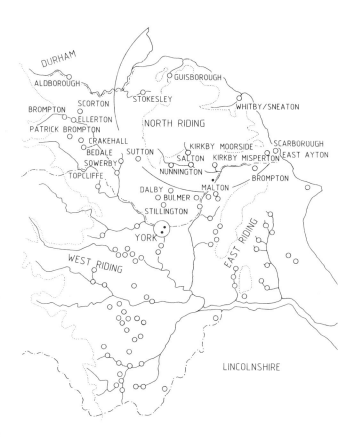

FIG 3. YORKSHIRE WATER MILLS RECORDED IN THE DOMESDAY SURVEY.

The region was also marginal in terms of Norman occupation. The winter of 1069-70 had seen the destruction of the holdings of those thought to be loyal to the Northumbrian Earls, an event which would later become known as the 'Harrying of the North'. Sixteen years later north east Yorkshire had still not recovered. Among the manors described as 'waste' by the Domesday Commissioners were those of the Count de Mortain (in Kilton, Tocketts, Lackenby, Eston, Normanby, Barnaby, Hilton, Carlton, Crathorne and Little Broughton) and those of Hugh d'Avranches, the Earl of Chester (in Coulby, Hemlington, Stainton, Thornton, Maltby, Thornaby, Stainsby, Loftus,

1

Hinderwell, Liverton, Upleatham, Marske, Kirkleatham, Lazenby, and Lackenby). Together these represented a big proportion of the settlements on the south side of the Tees estuary and along the north coast. Lands in the Esk valley were also waste. In the whole of the North Riding some 217 vills were wholly waste and a further 150 partly waste, approximately 58% of the total (D Hey, 1986, 27). Even in areas not described as waste the record quite often showed that values had declined since the time of Edward the Confessor. If corn mills had once existed in these wasted vills they would not have escaped destruction and the commissioners would have ignored ruined mills since their task was to record revenue producing assets. The information left by the commissioners has left unresolved the issue of how many mills, if any, there had been in north east Yorkshire in Anglo-Saxon times.

Within the relatively small number of mills in north east Yorkshire there were big variations in recorded values. The total annual value of all the mills in Yorkshire has been estimated at some 600 shillings (£30); on average, 6s each. The average value of the Swale group of mills was well below this. In the Derwent valley the mills at Dalby and Bulmer were each worth 2s, those at Salton, Brompton and East Ayton 5s each and that at Kirkby Misperton 5s 4d. Further west the mill at Sutton-under-Whitestonecliffe near Thirsk had no value. On the other hand, the mill at Sowerby, also near Thirsk, had the amazingly high value of 20s. In the wasted north and east the values of two of the three mills were also surprisingly high. The mill at Guisborough was worth only 4s but those at Stokesley and Whitby/Sneaton were each worth 10s, placing them among the most valuable in Yorkshire. The range of value for working mills in north east Yorkshire was such that the most valuable were worth ten times more than the poorest.

The variation in value could hold a clue as to the state of settlement in north east Yorkshire in 1086. Pre-Norman settlements had consisted of 'vills', or scattered townships with each dwelling probably using querns or hand mills for grinding its grain. After the 'harrying' the priority of the Norman lords must have been to re-group the surviving populations of their ruined holdings in new, viable communities. These re-grouped communities almost certainly lived in villages rather than in scattered dwellings.

The characteristic living unit in medieval new settlements was the 'toft', with a dwelling fronting onto a village green and a croft extending to a back lane. Beyond the crofts were the ploughed furlongs of the open fields. There are well-known examples of this distinctive settlement pattern in north Yorkshire, for instance at Guisborough, Appleton-le-Moors and Newton-on-Rawcliffe. The dating of these planned and 'planted' villages is problematic but they are normally thought of as post-Domesday. However, in north east Yorkshire, the relationship between one or two of the mills recorded in the Domesday Survey and their associated planned villages seems to suggest otherwise. Particularly interesting are the mills at Sutton-under-Whitestonecliffe, Stokesley and Guisborough, where it may be that the Domesday Survey captured a moment in time when Norman tenants-in-chief were already establishing new villages.

Sutton-under-Whitestonecliffe contains a manorial site (the Hall) and a well-defined single-row of tofts. There was also a mill in 1086, though its value was listed as nothing. The closely integrated relationship between the manor, the tofts and the mill cannot be co-incidental. At the time of the Survey there was either a surviving Anglo-Saxon manor with its mill still standing but not working or there was at least part of a new, Norman planned village with the mill being rebuilt or new-built to serve it.

Stokesley was a sizeable settlement in 1086 even though its value had fallen from £24 in Anglo-Saxon times to £8 at the time of the Survey. It has since grown into a small town round a big market place. However, the single row of tofts on the north side closely resembles the single-row plan at Sutton-under-Whitestonecliffe and these may have been the first to be established. The water mill of 1086 was probably on the same site as the later mill since, given the lie of the land and the floods that formerly plagued the town, there was no other feasible water-driven site. The close relationship between manor, church and mill might seem to suggest that all three were on Anglo-Saxon sites. On the other hand, the wide leat at Stokesley, which must have cost an incredible number of man-hours to cut, suggests it was designed to provide milling capacity for a projected new large township, even though this may have existed only in embryonic form in 1086.

The pattern is repeated at Guisborough. The smallest and most tightly grouped (and perhaps the oldest) tofts are on raised ground at the east end of the north side of Westgate (nearest the church). These plots are similar to those at Stokesley in their south-facing alignment, probably looking over an open green to a beck. The ancient street called Northgate, formerly *"Northoutgate"*, breaks off northwards through these tofts directly to the site of the mill at Howl Beck. This relationship seems to show that this former 'mill lane' was an integral feature of the original planning and that, therefore, this part of Westgate existed when the mill was recorded in 1086. This mill also had a very large leat.

Whitby, because of its river harbour, would also have been seen as a place where re-settlement was needed. Lands to the north and the south of the lower Esk, had suffered severe 'wasting', its value decreasing dramatically from Anglo-Saxon times. Yet the mill of *"Whitby/Sneaton"* was worth 10s and was one of the

A)

B)

C)

Fig 4. a) Sutton-under-Whitestonecliffe, b) Stokesley and c) Guisborough.

most valuable in Yorkshire. The site of this mill has not been identified. Today, Sneaton survives as a planned village at some distance from Whitby, but the description *"Whitby/Sneaton"* for the location of the mill is obscure. It was listed in the context of *"Sorebi"* (Sowerby) which has been identified as Sneaton Thorpe, now a small settlement near Sneaton (L Charlton, 1779, 70). The nearest surviving mill sites to Sneaton and Sneaton Thorpe are Cock mill and Rigg mill, both of which were named as early as 1102. The pattern of manor, church and mill is not apparent at Whitby.

The evidence of the Domesday Survey is slim but does seem to point to one or two new mills being established as a result of an urgent incentive to re-structure land holdings following the devastation of 1069-70.

Medieval expansion

Because of the relatively large numbers of mills existing in much of England in 1086 they are not likely to have more than doubled by the time of the Black Death (1349). In north east Yorkshire, where few mills existed in 1086, the situation was very different.

Historians of technology have explored the idea of a European-wide technological revolution in the early medieval period in which manpower and animal power were replaced by water and wind power for corn milling and also for cloth fulling and iron making etc (Lynn Whyte, 1962, 79; Jean Gimpel, 1976, 1). This view is supported by evidence from north east Yorkshire where the period from the Domesday Survey to the Black Death saw water driven sites established in large numbers. Indeed all but a very few such sites known today were already operating by the end of the medieval period. In addition, there was a substantial number of windmills.

Population growth does not, on its own, explain why hand milling was abandoned but it was certainly important. Figures for population growth within north east Yorkshire are not available but estimates for England, excluding Northumbria, Durham and Cumbria, taken from the Domesday Survey suggest a population of 1.4 million, whereas by 1300 there was a minimum of 3.25 million. Growth of this order resulted in pressure to put more land under the plough and, consequently, to increased corn milling capacity. This period of growth faltered at the beginning of the fourteenth century and came to an abrupt end when the Black Death reached north eastern England in 1349. The high death rate dealt a fatal blow to the old manorial system. There is evidence that following 'the mortality' the value of some demesne mills in north east Yorkshire had markedly declined and, elsewhere, there is some evidence that the number of mills declined as landlords concentrated on developing the better sites (R Holt, 1988, 165). The

Black Death can, therefore, be seen as marking the end of the two and a half centuries which had seen the introduction of water and wind driven corn mills to this region.

Historical evidence

There is surprisingly little documentary evidence for corn mills in north east Yorkshire for the first 100 years or so after the Domesday Survey. What has survived is confined to grants to monasteries (eg Ruswarp, Rigg, Cock, Fylingdales, and *"New Mill"*, all granted to Whitby Abbey in 1102) and a few boundary descriptions referring to mills (eg at Sproxton in 1145). All of these early sources taken together confirm less than 20 mills (Appendix 2) in addition to those listed in the Survey itself. This record is almost certainly deficient and the question arises as to how far it falls short. In the neighbouring county of Durham to the north the Boldon Book compiled for the Bishop of Durham in 1183 (D Austin, 1982) listed at least 36 mills. The Boldon Book did not cover the whole of the county but it is sufficient to establish that mills were common in Durham one hundred years after the Survey and at a time when there was no equivalent record for north east Yorkshire.

After 1270 information is more readily available, mainly from inquisitions post mortem (lists of possessions of a tenant-in-chief or sub-tenant prepared immediately after death). However, these late records cannot be taken as evidence for the date of building, since this would imply that water mills were being built in quite large numbers after an unbelievable delay of about two hundred years from the earliest record in the Domesday Survey. The inquisitions are important in tracing the subsequent history of the mills rather than in dating their establishment.

Taken together, the various records prove the existence of some 90 water mills in the region by 1368 in addition to the 17 or so listed in the Domesday Survey. The records do not include another eight built in monastic precincts (Appendix 4). Also there are no records of the three mills in Bilsdale and this must be seen as an interesting omission, since records have survived for mills in equally remote Bransdale and Farndale. Without making any claim for completeness it is clear that there were at least 115 water mills in the region by the middle of the fourteenth century.

The Lay Subsidy of 1301 listed many millers and is interesting because it provides a partial record of the situation towards the end of the manorial period. Each contributor had to pay one fifteenth part of his possessions as a levy to Edward I to support the war against the Scots (W Brown, 1896). In the North York Moors and surrounding lowlands contributions were levied from the millers of some 35 water mills and one or two windmills, including some mills which were not listed

FIG 5. WATER MILLS IN NORTH EAST YORKSHIRE AT THE END OF THE MEDIEVAL PERIOD.

in other sources (Appendix 3). However, it is not a complete record. Many other millers (at water mills documented pre-1301 and certainly still at work) were not taxed. These included the millers of Kildale, Great Ayton, Ingleby Greenhow, Skelton, Westerdale, Tocketts, Saltburn, Caldecotes, Upsall, Loftus, Scaling, Scalby, Cropton, Allerston, Brompton, Ellerburn, Levisham, Pickering, Gillamoor, Sproxton, Ampleforth, Foxton, Ingleby Arncliffe, Kirby Knowle and Sutton-under-Whitestonecliffe. The millers for Gisborough Priory and Whitby Abbey do not appear in the record.

Field Evidence

In this region, as in others, mills tend to occupy the best sites within the township boundaries, so it is safe to assume that in most cases steadings have not migrated by more than a few metres from their medieval sites. There is a clear relationship between mill steadings, medieval ploughed fields and planned settlements.

This is a varied upland and lowland region, the core being made up of high moors bounded in the north by sea cliffs and in the west by steep scarps (hence *"Cleveland"* or *"Cliff Land"*). Even the bigger dales have steep edges and comparatively little ground suitable for the plough. In contrast, some land around the Tees estuary was flat wetland, making good summer pasture but abandoned to the gales, the sea birds and the fishermen in winter. A network of tracks gave access to pastures and to the river bank but there were few permanent dwellings. Settlement was restricted to the raised fringes. During the medieval period there was much progress in draining, embanking and ploughing but this was no place for water mills and, consequently, windmills would be built instead. To the south, the broad flat valley of the Derwent, separating the North York Moors from the Yorkshire Wolds, presented similar difficulties.

The Derwent meandered across an old lake bed and on each side there were the 'carrs' and 'marshes' which were later reclaimed by cutting drains and building banks or levees. As with the south bank of the Tees most of the population lived in dry-point settlements.

Early cultivators looked for gently sloping, raised ground. Sometimes this was in the form of low, isolated hills, eg Stainsacre Rigg, Brock Rigg at Mickleby and High Riggs at Thornton Dale. Other areas of land suitable for the plough became known as 'flatts', derived from 'flat', Old Norse for a level piece of land, eg *"Cat Flat"* near Marske, *"Kiln Flatts"* in Bransdale and simply the *"Flatt"* near Newton-under-Roseberry. In addition to the riggs and the flatts, other sought-after areas were on the lower slopes of dale edges, particularly if they faced south 'into the sun'. Examples are the south face of Langbaurgh Ridge at Great Ayton, the south-facing lands of Barnaby along the southern edge of the Eston outlier and the area known as Skelderskew in Commondale. Riggs, flatts and south-facing slopes provided good conditions for the 8-ox plough teams since the soil dried out and warmed up during the spring of each year and the soil remained firm during the harvest period.

Today, the surviving evidence of medieval ploughing consists of three elements; field names, rigg (ridge) and furrow and reversed-S field boundaries.

Many medieval field names disappeared when the open land was enclosed but others survive, for example, *"Wandayles"* and *"Longlands"* (Danby Dale), *"Wand Hills"* (North Skelton), *"Woundales"* (Borrowby), *"Toft Hill"* (Hutton Rudby), *"Bydales"* (Marske), *"Town Field"* (Bilsdale), *"Town Lands"* (Newton Mulgrave), *"Swathlands"* (Burniston), *"Westfields"* (Barnby) and *"High Fields"* (Loftus). The map in R W Jeffery's history of Thornton Dale (1931) provides other examples.

It can be difficult to differentiate between medieval and later ploughing. In winter, when the snow is melting, almost every piece of enclosed land shows traces of post-medieval ploughing with horses or tractors and in some cases these overlie distinctively reversed-S curved, medieval rigg and furrow, created with oxen. Fortunately, some areas of medieval rigg and furrow survive untouched. They can be seen for example in the east field of Guisborough, on Lythe Bank near Sandsend and at the foot of Turkey Nab near Ingleby Greenhow, and there are great swathes along the southern margins of the Tabular Hills.

Even where the rigg and furrow has been ploughed out it is still sometimes possible to locate old fields from surviving boundaries following the curved lines of old ploughed strips. They can be seen for instance in the field system to the east of Westerdale village, and again in the 'fields' within Danby Dale, both areas which are interesting in the context of their water mills. Much more extensive areas of surviving field boundaries surround both Thornton Dale and Pickering.

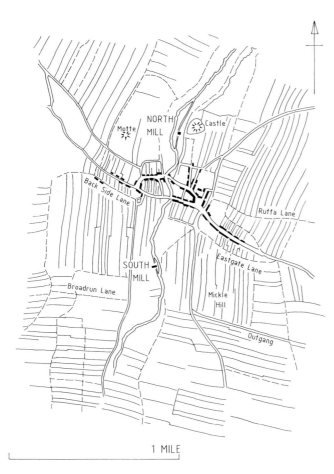

FIG 6. MEDIEVAL FIELD BOUNDARIES SURVIVING AT PICKERING IN THE MID-NINETEENTH CENTURY.

These open fields were typically very large. For instance, the east field at Guisborough is over a mile long and half a mile wide. In Danby Dale, Millwaite is over half a mile long and quarter of a mile wide and the adjacent Longlands is bigger. The individual ploughed strips at Thornton Dale vary from one third to half a mile long.

What crops did they produce? In one area of the West Riding the Lay Subsidy of 1297 records that tax was paid on 102 quarters of barley (*"ordeum"*), 24 quarters of maslin (*"mixtura"*), 3952 quarters of oats (*"avena"*) and 834 quarters of wheat (*"frumentum"*) and rye (*"siligo"*) (W Brown, 1894, YAS vol 16, Intro). Oats would remain the main crop of the wet Pennines and were also grown in north east Yorkshire, but the proportion of wheat and barley was probably much higher. For instance, the Hospitallers of Staintondale enclosed land in the time of King John (1199-1215) for both oats and wheat (F C Rimington 1988, 59), and in 1307 the Templars of Allerston had 114 acres of wheat (B Waites, 1997, 98). Even after the Black Death wheat was being sown on Whitby Abbey lands: 17 acres at Stakesby, 30 acres at Lathgarth and 30 acres at Whitbylathes for example in 1394 (B Waites, 1997, 94).

Medieval fields produced low yields. There was little animal manure and farmers relied on crop rotation, which meant that at any one time at least two thirds of the field was not producing grain. Medieval cropping may have produced as little as 10 bushels of grain per acre or just over a third of what became normal in the mid-nineteenth century. Early thirteenth century returns for the West Riding show yields of between three- and four-fold for wheat, three- and six-fold for barley and two-and-a-half-fold for oats (D Hey, 1986, 70). 25% of the crop was needed for seed for the next season and the villager also lost, typically, one sixteenth part of his crop in multure to the miller. A medieval village needed very large acreages to be able to feed few people.

These open fields provide a context in which to study early mills. Wherever such fields and their associated planned villages were established there must have been access to a water mill. Thus, open fields, Norman planned villages and water mills were interdependent and contemporary developments. Therefore, the relationships between them, dictated by the varying geographical conditions, provide an insight into the earliest history of the mills, even in some cases where historical evidence is missing, as for example at Faceby, Raisdale, Bilsdale and, remarkably, at Tocketts where the parish boundary runs along the ancient water leat and not along Skelton Beck which feeds it.

FIELDS AND MILLS

In early medieval times the most valuable lands in north east Yorkshire were in the Vale of Pickering, followed by those around the Tees estuary, then those of the Vale of York (roughly Stokesley to Thirsk), with those of the high coastal strip and the moorland dales trailing behind (B Waites, 1997, 74). This section looks at the different ways in which water mills relate to the remains of medieval open fields in four of these regions.

Pickering and Ryedale

Some of the region's best examples of medieval planned villages, Levisham, Newton-on-Rawcliffe and Appleton for example, each laid out around spacious greens and ambitiously planned from the outset, are situated high on the Tabular Hills to the north of Pickering and Ryedale. The lack of a mill in some settlements, eg Pockley, Carlton and Cold Kirby, might seem to raise a question as to the extent of early ploughing. However, it seems that it was normal for the villagers of the Tabular Hills to carry grain considerable distances to the mills. Grain from Pockley and Carlton, for example, must have been carried over two miles to mills at Helmsley while other villages used distant mills sited in narrow gorges of the Seven, Dove and Hodge. Raindale mill served Newton-on-Rawcliffe and Hold Cauldron mill served Fadmoor while, further west, Caydale mill

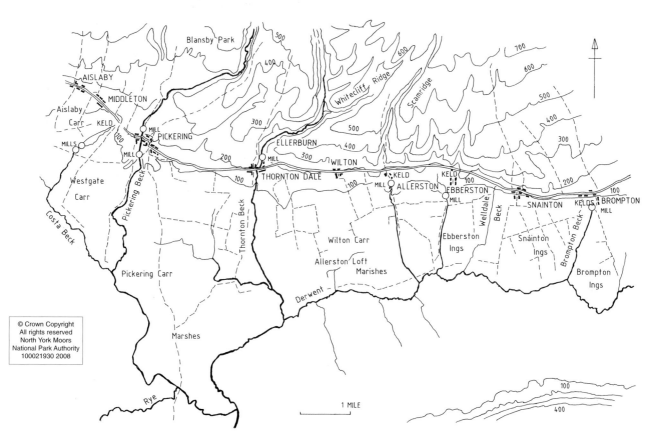

FIG 7. 'KELD' LINE MILLS TO THE EAST OF PICKERING.

served Old Byland. The mills of Levisham, Cropton and Appleton were also distant from the villages. From very early times, distance from the mill was not seen as a bar to settlement. Soon after 1086, for example, *"the site of a mill"* and three carucates of land at Appleton were given by Hugh son of Baldrick to St Mary's Abbey in York, and in 1141 Robert de Stuteville granted Gillamoor mill to St Mary's.

Along the foot of the dip slope of the Tabular Hills there is a line of villages with Anglo-Saxon names – Brompton, Snainton, Ebberston, Allerston, Wilton, Middleton and Wrelton. These lie along a horizontal geological boundary where a series of springs or 'kelds' emerge from where the permeable Corallian limestone dips under the impermeable Kimmeridge clay. Each has its elongated parish running from high up on the dip slopes to deep into the 'ings' and the 'carrs' of the Vale of Pickering and Ryedale. These 'keld' or spring line villages were larger than the villages on the Tabular Hills. The even bigger settlements of Thornton Dale, Pickering, Sinnington, Kirkby Moorside and Helmsley were sited where Thornton Beck, Pickering Beck, the Seven, Hodge Beck and the Rye respectively emerge from their gorges through the Tabular Hills. Waterpower for this fertile region varied enormously from the ample rivers to barely adequate 'kelds'. There were also one or two 'dry villages', for example Wilton and Wrelton. In general, however, and in contrast to the situation high on the Tabular Hills, the mills were very conveniently sited within the village boundaries as, for instance, at Brompton, Ebberston, Allerston, Thornton Dale and Pickering.

The western scarp lands

The prominent western scarps of the high moorlands are capped by sandstone to the north, eg in Arncliffe, and Corallian limestones to the south, eg in Whitestone Cliff. In any scarpland both surface and underground water will drain down the dip slopes and away from the scarp. Hence, in north east Yorkshire there was a shortage of water power for the rich ploughlands stretching away to the west. Only in Scugdale and in Cote Gill at Osmotherley were there good flows. At bigger villages, away from the scarps, there were much busier mills, at Great Ayton, Stokesley and Crathorne on the Leven, and at Thornton-le-Street and Thirsk on the Cod Beck.

By contrast some of the western scarpland villages had to share mills. Carlton and Faceby, about one mile apart, both retain tofts and open fields from medieval times. Each had drinking water from a small beck. At first glance, Carlton might seem to have been a double row village but in fact it is only the west side row which has crofts and a back lane and it seems that Carlton was, in its earliest days a single row village (B Roberts, in D Spratt & B J D Harrison, 1989, 84). Beyond the row and

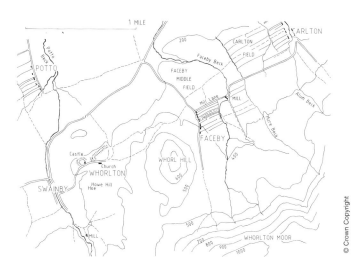

FIG 8. MILLS AT CARLTON, FACEBY AND WHORLTON.

the back lane the medieval 'Carlton Field' stretched out towards its neighbour, Faceby, which appears to have grown up along the old track or 'gate' leading up to the open moorland to the south. There are preserved crofts to the east of the dwellings and there is rigg and furrow of former open fields beyond. The land to the north of the road between Carlton and Faceby was the medieval 'Faceby Middle Field'. Thus the original centre of gravity of Carlton was to the west, towards Faceby, and the original centre of gravity of Faceby to the north and east, towards Carlton, and their open fields abutted each other. Faceby Beck was the strongest available water resource and was used for the mill serving both settlements. The field evidence points convincingly to an early mill to the east of Faceby.

Likewise, the village of Thimbleby shared the Bishop of Durham's demesne water mill of Osmotherley. In fact, the mill was named *"Thymbleby"* mill in a document of 1359 but the name changed as Osmotherley gradually became the dominant settlement. The mill is situated between the two and is actually nearer to Thimbleby. The open fields of Osmotherley were situated to the west of the village, at some distance from the mill, whereas part of the Thimbleby fields, still called the *"Fleers"*, is almost on the doorstep of the mill.

The linked settlements of Whorlton and Swainby also shared a mill. The hill-top settlement of Whorlton, overlooking the plains to the west, was dominant in medieval times, though today only the remains of its castle gatehouse, its ruined church and a couple of farms remain. The open fields of Whorlton lay to the south east, on land sweeping down into Scugdale, and to the south on the lower slopes of the scarp. There was no access to waterpower at Whorlton and the mill was sited in Scugdale. Later, when Swainby became the dominant settlement, the mill became known as Swainby mill.

9

The northern coastlands

Although the land along the north coast is high and windswept the survival of rigg and furrow shows that in medieval times much of it was used for growing grain. Peter de Brus, for instance, had 382 acres of arable at Brotton in 1272 (B Waites, 1997, 92). There was a lack of waterpower in some areas and the ready availability in others.

Robert de Brus acquired a huge holding of lands along the Tees and around Howl Beck (Skelton Beck) and Kilton Beck soon after the Domesday Survey. His descendants had windmills near the Tees estuary and water mills on Skelton and Kilton becks. When Peter de Brus, the last of the de Brus line, died in 1272 his inquisition post mortem listed *"... five mills with their suit worth £21 8s 0d"*. They were not named but in another inquisition from 1408 three were named as *"Holbekmyll, Saltbornemyll and Skinnengrefmyll"*; Skelton, Saltburn and Skinningrove mills (YAS Rec Ser vol 12, 143 and 194-5). The identity of the other two is not known. In addition to the mills belonging to the de Brus holding there was the old mill at Guisborough, listed in the Domesday Survey, which Robert de Brus had granted to Gisborough Priory and another, initially called Hutton mill but later known as the West mill of Guisborough.

These mills were evenly spaced down the beck, each adjacent to blocks of ploughed land:

- Hutton mill – the fields of Hutton and Pinchinthorpe
- Guisborough mill (later Howl Beck mill but not to be confused with 'Holbeckmyll' at Skelton) – the east field of Guisborough and also the North, Dunsley, Thornton and Wandells fields
- Tocketts mill – the south facing slopes below Upleatham and the fields of Tocketts
- Skelton mill – the fields to the south of Skelton and 'Wand Hills'
- Saltburn mill – the high fields of Brotton running up onto Warsett Hill.

The mills of Upsall, Loftus, Kilton, and Skinningrove in the same general area also conformed to the same pattern.

This ideal pattern of even spacing between mills was not possible on the neighbouring de Mauley estate on high coastal land between Staithes and Sandsend because of the shortage of becks. For instance, at the village of Hinderwell, sited on high-and-dry ground where the drinking water had to be raised via a well, there was no alternative but to carry the grain well over a mile to the mill on Staithes Beck (later known as Dalehouse mill).

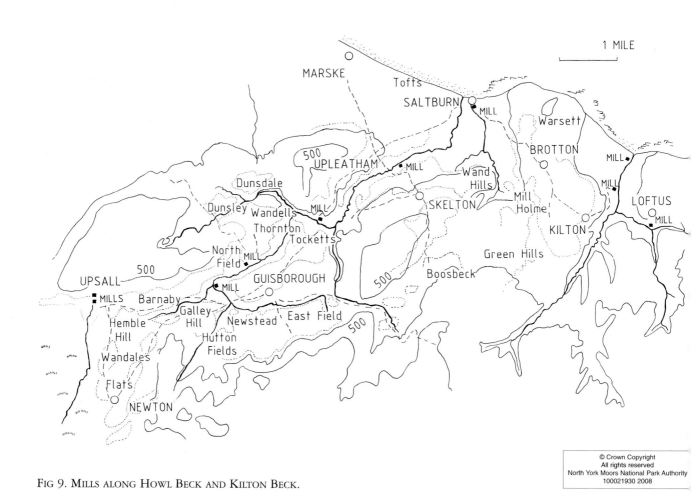

FIG 9. MILLS ALONG HOWL BECK AND KILTON BECK.

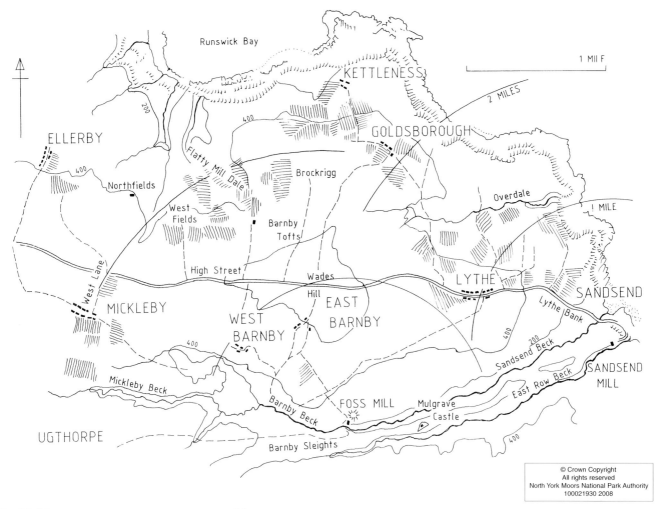

FIG 10. MILLS AND RIGG AND FURROW ON THE MULGRAVE ESTATE.

There was an even bigger problem to the east, on the high land centred on Wade's Hill where, to the north, a windy and treeless landscape slopes away to the sea cliffs and, to the south, the land sweeps down towards the 'griffs' (steep sided and wooded valleys) of Barnby Beck and East Row Beck. Most rigg and furrow has been ploughed out of the southern slopes but to this day the northern slopes retain great swathes of medieval furlongs; to the north of Lythe, around Goldsborough and Kettleness, to the north of Barnby and around Mickleby.

Mickleby lies to the south of the old ridge route known as 'High Street'. There is what at first appears to be a mis-named 'West Lane', which actually runs north east to former outfields, now Northfields Farm, and to the former West Field of Barnby, now Westfield Farm. In contrast with the obviously planned lay-out of Mickleby the scattered township of Barnby consists of the hamlets of West Barnby and East Barnby, with former outlying fields at Westfield Farm, Brockrigg and Barnby Tofts.

To the north and east are the fields of Kettleness and Goldsborough and the fields of Lythe extending to Overdale and to the cliff edge. This huge area was bereft of waterpower. All of the high fields of Mickleby, Barnby, Kettleness and Goldsborough are over a mile away from their nearest mills, at Foss and Sandsend, and some are over two miles away.

The inquisition post mortem for Peter de Mauley (1279) listed his holdings in *"Goldsborough, Lythe, Egton, Westingby"* (Westfield Farm*), "Miccelby, Newton, Barnaby, Sandeshend and Hotun"* (Hutton Mulgrave) and also *"four mills which yield yearly 20s"*. One of the four was Foss mill on Barnby Beck. The second was at Sandsend. The third may have been the mill at Dalehouse, near Staithes. The fourth is more obscure. First edition Ordnance Survey maps record *"Flattymill Dale"* to the north of Barnby. There is no surviving history of any 'Flatty mill', nor any trace on the ground. Any mill in this dale would have been poorly supplied with water and would have needed a dam and pond. It is unlikely that it would have been sited where the beck

11

reaches the sea because the griff is very steep and inaccessible. A more likely site would have been further inland on land now buried under the railway embankment. The evidence is slight but it is just possible that there was an early mill serving the outlying fields along the coast.

The water resources in the Percy holdings around the lower Esk were different again. There was ample water in the Esk but it was difficult to harness and it was used only for Ruswarp mill with its weir across the Esk at its tidal limit. The Norse-named villages of Sneaton, Sneatonthorpe, Ugglebarnby, Stainsacre, Hawsker and Aislaby each have high flatts which were ploughed in medieval times and were served by mills on tributary becks with reasonable flows and good gradients. Five water mills were granted by William de Percy and his son, Adam, to Whitby Abbey and they were confirmed in 1102 as *"Agge Milne, Cocchemilne, the molendinum of Risewarp ... the Novendum Molendina"* and *"Fieling Milne"* in Fylingdales. *"Agge Milne"* or 'Hagg mill' named after coppice woodland and later called Rigg mill, served the villages of Stainsacre and Hawsker. *"Cocchemilne"* or 'Cock mill', named after the woodcock found in the dale, served Sneaton village via the old 'Monks Walk'. *"New Milne"* served the high fields of Newholm and Dunsley. *"Fieling Milne"* served Fylingdales where a set of curved medieval field boundaries survives on the south-east facing ridge running from Fylingthorpe to what might be an embryo single-row village at Raw. The precise location of the mill is not known.

The moorland dales

In the dales within the moorland there were fewer places where open fields could be created, and a good guide for locating them is to look for land which catches the December sun. But it is curious that there are a number of such fields, with clear evidence of medieval ploughing and also with associated water-driven corn mills, which are not near any present day settlement. There is a contrast between the mills of the villages of Kildale and Westerdale, for example, and those of Bilsdale, Bransdale and Farndale which do not have a nucleated village.

Kildale is a wide, rolling basin surrounded on three sides by high moorland. In medieval times it was held by the Percy family. The mill was first recorded in a grant by William de Percy to the Canons of St John the Evangelist of Healaugh Park (c. 1262). This included lands in Kildale, a rent charge of two marks per annum out of his mill (*"molendino aquatico"*), the right to grind multure free and to have corn and malt for those visitors who came to stay at the chapel. This mill was built on the Leven under Kildale Force. Today, access is along the steep-sided bank of the Leven but the medieval track (now disrupted by the railway) can be

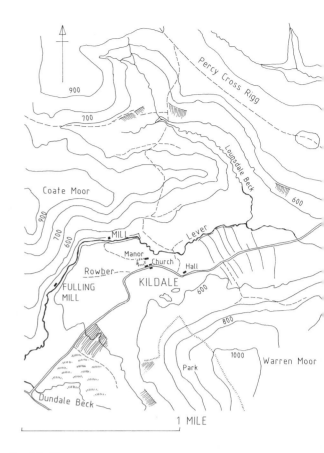

FIG 11. KILDALE AND ITS MILL.

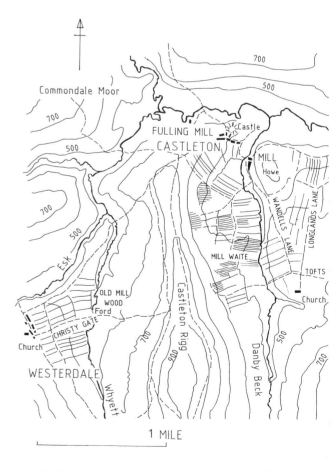

FIG 12. FIELDS AND MILLS OF DANBY DALE AND WESTERDALE.

raced along a field boundary running directly across the fields from the hall and church. The village itself is now re-aligned. All traces of rigg and furrow have gone from the land to the west of the village but regular field boundaries survive to the east. There is also evidence of population pressure in early medieval times in areas of rigg and furrow in the tributary valley of Lounsdale. Conversely, there are traces of rigg and furrow within the ditched boundary (or 'pale') around the north east corner of a later deer park where ploughing had been discontinued.

Danby dale had been partly settled before the Domesday Survey. The de Brus landlords established a defensive site on a steep-sided spur overlooking the Esk at the foot of the dale and this gave its name to Castleton. The castle never developed beyond the earth mound stage and in the inquisition 'post mortem' for Peter de Brus (1272) it was listed as worth only 6s 8d while, in contrast, two water mills held by Roger de Burton were worth £10. One of these, later known as Howe mill, at the foot of Danby dale, was served not by the Esk as might be expected but by a long leat from the tributary Danby Beck. There were good reasons. The Esk floods badly on occasions. More importantly, that part of Eskdale near Castleton is steep-sided and unsuitable for the plough while, on the other hand, Danby dale has well drained land on two low riggs, mid-way between the three old settlements at Castleton, Ainthorpe and near the old Danby church.

In 1307 the Knights Templar of Westerdale were about to be deprived of a hall with kitchen, brewery, chapel and a mill. From the evidence of carved stones in the buildings of New Farm it seems likely that the Templars' hall and chapel stood within the present village boundary. As at Castleton, the land sloping steeply down to the Esk was not good for the plough and, though not south facing, the lands sloping more gently away from the village to Whyett Beck were preferred. Surviving field boundaries trace the medieval reversed S strips running from the back lane of the village to the beck side. An old track called Christy Gate runs down through the middle of these strips from the site of an ancient cross on the back lane of the village to a stone-paved ford in Whyett Beck and then up to an old house formerly known as Miller's House (now Millinder House). The name "Old Mill Wood" was used on the first edition Ordnance Survey map to describe a patch of woodland in the dale below the ford. Although there is now no evidence of a building or leat, the association of curved field boundaries and old names is surely evidence of a medieval mill.

Not all early settlements in the dales prospered to become villages like Westerdale. In early medieval times the settlement now known as Chisel Hill in Bilsdale, for instance, had open fields and a mill with a very long leat, but development seems to have stalled at an early

date. At the beginning of the twelfth century the whole of Bilsdale was held by Walter l'Espec and a chapel belonging to Helmsley Church stood on the site now occupied by St Hilda's Church. The nearby Bilsdale Hall was not recorded until after l'Espec granted this part of Bilsdale to Kirkham Priory (between 1122 and 1130) after which it became the home of the lay administrator for that Priory (J McDonnell ed, 1963, 128-9). An ancient track across Bilsdale head runs east to west from Urra past Bilsdale Hall and Church, the *"Town Green"* and the water mill on its way to Raisdale and Carlton-in-Cleveland. The dwellings on the north side of the *"Town Green"* face south down the dale. William Calvert's Survey of Charles Duncombe's estate, 1781 (NYCRO ZEW 1/7 mic 1023) showed three parallel *"Town Garths"* and a *"Glebe"* running back from the dwellings and remains of other un-named tofts. An old track, now lost, ran from below the mill onto another rigg, called the *"Town Field"*, which still has medieval field boundaries. This place would have been a natural choice for a new village and the evidence suggests that it was planned, complete with mill, by l'Espec, probably in the eleventh century, but that further development was abandoned after the grant to Kirkham Priory. The mill, however, survived.

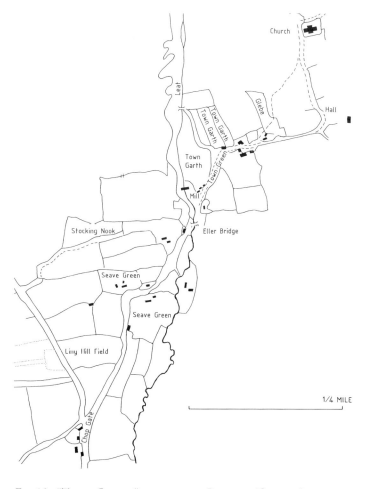

FIG 13. *"TOWN GARTHS"* AND MILL AT BILSDALE (CALVERT'S SURVEY).

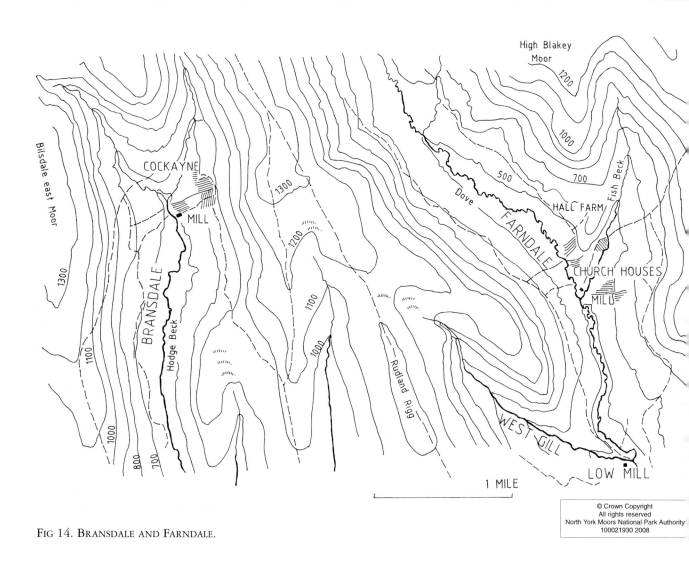

FIG 14. BRANSDALE AND FARNDALE.

Something similar happened in Raisdale, where the old township has disappeared, leaving only hummocks in the land and carved stones at the farmstead called 'Hall Garth'. This part of Raisdale was granted to Rievaulx Abbey and, again, the story may have been one of early development followed by later abandonment. There is no medieval documentation for the mill but, nevertheless, the elongated loop in the parish boundary specifically taking in its steading shows that this must have been a very early mill.

The pattern is repeated in Bransdale and Farndale, both of which have good land in the dale bottoms. The dale-head settlements of Cockayne and Church Houses failed to develop, though both had an early chapel and a mill. There is a 'Hall Farm' immediately to the north of Church Houses in Farndale. Cockayne and Church Houses were cut off from neighbouring dales by steep edges and moorland. Decline had set in by the time of

the Black Death and subsequently both dales were developed by assarting around the dale edges. These assarts, which form the origins of many of the present day farms, occupied steeper land and their crops consisted, in the main, of oats and hay. On their own they might not have generated the need for a mill but they did enable established mills to survive.

Interestingly, in Farndale and in Bilsdale, there are later mill steadings, known as either the 'low mill' or the 'nether mill', names which describe them as lower down the beck. The medieval Farndale Low mill stood on West Beck (not on the site of the surviving mill building), and served good land in West Gill and on the east side of Farndale. In medieval times there was probably no settlement. Bilsdale Low mill is also isolated though linked by old tracks to good land and a scattered settlement centred on Grange.

WATER POWER

Iorth east Yorkshire is drier than the other upland areas f northern England, and particularly so in spring and ummer. The Cod Beck valley and the Tees estuary have etween 500 and 625 mm of rain each year; Ryedale and he East Coast between 625 and 750 mm and the high noorlands something over 750 mm, figures which con-ast with the 1500 mm common across the Pennines. ronically, a climate suitable for growing wheat results in lack of waterpower for milling it. Water, like good nd, was a scarce resource in most of medieval north ast Yorkshire and by the end of the period most of it ad been harnessed. The vital function served by the

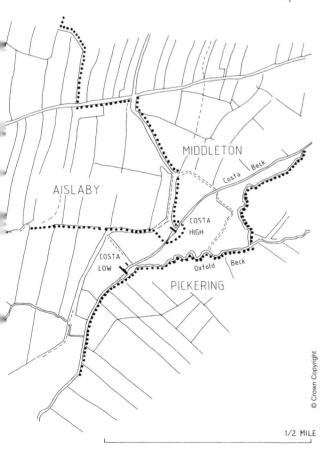

© Crown Copyright

1/2 MILE

IG 15. Parish boundaries near the Costa mill steadings prepared from Ordnance Survey 1st Ed, 6 inch map).

mill is sometimes demonstrated in distorted parish and township boundaries, deliberately deflected to take in a suitable source of waterpower (M Aston, 1985, 42). Such distortions are seen as evidence of very early mills. In north east Yorkshire they can be seen at Scackleton, Aislaby near Pickering, Spaunton and Raisdale.

The stonework of waterwheel pits in the northern peat moors is invariably stained black. In contrast, the wheel pits (and the waterwheels themselves) in and around the Corallian limestone hills are lime crusted. The becks of the northern moors run peat brown in win-ter and lightly hazed in summer whereas the becks from the Corallian limestones are crystal clear and as such were much prized for paper making. The contrast can be seen at Rievaulx Abbey where the Rye, flowing from the northern moors, was ignored and, instead, three ponds cut into the Corallian limestone edge above the Abbey buildings provided clear water for the precinct and were also used to drive the corn mill. However, it was the quantity and the gradient of the water and not the qual-ity that led to different forms of water engineering for corn mills. Within the northern moors, for instance, where there is more relief rain the mills tended to have leats whereas those in the lower and drier Corallian limestone areas tended to have storage ponds.

Leats

Clay soils in the dale bottoms of north east Yorkshire can become semi-fluid and unstable in times of prolonged wet weather or floods, and one important consideration in choosing a mill steading was to avoid clay founda-tions. Flooding can occur when heavy rain combines with melting snow in January and February. It can also be a serious problem in June and July when the water-courses are partly choked with vegetation, as for exam-ple in the flood of July 1930 when the 14 feet diameter waterwheel at Danby mill on the Esk was completely submerged. The arrangements at Commondale, where the mill was built on a shale ledge with a platform roughly hewn to shape and then lined with masonry, show that the medieval builders fully understood how

15

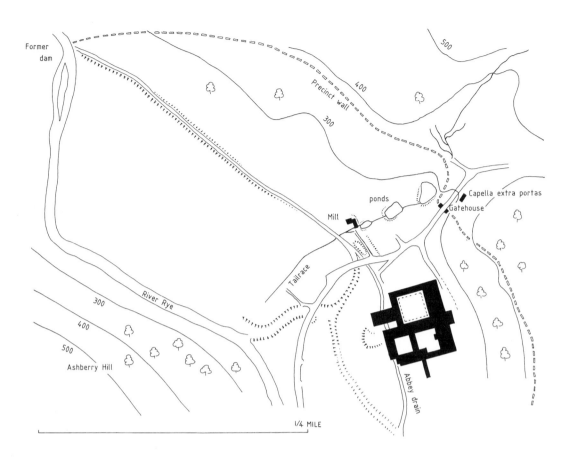

FIG 16. PRECINCT AND MILL AT RIEVAULX (PREPARED FROM VICTORIA COUNTY HISTORY, YORKSHIRE, VOL 1, P495).

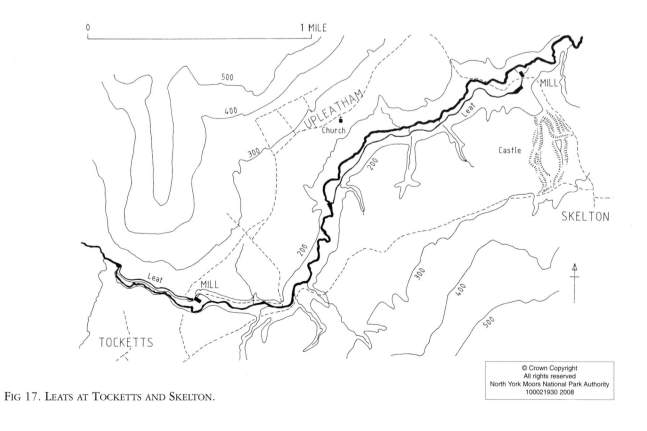

FIG 17. LEATS AT TOCKETTS AND SKELTON.

the turbulence of flood water could undermine clay foundations (J K Harrison, 1995). In other cases mills were built on dry terraces well clear of even the worst floods. At Tocketts, for instance, the leat made it possible to build the mill on secure foundations in a dale which is steep sided, clayey and unstable.

Leats were used where the gradient and flow were sufficient to drive a wheel without ponding. Although leats were expensive to construct they were used for the earliest water mills, for example, those listed in the Domesday Survey at Stokesley and Guisborough. Other early medieval mills at Bilsdale, Crathorne, Sandsend, Pickering High and Castleton also had leats between half and three quarters of a mile long, excluding the tail races which were deeper and even more expensive to cut. The longest of all, at over a mile long, was at Skelton where Robert de Brus established a castle, with major earthworks, soon after the Domesday Survey. The size of the leat at Skelton, with deep cuttings at some points and wooden troughs to bridge three small gills, indicates the scale of resources invested.

There was similarly major investment in the water engineering at Keld Head near Pickering, where the villagers of Cropton, Aislaby and Middleton farmed wide acres of fine south facing land. The shallow, marshy Ox Fold Beck was diverted into a straight, fast flowing leat, now called Costa Beck, to drive two separate water mills, one serving Aislaby and the other serving Middleton. A similarly ancient leat, from the Leven at Great Ayton, drove two mills, the East mill and the West mill, in tandem.

On the other hand, the inadequacy of some medieval leats serving the small mills in the dales is shown by the number which had to be augmented in later centuries, for example at Wilton, Guisborough, Cropton, Lastingham, Bransdale, Farndale High and Rosedale.

There was a quite different problem at Stokesley where the land lies flat, just above the 225 feet contour. How would it be possible to supply power for a water mill to serve the new town emerging at the time of the Domesday Survey? The solution was to dig a leat from a dam on the Leven, half a mile in length along the top of a long, low spur of land which became known as Mill Rigg, to lead water to the mill at a head of about 8 feet.

Forces

Waterfalls, known as 'forces' in the Norse derived dialect, would seem to have been an obvious source of power since the engineering works required were much less expensive. Foss mill in Mulgrave takes its name from such a force and there are 'force mill' names in other parts of the north. Force mills seem to have been established as early as mills with leats.

Cock mill, first identified in 1102, may have been the mill of Whitby/Sneaton listed in the Domesday Survey.

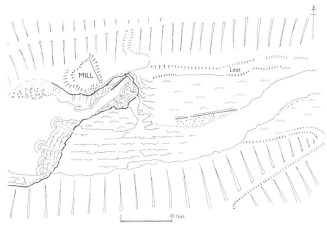

FIG 18. SITE OF KILDALE MILL.

By the nineteenth century it was attracting attention as a curiosity, "... *most picturesquely peeping from amongst the umbrageous multitude of leaves*" (Belcher, 1836, 20). Today the overwhelming impression left by a visit is the noise of the 20 foot waterfall and the dampness from the spray thrown up from the rocks below. The mill was built under the rock edge, on a hard shale platform well clear of floods. The water was drawn from a low dam built well back from the lip of the fall and led by a short leat and a wooden trough to the waterwheel. Above the fall the rock lip was used as a 'wath' or ford.

Arrangements were very similar at Kildale mill which was built under Kildale Force, later called 'Old Meggison', on the Leven. As at Cock mill, the water was drawn off by way of a low dam and short leat from a point well back from the lip of the fall. The mill was built on a platform half way down the fall, an arrangement which protected it from flood water from both above and below the fall. Access was via a doorway at millstone level in the rear wall. The waterwheel was set well above the lower water level in a roughly squared-up natural cleft. As at Cock mill the hard sandstone above the fall provided a natural wath for the mill track from the village.

Other examples of this arrangement, though later modified to take larger diameter waterwheels, are at Rigg mill and at Goathland. Force mills were always at the head of a gorge and therefore on natural crossing points. At Goathland, for instance, the original ford was successively replaced by a wooden footbridge and then by the extant bridge to the railway station. A similar wath at Foss mill has a timber bolted into the lip of the fall to prevent the wheels of horse-drawn carts slipping over the edge. Flood damage to foundations was less of a problem in force mills. For instance, the foundations of Foss mill were built level with the tail water but the bed of the beck falls away very steeply into a gorge and the water could get away. In any case, the masonry was securely founded in solid rock and would surely come to no harm.

Ponds

Ponds were constructed where the water supply was not good enough to drive a wheel continuously. For instance, the pond for the medieval upper mill at Upsall on the southern flank of the Eston outlier was fed by a very small spring. The water table in the Eston Hills was lowered by ironstone mining in the second half of the nineteenth century but, nevertheless, it is clear that there was always a water shortage. As demand for milling increased the only solution was to build a second mill with its pond collecting water from the tail of the upper

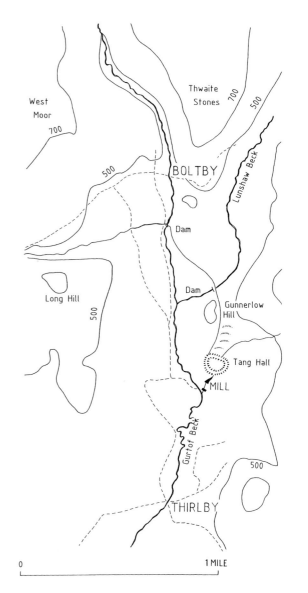

FIG 20. SITE OF RAVENSTHORPE MILL.

mill, a solution very similar to that used in some Scottish Highland 'Norse' mills built in series down a small burn.

At Allerston and Ampleforth on the dip slopes of the Tabular Hills ponds were made by digging into a natural slope and using the waste to raise an earthen dike round the hollow. At Ampleforth there are two ponds on sloping ground while at Allerston there is a dike along one edge of a shallow valley. In each case the water was carried from the pond to the wheel via a wooden trough. Many of these pond mills were short of water and in later times they could only work in the mornings and evenings.

Some mill ponds were fed by 'kelds' (springs). Perhaps the most remarkable example is at Brompton where springs feed directly into the pond. One account described the situation where "... *a river bursts at once from the caverns of limestone, and it is collected at its very source into a large mill pond ...*" (George Young 1817, 774). First-hand observation by the current owner

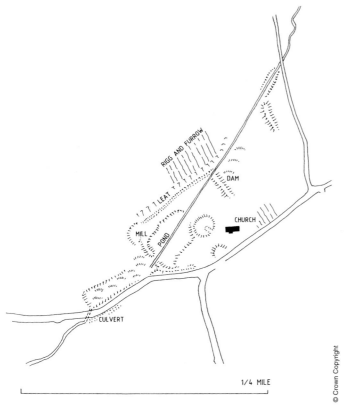

FIG 19. SITE OF MILL AT KIRBY KNOWLE.

has revealed some 17 springs feeding into the pond; most of them within 50 metres of the mill. At Ebberston the water comes to the surface at the foot of a dry valley immediately behind Ebberston Hall, north of the village, and flows half a mile as Bloody Beck to the large millpond at the low end of the village.

On one occasion, in later times, there was a conflict between two mills on a beck which went underground and then re-emerged as a keld. In this case, some of the water of the Hodge went underground near Kirkdale and re-emerged as the Howkeld Beck to the north east of Welburn Hall, where it filled the pond of Howkeld mill. Soon after 1704 there *"... being opposition between the millers"* (of Hold Cauldron mill) *"and those of Howkeld the millers of Hold Cauldron stopped up their sinks with lime and sand so the millers of Howkeld were unable to grind, their supply of water being cut off. ... Enraged by this aggravation a servant of Howkeld, Robin, went at dead of night with a fiery turf in his hand and set on fire the Hold Cauldron mill, consumed it to ashes"* (Parker, 1858; Ryedale Historian, 1980, 24).

Mills under the western scarps were also short of water. The shrunken hamlet of Kirby Knowle has a Manor Farm, church and a few houses. A mill was listed for the first time in the inquisition post mortem for Anketin Salveyn in 1291. It was supplied by a dam across a tiny beck via a leat around the edge of a large, possibly later, pond. The mill was burned down in the

seventeenth century and never rebuilt, almost certainly because of its poor water supply.

Problems caused by the small flows from the limestone scarps resulted in remarkable water engineering for the mill of Ravensthorpe, which served the village of Boltby. Ravensthorpe was granted by Odo de Boltebia to Rievaulx Abbey in 1142 and the chartulary described the boundary of Ravensthorpe as, at one point, passing to the place *"... where the water is withdrawn from its own course"*. The mill itself was first listed in the inquisition post mortem for Nicholas de Boltebi (1272) as *"one water mill worth 8 marks per annum"*. The watercourse of 1142 can still be traced. The water was dammed off from Gurtof Beck immediately to the south of the village of Boltby to flow across the marshy land, capturing Lunshaw Beck on its way and then skirting to the east of Gunnerlow Hill. This watercourse had a dual purpose. It fed the moat of Ravensthorpe manor (Tang Hall), an impressive ditch up to 15 feet deep, surrounding an area of some four acres. The overflow ran into a banked up pond for the corn mill.

The old manor of Bordelby formerly held by John de Inglebi was granted to Rievaulx Abbey then to Mount Grace Priory in 1381. It is thought that the square, moated area below the Priory, now incorporated into the landscaped ponds, is the site of the manor house. However, the statement that the old vaulted building to the west of the north end of the surviving seventeenth

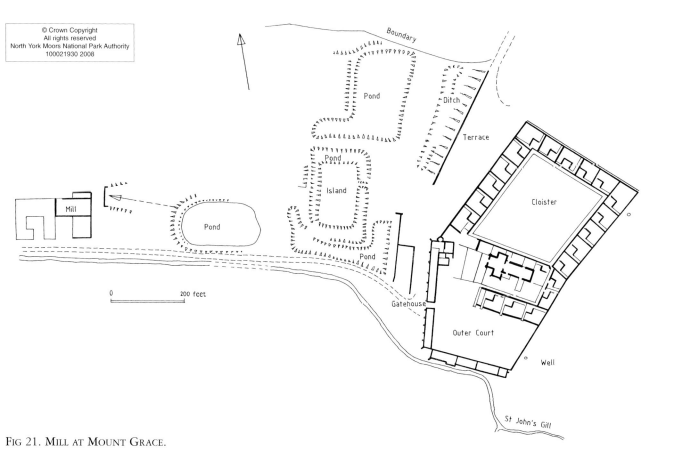

FIG 21. MILL AT MOUNT GRACE.

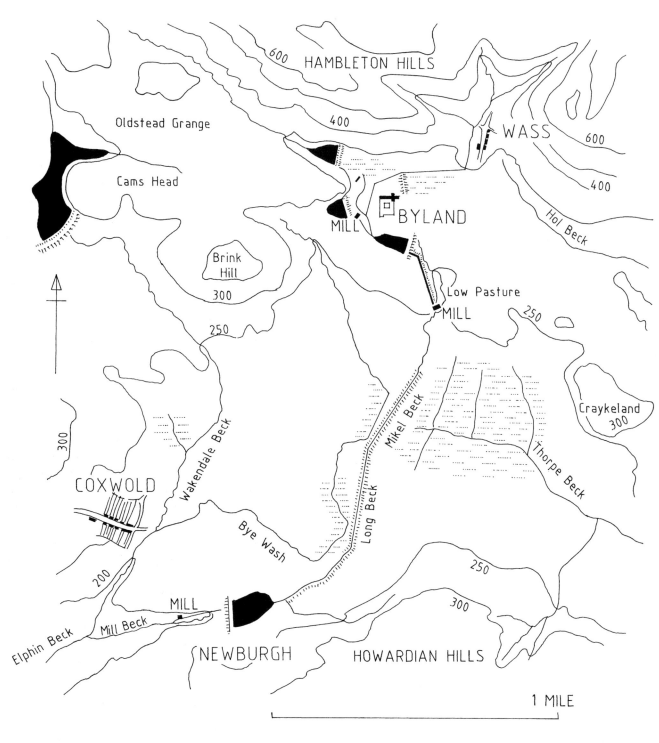

Fig 22. Water engineering at Byland and Newburgh

century house may have been the water mill may be incorrect (W Grainge, 1859, 348) since there is no feature to positively identify it as such. It is more likely that the old mill was on the site now occupied by the nineteenth century corn and saw mill at Mount Grace Farm. If so, there would have been a close parallel with the arrangements at Ravensthorpe, in using waste water from a moated hall to feed an embanked mill pond.

However, the water engineering at Ravensthorpe and Bordelby was far surpassed by the combined works at Byland Abbey and Newburgh Priory. At Byland, water flowing down the dale from Oldstead was dammed to make fish ponds before reaching the final dam which provided the head for the precinct mill (J McDonnell & M R Everest, 1965). A second source of water, the Holbeck, was diverted near Wass from its natural south easterly direction into an artificial course leading to the Abbey precinct (S A Harrison, 1986, 26-47). Below the precinct corn mill the combined flow was dammed to create more fish ponds, before driving the second Abbey mill at Low Pasture farm. The tail water from this mill was then diverted from its natural course via Thorpe Beck into a raised leat called Long Beck which led to the pond at Newburgh Priory and thence to Coxwold/Newburgh mill. This pond was listed in a description of the land taken by the canons of Newburgh, to the east of Coxwold and *"beyond the pond"* (1145) and was referred to as *"the Stanke"* in 1605 (NYCRO ZDV I, mic 1504). It had been drained by 1722 but was resurrected by 1827 and was enlarged in 1858 (J Hatcher, 1978, vol 2). The Stanke, though now modified, is the largest surviving medieval fish and mill pond in the region.

Weirs and tides

An early study of the mills listed in the Domesday Survey drew attention to the lack of mills on the *"great highway rivers"* (M Hodgen, 1939, 261-79). However, the hint that the deficiency resulted from a need to keep rivers clear of weirs for the sake of navigation was not the only reason why mills were not built on lower river courses. In fact, such sites would be difficult to manage because of flooding. Certainly no mill using a weir across a river existed in north east Yorkshire at the time of the Domesday Survey, but Ruswarp mill, sited on the tidal limit of the Esk ('warp' meaning silted tidal mud bank) existed by 1102. From the outset it must have used at least a wing weir to deflect water onto the wheel, and in later times a massive dam was built across the river. However, this mill was exceptional.

The situation on the Tees was different. The Tees is bigger and there was no equivalent river-mouth port. Until the Barrage was built in the 1990s the high tides of the Tees reached up-river as far as Worsall above Yarm, where there is still a distinctive change from a brisk flow over a stony bed to a sluggish (formerly tidal) flow between muddy banks. About a mile upriver from the tidal limit are the hall and earthworks of the shrunken village of Newsham. Bernard de Baliol granted a fishery at Newsham to the monks of Rievaulx Abbey, with the additional rights that no one else could take fish from this stretch of the river and that they could collect stones for building a dam *"... wherever they could find them"*. There was a condition that the dam would not stop the running of the fish. In one early document this dam was referred to as the *"milldam"*. It supplied the lowest medieval mill on the Tees. The dam survived until 1581 when it was demolished by sixty armed men hired by William Bowes of Streatlam Castle, on the grounds that it did indeed stop the running of the fish.

Conditions were even more difficult in the lower estuaries below the tidal limits. In the saltmarsh wetlands of estuaries a tide mill was the only possible solution. They were not ideal since they could not operate for more than between six and ten hours per day but a national survey of tide mills indicates that something like 37 were built in England before 1300 (W E Minchinton, 1979, 777). There were many more in France, particularly in Brittany, and others in Spain and Portugal. None of the listed English sites was in north Yorkshire. Though the tidal range on this coast is on average between 14 feet and 18 feet, quite adequate for a tide mill, it was not so much the tidal range that counted as the conditions on the ground. Tide mills were not built directly on a coast because neither the buildings nor the dams could stand the pounding of the waves. Instead, they were normally sited where a sluggish river flowed into an estuary, well clear of the coast. Such mills needed an embayment suitable for damming off to make a pond. In this respect, several sites in Hartlepool Bay and the Tees estuary would have been suitable.

Until the mid-nineteenth century there was at Hartlepool a large area of tidal mud-flats known as 'the Slake', which was sheltered from the north easterly winds by the Headland. The question of how the medieval townspeople of Hartlepool ground their grain has never been satisfactorily explained. When, during the Scots troubles in 1314, Bishop Kellow seized the town and leased it to Richard le Mason he listed *"... a bakehouse, watermills and the mill of Hart"* (C Sharp, 1816, 36). Clearly, any water mill at Hartlepool could not have been a river mill since the land is flat and the underlying magnesian limestone permeable. On the other hand, there was a suitable site for a tide mill on the northern edge of the Slake where Hart Beck meandered towards the mud flats. Interestingly, the old farm name, Dyke House, is related to the Dutch 'dike' meaning a wall for impounding water, though of course not necessarily for a mill.

There were other creeks in the Tees estuary which might have been suitable for tide mills, particularly Greatham Creek and Billingham Beck on the north bank and Caldecotes Fleet and the Coatham shallows on the south bank. There was a medieval mill at the tidal limit of Billingham Beck but it was not a tide mill. However, there may have been a partial tide mill at Caldecotes. Caldecotes had been given to Gisborough Priory by Arnald de Percy soon after 1119 and a piece of ground immediately to the west was granted by William Malbisse to Whitby Abbey for the purpose of setting up a cell in 1215. Part of the boundary between the Malbisse grant and Caldecotes ran from the point where *"... the headland of Radulph Longi reaches the Caldecotes Fleet and from there by the middle of the Fleet to the Fleet mill near Felebridge"* (J C Atkinson, 1874, vol 2, part 2, 12). Fele Bridge must have been across the tidal fleet (later called Cargo Fleet) which ran parallel to the Tees for some hundred metres. In early times the inhabitants of Ormesby had seen Cargo Fleet as a cold

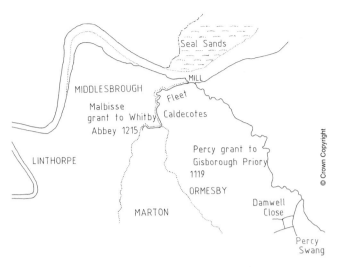

FIG 23. PLACE NAMES AT CALDECOTES.

place suitable only for summer grazing (hence the name *"Caldecotes"*) but the existence of the bridge in 1215 suggests that by this date it was becoming more heavily used. The Fleet is joined at its outflow by Ormesby Beck and the name *"Damwell Close"* near *"Percy Swang"*, on

an estate map of 1791, shows that this beck was also put to use to drive a mill (TA ZDM 77). There is hardly any gradient on this beck but a 'swang', an area of natural seepage, could have served as an additional reservoir for a tide mill on the Fleet itself. There are no later records of Caldecotes mill and its story may have been similar to that of some known tide mills on the Humber estuary which were abandoned before 1200, normally after serious storms, sometimes to be replaced with cheaper windmills.

At a later date there is a single reference to what may have been a tide mill at Yarm. Because the Tees was big and subject to flooding the town had been served by a windmill since before 1272. A list of the confiscated estates of Christopher Conyers (1539) included not only the *"… farm of the windmill there, Henry Gibson 26s 8d"* but also *"… the farm of the mill brini newly constructed by Henry, 6s 8d"* (NYCRO ZBA 5/1/13). The Tees at Yarm is tidal though not salty, but the term *"mill brini"*, though obscure in this case, would normally be used for a saltwater mill. This mill was worth much less than the windmill and may not have been a substantial structure.

MONASTIC WATER MILLS

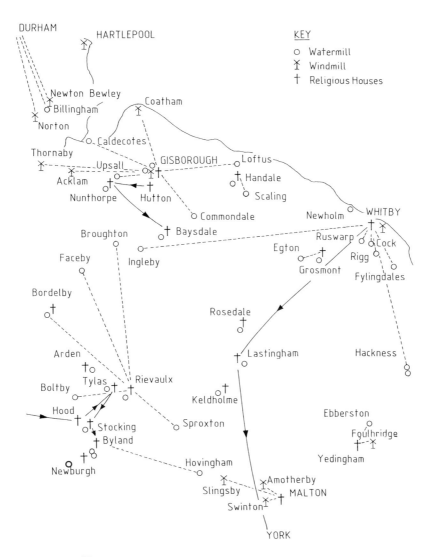

FIG 24. MONASTIC MILLS IN NORTH EAST YORKSHIRE.

Between them the various monastic orders eventually took over something like one third of the land area of the North York Moors. With regard to corn milling there was a significant difference between the houses. The Benedictines and Augustinians acquired grants of existing manorial mills, which they then either continued to operate like manorial mills or farmed out for a rental, whereas the Cistercians built their own very distinctive precinct mills.

The Benedictines of Whitby Abbey received a grant from William de Percy of a very large block of land around the lower Esk and extending to Fylingdales and to Hackness. This included seven water mills, *"Agge Milne, Cocchemilne, molendinum de Riswarp, Novum*

Molendinum, molendinum de Fielinga, villan de Hacknesse et duo molendina" (Whitby Chart, Surtees Soc, vol 64, 3). Thus, at a stroke, the Abbey gained a monopoly of milling around the lower Esk. Interestingly, a Roll of Disbursements from Martinmas 1394 to Martinmas 1395 recorded a cost of 33s for shoeing the horses of the bursar, the poulterer, the abbot's cook, the bailiff, the miller and the baker (G Young, 1817, 324). Later the Abbey received the mill at Ingleby Greenhow. This grant was confirmed in 1151 by Adam, son of Viel, including the provision that the landholder could still use the mill multure free (L Charlton, 1779, 115), an agreement which took care of his problem that he would otherwise deprive himself of the use of the mill as well as the income. Afterwards the rights were reaffirmed whenever there was a change of landholder. For instance, in 1205 a new holder, Guido de Baliol of Barnard Castle, confirmed the grant *"… lest by chance of times or devices of wicked men the benefactions which had been granted for ecclesiastical use should be in danger of being weakened or set aside"* (Whitby Chart, Surtees Soc, vol 64, 54). Five years later the Abbey farmed out the mill to Hugh de Baliol to be held on a yearly rental of 15s during his lifetime after which time it was to revert to the Abbey. Renting out was the solution to the problem of administering a distant mill.

The Augustinians also received grants of corn mills. For instance, in the foundation grant of 1119 Robert de Brus gave Gisborough Priory the mills of Guisborough with *"soc and molt"* and the additional right that *"… no other be allowed to build mills in Gisborough"* (Gis Chart, Surtees Soc, vol 86, 4). Unlike the situation at Ingleby Greenhow, de Brus reserved no rights with regard to milling to himself. At the same time he gave land in Commondale and, although not mentioned until the Dissolution, it is likely that the mill there was first established as the mill of Skelderskew grange (J K Harrison, 1995). The Priory received further grants. During the thirteenth century, for example, Robert de Tunstall gave the water mill at Upsall near Barnaby, along with *"soc and molt"*, and the grant was confirmed by Reginald, his son, and Hawyse, his daughter. Hawyse confirmed the grant *"with her corpse"*, or on condition that her body would eventually be buried in the monastery church. Also, Arnald de Percy gave the water mill at Caldecotes on the River Tees but later recovered it in exchange for land. In addition to these water mills the canons also obtained interest in a number of windmills on the south bank of the Tees estuary.

The Benedictines and the Augustinians may have built one or two water mills, for instance at Commondale, but this was unusual. It was very different with the Cistercians who were charged with the duty of maintaining themselves by farming and industry, using the labour of lay brothers. It is thought that some of the earliest communities on the Continent ground their grain in hand mills but in north eastern Yorkshire there is no evidence of this. At Rievaulx they received Sproxton mill from Everard de Ros in a grant which supplemented Walter Espec's original grant (Riev Chart, Surtees Soc, vol 83, 23), but this does not necessarily mean that they relied on it for flour for their own use. In fact, at all Cistercian houses domestic buildings such as the barn, slaughter house, pigsty, stable, smithy, hen house, dovecote, brew house, malt house, bakery and corn mill were built within the boundary wall of the precinct. They were in the outer court or 'curia' which the laymen might enter without having access to the nave of the church. The Cistercians followed St Benedict's rule that each monastery *"… ought, if possible, to be so constituted that all things necessary, such as water, a mill and a garden and the various crafts may be contained within it so that there may be no need for the monks to go abroad, for it is by means expedient for their souls"* (D Luckhurst, n d, 5). It was a standard layout that the tail water from the mill was used to flush out the main drain of the monastery. The water at Clairvaux, for instance, was used over and over again, in the corn mill, fulling mill and wash houses within the curia. The larger Cistercian houses of north east Yorkshire, at Rievaulx and Byland, had similar arrangements and even the smaller Cistercian nunneries had a water mill within or near the precinct. These precinct mills differed from the older manorial mills. Whereas the manorial miller extracted a multure to earn his keep the monastic miller was a paid servant who worked under the direction of the 'cellarer' (who catered for the house) and the 'granator' (who received the grain from the monastic fields and granges).

The best preserved Cistercian 'mill' in England, perhaps in Europe, is at Fountains Abbey. This building is 23 feet in internal span and over 100 feet long (David Luckhurst, n d, 10-12). First built before 1147 with buttressed bays and round arched windows it was changed and heightened in the thirteenth century with the insertion of lancet windows. At the Dissolution the building contained *"… two water corn mills under one roof"*. The Fountains building was in fact a very large multi-purpose service building which incorporated corn 'mills' (used in the original meaning of the word). A similarly large, multi-purpose building survives at Fontenay Abbey in France where it is today described as a 'forge'.

No such building survives in north east Yorkshire but something of the sort may once have existed at Rievaulx. The Abbey corn mill was built on a dry terrace and it took its water from three ponds fed by a spring emerging from the limestone of the dale edge. The siting conforms to the Cistercian standard, that is, within the precinct walls and quite close to the gatehouse, the last fragments of which can be seen in the roadside wall just below the 'capella extra portas' or 'chapel outside the gate'. The surviving tailrace takes the shortest route

A)

B)

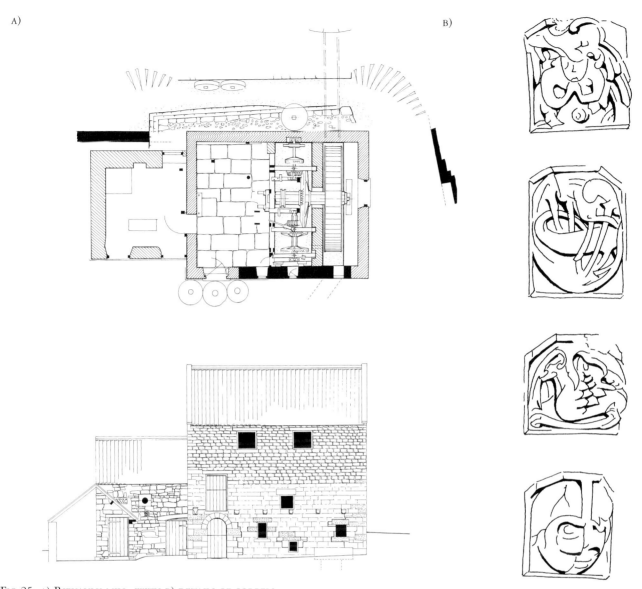

Fig 25. a) Rievaulx mill, with b) details of corbels.

across the flat dale bottom to the Rye but the original tail took a longer route through a culvert running east to the Abbey lavatories etc. The mill was re-equipped in the eighteenth century and extended upwards in the nineteenth but the front facade retains medieval limestone blocks. The much eroded corbels, two of which can be recognised as a praying angel and a winged beast, are of a style which is commonly found in twelfth century churches in France. There is no doubt that these corbels were carved by a craftsman from France working soon after the Abbey was founded in 1131. Whether they have been re-sited from another building is open to question. If they are in-situ then they are set too far apart to have supported masonry but they might have supported the sill of a timber framed upper storey. A re-used section of a mortised beam came to light during conversion of the mill to a house.

What is clear is that the medieval mill at Rievaulx was bigger than the surviving building. Levelling work car-

ried out with a mechanical digger at the time of conversion to a house uncovered old foundations extending further to the north and east. Also uncovered, outside the waterwheel end of the building, was heavy masonry probably associated with an earlier water system.

The second great Cistercian house in north east Yorkshire was at Byland. Savignac monks from Furness in Cumberland had first migrated to Hood Grange near Thirsk, then to Tylas on the banks of the Rye a short distance from Rievaulx, then to Stocking near Oldstead and finally to Byland, by which time they had been absorbed into the Cistercian order. Their early halts were quite short but they would have needed flour and they may have built mills at Caydale, near Old Byland, and at Oldstead. Mill buildings survive on both these sites. Their ultimate home, at 'Bella Landa', was built on marshy land and, before building work could begin, water engineering works were put in hand to drain the site and to create large fishponds. By the time of the

Dissolution there was a close parallel between arrangements at Rievaulx and Byland. Both had two water mills, one a precinct mill and the other a fulling mill. At Byland, the mill within the abbey precinct replaced the earlier corn mill at Low Pasture farm some distance to the south. All that survives of the precinct mill is the dry pond with its earth dam and a millstone used as the threshold of a later house. The mill at Low Pasture may have been the manorial mill of Wass, pre-dating the Abbey. By the time of the Dissolution there was a fulling mill on the site and, judging from the size and complexity of the water works, incorporating two separate dams and ponds, the mill had been extended considerably during monastic times. The current range of buildings, backing onto a large earth dam, may be on the foundations of a large medieval building.

In contrast with the wealthy monasteries the several nunneries in the region were recorded in Dissolution inventories as quite small and poor, with few remaining nuns and little income. In their earliest days, the nunneries belonged to no particular order but, later, Arden was known as a Benedictine nunnery and Handale, Baysdale and Rosedale were absorbed into the Cistercian order. They all lived by Cistercian rules, supporting themselves through agriculture, with a particular involvement in the wool trade. With the exception of Keldholme nunnery to which Robert de Stuteville gave the mill of Kirkby Moorside they built their own precinct mills.

The earliest possible record of a mill at Arden Priory is found in the resolution of a dispute between the nuns of Arden and monks of Byland. The monks had moved away from their Tylas site not long before the nuns arrived at nearby Arden but they still had lands there. In 1119 the Prioress, Muriel of Arden, and the Abbot of Byland appeared before Jeremy, the Archdeacon of Cleveland, for a hearing over rights of way over their adjoining lands. A settlement was made whereby *"... the monks condoned the nuns in regard to all dams, enclosures for animals, the rough words of their men and other irregularities, whilst the nuns conceded to Byland the free passage for the abbot and carriages over the nuns' land"* (VCH, vol 3, 113). The *"dams"* were probably for the mill at Arden. There was certainly a corn mill there by the time of the Dissolution. Ironically, although only a short length of wall of the Priory itself survives, encapsulated within the later house, there is still a complete water mill. The precinct grounds would probably have been enclosed in some way and there would have been a main gate. The mill site is close to where the gate must have been.

Handale, Rosedale and Baysdale nunneries were established in 1133, 1160 and 1162 respectively. Handale or *"Grendale"* was set up to the south of Loftus on open moorland (since enclosed), donated by William de Percy. The buildings are now demolished and the base of a stone cross, a carved coffin lid and the chamfered

plinth in the farm house built on the site are the only above-ground relics. Radiating from the site are three old trackways, one leading across Handale Beck to Liverton village, one across the fields towards Loftus and the third across the fields to Scaling where the nuns were given a moiety of Scaling mill. However, they also built a precinct mill. This, along with a bolting house and a kiln house, was described in a Dissolution inventory:

> *"Item. The brewhouse and bultynge house, conteyning in length xi ffoote and in bredith xviij ffoote, wherof xviij ffoote couered wt slates and xxij ffoote wt thack, dawbid walles, somwhat oute of reparacon.*
>
> *Item. The kilne house conteyning xi ffoote longe and xiiij ffoote brode, dawbid walles and couered wt thack.*
>
> *Item. There is a little overshot mylne goynge wt a little water, dawbid walles and couered wt thak"* (W Brown, 1886, 208-9).

This vividly describes a small, timber framed and thatched water mill set alongside malting, brewing and bolting houses not far from the church and cloister – all very hard to imagine on site today. However, traces of the water engineering survive. Water was drawn from a tiny tributary of Handale Beck via an open leat to a pond on the edge of a second tributary valley. From the pond the water passed by trough onto the wheel and then by culvert under the old road to Liverton. Nowadays the clay bed of the pond is sometimes dry and crazed. The pond does not seem big enough to have been capable of driving a waterwheel, even one *"... goynge wt a little water"*. The lower walls of a building, 47 feet long and with an obvious place for a waterwheel at one end, may be the remains of the mill, kiln house and brew house, a poorer version of the granary ranges at Fountains and Rievaulx.

The mill at Rosedale nunnery was recorded in 1330. In 1570 *"... the site of the late priory of Rosedale with all buildings ... with a water corn mill and four crofts called Kilnegarth, Mylnegarth, Barkerhousegarth and Kirkegarth"* was granted to Ambrose, the Earl of Warwick (NYCRO ZBA 5/1/13, cal). By 1830 little of the nunnery survived and in 1839 the remaining chapel was pulled down to make space for the new parish church. Soon suburban-style stone-built terraces, associated with ironstone mining, obliterated everything except part of a stone turret staircase. However, the roundabout layout of the present-day roads reflects the old precinct wall. A new water corn mill, built in 1853 on the monastic steading, was served by two water leats; one from the Seven and the other, which is almost certainly the original, from the smaller and more manageable Northdale Beck. It ran just outside the line of the west wall of the

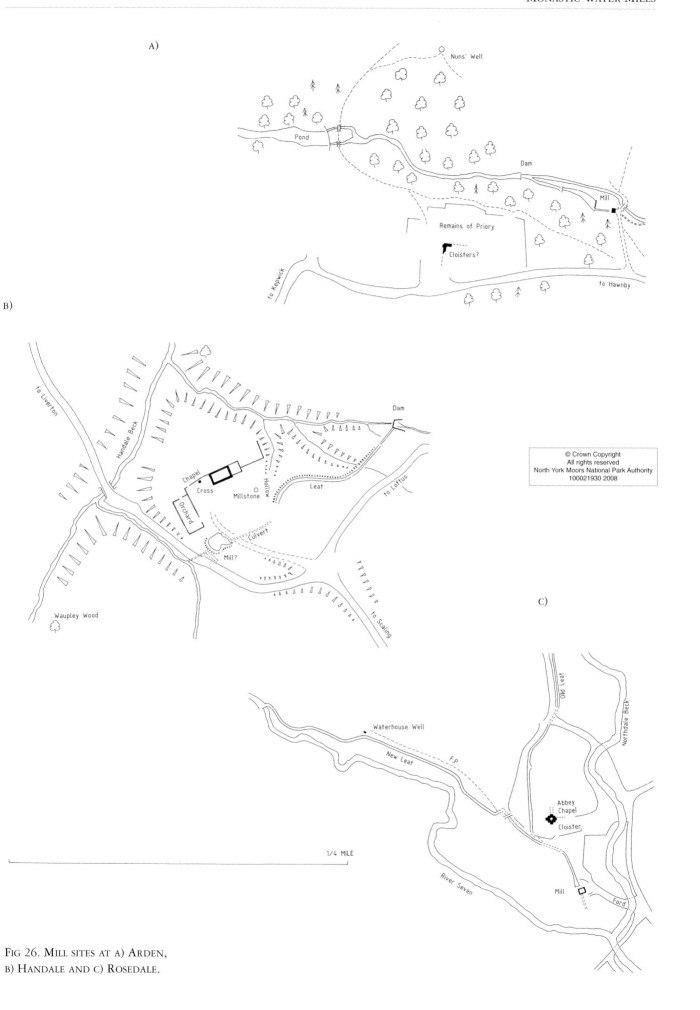

Fig 26. Mill sites at a) Arden,
b) Handale and c) Rosedale.

A)

B)

FIG 27. A) LEAT AND B) MILL AT ROSEDALE (PRE-1850).

graveyard and an engraving of before 1851 shows it running close to the then surviving chapel and the corner turret which still stands today (R H Hayes, 1985, opp 27). In another engraving, by William Richardson, the mill itself is shown, a few years before its demolition, as a low thatched building with overshot waterwheel and an attached mill house (W Richardson, 1855, published in Monasteries of Yorkshire, vol 2, York).

Baysdale nunnery was set up by nuns who had previously migrated from a house at Hutton, near Guisborough, and another at Nunthorpe. While at Hutton they used the mill granted to them by Ralph de Neville. Their arrangements at Nunthorpe are not known, though there is reference to a mill at Nunthorpe in 1231 some time after they had moved on. Their domestic buildings at Baysdale were described at the time of the Dissolution:

"Item. The brewhouse at the upper end of the halle, stone walles, coueryd wt thack.

Item. The kylne house wt a litle maltynge fflore and a little garner in th one ende, alle undir one roofe conteyning xxx ffoote long and xvj ffoote brode, olde stone walles, coueryd wt thak.

Item. The bakehouse almost downe, xxv ffoote longe, xvj ffoote brode, old stone walles and alle coueryd wt thack, decayed.

Item. The ouershot water mylne hardby the gate, xx ffoote longe and xiiij brode and part bordid and coueryd wt thack and the whole in decay so that the seid mylne goith not"

(W Brown, 1886, 327-8).

The fact that the mill was derelict reveals the straitened circumstances to which the Baysdale nuns had been reduced. Nothing remains of their mill, but the description *"hardby the gate"* is illuminating. The main gate probably stood immediately beyond the surviving medieval bridge which carried the old track from Nunthorpe and Great Ayton, via Battersby, into the Priory precinct. The site of the mill may be under the modern farm buildings immediately below the bridge. The course of the leat can be traced in times of very wet weather.

Grosmont Priory near the Murk Esk was set up by the Order of Grandmont in France with the help of a grant by Joanna Fossard (c. 1200) of 200 acres and a mill and fishery at Egton plus the right to graze 40 cows and 500 sheep on her pastures. Just as Handale Priory was not content to use its outlying mill at Scaling, the monks at Grosmont were not content with their mill at Egton, and they built a mill nearer to home. At the Dissolution only five inmates remained and their holdings, valued at £25 18s 6d, included:

"Item. A little ouershot water mylne ... couryd wt thack, which went not this ij yeres. Nota, decayed"

(W Brown, 1886, 213-5).

A further note described an *"olde halle"* by the court side and *"low garner at the ende of the halle ... garner floor over either the garner or the halle and ouershot milne by the same"*. This was another precinct mill, apparently integrated into the main ranges of buildings.

Records of Cistercian houses elsewhere in Yorkshire show that they too had malting floors, corn barns, bolting houses, bakehouses and hay houses within their precincts. In most cases two or more of these functions were contained within one large building. Water driven mills carried out the key process between the corn barn and the bolting house. At Grosmont it may have been integrated into buildings within the outer court. At Handale, Baysdale and Arden the mills were separate buildings near the gate, so that the grain could be delivered by cart without disturbing the peace of the church and cloister.

Today the isolation of the mill at Arden (also to be seen at Rievaulx and Byland where the settlements are later) is a direct result of the original function of the mill as a service to a closed community living in secluded premises. The Cistercians introduced a new form of corn mill in which siting was not determined by the normal medieval three-way relationship between fields, settlement and mill.

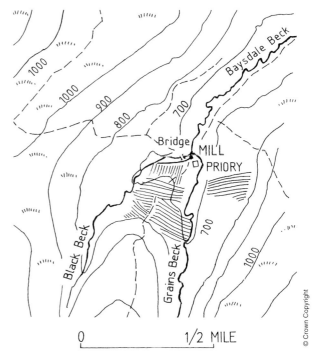

FIG 28. RIGG AND FURROW, BRIDGE AND MILL AT BAYSDALE.

MEDIEVAL WINDMILLS

The first records of north European windmills, variously described as *"molendinum venti", "molendinum ventum", "molendinum de vento", "molendino ad ventum"* or *"molendinum ventrico"*, appeared about one hundred years after the Domesday Survey. The earliest were found in documents from Normandy, Flanders and eastern England. Early English windmills were recorded at Amberley in Sussex and at Swinehead Priory near Boston (both c. 1181), and there is an unambiguous reference to a *"molendinum venti"* at Weedley, in the East Riding, which belonged to the Knights Templar in 1185. Briefly summarised, the earliest references date from about 1180 and there were at least 20 windmills in England by 1200. After 1200 the number of references increased, almost all to windmills to the east of a line from Newcastle-upon-Tyne to the Isle of Wight. This period of innovation lasted just under a century from about 1180 to about 1275. Over most of the country, though not in north east Yorkshire, far fewer new windmills were built after 1300 following a downturn in the weather and even fewer were built after the Black Death in 1349.

There was a close match between the siting of early English windmills and the reclamation of marshlands. For instance, by the end of the thirteenth century wind powered corn mills outnumbered water mills in and around the Fens of East Anglia, Cambridgeshire and Huntingdonshire by about 2:1 (R Holt, 1988, 22-27). It was impossible to build water mills on the sluggish Fenland streams and, as a result, wind power played an important role in supporting settlements on the margins of these former marshes. Windmills were less used on dry chalk and limestone uplands where they might also have been expected. For instance, only six windmills were listed in Bishop Hatfield's survey (1380) of his lands in Northumberland and Durham, a holding which contained what might appear to be good windmilling country on the magnesian limestone east coast.

North Yorkshire has never been regarded as windmilling country but, in fact, there were over two dozen windmills in the region in medieval times, most around

FIG 29. MEDIEVAL WINDMILL SITES IN NORTH EAST YORKSHIRE.

the Tees estuary but with a few on the east coast and in the Vale of Pickering.

The Tees estuary

The Tees estuary lowlands had high values per acre by 1292, meaning that there was a good deal of arable farming (B Waites, 1997, 74). Yet there were very few water mills and it was here that the biggest group of north east Yorkshire windmills was built. To the south of the river the old highway of 'Ladgate' ran from Yarm to Marske along the fringes of the flat land, linking together the villages of Stainton, Marton, Ormesby, Normanby, Eston, Lackenby, Lazenby, Wilton and Kirkleatham. Each has elongated township boundaries running north through the marshes to the tidal river bank. Some of these old established villages had windmills. The precise sites are generally not known but at Yarm, Thornaby, Tollesby and Marton (and elsewhere at Guisborough, Newton Bewley and Hartlepool) the windmills were built within their settlement boundaries.

On the other hand, probably the earliest windmill was built at some distance from the parent village of Kirkleatham, on the coast at East Coatham. The earliest references, thought to date from before 1200, occur in grants of salt works situated near the mouth of the Tees estuary (Gis Chart, Surtees soc, vol 89, 114-6). Several cotes had been granted to Gisborough Priory, including one by Roger son of William de Thocotes situated close to the "Mill". Hugh Delblel had also given "the site of his mill in Cotum and the mill itself". A slightly later document in the series referred to the "molendinum Prioris". At that time East Coatham consisted of a low spit of sand dunes, between the North Sea and the Tees estuary, which protected a number of saltwater creeks and lagoons with their salt cotes. Big fields had been created between Coatham and the village of Kirkleatham. The references do not specifically describe a windmill, but there was no flow of beck water for driving a water-wheel. It is possible, of course, that there may have been an early tide mill on one of the creeks, later found to be unsustainable. In any case, there was certainly a wind driven corn mill in Kirkleatham by 1340 and also at the time of the Dissolution.

Many references to windmills resulted from grants to monasteries, particularly on the south bank of the Tees estuary, where early windmills were granted to Gisborough Priory. Windmills appear to have been built not only by the powerful de Brus and Percy families but also by sub tenants such as Delblel. The windmill of Ormesby, listed in a Gisborough Priory Rent Roll (1280), was given to the Priory by a de Percy. Another Priory Rent Roll (c. 1300) included the tithe worth 2s per annum of a windmill in Acklam. In this case, the owner had retained the mill itself. A windmill at Thornaby belonged to William de Thorodby in 1275 but soon afterwards Gisborough Priory was recorded as holding the "manor of Thornaby" with "lands, tenements and wind-mill". Gisborough Priory also had a windmill in the town of Guisborough itself. It was first recorded in a document of 1346, which states that Philip de Garton, son of Sibilla, held one toft and one croft and three acres on the "north side of the vill of Gisborough" and half an acre in the "field of the windmill" (Surtees Soc, vol 86, 75).

The de Brus family retained at least two of the most valuable windmills on the south bank of the Tees estuary, one at each end of Ladgate. Their windmill at Yarm, on the lowest bridging point over the Tees, was worth the goodly rental of 30s per annum in 1272. This windmill had a continuous record for centuries and was shown, for instance, on Thomas Meynell's map of 1658 as "the manorial mill", standing on a rise to the north of the church and near the old Market Green (J W Wardell,

1957, opp 72). The de Brus family also kept their wind-mill at Marske. In 1272 part of the estate passed to Walter de Fauconberg and his inquisition post mortem (1304) listed four water mills and one windmill together worth 7s. The windmill was listed again in 1319, and in the inquisition post mortem for John de Fauconberg (1349) it was listed as being worth 13s 4d "before the mortality" (ie the Black Death). This windmill was probably sited on the flat lands to the west of Marske, possibly near Ryehills farm which is linked directly by Green Lane to a point called Mill Howl on the coast near Redcar. Further documents noted the "windmill of the Fauconbergs at Marske" (1349) and "the profits of a windmill called Rydkermyll, otherwise Leymilne" (1408). After the de Brus era this mill, too, was released to the Priory. A windmill in the 'West Field' of Marske was released at the Dissolution and soon afterwards the farm of a windmill on the estate of Christopher Conyers in Marske was reduced in value by one mark from 40s to 26s 8d.

There were also windmills north of the Tees estuary. The building of a windmill at Norton was referred to among payments listed in the Roll of Bishop Bec in 1307 and again in 1310 (Surtees Soc, vol 25, 25-8, 37). On the neighbouring lands of Billinghamshire John Fossor's accounts referred to a water mill at "Belu" (Billingham) and a mill at "Oventon Belu" (Newton Bewley) (L F Salzman, 1952, App A, 392-3). The latter, built presumably to serve fields on newly drained land to the east of Billingham, can only have been a windmill. It must have been built between 1341, when Fossor became Prior, and 1365 when the windmill at Newton Bewley was first mentioned in the Halmote Rolls (L Still & J Southeran, 1966, 48).

There was another windmill on the magnesian lime-stone outcrop at Hart, to the west of Hartlepool. The village of Hart and the township of Hartlepool had been added to the Skelton holdings by the second Robert de Brus. When he died in 1141, his lands were divided between two sons, Adam who got the Skelton estates in north Yorkshire and Robert (Lord of Annandale) who got Hartlepool. The Annandale branch kept Hartlepool until 1306 when Robert the Bruce had himself crowned king of Scotland and, for his pains, his lands in Hartlepool were confiscated and granted to Robert de Clifford. Clifford was killed in the battle of Bannockburn in 1314. Bishop Kelloe of Durham then seized the lands and let the farm of the town of Hartlepool and the "ovens, watermills, and mill of Hart" to one of his bailiffs, Richard Mason, at £84 per annum (C Sharp, 1816, 36). There is little water at Hart and the "mill of Hart" must have been driven by wind.

There was one more windmill, at Hartlepool itself. A Franciscan Friary had been established on the Headland of Hartlepool before 1240 but by 1380 the Friars had gone and the Bishop had taken over their possessions including *"herring house, common oven, windmill and tolls within the borough"*. There was still a windmill just outside the walls of Old Hartlepool in 1558 when a new owner, Cuthbert Conyers, left *"... the Freers (Friarage) and mill and lands in Hartlepool for life to his two sons ..."* (VCH vol 3, 264).

In summary, there were at least 11 windmills around the Tees estuary in early medieval times. One belonged to the Bishop of Durham and another to the Prior of Durham. Those on the south bank were built by the de Brus or Percy families or by lesser landholders, and most were eventually granted to Gisborough Priory.

South of the moors

The Knights Templar had a windmill at Foulbridge near Snainton in the Vale of Pickering. The Templars had arrived in Yorkshire by 1140 and are on record as having three of the earliest windmills in the country, at Weedley in the East Riding (1185), at Grimsby and at Dunwich in Suffolk (B A Lees, 1935, 131). At Foulbridge they had an *"empty windmill"* in 1273 (VCH vol 2, 428). The windmill was recorded again in 1307. Foulbridge was an isolated spot near the Derwent, surrounded by carrs which would have been wetlands when the Templars arrived. The name indicates that it was an early bridging point between the north and east Ridings.

A windmill at Appleton was mentioned in a claim made by Mabilla, the widow of Philip de Fauconberg, against St Mary's Abbey, York, in 1266. There is a problem with the location because there are three Appletons in the district. The only one with any supporting evidence is Appleton le Moors where a track leading to Lastingham passes over a steep scarp near Spaunton where two fields were still named *"Great Windmill Field"* and *"Little Windmill Field"* on the tithe map of about 1840 (R H Hayes, 1996, 11).

"Willelmo de Wyndmullen" of New Malton was taxed 19d in the Lay Subsidy of 1301 (W Brown, 1896). The use of the plural 'mullen' is interesting. Nicholas de Stapilton granted a messuage and half a carucate of land with a windmill in the vill of *"Lengesby"* (Slingsby) to Malton Priory in the mid-thirteenth century. They may have kept this mill for only a few years for in 1301 it was listed along with *"two watermills under one roof"* in the inquisition of a lay land holder. Malton Priory also had a large grange at Swinton where a windmill worth 13s 4d per annum was demised to Edmund Rasyn, the former tenant, after the Dissolution, and they had another windmill on their grange at Amotherby. In 1240 Walter son of Robert and his wife Avive granted to Henry the Abbot of Byland *"... the site of a windmill on their land in Leistorp so that the Abbot may build a windmill at his pleasure"* (YAS Rec Ser 67, 61-2). *"Leistorp"* is identified as a lost village on the site of Laysthorpe Lodge between Oswaldkirk and Stonegrave, to the south of Helmsley. In

1316 the Hospital of St Leonard in York granted a messuage and croft in Middleton (near Pickering) with a windmill for 5s per annum to Richard son of Thomas de Boynton (YAS, Rec. Ser., vol 65 Deeds 4, 107).

The late date of some north east Yorkshire windmills

The North East had particular problems during the early fourteenth century when Northumberland, Durham and Cumbria were repeatedly raided by the Scots. Stockton was attacked in 1325 and at various times the Scots reached as far south as Fountains Abbey, Knaresborough, Ripon and Byland Abbey. The crisis was not finally resolved until the battle of Neville's Cross in 1346. Some first references to windmills in the North East date from that half century and others from after the Black Death in 1349. These include windmills at Acklam (1300), Marton (1301), Marske (1304), Norton (1307), Hart (1314), Scarborough (1314), Kirklevington (1314), Whitby (1316), Middleton near Pickering (1316), Normanby (1324), Guisborough (1346), Newton Bewley (1341-1365), Hemlington (1353), West Coatham (1367), Eston (1368) and Hartlepool (1380).

Three of these windmills were built by the Percy family. No doubt the Scottish raiders would not hesitate to pick out the properties of the hated Percys of Northumberland and Yorkshire, including their water mills, for destruction. Percy resources were stretched. In 1321, for instance, their water mill at Kildale *"... was totally destroyed by a great inundation"* and John who was the son of Arnald de Percy was not able to rebuild it for two years *"... owing to the heavy price he had paid in ransom to the Scots"* (Gis Chart, Surtees Soc 68, 582). As a result, there was a dispute with Katherine de Meynill who had previously been given two marks per annum from the rent of this mill and now received nothing. In spite of the hardships, however, the Percys were building windmills at this same period. A windmill which Henry de Percy had in Scarborough at the time of his death in 1314 had not been recorded in earlier times. In the same inquisition he was recorded as having a windmill worth 26s 8d at Kirklevington, and this was almost certainly a new windmill because in 1281 two water mills had been listed but no windmill. The new windmill should be seen in the context of a substantial fall in the taxable value of Levington between 1301 and 1327, resulting from raids by the Scots (W Brown, 1896, 81-2).

The Percys were also at the heart of a dispute with the Abbot of Whitby over the water-driven Rigg mill, near Whitby (1316). The following is a translation of the final agreement:

"It being contained in a certain indenture made between the Abbot and the ancestors of the said

Alexander (de Percy) that the ancestors agreed to pay unto the Abbot and Convent of Whitby half a mark yearly for all that land reaching from Schalmeryg to Katewig ... and for keeping up the pond or dam for the water corn mill between Sethil and Rethrig: they were so far mislead by malice that they wholly threw down and took away the aforesaid mill, erected a gold mill (molendinum aurarium) in its stead. And thus was the said farm of about half a mark entirely lost for eight years or thereabouts. At length they humbly begged of the Abbot to allow them to build up again the aforesaid mill in its ancient place, and they would pay the usual rent as was reasonable, for ever. In which they were humoured and all arrearages being forgiven them, the mill was built and the aforesaid farm entirely restored at the Feast of St Martin in the winter, anno 1316" (L Charlton, 1779, 241-2).

Charlton went on to discuss the arts of making gold from other metals and also the craft of rolling gold leaf. However, he was mistaken in his translation of *"molendinum aurarium"* as '*gold mill*'. Some later authors have claimed that *"aura"* was derived from *"wind"*, not gold (G Young, 1817, 321). The term *"molendinum aurerium"* was noted in a list of old terms describing windmills by R Bennett and J Elton (1898, 237) and E J Kealey collected the term *"molendinum aurum"* from French descriptions of windmills (1987, 43-4). B A Lees collected a reference to *"Alexander de moledino aureo"* at Cogges, near Oxford in 1279 (B A Lees, 1935, cxix). On the other hand a modern translation gives *"aurarius"* as a noun meaning *"patron"*, ie someone who provided the resources for building a *"master's mill"* (R E Latham, 1965). The real story seems to have been that the Percys having given Rigg mill to Whitby Abbey in the early twelfth century and then rented it back were now at odds with the Abbot over the rent. They decided to abandon the water mill and to build another mill (*"molendiunum aurarium"*) both to save themselves the rent and also to raise revenue of their own. Of course, in doing so they deprived the Abbey of its rental for the old water mill. On the face of it the 1316 agreement seems to be couched in humiliating terms but in fact the Percys only agreed to rebuild the old water mill and were not asked to make good the arrears nor to dismantle their new mill. Since there is no other evidence of a new water mill in this region it is likely that the Percy's new mill was a windmill.

Other landholders were also building windmills in the troubled years of the early fourteenth century. For example, a windmill described as *"ruinous"* was listed in the inquisition post mortem (1367) for Ralph Bulmer of Wilton who is known to have fortified his old manor house (now Wilton Castle) against the Scots (PRO 135/192). If his windmill was ruinous in 1367 it is more than likely it had been built during the time of the raids. Since there is no subsequent history it is also likely that it was abandoned in favour of a much more powerful water mill near Wilton Castle after the troubles were over.

There were four other late windmills in the same area. A windmill worth 13s 4d was first mentioned as being in the possession of John de Blaby at Marton in 1301 and another windmill, in Normanby, belonged to the Wyrkesal family in 1324 and 1331. A *"weak windmill"* worth 3s per annum at Hemlington was listed in the inquisition post mortem for John, Earl of Kent (1353) and a windmill in Eston was listed in the inquisition post mortem for Hugh de Eston (1368).

Town windmills were also a feature in the North East at this period, particularly in Newcastle, Sunderland, York and Scarborough. For instance, the first parliament of Edward I (1272) put an end to the business of Jewish money lenders in York and, as a result, a windmill worth two marks annually, mortgaged by Walter Le Espec to Isaac the Jew, was seized by the King (G Benson, 1919, vol 2, 39). There was a windmill in Scarborough *"newly built"* out of the money of the burgesses (1320). A further reference in 1330 listed *"four watermills and a windmill, £16 per annum"* belonging to the burgesses of the town.

Windmills were probably built in north east Yorkshire simply because they were easily farmed or rented, thereby producing a guaranteed revenue for the lord. This would be particularly valuable for making good the losses caused by the Scots and, later, for compensating for loss of revenue after the Black Death. The values of most water mills did not decline following these disasters, but this stability was only achieved by farming them out rather than continuing to run them as demesne mills. Nevertheless, it may sometimes have been easier to build a windmill than to convert an old established water mill from manorial to rented status. In fact, the economics of building a windmill were quite favourable. The average cost at the end of the twelfth century was in the order of £10 (R Holt, 1988, 176-7) and with the returns then available outlay could be recovered within a decade. The late windmills in north east Yorkshire were not randomly placed. The two Kirklevington water mills had served one of the richest grain growing lands in the region and their replacement with one corn mill, one fulling mill and one windmill made good sense. The other late windmills were in the arable-rich Vale of Cleveland and near the ports of Whitby and Scarborough.

Mill Fields

The story of north east Yorkshire windmills has been built up from a limited number of contemporary records. One further source of information lies in field names on later maps. For instance, *"Mill Bank"* on the Headland at Hartlepool kept its name long after the Friars' windmill had disappeared. Similarly, the existence of *"unum molendinum ventricum"* at Ingleby Arncliffe listed in 1434 is confirmed by the reference to *"mylnehille"* at the same date and *"Mill Hill"* in later times. Other old 'mill' field names at Marton, Dromonby and Appleton-le-Moors are also associated with windmills known about from other sources. The *"Mill Hill"* in the marshes at Shepherd's House to the west of Newport, near Middlesbrough, appears on one map only; Dodds, *"Plan of Freholds, hereditaments belonging to Thomas Hustler Esq, 30 April 1860"* (TA U/S/274). The explanation may be that the field lay on a former track leading from a windmill at Ayresome to a landing point on the Tees at Newport.

A group of field names at Yearby near Kirkleatham was recorded in *"A Plan of the Parish and Manor of Kirkleatham"* made in 1774 when the old open fields were *"recently"* enclosed. These were *"Mill Flatt"*, *"Little Mill Flatt"* and *"Great Mill Flatt"*, adjacent to each other to the east of the village at NZ 605 212 (NYCRO ZMI 71). The mill was shown as a post mill with round house, though indistinctly, on the engraving of Kirkleatham c 1700 by L Knyff and I Kipp. *"Charles Turner Esqr, his seat att Kirkleatham in Cleveland in the County of Yorke"*. There is disturbance in these fields.

Field names at Newby and Tollesby identify windmills unknown from other sources. A particularly interesting group is recorded on the hill to the south east of the village, church and moated manor house at Easington in East Cleveland. The information is on a map of *"The Manor, estates of Easington, Boulby and also Grinkle Park, in the parish of Easington in the North Riding of the County of York"*, 1865 (Grinkle Estate papers, Watson, Burton, Cooper, and Jackson, solicitors, Newcastle-on-Tyne). The names were *"Mill Field"*, *"High Mill Field"*, *"South Mill Field"*, *"Long Mill Field"* and, not far away, *"Mill Pasture"*, *"High Mill Pasture"* and *"Low Mill Pasture"*. Also, on the steep sided valley on the flanks of High Rigg, separate from the rest, there was the name *"Mill Banks"*. The first group indicates a

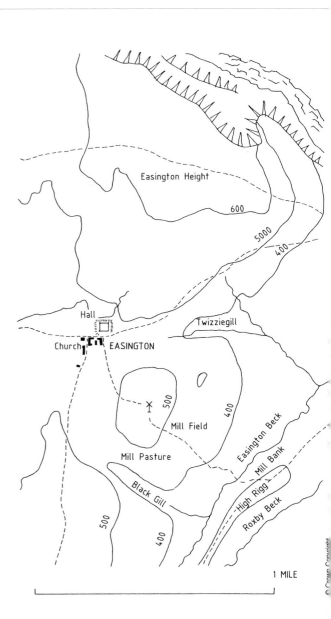

FIG 30. EARLY FIELDS AT EASINGTON.

large medieval open field (later divided into four). The second group marks the site of a medieval pasture. *"Mill Bank"* marks an old track across Easington Beck to the old routeway along High Rigg to Scaling. There is no other historical evidence for a windmill. Today the nineteenth century hedgerows of Easington have been rooted out and the landscape restored to its medieval appearance but the ploughing has also obliterated any sign of the windmill.

TECHNOLOGY

Mill lanes

Early nineteenth century engravings of packhorses, near Cock mill and Raindale mill, show scenes very similar to what must have been commonplace near every mill in medieval times. Although the corn (a still living seed) could be stored for a year or more, the broken meal would soon begin to deteriorate in the damp conditions of medieval dwellings and, therefore, grain had to be carried to the mill on a routine basis, at least once each week.

Consequently, mills would be built as near as possible to the village but, nevertheless, many villagers faced a long trudge along well-worn mill 'trods' or tracks. Today, some of these mill tracks survive as metalled roads. For instance, the modern roads of Hutton Rudby are laid on the old tracks from the medieval open fields to the village and mills (P Hastings, 1980, 13). Similarly, the roads of Commondale follow the ancient web of tracks converging on the medieval mill site (J K Harrison, 1995), and the network of roads linking Seaton, Hinderwell, Borrowby and Newton Mulgrave is centred on Dalehouse mill. The modern road from Newton-under-Roseberry runs across Green Hills to Pinchinthorpe and then via Galley Hill to the site of the medieval Hutton mill at the west end of Guisborough. Similarly, the old mill track from the centre of Guisborough to the water mill at Howl Beck is under the tarmac of Northgate and at Skelton the old track to the mill is now under the road leading from the north east corner of the Green to the mill site.

In other cases, mill tracks survive very much as they were in medieval times, for example, the old track from Fadmoor to Hold Cauldron mill running through a field still called 'Millgate' (R H Hayes, 1969, 9). Others have all but disappeared. The mill track at Kildale went out of use when it was cut by the railway and is now scarcely visible and the old track from Newton-under-Roseberry to the mill at Upsall is now no more than a line of field boundaries near Snow Hall and Spite Farm. One section of the lane from Handale to Scaling mill has almost disappeared.

The routes of some other old mill tracks have been preserved in a way which is distinctive, though not unique, to the North York Moors. In times of bad weather during autumn and winter the tracks would have been turned into quagmires if they were not to some extent drained and made up with stones. In later times, some were engineered into 'causeways', with heavy stone blocks set edge to edge and 'bridgestanes' over seepages and becks. One such causeway runs down Danby Dale from near the church to Howe mill. Another links the line of medieval assarts along Farndale East Side to Farndale Low mill. Yet another runs through Goathland village to Goathland mill. A fourth runs through the woods from the banks of the Esk to Cock mill. Of course, not all causeways were linked with mill sites and it could

Fig 31. Pannier way near Cock mill (Shaw Jeffrey).

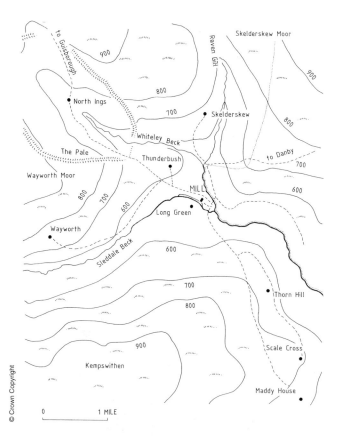

© Crown Copyright

FIG 32. MILL LANES IN COMMONDALE.

be argued that mills were often on natural beck crossing points which would, in any case, have attracted trackways. Nevertheless, it would be difficult to believe that some of these causeways did not originate in the medieval tracks used regularly by generations of villagers on their way to the mill.

Water mills

The medieval latin term 'molendinum' was made up of 'mola' (mill) and 'domus' (house) and a distinction can be made between the 'mylnes' which ground the grain and the 'mylne houses' which sheltered them (R Bennett and J Elton, 1898, 107).

The few surviving medieval illustrations of English water 'mylne houses' show them as built with either timber frames or stone walls. Roofs were 'thatched', a term which could sometimes include covering with stone slabs or tiles. Pits for waterwheel and cog wheel were lined with either timber or masonry. Floors were left earthen. Medieval mylnehouses probably needed constant repairs because of the water flowing past their foundations and the vibration from the gearing and top millstones. The frequency of repairs coupled with the difficulty of transporting heavy materials meant that stone and timber would be looked for as near the site as possible.

Only three descriptions of medieval mill houses have

been located for water mills in this region, all quite late.

● Handale Abbey (1538) *"... a little ouershot mylne goyng wyt a little water daubed walles couereyd wt thack"* (W Brown, 1886, 221).

● Baysdale Abbey (1538) *"... the ouershot water mylne ... xx ffoote longe and xiiij brode ... stone walles and parte bordid and coueryd wt thak"* (W Brown, 1886, 327).

● Norton (1538). Costs for repairs to mill included 4d for *"part of wall wattled"* (Bennett and B Vyner, 1979, 17).

Both Handale and Norton mills were timber-built and daubed while Baysdale mill had stone walls. In the moorland dales, where sandstone outcropped in every edge and where foundations could be found to support heavy walls, mills would be built of stone while timber framed mills would be built where stone was not available and where foundations, on boulder clay for instance, were less secure. The mill at Caldecotes on the banks of the Tees estuary would certainly have been timber built and the mill at Howkeld in Ryedale is known to have been timber framed in the eighteenth century.

Today, early timber framed domestic dwellings survive only to the south and west of a boundary more or less along the southern and western edges of the North York Moors. Most are in the Vale of York. In the region covered by this survey the only mill which contains any timber framing is at Thornton-le-Street, and this only for part of a post-medieval internal wall between the waterwheels and the hurst. To the north and east of the 'timber framing' boundary, north east Yorkshire and south Durham falls within the region where houses were cruck-built in medieval times (and later). These had an internal structure of A-frames, made up of pairs of crucks or siles, which was independent of the non load-bearing walls built round it. The word 'sile' is a north of England term for 'cruck' or 'crooked blade'. The mill at Osmotherley was re-built with siles in 1602. Re-used crucks survive in Arden mill and formerly at Great Ayton Grange mill while in-situ crucks survive in the mill house at Costa High mill.

With a width of 14 feet and thick dry-stone *"walles"* the span at Baysdale mill would be about 10 feet. This would have been adequate for a single set of millstones, but a waterwheel of between 10 and 12 feet could not have been fitted inside the span and would therefore have been set outside the building, on either a long wall or a gable wall. The nicely documented 10 foot span at Baysdale can be used as a yardstick when looking at one or two other mill buildings. For instance, the outside dimension of the surviving building of Cock mill is 11 feet 6 inches and the original span (before its conversion to a dwelling) would, therefore, have been less than 10 feet. The span at Kildale would also have been small,

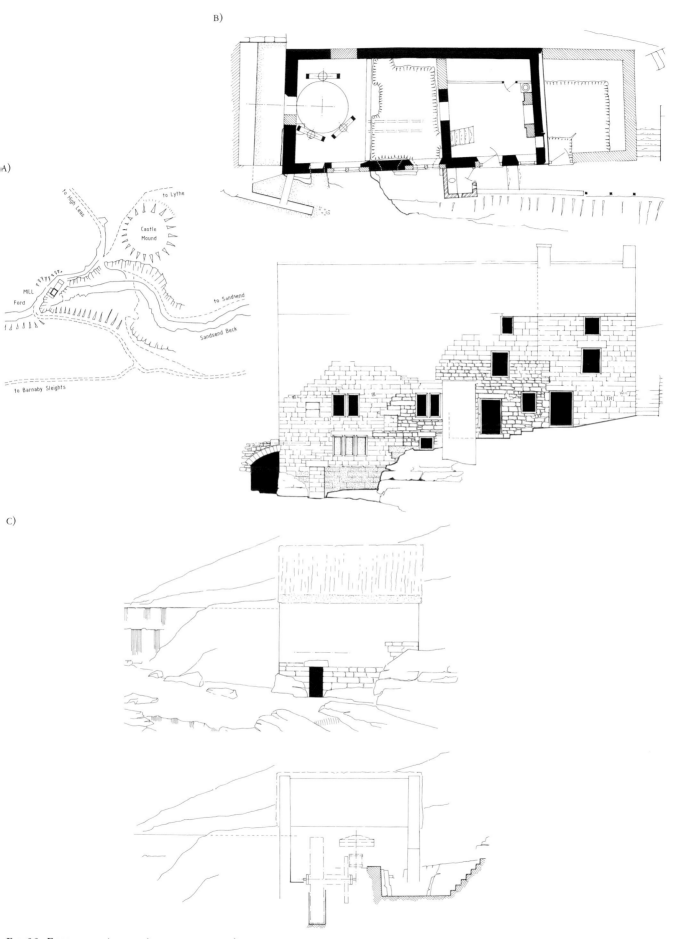

FIG 33. FOSS MILL, A) SITE, B) REMAINS, AND C) CONJECTURED DEVELOPMENT.

since the platform on which it was built is roughly 15 feet square and tightly constrained between steep banks on two sides and shale faces down to the water on the other two. Goathland mill was enlarged during the nineteenth century by extending the building over and beyond the old wheel pit but the ground plan of an earlier mill can still be detected as a chiselled bedrock ledge 15 feet 4 inches by 12 feet 6 inches.

Even the oldest standing stonework in mills in north east Yorkshire cannot be positively identified as medieval. Five or six stepped courses of good-quality dressed masonry in the facade of Foss mill are clearly very old. As built, this wall was not more than 16 feet long with a narrow tail opening (now blocked) for a small external waterwheel at one end. At the other end, now buried inside the later range of buildings, there is an ancient set of stone steps. This now leads from the ground floor of the mill into the house, but it was originally outside the mill, leading from an external doorway. Perhaps these features were part of the medieval mill.

In contrast to the cramped ground plans at Handale, Cock and Kildale mills the space at Cistercian precinct mills may have been more generous. Surviving spans at Lastingham (14 feet 9 inches), Arden (16 feet), Caydale (16 feet 3 inches), Coulton (19 feet 3 inches), Rievaulx (21 feet 9 inches, and originally much bigger) and Oldstead (22 feet 3 inches) are all more generous than would have been needed for a single pair of millstones. There is no proof that the walls of these mills stand on the medieval foundations but on the other hand these survivors are clearly ancient and, taken as a group, the evidence is suggestive.

Windmills

The many medieval illustrations of windmills show a standard design consisting of a wooden 'buck' or cabin pivoting on an upright post which was either sunk into the ground or supported on a trestle of 'cross trees' and 'quarter bars' (stays). Bucks were manhandled into the wind by means of tailpoles. Wind shafts were shown as horizontal. The sails were short and squarish, framed in wood and covered with canvas. The uniformity in content and style of these illustrations suggests that they were copied one from another rather than drawn from real life. Likewise, the fragment of carved stone cornice at Rievaulx Abbey showing farmers approaching a windmill is more likely to have been copied from a manuscript illustration than drawn from any windmill owned by the Abbey.

The first European windmill post-dated the first Roman water mills by at least 1200 years, yet most of the techniques were transferable. The jointed wooden frames of the bucks were little different from those used in timber-framed water mills, while the cog-wheels and lanterns, though over the millstones rather than under,

FIG 34. POST MILL CARVING FROM A FRIEZE AT RIEVAULX ABBEY.

were borrowed without modification from water mill practice. The wind is a more fickle and dangerous source of energy than water and there were no precedents for the techniques for handling the variable speed and direction. The canvas covered sails were unlike anything which had gone before and so were the pivoting bucks.

Windmills were highly vulnerable. At best they had a life-span of, perhaps, fifty years between rebuilds, though the main post might be used over and over again. At worst they could be blown down in heavy gales. A mill lost in this way would end up as firewood and the only archaeological evidence left would be its millstones and, perhaps, the cross trees buried in the ground. As a result, archaeological evidence of medieval windmills is scarce (J R Earnshaw, 1973, 19-41). What little is known about medieval windmills in this region is derived from a limited amount of historical evidence; the surviving windmill platform on Thornaby Green, a possible windmill mound at Pinchinthorpe and the relics of an early, but post-medieval, windmill at Elwick.

In 1588 the Dutch surveyor, Roberto Dromeslawers, made a pictorial map of the harbour of Hartlepool for the benefit of navigators (BM Maps 186 h 1 (4)). This showed the old walled town on the Headland and two post windmills, one the Friarage mill and the other across the Slake, on the sand spit known as Stranton (later Middleton). Thirty years later, in 1618 John Gibbon's *"Plan of the Scite, Cell and Towne of Middlesborugh"* showed a post windmill with squarish sails, in Ayresome to the south of the hamlet of Middlesbrough, near a track crossing at *"Belwether Cross"* (PRO MPE 524; Middlesbrough's History in Maps, CTLHS, 1980, 1). Unlike the Hartlepool mills this was shown to be standing on a mound. Such mounds may have resulted from burying the cross trees for stability or they may have been made to provide a dry platform round the mill. At Thornaby there is a platform, roughly 45 feet in diameter, surrounded by a drainage ditch. The windmill at Whitby Abbey was described as *"supra montem"* (G Young, 1817, 93), sometimes translated as being on a mound. However, a contemporary reference to Thornton-on-the-Hill, in which Richard Cholmley of Bransby *"... made entrye in the manor house of*

Thornton super montem" shows that the description may simply have meant 'on the hill' (Memorandum Book of Richard Cholmeley of Bransby, 1602-23, NYCRO pub 44, 1988, 48).

The Halmote Court Rolls of the Prior of Durham contain information on the sails used at Newton Bewley windmill (L Still and J Southeran, 1966, 35). In 1368 John Miryman and Robert Milner of Norton were confirmed as the new tenants of the water mill at Norton and the windmill at Newton Bewley for a customary rent of £23 per annum. Part of the agreement was that they were to find the *"sailclathes and what pertains to the farmers"* and *"the lord* (Prior) *shall find the rest"*. In 1370 it was agreed that the sailcloths the Prior had recovered from the previous tenant, John Fair-jon, for 20s had deteriorated to the extent of 4s. Therefore, the new tenants, Miryman and Milner, were to pay the reduced sum of 16s for them (L Still and J Southeran, 1966, 52). Canvas sails were clearly a costly item and at Newton Bewley the tenants were required to provide them.

Only one site has revealed early relics which may have been similar to those of medieval times. The words 'stob' and 'stoup' were north eastern words for a heavy post. They have the same origin as the term 'stubbekvarn' (literally post querns) used for post windmills in Sweden. The word 'stob' was used at Elwick and at Yarm (J W Wardell, 1957, 176) to describe post windmills. Relics of the 'stob' mill at Elwick, still standing in the 1930s, consisted of the post, cross trees, quarter bars and crown tree. Elwick 'stob' was an object of curiosity and was, for example, painted by Carl Wood soon before it was pulled down (Usher Gallery, Lincoln). Several local people remember an early date carved into one of the quarter bars. After demolition the Elwick timbers were

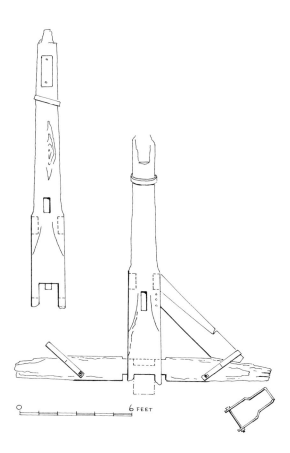

FIG 36. TIMBERS FROM THE 'STOB' MILL AT ELWICK.

dragged away and left under a hedge and when examined many years later there was no sign of the dated timber. However, there was other evidence pointing to an early date in that the remaining timbers were considerably smaller than those of surviving old post mills in other parts of the country. The fact that millers and farmers with their horses are depicted as very large in medieval illustrations has always been put down to artistic licence but this may be only partly true. These mills may, in fact have been very small. Surviving early post mills, for instance at Bourn, Madingley and Great Gransden in Cambridgeshire have cross trees of 21 feet in length, give or take a few inches. By contrast the Elwick cross trees were only 14 feet long. The stob was correspondingly small, with a length of 14 feet, as compared with 14 feet 6 inches at Bourn, 15 feet 6 inches at Six Mile Bottom and 17 feet 6 inches at Madingley.

Materials

The shaft for a medieval waterwheel was probably some 12 feet long and 20 inches square. The wind shaft for a post windmill was similarly massive while the main structural post might have been up to 15 feet long and 2 feet 2 inches square. Taking into account the diagonal measure of a square-section shaft and allowing for the cutting away of bark and sap wood then the millwright had to find an oak trunk of about 3 feet in diameter,

FIG 35. WINDMILLS AT HARTLEPOOL AND MIDDLETON (DROMESLAUER) AND AYRESOME (GIBBONS).

straight grained and free of big knots. Observation of surviving woodland in the North York Moors reveals that today there are few standing trees big enough to provide such a timber. In fact, such 'standard' trees suitable for providing 'great timbers' were probably quite rare even in medieval times and, as such, like all other natural resources would be subject to manorial control. For instance, 'great timbers' were taken from Spaunton Forest to repair Kirkby Misperton mill in 1140 (YAS Rec ser vol 1, 476). At Baxby in 1275 *"Henry II granted one oak yearly from the Forest of Galtres for the repair of* (the) *Mill"* (Yorks Inq p m, YAS I, 166). Another document shows that where suitable stone was not available timber was also used for dams. In 1226 Richard de Sproxton *"... by view and delivery of the Abbot's foresters may have timber in that wood for building and repairing the mill dam of Sproxton, as much and as often as necessary ..."* (Riev Chart, Surtees Soc, 383, note 35). Another document gave him a similar right in the woods to the west of Helmsley except that he was not allowed to take oaks, holly, sycamore or ash trees (YAS Rec Ser 62, Yorkshire Fines, 1218-31, 82). Joanne Fossard's grant of Egton mill to Grosmont Priory was confirmed by her husband Robert de Turnham, also granting *"... out of his forest at Egton sufficient main timber, both oak and alder, for the necessary repairs to the sd mill"* (J Graves, 1808, 287-8). The Roll of Bishop Beck of Durham records Robert de Teviedale *"... plying his trade in the moving shadows"* at Norton (1307), a mysterious activity which seems to be explained three years later when there was a payment of 20s to the same Robert from the Bishop's purse for cutting wood for *"... making a mill to go by wind"* (Surtees Soc, vol 25, 25-8, 37). *"Teviedale"* was an old name, derived from an association with the Percys of Northumberland, for land near Clack Lane at Osmotherley where the Bishop owned woodland. These timbers were being transported some 16 miles to the new windmill. The average cost of building a windmill in the early fourteenth century was about £10 and so Robert received one tenth part of this for the timber. Much later, in 1562, William Methan *"... felled and caryd awaye in Dawby (Dalby) sixe Timber trees of oak"* for the *"... Reparinge of the Queen's nether mylne of Pyckeringe and by warrant of John Braddel, Surveyor of the Queenes woodde there"* (R W Jeffrey, 1931, 289-90). Still in the old tradition, in 1602, Tobias Matthew the Bishop of Durham wrote an instruction to his woodman that *"These are to require and authorise you to deliver unto Thomas Todde, bearer hereof, out of my woods of Osmotherley called Clack Wood, two trees such as shall meet for his use reserving the trees lately marked there and also one crooked tree growing in the loning"* (lane) *"there meet to be a pair of siles. Given at Awkland Manor, 19 May 1602. To my keeper of Clackwoods or his deputy"* (Durham Univ Lib, ASC CCB Box 92 29,220830.8). These timbers were

for the Bishop's mill at Osmotherley. The document shows that a new set of crucks was being set up at the mill. Soon after, there was a second authorisation, *"To the Keeper of my wood in Clack or his deputy. These are to require and authorise you to deliver out of my woods in Clack unto Thomas Todd, fermour of my water corn milne of Osmotherley, three old dryed crab trees and one crooked oak tree fit for the trindler and bucket bordes and one eller tree for bushes toward the repairs of my said mile"* (Durham Univ Lib ASC CCB). In the case of the crab wood, probably for making cogs, the time of year for felling, normally late wintertime, did not matter since the trees were already dead. The crooked oak, in this case, would be used for the felloes of the water-wheel.

Waterwheels and wind sails were small and may have lacked the power to drive heavy millstones but, on the other hand, single stage gearing made it difficult to drive millstones at an adequate peripheral speed. One solution might have been to use large diameter millstones but with the runner stone tapered from the eye to the edge to provide a large diameter but with manageable weight. A fragment of a stone recovered from Commondale mill has a funnel shaped eye with a raised ring around it and it tapers away to the edge of the stone. Suitable stone is scarce in this region. The thick bed of deltaic sandstone underlying much of the northern moors is too soft. It seems that better quality stone was available near Scarborough. At Goathland the right of *"... chiminage in the hay of Scalleby, with millstones ..."* was granted in 1298 (YAS Rec Ser vol 31, 73-4), and in 1322 the Lord of Pickering had *"3s 4d from stone for millstones and tombs"* from the foreshore at Fullwood (Scalby) and on Cloughton Moor (Hon of Forest of Pickering, N R Rec Soc, new series, IV 200; VCH vol 2, 477). Also, the Lords of Cropton had *"the woods called Frith and Holthwaitbank ... in these woods they had the right to bees and honey and millstones and turf, bracken and heather for themselves and their tenants"* (Hon of Pickering III, 160; VCH vol 2, 456). Outcropping stone exposed on the surface was the preferred source. On Kildale Moor there is a 6 feet 11 inches diameter stone, possibly a millstone, shaped from an outcropping rock but abandoned after a flaw appeared when it was wedged off the mother rock. The costs of millstones varied considerably according to local availability but records from Buckinghamshire suggest an average cost for English stones of between 10s and 15s each (R Bennett and J Elton, 1900, 98, 99). Records of work done at the Bishop of Durham's mill at Norton show that a new set of millstones were 'laid' during the 1477-8 season. A new pair was transported in 1541-2 and another pair in 1552-3 and the cost of yet another pair in 1554-5 was 33s 4d (J Bennett and B E Vyner, 1979, 16).

The millstone spindle was the fastest running shaft in

FIG 37. ABANDONED POST-MEDIEVAL MILLSTONE (?) AT KILDALE.

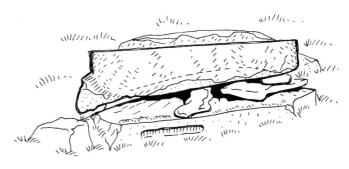

the mill and it also carried the full weight of the top millstone. Made from bloomery iron with many slag inclusions, these spindles were probably prone to splitting under the vibration and torque and they would wear at the bottom bearing. They would also wear at the fork for the 'rind' or 'rynd' or bridging iron, made from a flat iron bar flared at the ends or two pieces hand welded together to form a cross, leaded into the top stone. In France a spindle was called a 'fer'. Forged from many small pieces of iron welded together the spindle was an expensive item. In 1246 Ralph Bolbec took Thomas de Haugesgarth to court over a rent of 20s in Levisham. The ensuing agreement included a clause that Ralph give Thomas half a mark yearly rent of his mill at Levisham but with power of distraint on *"the iron of the said mill"* in case of default of payment at any term (Ft of F, 264, File 46 121, York Ref Lib). At Norton mill, spindles were either bought or repaired in 1394, 1421, 1458, 1469, 1476, 1513 and 1553 at costs varying from 6d to 3s 2d (J Bennett & B E Vyner, 1979, 15). Though there is no documentary evidence of the source of this spindle iron it was, in fact, readily available in the North York Moors where the remains of some hundred or so bloomery 'cinder hills', in Glaisdale and Bilsdale for example, provide evidence of medieval iron smelting.

Smooth-grained, hard-wearing stones suitable for journal bearings for waterwheel and wind shafts, and thrust bearings for millstone spindles were also available locally. They could be made from cobbles of volcanic basalt from the whinstone dike, which cuts diagonally across the North York Moors from Great Ayton to Goathland. Two post-medieval stone journal bearings made from whinstone have been located, one at Kilton

mill, the other at Danby mill. Two thrust bearings were recovered from Commondale mill but the origin of the stone has not been determined. It seems that stone bearings have survived much more commonly in the Lake District (M Davies-Shiel, 1978, 17), Cornwall, Wales and the Isle of Man (A Stoyel, 2000, pers comm) and their loss in north east Yorkshire probably indicates the scale of rebuilding at the beginning of the nineteenth century.

In the eleventh century milling technology was probably most advanced in France where evidence suggests that the earliest wheels were driven by water brought on wooden troughs (T S Reynolds, 1983, 54-5). However, this is not quite so helpful as it might appear since a wooden trough could be arranged either horizontally to deliver water to the top of an overshot wheel or sloping downwards to deliver water low down to a backshot wheel. The sloping trough would have 'jetted' the water, resulting in a livelier, and probably smaller, wheel. There are no illustrations of overshot wheels pre-dating the thirteenth century. However, the wheel at Handale was described as overshot in 1536.

It has been suggested that medieval millstones may have been driven clockwise or 'with the sun' following an earlier tradition in the use of hand mills (A Stoyel, 1992, 18-24). The orientation of furrows on Anglo-Saxon and early Norman millstones supports this idea, as do early illustrations of water mills. It might seem easy to prove or disprove the theory by looking at the relationship between watercourse and waterwheel but, in fact, this can only be done by making an assumption. Assuming a horizontal trough to an overshot wheel then the arrangements at Kildale, Cock, Tocketts, Rievaulx, Farndale High, Lastingham and Scaling, for instance, would indeed be correct, but equally, those at Castleton, Raisdale, Arden and Goathland would not. Assuming a sloped trough to a backshot wheel then the converse would be true. If there is any validity in the clockwise hypothesis then both overshot and backshot waterwheels were used in early mills in the region.

There were only two assemblies of 'going gears' in a medieval mill. The heaviest and slowest was the horizontal shaft carrying the 'water' wheel at one end and the 'cog' wheel at the other in a water mill; (also known as the *"out wheel"*, *"in wheel"* and *"tree axle"* (M L Armitt, re Rydall mill; see M Davies Shiel, 1978, 77). The equivalent in a windmill was the windshaft carrying the sail stocks at one end and the brake wheel at the other. There was a strong similarity. Medieval waterwheels were built on compass arms mortised at right angles through the shaft in the same way as the sail stocks were fitted to their mortised wind shaft. In both water mills and windmills the cog wheels, also known as 'face wheels', were also of compass arm construction, with cog mortises cut through the felloes. At Norton mill the waterwheel was renewed, the bay (part of the dam) repaired and the bridge repaired for £4 in 1513-14 and in 1553 there were repairs to the wheel and the bay costing £13 10s 11d (J Bennett & B E Vyner, 1979, 17). It would be rash, however, to assume that the waterwheel had lasted for forty years without other repairs.

The second and much faster running assembly was the millstone, spindle and lantern gear. The step-up in speed was provided by a 'lantern' made up of two stout wooden discs, wedged onto the spindle, with 'rungs' or 'staves' meshing with the cogs on the cog wheel. Repairs to the cogs and the rungs at Norton mill were carried out in 1476, 1493-4, 1509 and 1543-4 at a cost ranging between 2s and 2s 4d (J Bennet & B E Vyner, 1979, 15).

Other requirements were a hopper, shoe and agitator for feeding the grain into the millstones, a lever system for 'lightering' or lifting the top millstone to regulate the gap between the two, and a 'kist' or chest for collecting the meal. The latter needed to be secure, because medieval millers did not live in their mills. In a Survey of Harome of 1584 Thomas Bared left his title in *"Harome mylne"* to his wife, and *"... to my son Christopher all my working towilles (tools), cogges, trundle heads, spindels and two chests, one with a lock and one other that do want a lock but there is a lock in Robert Scott's chest which I give to Chris"* (R H Hayes and M Allinson, 1988, 18-38).

The use of bolters to separate fine white flour from coarser bran by shaking the meal through a woollen cloth sieve was recorded locally only in monastic mills. A Roll of Disbursements for Whitby Abbey dated 1394 noted *"Itm. Th Lewis p. i bult clath duo Abbi, viiid"* (G Young, 1817, 924) and at the Dissolution there were bolting houses at Handale (*"brewhouse and bultyng house"*), Baysdale and Grosmont (W Brown, 1886, 208-9, 213-5). References to bolting houses under the same roof as a brewing house and to a bolting house next to the bake house seem to show that bolting was done by hand as part of the baking process rather than by water as an adjunct to the milling process.

Carpenter millwrights

The standard tools available to the medieval carpenter, the axe and adze for the main timbers, framed saw for the tenons, mallet and various forms of 'bill' for mortising, and augur for boring holes for wooden pegs or 'trenails' were all that were required for mill components. What separated the mill carpenter from the common carpenter was his ability to cope with circular measure, involved in marking out the cog mortises in the felloes of the cog wheel and the centres of the rungs in the lantern gears.

During the thirty years from 1341 in which John Fossor was Prior of Durham his officers compiled a list of building works carried out. These included a healthy investment in water mills at Durham, Pittington, Rainton, Heworth, *"Wybestow"*, Billingham, Wolviston, *"Bermpton"*, Ketton, *"Fery"* (Ferry Hill), Merrington, *"Aclif"* (Aycliffe), and Scaltock and windmills at *"Oventon Belu"* (Newton Bewley), Southewick and Hesildon (L F Salzman, 1952, 392-3). In view of the large numbers of water mills and windmills built in north east Yorkshire between 1086 and, say 1350, it is reasonable to suppose that there were carpenters specially skilled in mill techniques. The separate title of 'millwright' did not exist at this time and, sadly, the names of these highly skilled craftsmen were not recorded.

MEDIEVAL ORGANISATION

In the early medieval or Norman period a few major feudal landholders, such as the de Brus, the Percy and the de Mauley families held the right to milling soke, a privilege which included the right to prohibit the building of mills other than manorial mills and the right to compel everyone living in the manor to grind their grain at the lord's mill. Milling soke was never written into national law and in early times there were few references to it. In the later medieval period, particularly after the problems of the early fourteenth century leading to the breakdown of the manorial system, mills tended to be rented or farmed out and there are many examples of the old customs being written into agreements between landlord and tenant. There was clearly a determination to maintain soke rights in the face of changing conditions. Throughout medieval times milling was a strictly regulated activity which was exploited to produce a guaranteed income for landholders.

The following is a list of known values of some North Yorkshire water mills:

		C11	C12	C13	C14
LEVEN					
Kildale	1280			£1 6s 8d	
Stokesley	1086	10s 0d			
Great Ayton					
(West)	1282			£5 6s 8d	
(East)	1282			10s 0d	
Ingleby	1211			5s 0d	
Rudby	1368				£6 13s 4d
THE NORTH EAST COAST					
Hutton	1298			£2 0s 0d	
Guisborough	1086	4s 0d			
Skelton/Saltburn/Skinningrove					
+ 2 others	1272			£21 8s 0d	
Kilton	1344				£1 10s 0d
Liverton	1336				£1 13s 4d
Seaton	1299			3s 4d	
Foss/Sandsend + 2 others	1279			£20 0s 0d	
LOWER ESK					
Rigg	1308				6s 8d
Cock	1396				£1 0s 0d
Ruswarp	1396				£3 6s 0d
New	1102			8s 0d	
Fylingdales	1190			6s 8d	

			C11	C12	C13	C14
THE DALES						
Bransdale	1276				£1 13s 4d	
Farndale (2)	1276				£7 7s 0d	
Castleton(2)	1272				£10 0s 0d	£6 0s 0d
Lealholm	1336					£3 0s 0d
Goathland	1298				5s 0d	
Westerdale	1307					£5 6s 8d
VALE OF PICKERING						
Scalby	1164			£6 0s 0d		
East Ayton	1086		5s 0d			
Brompton	1086		5s 0d			
Ebberston	1202				10s 0d	
Cropton	1349					£4 13s 4d
Pickering (2)	1298				£20 0s 0d	
Thornton Dale	1335					£2 13s 4d
Kirkby Misperton	1086		4s 0d			
RYEDALE						
Kirkby Moorside	1086 1276	4s 0d			£18 0s 0d	
Helmsley (2)	1285				£12 9s 0d	
Sproxton	1298				£1 6s 8d	
Nunnington	1086		5s 0d			
Ampleforth	1295				£1 3s 0d	
WESTERN SCARPS						
Whorlton	1340					£8 0s 0d
Foxton	1240				£11 13s 4d	
Kirby Knowle	1291				£2 0s 0d	
Ravensthorpe	1272				£5 6s 9d (8 marks)	
Sowerby	1086		20s 0d			

The few known values of windmills were as follows:

		C11	C12	C13	C14
Yarm	1272			£1 10s 0d	
East Coatham	1340				£4 0s 0d
Marske	1349				
Scarborough	1314				13s 4d

Predictably, the value of a mill was related to the size of the population in the township. The most valuable mills were in the towns and villages on the lowlands, for instance, at Great Ayton, Brompton, Pickering, Kirkby Moorside and Helmsley. The mill at Scalby, which served the port and castle of Scarborough, was valuable but, curiously, the mills of the lower Esk, which served the port of Whitby, were not. Within the moors, Castleton and Westerdale mills were both valuable, reflecting the good ploughland available in these two dales while in the narrower dales such as Kildale, Goathland and Ingleby the values were less. There was already a distinction between the dales mills and the lowland mills, a distinction which would develop through the seventeenth, eighteenth and nineteenth centuries.

A second trend was that the income from the mills increased as the period wore on. The breakdown of the manorial system did not always lead to loss of income from mills.

The early medieval period

Early medieval villages were self-sufficient, closed communities but what is not clear is how far the villagers valued the lord's mill. Would they rather have ground their own grain at home in hand mills? At what period did grinding grain at the lords' mills become compulsory? Though there have been many discoveries of early but not easily dated querns, few hand-mill stones have been found in north east Yorkshire, even in those villages where there were no mills. In only one case, in the grant of the mills of Ormesby to Gisborough Priory in the thirteenth century, is there documentary evidence that tenants were *"... not to possess querns or hand mills"* (Gis Chart, Surtees Soc, vol 86, 279n). The evidence points to an early imposition of milling soke.

In fact, the soke system may have been in place in the Anglo-Saxon period and it was certainly entrenched throughout the country by the twelfth century (R Holt, 1988, 38). There are no early recorded examples of fines for non-compliance within north east Yorkshire, though these are fairly common elsewhere. However, there is evidence that villagers had to contribute to the upkeep of the demesne mill, and this obligation would hardly have been enforceable if the villagers were not actually using it. In particular they had to help in the on-going and never-ending task of cleaning out dams, ponds and leats, constantly choked with leaves in winter and growing vegetation in summer. Also, they were bound to help with transport to the mill site on those occasions when new millstones and great timbers were needed, sometimes entailing a lengthy journey.

These two obligations first appear at an early period. For instance, when Adam de Ingleby (Greenhow) granted his mill to Whitby Abbey (1151) he retained the right to continue to have his own corn ground there multure free provided his homagers would *"... repair the mill dam, bring the main timbers and millstones (petras molendas) as in his own time"* (Whitby Chart, Surtees Soc, vol 64, 53n). Similarly, Robert de Turnham's confirmation of Joan Fossard's grant of the mill at Egton to Grosmont Priory bound *"... his homagers to perform all manner of services to the same, not only in carrying the stones and main timber, but also in every repair necessary from time to time to be made"* (J Graves, 1808, 287-8). In 1265 the inhabitants of Hackness had to *"make the millpond"* and carry millstones and the bondmen of nearby Silpho had to *"carry timber to the mill if broken and roof the mill"* (Whitby Chart, Surtees Soc, vol 72, 365-70). The *"bondmen of Neuham"* (Newholm, near Whitby) had to make the mill pond and the mill and carry millstones and timber. Likewise, at Pickering in 1298 the bondmen and cottars had to repair the mill pond of the two mills belonging to the Duchy of Lancaster (YAS Rec ser vol 31, 734). At Salton, in 1430 the services of the tenants of the Priory of Hexham included *"... buying a palfrey for each new prior and carrying provisions for him and his suite while they travelled in Yorkshire. They were also bound to convey all timber and other material necessary for the repair of the manor houses and the prior's mill, at which they ground their corn"* (Prior of Hexham, Surtees Soc, ii, 76; VCH vol 1, 552).

The later medieval period

Farming or renting of mills started quite early in the case of some town mills. For example, Stokesley mill was farmed in 1250. By the beginning of the thirteenth century almost all outlying monastic mills were also farmed. Many other mills were farmed after the Black Death. Under the new system long standing custom and practice increasingly became the subject of written agreements. The duties of the tenants of Salton were a case in point (Gazetteer p224). Some landholders attempted to re-affirm their soke privilege after the Black Death. This attempt to offset the inevitable decline in the manorial system is evident north of the Tees where the effects of the Scottish incursions were very severe and where the ecclesiastical landlords, the Bishop of Durham and the Prior of Durham, were particularly powerful. The Hatfield Survey (1377) records that *"... the copyholders of Norton, Stockton and Hartburn ... are bound to bring either the millstones or wood ... tenn miles and not above, the owners of the mill allowing 4d per mile for expence for every draught. Norton to find one half of the draught and Stockton and Hartburn one quarter each. The copyholders within the township of Stockton are to maintain all that part with mortar and straw from the middle of the dam on the south side to the wood worke on the same side at the west end of Norton Mill. The cavells or parts of Norton-mill dam belonging to the copyholders of the township of Stockton, to scour where they lye and of whose cavells or parts they adjoin"* (J Brewster 1829, 90). These cavells were sections of the mill leat and the copyholders were bound to clean the cavells adjoining their own holdings. John Elvet, William Shepherd, Robert Slowbek and William Townshende, all free tenants of the Bishop, were bound to strengthen the mill pond and the race of Norton mill, as also was John Layham a free tenant of Hartburn. Also, John de Holleston and John Sandy, free tenants of Norton were to *"... strengthen the millpond and race and carry timber to the said mill ... for rebuilding and repairing as often as necessary and find millstones for the mills of Norton and Stockton and roof the water mill of Norton at their own expense and grind their corn at the said mill"* (T Sowler, 1972, 435-9).

The duties of the tenants of the Prior of Durham were recorded in the Halmote Rolls (L Still & J Southeran, 1966, 44-5). In 1365, for instance, *"... all the tenants of the vill are ordered to repair the millpond (at Wolviston) and also to send sufficient men for the work there under penalty of 40d".* In 1381 some anxiety was expressed when it was ordered that the tenants of Billingham *"... shall not send boys to the work of the millpond ... under penalty of 40d".* There was a hint of irritation in 1383 when it was ordered *"... to all tenants of the vill whosoever of them shall carry stones and millstones should DO SO".*

The duties of the townsfolk of Stockton were still a topic for discussion as late as the seventeenth century. It might be expected that work formerly done on a boon day basis by the villagers would now be done by hired men. However, in a Survey of Stockton (1647) it was claimed that the copyholders are still to *"... repaire the sd. Milne (at Norton) with Thatch and Wall and to scour the Race and Dame when need requireth and to fetch such timber from time time from Clarke Wood (Clack Wood near Osmotherley) or elsewhere within twelve miles distance from the sd milne and also the millstones for the use of the sd. Milne from Raley Green or Walker Field. For this service every draught is to have 4d per mile and their mens' dinners paid by the tenant"* (W Fordyce, 1857, 153).

The monopoly on milling was also reinforced in the Halmote Rolls. In 1364, for example, it was ordered that the tenants of Billingham *"... shall not grind corn beyond the domain while the mill of the Prior can grind, under penalty of 20s"* and *"... the bailiff and judge to prevent corn being carried beyond the domain with horses and carts".* In 1265 the tenants of Cowpen Bewley were ordered *"... not to grind elsewhere than at the* (wind) *mill of Newton, while the wind suffices, under penalty of half a mark".* In 1368 it was again ordered that the tenants of Billingham *"... shall not grind elsewhere than at the mill at Billingham except at the mill in the next parish of Wolviston",* which of course also belonged to the Prior. In 1380 the tone stiffened when it was ordered that *"... the tenants of the vils of Billingham, Cowpen, Wolviston and Newton Bewley to grind at the mills of the lord* (Prior) *under the penalty of losing horses and grain".*

The millers

There is evidence from the Domesday book that a few millers paid their rent in kind with eels, grain (sometimes specifically wheat), malt, a pig, or honey (R Lennard, 1959, 282-3). There is no similar record for north east Yorkshire where the value of the mill was given in money terms even though the rent may have been paid in kind. The miller took his due, or multure, from the villagers by taking a proportion of the grain. The relationship between the amount of grain taken and the rental value of the mill may have varied from mill to mill, though clearly the multure had to cover the living

costs of the miller as well as the rent he paid to the lord.

The proportion of grain taken for multure (variously referred to as 'molt', 'molta' or 'mouta') may have varied between different parts of the country (R Holt, 1988, 6) but in north east Yorkshire a much more noticeable variation was associated with the status of the customer. At Ingleby Greenhow in 1151 Sicily and Wymare confirmed the grant of the water mill to Whitby Abbey but retained the right to have their own grain ground multure free. Conversely, when William de Percy granted land at Kildale to the canons of Healaugh (1290) he kept the mill for himself but allowed the canons to grind multure free (L Charlton, 1779, 115). Such privileges were only for the few, however, and lesser folk were forced to give a proportion. For instance, in 1235 Agnes de Norton was privileged to be able to grind her corn at Sproxton mill *"... to the twentieth measure"* and *"... she shall grind first after whoever she finds grinding there"* (YAS Rec ser, vol 67, 235; Yorks fines, 1237, 46, 31). In 1397 Thomas Davison was to grind his grain to the twentieth measure at Castleton. In the agreement between William de Percy and the Canons of Gisborough over the mills at Ormesby and Caldecotes the tenants were to pay one sixteenth measure ("sextum decimum") in multure while the corn of the Canons had to be ground multure free (Gis Chart, Surtees Soc, vol 86, 279). Both Robert de Thorpe and the lepers of Hutton Hospital near Guisborough were to grind their grain to the sixteenth measure at the mill of Hugh de Hotun (Gis Chart, Surtees Soc, vol 68, 171-3). Richard de Bradeley and all other cottars of Hackness and bondmen of Silpho at the Abbot of Whitby's mill at Hackness paid to the thirteenth measure (Whitby Chart, Surtees Soc, vol 72, 448-50). *"The men of Burniston"* also gave the Abbot of Whitby *"... tol and tac, merchet and one thirteenth measure of the grain they ground".* This inequitable system where cottars paid more than tenants may not have been quite so unfair as appears at first glance. It may have been considered more costly to mill in small batches. Also, poorer people would tend to bring more oats and rye (as compared with wheat) and the higher toll was needed in order to make up the shortfall in the value of the grain taken in multure (R Bennett & J Elton, 1900, 154-7).

Except in the case of certain privileged individuals like Agnes de Burton at Sproxton, the miller was normally bound to grind each man's corn in order as it arrived at the mill so as to avoid disputes. This meant that the miller had to keep his mill in running order at all times, except in severest conditions of frost or flood, and he had to carry out all repairs except where great timbers and millstones were involved. Nor did the landholders necessarily accept a reduced rent if the mill was not working. In a demise by Abbot Savary to Peter and Hugh, clerks of the mill of Kirkby Misperton (1145-55) there was to be *"... no reduction of rent in case it be broken down or burnt, but timber will be provided from the Forest of Spaunton for its repair*" (Chart St Mary's Abbey, Dean and Chapter, York). After the farming of mills became more common this may have become unacceptable to the tenant and written agreements covered this point. At Norton, for instance, the miller was granted an allowance on his rent proportionate to the number of days it was idle (J Bennett and B E Vyner, 1979, 12).

After the Black Death landholders lost their hold on boon day labour and they then needed clear undertakings from their mill farmers. Thus when the corn mills at Castleton and Lealholm, formerly in the tenure of Richard del Howe, were demised to new tenants, John Robynson and Robert Leventon (1431), there was the condition that the tenants would be responsible for the upkeep of the fabric "*... except great timber which the Lady shall find for them*" (Acc of John Forster, keeper, to the Countess of Cambridge, Sheffield City Library). In 1539 the estates of Christopher Conyers at Yarm included the farm of a windmill there ... for which Henry Gybson paid 26s 8d per annum and "*... he makes all repairs except, timber, millstones and iron*" (Confiscated estates of rebels, PRO SC6/4281). At an even later date the tenant's agreement with James Pennyman for the new mill at Marske (1640) included the condition that "*... the tenant to bring the great timbers and stones as shall be needed*" (NYCRO ZNK V/3/3/109 mic 1251). In 1677 the tenant's agreement with Anthony Lowther for the same mill included the terms that "*... the lessor to maintain the milldam and find the millstones and to lay them on the mill green*" and "*... the tenant to carry the timber*" (NYCRO ZNK V 3/3/127 mic 1251). As late as 1778 the tenant of Osmotherley mill was given "*... free liberty to dig turf for the reparation of the dams*" (Deeds of Osmotherley mill, BX 42 68).

In spite of their central role in village life early medieval millers were no more than manorial servants and their names have not been recorded. In the later period one or two personalities emerge. The descriptive Latin surname 'molendario' had appeared before 1300. "*Simon Molendario*" of Farndale paid 7s 9d (one fifteenth of his total wealth which of course excluded the mill itself) in the 1301 Lay Subsidy of Edward I (W Brown, 1897; see Appendix 5). In fact, Simon paid more than anyone else in the dale, which contributed in all £37 7s 4d from 34 taxable men and one widow. He was clearly a wealthy man and the farmer of the mill(s) in Farndale and perhaps Kirkby Moorside rather than a working miller. He was the exception. Roger of Goathland paid only 1d while other millers, for instance at Kildale, Ingleby Greenhow, Skelton, Westerdale and Gillamoor did not contribute at all. The contributions

show that, in general, millers in north east Yorkshire were no more prosperous than men in other crafts and trades. In the prospering town of Yarm, for instance, "*Giliot Molendinaria*" paid 1s 8d, which was a good deal less than the 15s 2d paid by Henry the Tanner and the 12s 2d paid by "*Galfrido the Dyer*" and less even than the contribution of "*Radulph the Glover*". The only windmiller specifically described was "*Willelmo de Wyndmillen*" of New Malton, but Giliot of Yarm, Roger at Marton, John and Stephen at East Coatham and William at West Coatham must also have been windmillers. Ricardo at Kirklevington had two water mills and a windmill. These windmillers all paid roughly the same amount, varying from 1s 4d at Marton to 1s 8d at Yarm.

The career of one named miller/farmer can be pieced together from entries in the Prior of Durham's Halmote Rolls. John Miryman was a free tenant of the village of Billingham. In 1366 he and other tenants were fined for mowing nine acres of land which was actually held by bondmen. In that same year there was a fire at Billingham water mill and Miryman, Gilbert de Hardegill and other tenants were charged with the task of taking out the main timbers of the burned mill and storing them in a safe place (*"quad meremium del Brantmyln extrahatur et ponatur in loco tuto et securo"*). Rebuilding would be started straight away and was referred to in Prior John Fossor's Accounts (L F Salzman, 1952, 392-3). In 1368 Miryman and Robert Milner of Norton were confirmed as the new tenants of the rebuilt water mill of Norton and also of the windmill at Newton Bewley for a rent of £23 per annum. Miryman was appointed Bailiff to the Halmote Court in 1374 and in the same year he stood as security to safeguard the inheritance of a minor of the village. By 1376 he had become tenant of the garden of the manor of Billingham and of the Prior's fishpond. In 1379 he stood surety for the good behaviour of John del Toune who was a junior member of another family of free tenants of Billingham. This may have been the high point in his career. He had given up the tenancy of the mills by 1379. In 1381 he was fined 40s for refusing hospitality to Agnes Souter, even though the Prior had demanded his co-operation, and in 1383 he was fined 40d because he had not "*... cleared the watercourse of Billingham*". Was he out of favour or had he simply grown old? However, in that same year he was allowed officially to take a messuage and land which he had held without license from the Prior for the past six years. That was the last reference to Miryman and the Halmote Rolls finished a year later. Overall the impression is that Miryman was a man of enterprise with many activities in addition to holding the farm of the water mill at Billingham and of the windmill at Newton Bewley.

EARLY FULLING MILLS

This short section is included because water driven fulling mills cannot easily be disentangled from the older technology of corn milling. For instance, some medieval fulling stocks were housed in the same buildings as corn mills. In other cases, in the late eighteenth and early nineteenth centuries, old fulling mill sites were re-used as flax mills and, later, for corn milling.

By the late thirteenth century Rievaulx, Byland and Whitby Abbeys and Gisborough, Arden and Rosedale Priories had at least 33,000 sheep and lay landholders had nearly as many (B Waites, 1998, 86-145). Place names such as Ewe Cote and Wether Cote in Bilsdale and near Old Byland, relate to the former sheep runs, and the base of a stone column from a two-storey wool-house is preserved in a farm building at Laskill. Most of the wool was exported in the raw state via Hull and York to Flanders and Italy, much of it for making tapestry wall hangings. However, some was processed locally and eventually spinning and weaving became established as cottage industries. Fulling mills would follow in due course.

Woollen cloth straight from the weaving frame was harsh and uncomfortable to wear. The process of fulling consisted of pounding it in soapy water to cleanse it of the natural oil from the sheep's back and also to matt and to felt it to make it soft to the touch. At first fulling was done by hand or by 'walking' the cloth under foot, processes which were labour intensive and unpleasant. The development of mechanical fulling seems to have taken place in the Alps and in Normandy, the first unambiguous reference dating from the late eleventh century. Early fulling stocks consisted of two or more heavy wooden pendulum hammers which were raised in turn by means of cams on a waterwheel shaft and dropped onto a sodden length of cloth which turned over steadily in a curved wooden trough under this pounding action.

An early reference dates from 1185 when the Knights Templar had two fulling mills, one at Barton, near Guiting in Gloucestershire and the second (a *"molendinum fulerez"*) at Temple Newsham near Leeds. This reference is from the same source as the record of one of the earliest windmills in England (B A Lees, 1935, 50 127). Subsequent diffusion of the fulling mill was nothing like as quick as for the earlier water-driven corn mills but records survive for over 130 English examples from before 1337 (E Carus-Wilson, 1941, 39-60).

It seems that fulling came to the North York Moors later than to other upland areas like the Lake District Wales and Cornwall. Distinctive personal names, such as *"Tinctor"* (Dyer), *"Fullo"*, *"Fuller"* and *"Walker"*, were listed in the Lay Subsidy of 1301, but most were in towns, for example, Yarm, Stokesley, Skelton, Whitby Scarborough and Pickering and most of them made only modest contributions, indicating that they were probably fulling by hand for town-based weavers. As the market demand for woollen cloth increased enterprising wool merchants turned their attention to these small-town weavers, and landholders began to see the potential of water driven fulling mills.

The fulling mills of north east Yorkshire were built too late to be included in a national survey of fulling mills up to 1337 (R A Pelham, n d, map derived from the Carus-Wilson survey). This introductory account, along with a list of some 40 sites, covers a slightly later period. The first unambiguous record for this area is for a *"molendinum fulreticum"* occupied by Robinson worth 20s at Ellerburn in 1335, (Inquisition post mortem for William Latymer; N Riding Rec Ser, new series, II, 273) However, it may be that fullers at Hackness and East Ayton were using waterpower even earlier. Bartholomew, the fuller at East Ayton, was taxed 6s and Matthew the fuller at Hackness paid 8s in the Lay Subsidy of 1301 when most other fullers paid tax in pennies rather than shillings.

Following the Black Death, evidence shows that some water-driven corn mills were taken out of use and the available water power used for fulling. For instance the fulling mills at Castle Levington (1350), Great Aytor (1352) and Farndale replaced former corn mills of higher value about this time. At Castle Levington there were two water corn mills in 1281 and 1337 but the inquisi

FIG 38. FULLING MILL SITES IN NORTH EAST YORKSHIRE.

tion post mortem for John de Meynil (1350) listed *"a water mill and one fulling mill and it is demised anew for 8s per annum"*. Evidently one corn mill had been sacrificed. There was a similar story in Great Ayton. There were two corn mills in 1282 but the inquisition post mortem for John, Earl of Kent (1353) listed *"... one fulling mill and one water mill worth 26s 8d and not more on account of the lack of tenants and the weakness of the soil"*. He also had two water mills in Farndale, worth 60s *"... and there is a fulling mill worth nothing on account of the deficiency of the tenants and workers"*. In Bransdale he had *"... one water mill worth ... and not more on account of the mortality"* but there was no mention of a fulling mill though there is a 'Tenter Garth' field name near Moor Houses on the East Side of the dale. The Fauconbergs of Skelton had three water mills in 1349 of which one was *"weak and ruinous, worth £4 before the Death"*, but by 1408 one third of the farm of a fulling mill was given to Joan, the widow of Thomas de Fauconberg. A fulling mill at Harome was recorded in 1430, another at Castleton in 1432, and the Hastings family had a fulling mill at Allerston in 1436. In fact, the evidence confirms that after the Black Death, landlords were turning their attention to returns from cash rentals rather than from the old system of manorial multure. As

new devices, both windmills and fulling mills were free from the old ties and could easily be rented out.

Guaranteed rentals were sought not only by lay landholders but also by the monastic houses. Dissolution documents show that the monasteries owned either eight or nine fulling mills, most of them of high value.

Whitby Abbey Accounts (1344) confirm the high value of a fuller at Hackness but in 1550 there were *"... the said 2 water mills in the occupation of Ingram Proctor for 60s 0d per annum and the walkemylle in the occupation of Henry Braidthewhate and Maulde for 6s 8d"*. References to the fulling mill or mills at Ruswarp (and Newholm) can be found, for example, in the Bursar's Accounts (1396). References to the *"molend. fullonic, xxxvjs vijd"*, appear to relate to Newholm, to Stakesby or to Ruswarp (Whitby Chart, Surtees Soc, vol 72, 572, 581 & 588). At Ruswarp the *"water of the Esk with Mill"* was worth £3 6s 8d and the fulling mill £1 16s 8d. There may have been only one fulling mill. A Dissolution inventory for Whitby Abbey listed the *"Rent of 1 tenement in Risewarp Carrs called Walkemylne in the occupation of John Pearson, 30s 0d"* and the *"Farm of the Fulling Mill demised to William Proctor, 6s 8d per annum"* (NYCRO ZF4/3/1).

49

Gisborough Priory had a fulling mill at Commondale. It was listed under an entry *"Colmandale. one cot, two small closes and a water miln, William Bennyson, 10s 8d. A fulling mill, Rob Doncaster, Henry Rowe, Rob King, 20s 0d."* (1535). The relative values of the corn mill and fulling mill, the reverse of the situation at other sites, shows that in this remote moorland dale little grain was grown at this period. The entry also provides an early example of multiple tenancy, a practice which would later become widespread. Probably Doncaster, Rowe and King were all local weavers sharing the fulling mill between them on a day-by-day basis.

The fulling mill at Rievaulx was part of a bigger industrial enterprise. An inventory taken at the time of the Dissolution includes the following entries:

"Farm of a mill called le Yron Smithie within the said site lately in the tenure of Lambert Semer, 26s 8d per annum.

Farm of a mill called le Walke Milne within the said site lately in the tenure of Lambert Semer 60s 0d per annum

Farm of a corn mill within the said site 6s 8d per annum"

(Rievaulx Chart)

The Frenchman, Lambert Symar (later Semer or Seimar) first came to England about 1496 to set up a water driven smithing hammer near England's first blast furnace recently built at Newbridge Ironworks in the Weald (H R Schubert, 1957, 148, App VII). Forty years later this same Symar, by now quite an old man, was the tenant of both the smithy and the fulling mill at Rievaulx. His iron making activities at Rievaulx are quite well known but in 1538 the fulling mill was rented at over twice the value of the iron smithy. In 1540 the Earl of Rutland's inventory of his new possessions at Rievaulx included *"... on the southwest there of a peace of grond belongyng to the walk myll cont. di rod and at the south west thereof standyth the walke myle with a garth adioinyng ..."* (Belvoir Castle, Misc m s, no 196). The site is roughly half way between the abbey church and Forge Farm. Today there remain the earthworks of a pond and a dam across the lower part of the 'canal'.

Byland Abbey had at least two fulling mills at the Dissolution, one near the Abbey and the other in Caydale. Near the Abbey site it seems that an old corn mill at Low Pasture Farm was converted into a fulling mill when a new corn mill was built close to the Abbey gates (J McDonnell and M R Dom Everest, 1965). The hollows of two ponds and a large earth dam close to the mill site can still be seen. The fulling mill in Caydale was on land which had belonged to the Byland monks. It was listed in 1539 (Augmentation Roll) at a value of less than £2 and it was described as the *"Walke Mill"* with

"Tenter Banke" in a patch of land called the *"Newe hag in Caierdale"* on Christopher Saxton's Survey of Old Byland (1598).

St Mary's Abbey in York also had a fulling mill in north east Yorkshire. At the Dissolution Thomas Burton paid *"10s farm of a fulling mill formerly St Mary's"* at Appleton. A few years later a *"water mill called Appulton Myll"* was in the tenure of John Bonnell and a fulling mill in the tenure of Hugh Burton (1566). The latter is still commemorated by the name *"Tenter Hill End"* on the wooded brow overlooking the corn mill.

The small Cistercian nunneries in and around the North York Moors are not on record as having fulling mills and must therefore have sold their wool raw. On the other hand, the alien monastery at Grosmont had a *"molendinum aquaticum"* and a *"molendinum fullonicum"* along with the associated *"stagna, fossatas, riuos riuulos and aquarum cursos cum lez slues and mylledammes in Egton"* on the Esk, all in the occupation of *"Roberto Gray"*. After the Dissolution this fulling mill was rented and then granted to Edmund Wright, *"formerly a Captain in the Scottish wars"*.

Field and architectural evidence

In addition to the early fulling mills listed above there were at least 26 later fulling mills in north east Yorkshire. They are listed in Appendix 5 and in the Gazetteer and one or two are mentioned in this section.

The detergent used for taking grease from the cloth was fullers' earth, a naturally occurring, highly absorbent clay found in the South West, the Midlands and south Yorkshire. Its absence in North Yorkshire might have been one of the reasons for the delayed start to water-driven fulling. Alternatives were either stale urine or 'lye' prepared from the ashes of bracken. There is no evidence that urine was used in north east Yorkshire but the production of 'brack ash' has left field names such as *"Kiln Garth"*, *"Kil Field"* etc in the vicinity of known fulling mill sites. Kilns were also, of course, used for burning limestone either from the Tabular Hills or brought by coastwise shipping from Northumberland but there are other field names which cannot be associated with lime-burning. For instance, a *"Kill Field"* is marked on the Tithe Map for Commondale, close to the site of Commondale fulling mill. There was another *"Kiln Garth"* at Upleatham where there was certainly no lime burning. Other descriptive field names have survived from the process in which woven cloths, shortened and thickened by the fulling process, were stretched on rows of tenterhooks on wooden frames. 'Tenter Fields' are found, for instance, in Laskill, in Bransdale and near Farndale Low Mill.

The remains of East Ayton fulling mill were uncovered when a site under a cliff alongside the Derwent (still named *"Banks Fulling Mill Garth"* in 1768) was

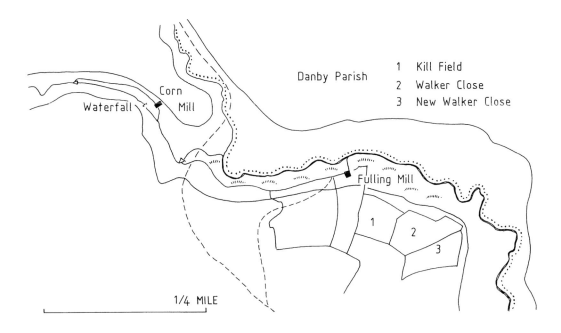

FIG 39. FIELD NAMES IN COMMONDALE.

excavated (F Rimington, 1964, 23-31). There were two boiler settings with fire grates beneath and, behind them, a fuelling point with pieces of coal which had been tipped over the cliff edge from the track above. The tops of the boilers were level with a cobbled floor but underneath the cobbles was a layer rich in sherds of the thirteenth and fourteenth centuries. Strada's engraving of German fulling stocks (1617) shows a similar boiler near to the fulling stocks, probably used for preparing the lye which was poured onto the cloth at something below boiling point in order to lift the grease out of the wool (Jan de Strada, c. 1617).

A pair of early fulling hammers needed roughly the same amount of ground space as a single pair of millstones but they were worked from ground level and did not necessarily need as much height. Fulling mills had no gearing and were therefore cheaper to build. Waterwheels were also smaller. For example, measurements of wheel pits of seventeenth century corn mills and 'tuck' mills in Ulster showed that waterwheel pits for corn mills averaged 14 feet 6 inches long and for tuck mills 12 feet (H D Gribbon, 1969, 20). The waterwheels of medieval fulling mills would have been smaller still.

In several cases there is a contrast between good documentary evidence with the lack of evidence on the ground. There are no signs of leats separate from corn mill leats at, for instance, Skelton or Castle Levington. The most likely explanation must be that the fulling stocks were added onto existing corn mills. They may

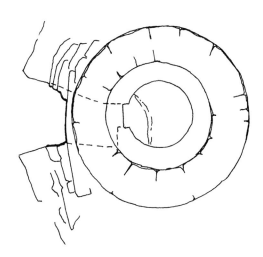

FIG 40. BRACKEN KILN AT TARN HOLE IN BILSDALE.

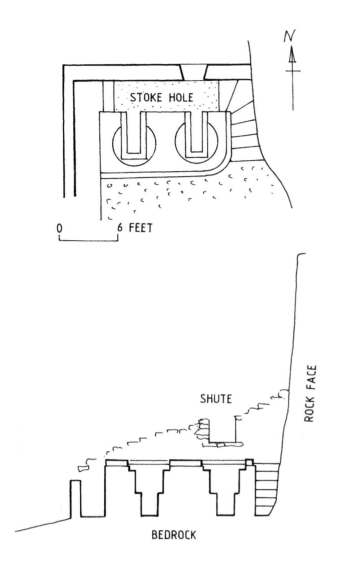

FIG 41. EAST AYTON FULLING MILL (AFTER F C RIMINGTON) COMPARED WITH SEVENTEENTH CENTURY FULLING STOCKS (DE STRADA, 1617).

have been housed in a long building under one roof, aligned across the leat, or alternatively in two separate buildings, adjacent but on the opposite sides of the wheel pit. The arrangement was described in a mill at Chartham in Kent which noted the *"... tayle of the middle water wey through the mills ..."* (L F Salzman, 1952, 509), and it is likely that such an arrangement existed at Great Shelford, Cambridgeshire, in 1387 (R Holt, 1988, 162). In these combined corn/fulling mills the waterwheel pit was near the centre of the building with one waterwheel and the corn milling machinery to one side and a second waterwheel and fulling stocks to the other. In relics of seventeenth and eighteenth century examples in Oxfordshire, Berkshire and Gloucestershire the corn mill is the more important structure with a smaller house for the fulling stocks on the opposite side of the waterwheel pit (A Stoyel, 2000, pers comm). It is noticeable that the corn mills at Lowna and Costa, formerly fulling mills as well, have wide waterwheel pits with working space on both sides, a feature not

seen in other local corn mills. At Costa High a redundant second arched escape-way survives in the downstream wall. Where such evidence is not to be seen a useful indicator may be the amount of water power available. There would have been little point, for instance, in cutting a second leat at Skelton, since the old corn mill leat would certainly have been strong enough to drive fulling stocks as well. There was also ample capacity in corn mill leats at Great Ayton, Castle Levington, Crathorne, Ruswarp and Hackness.

However, the fulling mills belonging to the monasteries at Commondale, Rievaulx and Byland were in separate buildings with their own leats. The same applies to later fulling mills belonging to lay owners at Rosedale, Kildale, Castleton, Staithes, Harome, Swainby, Osmotherley, Laskill, Oldstead, etc. At Rosedale the foundations of a building, 22 feet long and 16 feet wide, is aligned along the leat cutting across a loop in the Seven. The foundations at Kildale are obscured by those of a later flax mill but they too sug-

A)

B)

C)

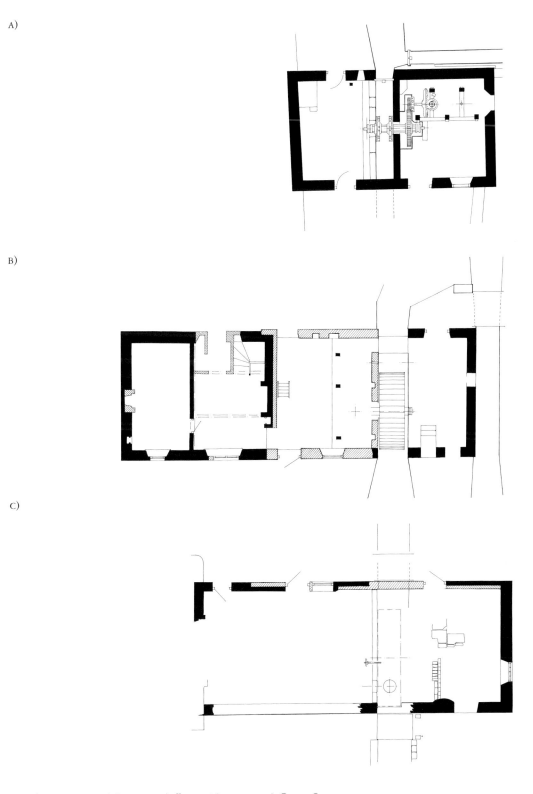

FIG 42. PLANS AT A) LOWNA, B) COSTA HIGH AND C) COSTA LOW MILLS.

gest a building aligned along the leat and similar in size to that at Rosedale. There must have been a problem in setting up these new fulling mills because the best sites were already occupied by corn mills. These later fulling mills had to be built on second-best sites where there was often a lower head of water and sometimes an increased risk of flooding. At Commondale, for exam- ple, the old corn mill was built on sound shale while the later fulling mill was sited on soft ground with a long leat to maintain. The fulling mills at Castleton and Glaisdale were built on the banks of the unruly Esk where inevitably they were flooded on occasions.

The fulling mill at Staithes was built on an even more difficult site, in the neck of a loop in Staithes Beck below the old Dalehouse corn mill. 'Tenter Hill' within the loop and surrounded by steep shale banks is 20 feet above the water level. Where the beck approaches the loop the cliff has been breached either by a tunnel or by a deep cut (bridged for access) to lead the water to the mill. This mill should be seen as one of a group of later industrial enterprises, (like, for instance, the Roman cement mill at Sandsend) which made use of the coastal creeks for transporting their products. The 'glazing' mill at Skinningrove was another. The term 'glazing' is associated with several industries, eg paper making. However, a *"Bleach Garth"* adjacent to the mill is shown on Bradley's Map of 1815 (NYCRO ZNK V 3/1/28) proving that this was a flax mill.

Paper making in north east Yorkshire is not part of this survey. Briefly, the earliest references are to the con-version of a paper mill at Stocking into a *"mall mill"* (1610) and to the fact that John Blanchard held a paper mill of the King at the old fulling mill site in Caydale (1619). Up to the middle of the seventeenth century most paper used in this country was imported from the Netherlands. There were two reasons why the industry was eventually started in north east Yorkshire. The first was the exceptionally clean, crystalline water flowing from the limestone Tabular Hills, which was suitable for processing cotton, linen and even silk rags into high-quality white paper, for instance at Ellerburn and Pickering Vivers (pre 1770). The second was the availability of large quantities of worn sails, rigging and ropes from the sailing vessels using the Tees and the Esk. These were suitable for the production of coarse or brown paper, which was made, for instance, at Hutton Rudby (1759), Lealholm (1762) and Egglescliffe.

Sixteenth and Seventeenth Century Developments in

CORN MILLING

The late sixteenth and the seventeenth centuries saw population growth. River ports prospered through trading with London and the Continent and, elsewhere, industry was established; alum making at Loftus and Guisborough and textiles at Thornton Dale, Pickering, Kirkby Moorside and Helmsley. From the time of the Black Death the soke right of mills was no longer seen as valuable and most mills were either farmed out or sold. Eventually, this loosening of control led to some mills being developed because of the increased rents they could then command.

The Dissolution (between 1536-40) provided a further stimulus. Typically, Henry VIII first leased the properties of the monasteries and then, after a few years, made a grant. For instance, the lands and mills of Guisborough were at first administered by an official, Robert Trystram, then leased to Thomas Legh and finally sold to Thomas Chaloner in 1547. Arden Priory and precinct mill went to Thomas Welles of the King's Household in 1536 and to Thomas Culpepper in 1540. Rievaulx Abbey mill went to Thomas Manners, Earl of Rutland, and the mill at Egton Bridge, formerly belonging to Grosmont Abbey, to Edmund Wright, a Captain in the Scots Wars. In other cases Henry looked to long term benefits by retaining mills for future disposal. These were still in the hands of the Crown when James I came to the throne. James sold them off. Some ninety of them went to Edmund Ferrers ('*mercer from London*') and Francis Philips ('*gentleman from London*'), speculative purchasers who seem to have dealt in mills only and who were to become the biggest mill owners in the country with an ownership never before surpassed except by the King himself.

The following ex-monastic mills in north east Yorkshire belonged to James I in 1608:

"Gisborough monastery. Windmill in the east Field of Marske in the tenancy of Robert Rookbie £0 6s 8d Whitby monastery. Mills in Ibwinedale (Iburndale) and Estdaleside £0 10s 0d Watermill in Branesdale (actually Ramsdale) in the parish of ffylinge £0 10s 0d."

A year later in 1609 James 1 began his disposal of mills:

"Water mill, Claughton (Cloughton) *£1 3s 0d Two watermills at Scauby* (Scalby) *£1 3s 4d One watermill at Longdale Ends on Scalby Beck £1 13s 6d Scalby £0 13s 4d."*

Nor were the disposals limited to ex-monastic mills. At least two were disposed of in 1611 from the Duchy of Lancaster:

"North Watermill and South Watermill, Pickering £13 0s 0d."

These two went to two other speculative purchasers, Felix Wilson and Robert Morgan (R Bennett and J Elton, 1900, 17-18, 21, 26, 42-3).

There were two important innovations in the late sixteenth and the seventeenth centuries; the introduction of the horse driven flour or malt mill and the development of the 'double' and even 'treble' mill in which two or three waterwheels were housed in a single building. In every case these new mills belonged to large settlements situated around the margins of the moorland.

A)

B)

FIG 43. A) HORSE DRIVEN CORN MILL (RAMELLI, 1588) AND
B) MILL WITH TWO WATERWHEELS EACH DRIVING A SET OF
MILLSTONES (DE STRADA, 1617).

Horse Mills

The relatively few documentary references to horse
driven corn mills in England may mean that few were
actually built (J K Major, 1978, 57). That is certainly the
case in north east Yorkshire where the few examples
enable only two conclusions to be drawn. First, they
were situated in or near towns (Whitby, Pickering,
Kirkby Moorside, Stockton and Scarborough) and, second, they were associated with the activities of bakers
and maltsters rather than millers. Increasing town populations meant that bakers had to produce more bread
and, furthermore, the unvarying daily demand meant
that the supply could no longer be subject to disrup-
tion by flood or storm. Illustrations of continental horse
driven corn mills date from the late sixteenth century
(A Ramelli, 1588, and G A Bockler, 1661) and there is
evidence that such mills, known as 'gruttrij' or groat
mills, were widely used as an adjunct to the baking
process in many towns of the Netherlands. A fine
example from Wormerveer is preserved in the Arnhem
Open Air Museum, Holland. Dutch mills had a large
diameter horizontal spur wheel driving individual sets
of stones each equipped with its own bolter, or flour
sieve. Some were used for milling buckwheat for making pancakes. In this country the finest surviving horse
driven corn mill is at Woolley Park in Berkshire.

However, horse mills had an early ancestry. In fact,
the earliest reference to a horse mill in the north east
of England (and possibly the earliest in England) is
found in a record of the labour and money due to the
Bishop of Durham. The reference, to an area now
known as Oxen-le-Flatts in a loop in the Tees to the
north west of Darlington, reads:

> *"William holds Oxenhalle, viz. one carucate and
> three portions of tillage within the territory of
> Darlington … He ought also to have a horse mill
> and is quit of multure, he and his land, and of the
> service at the mill, and renders 60s per annum …"*
>
> (Boldon Buke, 1183, ed J Morris, 1982).

It is not clear why William should have been granted this exemption from milling soke, and the exemption was clearly unusual. Two hundred years later it
was not the same at Kirkby Moorside where there was
a clear challenge to the manorial soke. During the
reign of Edward III (1327-77) *"… the lessees of the old
manorial mill on the banks of the Dove undertook proceedings against the owners of a horse mill in the town
of Kirkby Moorside on the grounds they were grinding
the corn of the tenants of the manor and reducing its"*
(ie the water mill's) *"lawful profits"*. This dispute must
have been seen as an important issue since it was
referred to in the much later Exchequer Depositions
during the reigns of both Elizabeth I and James I (Exch

Dep Trin 37 Eliz, No 9 and Easter 19 James I, No 2; VCH vol 1, 511).

The majority of horse mills came much later. By the time of the Dissolution horse mills had been used as monastic precinct flour mills in the East Riding. One, at Swine Priory near Hull, was described at the Dissolution as:

> *"Item. In the utter yarde the mylne house wt a horse mylne, the bakhouse, the bultynge house under one roofe, conteyning in length 1 ffoote (sic) and in bredth xx ffoote, olde dawbid walls, coueryd wt tyle, decayed"*
>
> (W Brown, 1886, 328-9).

Another, at Bridlington was described as:

> *"On the north side of the same bakehouse and brewehouse standyth a ffayre horse mylne newly buildyd and covered wt slatt"*
>
> (R Bennett & J Elton, 1900, vol 3, 61-2).

Horse mills were not needed at north east Yorkshire monastic sites, where water power was readily available.

Most horse mills were, however, built to serve towns. At Whitby there was a horse mill in Collyers Goyt, formerly Horse Mill Goyt, at the end of Baxtergate near the northern end of the bridge. No pre-Dissolution date is on record but in 1540 Gregory Conyers left Bagdale Hall and his horse mill to his son George (VCH vol 2, 520). The horse mill may well have been set up before the Dissolution. It was mentioned in 1626 when *"one mill called Horse Milne"* along with a water mill and a windmill were seized by the sheriff in order to cover debts of Sir Robert Cholmley (NYCRO ZPK 13 mic 1628) and in 1666, in the marriage settlement of Sir Hugh Cholmley (Burnett coll 1552). It was described retrospectively as a *"horse mill for grinding malt"* (G Young, 1817, 373), but Young gave no evidence for his description. In fact the demand for flour for bread and for ships' biscuit would have been at least as pressing as the demand for malt.

At Stockton where the nearest mill (at Norton) was two miles away, the need to break out of the inconvenient medieval milling soke had been recognised by the fourteenth century. In response to a request from the Mayor of Stockton for information as to the rights of the burgesses (1344) the Mayor of Newcastle confirmed the legal situation that the burgesses of Stockton had the right to the same privileges as those at Newcastle:

> *"Every burgess may have a mill of his own upon his own land, house mill, water mill, windmill or hand mill. He may also have an oven or furnace but not to bake bread to sell ... Every burgess may send his corn to be ground at whatever mill he will ..."*
>
> (T Richmond, 1868, 14-15).

Later, there were two horse mills at Stockton, the earlier a corn mill belonging to the castle and the later a timber sawing mill. Following the death of Bishop Pilkington of Durham in 1574 a survey was made of Stockton Castle to assess the likely costs required to put it in good order. Behind the massive moat of the castle ruins and its staithe along the riverfront there was a group of substantial but decayed buildings. They included a hall fortified by walls and towers, a large buttressed barn, a kitchen, kiln, malting house, combined brewhouse and bakehouse and *"... one House for a Horse Milne, the walles being xvj yardes longe, xiij yardes brode, iiij yardes high and ij foote thicke, which hath had a roufe of tymbre covered with slate and guttered rounde about wt lead, all decayed and downe. To be repaired in tymbre, slate, leade and stone coste lxxiijli xs iijd"* (T Sowler, 1972, 441-2). It survived to be listed in a further survey made in 1647 as a *"milne house within the castle walls ... but (pittie) all in ruins"* (T Richmond, 1868, 38). This, then, was a big, wide-span, stone-built and slate roofed building which was already old.

By 1629 the open fields to the north of Egglescliffe, on the Durham side of the ancient Yarm bridge, had been enclosed and there were three corn mills. The first was a water mill situated on the Cod Beck (later called Nellie Burdon's Beck), the second a windmill on the rise overlooking the bridge and the third a horse mill situated immediately to the west of the road leading to the bridge (B J D Harrison, 1978, 1-11). All three were let as a group to the millers, Thomas Scott (1644) and Richard Nicholson (1670). There was a problem with milling at Egglescliffe since the Tees is tidal at this point and the Cod Beck is small. There is no suggestion of a dispute in this case since all three mills were described as manorial mills; the windmill and the horse mill must have been built to supplement the water mill.

In 1649 Joseph Pennyman of Ormesby sold to Dame Ellinor Lowther *"one third part of the manor of Marske, Upleatham and Redcar ... with windmills, horse mills and watermills"* (NYCRO ZNK). This is tantalising since there is no other seventeenth century record of a horse mill in these townships. The phrase may have been merely a legal convention. However, over 60 years later, included in land leased by Sir James Pennyman of Ormesby Hall to Ralph Grange (1718) was *"all that Mill House and Horse Mill which stands near the Hall ... in Ormesby"*. In the same lease Pennyman undertook to build, in Ormesby village some distance away from the Hall, a brew house and a malt house *"... with a cistern*

FIG 44. PICKERING HIGH MILL (GEORGE NICHOLSON, REPRODUCED BY PERMISSION OF YORK CITY ART GALLERY).

which will contain and steep at one time 80 bushels of bigg (barley) *with floor kiln accordingly in proportion to work and dry the same and also one Stable to hold well-turn horses and also one pump well and pump"* (TA U/PEN 5/23). It seems that Pennyman was about to dismantle the old horse mill in order to make space for an extension to the hall and that he was agreeing to build a replacement in the village (D W Pattenden, 1991 and 1994).

Another horse mill was noted in the Corporation Records of Scarborough in 1656, when *"Ralph Hall undertakes not to grind any more wheat for the towne with his horsemill except with the leave of the bailiffs"* (J B Baker, 1882, 257). The explanation was that the water mills between Falsgrave and Scarborough *"... often stood idle in summer when the beck dried out and corn was therefore taken to Scalby and to Cayton Cliff mills and also, although disturbed by the bailiffs, various people in Scarborough erected horse and hand mills"* (Exch Dep, Hil 12 &13, Charles II no 1; VCH vol 2, 553). Excavations within the castle bailey in 1921-5 uncovered the paved, circular path of a horse walk actually within the foundations of the Norman chapel (A Rowntree, 1931, 146 & figs 26 & 46). This horse mill would hardly have been constructed until well after the former use of the building had been consigned to history. There is a possible explanation. Scarborough Castle had been held by Sir Hugh Cholmley of Whitby during the Civil War, and some 800 men were quartered there. When the Parliamentary forces arrived in 1645 they made short work of the town but a three-month siege was needed before the castle defenders gave up. During this time the defenders had access neither to the water mill in Scalby nor to the windmill in Scarborough and a horse mill might have been set up as an emergency measure.

Double and 'treble' water mills

Some water driven corn mills were re-built either at the end of the sixteenth century or during the seventeenth century to accommodate more than one waterwheel within a single building. The term 'double mill' is normally applied to two separate sets of corn milling machinery. There were three types. In one there were two waterwheels side-by-side with separate sluice gates and each driving a single set of millstones in its own building, one on each side of the watercourse. Sometimes, the two wheel pits were roofed over to make a single building. There was a second type consisting of a long building with a waterwheel at each end, for instance in the North York Moors at Howkeld mill (1649) and Kirby Mills. This second type of double mill might be described as 'two mills in one building'. In a third type the two waterwheels were in tandem, but offset, in a big wheel pit, with two pairs of mill-

stones in a long building alongside the pit.

"Two water corn mills under one roof" were recorded at Fountains Abbey at the time of the Dissolution and others were listed among the King's mills in 1608, particularly in the bigger towns of the West Riding (R Bennett and J Elton, 1900, 20-3). Another was intended in a specification of 1591 in which *"John Jackson of Gatenby covenants with Richard Stapleton to erect before the coming Michaelmas a mill house of six posts and two water corn mills on the site of the former mill of Bedale, walling the house with stones and covering the same with stone and slate. The said mill is to be large enough for two pairs of millstones ..."* (NYCRO ZBA 5/1/28). In addition to these documented examples there are also some surviving relics of the tandem layout in the lowlands between the Pennines and the North York Moors. In north east Yorkshire the few double and treble mills were restricted to the more prosperous margins of the North York Moors, with relics at Pickering High mill, Stokesley, Crathorne, Osmotherley, Borrowby (possibly), Marske and Dalehouse, and much more complete remains at Thornton-le-Street and Newburgh. Pickering High mill survived as a large pantile roofed building with two external clasp-arm waterwheels in 1810.

When, in 1602, the Bishop of Durham authorised the cutting of oak timber for 'siles' (crucks) for his mill in Osmotherley this may well have been for the building of a double mill, part of which survives (Durham Univ Lib ASC CCB Box 92,29 220830 8). Overbuilt in the north-facing wall is an early thatch-pitched gable wall which originally supported a roof over the mill house alongside the external wheel pit. The wheel pit would have been divided longitudinally by stone walling for two narrower wheels.

At Marske *"Two watermills standing on one parcel of*

Fig 45. Overbuilt seventeenth century gable in rear wall at Osmotherley mill.

ground called the Oxe Close ..." were listed in the tenancy agreement between James Pennyman of Ormesby, the owner, and Philip Hesseltone, in 1649 (NYCRO ZNK V 3/3/109 mic 1251), and *"Two water corn mills and the Rifts ..."* were leased by a new owner Anthony Lowther a few years later (NYCRO ZNK 3/3/123). This mill was rebuilt at the beginning of the nineteenth century and is now largely demolished but the hole for one of the early waterwheel shafts has survived in the wall between the waterwheel and the hurst.

Crathorne mill was described in 1672 as *"2 water corn mills built under one roof in Crathorne, with all soake, sucken, toll, moulture and other profits ..."*. By 1717 one of these mills was a fulling mill. Pickering High mill was illustrated by George Nicholson of Malton in 1810 as an old building with two waterwheels and sluices supported on a wooden frame. In 1832 it was described in a sale notice as having *"... two water wheels, a plentiful supply of water and machinery suitable for driving three pairs of stones"* (Yorks Gazette, March 10). Water still flows through the wide waterwheel pit which is quite different from those of old mills with single waterwheels.

The foundations of another early double mill exist at Dalehouse near Hinderwell. Here was an early double mill with an attached dwelling house, with fireplace window and cupboard, on the east side of the wide waterwheel pit and a nineteenth century mill on the other side. By the nineteenth century both mills and the dwelling were overbuilt into one large and complex building straddling the wheel pit. The building was demolished earlier this century. Foundations included two small hurst pits for the older mill, each for driving a single set of stones. Two narrow waterwheels, in tandem but offset, would have been separated by a thin wall, later demolished to make way for the much bigger nineteenth century wheel.

A mill at Thornton-le-Street on the Cod Beck near Thirsk was recorded in 1572 but, according to the date carved on the sundial built into the south west corner of the building (noted by Mitford Abraham and other observers but now weathered away), the mill was rebuilt in 1666. The near-ashlar quality of the stonework, the fine verge copings, corner finials and mullioned windows of this mill compare well with those in manor houses of the period. The building is elongated along the water leat and is divided into two roughly equal sized chambers, one for the waterwheel pit and the other for the driving gear and millstones. The wheel house has a narrow, four-centred arched doorway for access while the latter has had a very wide doorway (now blocked by a later building) which was suitable for carts or waggons. There are two mullioned windows under rises in the drip course of the gable walls to light the original hurst platform and two more

windows, high up in the gables, which show the wheel chamber was originally lofted over for extra storage. Today this fine building houses a single waterwheel with a nineteenth century drive system and three pairs of stones but there is evidence of two waterwheel shafts and a further hole for a water control shaft in the stonework of the dividing wall. A drying kiln was referred to in 1734 when the mill was described as *"a water corn mill called Thornton Mill, with house, kiln, stable and out-buildings"* (NYCRO ZQM IV 1/4 Cal). The kiln was built over the position of one of the former waterwheels, proving that at least part of the 1666 system had gone by then.

A smaller seventeenth century double mill, now known as Newburgh mill, survives at Coxwold in the south of the region. The surviving buildings consist of a modified seventeenth century mill with a nineteenth century granary built onto its facade. Originally there were ground floor and first floor entrances to the mill, one of which survives. The lower walls of the mill are of coursed rubble stone with good quality quoins up to the moulded string-course and the two steeply pitched gable walls (later raised to create a dwelling above) are of hand-made brick. As at Thornton the roof covered both the mill and the wheel pit. Inside the building the wheel chamber now contains a single mid-nineteenth century wheel but there are circular axle holes for two earlier wheels. The masonry at the head of the wheel pit shows that originally it was divided longitudinally for two wheels, about 11 feet in diameter and 3 feet wide. *"Two mills at Newburgh"* were mentioned in estate accounts in 1684-5. Michael Barehead made *"two new waterwheeles for Newbrough mills ..."* in 1689 and Robert Waters was paid £2 4s *"... for 24 days cutting, sawing, fitting and making a New Cogg wheele"* in 1689 (NYCRO ZDV). In 1813 the mill was described as having an *"overshot wheel and three pairs of stones"* (NYCRO ZDV mic 1285). The old machinery had already gone by then but the lay shaft for three stones and the larger waterwheel from this era survive.

The two major developments of this period, horse mills and double mills, came together at Stokesley mill. Stokesley was a prosperous and growing market town, but its mill was sometimes stopped because of backwatering when the Leven flooded. A survey of the estate of the recusant William Peirson (1717) included *"... All those three water corn milnes and one horse milne all within the one house, with the said milne house, two stables, curtillage and a little garth thereunto belonging ..."* (Quarter Session Records, N R Rec Soc, vol 8, 12). The property was described again in 1730 in similar terms (N R Rec Soc vol 8, 85 & 96). These eighteenth century descriptions tallied with relics of the 'mills', surveyed and recorded in 1974 (J K Harrison, 1974). The lower walls of the octagonal horse wheel house, suitable for a 20 foot diameter wheel, and the longitudinally divided waterwheel pit suitable for two wheels had been incorporated into a later and larger building. These features were easy to explain but there remains the problem of resolving the description of the *"three water corn milnes"*. This problem cannot be resolved in terms of the milling technology described so far. It seems that at Stokesley there was a very early example of a type of mill in which a single waterwheel was geared to drive two separate sets of millstones. From the few references located so far it seems that any late seventeenth century or early eighteenth century mill equipped with three pairs of millstones, might be referred to as a 'treble', 'threble' or 'threbble' mill (See also Ruswarp Country Mill, 71).

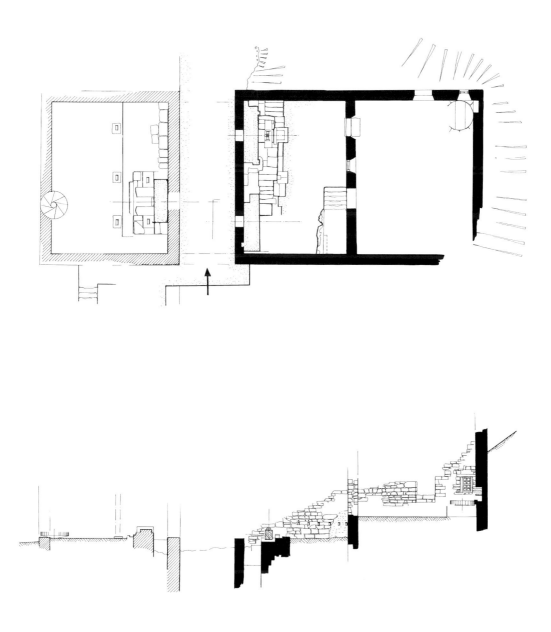

Fig 46. Foundations of a double mill (in black) at Dalehouse.

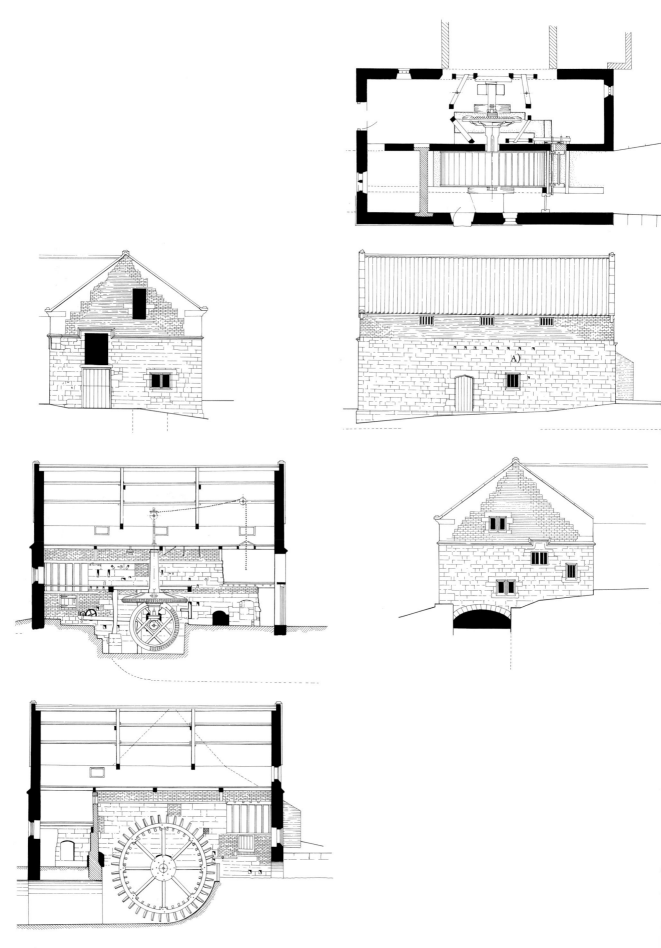

Fig 47. Thornton-le-Street mill.

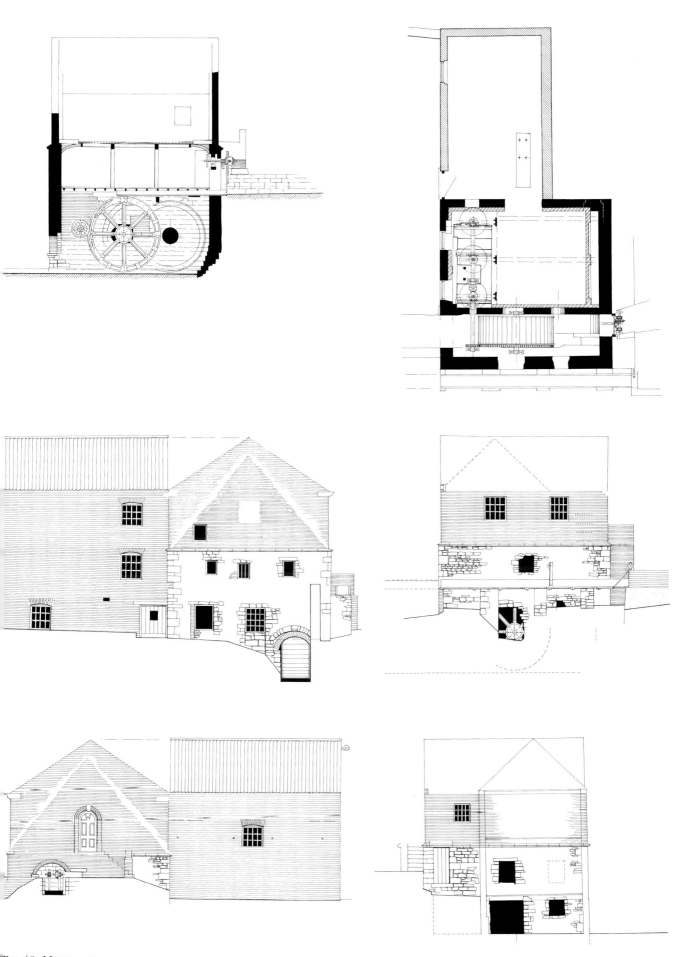

Fig 48. Newburgh mill.

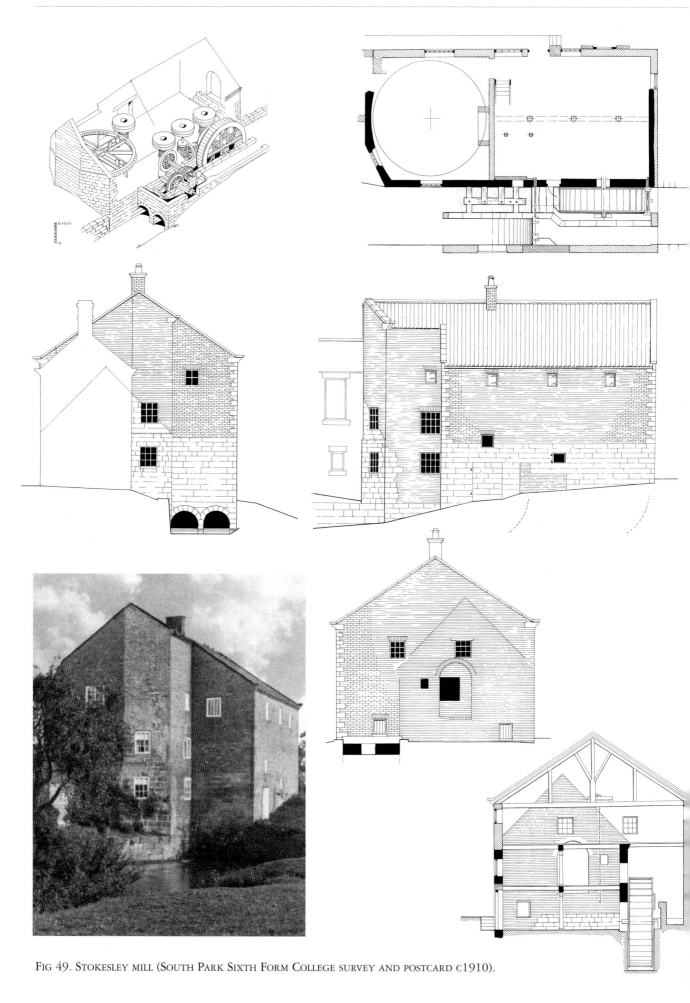

Fig 49. Stokesley mill (South Park Sixth Form College survey and postcard c1910).

EIGHTEENTH CENTURY DEVELOPMENTS

At the beginning of the eighteenth century there was an increasing demand for oatmeal and also for flour for the expanding villages, towns and ports. At the same time there was a new pressure arising from a fashion for white bread, lately taking root in wealthy social circles. There would be two fundamental changes in milling practice in north east Yorkshire. First, new types of millstone were introduced and, second, gearing systems were developed to allow more than one set of millstones to be driven from one waterwheel. In north east Yorkshire some millers turned from locally available sandstone outcrops to the Millstone Grit series of the Northern Pennines, for example from Summerbridge in Nidderdale. Mills in the margins of the Pennines were also so equipped. In 1629, for instance, the Slingsby family of Knaresborough bought millstones and paid £16 for "... *foure paire ... brought from Braisty Wood to the milne door*" (Blacker J G, 1993, 3,4).

Formerly it was only the wealthy who were able to enjoy the pleasures of soft white bread, variously known as 'pain de main', 'payndemayn' or 'manchet (manger?) loaf', baked from flour with the bran removed. Others made do with coarse brown loaves made from maslin (a mixed crop of wheat and rye), rye, barley and/or peas. However, coarse bread had a reputation. "*Browne bread made of the coarsest of wheat having in it moch branne, fylleth the belly with excrements, and shortly descendeth from the stomacke ...*" (Thomas Cogan, 1584; J C Drummond and A Wilbraham, 1958, 74). The bran was seen to be indigestible and, in particular, was thought to cause 'wind' ... perhaps beginning to be seen as a problem in polite society! High fashion was turning against keeping the bran in the flour. Hence, Andrew Boord (1542) enthused over "... *manchet (white) bread ... thoroughly baked, the bran abstracted and thrown away ...*"

Producing fine flour for white bread was a two-stage

process, milling under blue stones followed by bolting. An account by Gervase Markham stated that "... *your best and principal bread is manchet, which you shall bake in this manner; first your meal being ground upon the black stones, if it be possible, which makes the whitest flour, and passing it through the finest boulting cloth ...*" (Markham G, 1615; E David, 1977, 335). With regard to grinding it was Thomas Muffet who added the key to understanding the eighteenth century changes in milling technique when he stated that "*The meal must be neither so finely grinded least the bran mingle with it, nor too grossly, least you may lose much flour, but moderately gross, that the bran may be easily separated, and the fine flour not hardly bolted*".

In 1641 Henry Best, a prosperous farmer of the village of Elmswell near Driffield, sent best wheat to the mill for making "... *bread for the family*" and massledine

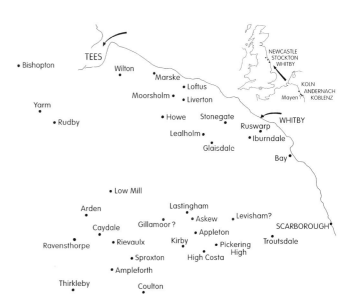

FIG 50. GERMAN BASALT MILLSTONES IN NORTH EAST YORKSHIRE.

for the "*pye crusts for the folkes*" ie people working on the farm (Surtees Society, 1857). "*... after-loggings of wheate*" (left-overs from bolting) were ground for pies for the servants while the "*Poore folks*" (of the village) received mixed peas and rye or massledine "*... and say that these make a hearty bread*". The difference between "*tempsed bread*" and "*hearty bread*" was a measure of social standing. Rye was the staple diet across the whole of northern Europe, where it was grown because of its ability to ripen between a fortnight and a month earlier than wheat, but the most common way in which it was grown in north east Yorkshire was in the form of maslin, a mixture of rye and wheat. It was claimed that this mixed crop was never affected by mildew. Wheat on its own was a preferred cereal but it could only be grown in Cleveland, around Thirsk, in Ryedale and around Pickering but not in the moorland dales.

Blue or 'cullin' stones

As Markham pointed out, the 'black' (blue) stones were used for making fine flour. Sandstone and grit millstones are both composed of coarse, hard grits cemented together in a softer matrix. The matrix will always wear away more quickly than the grits and two gritty surfaces rubbed together will break up the husk of the grain into a coarse powder. Lava stones, on the other hand, consist of frozen lava and, like pumice, filled with gas holes. In use, wear exposed fresh cavities to form new cutting edges but there was always a flat and smooth surface on the 'lands'. The hard flakes of bran could slide outwards through the tiny gap between top and bottom millstones without being broken up. Light in weight and with a comparatively big surface area, these flakes could be separated out from the heavier and finer flour by sifting and/or fanning.

Blue millstones were imported from a region called Meyer Mendig, via Cologne to Hull and, possibly, Whitby. They were smaller in diameter than the older millstones and were cut to a very precise pattern of furrows, normally with 13 harps. There is little evidence of their early use in named mills in the north of England, where research has located only 18 firm references from before the end of the eighteenth century and of these only five date from before 1750 (Harrison J K, 2005, Appendix 2).

Blue stones were installed where there was a 'big house' (Arden, Helmsley, Castle Howard), near the market towns (Malton, Pickering) and near the coastal towns. The earliest in north east Yorkshire dates from 1681 when Sir Thomas Mauleverer leased "*All those two water corn mills ...*" of Boroughbridge to Ambrose Jackson, miller. For his part Jackson was to "*... keep the said mill and implements in good repair, and also, ... if any of the blow stones (sic) or any other of the stones be broken he will replace them*." (Lawson-Tancred, 1937,

162,163). Boroughbridge is sited at the highest navigation point on the Ure; navigation in fact being blocked by its mill dam. By this early date, at least one pair of blue 'Dutch' stones had made the journey.

In 1706 Thomas Stent recorded a payment in his Account Book for the Duncombe estate: "*To Edward Sadler for work done to Sproxton mill and for Blue Stones £50 0s 0d*" (NYCRO ZEW X IV 6/3/1). Sir Charles Duncombe was at the heart of London politics during the reigns of Charles II and of William and Mary. Often described as a goldsmith, his actual business lay in tax collecting for the King and, operating as a bank, accepting deposits and using the money as loans to the Crown. He became Lord Mayor of London and when, in 1689, he bought the Helmsley estate in North Yorkshire from the bankrupted Duke of Buckingham he was described as "*the richest commoner in England*" (Duncombe P, 2001, 128). In 1697 he spent £15 10s on a new pair of millstones for Helmsley mill and, although the account does not state what kind these were, the very high price strongly suggests they were blue stones from abroad. At first Duncombe lived in the old house in Helmsley castle yard but in 1706 he bought a neighbouring estate called West Newton and spent considerable sums of money on up-grading the house and the nearby Sproxton mill. Duncombe was bringing London fashion to his country estate.

The most important house in north east Yorkshire was Castle Howard. In 1727 Ralph Fowler, millwright to the Earl of Carlisle at Castle Howard, wrote, "*... the blue stones from Holland are become most general, they being cheaper, on account of lasting 40 or 50 years ... they commonly sold at the Sea-side upon the Northern Coasts*" (Lawrence E, 1727, 161-2). Thereafter, there was a pair of blue stones in Ruswarp mill in 1765, and there are early dated stones with incised lettering at Liverton (17??) and Thirkleby ("May 12 1774").

Two-stage gearing

At the beginning of the eighteenth century small water mills still consisted of single pairs of millstones each driven by its own waterwheel and cog-wheel. Where extra capacity was needed an additional water wheel with its own pair of millstones was installed. There was change with the introduction of blue stones. These were generally thinner and smaller in diameter than the older millstones and to have driven a blue top stone on a spindle directly from the pit wheel, even with a smaller diameter lantern, would have meant that the peripheral speed would have been too low. This was the problem solved by the type of gearing first illustrated in an engraving made by Henry Beighton in 1723 of a "*Water Mill for Grinding Corn at the Barr Pool by ye Abbey in Nunn Eaton in Worwickshire*" (published Desaguler J T, 1744, vol. 2, plate xxxii and 450-53) in which, for the first time, two different types of millstone were driven at different speeds from the same waterwheel.

The Beighton engraving shows a pair of large-diameter millstones suitable for grinding oatmeal but with an additional smaller pair set on the same hurst frame. The oatmeal pair was driven directly from the pit wheel while the second pair was driven by a short horizontal shaft. At Nuneaton the top stone of the second pair "... *which stones are used for grinding Wheat for fine flower* ..." would have revolved over two and a half times faster than the centre pair used for coarser meal. This was what is essentially a traditional mill for coarse meal with a pair of bakers' millstones tacked on.

Beighton claimed that the water mill at Nuneaton

"... *is by most People accounted as good a one as any the Country affords, for dispatching as much Business in the time, and doing it well*". It was not claimed as a 'first'. There may have been others. The description of three pairs of millstones driven by two waterwheels at Stokesley mill, for instance, pre-dates Beighton's engraving by six years. There is also evidence that the system may have been in use in Ruswarp Country mill as early as 1682. A survey of between 1000 and 2000 English water mills (D Jones, 1969, TIMS) located the relics of several similar mills, by far the best preserved being the almost complete Arden mill in the North York Moors.

The surviving relics at Arden mill are worth describing in detail. In 1536 the "... *scite of the late Priory*

FIG 51. HENRY BEIGHTON'S ENGRAVING, 1723.

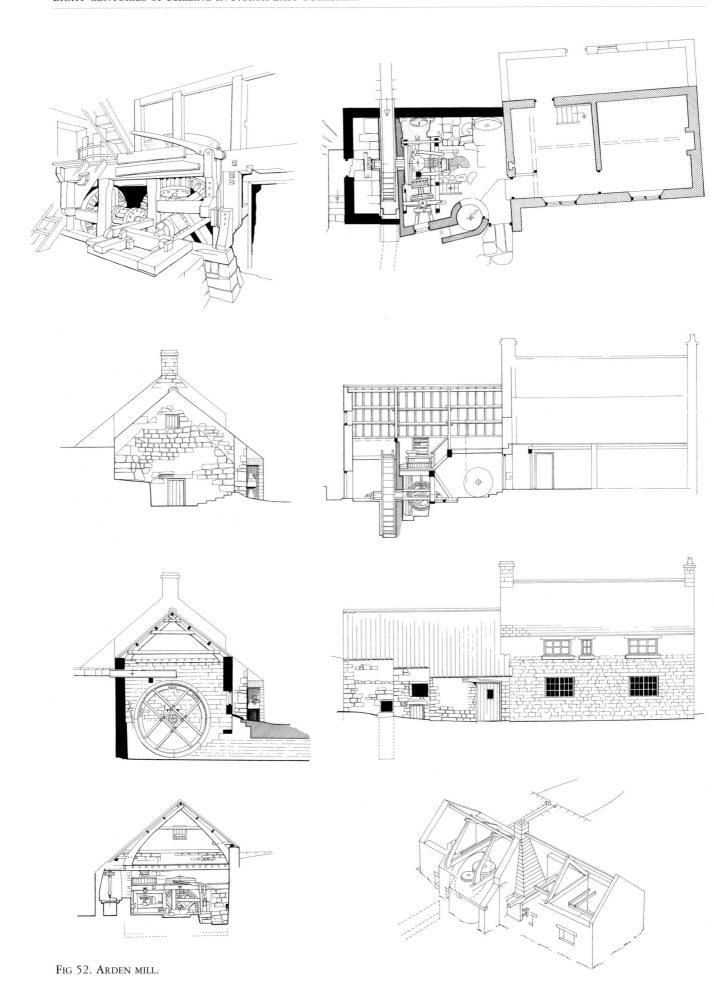

Fig 52. Arden mill.

including one water mill with one acre of meadow to the same adjacent" was leased to Thomas Welles, a member of the King's Household, and there is a continuous record thereafter. There is a striking similarity between the virtually intact machinery at Arden and that at Nuneaton illustrated by Beighton in 1723. Arden mill is an amazing survival. The range consisted of a one-and-a-half storey mill (formerly one storey) and a two-storey mill house (formerly one-storey with loft). The mill has an internal waterwheel, two sets of millstones and a later oat roasting plate. Part of the front wall of the mill has been rebuilt to accommodate the oat roasting kiln and the roof has been raised, re-using the old cruck blades.

Thorodale Beck was dammed to fill a pond from where the water was led into the mill by a trough. The wooden overshot wheel is only 2 feet wide, with 40 buckets and a single set of clasp-arms round a square-section wooden shaft. The hurst and hurst gearing are also relics from the time when wood was the main material used by millwrights. Like the waterwheel, the pit wheel is of clasp-arm construction, but later modified with cast-iron gear segments bolted over the old mortises. It drove one upright lantern gear for the centre millstones and a horizontal lantern for the shaft to the blue stones. The original top stone of the centre set is now propped against a wall, having been replaced with a smaller top stone. The tentering of the centre stones was by lever or 'lighter' staff, an old system with the advantage of requiring no expensive screw thread. The system for disengaging the blue stones was similarly primitive, by sliding the bearing of the shaft sideways to disengage its lantern from the pit wheel. Also rudimentary is the wooden wedge adjustment for the woodwork supporting the inner bearing of the waterwheel shaft. Missing is a second, possibly later, lying shaft on the upstream side of the pit wheel, which may have driven a grain cleaner. Another drive consisted of an endless rope from the waterwheel shaft running through pulleys set inside mortises in the hurst beam to the rotating paddle of the oat plate.

The building is no less interesting. Sadly the house has now been destroyed by flood but the present walls of the mill, except for the front wall and the kiln, probably stand on the medieval ground plan and the south gable wall incorporates a lower gable wall of early date. The extant wall between the hurst and the waterwheel is the newest wall in the mill and this places a question mark over what might originally have separated the waterwheel from the gearing. One of the most striking features is the large size of the hurst pit, necessary to house the bulky wooden pit wheel, the horizontal shaft with its cog wheel, and the timber-framing supporting the millstones. A bad feature of such a pit was that the feet of the hurst posts were set in the floor of the pit where very wet conditions caused rotting. Nevertheless, such large pits are a feature of other surviving early mills in the area and were

no doubt common in the eighteenth century.

Arden mill was not the only one of its type. Earlier this century there was a similar set of machinery at nearby Caydale mill, immediately to the north of Old Byland. Where the narrow road from Old Byland fords the beck the water was diverted along a leat to a pond, from whence it rushed either down an escape leat now known as the 'waterfall' or into the L-shaped range of buildings. The combined mill and house range has a 16 foot span with walls 2 feet 3 inches thick. The spacious waterwheel house has a pit for a waterwheel 14 feet in diameter and 3 feet wide. The mill had a low access doorway to the hurst and a wide doorway, which formerly gave access to the house as well as the mill. The house still contains a smoke-hood and bread oven. The second 'wing' of the range, at right angles to the first, may have been garner storage, etc.

The known history of *"Caierdale Mill"* dates from its inclusion on Christopher Saxton's Survey of Old Byland in 1659 but the mill may have been much older. It was stripped of its eighteenth century hurst and gearing in November 1928 by its owner, the mill enthusiast Mitford Abraham, who donated the pearl barley machine to the Kirk Collection in York Castle Museum. Abraham was a keen photographer and left a set of photographs showing a clasp-arm waterwheel and driving gears which could well have been made by the same carpenter as those at Arden. At Caydale, however, the original lay-out had been modified and, for instance, the lanterns had been replaced with cast-iron bevel pinions. The old hurst beam, now re-located as a mantel beam over a new fireplace, is a remarkable piece of woodwork with separate carved boards attached to its front face over the meal spouts of the three sets of millstones. The spout for the centre set of stones is incised with "S B FECIT ANO 1729", that for the blue stones "I K + R H FECIT 1750" and additionally "R 1841" and there is a third spout marked simply with the initials "T F". The earliest date is six years later than that on Beighton's engraving. However, the dimensions of the shaft lay-out which survived until 1928 did not line up with the hurst beam spouts. The gearing had been modified.

Another mill of the type illustrated by Beighton, now demolished, stood on the north bank of the lower Esk at the upper tidal limit. It was owned by the Cholmley family, which derived much of its income from the harbour of Whitby. From 1632, when the first pier was built at Whitby, the Cholmleys had improved the navigability of the river for the sailing vessels trading between Whitby and London, and by the mid-eighteenth century they had added wheat milling and flour exporting to their other interests. Their 'Bolting Mill', built in 1752, at the lowest weir on the Esk is a large and handsome Georgian brick structure. It was built alongside the older stone-built mill which became known as the 'Country Mill' because it continued to deal with the local trade of the farmers. As

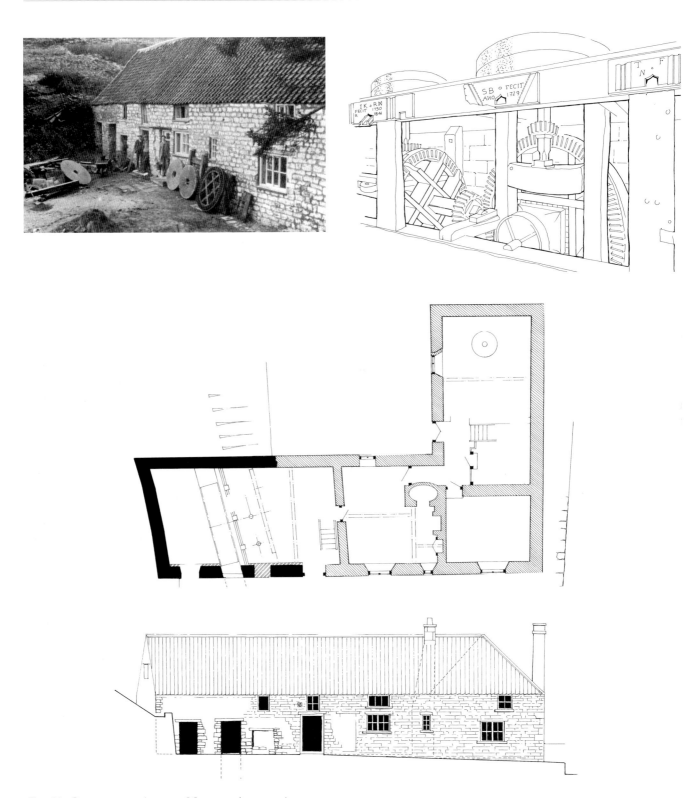

FIG 53. CAYDALE MILL (PHOTO, MITFORD ABRAHAM).

a result of a court case in the York Summer Assize of 1768, quite a lot is known about the machinery in the 'Country Mill'. Soon after the completion of the new bolting mill the lower river and the harbour at Whitby began to silt up as a result of waste shale being dumped into a tributary beck by John Matthews and Samuel Howlett of the Iburndale alum works. Nathaniel

Cholmley, as holder of the river and harbour dues and owner of Ruswarp mill, sued Matthews and Howlett on the grounds that they:

"... *wrongfully and injuriously laid placed threw and conveyed into and in a certain beck or rivulet in ye parish of Whitby called Ibrondale Beck and to be carried washed and conveyed in down and along ye stream and channel ... into ye river Eske diverse great quantity of Alom Slam Shail and other rubbish that is to say 300 000 tons of Alom Slam, 300 000 tons of Alom Shail and 300 000 tons of the rubbish arising from and coming from certain works or Mines of Alom ..."* and that this rubbish had *"... filled loaded obstructed choaked and stopped up in divers parts ... the river Eske and thereby hindered the working of the mill"*

(Chancery Court Records, Percy Burnett coll, no 1558; see also J Richardson, 1812, Reports of the late John Smeaton, 230-3).

The plaintiff claimed that before this time the two mills together could grind and dress 150 quarters of corn through every season but afterwards they could grind no more than 20 to 30 quarters. To make matters worse, it had become impossible to use small boats to carry the flour down-river to the waiting ships. This was indeed a disaster. In the event judgement was given against Matthews and Howlett. They were ordered to clear the river as best they could. Also, in what has subsequently been described as a 'judgement of Solomon' they were to rent both the old and new mills at Ruswarp on an annual fixed rent, calculated as the equivalent of the average annual profit of the two mills over any three years of their life before silting up. This safeguarded Chomley's income. Subsequently a lease was drawn up, accompanied by a schedule and inventories for both mills (Burnett coll, no 1700). The inventory for the 'Country Mill' reads as follows:

"The country water wheel from outside to outside thirteen feet six inches diameter and four feet wide, the diameter of the axle tree twenty two inches

The main wheel on the same axel tree eight feet nine inches and a half diameter

The trunnels for the centre stones one foot eight inches and a half diameter

The walloes two feet two inches diameter with iron staves

The counter and threble wheels six feet one inch diameter

The counter wheels two feet and half an inch with iron staves

The trunnels for the Blew Mill one foot eleven inches diameter with iron staves

The centre grey stone four feet eleven inches diameter with...

The Counter grey thribble stones four feet diameter...

Ragg wheel and blocks for taking up the stones, with cases, hoppers, truss and all things suitable for them with iron cannels

Three moulter boxes

One large corn chist. One dusting seive for shilling

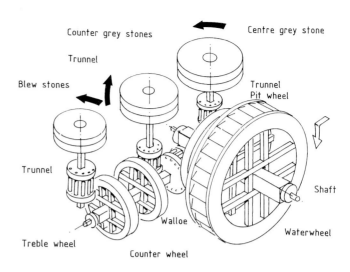

FIG 54. RUSWARP COUNTRY MILL (CONJECTURED DRAWING BASED ON INVENTORY DESCRIPTION).

oates

One iron bar to raise the water clow. One large iron crowe. One small iron crowe. Two bush chizels. One hammer. One iron scale balk four feet long. Four plates for drying oates, seventeen pickes and seven bills ..."

This inventory is difficult to interpret. However, it clearly describes a centre-driven pair of grey millstones and two other pairs, called *"the counter grey stones"* and the *"blew or thribble stones"*. The term *"centre grey stones"* is self-explanatory. But also driven from the pit wheel was the *"walloes"*, which can only have been on a horizontal shaft. The use of the term *"counter"* to describe the second pair of grey stones probably indicated that the top stone rotated in the opposite direction to the other two. This could easily have been achieved with a horizontal shaft. It is likely that early eighteenth century millwrights did not think in geometrical terms when describing shafts, and the terms vertical and horizontal might not have been in common use. The more homely terms, *"upright"* and *"lying"* were probably preferred, but even these were used sparingly. In retrospect, though not in line with later use of the term, it is tempting to use the term 'countershaft' for the lying shaft with its two face wheels set back-to-back to deliver the counter-rotation to the two millstones.

Evidence for dating this type of gearing is not plentiful. Unfortunately, the gearing at Arden mill has not been dated. The 'Country Mill' at Ruswarp was described as *"All those three water corne mills called Riswarpe Mill ... together with soake and sucken"* as early as 1682 (Assignment of Mortage; Burnett coll, 1424). Stokesley mill was described as three mills within the one building in 1717.

The hurst beam at Caydale has three meal spouts, the earliest dated 1729. There is further evidence from datestones, dated millstones, etc, that at least another seven mills in the region were rebuilt about this time:

Rosedale mill, relocated date stone in back wall, "1667"

Kilton mill, relocated date stone in back wall "D G T 1701"

Goathland mill, relocated date stone in gable wall "I W 1716 R R"

Stonegate mill, relocated date stone "I K 1735"

Marske mill, dated lintel recovered during excavation "173-" and "IRW IR W"

Vivers mill, relocated date stone "1744"

Raisdale mill, relocated date stone in back wall "W G 1769"

The discovery of such eighteenth century relics in what is essentially a moors and dales region, initially at Arden and Caydale, might lead to a view that these mills had formed part of a wider group of 'upland' mills. This is not the case. An upland mill can be seen as one concerned with grinding oats and barley, commonly in areas of high rainfall, such as the Highlands of Scotland and Wales. It would not be equipped with blue millstones for grinding wheat; it might well be equipped with a grain drying kiln for oats. The mills as Arden and Caydale, though situated in deep dales, are in fact surrounded by high-lying, well-drained fields, good for growing wheat.

'Grey' millstones

'Grey' millstones were cut from outcrops of Millstone Grit throughout the length of the Pennines. The 'centre grey' stones at Ruswarp recorded in 1765 were early examples and, at that time, greys were certainly much less common in records of north east Yorkshire mills than German blue stones. However, two even earlier records very likely refer to 'greys'. In *"An exact survey of the manor of Stockton, … taken by Edward Colstone and George Daile"* by order of Parliament (1647) it was recorded that *"… the copyholders within the s'd several townepps, by custom of the s'd man'r are to … fetch … the millstones for the use of the s'd milne"* (Norton mill) *"from Raley Green and Walker-field"* (T Richmond, 1868, 37). The most likely location of Raley Green is the Millstone Grit outcrop at Railey Fell in the Pennines, immediately to the north of Ramshaw near Bishop Auckland.

There can be no doubt about the notes kept by Timothy Mauleverer, landlord of Ingleby Arncliffe, about the transport of a set of greys across the Vale of York from the Yorkshire Pennines (NYCRO Transcript TD 38). In 1694 he was thinking of upgrading his water mill, where the millstones were worn too thin, and he began

to collect relevant information. For instance, he noted that *"… good millstones are got and to be sold besides Pateley Bridge, says Mr Edward"* and a little later that *"… the best millstones, large and fit for this mill may be found at Braceby Wood, 6 miles beyond Ripon for £10 a pair, and they'l bring them at that price, and a foot thick at the edges and 2 foot at the eye or crown, says John Pierson's father … The millstones should be two yards over …"*. With regard to dressing the stones Mauleverer noted that *"Says John Pearson, pick the upper stone line contrary to the lower stone in the line edges … the strait long lines are pickt but once a year, but the little small dimples picked are picked full and throng every month or two, and especially near the edg of the stone and so to a foot from the edg round …"*.

Mauleverer eventually bought two stones from Thomas Lasselles. His note shows that he was under the impression that the price included the cost of delivery (just over 30 miles) but this proved not to be the case. By mid-October he was in dispute with his carrier, John Smith, to whom he had paid 20s to transport the stones. Smith had four oxen and two horses of his own and a further three horses on loan from Mauleverer to cope with the task of hauling these massive millstones but there was still some sort of problem. A wayleave, needed before he could carry the stones across land at Romanby, near Northallerton, had been delayed for an hour and for some reason Smith walked away from the job leaving a very disgruntled employer. Incidentally, nothing is noted of the method of transporting the stones. An account from north east Scotland described how a pole was wedged through the eye of a millstone and set into a wooden frame either on wheels or runners (W Alexander, 1877, 120-1) but it is more likely that the Pateley millstones were carried on a heavy waggon. Whichever way, it is clear that there were formidable problems in getting better quality millstones for mills in north east Yorkshire.

The most likely location of 'Braceby Woods' is Braisty Woods above Summerhouses near Pateley Bridge (SE 205638) where the Millstone Grit outcrops in a prominent edge. Here at least four old millstones lie where they were abandoned, probably after flaws were discovered. The diameter of two of them is 6 feet (matching Mauleverer's note). A neat feature of two of the stones is that the edges were left rounded in cross section (over and above the nominal diameter), to protect the vulnerable edges while they were being rolled to the roadside.

Mauleverer's notes describe a method of dressing with inscribed furrows and 'pecking' in the 'lands' between, a technique which was also used on early sandstone millstones at Commondale and Kildale where the roughly incised furrows are set in crude and irregular 'harps'. These Pennine greys were dressed in the same way as the older sandstones, the crudeness of this traditional form contrasting markedly with the precision found on German blue stones of the same period.

Although greys were to become common in north east Yorkshire in the nineteenth century, little is known about their earliest use. Four local grey millstones have eighteenth century dates incised into them; Ruswarp ("1720"), Ingleby Greenhow ("1767"), Sutton-under-Whitestonecliffe ("I B 1768") and Liverton ("17—", obscured). There are one or two slightly later documentary references, in particular to a payment of *"... sundries to Henry Mills, pr of grey stones, £9"* for Howl Beck mill (1807) and the payment for *"... a new Grey Millstone and fitting up ... £12"* for Danby Howe mill (1819).

Opposed lying shafts

In addition to mills with centre-driven stones as at Arden, there are also relics in north east Yorkshire of a variation in which the centre-driven stones were dispensed with altogether. In this system, either two or three sets of millstones were driven by a single lying shaft or by two opposed shafts, one on each side of the pit wheel. In the three surviving examples of this arrangement two have two sets of millstones downstream of the waterwheel shaft and one upstream while in the third there are two sets only, downstream of the shaft. In all three the downstream stones were arranged to counter-rotate, one clockwise and the other anticlockwise, to even out the end thrust on the shaft bearings. A rather similar system of opposed lying shafts was illustrated in the encyclopaedia of Denis Diderot (1763) but in that case they drove ancillary machines only and the millstones were still centre-driven.

The introduction of blue stones alongside the larger sandstones has already been explained in terms of increasing demand for wheat and rye flour but this does not explain the mills with no centre-driven millstones. Probably the answer lies in the introduction of grey millstones. Unlike Mauleverer's set, most grey millstones were probably smaller in diameter than the traditional sandstones and they would need, therefore, to rotate more quickly, certainly at a higher speed than the old single-stage trundle gear could deliver. Two-stage gearing was now needed for both oatmeal and flour milling.

The best examples of this form of drive in north east Yorkshire are at Rievaulx, Coulton and Lastingham. There are a number of documentary records of mill improvements for this period. For instance, after Charles Duncombe, London City banker and formerly Lord Mayor, bought the Helmsley Estate from the Dukes of Rutland, the following entries were made in an estate book by his accountant, Thomas Stent:

"1697 Pd. for a pair of millstones at Helmsley Mill £15 10s 0d

1703 Pd. Ed Sadler for repairing the Mill and a pair of new Millstones £20 18s 4d

1706 Pd. Edw. Sadler and others repairing Helmsley Mill and Sproxton Mill £19 0s 4d

1706 Pd. Edwd. Sadler for work done to Sproxton Mill and the Blue stones £50 0s 0d

1706 Pd. Geo. Tayler for rebuilding Rievaulx Mill £43 0s 0d"

(NYCRO ZEW IV 6/3/1 mic 2952/803; J McDonnell ed, 1963, 167).

This was a healthy ten year investment in three water mills. Further developments were also considered but not implemented. In 1719 Duncombe sought Council's advice as to the legality of building two new water mills, one at Keldholme near Kirkby Moorside and one downstream from the Abbey ruins at Rievaulx. The advice received was that *"Mr Duncombe may erect a new mill or mills in his Mannor of Rivis* (Rievaulx) *being below his other mill so as no detriment by diversion of water can be pretended"*. In fact this mill was never built. With regard to Kirkby Moorside, Council's opinion was that there was no customary soke right in Kirkby Moorside *"... which was exclusive to existing mills"* and *"... although there was a soke right in general terms it would certainly be possible to challenge it in court of law if the need arose"* (NYCRO ZEW VI 20/2 mic 1307). Further, at one stage the town had been taken from the Earl of Westmorland by attainder into the hands of the King but it was Council's opinion that this did not constitute a right to special claims on the grounds there had been a King's Mill. In other words, Duncombe was on fairly safe ground if he wanted to build new water mills.

From Stent's accounts it seems that the old Abbey mill at Rievaulx was rebuilt in 1706. The general arrangement of the hurst and gearing still survives though, as in all old mills, there have been later modifications. In particular, a new waterwheel was installed in 1857. The original wooden pit wheel and counter wheels have been replaced in cast-iron, and the old tentering system has been replaced by hand wheels and bell cranks. Surviving eighteenth century features include the very large hurst pit, the lying shaft lay-out with two counter-rotating millstones on the downstream shaft and the system for engaging the stone nuts by means of forked levers. Also, the sack hoist is the only unmodified survivor in the region of a type which may have been common in the eighteenth century. A crude wooden pulley made up of segments nailed to the waterwheel shaft drove a rope, later replaced by a chain, to the pulley on the hoist drum shaft. The sacks were lifted through a raised box hatch alongside the hurst steps while the short set of steps from the hurst platform to the first floor actually ran between the driving chains, an arrangement which seems highly dangerous by modern standards. The hoist must have been very slow in action but this mattered little since before 1875 the mill was essentially a one-storey structure.

A similar set of gearing survives at Coulton mill on Marr Beck, between Scackleton and Coulton. In 1725 this mill was in the hands of the Fairfax family of Gilling and was, apparently, changed from an undershot to an overshot mill (J Rushton, nd, 74). This would have entailed digging a new water leat with a new dam. The work may have become necessary because more power was needed to drive a second pair of stones. Surviving eighteenth century features at Coulton include the massively constructed clasp-arm pit wheel, the downstream lying shaft and pieces of the blue stones in the threshold of the mill and in the wall above the pen stock. Again, there have been modifications. For instance, the waterwheel is of nineteenth century design (but rebuilt in the twentieth century). The roof and its main timbers have been replaced this century so the sack hoist is lost. A new hurst frame has been installed in front of the old so that the original is hidden away from all but the most persistent searchers. The upstream lying shaft is missing

and one gear wheel is missing from the downstream 'countershaft'. A wooden pulley for a flat belt was added to the downstream shaft to drive a flour dresser which hung from the joists of the first floor. But many original features have survived, including the very large hurst pit running the full width of the mill and the two sets of counter-rotating stones on the downstream shaft. The dimensions of the lying shafts are almost identical with those at Rievaulx. One variation is that the wooden rope pulley for the hoist drum is on the downstream lying shaft and not on the waterwheel shaft, the advantage being a quicker hoisting action.

The third example, Lastingham mill, is small and there was no opposing lying shaft on the upstream side. At Lastingham there are also traces of an even earlier centre-driven set of stones in the inner leaf of the wall between the waterwheel and the hurst, and the centre line of an earlier waterwheel is in line with this earlier set of stones. Surviving relics of the eighteenth century system are very similar to those at Rievaulx and Coulton, in particular the dimensions of the wooden 'counter-

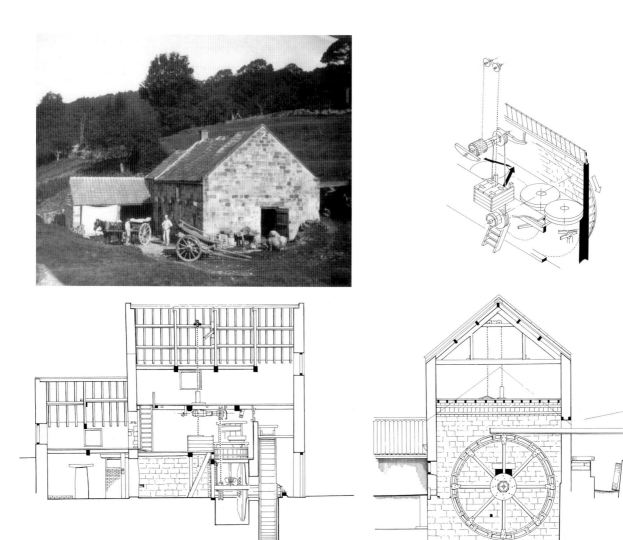

FIG 55. RIEVAULX MILL (PHOTO C1875). SEE ALSO FIG 25.

FIG 56. COULTON MILL (PHOTO,
MITFORD ABRAHAM).

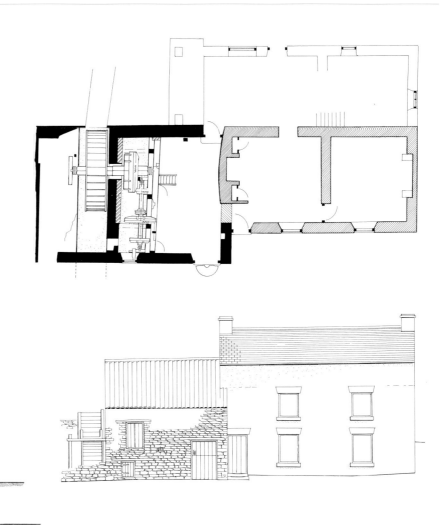

shaft' with its two wooden face wheels. The wallower is of cast-iron. The stone nuts were disengaged with wooden forked levers. Until the 1980s, there was one blue stone in the yard outside. Tentering by nuts on top of the hurst beam with hangers down to the tenter beam was a later system. As at Rievaulx the rope pulley for the hoist is on the waterwheel shaft. Though no longer complete this tiny mill is a remarkable survival. The front wall has been raised from the original thatched pitch to give a little extra space but the back wall has not. The cramped conditions which must have been a feature of many early mills is preserved here as in no other mill in the region.

Bolting

The mills described so far were humble buildings. However, this should not be taken to mean that it was only the smaller dales' mills which were equipped with blue stones and two-stage gearing. The bigger mills in the lowland margins of the moorland were almost certainly equipped in the same way.

One example is the 'bolting mill' at Ruswarp. This was an exceptional building for its time, built at the highest tidal point on the Esk as a grain store as well as a corn mill. It is a very large building, built in the Georgian 'polite' style with large windows and string courses at each floor. It is six bays long (52 feet by 36 feet wide) and four storeys high with two lofts above the eaves, the upper one lit on both sides. There were four separate chimneys. The mill represented a major investment by the Cholmley family and the man in charge of the project was acknowledged by a plaque which reads "THESE MILLS WERE ERECTED AT THE EXPENCE OF NATHAN^L CHOLMLEY ESQ^R BY PHILIP WILLIAMS ENGINEER 1752". This is a very early use of the term 'engineer'. Williams would have seen himself as a civil engineer rather than a mechanical engineer and he would have been responsible for the overall project, employing builders and carpenters as well as millwrights. This corn mill pre-dated the big cotton mills built by Arkwright. Indeed it pre-dated the similarly big Albion Steam Mill in London (1785) and Abbott's Mill in Canterbury (1792).

Removing the flaky bran from the meal was the second stage in producing fine flour. In the early eighteenth century it is likely that most bolting was still being carried out in 'hutches' in the bakery in big houses and in towns. This was a slow and laborious process. Bolters

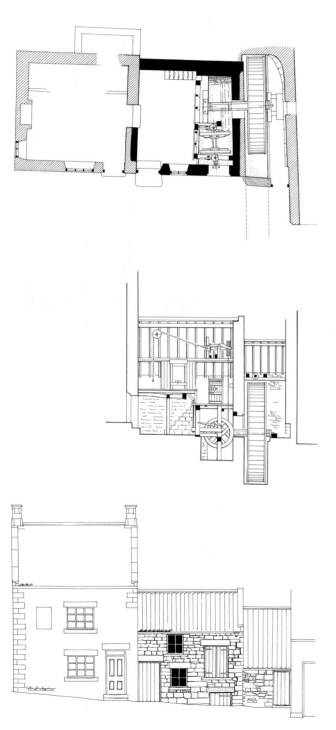

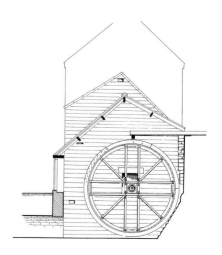

Fig 57. Lastingham mill.

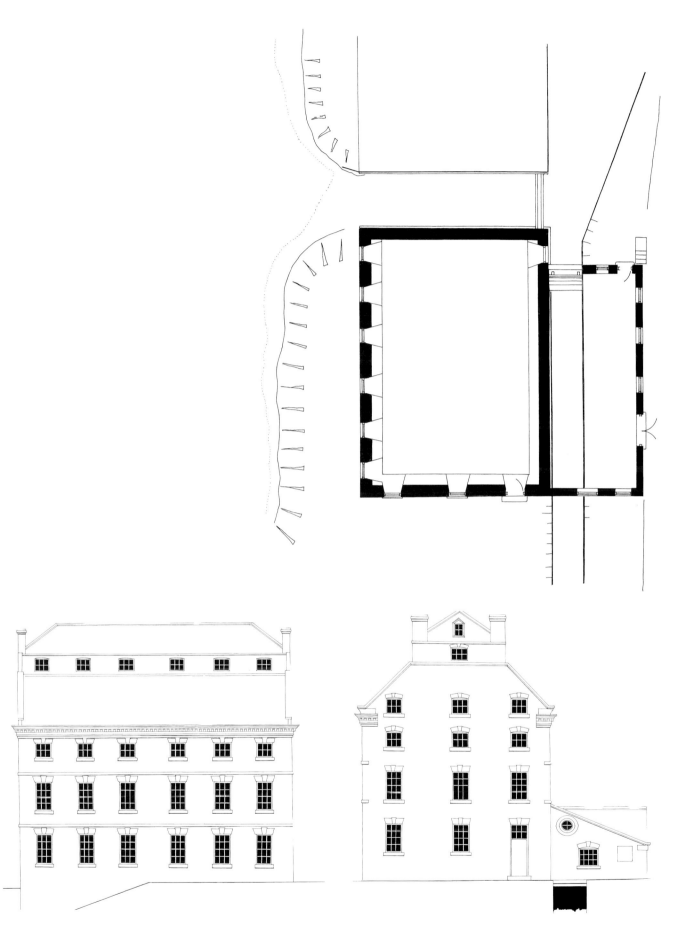

Fig 58. Ruswarp bolting mill.

attached directly to millstones were illustrated by Ramelli (1528) and Bockler (1661). In south Germany and France 'bag bolters', in which the meal was fed from the millstones into a woollen cloth bag and beaten out by a wooden beater bar driven by a cam on the millstone spindle, were known from the beginning of the sixteenth century. The flour passed through the weave and was collected in a chest; the bran flowed to the 'tail' of the bag.

By the eighteenth century bolters were separate machines, capable of coping with the product of several pairs of millstones. 'Bolting' mills in England were built specifically for the flour trade, normally sending the product to an urban centre. Ruswarp bolting mill was one of these.

A summary of the inventory which followed the Cholmley-versus-Matthews and Howlett case at Ruswarp provides a picture of the general arrangement in the new 'bolting mill':

"Floor 6 Loft with sack tackle

Floor 5 Loft used as granary

Floor 4 Corn chambers

Floor 3 Corn chambers, flour chambers, stoving room

Floor 2 Flour chambers, corn chambers, stove chamber, screens

Floor 1 Three pairs of French stones, joggling screens, bolter

Cellar Drying stove, water wheel, centre stone drive, countershaft and lower end of a vertical shaft"

(Burnett Collection).

This exceptional building housed three pairs of French stones with a bolter on Floor 1. One pair was driven directly from the pit wheel and the others by lay shaft(s). The vertical shaft would drive the sack hoist.

Mill houses

In the eighteenth century mills were no longer isolated buildings to which the miller walked each working day. There were clear advantages in being able to live on the premises. Building mill houses became a part of the 'great rebuilding' movement of the seventeenth and eighteenth centuries. Early daubed and thatched dwellings were swept away, to be replaced by stone-built 'longhouses', in which cows and people were housed under the same roof but separated by a cross passage. Superficially, some of the eighteenth century mill/house ranges look very much like 'longhouses', with the mill in place of the byre. In fact, this is deceptive.

Perhaps the earliest surviving mill house in north east Yorkshire is the seventeenth century, two-storey, gable-entry house at Commondale mill (J K Harrison, 1995, 197-210). It has finely dressed masonry and deeply chamfered mullioned windows. Curiously, the doorway is of very poor quality masonry compared with that of the windows. Though there was neither cross passage nor low end at Commondale the doorway was still left plain in the traditional way.

Commondale mill house was built about 100 metres from the mill because there was no room at the mill site, but on more spacious sites houses were built onto the ends of formerly isolated mills. The normal method was to demolish the gable wall furthest from the water-wheel, and to build the gable wall of a new house on the foundations. In other words, this gable wall was turned 'inside out', so to speak, to become the fireplace wall of the house. As at Commondale these mill houses had no doorway in the front façade. The millers entered the house via the old mill door and the mill, in effect, became the 'low end' of the range. This was the original arrangement at Lastingham, Coulton, Osmotherley and Oldstead but these have been modified by knocking through later doorways. Access through the mill into the house was still a feature of life at Tocketts mill in the 1960s and at Arden until 2005. Interestingly some of these mills have a first floor doorway between the loft of the mill and the chamber of the house, showing that at least part of the chamber was used as a garner floor for grain storage.

Many old mills have wide spans, in some cases increased in the eighteenth century to accommodate the longer hurst required for the lying shafts. By contrast, the new gable-entry mill houses were two storeys high and not as deep. There are examples of this mismatch between a squat and wide-plan mill and a taller and narrower mill house set end-to-end at Arden and Coulton.

At Osmotherley the fireplace wall has survived intact and there is also a small fireplace window, a regional feature of old houses originally fitted with a smoke hood. After severe flood damage at Arden, in 2005, most of the house is lost but the fireplace wall has survived together with the beam for the fire hood, spice cupboard and salt box.

Summary

The characteristic features of a small eighteenth century water mill in north east Yorkshire, can be summarised as follows:

- Lofted one-and-a-half storey building with a wide ground plan
- Wide doorway for access and a small wooden door leading to the hurst gearing (Arden, Coulton)
- Windows lighting the ground floor and the hurst platform (Arden, Lastingham)
- Clasp-arm waterwheel and pit wheel mounted on square-section wooden shaft (Arden, Caydale, Lastingham)
- Wide hurst pit extending the full width of the mills to accommodate the lying shafts (Rievaulx, Lastingham, Coulton, Bilsdale Low)
- EITHER a centre-driven stone with a secondary blue (Arden, Caydale)
OR a row of greys and blues driven by either a single 'countershaft' or two opposed lying shafts (Rievaulx, Coulton, Lastingham)
- Attached two-storey, gable-entry mill house with fireplace wall backing onto the mill and access to the house through the mill (Arden, Coulton, Oldstead, Osmotherley, Tocketts).

The introduction of blue and grey millstones with two-stage gearing was a radical change in milling.

It seems that field recording and research in the North York Moors, where most mills are smaller than those in the south east for instance, and built of stone, may have uncovered significant evidence concerning the introduction of blue millstones into this country, the development of new forms of gearing and the evolution of mill buildings and houses. (J K Harrison, 2005, SPAB).

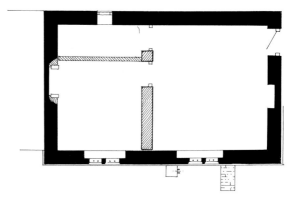

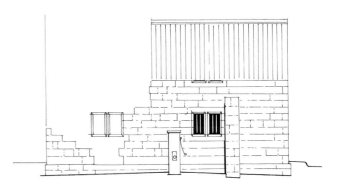

FIG 59. REMAINS OF SEVENTEENTH CENTURY MILL HOUSE AT COMMONDALE.

EARLY NINETEENTH CENTURY
FLOUR MILLING

The coastwise grain and flour trade

The last decades of the eighteenth century saw the start of a major shift in the grain trade in north east Yorkshire. The old pattern of localised grist and flour milling on the one hand and the 'export' of untreated grain from the Tees on the other gave way to large-scale milling of flour for coastwise shipping via the Tees and Esk.

The Tees was well suited for trade with east coast towns, from Edinburgh to London, as well as continental ports and it had long been an important grain exporting river. By the end of the seventeenth century the Collector of Customs for the Port of Stockton, which included Hartlepool, was recording the export of 11,000 quarters of wheat, barley and oats per annum, some of it to Rotterdam but most to London. The trade grew steadily throughout the eighteenth century. In 1794 the wharfs at Stockton town alone shipped 12,927 quarters of wheat and 16,212 quarters of oats (J Brewster, 1829, 200). In addition, a number of new berthing places were established along the shallow and winding Tees, each equipped with warehouses and granaries. For instance, William Hustler had built a big granary at Newport before 1695 where *"... the small ships discharged part of their cargo onto small barges and lightened their burthen before venturing higher up; and on their way back to the sea, received from the packhorses the consignment of grain which the Cleveland and south country* (Durham) *farmers must formerly have shipped at Yarm"* (R L Kirby, 1900, 139). His nephews, Robert and Thomas Peirse, built a warehouse at the tidal limit at Low Worsall and Charles Turner built warehouses at Coatham before 1771. Wharfs and warehouses were built at Cleveland Port (Cargo Fleet) which by 1798 shipped out large quantities of wheat and oats. Whitby was an exporter of oats at the turn of the century but there was no mention of wheat (G Young, 1817, 562). Scarborough was less important because of its poorer harbour.

FIG 60. NEWPORT WAREHOUSES (KIRBY, 137).

From the middle of the eighteenth century the increasing exports had resulted in tension in the local townships after seasons of poor harvests. In 1740, for example, *"... immediately after a very severe winter the prices of corn rose considerably and a great scarcity was apprehended. There were riots at Newcastle and at Stockton, where the mob rose when they saw some corn shipped"* (W H D Longstaffe, 1854, 157). Thirteen years later, on 27 September 1757, Ralph Jackson reported on his contact with *"a crowd of 100 poor people"* who intercepted horse-drawn carts carrying corn to the East Row flour mill at Sandsend because they suspected (correctly) that the grain or its badly needed flour would be sent out by boat (R Jackson, 1757, TA U/WJ/13). The next day a crowd seized what was claimed to be seed corn being delivered to Tob Taylor of Skelton, a man who Jackson described as *"... charged with Shipping Corn clandestinely on board Smuglers"*. The next day *"... the mob went down to Mask to stop one Dalton? there from shipping any more corn ..."*

By the end of the century the shortfall of grain and flour was a permanent fact of life. The population of

England, Scotland and Wales doubled between 1750 and 1821 and, although the production of grain was increasing fast, it still did not satisfy demand. Exports of grain gave way to imports. Grain was brought to the west coast of the country from Ireland while wheat was brought to the east coast from the Baltic. The price of wheat became a sensitive indicator of the state of the market. Nationally price was dominated by the demand in London but in the north it was also influenced by demand in the coal ports of Newcastle and Sunderland and in the West Riding textile towns. The waterlogged harvest of 1794, for instance, left some grain in the fields and some which had been harvested too wet to be threshed. Something like a quarter of the crop was lost. In the following July very high wheat prices, blamed on the activities of *"vile speculators"*, were recorded at Darlington (W H D Longstaffe, 1858, 158, 310). One result was that a group of Darlington people raised a subscription of £296 5s 0d to buy corn to sell to the poor at reduced prices (T Richmond, 1868, 94). There were drenched harvests again in 1799 and 1800 and the poorer people, by this time accustomed to a diet of wheatmeal bread, were forced back onto oat gruel, barley and potatoes.

But the switch from grain export to import led to a new vulnerability. The war with France (starting in 1792) coincided with other conflicts between the Baltic States. It was symptomatic that in November 1800 Tsar Paul of Russia suddenly broke off diplomatic relations with Britain and placed an embargo on some 200 ships (the biggest group from Whitby). These were trapped in the Baltic ports for six months so that both the timber and the corn trades were badly affected (R Barker, 1990). Supplies from the European plain were at risk at a time when demand for flour was increasing. Wheat prices rose from 110s a quarter in September 1800 to 145s in December and the following January. The average price of wheat remained high until 1812. Thereafter the price gradually fell to 76s 8d and then stabilised at roughly pre-war levels.

The price rises led to an expansion in land under the plough in north east Yorkshire and elsewhere, and also to a big expansion in flour milling capacity. The coastwise shipping of wheat flour from Stockton rose from 2278 quarters in 1785 to 4954 quarters in 1794 (J Brewster, 1829, 200), demonstrating that a new trade had begun. This would lead to the widespread improvement of old water mills and the building of big tower windmills around the Tees estuary and at Whitby and Scarborough.

Agricultural improvements

Arthur Young, later to become the secretary of the Board of Agriculture, visited the Duncombes of Helmsley and Sir Charles Turner of Kirkleatham and Kildale during his six month tour of the North of England. He wrote critically about the small size of many of the farms and of the small rentals got from them. The farmers on the Duncombe estate were described as a *"... poor and retched set of people"* and their land was full of *"whins, brakes* (bracken) *and other trumpery"*. The remedy he proposed was to raise the rents *"... first with moderation, and if that does not bring forth industry, double them ..."* (A Young, 1771, vol 2, 78-88). On the other hand, he commented favourably on Turner's ambitious scheme to cultivate a barren, peat-and-heather moorland rigg called Kempswithen on the Kildale estate which had been deep drained, the heather pared off and burned, and the land ploughed and seeded with grain. If such treatment could be successful at Kempswithen then there were thousands of acres of similar moorland which might also be treated. Though the project would ultimately fail there is no wonder that it attracted attention at the time. Young was also impressed with Turner's improvements at Kirkleatham where, for instance, he had built a large house with granaries and warehouse on the sea coast at Coatham, *"... a proper place for the farmers to lodge their corn etc ready for shipping, and to enable the merchant to speculate in the corn trade"* (A Young, 1771, vol 2; J Graves, 1808, 403). Wartime shortages and price rises led to further changes, many of them recommended by the Board of Agriculture. Two farms in Danby, which had been let in 1776 for £54 per annum, were let for £210 per annum by 1808 because of the improvements by Mr Newburn in the form of *"... draining, casting new fences and erecting farm buildings on a new plan viz. a square farm with a fold yard in the centre and an outlet from the low byres for the liquid manure to mingle with the heap outside"* (J W Ord, 1846, 340).

Above all the Board promoted enclosure as a means of increasing production. In north east Yorkshire a great deal of land had already been enclosed by common consent, or at least by acquiescence, long before. On the other hand, Parliamentary Enclosures, which peaked nationally between 1793 and 1817, certainly affected Spite mill at Osmotherley, and Vivers and Low mills at Pickering.

Crops

Early nineteenth century reports stated that *"Wheat may be regarded as the staple crop of Cleveland and oats that of the Vale of Pickering"*, that barley, rye, beans and peas were also grown but *"... they are by no means general"* (Young, 1817, 802-3). Indeed, *"... no other part of the North Riding, or perhaps, northern England, produced so much good quality wheat in proportion to its size as Cleveland"* (J Tuke, 1800, 116). Even in the Vale of York, where there was less ploughland than in Cleveland, the cropping had changed from rye, maslin and oats in the mid-eighteenth century to wheat by the mid-nineteenth. The situation was different in the moorland dales, for instance in *"... the vale called Danby Dale* (where) *the soil is particularly adapted to the growth of oats"* (J Graves, 1808, 277). Dales farmers concentrated on oats, barley, rye and maslin. Nevertheless, bread made from wheat or maslin flour was eaten by families of all ranks at the turn of the century. Only the industrial workers of the Pennines of the West Riding still ate oaten bread.

An Act of Parliament (1794/5, 35 Geo III cap 102) required that Chief Constables should enquire into the provision of weights, measures and toll boards in local mills. This resulted in a series of returns compiled in 1800 on mills in the various wapentakes in North Yorkshire. These throw light on the state of the mills at that time (NYCRO QAW). They show that almost every mill had the facilities for milling a variety of cereals and that prices for the different types of milling were normally displayed on a toll board. Almost all were able to mill wheat (differentiated sometimes between *"old"* and *"new"* wheat, the former being less expensive), barley, rye (presumably in the same set of stones as wheat), peas, beans and oats. In addition, a small number had a price for maslin (either a mixture of wheat and rye or barley and rye) The price for milling wheat was normally about twice the price for milling oats, because the wheat was ground fine and therefore more slowly. Rudby, Hutton, Leven Bridge, Scalby, Cayton, Brompton, Helmsley and Thirsk mills all had a price for grinding *"corn"* (oats, not maize).

Threshing machines

The Board of Agriculture also recommended the new 'Scotch' threshing machine. In primitive cultures, the edible berry was separated from the chaff and straw by knocking the sheaf against a stone or a log. In the highlands of Scotland and west coast of Ireland small batches of barley were threshed by hand for each meal. In Mediterranean countries threshing was done by oxen dragging a stone or sledge over the straw within a circular threshing platform. In England and northern France the separation was done by wooden flails on threshing floors, either in the open or in threshing barns with facing doors to create a through draught to blow out the light chaff and dust from the heavy grain. However, the end of the eighteenth century saw the introduction in East Lothian of threshing machines. There had been several attempts to develop a practical threshing machine, culminating in the first really successful machine, with beater bars on a high-speed drum, built by the Clackmannanshire millwright, Andrew Meikle. His first machine was set up for Mr Stein of Kilbagie in Clackmannanshire in 1787. It was immediately successful and the system was patented in 1788 (Patent No 1647).

Within a decade these threshers, most horse driven, were found throughout the east of Scotland, Northumberland, Durham and North Yorkshire. The first threshing mill in north east Yorkshire was built in 1790 by the Northumbrian millwright John Rastrick (Meikle's arch rival) for Mr E Cleaver of Nunnington Hall (J Tuke, 1800, 81-2). A threshing machine at Hough Hall near Durham was described by its owner, John Lewkup (J Grainger, 1794) and another was noted in the East Riding in the same year.

Although there was a thin scattering of threshing mills in some other counties, particularly Cornwall, they were mainly found to the east of a clearly defined boundary. In Scotland this boundary was the Highland Line; in England it ran round the Lake District, down the eastern flank of the Pennines and along the Humber estuary (K Hutton, 1976). To the south and west of this line threshing mills were hard to find and it has been suggested that the threshing mills were destroyed in the widespread acts of incendiarism and machine breaking of 1830-2, known as the Captain Swing riots. However, contemporary newspaper accounts mention the destruction of only 403 threshing machines in the whole of the Midlands and southern England (E J Hobsbawm and G Rude, 1969, 167), a total which contrasts with the 575 wheel sheds estimated to have been built in Northumberland alone (J A Hellen, 1972, 144). Clearly such numbers of threshing machines had never been built south of the Humber. This view is confirmed in the 1799 report to the Board of Agriculture stating that *"... strange to tell they (the horse drive threshing machines) are scarcely known in the southern and best cultivated parts"*. In the north it was a different story. Indeed, barn threshers continued in common use for almost another century.

The reason for the lack of threshing machines in the south was probably that threshing was an autumn and winter task, which largely determined the number of permanent hands a farmer would employ. Casual labour from Ireland and Scotland and mechanical threshers between them represented an acute threat to jobs in regions where there was little alternative employment in industry.

Horse wheel sheds, known as 'gin gans' in Northumberland but simply as 'wheel sheds' in Yorkshire, are now a distinctive part of the built heritage. The horses were yoked under heavy wooden arms radiating from the central upright shaft with starts reaching over the horses' shoulders. Triangular, square or pentagonal frames were bolted onto the tops of the starts to brace them and to carry the segments of the ring gearing which drove the pinion on the horizontal 'tumbler shaft' which carried the drive through the barn wall to the thresher. Ring gears were at least 10 feet in diameter while the tumbler pinions were very small, providing the first stage in the step-up required to drive the threshing drum at the necessary 1000 revolutions per minute.

Sheds in north east Yorkshire were built with a number of variations but mainly square or hexagonal in plan (A and J K Harrison, 1973, 258-60). A more recent view is that the main distinction is between those sheds which have the roofs resting on separate columns leaving the horses exposed to the wind and those in which the horses worked within masonry walls, with only two entrances. When Rastrick built the first recorded threshing mill at Nunnington he charged for the mill *"... exclusive of a roof to cover the wheel and horses while at work"* but this wording simply indicated a division of cost between millwright and builder. The wheel and the roof were not independent of each other. The horse wheel needed a heavy horizontal beam between stone or brick piers to support its top bearing. To make the 'shed' additional piers were built in a circle round the wheel and common rafters thrown up to a central apex. This primitive form of shed with facetted roof, illustrated in Agricola's De re Metallica two centuries before, was probably the first to appear in north east Yorkshire.

In 1843 four wheel sheds with thatched roofs were listed in *"A Survey and Valuation of the Whorlton Estate, 1842-3"* (NYCRO Z02), and to this day one surviving shed near Swainby has staining on the barn wall which confirms that it was originally thatched. This shed is hexagonal in plan and completely open-sided. At the turn of the century pantiles were being introduced, initially from Holland, then from Hull and later from Pickering and other local clay pits. In spite of the difficulty in cutting and fitting the rectangular pantiles to the triangular facets of wheel shed roofs they were widely used for this purpose. In appearance they resembled the wood shingled roofs illustrated by Agricola.

The 'Scotch' threshing machine led to a new weekly routine on the farms which in turn contributed to a change in the design of water-driven corn mills. Threshing by hand had always been a slow process. Medieval farmers had threshed out a small amount of grain and brought it to the mill to be milled there-and-then while they waited. The threshing machine cut across this older practice. It was claimed for Mr Cleaver's machine at Nunnington, for instance, that *"... another great advantage arising from this machine ... that of being able to get corn to his market whenever there is an advance in price"* (J Tuke, 1800, 81-2). His machine could thresh 12 to 15 quarters of wheat in 12 hours. Now, after a day's work, a farmer could take a cart load or a waggon load of threshed grain to be left at the mill for the miller to deal with in his own good time during the following week. But this left the miller with a new problem. He now had to store a week's supply of grain and flour from a number of farmers. The old one-and-a-half storey mills were no use for this purpose and many were extended upwards with the addition of garner floors. This, in turn, generated further change since the additional storage space gave the miller the opportunity to speculate in buying grain when it was cheap and selling flour when the price rose and also to supply local smallholders with pig and hen feed made from bought grain.

A)

B)

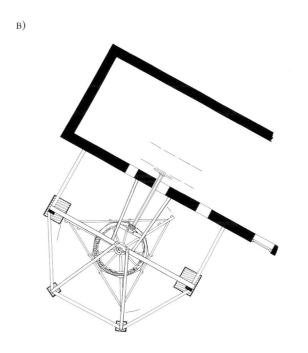

FIG 61. HORSE WHEEL SHEDS AT A) TIDKINHOWE (GUISBOROUGH) AND B) URRA (BILSDALE).

Oil mills

Increasing seaborne trade threw up another type of mill, apparently new to this country but well established from the sixteenth century in Holland, France and Germany. The export of lead and butter from the Tees estuary drew in imports of flax in return and, particularly during the French Wars, the fibres of this plant were spun and woven into linen and sailcloth in flax mills at Brompton near Northallerton, Bishop Monkton near Ripon, Hutton Rudby, Stokesley, etc. An offshoot of this industry was the extraction of linseed oil from the flax seed and, to a lesser extent, rape oil from locally grown rape seed. During the French wars the oil pressing industry was protected by import duty. Smeaton produced a design for an oil pressing windmill and the process became quite widely used in Newcastle-on-Tyne for pressing seed from the Baltic. Locally, six mills at least were set up for oil extraction. There were tower windmills at Stockton c.1785 and two near Whitby (pre-1796), two water mills at Great Ayton (one pre-1765 when Ralph Jackson visited *"Mr Richardson's oyl mill"*), one at Fryup Hall and finally Caleb Fletcher's mill at Keldholme (G Young, 1817, 819). As was common practice in Holland two of these mills were dual-purpose, designed for grinding grain as well as for extracting oil. The oil extraction plant consisted of a set of edge runner stones to break down the seeds, a heating plate with a power-driven stirrer and some form of press which squeezed the oil from the hot 'seed meal'. Linseed oil was used for oil paint and varnish, and the residual cake was used for cattle food.

The linseed oil process used at Great Ayton in Philip Heselton's old mill was vividly described when the mill was taken over by the Ayton Agricultural School:

"Adjoining the school premises was a mill known as the Oil Mill, the wheel of which was driven by the River Leven ... the oil mill buildings were very old, said to have been first a brewery ... afterwards a flax mill ... When we came to the village in 1841 it was used for expressing oil from linseed.

A pair of edge stones crushed the seed which was heated in small iron pans over a slow fire, and kept from burning by revolving knives inside the pans. When hot it was put into hair bags and placed between wedges made of beechwood, the upper ones driven by heavy stampers lifted by a revolving shaft and then allowed to fall on the wedge. When this was driven home the bag was taken out and the crushed linseed was found pressed into a flat mass called oilcake, sold to the farmers for feeding their cattle. The oil ran down into tanks below the wedges. In this state it was called 'raw linseed oil' ... This oil when pumped into cauldrons and boiled with sulphuric acid was called boiled linseed oil, and was in great demand for mixing with paint ..."

(G Dixon, 1891, 88).

The description fits the operation which was carried out in horse mills, windmills and water mills all over the Low Countries, where several sets of stamps have survived in preserved mills, for instance at Het Pink windmill at Koog aan de Zaan in Holland.

The process for extracting rape oil was similar. Rape was widely grown in the polders of the Low Countries and was introduced into the Fen counties where it grew well on the damp peaty soils. It was also grown as a 'break crop' on more open land. Arthur Young reported that Mr Turner of Kirkleatham used rape *"... for breaking up old pastures over-run with rubbish; pared and burned and sown in one ploughing"* (Arthur Young, 1771, vol 2, 134-9). Most rape was used as sheep fodder as an alternative to turnips but some was allowed to ripen to be cropped for its seed. Rape seed was grown near Pickering in 1788 and sold at the market at Malton for transport to Hull (H W Brace, 1960, 28). Rape oil was mainly used as lamp fuel. Rape oil cake was rejected by cows and was either given to sheep or ground up for fertiliser.

The only recorded example of a rape seed mill in this region was that built by the Downe estate at Fryup Hall for their tenant Matthew Agar at some time before 1786, when it was first reported that lamp oil was produced in Fryupdale. The mason and diarist Daniel Duck recorded that his elder children went to watch Matthew Agar's rape threshing in 1788, making it clear that this was something of an 'event' (J Davison, 1967, Diaries of the late Daniel Duck, Whitby Gazette, 20 Oct). Below Fryup Hall the valley bottom is flat, damp and low-lying, an ideal place for growing rape. Threshing was carried out on canvas sheets, up to 20 yards square and weighing more than half a ton (J Tuke, 1800, 130-45), normally using the flail, sometimes by treading out under horses' hooves and at a later date by threshing machines similar to those used for oats and wheat. The process was delicate since the seed, once ripe, would be lost if the plant dried out. The rape had to be got onto the threshing floor early in the morning while the dew was still on it. The water-driven oil mill at Fryup was also used as a corn mill. Matthew Agar still paid £5 per annum rental for the mill in 1828 but it was defunct by the 1850s and derelict by 1877. The reason was the decline in the demand for lamp oil in London following the widespread adoption of coal gas lighting from about 1840.

Coastwise trading flour mills

In the early nineteenth century the coast of north east Yorkshire was becoming a busy place. Limestone for burning was being brought in from Northumberland. Coal was being brought in from County Durham to be used in the alum works while alum was being shipped out to London and the Continent. Willow saplings were being collected for making corves for winding coal in north eastern pits. There was a fulling mill at Staithes and a 'glazing' mill at Skinningrove. In addition, flour was being shipped from a group of big new tower windmills around the Tees estuary, at Whitby and Scarborough, and from a number of new or rebuilt water mills engaged in coastwise trading. The earliest of these, Nathaniel Cholmley's bolting mill at Ruswarp, has already been described. There were others at Leven Bridge, Saltburn, Larpool and Robin Hood's Bay.

There had been a corn mill at Leven Bridge since before 1718. It was probably enlarged and up-graded in the time of Thomas Simpson, who was miller there by 1800, when, according to the Lieutenancy Returns, *"No other corn ground under any terms"*, ie he ran a commercial rather than a local mill and he was not interested in multure. His eldest son, William, was miller in 1822 and his grandson, Robert, was miller in 1830. The foundations of the Simpson wealth had been based on grain exporting but they expanded into the export of flour. They took the lease of the Hustlers' granary at Newport in 1818 and Robert took over a schooner called the 'Newport' in 1838. In its hey-day Leven Bridge mill was a brick-built range of eight bays and three storeys, with a wide wheel pit for two waterwheels in the centre. North of the wheel pit was the flour mill and south was the provender mill. Close by, where the Leven flows into the Tees, there was a wharf for loading the flour boats.

Larpool mill, on the Esk, was also built to send out flour by boat via a landing stage. This building has hardly any recorded history. It had become the Glen Esk Tearoom by the 1870s and there is little evidence on site to show that it was once a corn mill.

The most interesting survivor is Bay mill near Robin Hood's Bay, which carries a plaque over the main entrance; "THIS MILL WAS REBUILT AND NEW MACHINERY PUT THEREIN AT THE COST OF G J FARSYDE ESQ, AD 1839. CROSBY, BUILDER SCARBOROUGH". Though now stripped of its machinery and used as a youth hostel there is much to be seen. Older masonry in the upstream wall shows that there was an early mill but it is the mill built in 1839 which largely survives. A large dam (rebuilt in 1858) on the lip of a natural fall in a narrow shale gorge sent water through a masonry lined tunnel, said to have been dug by local jet miners, to a big pitch-back waterwheel. The building is a spacious three-storey structure with internal support from cast-iron columns. A ring gear on the arms of the waterwheel drove a pinion on the end of a lay shaft to four pairs of stones, two grey and two French. The remains of two loading doors in the beck-side gable wall show that sacks of meal were lowered down the outside of the building into carts standing in the bed of the beck at low tide. From there it would be led to a small sandy landing place about 40 metres beyond the sea cliffs for loading into wooden ships. This mill and its water works was a very expensive project, clearly intended for coastwise trading.

Only the smallest of wooden ships could have penetrated the Tees as far as the confluence of the Tees and the Leven. Ruswarp mill was said to have been visited by *"lighter boats from Hull"* and it is likely that all of the mills on the lower Esk and Tees were serviced by boats which loaded the London bound sailing ships nearer the river mouths. Scalby Low mill probably used boats for carrying flour to Scarborough. On the other hand, the mills on the coast, at Saltburn and Bay, were built near sandy beaches and small wooden sailing ships (called *"Billy Boys"* at Bay mill) were loaded from horse-drawn carts, as they lay beached at low tide. None of these coastal mills had sea walls to protect this operation from the vicious north easterly gales and there would be many winter days when the mills could not be approached.

IMPROVED WATER MILLS

The rapid growth in the flour trade of north east Yorkshire in the last decade of the eighteenth century and the early years of the nineteenth resulted in technical developments in both water mills and windmills. Old water mills were 'improved' and many new windmills were built. French burr stones were introduced for grinding flour. Cast-iron was introduced for some shafts and gearing and in water mills there were two new gearing systems.

From the surviving structures it seems that the majority of mills in north east Yorkshire were 'improved' at this period. However, actual dating has been possible in only a few cases. One of the earliest was the old mill at Appleton. This came into the hands of John Thompson at some time between 1760 and 1776 (Appleton mill deeds in possession of J & M Allison). In 1778 he negotiated a mortgage for £110 from the local landowner, Thomas Grundall (whose ancestors had formerly owned the mill) and the sum was paid on the security of *"… that newly erected messuage and corn mill in the ownership and occupation of John Thompson and George Lynas"* in 1780. A year later Thompson took out a second mortgage, this time for £250, from Christopher Wood, gent, Welham, on the security of *"a close and newly erected corn mill"*. Thompson had built up a considerable estate by the time he redeemed the mortgage in 1794 when he sold the house, mill and various closes to Thomas Hill, yeoman, of Farndale for £1000. The security for these mortgages was provided by the newly-built mill house and corn mill, a plain two-storey building in coursed limestone blocks. The hurst and gearing are lost but the surviving waterwheel, renewed in 1929, still retains the late eighteenth century cast-iron nave plates.

A few years later a mill was built on a new site near Guisborough, at Swathey Head, a small parcel of land near a wooded valley on the boundary between the Chaloner (Gisborough) and Skelton estates which had been sold off from the former in 1587 (J K Harrison, 1980). In 1787 it was conveyed to Thomas Jackson, miller, of Guisborough who *"… afterwards erected and built a water corn mill on part of the said premises"*

(NYCRO ZFM 4). The venture was evidently not a success and in 1794 Jackson sold it to David Dixon, a toll keeper at Stockton Bridge. Party to the purchase was Robert Dixon, gentleman, of the Tyne Toll Bridge in Gateshead. The toll keepers were no more successful and in 1796 Dixon sold out to Emma Chaloner, acting on behalf of Robert Chaloner who was a minor, thus reuniting the land with the Gisborough estate. At the time of the sale the mill was in the occupation of William and Charles Pollard and these two stayed on as millers for the new owners. Their rental increased from £15 per half year to £19 per half year in 1801 but there were no further records and it must be assumed the mill had stopped work. As revealed by excavation (J K Harrison, 1980) the mill was very small, merely 14 feet by 16 feet internal dimensions, with an external waterwheel pit capable of holding a wheel 14 feet in diameter and 4 feet wide. In 1800 this mill was equipped to grind wheat, barley and rye but not oats (NYCRO, QAW mic 1203). This could have been achieved on a single set of stones.

Soon there was to be a much bigger mill in Guisborough. There had been two water-driven corn mills in the town since medieval times, one at Howl Beck and the other to the west of the town. An entry in the Gisborough estate agent's accounts for 1773 recorded a payment in cash for *"lonans when Harvey's Mill was on fire"*. What the entry means is obscure but it may be that the 'lonning' or lane had been hastily repaired to get fire fighting equipment to the mill. The West mill disappeared from records about this time and by the middle of the nineteenth century nothing but the leat was visible (J W Ord, 1846, 170). The estate made do with its one mill at Howl Beck and then purchased the short-lived Swathey Head mill. In 1804 they started to rebuild Howl Beck mill. James Wilson, the millwright, worked with a cooper, carpenters, stone masons, a glazier, a blacksmith and a number of local men who acted as labourers and carters. Unfortunately, the machinery at Howl Beck mill was dismantled over a century ago and there is no archaeological record. However, the accounts prepared by Joseph Hickson, agent to Robert Chaloner,

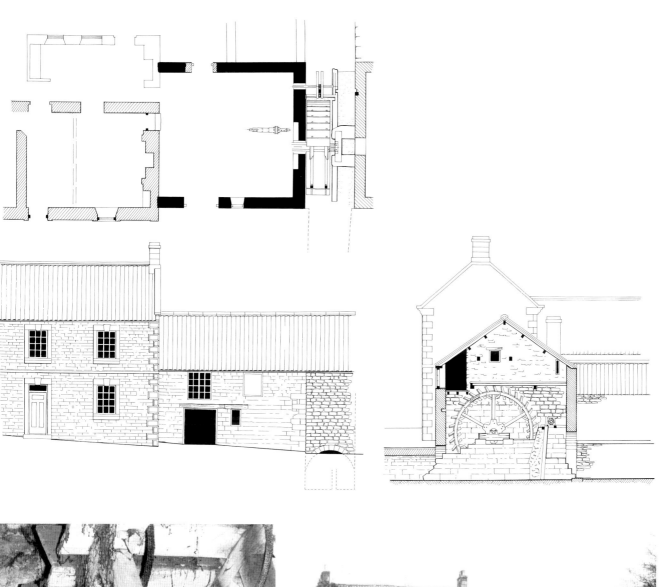

FIG 62. APPLETON MILL AND HOUSE (PHOTOS, JKH & MITFORD ABRAHAM).

1796-1806, have survived (NYCRO ZFM 87 mic 1415):

"An account of sundry expenses attending the rebuilding of Howl Beck Mill by James Wilson.

1804

Jan 27 – Aug 25.	*Thomas Wilson (carpenter)*	*£6 7s 10d*
Aug 25.	*Messrs Todd and Campbell, for millstones*	*£33 0s 0d*
Sept 1.	*Thos Wilson, watching for files?*	*7s 2d*
Sept 17.	*Wm Harpley, sawing planks*	*3s 4d*
Sept 22.	*Thomas Wilson (carpenter)*	*11s 8d*
Nov 6.	*Wm Portus, for nails.*	*£10 14s 0d*
Nov 7.	*Wm Portus, for nails*	*10s 4d*
	Roger Sanders and Cooper (labourers)	*£16 14s 10d*
	Mr Danby, for paint etc	*£2 19s 4d*
	Robert Knaggs, leading	*£11 0s 0d*
	Robert Walker, for leather (?)	*15s 9d*
	John Lincoln,	*£2 14s 4d*
	Wm Carter, for leading	*£1 9s 0d*
	TOTAL	*£89 1s 1d*
	Thomas Bulmer Robert Dunn, for lime etc	*£2 18s 4d*
	Thomas Wilson (carpenter)	*6s 4d*
Nov 29.	*Jona Wilson (carpenter)*	*£1 18s 0d*
Nov 30.	*John Aibblewhite of Stockton, for cast iron as per account*	*£58 5s 4 1/2d*

1805

	Martin Kirtley of D., for ironwork	*£67 15s 2 1/2d*
Jan 2.	*Geo Havelock (stonemason)*	*£60 9s 10d*
5.	*Wm Postgate (labourer)*	*£9 15s 0d*
	John Wilson (labourer)	*18s 6d*
	Thomas Smith (labourer)	*£1 5s 0d*
	Thomas Nicholson (labourer)	*£2 11s 3d*
	Isaac Postgate (labourer)	*5s 0d*
	Geo Mills (labourer)	*£5 8s 0d*
	Richd Pretty (stonemason)	*£9 3s 0d*
	Wm Fletcher (stonemason)	*£3 6s 0d*
	Thos Wilson (carpenter)	*18s 0d*
	Richd Ripley,	*£6 19s 2d*
	Mr Danby, for tar etc	*16s 0d*
	Lawrence Wilson, for lime	*£11 8s 0d*
Jan 20.	*Ralph Pulman (blacksmith)*	*£2 6s 0d*
26.	*Thomas Wilson (carpenter)*	*5s 0d*
	James Wilson (millwright)	*£163 11s 6d*
	TOTAL	*£499 9s 7d*
Jan 27.	*James Wilson, for nails*	*3s 2d*
	James Wilson, for nails	*£1 0s 8d*
	James Wilson, for turning patterns	*6s 0d*
	Thomas Wilson (carpenter)	*£7 7s 10d*
	Wm Potter, for leading stones	*£21 0s 0d*
Feb 2.	*Jona Wilson,*	*£2 7s 0d*
Mar 9.		*£2 9s 0d*
Apr 29.	*John Aibblewhite, for cast iron*	*£3 6s 7d*
	Martin Huntley, for iron work	*£2 3s 2d*
	Geo Havelock (stonemason)	*£7*
	Richd Wilson (glazier)	*£2 10s 11d*
	Ralph Pulman (blacksmith)	*17s 8d*
	Wm Pulman, for bricks and tiles	*£10 5s 6 1/2d*
	Thomas Bulmer, sundries	*£2 4s 3d*
May 17.	*T Heselton, for wood for patterns*	*£11 11s 0 1/2d*
	Agreed with Henry Mills, for building of stable as dimension	*£56 14s 4d*
	Henry Mills, for bringing the water over the moor	*£21 0s 0d*
	TOTAL ACCOUNT OF EXPENSES AT MILL	*£652 4s 9d"*.

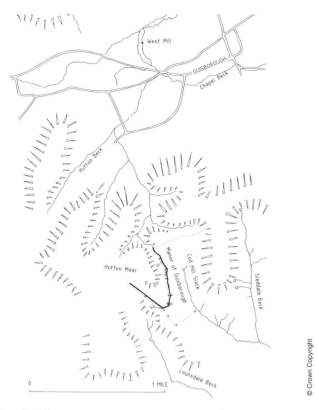

© Crown Copyright

FIG 63. MOORLAND WATERCOURSE FOR THE GUISBOROUGH MILLS.

The amount involved shows that this was a complete rebuild. Significantly, an expensive set of millstones was bought from Todd and Campbell of Hull, and payments were made to John Aibblewhite of Stockton for cast-iron and to James Wilson for *"turning patterns"*.

The payment of £21 to Henry Mills, the miller at Howl Beck for *"bringing water across the moors"* came about because Hutton Beck did not deliver enough water for the enlarged mill. Mills, of course, had no work to do while his mill was being rebuilt, and the estate paid him to cut water courses across the moors, three feet wide and three feet deep up to a mile long, starting some two and a half miles away. These were to divert water formerly flowing south to the Esk. The amount would not have been great but it might have been sufficient to drive an additional set of stones and it would certainly have been useful in dry seasons. The predictable result was a trial at York Assizes in which the plaintiffs were the various millers on the Esk (Burnett coll no 1558). It was claimed that business at the Bleach mill at Commondale, for example, was damaged to the extent of £1000 and that the paper mill at Lealholm could only work two thirds of the normal hours. These were exaggerated claims and it was stated that in a previous assize *"… the verdict had been given in favour of the defendant"*. The estate was anxious to recover its costs and the rental for Howl Beck mill was increased from £46 per annum to £90 per annum, a change which no doubt contributed to the bankruptcy of the unfortunate Henry Mills in 1812 (London Gazette, 4 & 7 January).

Spur wheels and upright shafts

The documents from Appleton, Swathey Head and Howl Beck mills contain little information about the gearing and millstones installed and, unfortunately, the archaeological record is also thin.

However, when Charles Slingsby Duncombe had *"Coulson's mill"* (almost certainly Bilsdale Low mill) rebuilt and the dam repaired in 1785-6 he was put to *"… the expence of a spur gear wheel and other articles, which was unnecessary for a mill so situated"* (NYCRO, ZEW X, mic 1427). This is the first evidence of an entirely new type of driving gear in north east Yorkshire. Bilsdale Low mill is a small two-storey plus loft building. The lower walls and the very large hurst pit are part of an early mill while the upper walls, wooden upright shaft and the wooden crown wheel are part of the 1785 rebuild. The upright shaft also carries a simple rope pulley, which may originally have been used for driving an oat roasting plate. The surviving clasp-arm waterwheel is a copy of the original, though fitted with cast-iron shroud plates marked "BUTLER HELMSLEY" in the nineteenth century. The cast-iron pit wheel, wallower and spur wheel are replacements.

There is also good evidence for this new type of gearing at Scaling mill, in the north of the region. In 1792 *"… all that messuage Dwelling House or Tenement and all that water corn mill lately erected and built by John Wallis upon part of the said close or parcel of ground called the Low Close, otherwise Low Botton … situate lying and being within the Hamlet Township or territories of Scaling …"* was sold to Gilbert Sturdy, formerly a miller at Kilton (NYCRO ZMP 1/4 mic 1643 182). The mill was mortgaged to Daniel Duck, late of Osmotherley, for £200. The relatively small amount probably indicates that the *"lately erected"* meant that new machinery was put into an old mill. The archaeological record bears this out. Before 1792 it had been a two-storey building, housing both mill and a dwelling. The improvement involved raising the building by two courses of masonry and installing a new waterwheel on a wooden shaft along with pit wheel, wooden upright shaft, wallower and spur wheel. All except the waterwheel survived until the 1970s. The pit wheel was of clasp-arm construction while the spur wheel was of compass-arm construction. The bench hurst carried two pairs of millstones, but there was some evidence that a third set had been added to the front. The stubby upright shaft was lathe-turned above floor level and square-section where the wallower and spur wheel were fitted. There was a primitive rope pulley, very similar to that at Bilsdale Low mill and also at nearby Loftus mill. Every feature of this drive system fits comfortably with a 1792 date.

The mill at Easby carries a keystone inscribed "I M 1799" over the main door. This was evidently another improved mill but more handsomely built than either

89

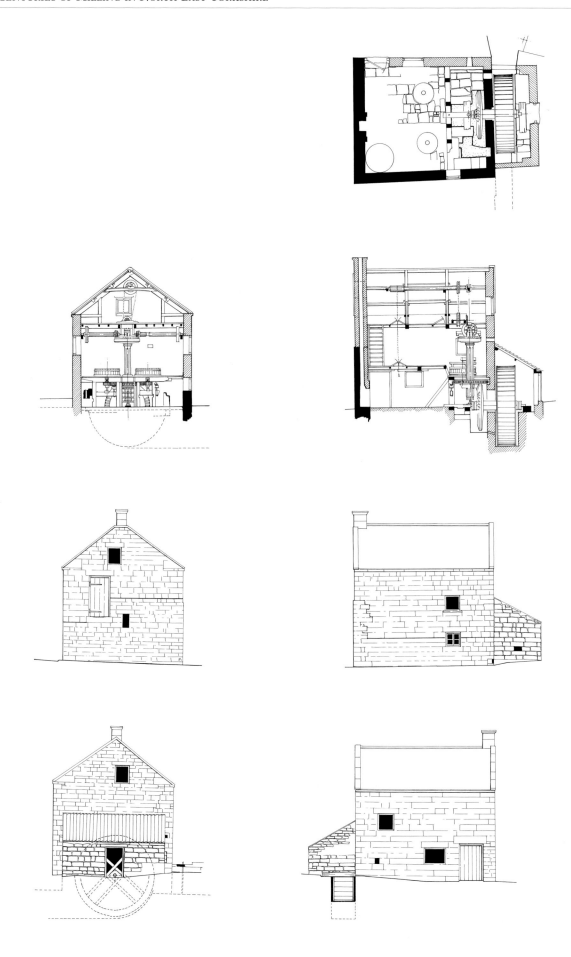

FIG 64. BILSDALE LOW MILL.

FIG 65. SCALING MILL.

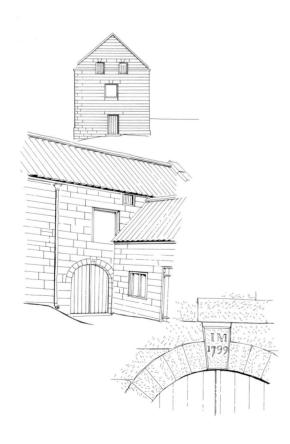

FIG 66. EASBY MILL (PHOTO, A STOYEL).

Bilsdale Low or Scaling mills. It was perhaps the earliest example of a style which would later become standard – arched entrance doorway to the ground floor, a second doorway at the first floor and small vents under the eaves to light and ventilate the spacious loft or garner floor under the roof timbers. The hurst posts, now missing but recorded in 1979 (A Stoyel, 1985, pers comm), indicated an upright shaft drive to either two or three sets of stones.

Danby mill was built a year later. At the end of the eighteenth century Danby End was a new settlement with dwellings mainly for colliers who worked the moorland pits. In 1801 Thomas Weatherill completed his new mill on his own land at Danby End *"... no mill of any kind being there before"*. In so doing he created an immediate conflict of interest. The land on the opposite bank of the Esk belonged to Robert Harrison, who was incensed because the backwater from Weatherill's new dam invaded a traditional cattle watering place. It was submitted in court that the mill had been discussed between the two men before work began and Harrison *"... wishing to be a good neighbour ..."* had agreed to the building of the dam provided that it did not raise the water level by more than 2 feet. However, this was only a verbal agreement. Weatherill's dam eventually raised the water by 4 feet 6 inches so that Harrison's cattle *"... one day went to drink as normal but instead were forced to swim for their lives"*. Under pressure, Weatherill agreed in 1802 to lower his dam by 18 inches, but this was another verbal agreement which was never carried out. Harrison then tried to take matters into his own hands. He cut a trench across his own land to drain the dam and when this failed he pulled down part of the dam itself where it abutted onto his land, letting the water down to its original level and putting the mill out of action.

By this time Weatherill had let his mill to a miller called Thomas Thompson and it was Thompson who brought an action against Harrison. Harrison sought Council's advice and it is this preserved document which contains the story (NYCRO ZEL 2/2/200 mic 1119). In Council's opinion the backwater also affected the ancient ford and footbridge on the road to Castleton

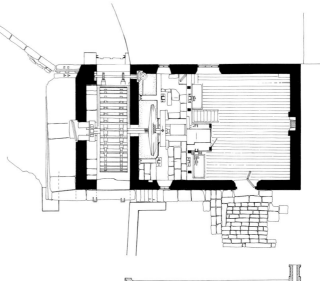

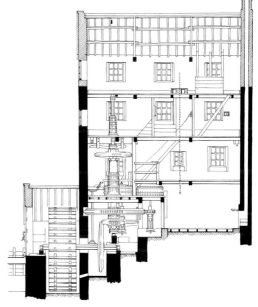

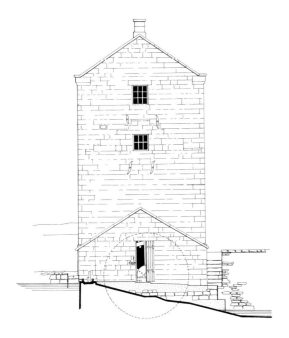

FIG 67. DANBY MILL.

half a mile upstream. The ford had become impassable and the footbridge deck was 2 feet under water, even in dry weather. Council felt that this was a public nuisance against which any of the King's subjects could take action. The dispute must have been settled in such a way that Thompson was able to carry on working his mill. Today, the dam still raises the water by at least 4 feet 6 inches and the flooded ford and footbridge have been replaced by a low, lintelled, road-bridge. Furthermore, the Thompsons were successful millers at Danby until after 1895. One problem could not be solved, however. Sited on the very banks of the Esk, Danby mill has seen many floods. For instance, in the floods of 1930 and 1931 the Esk rose so high that the waterwheel was completely submerged. Jack Petlar, who worked at the mill many years ago, said that the stone nuts were disengaged whenever there was a flood and the wheel simply allowed to run free.

The fact that there is a known date for this mill makes it particularly interesting. Although to some extent modified Danby mill typifies good practice of its period. The most radical modifications have been to the building. It has been raised by two storeys, the original roof timbers being re-erected two storeys higher, and the attached mill house was built after 1864 when the Esk Valley railway was cut through between the mill and the old mill house. There have been fewer modifications to the machinery. Only the hurst frames, millstones and crown wheel have been replaced. Otherwise the mill is vintage 1800. The waterwheel is a low breast wheel 14 feet in diameter and 5 feet wide, built on a square-section iron shaft with cast-iron nave plates and wooden arms, felloes, starts and paddles, very much like some designed by Smeaton. The facetted and lathe-turned upright shaft is a fine example of its type, protected by a cooper-made ringing at first floor. The wooden spur wheel is built to the compass-arm construction, as at Scaling, but it is bigger and has six arms. The stone nuts are of cast-iron, with very coarse pitch to match the wooden cogs in the spur wheel. It is probable that the matching set of pit wheel and wallower is original. The original millstones were replaced about 1880 but an old set of blue stones has survived on site, formerly in the floor of a building in the fold-yard. Interestingly, a basalt waterwheel bearing now built into a window opening in the hurst may well have been installed in 1800, showing that some elements of older technology were still thought to be serviceable.

Not far from Danby, William Wilson, the tenant miller for the Downe estate at the old Howe mill, must have watched with dismay as Weatherill built his new mill. The seemingly unlimited water supply from the Esk and the up-to-date equipment must have seemed threatening. When the result of the dispute between Thompson and Harrison went in favour of the new mill it was time for action. The old Howe mill was rebuilt in 1807. Accounts have survived (NYCRO ZDS 14/6 mic 1120/6599):

"The cost of Building a Water Corn Mill by Wm Wilson of Danby, 1807.

July 27.	*Paid Thos Garbutt, for millwright work*	*£105 4s 8d*
25.	*Mr Barker, for timber*	*£35 7s 6 1/4d*
Aug 6.	*Geo Thompson, for Mason work*	*£42 6s 6d*
15.	*Arthur Gibson, for iron work*	*£14 1s 2d*
	Jonathan Webster, for plumbing and glazing	*£3 12s 5 1/2d*
	... ...	*£38 8s 0d*
	John Hall, for nails	*£1 10s 3d*
	Joseph Handswell, for Blacksmith work	*£32 4s 1d*
	Norman..., for 1 pair of Blue Millstones	*£38 17s 0d*
	Joseph Handswell, for blacksmith work	*£5 3s 8d*
	John Rose, for carpenters work	*£14 0s 0d*
	William Teasdale, for labour	*£12 0s 0d*
	Ale to the workmen	*£14 0s 0d*
	Sundry small bills	*£12 8s 0d*
		£369 3s 4 1/4d

A new Grey Millstone and fitting up 21 Feb 1819
£12 0s 0d".

Significantly, the mill was equipped with one set of grey stones and one set of blue stones. The partly illegible entry for the blue millstones should probably read "Norman and Smithson", millwrights in Hull. Oats would have been grown in Danby Dale but wheat would have been more important. Arthur Gibson who supplied "ironwork" was almost certainly a blacksmith. The building survives, though modified and without its machinery. The centre line of the well-masoned waterwheel pit is on the centre line of the mill, indicating that there had been an upright shaft drive. As at Danby End there was no attached mill house, the fine house of the Wilsons standing on slightly higher ground some hundred yards away.

According to the dated lintel over the main door the ancient mill at Ingleby Greenhow was rebuilt in 1817, presumably by the then lord of the manor William Foulis. This fine example of an improved mill was recorded before dismantling (A Zealand and J K Harrison, 1968). There was a first floor doorway immediately above the main doorway, Yorkshire sliding sash windows on the ground and first floors and vents for the loft. The roof couples incorporate curved 'knee braces' from the tie beams to the rafters. The machinery of 1817 had survived with little modification. The cast-iron nave plates of the waterwheel set on the wooden octagonal section 12 feet long shaft were original but the cast-iron

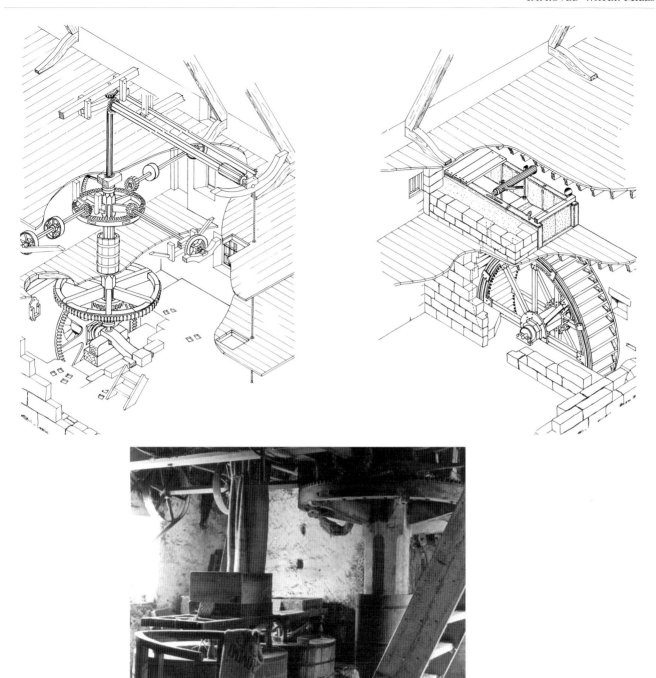

FIG 68. INGLEBY MILL (PHOTOS, A STOYEL).

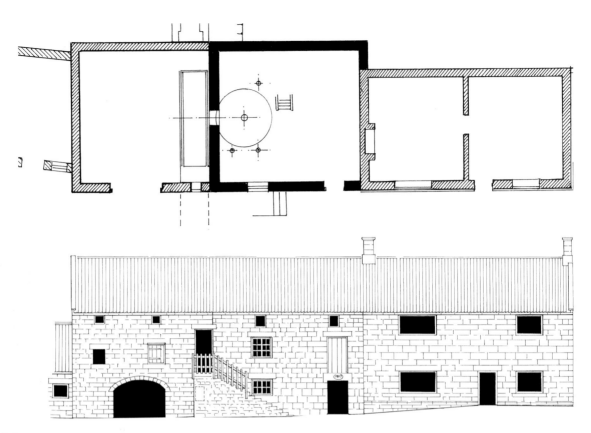

FIG 68. INGLEBY MILL.

shroud plates may have been reversed or replaced when the wheel was altered from overshot to pitch-back at some unknown date. The 15 feet long hexagonal section upright shaft and the compass-arm spur wheel were similar to those at Danby.

Two years later it was the turn of the Marquis of Aylesbury's mill at Swainby to be rebuilt. In an Estate Book of 1806 the Agent had described it as follows:

"Swainby Mill, Stephen Coulson ... Rent £50. The buildings consist of an overshot Water Grist Mill, two pairs of Stones in very bad repair. Also a messuage adjoining, stone and tile. This mill must be re-built, it is of great use and convenience to the tenantry, but it is of a very old and inferior construction and quite worn out"

(NYCRO, ZJX 4/44 mic 915).

John Claridge of Pall Mall reported that *"... the Mills are also in a very decayed and delapidated state and want not only thorough repair, but should be taken down and rebuilt, which would pay very good interest for being done, if effected in a frugal plan"* (NYCRO ZJX 4/44 mic 915). However, another decade would pass before action was taken. The new mill was included in a *"Survey and Valuation of the Whorlton Estate"* made in 1842-3:

"Swainby Mill ... Stephen Coulson, Tenant, Rent £76. The Buildings consist of a good Dwelling House, tiled, a Granary and Cart House, a 2-stalled and 3-stalled Stable, 2 Pigsties and a Cart House all tiles; also a Water Grist Mill with 3 pairs of stones, erected or increased and enlarged about the year 1819 at the expense of the Marquis of Aylesbury ... Lord Aylesbury found one pair of grey stones in 1818, one pair of French stones in 1819 and one pair of French stones in 1835 ..."

(NYCRO, ZJX 4/45 mic 915).

Selected items from a set of payment vouchers are given below (NYCRO ZJX mic 1549 & 152):

"W Greathead (Brick and Tile Manufacturer of Yarm), 2100 tiles for the mill £9 9s 0d, 500 bricks 12s 6d

John Temple, Digging the Foundations for a new Water Work at Swainby Mill, widening the Old Race for the Mill and digging the Space for the Water Wheel £50 7s 6d Wm Taylorson, 2 Door Latches, 2 Chamber Door Latches, 1 pr T Hinges, 4 Pair Dove Tail Hinges £10 7s 4d

John Temple, To cash paid Thos Tyerman for assisting to load Waggon with stones for the Mill, 7 days 14s 0d

Richard Fairweather,

For Iron Work at Swainby Mill £1 4s 7 1/2d

3 New Gavelicks wt. 45 1/2 lb £1 7s 9d

To Hacks sharping, lying and mending £1 1s 0d

To Iron Work at the Stone Sledges 14s 4d

To Iron Work at the Stone Waggon 12s 10d

To Iron Work at the Rully 15s 9d

To Hinges and Spar Nails and Screw Bolts £3 5s 8 1/2d

TOTAL £17 12s 0d

John Milburn, Stokesley

To 108 Squares of Glass 8 5/8 by 11 5/8 £7 8s 0d

Thomas Nelson, £30 0s 0d

Thomas Harland, 13 and a half days Walling at the New Water Mill at Swainby £2 7s 3d

Jonathan Hughill, To leading 20 loads of lime from Piersbridge near Darlington to the New Mill at Swainby £28 0s 0d

John Temple, Cash pd for Boon Work at 1s per day (Various local men, a total of 142 days) £8 2s 2d

Messrs Wass, Johnson and Todd of Stockton, various Memel and Pine timber, planks and deals and tiling lathes

John Jackson, for Gudgeons, carriages, brass steps, flanges, Boxes

Pit Wheel £18 15s 4d

Crown Wheel £4 7s 0d

Wallier Wheel £2 6s 0d

Mortus Wheel £13 1s 4d

Wheels, carriages and shaft £4 6s 4d

3 plates to casting pit wheel and Wallier £2 10s 8d

TOTAL £68 13s 9d

Allowed for old plates £1 6s 10d

BALANCE £67 6s 7d

Aaron Peacock, Stokesley, for general smiths work.
Numerous screws, bolts, gudgeons, hoops, cold chisels, drills, *"4 hoops for Water Wheel"*, brasses, *"33 bolts for warter wheel"*, *"20 bolts for Pit Weel"*, *"1 Rowler"* and *"to turning rowler and fitting"*, *"to one gudgeon for upright shaft"*, *"to one lead screw for rising stone and key for same"*, *"to 1 striking ring for Blew Mill"* etc. *"To 7 bolts and 1 plate for Clowes, to Shrinking Ring for grey Mill, to universal joint and spindle, to one dozen hooks for Silinder"*. *"To 2 cast steel Chisels, to 1 chean and 2 staples for hoist, 1 Rowler and 2 Cheakes for Clowes"*.

£44 13s 0d".

The account shows that the mill was built of stone led from the dale edge on the *"stone waggon"* or sledges by local men, no doubt tenant farmers. The stone mason is not identified and we can assume that he was an estate employee. The roof was covered with pantiles brought from Stockton. The 500 bricks were probably for a chimney-stack. In contrast with the dark, sometimes windowless, mills of former days, Swainby mill had 108 panes of glass. The waterwheel pit was enlarged and fit-

ted with a *"clowe"* gate, running between *"cheakes"* and raised by a *"rowler"*. By omission in the list of castings it seems that the waterwheel was of wood – part of the wooden shaft survived into the 1960s. The upright shaft had a gudgeon supplied by Aaron Peacock and must therefore have been made of wood. The mill was equipped with one pair of blue stones, at least one pair of greys and a cylinder. The stone nuts were engaged by a *"striking ring"* and tentering was by *"screw"* jack. The millwright work was very like that at Danby and Ingleby.

Costa High mill was rebuilt in the same year as Swainby mill and carries the inscription "I S 1819" over the entrance. At ground level this mill reveals its previous existence as a combined corn mill and fulling mill but above ground level the mill is entirely of 1819 rebuild with the standard two-and-a-half storey 'improved' arrangement though, in contrast to Swainby mill, it is poorly provided with windows. In recent times the clasp-arm waterwheel, on its square-section wooden shaft, has been repaired by the National Rivers Authority (now part of the Environment Agency) to its original design. The wooden upright shaft, chamfered from a 14 inch square-section timber, rests on a wedged footstep bearing very similar to that at Ingleby Greenhow. Unlike at Ingleby and Danby the coarse-pitched cast-iron wallower was designed to mesh with a wooden pit wheel, and recently a new clasp-arm pit wheel, to the old design, has been installed. The broken crown wheel is not the original. Other machinery is now missing, but records of 1965 show that there had been a hoist, grain cleaner, three pairs of stones and a flour cylinder.

The following is a list of these well-documented early upright shaft driven mills described so far, together with additional examples for which there is fragmentary evidence:

FIG 69. COSTA HIGH MILL.

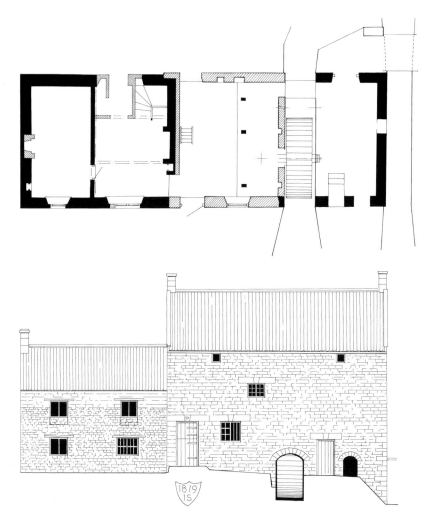

Fig 69. Costa High mill.

1781 Hold Cauldron, Charles Slingsby Duncombe

1785 Bilsdale Low, Charles Slingsby Duncombe

1789 Stonegate

1792 Scaling, John Wallis

?   Loftus, Sir Thomas Dundas

1799 Easby, "I M" (John Marr)

1801 Danby End, Thomas Weatherill

1804 Howl Beck, Robert Chaloner

1807 Danby Howe, William Wilson

1817 Ingleby Greenhow, William Foulis

1817 Farndale Low, Charles Slingsby Duncombe

1819 Swainby, Marquis of Aylesbury

1819 Costa High, "I S 1819"

1824 Sutton-under-Whitestonecliffe

Beyond this, it is clear from surviving remains that many other local water-driven corn mills were re-fitted with spur wheel and upright shaft drives during the first quarter of the nineteenth century. Very good buildings of this early period, all with excellent masonry, survive, for instance, at Kepwick, Glaisdale High and Littlebeck.

Waterwheels and gearing problems

The increased throughput in these mills highlighted the old problem of shortage of waterpower. John Smeaton had pointed to the importance of measuring the power available on a site before building a mill and he produced experimental data as to the gallons per minute required for grinding wheat and other cereals. Wheat needs more because of the fine gap between the millstones and the higher speed of rotation. Smeaton quantified what every practising millwright must have known from experience – that overshot wheels working by gravity were more efficient than undershot wheels working by impulse, 63% and 22% respectively (J Smeaton, 1759). However, in practice, the choice of waterwheel was dependent on the gradient and flow of the beck or river rather than on the theoretical advantage of overshot wheels, and since most mill steadings had been established in medieval times they were now short of water. There were at least three early attempts to tackle the problem by extending the natural catchment area into neighbouring dales. During the eighteenth century the old leat from Hole Beck to Lastingham mill was replaced by a watercourse, over a mile and a half long, from

Loskey Beck in an entirely different dale. In 1800 a long watercourse was cut in the moors above Hutton near Guisborough to catch water for Howl Beck mill, and another course, over a mile and a half long, was cut from the Moordale Beck to serve the mill at Wilton (pre 1803). Another approach was to dig supplementary leats to harness a second beck, for example at Rosedale, Cropton, Bransdale, Farndale High and Moorsholm mills. At Bransdale the leat was raised to drive a larger diameter waterwheel and at the same time a second small beck was captured. At Farndale High mill a second leat from the Dove was cut to supplement the old supply from Fish Beck. Rosedale mill was driven from Northdale Beck until a bigger leat was cut from the Seven. Cropton mill had leats from Little Beck, probably the original, and from the Seven. At Farndale Low mill the old steading on the small West Gill beck was abandoned in favour of a new steading set up on the more ample Dove. Yet another approach was to raise the head of water by building a new dam further up the beck, as at Foss, Rigg and Goathland. At Rigg and Goathland the water level was raised to allow an increase in the diameter of the waterwheel. At Foss it was raised merely to increase storage capacity of the dam.

The extent to which available waterpower had already been harnessed in previous centuries is shown by the fact that new water mills on new steadings were not common. Their water supply tended to be less manageable. At Danby End (1800) there was a problem with flooding and although there was an ample flow there was only a low head, and there was no alternative but to use an undershot wheel. Where undershot wheels were unavoidable Smeaton recommended that the masonry of breast walls be fitted as closely as possible to the curvature of the wheel, and the high quality of breast work is a feature of both new and improved mills of this period. At Costa High, for instance, a segment of masonry stands proud of the walls to hug the paddles as they swept round the inside of the pit. At Danby End similar proud masonry incorporated stepped ledges, used for boards set across the wheel pit when the waterwheel was being repaired.

During the eighteenth century most waterwheels had been built on square-section wooden shafts using the clasp-arm construction illustrated by Agricola and widely used throughout northern Europe. They were cheap to build and they were robust, particularly in small and medium-sized wheels. An unusual variant on the clasp-arm construction is to be found in three mills in north east Yorkshire at Coulton, Hold Cauldron and Raindale. In these the wooden shaft is hexagonal in section rather than square and the clasp-arms are locked together in a hexagonal pattern thus providing more support points to the felloes. The disadvantage was that the arms could not be fitted together with simple cross-halving joints, so the wheels were more difficult to construct. This can be

seen in the wheel at Coulton, which was assembled by splitting one set of arms lengthwise and then bolting together the two halves over the other two sets. Smeaton used traditional clasp-arm wheels but he also pioneered the use of more durable wheels with cast-iron shafts and cast-iron nave plates. The arms were fitted into slots in the casting and were therefore better supported at their weakest point. In north east Yorkshire cast nave plates were applied to both iron shafts (Danby End) and wooden shafts (Ingleby Greenhow).

Most new mills were fitted with large diameter spur wheels on elegantly crafted wooden upright shafts which took the drives up to the first floor. This system represented the pinnacle of the 'high millwrighting' practice developed from the work of Smeaton and other millwrights of the late eighteenth century. The shafts were lathe-turned or multi-facetted above floor level but left square- or hexagonal-section in the hurst where the arms of the wallower, spur wheel and crown wheel were fitted. They were more finely crafted than the upright shafts of early horse wheels and equal in quality to those in tower windmills. Typically, they ran through two floors, from a footstep bearing on wedged wooden blocks at ground level up to a bearing framework set in the floor beams above the first floor.

Upright shafts were illustrated by Agricola (1556), Ramelli (1588) and Diderot (1763), but not in corn mills. The earliest illustration of their use in a corn mill was published in 1735 (Beyern, Theatrum Mechinarum Molinarium). The earliest surviving English example may be the lathe-turned shaft in James Brindley's mill in Leek, Staffordshire (1752) which has 12 mortises for a multi-spoked spur wheel and 10 mortises for a crown wheel. Smeaton's design for Sir Lionel Pilkington's flour mill (1754) had an upright shaft with wooden lantern and spur wheel to three sets of stones (Joshua Richardson, 1812, vol 2, 430-1). Thirty years later illustrations became more common (see, for example, James Ferguson, 1784, Lectures on Select Subjects) and from that time spur wheels and upright shafts were installed throughout most of England.

The spur wheel was a very large diameter wheel with cogs set around the outer edge of the felloes, like the rowels of a spur. It was used to drive two, three, or, more rarely, four sets of stones set in a circle around it. The advantage was that the large diameter enabled a high gear ratio suitable for the fast rotation needed for milling wheat. Setting the spur wheel on an upright shaft avoided the problem that a spur wheel on a lying shaft would have entailed a second deep wheel pit in the hurst, and the increased number of millstones meant that there was greater flexibility for milling wheat, as well as oats, barley, peas and beans. It was also true that the hurst frame was tidier and the gearing more accessible. The out-dated large hurst pits needed for lying shafts could be closed up to provide a hurst floor which

Fig 70. Upright shaft gearing (Beyern, 1735).

Millwrights turned to the much heavier wooden upright shaft.

The new system highlighted the inadequacy of the old face-wheel and lantern drive. The small diameter lanterns set up heavy resistance to the cogs, a problem aggravated by the very coarse pitch of the cog mortises in the wooden felloes of the pit wheel which meant that few teeth were in mesh at any one time. The pitch could not be reduced because of the short grain between the mortises. Also, the cogs in the face of the pit wheel moved with a rolling action across the rungs of the trundle and this resulted in abrasive wear to both cogs and rungs. These problems were recognised by Smeaton, who suggested cast-iron staves with a *"flattish or oval figure"* for the lanterns (J Smeaton, 1766, 248-51). A further problem with wooden cog wheels is that they tended to go out of true as the curved felloes straightened out with shrinkage over the years. Taken together these problems in the primary drive could never be properly resolved using face wheels and lanterns.

However, they could be solved by bolting segments of cast-iron gearing to the face of the old wooden pit wheel, as at Costa High mill, and by scrapping the old lantern gear in favour of a cast-iron wallower. This system had been installed, by William Hazeldine of Shrewsbury, in mills in Shropshire and Staffordshire by 1789. The earliest dateable example in north east Yorkshire is at Danby End mill, built in 1800. At Costa the cast-iron wallower has only 28 teeth with a very coarse 4 inch pitch, designed to run against the wooden cogs of a clasp-arm pit wheel. However, the best solution was to put in a matching pair of cast-iron bevel gears.

Spur wheels were still usually built of wood. Some were of compass-arm construction, four arms at Scaling and six arms at Danby and Ingleby Greenhow, while at Oldstead, Thornton-le-Street and Ellerbeck they were of clasp-arm construction. As a general rule the coarser the pitch and the longer the cogs, the older the wheel (A Stoyel, 1995). Smeaton had recognised the need for finer pitch teeth for the fast-running secondary drive from the spur wheel to the millstone spindle as early as 1778 when he installed a cast-iron mortise wheel with wooden cogs for Brook Mill at Deptford. With cast-iron it was possible to reduce the spaces between the mortises and the finer pitch produced smoother and quieter running. However, there is no early example of a cast-iron spur wheel in this region though there is a later example at Tocketts mill.

was drier and easier to work on. The increased weight and speed of millstones, commonly by this time 120 revs/min, required more power. Many mills were now equipped with ancillary machines such as grain cleaners, flour dressers and sack hoist. Upright shafts, reaching through two storeys with a spur wheel for driving three or four pairs of millstones and a crown wheel above for driving light machines, were perfectly adapted for the new demands. Also, the torque from new powerful waterwheels could not be transmitted through the old-fashioned light-section horizontal shafts.

New buildings

The new and 'improved' mills were built to a two-and-a-half storey, or two-storey-plus-loft, arrangement; one storey higher than most mills of the early eighteenth century. These mills were much more spacious inside. Ground floors were more spacious because the millstones were placed on the first floor rather than on a bench hurst. Stone floors were made taller to accommodate the lay shafts from the crown wheel. The lofts, used for storage, were low at the eaves but roomy under the roof ridge. The raising of the rafters above the tie beams in such half floors created structural problems because there was no direct joint between the rafters and tie beam and this was solved by knee braces at Ingleby Greenhow, or uprights and cross braces in later mills at Kilton and Raisdale.

These new taller mills became a more easily recognisable feature of the landscape. Most still had the eighteenth century feature of glazed windows lighting the stone floor and the ground floor. At Bilsdale Low mill and Scaling mill these were small but in the later mills at Danby and Ingleby Greenhow they were much larger. Other window openings were smaller and irregularly spaced, in most cases no more than vents under the eaves to light the loft or roof chamber. Ground floor doorways could now be arched because there was plenty of headroom inside the mill. Sections of machinery could now be got into the hurst through the front of the hurst frame and there was, therefore, no further need for the small hurst doorways which had been a feature of early eighteenth century mills. Date-stones were no longer tucked away on back walls but were much more consciously styled and placed above the front entrance.

There was one regional variation. In the Tabular Hills and the Vale of Pickering, mills were built of coursed rubble blocks or 'moorstones' from the Corallian Series. They were used undressed, just as they had been prised from the beds in the quarries. Timber lintels, or sandstone lintels brought from elsewhere, were used to make doorway and window openings. By contrast, mills of the northern moors were built of 'quarry worked' and herring-bone dressed blocks from the Deltaic Sandstone which outcrops in every dale edge. The blocks were wedged off the quarry face and dressed with masons' picks to standard 9 inch, 10 inch and 12 inch courses. Contrary to common belief, it is by no means the case that buildings were always built with the thickest course near the ground, since the thickness of the courses was determined by the need to accommodate the window openings in the appropriate levels. The resulting buildings have a sturdy, functional, no-nonsense quality, which is also pleasing to the eye.

New materials also affected roof design. The humped thatched roofs of former times were replaced with brash red pantiles, carted from tileries at Pickering or from the

A)

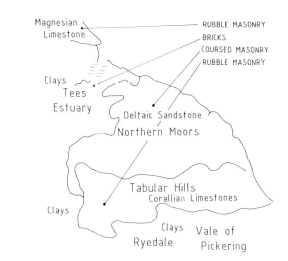

B)

FIG 71. A) BUILDING MATERIALS IN NORTH EAST YORKSHIRE AND B) EVOLUTION OF ARCHITECTURAL TREATMENT IN THE NORTHERN MOORS.

ports of Whitby and the Tees estuary. Roof pitches became flatter, making more space near the walls in the garner lofts. Tiles did not harbour rats and mice and therefore gave a cleaner cover for the stored grain. The new pantile roofs demanded new masonry techniques. Vulnerable tops of walls were thickened by oversails, for strength and to support guttering brackets. The top rows of pantiles were held down by a row of stone ridge copings while the gable-end pantiles were held down by stone verge copings which in turn were prevented from sliding down the roof slope by moulded 'kneelers' or stone corbels (see Easby mill).

Many new mills, for example Danby End, Danby Howe, Costa Low and Kepwick, had the previously unknown luxury of a fireplace for the comfort of the miller. Ground and first floor windows were glazed with panes of standard 'Georgian' proportions normally fitted into Yorkshire horizontally sliding frames. These floors were essentially working floors needing good light but with protection from draughts. Lofts, on the other hand, were essentially storage or garner floors needing ventilation rather than light and the vents were fitted under the eaves, with sliding slatted windows or hinged shutters. Doorways were fitted with half-doors in which the top half could be opened to let in light while the bottom half kept out the hens and provided an elbow rest for the miller as he smoked his pipe and contemplated the prospects for business. The stonework around the door became worn where he sharpened his pocketknife and his sickle.

Lay-shaft mills

The spur wheel and upright shaft drive was essentially the culmination of the old millwrighting tradition. By contrast, this same period also saw the introduction of the lay shaft drive, based on engineering practice used in the textile mills of Lancashire and the West Riding. In this the pit wheel drove a pinion on a horizontal or 'lying shaft' which was parallel with the waterwheel shaft. Either two or three sets of millstones were driven with bevel gears, not lanterns, and normally mounted on iron shafts. With this system there was no need for the awkward right-angle in the heavily loaded primary transmission and the geometrically complex bevel gearing was used only for the more lightly loaded millstone spindles.

Lay shafts were illustrated by Agricola (1556) but only applied to waterwheels and treadmills driving slow running shafts for water pumps etc. They were also illustrated by Agostini Ramelli (1588). In corn mills the gearing had to speed up the output shaft and the loading was therefore much heavier.

The lay shaft drive became more common in north east Yorkshire towards the middle of the nineteenth century (at West Ayton and Sinnington, for example) but there are four probable early examples. It is impossible to read much into the evidence from these few early examples but, rather surprisingly, the first may have been installed in the 1780s, contemporary with the earliest upright shafts. In contrast to the finely crafted upright shaft mills the lay shaft mills are humble one-and-a-half or two-storey structures. They were more cramped in the garner and sometimes space in other buildings was used for storage. Unlike the easily recognisable upright shaft mills, some early lay-shaft mills might easily be mistaken for farm buildings.

The earliest example, Spite mill near Osmotherley, was new-built in 1781 (Bell J, 2003, pers comm.). The advanced technique probably derived from work by millwrights at the nearby new textile mill at Cote Gill on land newly enclosed by Parliamentary Enclosure. The waterwheel, running gear and three sets of stones were dismantled long ago but in the 1960s the surviving hurst posts, tenter-beam brackets and hand wheel/bell crank tentering system were clearly relics of a lay shaft arrangement. In 1837 all three sets of stones were listed as French burrs.

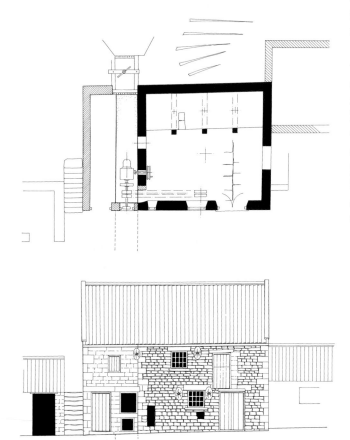

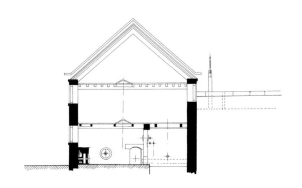

FIG 72. SPITE MILL, OSMOTHERLEY.

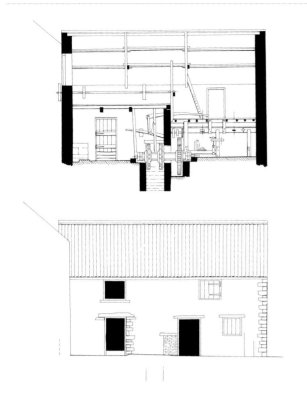

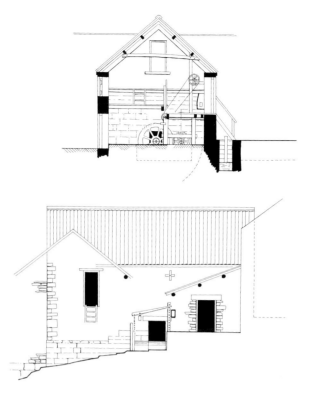

FIG 73. LOWNA MILL.

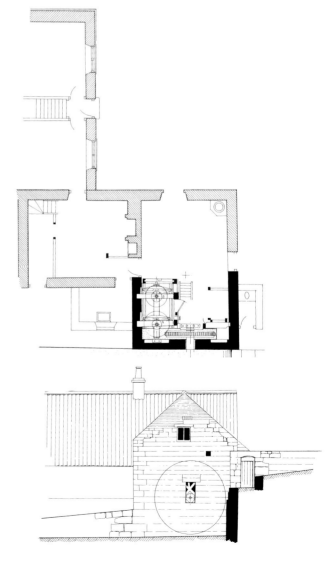

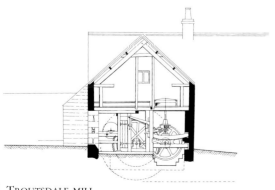

FIG 74. TROUTSDALE MILL.

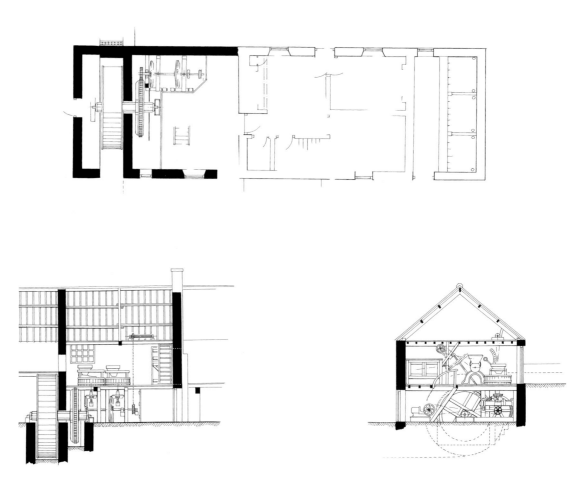

Fig 75. Liverton mill.

The other datable example is Lowna mill near Gillamoor. In 1790 the old fulling mill site at Lowna passed into the possession of Dinah Moon, who was still a minor. By 1801 she was married and she sold the mill, described as a fulling mill but still retaining an old corn mill *"sock, sucken and multure"* to the occupant, Thomas Baxter, who was described as a skinner and wool merchant. It was Baxter who developed the still surviving tan yard. The corn mill within the tan yard complex was working in 1813 (J T Capron, 1967, 42-44). The waterwheel is now missing but was, in any case, a later rebuild on the old shaft, by Butlers of Helmsley. The surviving pit wheel, pinion and lay shaft are of iron. Formerly there were one set of grey millstones and one other unknown. Stone nuts were engaged and disengaged by forked lever.

Two other lay shaft mills can be dated, tentatively, on stylistic grounds. At Troutsdale the range of buildings consists of a one-and-a-half storey mill with an eighteenth century longhouse built across the front of it and a nineteenth century house added to the front of the longhouse. The waterwheel is missing but an old painting shows it to have been of the out-dated clasp-arm

construction. The surviving pit wheel is also of clasp-arm construction. The lay shaft, now missing, was of wood and it was fitted with cast-iron bevel gears for driving the stone spindles. The cramped hurst platform carried one set of sandstone millstones (later replaced with a set of emery stones from a farm mill) and one set of bluestones. The stone clutches were engaged by forked lever and the tentering was by lighter staff. Even though much is missing Troutsdale mill is a rare and interesting survivor.

At Liverton mill the range of buildings looks rather like a traditional Yorkshire longhouse range with the mill steading at one end, the house in the middle and byre at the other end. This is deceptive, however, because the mill steading is medieval and the house and byre are much later. The waterwheel with its cast-iron naves and shrouds is mounted on an older square-section wooden shaft with an antiquated clasp-arm pit wheel. The two sets of millstones were driven by an iron lay shaft. The bedstone of a set of greys has a half obscured "17.." date incised in the lower surface and the top stone is inscribed "W W 1807". As at Troutsdale the second set are blues.

Ring-gear mills

A developed version of the lay shaft drive had a cast-iron ring-gear bolted onto either the arms or the shrouds of the waterwheel, taking the place of the traditional pit wheel. The wheel shaft could be lighter and shorter because it did not transmit the torque. The advantage had been recognised by Thomas C Hewes of Manchester, and ring gears were quite commonly used in textile mills by 1806 (T S Reynolds, 1983, 292). Later they were used in corn mills. The earliest ring-gear in a corn mill in north east Yorkshire may have been that at Newburgh but the earliest detailed record is for Rigg mill. A specification for a complete rebuild has survived from 1822 (Burnett Coll, 2255-57). The new mill stands tall and tower-like on a small base and it is distinguished from all other mills in this district by the very thick walls at ground level. The agreements made

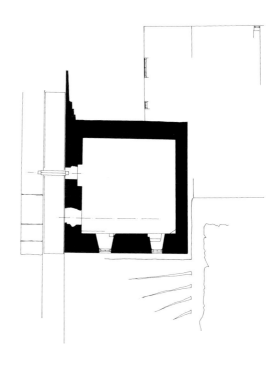

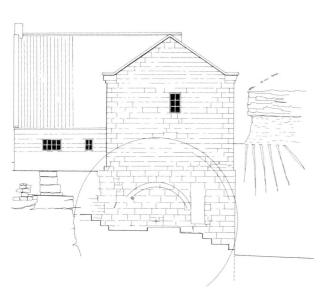

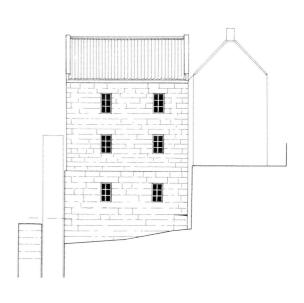

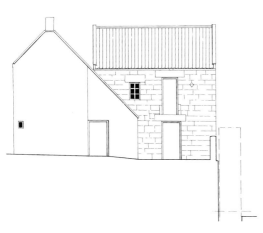

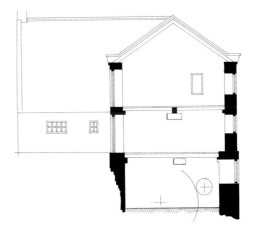

Fig 76. Rigg mill.

105

between the Sneaton estate and the various contractors read as follows:

First, with John Smith who was a mason:

"4 Sept 1822. Plan, Elevation, SPECIFICATION & AGREEMENT FOR BUILDING RIGG MILL AND DWELLING HOUSE.

Contractor to find everything but wood which is to be found by Mr Wilson ... labour to be found by Contractor as well as other materials ... lime, stone and sand, hair, nails, hinges, good locks and all other iron work, glass for all windows both mill and dwelling house ... all other materials to be worked up in a most careful manner. Parping walls to be nine inches thick which face up the lower part of the rock and to be carried the full height at the end across the house wall so as to make the end wall next the house strong. The walls of the dwelling house to be raised eighteen inches according to plan, both mill and dwelling house to be covered with Pickering tiles. A new chimney to the house as far as it is necessary with a new kitchen range and oven. The floor of the dwelling house to be neatly paved with flags. The headstock wall for the wheel to be faithfully built of solid masonry work to the proper height of 4 or 5 feet in breadth and to run up to this on solid rock towards the lane with solid Battlements and to extend past the mill as far as may be found necessary. The mill race to be properly paved with flags the full length of the stock wall as far as the tree pointed out and the lower or other part of the race for the backwater to be left properly opened up to a proper depth so as to take off the backwater, to the satisfaction of James Wilson. All wood work to be painted. The small drying house to be completely repaired and the ridging for all the buildings to be of good cut stone. Also the door and window heads and sills to be of cut stone with all necessary Battlements. Contractor to find the proper lead gutters. The Mill Race to be cut to the full length of the stock wall in line with the tree pointed out to a proper depth for a wheel twenty feet in diameter. Race to be faithfully walled on the opposite side as far as the stock wall runs down. Stone stairs from lower mill floor and a neat small staircase for the dwelling house as pointed out by James Wilson.

We agree to complete for £134.

John Smith.

(£134 paid 4 Nov, 1823)".

Then the millwright William Booth:

"4 Sept 1822. Wm Booth's Agreement with James Wilson Esq. to BUILD A NEW MILL AT RIG MILL ON THE SNEATON ESTATE.

I will engage to do all the mill wright work at Rig Mill ... to find all Materials of every description, wood excepted, which is to be found by you and laid on the spot. The water wheel is to be twenty feet in diameter, a cast iron axel, to be faithfully made and bolted in a worklike manner. All the machinery to be of the best cast iron, which with every other article, wood ecepted. I engage to find, such as nails, boltes and all other wrought iron that may be wanted, all brass work ... so as to complete in every respect a faithful working mill with two pair of stones on the best construction. The pair that is now in use to be allowed as one and the other to be found by me which are to be a prime pair of four feet diameter French burrs 6 inch thick in the burr and nothing less throughout and in every sense complete.

I am also to find a new cylinder complete in every respect with a proper sack tackle ... for hoisting and lowering sacks ...

... subject to survey.

When the mill is faithfully finished I am to have a dft for £150 ... in full payment for completing ...

(Settled in full, 18 Sept 1823)".

Finally with William Stockill and Thomas Headlam, labourers:

"27 Dec 1822. Agreement for cutting Rigg Mill Dam ...

We agree to cut the tail race for Rigg Mill to commence at a certon whole now in the rock and to cut it through the rock and from there to where it is already cut near the mill. The cutting to commence leavel with the top of the rock in the beck botom opsite the above mentioned whole and to be cut leavel as far as we have it to cut. The whole of the race boath through the rock and in the open cutting to be three feet three inches wide at the bottom and we allso agree to build a strong and sufficient wall between the beck and the above race from the point of the rock to a tree now growing in the back side, the wall to be suffient height and well backed up with earth to continue the present footpath leavel from the mill to the above mentioned rock and to prevent the beck at any time breaking into the above race ... for the sum of £8 8s 0d.

(£8 8s 0d paid 22 March 1823)".

Coupled with the archaeological evidence William Booth's agreement is revealing. The extensive use of

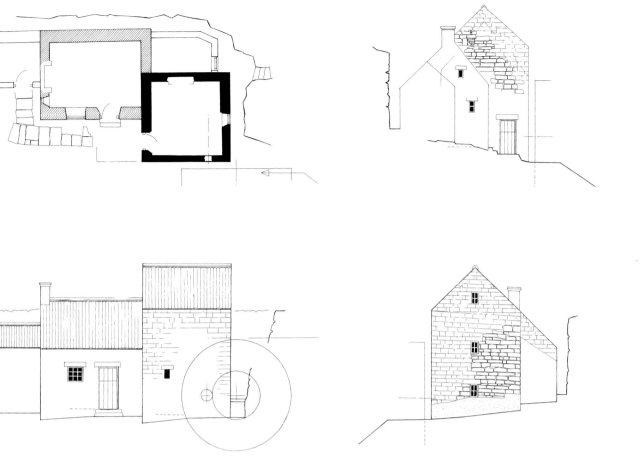

FIG 77. COCK MILL (PHOTO, WHITBY LITERARY AND PHILOSOPHICAL SOCIETY).

cast-iron shows that this mill was of advanced design. Booth could properly be described as a millwright engineer. Perhaps he was related to James Booth of Malton who rebuilt Tanfield mill in 1822. It is clear from old photographs that this was a ring-gear mill. The very large waterwheel was built onto a short iron shaft and the ring-gear was bolted to wooden arms. Nevertheless this project may not have been entirely successful to begin with. Even though there were only two sets of millstones the mill seems to have been short of power. In later years a wooden trough was built to take the water from higher up the beck and the waterwheel was rebuilt from 20 feet to 27 feet diameter in order to increase the torque.

The neighbouring Cock mill was also refurbished as a ring-gear mill, also with two sets of stones and a good deal of cast-iron and a narrow but large diameter waterwheel. Again the waterwheel shaft was very short. At both mills the ring-gears were about two thirds of the diameter of the waterwheel. Both wheels were set with their axis outside the line of the mill walls so that the ring-gear could drive a pinion on the end of the lay shaft running through the wall directly into the hurst.

A)

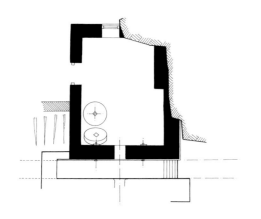

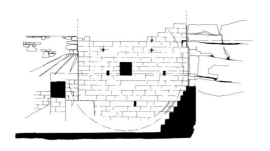

B)

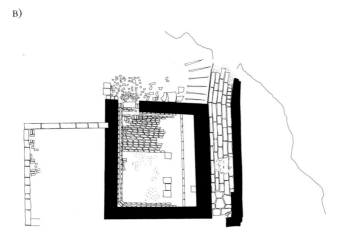

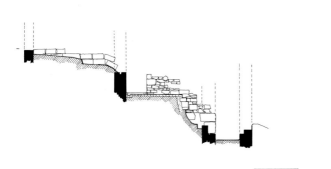

FIG 78. SQUARE GROUND PLANS AT A) ROXBY AND B) SWATHEY HEAD.

Summary

The following early lay shaft and ring-gear mills have been located:

Lay-shaft mills:
> Spite (1792), 3 pairs of stones, all French
> Troutsdale, 2 pairs, the second pair blues
> Lowna (1801 – 1813), 3 pairs, the first pair greys
> Liverton (1807?), 2 pairs, one grey and one blue

Ring-gear mills:
> Newburgh, pre 1813, three pairs
> Cropton (1822), three pairs
> Rigg (1822), two pairs
> Cock, two pairs
> Bay (1838), four pairs

In north east Yorkshire the best quality millwrighting practice was only installed at newly-built mills; Spite mill and Rigg mill, where the shafts and gearing were of iron. By contrast the machinery at both Troutsdale and Liverton appears to be hybrid, combining, for example, a lay shaft with an old-fashioned clasp-arm pit wheel.

Rigg mill and Cock mill both have small square ground plans and therefore appear tall in elevation. This characteristic is found in four other mills along the north coast; at Glaisdale High, Littlebeck, Roxby and Swathey Head, not all fitted with lay shafts. It is very noticeable that medieval mills at Howl Beck, Tocketts, Skelton and Saltburn had wide-span ground plans while these much later mills had much smaller, square plans. Constricted sites under waterfalls may have had an influence, but it is unlikely that this was the only reason. The efficient use of space points to an entirely new concept of how to provide storage space on top of the ground and stone floors.

Conclusion

Today, the surviving relics of these fine new mills, driven by upright shafts, lay shafts or ring-gears, completely eclipse the relics of earlier days. If any kind of water mill can be seen as representing a distinct north east Yorkshire type then it is these neat, beautifully built and functionally efficient mills.

TOWER WINDMILLS

A mid-eighteenth century "*Prospect of Newcastle-upon-Tyne*" by N & S Buck showed seven windmills to the north of the city. Had there been another engraving from the same spot at the end of the first quarter of the nineteenth century it would have shown a forest of arms. Mr Brown of the Newcastle Steam Mills reported to the British Association in 1822 that in Newcastle "*… 37 windmills, containing 99 pairs of stones ground weekly 1110 quarters of wheat*" (J Collingwood-Bruce, 1863, 269). Most were situated in a ring around the built-up area. By the same date there was a smaller 'wind farm' on the banks of the Tees estuary and by the middle of the century there were at least 45 windmills around the estuary and along the north coast. These new mills were bigger and more powerful than the old wooden post mills. The machinery was housed, not in a buck on a wooden trestle, but in a stone or brick tower varying in height from the humble three storeys at Ugthorpe to the mighty 12 and 13 storeys at Yarm and Pickering. Most post mills in north east Yorkshire had gone by the middle of the eighteenth century and it is not at all clear that there was continuity between them and the later towers. Certainly, they can be regarded as largely distinct, both historically and technically.

Tracing the history of local tower windmills is tantalizingly difficult. The archaeological evidence is thin since there are now the remains of only 11 towers and of these only Hart and Elwick have machinery in-situ. To make matters worse, the historical record for windmills compares badly with that for water mills. Many water mills remained in the ownership of landed estates, which tended to keep their archives. On the other hand, most windmills were built by individual entrepreneurs and when a windmill was given up at the end of its working life few documents were kept. Particularly frustrating is the lack of information on the dates of building. Considering the stir there must have been when the sails of a new mill turned for the first time newspaper reporters seem to have been blind or housebound.

Nevertheless, it is possible to tease out a few patterns:

● Industrial windmills were not a feature of north east

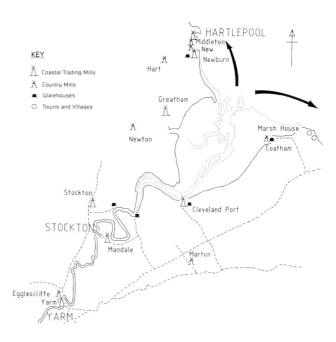

FIG 79. TOWER WINDMILLS ROUND THE TEES ESTUARY.

Yorkshire and south east Durham. Almost every windmill was a corn mill. The exceptions were two early oil mills and both of these were milling corn by 1800.

● The 'improved' water-driven corn mills of the late eighteenth and early nineteenth centuries, the contemporary tower windmills and the horse-driven threshing machines were all part of the same movement.

● The geographical distribution of the new tower mills was similar to that of the earlier post mills. However, the reason was different. The new mills were built not so much because of the lack of water power, as was the case in medieval times, but to serve coastwise and continental trading and, later, the new industrial towns such as Middlesbrough and North Ormesby.

● Though some of the new tower mills were quite small, some of the earliest, eg Cargo Fleet, Union mill at Whitby, Appleton's mill at Yarm, John Middleton's mill at Hartlepool and the short-lived mill at Pickering were among the biggest in England.

The last of the post mills

The survival of wooden post mills depended on regular repairs and if for any reason these repairs stopped the mill quickly became derelict. Some windmills went out of use at an early date. For example, the windmill at Whitby disappeared from the record after the Dissolution. The last recorded dates of other post mills include Coatham (1613), Ayresome (1618), Egglescliffe (1670), Marton (1675), Scarborough (1723) and Redcar (*"fallen into disrepair"*, 1726) but how far these reflect the end of working life is not clear. It seems inevitable that during the eighteenth century windmillers would have come under pressure to install blue stones for milling flour but there is no evidence to show how they responded.

A successor of the manorial windmill at Yarm, first listed in the thirteenth century, still stood on a rise to the south of the church, near the old Market Green, when the Enclosure Map was drawn up in 1658 (J W Wardell, 1957, opp 72). It had gone in 1837 when the tithe system in Yarm was replaced by rent charges and a Schedule of Titheable Lands in the Parish of Yarm recorded *"Stob Mill Field"* in the occupation of William Kilvington and Robert Southeran and *"Mill Scite"* in the occupation of Thomas Wastell (J W Wardell, 1957, opp 88 and 176).

The post windmill at Hartlepool stood just outside the town walls. It was illustrated on a map of the harbour and town, drawn by the Dutchman, Dromeslawers (1585), and it was evidently still at work in 1666 when the townsfolk were forbidden to cross the wall to go to the *"North Sandes Wind Mill"* under penalty that *"He or she shall pay for every tyme of doinge to the use of the towne xiid or he or she be punished at the direction of the Manor"* (W Boagey, Notes on Stranton, Hartlepool Museums).

In 1641 the inhabitants of Thornaby raised a petition against the heavy-handed treatment meted out by troops based at Stockton Castle when Scottish raiders were roaming through the County of Durham. The soldiers, under the command of James Livingstone, were crossing the river, using the meadows for their horses and had *"... broken a windmill nighe the towne and doe assault and draw their swords upon your peticons"* (T Sowler, 1972, 72-3). The mill must have been repaired since it stood in 1684 (Ft of F, York 24-5, ch 11). The circular platform can still be seen on the village green, 70 metres north of the church.

In 1653 the trustees of the Ormesby estate which had been *"... forfeited to the Crown for treason"* sold it to William Tooms of the parish of Hackney. Included was a *"... cottage in Normanby and a close of pasture ground adjoining called Milne Lease ... and a windmill standing on it ... now in the tenure of William Dickyson ... Also a cottage in Normanby, now or late in the tenure*

of Bartholomew Nicholls and the parcels of ground belonging to it ... Windmill Close along with the windmill standing on it ..." (TA U/PEN 179/80). Two separate windmills and horse mill were referred to in a lease and release of 1712 (TA U/PEN 1/169). However, in 1723 the field names were listed but not the windmills.

Only three post windmills can be said, with any confidence, to have survived into the nineteenth century. There had been a windmill at Hart for 500 years on the limestone scarp overlooking Hartlepool Bay, exposed to every wind, particularly the vicious north easterlies. To anyone who knows the site, it will come as no surprise to learn that on 16 December 1814 there was a *"... tremendous gale of wind ... At Hart the windmill was blown down with three men in it"* (T Richmond, 1868, 309). The wording is that which would have been used to describe the felling of a tree and leaves little doubt that it was a wooden post mill which had been laid on its side.

The second late survivor was at the tiny settlement called Newburn Rawe near Hartlepool. Records of its millers date back to 1631. In 1762 Rawe mill was illustrated as a post mill (though incorrectly named) on Joseph Dobson's plan and it also appeared as a post mill on Palliser Thompson's map of 1815. But by 1848 it had been replaced by a tower mill. The third survivor was the 'stob' mill at Elwick but it is not known when it stopped work. These three windmills may well have been the only ones still at work when the first tower mills were built.

Common-sail tower windmills

Tower windmills were known in the Mediterranean lands and the Iberian peninsular in the fifteenth century. Very old windmills in La Mancha in central Spain have massively built stone towers, stepped on the inside rather than tapered on the outside and with spiral staircases built into the inside of the walls. They were equipped with a single very large set of millstones. Most Mediterranean windmills were, broadly speaking, of this type. However, engravings by Ramelli (1588) and Strada (1600-17) show that by the end of the sixteenth century another type of tower mill was in use in northern Europe. The towers were still stepped on the inside rather than tapered on the outside but they were slimmer, which meant that there was space only for ladders rather than spiral staircases. Remains are found in the west of France, and there was a special variant called the 'petit pied' in Brittany. In the Low Countries, they coexisted with post mills. There was a scatter of small vertical sided windmill towers in south west England (mainly in Somerset) and a few others in Wales, Ireland and Scotland.

A later and bigger type, found in Anglesey, and north west and north east England, could accommodate a sec-

A)

B)

C)

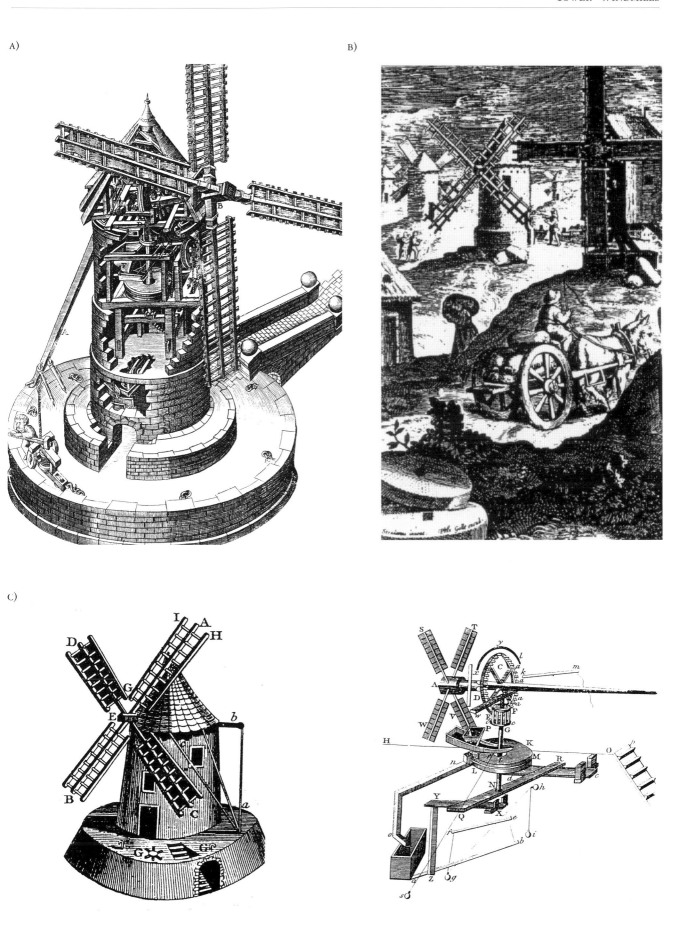

Fig 80. Early tower mills, a) Ramelli, b) de Strada and c) Johnson's Encyclopedia.

111

ond set of millstones and had battered walls which meant they were sturdier than the vertical-sided towers. Most were so stumpy that their common sails could be reefed from the ground or from reefing mounds round the base of the tower. Some of these mounds were high enough to need stone revetting and this gave the extra advantage of keeping animals away from the sail tips. Most were stone-built with four storeys; the hurst on the

first floor, millstones on the second, bin and hoist on the third and windshaft on the fourth. Like the earlier types they were equipped with common, or canvas covered, sails and endless chain winding wheels for turning the caps into the wind. The miller reefed the sails and turned the cap into the wind while standing on the ground.

There have been some twenty examples of these humble mills in the County of Durham. All but one or two were built on the magnesian limestone, which outcrops from Sunderland on the east coast. Whereas medieval ploughmen had preferred heavy soils because they regenerated more quickly in fallow years, the new ploughmen, working with horses, preferred lighter soils which could be turned more easily. Limestone lands were very suitable.

Engravings of the medieval town wall of Hartlepool show, in the background across the entrance to the Slake, a three-storey tapered tower windmill with four sails and no fantail. About 1770, a much bigger windmill was built alongside, by John Middleton. In September 1771 Ralph Jackson wrote in his journal that *I rode with Mr Wilson round Seaton Snuke before Dinner and after Dinner we looked through Jno Middleton's Wind Mill* (Ralph Jackson's diary, m s. TA U WJ/13). The mill was described in an insurance schedule:

> *"3 March, 1792. John Middleton of Hartlepool in the County of Durham ... on his dwelling house called Middleton House, situated aforesaid £200 ... Wind Corn Mill near, separate, stone and timber £100. Utensils and stock and standing and going gears and machinery therein £200. Shelling Mill and granary under one roof, a communication between the two mills by wooden axle tree £100. Utensils and stock therein £300"* (Sun Fire Insurance).
>
> (Cuthbert Sharp, 1816, opp 149 and opp 152).

FIG 81. MIDDLETON'S MILL (CUTHBERT SHARP).

Another, at nearby Stranton, was built before 1815. Ninian Sheraton of the nearby post mill died in 1790 and his widow, Ann, married another miller, William Knowles, who came from Yorkshire and took over the mill in 1799. Dodd's Chart of Hartlepool Bay (1802) showed a post mill but Palliser Thompson's Chart (1815) showed a tower mill. Cuthbert Sharp used an engraving of the mill as the frontispiece for his History of Hartlepool (1817). It was a three-storey tower on a stone-walled reefing mound, with common sails supported by rope ties to a pole extending from the front of the windshaft. The artist clearly did not understand the winding mechanism. The mill was variously called 'Knowles' Mill', 'New Mill' and 'White Mill', the term white referring to the magnesian limestone from which it was built. Robert May's engraving (1822) shows the mill against a backdrop alive with sailing ships in the

A)

B)

FIG 82. STRANTON MILL
A) BY CUTHBERT SHARP, 1816,
AND B) AFTER ROBERT MAY.

West Harbour and fishing boats on the sandy beach.

To the south of Hartlepool the magnesian limestone gives way to the clay of the Tees basin and the liassic series of the North York Moors. There were other common-sail windmills of the same general form as those on the magnesian limestone but built of locally available materials. For instance, when Mitford Abraham visited the old manorial windmill at Egglescliffe in 1932 he described it as *"... formerly a stage mound mill which has evidently been raised"* and one of his photographs

shows that it had been a low brick tower, later raised and fitted with an ogee cap.

Another small tower mill still stands at Ugthorpe and it is held locally, on the basis of a date carved into a timber removed from beneath the first floor, that it was built in 1796. However, the will of Mathew Cook shows that a mill existed in 1776 (Borthwick Inst, Exchequer Court Wills, Feb 1777). The outside diameter of the tower at its base is 22 feet 6 inches with a plinth around the base and there is a very pronounced batter. The tower now

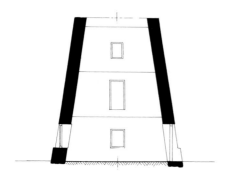

FIG 83. UGTHORPE MILL.

windshaft in John Smeaton's drawings for Chimney mill in Newcastle-upon-Tyne, although Chimney mill was bigger (Joshua Richardson 1812, vol 2, 396-7). There is an important difference however. At Chimney mill there was a forward strut for rope stays to the tips of the wands and the wands carried common sails, whereas at Hart the shaft has been bored, not quite accurately, from both ends. The drilling of windshafts for striking rods was first tried out by Captain Stephen Hooper for his roller reefing sails in 1789 and became much more common after William Cubitt combined Meikle's shutter sails and Hooper's striking rod to produce the true 'patent sail' design in 1807. Cubitt's patent meant that all of these sails were built under license until 1821.

stands 24 feet tall, but it may have been cut down slightly when the curb was taken off. It is built of rubble stonework with large sandstone window and doorway quoins, now obscured by rendering. Ugthorpe mill was clearly built as a common-sail mill which was reefed from the ground, and the old sad story about the donkey tethered to the tip of one of the sails on a deceptively calm day is told about Ugthorpe mill. Later it had reefing sails.

By 1796 there were two more common-sail windmills in the open fields of Low Stakesby to the north west of Whitby. Bagdale mill was the earlier of the two but no reliable illustration has survived. Stakesby mill was described as a *"Wind Corn Mill"* in the occupation of Elizabeth Knaggs and James Lewis in 1778 (Burnett coll 4572) but according to another source it had been built as an oil mill (G Young, 1817, 819). An engraving of Stakesby mill (R T Gaskin, 1909, 228) shows it with tapered tower, three floors, pitched cap roof, common sails and an endless chain winding wheel. In this case, however, it was built of 136 courses of brick, rather than of stone.

The problem of identifying common-sail mills is illustrated in the case of Hart mill which has the common sail proportions, but all surviving illustrations show it with patent sails. It is built of magnesian limestone and the cap had a flattish domed roof, carvel-built and covered with tarred canvas, not very remarkable for an area known for boat and ship building. In common with some water mills of this period, there was a fireplace, the smoke from which escaped through a flue in the tower wall (now covered with rendering). It has no reefing gallery. The short windshaft rests on a tail bearing fitted to the sprattle beam immediately behind the centre of the tower. The reason for this short windshaft may have been either that it was still seen as difficult to make a sound casting long enough to straddle the walls of the tower, or that the wind shaft was designed to be drilled to take a striking rod for operating patent sails. In fact the dimensions for the windshaft at Hart mill are similar to those for the main part of the

FIG 84. STAKESBY MILL.

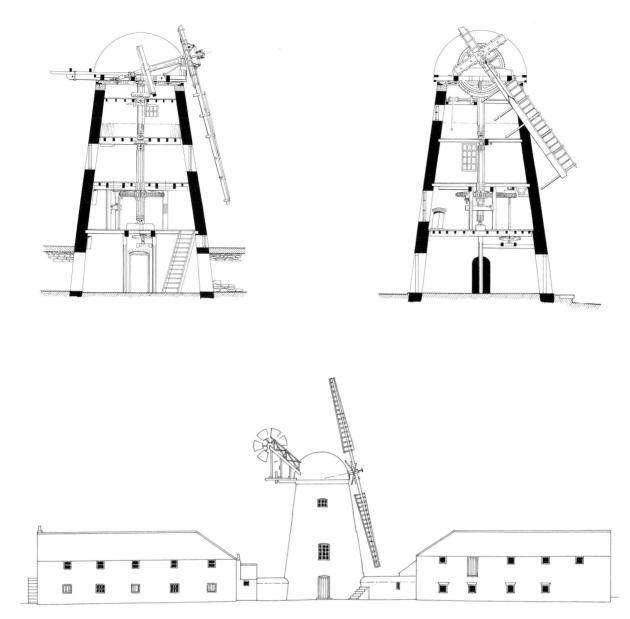

NOT TO SCALE

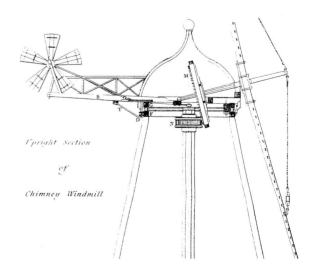

Upright Section

of

Chimney Windmill

FIG 85. HART WINDMILL AND, FOR COMPARISON, SMEATON'S
CHIMNEY MILL, NEWCASTLE (JOSHUA RICHARDSON 1812,
REPORTS OF THE LATE JOHN SMEATON).

Coastwise trading windmills

For centuries sailing ships had berthed in the sheltered tidal creeks behind the sand bar at Coatham. In 1771 Arthur Young visited the Kirkleatham estate of Charles Turner and wrote enthusiastically about *"… a house near the sea with spacious granaries, warehouses etc designed for and let to a merchant, by way of fixing a trade at this place, or at least providing such conveniences that farmers may be sure of proper places for lodging their corn ready for the sea, and also enabling the merchant to speculate in the corn trade at Kirkleatham …"* (A Young, 1771, vol 2,134-9). Had Young re-visited East Coatham three years later he would have been even more impressed, because a windmill had been built (Thos Atkinson, Plan of the parish and manor belonging to Charles Turner Esq; NYCRO ZMI DN 88). Quarter Sessions records of 1801 show that much more flour was being produced than was needed locally.

From 1775 a new generation of windmills was built around the Tees estuary, much bigger than anything built before and towering over the flat estuary landscape and the rooflines of Whitby and Scarborough. Most were built by millwrights from outside the region. The reason was that troubles in France, culminating in the French Revolution of 1789, pointed to a need for Britain to secure its grain supplies. The price of wheat rose from 62s/quarter to 128s in 1801, a cause for serious concern. As a result, Chief Constables of each county had to compile returns on the prices charged by each miller in their area. The result was that by 1828 *"… there are upwards of twenty windmills many of them recently erected between Yarm and the mouth of the River Tees"* (J Brewster, 1829, 271-2). After the turmoil in France the big windmills continued to serve the growing market in London as well as the local demand. During that period the following big windmills were built.

Stockton Old Mill, 1786

Scarborough Common, pre 1787, 7 floors

Middleton, Hartlepool, 1791

Mandale, 1800, 8 floors

Greatham , c 1800, 5 floors

Whitby Union, 1801, 7 floors

Cargo Fleet, c1803, 6 floors

Dovecot, Stockton, c 1814

Yarm, pre 1815, (said to be 12 floors, *"the loftiest building of its kind in England"*)

Knowles, Stranton, pre 1816

Redcar, 1816, 6 sails

Scarborough, Albion, pre-1819, 6 floors

Mount Pleasant, Stockton, before 1825

Hinderwell, 1827, 7 floors

Pickering, 1827 (*"lately erected"*), 13 floors.

The Halmote Court Rolls for 1786 noted that William Smith of Stockton, miller, lost his copyhold land on the Stockton to Norton Road for digging clay (T Sowler, 1972, 483). That same year Smith built a windmill on the west side of Stockton, on Browns Haugh, high ground south of Bishopton Lane near Browns Bridge. There had been a windmill here since the time of the Commonwealth, when the inhabitants of Stockton were no longer tied to grind their corn at the Bishop's watermill at Norton. This site was not far distant from the main turnpike road from Stockton to Sunderland, which had become increasingly important after 1769 when the bridge at Stockton was built across the Tees. It also had access via Portrack Lane to the river at Portrack, where a wharf saved some two miles of torturous navigation through the Mandale loop down-river.

A sales notice described Smith's new mill as *"… adapted for the flour and oil trade, with a dwelling house and out-buildings. The mill stands well for the wind and has a cast metal axle tree, three pairs of stones, and stands within half a mile of Stockton"* (Yorkshire Herald, 9 Oct. 1790). In an insurance document of 1791 it was described as a *"… corn mill with going gears and machinery therein and warehouse under, brick with a cone of timber, built and known as Stockton windmill"* (Royal Exchange Fire Insurance no 124935). A painting of about 1840 shows that it was in fact a smock mill. Although its lower part and outbuildings were of brick, the tower appears to be entirely built of timber. This is presumably the 'cone' referred to in the insurance document. (William Wheldon, *A View of Stockton …*, Stockton Borough Council)

Another insurance document of 1794 shows that by that time the mill belonged to Henry Richardson, from the landowning family which had a water-driven mill at Great Ayton. In 1832 the mill was purchased by Thomas Wren.

Hartlepool, surrounded by fine corn country, had *"… two extensive flour mills that manufactured great quantities which is conveyed to Newcastle and Sunderland by water; each having a vessel for that purpose"* (William Tate, 1816, Hartlepool, Seaton and Stranton). About 1760 John Middleton, a millwright from Guisborough, acquired an estate across the Slake from Hartlepool (Milburn G E, 1983, 81). Between 1791 and 1799 he was handling cargoes of corn and wheat out of the Tees in a sloop called the Dove (NYCRO ZK 4958-60). About this time he built a big windmill close to his old common-sail tower mill. A sales notice of 1793 described it as working four pairs of stones, a barley mill and two flour machines (Yorks Herald, Aug 24), and when Middleton tried to sell or to let it in 1798 the mill was capable of *"… manufacturing 6000 sacks annually. Its situation is particularly well adapted for the shipping of grain and flour, being in the immediate vicinity of the Town and Port of Hartlepool, and the tide flowing* nearly up to the granaries. There is also a kiln for drying grain, a coach house, cart house, workshop and stabling for six horses" (Newcastle Advertiser, July).

More detail is contained in an insurance valuation of 1800: "On a corn windmill house near (to Middleton House) £350. On the wooden moveable top, standing and going gears thereon £850. On the shelling mill, communicating by an axle with the above £100. On the machinery and going gears therein £100. All that brick tiled and slated except for the wooden top of the windmill" (Royal Exchange Insurance, no 174785). The values were much higher than those of older common-sail mills. The contrast between the two can be seen in an engraving of 1839 (W Finden). The small mill had gone by 1857 when Middleton was described as having one windmill only (Fordyce, 1857, 293). The big mill was a tall eight-storey tower with a round cap, patent sails and a fantail.

Mandale windmill, in Thornaby, was built in 1800 on a steep bluff overlooking the Mandale loop, downriver from Stockton and part of an estate belonging to Lord Harewood of Harewood House near Wetherby. The windmill was described in 1801:

"MANDALE near Stockton-upon-Tees. To be Let and entered upon immediately, a new erected wind corn-mill, situate at Mandale in Cleveland in the County of York, with Three Dwelling Houses, the Granaries, a Kiln and other suitable conveniences and about Four Acres and a Half of Land occupied and employed therewith, the property of Lord Harewood. Mandale is situate on the banks of a Navigable part of the River Tees, in an excellent Corn Country and is a short distance from the several market towns of Stockton, Darlington, Stokesley, Guisbro' and Yarm. The Mill is built upon a new and much improved construction, will contain about 600 sacks of flour, and is calculated to grind 150 quarters of Corn in a week in its present state, but at an inconsiderable expense may be made to grind double that quantity, and the granaries adjoin the river and will contain 2,000 quarters of corn. For further particulars apply to Mr Raisbeck, at his office, in Stockton.

Stockton, September 22, 1801".

The owner hoped to sell flour in the market towns on the various roads running out from Stockton Bridge but, from the siting of granaries on the river bank, it is clear that he also looked forward to shipping flour out by river. No millwright's name appears in the Harewood Papers dealing with the early years of the mill (West Yorkshire Archives, WYL 250/1/368). Sowler suggests Andrew Brown, a Scotsman (T Sowler, 1972, 349). However, born in 1777, he would have been very young to have been in overall charge of such a project. Brown settled in Stockton and by 1806 was one of the proprietors of an iron foundry, a business which under his sons became the Portrack Lane foundry and engineering works.

It is hard to imagine what the loop in the river at Mandale looked like when the mill was built. Sailing ships could not move easily against tide and wind through the shallow reaches and many had to transfer part of their load to smaller boats before they could make their way upriver. It was this that led to problems for the windmill when a committee of townsfolk from Stockton and Darlington commissioned a Newcastle engineer, William Chapman, to prepare a survey and a report for cutting out the tedious Mandale Loop altogether. Chapman presented his report in 1805 recommending that a 200 yard 'cut' could save over two miles

FIG 86. MIDDLETON MILLS, AFTER W FINDEN, 1839.

117

FIG 87. GREATHAM WINDMILL.

over a period of two years. According to later description this was *"A capital and complete windmill upon an improved construction built of brick and covered with lead, with dressing mills and machinery surpassing most other corn mills in the kingdom"* (T Sowler, 1872, 349).

Greatham windmill was built about 1800 at the hilltop village not far from a muddy tidal inlet called Greatham Creek, on the north bank of Tees Bay. It was a six-storey mill with an ogee cap roof with an exceptionally tall finial, fantail and a reefing gallery at second floor. It appears to have been built of local bricks. By the beginning of the twentieth century it had four sails, rotating anti-clockwise, and an eight-blade fan.

Another big windmill on the Tees was built downriver where the Cargo Fleet cut through the mud banks to join the main tidal flow. At the beginning of the eighteenth century this was part of the eastern half of the estate of the Pennymans of Ormesby. It was sold off in 1715, bought back by Sir James Pennyman in 1771 and placed into receivership in 1779 (D W Pattenden, 1985). By this time a wooden wharf and two warehouses had been built at what was now known as Cleveland Port. For a time, the port was rented as a timber stocking point by Thomas and Richard Peirse of Low Worsall. Then, from 1794, it was rented by Messrs Richardson of Great Ayton for £100 per annum (D W Pattenden, 1985). In 1798 it was reported that *"... considerable quantities of wheat, oats, beans, butter, bacon and cheese were shipped from Cleveland Port for the coal country near Newcastle and for London and coals and other necessary articles were brought in return"* (J Tuke, 1800, 310n). 5000 quarters of wheat and 30,000 quarters of oats together worth about £40,000 were shipped from Cleveland Port in that year. Interestingly, it was suggested that the figures were lower than in the previous years because of *"... the great quantity that was made into flour and shipped to different ports"*.

Nicholas Richardson, the then tenant, died in 1801 and the tenancy was taken over by Philip Heselton, also from Great Ayton, who had married Richardson's niece. Two years later the rent jumped from £100 to £300 per annum (D W Pattenden, 1985). Such a rise might be explained by the building of a large windmill. By 1808 turnover at Cleveland Port had reached £1000 per day throughout the year (J Graves, 1808, 450). Palliser Thompson's chart of 1815 showed the Cleveland Port windmill as a big six-sail tower mill but this was probably a stylised drawing (British Library, maps, 1202.29). There is an accurate illustration of Cleveland Port, drawn from the mud bank between the Fleet and the river, in a vignette included on *"A map of Middlesbrough"*, c 1840 (TA U/OME 8/7). The scene is reminiscent of East Anglia or Holland, with a ship and a barge tied up beside the windmill and granaries. The windmill was a splendid eight-storey tower with a gallery at the fourth floor, five sails, ogee cap roof and fantail. At that time it was run by a Master Corn

of navigation. The main obstacles to a bill in Parliament arose from land ownership and, of course, the fact that Lord Harewood's windmill, left isolated in a severed loop of the river, would be cut off from the sea. At first Harewood resisted all offers of compensation but in the end he capitulated and accepted an offer of £2000 to be paid when the new cut became navigable. In addition, he would receive some of the land which was reclaimed by filling in the old river bed (T Sowler, 1972, 237). The bill received the Royal Assent in May 1808 and the Mandale Cut was formally opened on 18 September, 1810. The Navigation Company was authorised to raise a capital of £7000, with an option to raise a further £5000 at a later date, and the £2000 offered to Lord Harewood had taken a considerable slice out of this total.

But by 1814 the modest five-storey tower was found to be leaning out of plumb by 11 inches at the height of the gallery, 44 feet above the ground. An estimate for levelling the foundations and righting the tower at a cost of £407 was prepared by Andrew Brown, but was found to be unacceptable. Instead, a drawing for an eight-storey, 74 feet high windmill, re-using some of the older machinery and shortening the windshaft, was prepared by the millwright James Booth of Malton (Harewood papers, West Yorkshire Archives, WYL 250/1/368). His estimate of £894 was accepted and the mill was re-built

Fig 88. Cleveland Port ("*Map of Middlesbrough*", c1840).

Miller and two journeyman millers and it had been fitted with auxiliary steam power within the previous ten years. Trade declined, however, and soon afterwards the site was overwhelmed by the Ormesby Ironworks.

Another windmill (Mount Pleasant) was built, pre-1824, on the highest ground within the Stockton town boundaries, a short distance from the turnpike road north from Stockton to Norton and conveniently situated for Portrack Lane, which led directly to the river wharf at Portrack. In its later days Mount Pleasant mill was an eight-storey tower with an ogee cap and a reefing stage on iron brackets, anti-clockwise sails and a fantail on a tall frame (M Heavisides, 1906, In and around picturesque Norton).

In 1815 Palliser Thompson showed Newburn mill, near Hartlepool, as a wooden post mill. In 1827 it was owned by James Sheraton and his brother, John, and about this time they built the new tower mill with large warehouses which were illustrated in Thomas Thorpe's engraving (1848). It had a fairly short working life. Access to the sandy shore where sailing ships could be beached in fine weather was reduced to a low tunnel when the Stockton and Hartlepool Railway was built in 1841 but, unlike its neighbour, Knowles mill, it was not immediately dismantled. It was last recorded in the late 1850s.

The five-arch bridge built at Stockton in 1762 blocked navigation to Yarm. Nevertheless Yarm continued to develop corn milling. The family name of Appleton appeared as early as 1753 when James Appleton *"miller and maltster"* claimed a refund on tax paid on a quantity of grain which had subsequently been lost in one of the disastrous floods which plagued the town. Richard Appleton was variously listed as *"miller"*, *"corn factor*

and corn miller", *"corn miller"* and *"corn miller and merchant"* between 1822 and 1848. His second son,

Fig 89. Mount Pleasant mill (Heavisides).

119

FIG 90. NEWBURN RAWE WINDMILL, T THORPE, 1848

Richard Henry, became a national figure in milling and in his later career provided a brief note on his father's background:

"The Agricultural produce of Yarm district was bought up by merchants for shipment. Mr Richard Appleton being one of these, and seeing the advantage which would result in sending the wheat in manufactured product of flour to Newcastle, Sunderland, London and Scotland, he built a windmill at Yarm. The site being low it was found necessary in order to utilise the motor to best advantage to carry the mill twelve storeys high. Consequently, when completed, the erection was said to be the loftiest building of its kind in England"

(The Miller, 2 July 1889, 347).

Richard Appleton must have used lighter boats or barges to carry his product under the bridge at Stockton. Unfortunately, Appleton did not give a date for building the windmill. It is known that a windmill in Yarm was *"burned"* in 1815 (T Richmond, 1868, 124) and that Appleton's windmill was partially converted to steam in 1827, two years after the opening of the short branch railway line into Yarm. It is also known that Richard Appleton's mill was destroyed by fire on 11 March 1848 (T Richmond, 1868, 204).

The millers of the big, capital windmills would no doubt be prepared to grind corn for local villagers and townsfolk, for ships biscuit making as well as for *"export"* but, technically, the very large, capital windmills were quite different from their common-sail neighbours. A third group of windmills, mostly later, which served the growing towns of Whitby, Scarborough, Pickering and Brompton and the new iron making towns along the south bank of the Tees estuary are described in the next chapter.

THE MID-NINETEENTH CENTURY

After the end of the Napoleonic Wars (1815) the price of flour gradually reduced. Across north east Yorkshire cattle grazing increased again and much of the remaining ploughing was concentrated around the Tees estuary, Pickering, Ryedale and the Vale of Mowbray. On the other hand, the population of the country was still increasing and Britain was no longer growing the whole of its grain requirement. In north east Yorkshire the effect of these opposing trends was that some mills developed while others stagnated.

In the early nineteenth century north east Yorkshire had supplied flour to industrial populations elsewhere while itself remaining rural and agricultural. Spite mill at Osmotherley (1792) and Brompton windmill (pre-1806) were exceptional in that they were built to serve populations of flax workers. However, the next fifty years saw proposals for improvements in communication, in two cases canals but more particularly railways. Such projects stimulated activity in rural towns and villages. After the mid-century the region developed its own large-scale industry, based on ironstone mined from under the northern Moors. Twenty years later, the Cleveland iron making district was one of the largest regional producers in the world. It drew in large numbers of ironstone miners, into Eston, Guisborough and East Cleveland and also into smaller mining areas such as Rosedale. It also drew in blast-furnacemen, puddlers and rollers who settled in new grid towns like Middlesbrough, North Ormesby and South Bank. This extraordinary rise of industry led to the building of town windmills and to the re-building of one or two old water mills.

Threshing mills

Towards mid-century, barn threshing machines spread from the lowland wheat farms to marginal upland farms where oats were grown. In 1839, for instance, the old barn at Mountain Ash farm in Glaisdale was blown down and William Lister built a new barn and threshing set at a total cost of £105 3s 1d (P Burnett, 1946, 29-31). The horse wheel shed is a handsome five-sided building with a wide doorway for horse access. The preserved wheel and square-plan wheel shed at Drummer Hill farm near Ingleby Greenhow were built about 1850 (M Shotton, 1973, pers comm). These later wheel sheds tended to be roofed with Welsh slate and most were built with enclosing walls. It is noticeable that most of the open-sided sheds are situated on the wheat growing farms of Cleveland and along the north coast while many of the square, enclosed sheds are on dale-edge farms.

Other farmers installed cast-iron horse wheels bolted onto wooden frames set in the centre of a horse walk and driving the thresher via a small diameter iron shaft running at ground level. They were obviously cheaper than the shoulder start wheels since they did not need a support for a top bearing or a covering shed. Sometimes they were known as 'tenants' wheels' because they might be moved from one rented farm to another when the tenant moved or, if not, their value might be taken into account by the owner. One wheel, for example, was moved from Glebe Farm, Easington, to Scale Foot Farm, Commondale and then to Warren Moor Farm, Kildale (Matthew Simpson, 1973, pers comm). Several firms manufactured them, for instance Yates of the Derwent Foundry in Malton in the 1840s, and Christopher Carter of the Ryedale Foundry in Kirkby Moorside advertised his *improved threshing mill* at prices varying from £48 to £84 (Malton Messenger, 1856 and 1857). All that remains of these wheels today are one or two circular horse trods, for example at Barnby, Millinder House in Westerdale and at Hayburn, but the most impressive is at Long Causeway Farm in Farndale where the trod has been revetted into a raised circular platform. Most of these cast-iron horse wheels were installed on dales

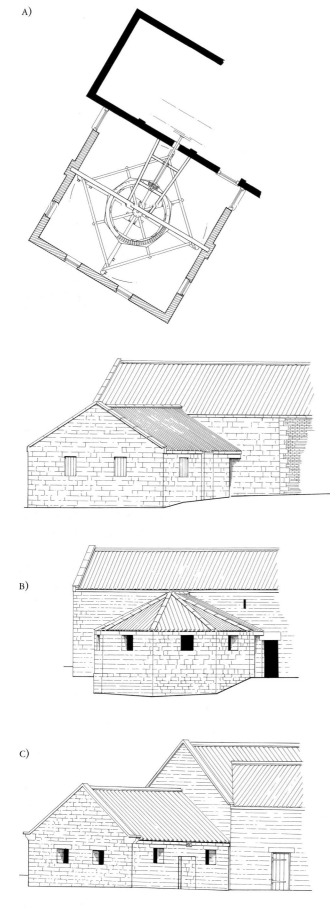

FIG 91. HORSE WHEEL SHEDS AT A) DRUMMER HILL,
B) MOUNTAIN ASH AND C) FAIRY CROSS PLAIN.

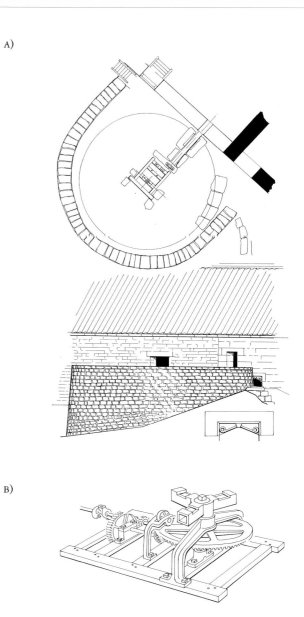

FIG 92. A) HORSE WALK AT LONG CAUSEWAY AND B) CAST IRON
HORSE WHEEL FROM STORK HOUSE.

farms, many above the 150 metre contour. One preserved horse wheel of this type, now in the Ryedale Folk
Museum, was used at Stork House, a remote farm on the
western edge of Bransdale where two large fields were
carved out of the natural heather moorland and put to
the plough.

One or two barn threshers were driven by single-
horse 'paddlers', in which the horse tramped on a moving belt. The belt was clamped with a brake while the
horse was led on and tethered and then the brake was
released! This was an American invention but was also
used in France. It was, in fact, very rare in England and
in north east Yorkshire was confined to two or three sets
installed at Thorgill in Rosedale. The shed which housed
one of them, at Gillbank Farm, still stands though the

A)

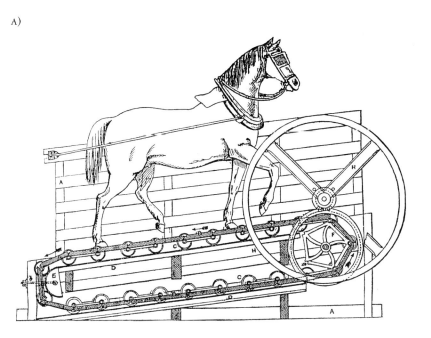

B)

Fig 93. a) 'paddler' (Agricultural Gazette, 27 June, 1857) and b) 'paddler' shed at Gill Bank, Thorgill.

paddler itself has gone. Isaac Hartas of Pickering exhibited a paddler, suitable for driving threshers and chaff cutters, at the Ripon Meeting of the Yorkshire Agricultural Society in May 1857 and there seems little doubt that the Thorgill paddlers were made by him (The Agricultural Gazette, 30 May 1857). One dalesman who could remember one of the Thorgill paddlers at work recalled the wooden blocks which made up the tread-mill belt as *"choggs"* (Arthur Champion, c. 1980, pers comm).

Other threshing machines were driven by water, normally alongside a set of millstones in the same barn. Examples include those at Under Park (Lealholm), Broad Gate Farm (Westerdale), Low Fair Farm (Grosmont), Low Askew (near Lastingham) and the Dell mill (Lealholm). Water was taken from ponds fed by small becks, field ditches and drains. One or two late threshing machines, in areas near railways, were driven by steam engines, but these were not nearly as common as in Northumberland. The frame of a small 'Crowther' patent inverted vertical stationary steam engine survived at Green Hills Farm near Brotton in the 1970s and there was another stationary steam engine at Kilton Thorpe. A square chimney surviving at Wheatlands Farm near Marske in the 1970s took smoke from a portable engine driving a thresher.

These late developments in threshing seem to indicate that, between the end of the Napoleonic Wars and the mid-century, the decline in grain farming was neither sudden nor universal. Where appropriate, estates and farmers still continued to invest in their farms.

Town windmills

Flour ranked alongside water as one of the first requirements of a new industrial village or town. Around the Tees estuary a very rough rule is that in each town there was one windmill for every thousand inhabitants. Variations from this rule can easily be explained. If there were more windmills then the surplus capacity was going for coastal trading. If there were fewer then there was a steam mill not too far away.

The windmill on Scarborough Common was built to serve a town which had grown steadily on coastwise importing and exporting, catching fish and providing the spa waters and sea bathing for 'persons of quality'. The population increased threefold from the middle of the seventeenth century to the middle of the eighteenth and continued to expand rapidly in the nineteenth. The old post mill on common land just outside the town moat to the north west of the Newborough Bar was still standing in 1725 (*"A new and exact plan of the Town of Scarborough"*) but in 1784 Thomas Robinson petitioned Scarborough Common Hall for permission to build a new windmill (NYCRO, DC/SCARB C43). It was complete by 1787 when it was referred to as *"a noble windmill"* (J Schofield, 1787, Guide to Scarborough, 12). This very large brick tower mill, known as the Common Mill, was among the first tower mills to be built in north east Yorkshire. The tower is preserved as a townscape feature.

An even more splendid windmill was built at Whitby. In the late eighteenth century one way for townspeople to meet the problem of feeding the poor in times of grain shortage was to raise a subscription. Associations

FIG 94. UNION MILL (PHOTO, F M SUTCLIFFE, WHITBY LITERARY AND PHILOSOPHICAL SOCIETY).

were formed to buy wheat, rye and oats at market prices and to sell to the poorer townspeople at reduced prices. When price rises became a permanent fact of life after 1795 further measures were called for. In some towns groups of subscribers came together for the purpose of buying or building corn mills in order to undercut the prices of commercial millers. The system was a mix of philanthropy and self-interest. The cut-price flour would be sold to the poor and to the subscribers as well, and profit made in good years was shared between the subscribers. The earliest subscription mills in Yorkshire were all windmills; the Anti-mill at Hull (1797), the Subscription Mill at Hull (1801) and the Union Mill at Whitby (1801) (R Gregory, 1985).

The first meeting about a proposed subscription mill at Whitby was held at the White Horse and Griffin on 10 March 1800. The aim was to relieve the *"... suffering of the poor ... considering the very high price of wheat and the frequent practice of grinding inferior grain* (so) *that good bread was difficult to procure"*. It was said that *"... as the people of Hull have found much relief by such an institution it is hoped the GENTLEMEN of Whitby and its environs will be ready to promote and forward such an undertaking, as well by donation and subscription as by taking an active part in the business ... In as much as you have done it to one of the least of these thy brethren ye have done it to me ..."* (Pamphlet, Whitby Museum). At the first public meeting it was suggested that there should be a subscription of 26 shillings per member and that each member would be committed to additional subscriptions up to 9s if needed. The number of members was to be restricted to 1100. The original intention was to buy an old mill in which to start operations. Among the articles and rules were:

● The Committee would be responsible for hiring the miller, clerks etc

● Not more than twelve and not less than three respectable gentlemen were to become Trustees and they were to hold the property in trust for the Society

● Each member to pay 1d for a copper-plate ticket which shall contain the name, number, occupation and place of abode

- No master miller should be a member of the Society
- The Committee was to hire an agent to buy corn
- Scale beams, scales and weights should be provided for the Agent by the Committee (Pamphlet, Whitby Museum).

There was a good response and soon there were 900 members. They quickly agreed to abandon the idea of taking on an old mill in favour of building a new windmill and the foundation stone was laid 16 June 1800 by T Fishburn and T Broddick Esq (Whitby Museum). An additional subscription of 13s was raised. This in theory raised some £1756, enough for a handsome windmill. The insurance valuation read as follows:

"19 March 1803 Thomas Fishburn Jnr, Esquire, and the Trustees ... On a Corn Wind Mill called the Union Mill, with granaries, dwelling house and drying kiln all (in) communication, brick and stone built, and tiles, situate in the township of Ruswarp in the parish of Whitby aforesaid £500. On the standing and going geers, millstones, wire machines, dressing mills etc therin, £499. Warranted no steam engine ... To commence 25 March."

(Exchange Fire Insurance).

The Society was successful and the cost of building was quickly paid off.

The magnificent windmill was built into the middle of a three-storey brick-built granary, eleven bays long with a pedimented central feature and a chimney stack at each end. The tower was nine storeys high with reefing gallery at the sixth floor and a tall ogee cap roof. At the end of the century it had five single patent sails set on an iron 'cross' and an eight sail fan on a tall frame. The name of the millwright has not been located but few firms could have tackled such a project. Since the inspiration for the project came from Hull the millwrights may also have come from the East Riding. The firm of Norman and Smithson of Hull has been suggested (R Gregory, 1996, pers comm).

Within five years another big windmill was built at Brompton near Northallerton to serve a population of flax workers. In 1806 William Elgie the miller insured the *"... stock in trade including bolting cloths and all movable utensils in his corn windmill house and chamber all in the one building, brick and timber built, situated at the East End of Brompton aforesaid, £800"* (Royal Exchange Fire Insurance). Today only the stub of this windmill tower survives.

Stockton's second windmill was opened on 10 January 1814. This, *"The new corn mill at Stockton"*, stood on an extension to Dovecot Street to the west of the town. John Tweddell, millwright, built the tower and installed the machinery (T Richmond, 1868, 121). W Murphy's map (1826) shows the mill with a granary and house in the possession of *"Mr Hugil"*, and Brewster's map (1829) shows it on the north side of what had become known as Mill Lane. An early photograph shows the derelict mill as a seven-storey, brick-built tower with a wooden gallery at fifth floor, by then overtaken by later development (Stockton Reference Library).

Newholm windmill (also known as Skelder mill and Burnt mill) was built on the roadside to the north of Whitby conveniently close to the town and port. It has a recorded history lasting from before 1822 when it was rebuilt after *"William Appleton's Mill was totally destroyed by fire ... nothing but bare walls left standing"* (Stamford Mercury, 19 April) to about 1913 when it was still in the hands of the Appleton family. The five-storey tower, with gallery, four anti-clockwise roller-reefing sails and a fantail was photographed at the beginning of the 20th century.

A much bigger windmill was built at Pickering in, or immediately before, 1827. Pickering was a prosperous town involved in textiles and corn milling but still relatively isolated. When, in 1826, the people of Whitby began to become aware that their port was hampered by its small hinterland around the lower Esk they looked at

FIG 95. NEWHOLM MILL.

Fig 96. Hinderwell mill.

two options for building railway links to the outside world. The first was to build a line through the Esk valley to join the Stockton and Darlington Railway somewhere on the banks of the River Tees. This scheme was rejected (although taken up later). The second was to build a much shorter line to Pickering, picking up freestone and whinstone on the way. The enabling Act received the Royal Assent in May 1833, and the railway opened in 1835. As was the case with other inland towns even the prospects of a link to a port stimulated development. The projected railway was almost certainly one of the reasons why William Hodgson built a large tower windmill. However, it was not a success. Perhaps the most dramatic way of telling its story is to quote directly from references collected by H E S Simmons:

1827 *"To be sold by auction. A Wind Corn Mill at Pickering, with the steam engine of Nine Horses power attached all lately erected and in good condition. The Mill is unusually large and powerful, having 13 floors and containing 4 pairs of flour stones and one pair of shelling stones, and is replete with every description of machinery necessary for the grinding and dressing of corn. Late the property of William Hodgson, bankrupt"*

(Yorks Gazette, 24 March).

1827 *"To be sold by auction under a Commission of Bankruptcy warranted agent … William Hodgson, now or late of Pickering. A dwelling house with a brewery adjoining occ. by the sd. bankrupt, also the Wind Corn Mill."*

(London Gazette, 27 March).

1837 *"To be sold by auction by order of the executors of the late Mr Josh Wardell, deceased … 5 new pressure sails … four pairs of flour stones and one pair of shelling stones. Situated within 200 yards of the termination of the Pickering and Whitby Railway"*

(Yorks Gazette, 4 November).

1839 *"Gale damage on Monday last … the owner of the windmill will be a great sufferer; the sails which were put up by the late Mr Wardell a short time ago, at considerable expence, are partially destroyed the wind carrying the fragments a great distance …"*

(Yorks Gazette, 12 January).

1839 *"To be sold. To be taken down. An excellent modern brick-built tower Windmill … having five pressure sails 36 feet long and 8 ft 6 inches wide"*

(Yorks Gazette, 2 February).
The machinery was described as *"… but little*

used and will be disposed of at considerable sacrifice".

Pickering windmill was one storey taller than the windmill at Yarm and it was certainly among the tallest in England. The extraordinary height must have meant that any repairs to the sails would be very expensive. It seems likely that her first owner was bankrupted by the cost of building. Her new owner Mr Wardell had bought a new cross with five *"pressure sails"*, then lost heart and tried to sell them and finally placed them on the tower only to have them destroyed by a gale. The windmill then disappeared from the record and was presumably demolished soon after 1839.

Hinderwell windmill was built in 1828. It may have been partly as a response to population growth in the nearby fishing village of Staithes but the builder must also have been aware of Joseph Bewick's survey of ironstone in the coastal cliffs from Saltburn to Scarborough, published in 1827-8, which pointed to the potential for large-scale extraction. A description of the mill is contained in a sale notice of 1830:

"To be sold by auction. A recently erected wind corn mill 7 storeys high and in complete working order, with 2 pairs of French stones, cylinders etc. situate on a parcel of ground fronting the town street of Hinderwell on the road leading from Whitby to Guisborough. The beautiful and substantial stone built tower has only been erected about two years and the machinery was executed by a first rate workman without regard to expense"

(Yorks Gazette, 22 May).

One or two photographs of the disused windmill show that although stone-built the tower was in fact a very slender structure, seven storeys high. There was a reefing stage at the fourth floor, four sails on an iron cross and a fantail.

There were two windmills at Coatham and Redcar, where again, population was growing and further development expected. The old tower mill near Marsh House in Coatham was burned down in 1815 and was not replaced. Instead, new tower mills were built, one within the Turner estate village of Coatham and the other in the Zetland village of Redcar. Robert Coulson was recorded as a miller in Redcar in 1822, showing that at least one new mill had been built. The earliest unambiguous recorded date of both windmills is 1832 when they were illustrated in stone engravings made by L Haghe of Lincoln Inn Fields, London, to illustrate W A Brooks' paper on his proposals for a ship harbour called Port William to be built over the scars at Redcar and for a ship canal from Cleveland Port (W A Brooks, 1832, Observations on Port William at Redcar). At the time

A)

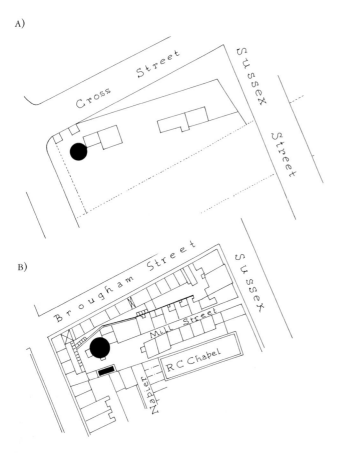

B)

FIG 97. MIDDLESBROUGH WINDMILL, A) C 1840 AND B) 1858.

coastal merchant ships off the north east coast had no harbour of refuge from north easterly gales. Brooks proposed Redcar as a new naval port, with firing ranges on the sands to the east, a harbour suitable for first rate men-of-war, coaling facilities supplied by the Stockton and Darlington Railway extension line and also anchor forges and foundries. Coatham windmill was shown on the Haghe engraving as a tall tower windmill with four sails, a gallery at second floor level and a domed cap roof. Redcar windmill was shown as having six sails.

It was the expanding railway network which led to the building of a windmill at Middlesbrough. The land on which the town would be built was bought by the Owners of the Middlesbrough Estate in 1829, and the extension to the Stockton and Darlington Railway to the coal staithes was opened in January 1831 for the purpose of shipping coal from pits near Bishop Auckland. With coal shipping established the Owners drew up designs for a new grid pattern town with a church and market square at its centre. Soon there was a sailcloth manufactory, a pottery and a gasworks, and the first sales of domestic building plots took place. In 1838 the Duke of Sussex was pulled in style by a group of sailors through the muddy streets, one of which was then re-named Sussex Street. The windmill was built between 1832 and 1840 within a few metres of Sussex Street at the inter-

section of Cross Street and Wellington Street. The plot on which it was built was one of the first to be sold and in 1840 the windmill and its granaries stood isolated among the other building plots which were still under grass. The old 'Mill Lane' had become a street by 1853 and the windmill was completely surrounded by houses, and no doubt seen as a nuisance. It is interesting to see how Middlesbrough windmill was downgraded. By 1858 Cross Street had been narrowed down and re-named. The space recovered was occupied by a row of houses with their outdoor privies backing onto the boundary wall of the windmill ground, which also now contained a row of houses. A boiler had been installed to the south of the tower and one of the outshot buildings at the foot of the tower may have housed a steam engine. In the next lot to the south the Roman Catholic Cathedral had been built. In 1869 the tower was gutted and used as the camponile for this.

The dates of the adjacent and very similar windmills, at Sober Hall and High Leven in Ingleby Barwick near Thornaby, are also unknown. The 1848 Tithe Award refers to a *"Little Church Field south east of the windmill"* near Sober Hall. Both were marked on the first edition 6 inch Ordnance Survey map (1857). They were probably built to exploit the needs of Stockton and possibly the new industrial town of South Stockton (Thornaby). The group of buildings at Sober Hall is interesting in that there is a big granary served by both a windmill and a horse wheel, both of which seem to post-date it. The windmill may have failed in the face of competition from steam mills in South Stockton and the granary with the adjacent horse wheel may have then become a threshing barn. The tower of the neighbouring High Leven mill was seven storeys high.

With the arrival of railways a windmill was built at North Ormesby and three others at West Hartlepool. Ironically, a railway was probably also responsible for the building of the Church mill at Stranton. It was built to house machinery from the Old Stranton windmill which was dismantled to make way for the Stockton and Hartlepool Railway (1841).

Some speculative windmill building was probably not successful. For instance, the Beacon windmill at Ravenscar, completed in 1859, was probably built too late to be profitable, by a landlord who was new to the area. William Hammond, described in the deeds as an auctioneer of Bell Yard, Middlesex, bought the Raven Hill estate consisting of three or four farms, ten cottages, various enclosures and Raven Hall manor house. He advertised in August 1857 for a windmill builder and in 1858 he held part of a wedding reception for his daughter in the incomplete tower (F C Rimington, 1988, 77). The stonework came from the sandstone overlying the alum shales, each block dressed in a rusticated style and most showing the tong holes which were used when they were hoisted into place. However, the population of

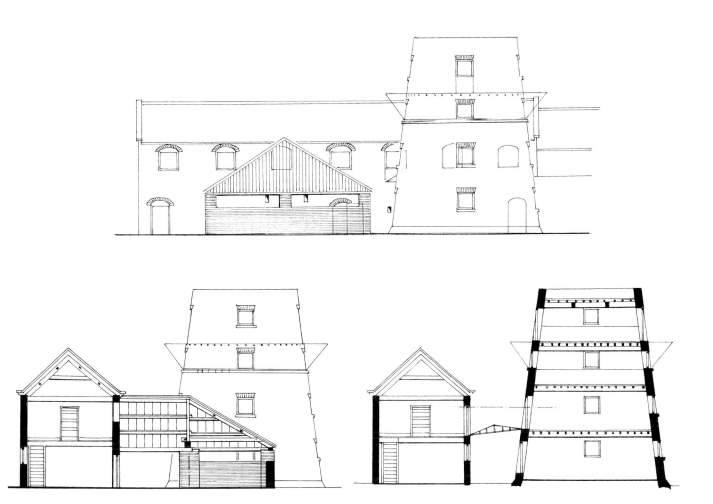

FIG 98. SOBER HALL WINDMILL AND WHEEL SHED.

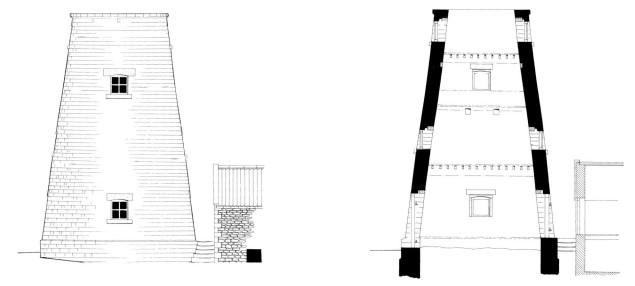

FIG 99. BEACON WINDMILL, RAVENSCAR.

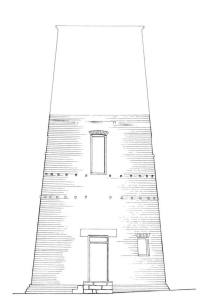
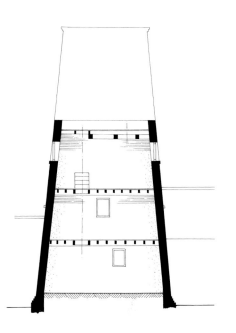

Fig 100. High Hawsker windmill.

Raven Hall and Staintondale was only 343 persons of whom 40 were classed as alum workers. Hammond eventually bought the Peak Alum works in 1862, nominally in good order but actually standing idle. The population base was too small to support a windmill. Hammond seems not to have recognised the permanent decline in the alum industry and he may have planned for a population growth which did not happen.

High Hawsker windmill was built about 1860 by George Burnett, lately manager of the Union mill in Whitby. Its advantage was that it was close to Whitby. It was an elegant six-storey mill, 64 feet tall, and in contrast to the heavily built tower at Ravenscar, it was lightly built with 14 inch thick brick walls. It had three pairs of millstones. A mortgage deed provides more detail:

> *"Geo Burnett, Hawsker, miller to Richard Parkin, Thorpe, Fylingdale, gent 2 cottages, yard attached with newly erected messuage and windmill, corn out house and premises lately erected by George Burnett upon some part of garden in Green Gate ..."*
>
> (NYCRO Deeds Reg IY, 1862—3).

In August of 1868 the mill, described as *"a solid structure, built of brick only a few years ago"*, was destroyed by fire and *"... the mill wands fell and were broken to pieces"* (Whitby Gazette, 4 September). Photographs show that it was re-fitted with double patent sails, an ogee cap and tall fantail stage.

The date of Elwick windmill, to the north of the Tees, has not been firmly established. According to some sources it was built about 1820. However, according to parish registers the address of the miller, John Hutchinson, up to 1859 was *"Elwick Mill"* but by 1860 it was *"Elwick New Mill"*. If so this would have been the last windmill to have been built in the Tees valley. The first unambiguous record comes from a newspaper of 1864:

> *"A WIND CORN MILL containing three pairs of stones and about 9 acres of land attached, situate near Elwick ... now occupied by Mr William Jobson"*
>
> (Stockton and Hartlepool Mercury, 9 January).

The windmill is a handsome eight-storey brick tower with flat arched windows and a reefing stage at fourth floor. What remained in the early 1990s survived unaltered, a fact which supports the argument for a late date of building. The cross, windshaft, brake wheel, the gearing and the quants of the overdriven stones were all of cast-iron. The sails were of double patent, anti-clockwise type, operated by striking rod and spider. There were three pairs of French burr stones each equipped with a centrifugal governor. Elwick windmill was purely and

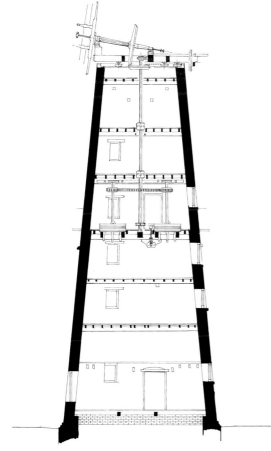

FIG 101. ELWICK WINDMILL.

131

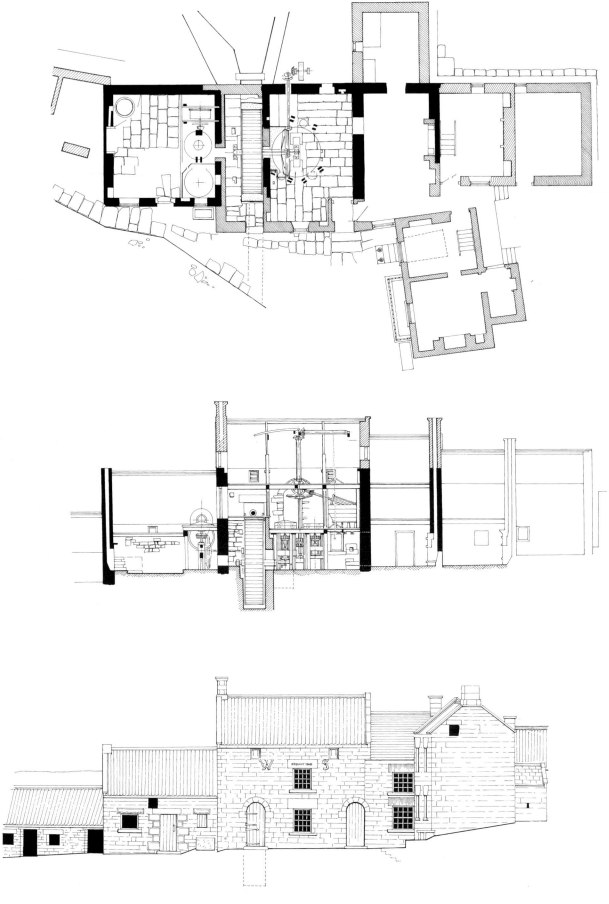

Fig 102. Bransdale mill.

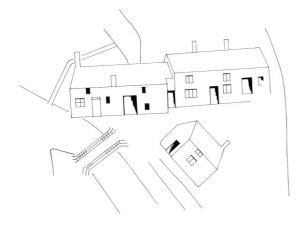

simply a flour mill, built no doubt to exploit the rapidly growing port and industrial town of West Hartlepool.

There are some disadvantages in classifying town windmills as separate from the common sail mills and coastwise trading mills, since the functions of all three different types were probably flexible and overlapping. The Redcar windmills, for example, almost certainly sent out flour from the coast when weather conditions were right. Nevertheless, it seems that men of enterprise were prepared to invest in the hope of benefiting from urban industrial development.

Dales water mill hamlets

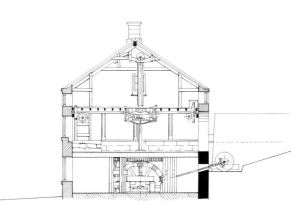

Also at mid-century, one or two new water mills were built in the dales where they served a purely agricultural economy. Estate owners and their agents tended to place enterprising and energetic tenants in their mills and in one or two cases the partnership between estate and miller developed a mill as a centre for a range of services. In two cases, at Farndale Low mill and Hawnby, the mills spawned small hamlets. The Duncombe estate in Helmsley was active in this but so too were smaller owners such as William Strickland at Bransdale and George Wilson at Rosedale.

Bransdale mill was re-built by William Strickland in 1842. The project seems difficult to understand but it should be seen in the light of a population peak in Bransdale of some 400 people in the early nineteenth century. On the other hand, by the 1840s coal mining on

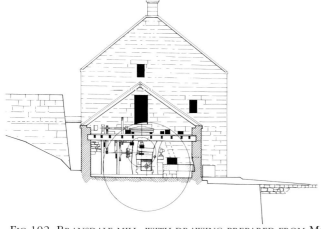

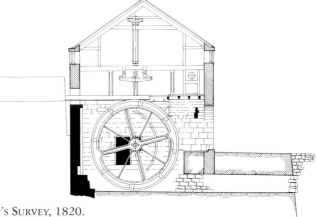

FIG 102. BRANSDALE MILL, WITH DRAWING PREPARED FROM MOON'S SURVEY, 1820.

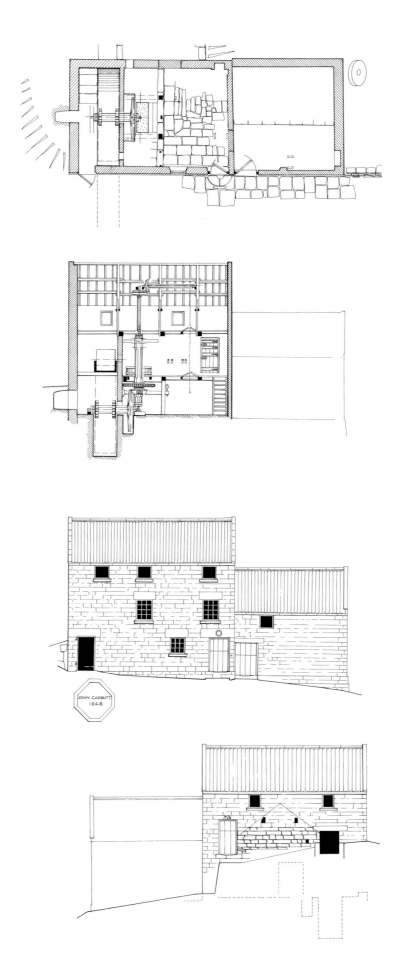

FIG 103. RAISDALE MILL.

the nearby Rudland Rigg was already past its peak and the population of the dale was declining again. Nevertheless the people of such an isolated dale needed to be largely self-sufficient. After moving from Farndale in 1817 Strickland had built a smithy and, if the cellar with outside trap door under one of the houses is anything to go by, an inn as well. His last improvement, the new mill, was built with facilities not only for wheat milling but also for oat shelling, roasting and milling, and also for producing pearl barley. The machinery was a curious mix of old and new. There were old fashioned

wooden hurst posts and forked levers for disengaging the millstone pinions alongside all-iron gearing and shafts and a waterwheel with two cast-iron arms on each side with tension arms between.

There is a similar mill complex at Raisdale, where the Garbutt family had the mill from the Feversham estate continuously from 1721 and left a number of datestones. A re-used lintel built into the back of the mill is inscribed "IIGG 1775". There is a smithy dated 1779 and, according to inscriptions over the doors, William Garbutt built the fine new house in 1810 and John Garbutt rebuilt the mill in 1848, equipping it with a barley mill for pearl barley as well as millstones for both oats and wheat. The number and variety of finely crafted buildings indicates that Raisdale mill was intended to occupy a key role in the dale. Precisely the same can be said of the fine complex at Farndale High mill, probably built by John Strickland, brother of William at Bransdale.

A more highly developed 'mill hamlet' takes its name from Farndale Low mill. The old mill on West Gill Beck had been pulled down many years before and a handsome new one was built in the early nineteenth century, using the more ample waters of the Dove. Eventually there was a saw-pit, a joiners' shop and smithy in Low Mill hamlet. There is another such hamlet at Hawnby where a small secondary village grew up around the corn

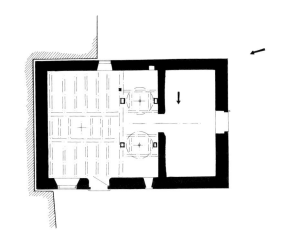

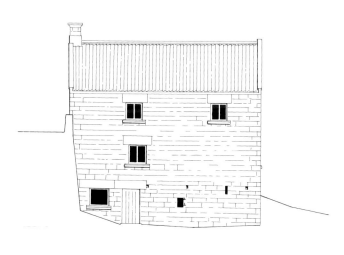

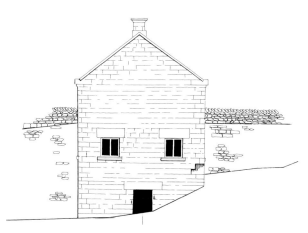

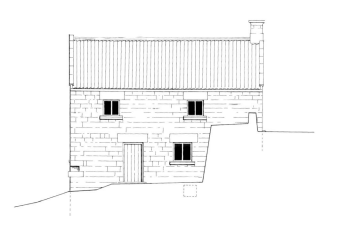

Fig 104. Farndale Low mill.

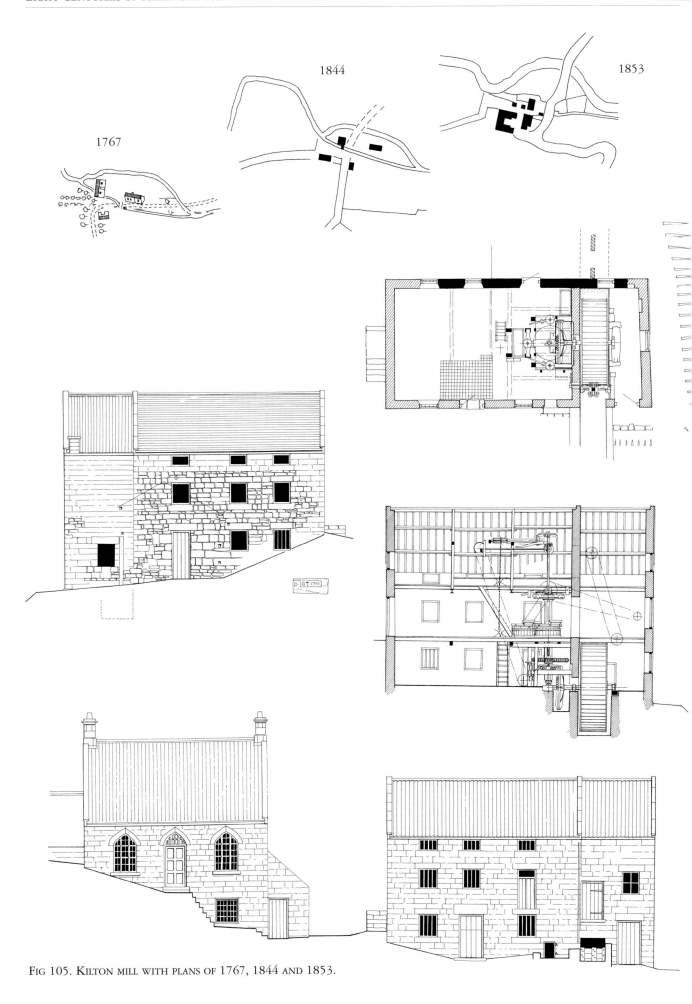

Fig 105. Kilton mill with plans of 1767, 1844 and 1853.

mill and old fulling mill about half a mile from the parent village. After the mills at Hawnby were demolished the water power continued to be used to drive a set of bellows for a smithy.

Water mills for new industrial villages

Some other new water mills were associated with the discovery of ironstone. Some were built in anticipation of major population growth, an indication of the typically Victorian faith the landowners had in the benefits of industrialisation. A map of the Skelton estate by R Richardson (1767) showed an early arrangement of buildings at Kilton mill near Skelton (J Ryder, 1992, 69). This arrangement was still evident in the Tithe Apportionment Map of 1844 but the 6 inch Ordnance Survey map of 1853 has the present-day lay-out, show-

ing that the mill had been rebuilt. Supporting evidence is that one set of millstones has a cast-iron eye ring inscribed "MAKER, JAS SAVERY, STOCKTON-ON-TEES, 1847". Kilton mill seems to have been built all-of-one age as a neat structure with evenly spaced windows, with good quality blockwork at the front but rubble masonry at the rear. The waterwheel, on its iron shaft, is part of the rebuild but the upright shaft and its wooden crown wheel have been re-used from an earlier arrangement. The timing of the rebuild coincided with intense interest in the potential for ironstone mining in the Skinningrove valley. Blast-furnace plants in the County of Durham were in trouble because supplies of local ore were insufficient and the search for new supplies had resulted in small-scale extraction from the cliff faces at Staithes and Kettleness in 1837. During the spring of 1848 ironstone was being picked up from the beaches

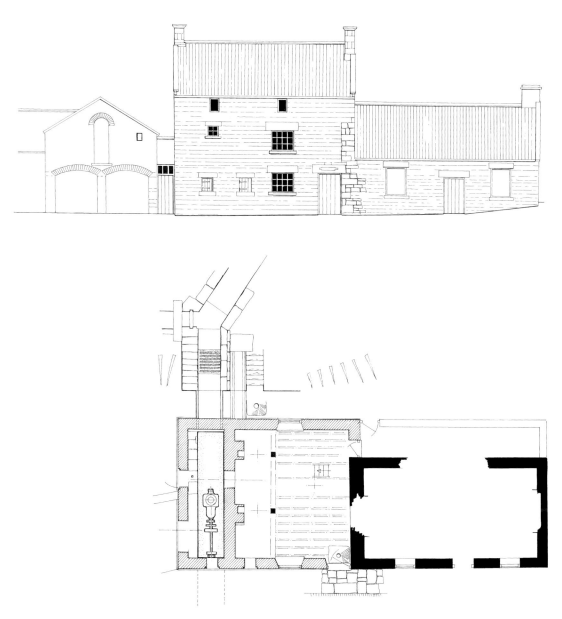

Fig 106. Rosedale mill.

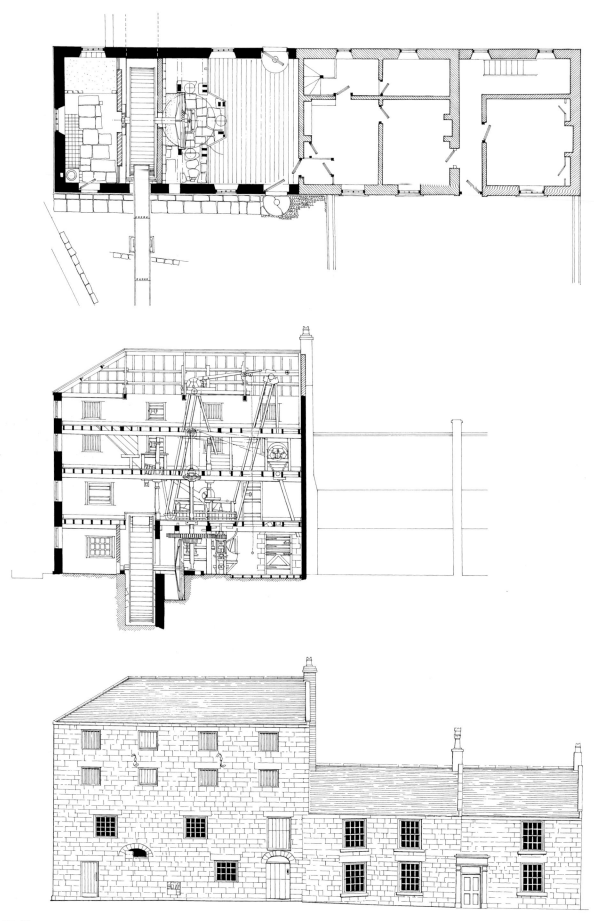

FIG 107. TOCKETTS MILL.

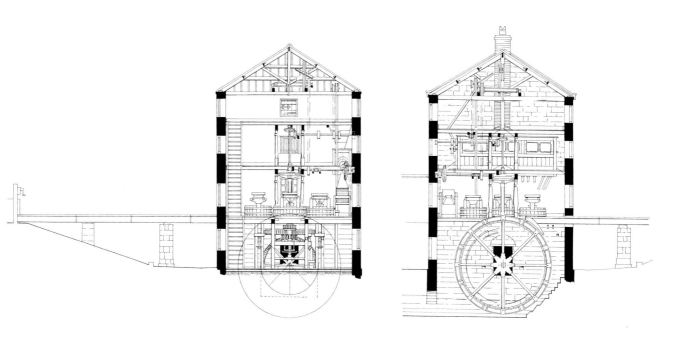

FIG 107. TOCKETTS MILL.

where it had fallen from the cliffs between Staithes and Skinningrove and in the same year the local landowner, A L Maynard, drew attention to the possibility of good seams of ironstone under his land. By autumn some baring had been carried out in preparation for quarrying and by July 1849 the prospects looked so promising that the operation had been taken over by the ironmasters, Bolckow and Vaughan of Middlesbrough and Witton Park. This was precisely the time when the elderly Kilton mill was rebuilt, and fitted with a pair of ready-made millstones from Stockton.

There was a similar story in Rosedale. By the beginning of the nineteenth century the ruins of the medieval Rosedale abbey were all but gone. Why then did George Wilson demolish the old thatched mill in 1853 and build a new mill on the site with a new leat from the Seven to supplement the old source from Northdale Beck? Logically, such a project can only be explained by the discovery of magnetic ironstone in the dale but standard histories of the dale place the beginning of large-scale development and population growth at about 1856. However, more recent research suggests that the ironstone had been discovered as early as 1845 (J S Owen, 1975, CTLHS Bull 28, 1-11). Thus, the reason for the rebuild of the corn mill becomes much more understandable.

Tocketts mill was raised by two storeys and re-equipped, also at mid-century. The upper floors have regular spacing of windows and the roof is of Welsh slate. In the 1850s the owner was the Zetland estate of Upleatham Hall, which could confidently expect large-scale returns from the newly discovered Main Seam of

Cleveland ironstone under the Upleatham outlier. The same seam had already been exploited with spectacular success under the nearby and similar Eston Hill. Mining was also beginning at nearby Guisborough, in Cod Hill (1853) and Belman Bank (1854). There were no ironstone miners in the Guisborough area in 1851 but by 1861 there were 412 miners and also 102 railwaymen. They needed flour for bread and oats for the horses. In 1854 George Heseltine, formerly miller at Skeeby mill on the Zetland estate near Richmond, came to Tocketts, almost certainly to work the new machinery. The water-wheel pit had been deepened and a more powerful pitch-back wheel replaced the old smaller diameter overshot wheel. Also, a cast-iron upright shaft and fine pitch gearing were installed to drive two pairs of French stones and one pair of greys.

New mills to the south of the moors

In the south of the region, the development of milling in a few larger units is demonstrated in the new mills at West Ayton, Allerston, Sinnington and Nunnington. For these mills the owners used the skills of millwrights from outside the region. For instance, when West Ayton mill was rebuilt in 1843, as a Georgian-style building with two wings, it was equipped with lay-shaft drive by Harkers of Driffield. A similar set of machinery was installed by Harkers at Seaton Ross Steam Mill south of York about the same time. A year later, a much bigger mill was built by Thomas Hartas, on a new site at Sinnington Grange, with a large waterwheel, an auxiliary steam engine and machinery by "WILLIAM WESTWOOD AND SONS, MILLWRIGHTS, 1845, LEEDS". The architect

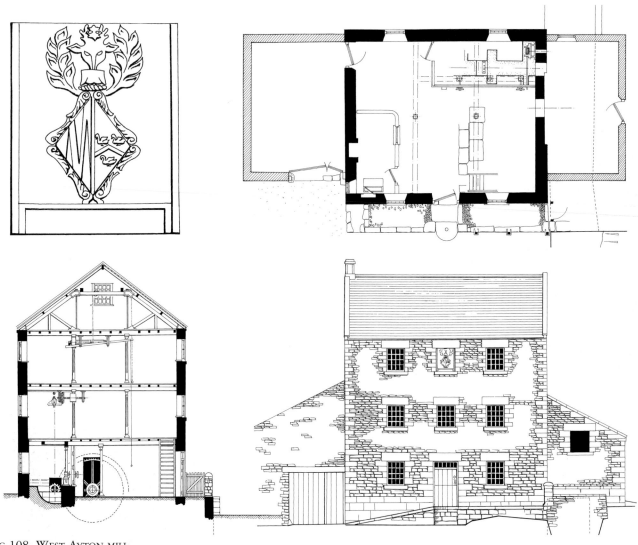

Fig 108. West Ayton mill.

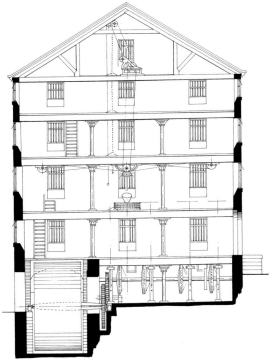

Fig 109. Sinnington mill.

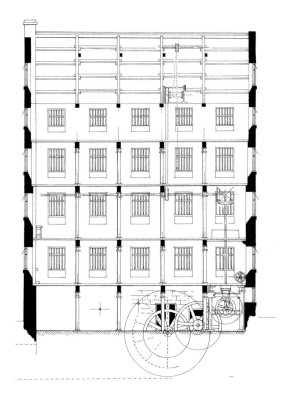

FIG 109. SINNINGTON MILL.

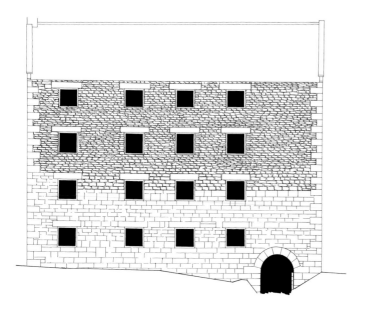

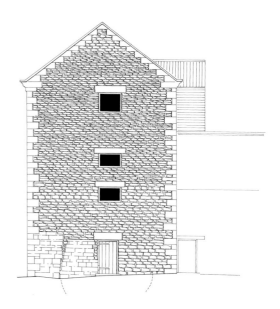

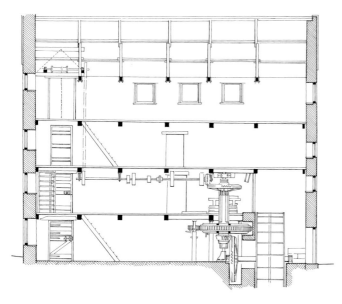

Fig 110. Nunnington mill.

was named Burton. Sinnington mill was built of brick, with eight cast-iron columns supporting each of the four floors. The waterwheel drove an intermediate step-up shaft to a lay-shaft driving six upright spindles (five pairs of millstones and one ancillary vertical shaft).

The last upgrade was at Nunnington mill. Documentary evidence has not been located but local historians refer to a rebuild in 1874 and the evidence within the building tends to confirm this date. There are three pairs of millstones, one French by "W J & T CHILD, HULL & LEEDS" which was fitted with a silent feed system with a sheet iron hopper, consistent with the late date. The other two are greys, consistent with the verbal information that the mill was to be used for grinding oatmeal for racehorses. The stones are on cast-iron hurst frames by "J HAUXWELL, MILLWRIGHT, YARM,

1870". It is not likely that Hauxwell changed the date on his patterns every year so again the date is consistent. Some old hurst timbers were re-used as inner leaf window lintels, showing that the building was changed at the same time as the hurst. The waterwheel is said to have been built by a firm from Manchester, the components having been delivered by rail. As it stands today the building displays its intended purpose as a grain store as well as a mill, almost certainly intended to exploit the railway which reached Helmsley in 1870.

These new millwrights, Harkers, Westwood and Hauxwell, were engineer millwrights. They had moved a long way from the ancient craft of carpenter millwrights, who had relied on experience and 'feel' to estimate efficiency. The engineer millwrights had mathematical skills but, more importantly, a much wider range of technique, particularly in the use of iron instead of wood.

There were, in addition to the new-built mills, one or two conversions from flax mills. For example, in 1813 Esk mill at Castleton was a flax spinning mill described as "lately erected" (NYCRO, Deeds Reg, DP 528 674 mic 316). It employed 21 persons by 1836 but there was decline during the 1840s and by 1853 it had been equipped with three pairs of millstones. An interesting feature was that the gable wall overlooking the external waterwheel shed had large windows, a feature never seen in purpose-built local corn mills, because of the likelihood of damage caused by vibration from the gearing. Another flax spinning mill, built at Balk near Thirsk about 1790, is a large building with a 30 feet by 40 feet ground plan. It was built of hand-made bricks and originally set up with distinctive cast-iron window frames. The mill had its own hamlet of housing for the workers. As at Castleton this mill was converted to corn milling at mid-century.

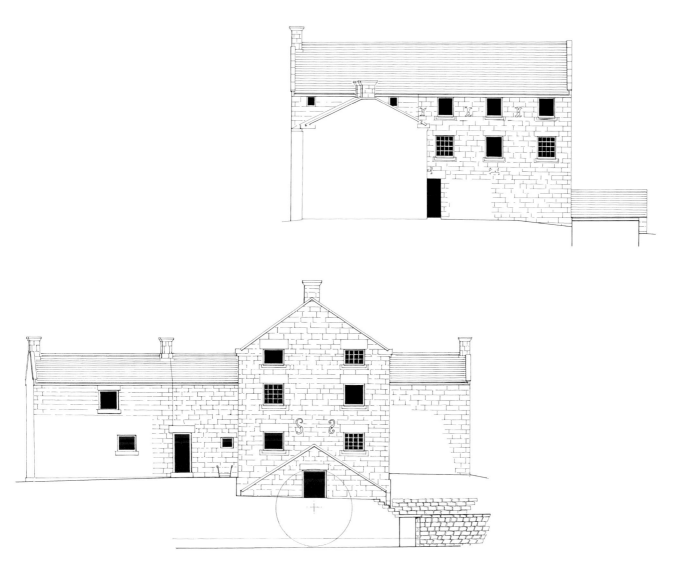

FIG 111. CASTLETON MILL.

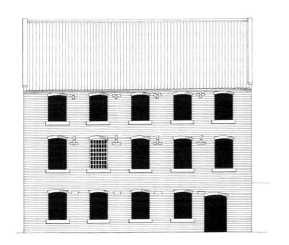
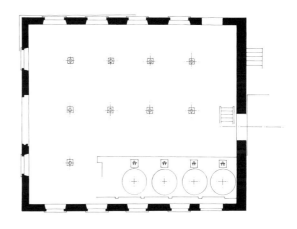

FIG 112. BALK MILL.

143

Buildings and machinery

The mills of this late period contained a mix of driving systems; upright shafts at Raisdale, Kilton, Castleton, Levisham, Farndale Low and Bransdale; lay shafts at Sinnington, Allerston and Balk; and ring gears at West Ayton and Ramsdale. Some building features were borrowed from textile mills, such as evenly spaced windows (Tocketts and Kilton), memel timbers from the Baltic (Tocketts), thick floor boards (West Ayton and Nunnington), collar beam roof couples (Allerston, West Ayton) and Welsh slate roofs (Tocketts, Kilton, West Ayton). Some features of millwrighting were borrowed from textile mill technology, particularly sheet iron buckets on waterwheels, which gave a much smoother flow of water into the bucket and which carried more water than traditional wooden buckets (Kilton, Bransdale, Sinnington). Taken as a group, these mills do not represent the high point of the millwrights' craft. For instance, one or two incorporated old components. The upright shaft and crown wheel at Kilton are older than the building. The upright shaft and wooden gearing at Nunnington were also retained during the 1874 rebuild. The handsome new building at High Farndale had an old-fashioned clasp-arm waterwheel. The wooden hursts at Bransdale and Tocketts contrast with the fine pitch cast-iron gearing. It seems almost that owners still felt the need to invest in corn milling but they were sometimes prepared to cut corners. Only at West Ayton, Allerston and Sinnington was there that harmony between function, building and machinery which had been a hallmark of the earliest years of the nineteenth century.

Some millers in Ryedale and the Vale of Pickering tried a completely new direction. Roller mills were set up at Allerston (Simons, 1922), Thornton Dale (Simons), Sproxton and Howkeld. Turbines for corn milling, as distinct from generating electricity, were installed at Brompton, Ebberston, Kirkby mill (Haswell's Hercules),

Old Helmsley (Charles Louis Hill, 1889), Spite mill at Osmotherley, Rosedale (Gilkes, 1914), Farndale Low, Harome (Gilkes, 1923), Howkeld (Hercules, 1878), Sutton-under-Whitestonecliffe and at Malton. The late nineteenth century advert for Old Helmsley mill was almost wistful:

"The Old Helmsley Corn Mill which for six centuries has ground and supplied flour, meal etc to the surrounding inhabitants, has during that time had various kinds of machinery introduced to keep pace with the times, the latest being a Turbine water-wheel, for the Motive Power, and a complete Roller Plant on Simons' system for the maufacture of flour. George Rivis the Present Proprietor, sincerely thanks the inhabitants of Helmsley and the tenants of the Duncombe Park Estate, generally for the liberal support he has received and trusts there will always be a tenant at the Old Mill who will endeavour to keep up the old landmark –

THE OLD HELMSLEY CORN MILL"
(c. 1890, undated local guide book).

Roller milling was not a new concept. Oat crushing rollers had been in use at least since 1651. However, there was a good deal of difference between the relatively crude and slow-running oat rollers and the precision turned and hardened rollers which were used in the gradual-break system for reducing wheat to a fine flour. There had been experiments in France in the 1820s and the process came to commercial success in Switzerland in 1833. It was developed in Hungary, where it first began to pose a threat to traditional milling with millstones. In addition to the small-scale plants installed in old water mills some very large roller mills were built in Teesside, but these were driven by steam engines and they were a far cry from the traditional water mills.

EQUIPMENT

By this time traditional local milling gave way to commercial milling for money and weighing had replaced measuring by volume, but, in the nineteenth century the most important innovation was the introduction of French burr millstones in place of German basalt stones for grinding wheat.

Grain cleaners

The Compotus of brother Stephan de Ormesby and William de Dalton listed a gift to the church of Great Ayton of *"iii quart. ordei et u quart. ffallings, ..."* (Whitby Chart, vol 72, 568), The editor, writing in 1881, described *"ffallings"* as *"... inferior grain falling away from the better and weightier corn, in the process of 'dressing' ... to this day called in Cleveland 'offal', itself depending on two words off and fall ... the equivalent word in more southerly districts is tail corn"*. He went on to say that offal was sometimes referred to as hen meal. Grain dressers at Tocketts and Bransdale consist of woven wire mesh cylinders with sweepers inside and a fan to blow out the dust. Sometimes, in Yorkshire *"... wheat was passed through the machine twice while oats, barley were seldom dressed more than once"* (Marshall, 1788, The rural economy of Yorkshire, vol 1, 400-1).

French burr millstones

French burrs were made of a fine-grained white/grey chert quarried in the area of La Ferte-sous-Jouarre in the Paris basin. Beds thick enough for monolithic millstones were rare. Stones were made up of individual pieces, or 'burrs', accurately cut to form the circular cutting face, banded together with iron hoops and then heavily cemented on the back with Plaster of Paris. The burrs themselves were only about 5 to 6 inches thick but the complete stone was built up to about 12 inches to provide the weight required. They were expensive.

In 1748 Walter Lutwidge, a Whitehaven tobacco magnate, instructed his factor in Bordeaux to buy a pair of French millstones *"... fit for a wheaten watermill"* of his at Whitehaven. He was probably thinking of lava millstones from near Berjerac on the Dordogne. However, he was advised that his millstones would be best obtained from *"Roan"* (Rouen) (A E Hughes, 1965, vol 2, 25), to where stones might easily have been transported down the Seine from La-ferte-sous-Jouarre, near Paris. Records for mills equipped with three pairs of French stones, and which can truly be classified as flour mills rather than grist mills, survive for Moor Mill at Lamesley in Gateshead (1754) (Newcastle Courant, 26 October), Ruswarp on the lower Esk (1752) and Waren, on the coast at Budle Bay in Northumberland (1783). Each was well-placed to provide flour for an expanding urban centre. By 1798 William Hazledine of Shrewsbury was making French burr millstones, 4 feet in diameter, at £20 a pair and Thomas Telford was of the opinion the *"... French burrs answer all the problems of fine work better than any other which has yet been used in this country"*. In 1802 Svedenstierna reported on their availability in Newcastle: *"Although one could certainly obtain good millstones here they are as yet imported from France from the so-called Pierrre de Moulin near Paris. A pair of these stones cost up to 60 guineas during the war. The normal price was otherwise 30 guineas for stones of ordinary size, however, this high cost was mostly traced to the high duty. These stones were considered to be better than the Rhineland ones"* (ie the Blue stones) (Svedenstierna F T 1973).

French millstones supplanted blue millstones because they had better resistance to abrasion. Robert Townson commented that German lava was *"... admirably adapted for millstones ... but being of basalt or lava, stones of very inferior hardness, it can by no means come as competition with the French burrs. It wears away fast, and as it gives a dark powder it does not turn out a white flour"* (Townson R, 1799, 226). Tainting the flour would certainly have been undesirable but it was also important that they did not need to be dressed as frequently. This explains why the possession of French stones was widely advertised when windmills and water mills went on the market.

The earliest records of French millstones in the North East date from 1752 and 1754. First records in Norfolk date from 1759 (H Apling, 1984, 14). Most were imported from the 1840s to the 1880s (O H Ward, 1982). Hardly any came as monolithic stones but some 15,000 pieces (burrs) were imported each year. At Tocketts mill a runner millstone made in the 1870s has 16 burrs and, taking this as an average, the annual production would be something under 500 pairs of stones. By the mid 1860s it has been estimated that there were some 24 millstone manufacturers in England, all assembling stones from imported burrs. From the import figures it is clear that most were very small concerns. It has been estimated that one skilled man could cut and assemble eight to twelve stones in a year (D G Tucker, 1987, 172). In the later years, but before the onset of roller milling, most of the production was probably installed in large steam mills. In country mills such stones would last for a very long time. In fact, with the decline in rural flour milling it is likely that few of the French burrs installed in country mills were ever worn out.

In north east Yorkshire the earliest record is in the inventory of the two mills at Ruswarp, dated 1767, which listed "3 pr of French stones 4 feet in diameter" in the new bolting mill. The example was not followed, for instance, in the new mill at Danby (1800) nor in the rebuilt Danby Howe mill (1807). On the other hand, a pair of stones costing £33 was supplied to Howl Beck mill by Messrs Todd and Campbell in 1804 and from this high price it seems likely they were burrs. Though there is no evidence of a prohibition against the export of millstones during the French Wars, there was probably an increase in the use of French burr stones after 1815. Thereafter, every surviving valuation, sale notice and agreement seems to include a mention of French stones. At Swainby mill the Marquis of Aylesbury "... put in one set of greys in 1818 and one set of French stones in 1835". When Rigg mill was rebuilt in 1822 William Booth agreed to find one pair of "... four feet diameter French burrs 6 inch thick in the burr". The Albion windmill in Scarborough had three pairs in 1821 and Pickering windmill had three pairs in 1827. Hinderwell, Stainsacre and the Scarborough Common mills each had two pairs. Stockton windmill had three pairs in 1857. Spite water mill at Osmotherley had three pairs in 1826. Pickering High mill had one pair in 1832 and in the same year Rudby mill had three pairs. In 1842 Wilton mill had three pairs and Bay mill had two pairs. In 1851 Borrowby mill had three pairs and in 1865 Costa High had two pairs.

None of these records includes the name of the millstone makers. Indeed, many surviving millstones have no identification but some manufacturers fitted named and dated cast-iron rings around the eye of the top stone. The earliest surviving example in north east Yorkshire was made by George Maris of Hull in 1838.

1838	Oldstead, George Maris, Hull
1842	Bransdale, George Maris, Hull
1846	South Kilvington, Knowles, Thirsk
1848	Kilton, Jas Savery, Stockton-on-Tees
1849	Bilsdale Low mill, Jas Savery, Stockton-on-Tees
nd	Mount Grace, Savery, Stockton and Leeds
1850	Bishop Monkton, George Maris, Hull, Maker
1870s	Tocketts, Mountain & Sons, Newcastle upon Tyne
nd	Marske, Mountain & Sons, Newcastle upon Tyne
nd	Kilton, Mountain & Sons, Newcastle upon Tyne
nd	Danby End W J & T Child, Hull and Leeds
nd	Rievaulx, W J & T Child, Hull and Leeds
nd	Nunnington, W J & T Child, Hull and Leeds
nd	Hold Cauldron, W J & T Child, Hull and Leeds
nd	Loftus, W J & T Child, Hull and Leeds

In the late 1830s and 1840s the supplier was George Maris, who started business at some time between 1821 and 1834 and had workshops in both Hull and Leeds until the end of the 1840s. Purchasers then turned to two local firms. "James Savery, millstone maker, Castlegate, Stockton" first appeared in a local directory in 1848 (Slater's Royal National Commercial Directory of Topography, 246n). In addition to the stones listed above he supplied stones to Shildon mill in County Durham and to Kirk mill in Richmond, both dated 1847. By 1853 he had a new address in 5 Wade Lane, Leeds and the Mount Grace stone must date from this period. He probably made the pair of millstones worth £4 which were included in Brown's Export List from Stockton (W Fordyce, 1857, 196). Thereafter his name disappeared from the record. In 1846 South Kilvington mill was equipped with a set of burrs by W Knowles of the Norby Foundry in Thirsk. Another set by Knowles survives at Crakehall mill near Bedale.

The three sets of stones by Mountains of Newcastle are not dated but W Mountain was listed as a "grindstone maker" in 1875 and it is thought that he operated for only a few years around that date (D G Tucker, 1987, 185). The stones by Childs were not normally dated but John and Thomas Child worked as millstone makers from Nelson Street, Hull and Cross Street in Leeds from 1851 and the name of the firm remained unchanged until 1892. The hurst at Nunnington mill was refitted by John Hauxwell of Yarm in 1870 and the pair of stones almost certainly dates from the same time. The stones at Danby End almost certainly date from the rebuilding of the hurst by John Hauxwell in 1880. Hauxwell put a pair of French stones into Grange Mill, Great Ayton, in 1891.

The top stone of a pair of sandstone millstones would have been raised for dressing by lifting it slightly with a crow bar or 'gavelock' and then threading through a loop of rope to a curved piece of wood called a 'dog leg' acting as a toggle across the eye of the stone. Grey stones and blue stones had a dovetailed mortise chis-elled in the edge so that a set of iron wedges, known as 'lewises', could be fixed. French burrs always had a threaded iron nut leaded into the side of the stone, into which a ring could be screwed. Today there are no examples of lifting cranes in north east Yorkshire where block and tackle were used instead.

Cylinders

The hand bolting sieve, used by bakers, was eventually fitted up so that it could be driven by a waterwheel. Thomas Machell of Kirkby Thore in Westmorland described *"... a dressing sieve which moves by the wheel and water as of itself"* at Bridge End Mill in Old Hutton near Kendal at some time during the last quarter of the seventeenth century (M Davies Shiel 1978, 73-4).

Just as the process of bolting had responded to demand for fine flour in earlier times then the increased quality offered by French millstones led to further improvements in bolting. Early types of bag bolter gave way in England to a rotating cylinder covered, in the early days with woollen or horse-hair cloth and later with silk.

In 1754 Angerstein described a bolting machine, *"made in Birmingham"*, in Mr Hall's water mill at Newcastle, in which the meal was tumbled inside a revolving, cloth (silk)-covered reel with sifting cloths of varying degrees of fineness to sift fines, middlings, pollards and bran. The mill was described as having been built a few years ago (Angerstein R R, 1755, 255-257). An early local example was at Ruswarp Bolting Mill on the tidal limit of the Esk near Whitby, built in 1752. There is a good example in Tocketts mill.

John Milne patented his wire-dressing machine in 1765 and a drawing of Keighley mill dating from 1772 with the note *"... flour machine supplied by John Milne & Co at a cost of twelve guineas"* shows that there was some early take-up (Worsborough Mill collection; see Watts M, 1994, 9). William Hazledine was installing wire machines with brushes in 1789.

Eventually cylinders were used for two different purposes; for cleaning dust and chaff from the grain before milling and for separating the different grades of flour after milling.

'Weigh and weights'

The bushel, a measure of volume equal to eight gallons, was normally a cooper-made wooden bowl, some 18 inches in diameter and 8 inches deep. The peck measure had an internal diameter of about 12 inches and a depth of 6 inches. By the end of the nineteenth century millers were beginning to deal in weight rather than volume and most acquired 'baulks' or 'beams' with standard weights. In 1796 there was a statute requiring that *"... every miller shall have in his mill a true balance and proper weights"* and *"... every miller shall put up in his mill a table of prices for grinding or of the amount of toll required"* (R Bennett and J Elton, 1900, 168).

Until the end of the nineteenth century one of the duties of the Justices of the Peace was to oversee weights and measures. From 1797 they were required to appoint inspectors and they often used their local Chief Constables for this purpose. A series of returns for local mills was made in 1800 by Chief Constables for the various wapentakes of north Yorkshire (NYCRO, QAR). Most mills were recorded as having a price for milling oats and barley as well as wheat and many were prepared to grind rye and maslin, particularly in the Pickering and Ryedale region, as well as peas and beans. Milling wheat was invariably more expensive than milling the other grains, reflecting the slow rate of feeding of the millstones needed for flour milling. The ancient practice of taking payment by multure still persisted but most millers had already adopted weights and many displayed toll boards which showed the costs of milling each type of grain by weight rather than by volume. Returns varied in format to some extent. For instance, John Young of Whitby, made meticulously neat returns for the mills for the lower Esk but he did not record whether each had weights or tables. Sixteen out of over 80 mills covered by this survey were recorded as having a toll board while fifteen were recorded as not having such a board. There is no information on the rest. Similarly 28 were recorded as having proper weights and two were recorded as not having proper weights. Thomas Farmer of Castle Leavington reported defensively that his weighing machine was *"... at home getting repaired"*.

At the big new windmill at Mandale Thomas Langdale had a display board and proper weights and he stated that *"... no other corn ground upon any terms"*. In other words, this was a commercial mill and Langdale was not interested in milling for multure. At Pickering Low mill Joseph Rowntree also stated that *"... none ground for toll"* and at Leven mill the miller also ground commercially. On the other hand many of the older mills still depended on country trade. Thomas Galloway at Ingleby Greenhow had weights, etc, but would also grind for a one sixteenth measure. John Fidler at Little Broughton, Joseph Ayre at Great Ayton, Richard Park at Ellerbeck, James Metcalf at Thornton-le-Street, Thomas Hind at Rudby mill and William Watson of Brompton would all grind to the sixteenth measure provided the farmers led the grain to the mill. Mary Robinson of Cloughton mill would do the same but with a curious mixture of weights and measures so that *"... if moulter taken five pound per bushell"*.

The survival of medieval milling practice into the nineteenth century may seem surprising but, in fact, the practice survived in the memories of some local millers and farmers still living in the 1960s and even today a bushel measure survives in Allerston mill. Early 'baulks' with their sack cage and weight platform are also rare but there is a complete example at Thirkleby mill. Otherwise surviving 'weigh and weights' are the smaller machines with the levers under the platforms, many of them made by Avery of Birmingham.

Oat roasting plates and drying kilns

Highlanders and islanders of western Scotland formerly used a primitive process for preparing 'graddan' oats by setting fire to a small heap of complete grains and burning off the husk. The scorched grain was broken down into meal under a quern or hand mill and then baked into bannocks. In the remoter parts of Ireland the same process was known as 'burning in the straw'. Oats have a higher fatty content than other grains and once they had been heated they had to be consumed quite quickly to avoid the fat going rancid. The process was carried out virtually a meal at a time.

Many farm steadings in Shetland, Orkney and the north and east of Scotland had drying kilns, one-and-a-half storey stone-built conical structures with a fireplace in the base and an inner ledge for a platform of sticks and straw on which to lay the grain. The temperatures reached were quite low and these kilns were used simply for drying damp grain ready for the millstones. Oats, in particular, needed to be dry so that the hard shell could be removed before grinding to oatmeal.

A third process, involving an iron 'girdle' or circular iron plate with a fire underneath, was used in Scotland and the north east of England for oat roasting. The grain was prevented from burning onto the plate by a rotating scythe-shaped scraper. Roasting gave a distinctive flavour to the oats and also conditioned the grain so that after milling it could be made into porridge simply by pouring on boiling water (the so-called 'English method') whereas Scottish porridge was normally made by prolonged cooking in a cast-iron pot.

In Scotland roasted oats were used for porridge and also for 'brose', an oatmeal porridge or broth which was served with vegetables or meat. The brose could be prepared either by pouring boiling water onto the meal or even by allowing the meal to ferment in a wooden 'hoggin' or small barrel, as carried by shepherds in the Highlands (Dorothy Hartley, 1973, 527). In England, roasting plates were restricted to the north and relics have been found in Northumberland, Cumbria, Durham and North Yorkshire. An oat kiln worth 2s 6d rental belonged to Matthew Foord at Hold Cauldron mill in 1741 and to Joseph Foord in 1772 (NYCRO ZEW IV 5/6 and NYCRO, ZEW IV 5/8). Oats were dried at Ruswarp mill where *'four plates for drying oats'* were listed in an inventory of 1756 and at Faceby mill where there was a charge of 9d/bushel for *"drying and shelling oats"* in 1800. Complete oat roasters survive at Arden and Ravensthorpe, and relics of others at Bilsdale Low, Bransdale, Thirkleby, Larpool, Dalehouse, Loftus and Liverton mills.

The larger type of drying kiln with a perforated earthenware tiled floor, commonly found in Scotland, the Pennines and the west of England, is rare in the north east where the climate is drier and the grain more likely to be ready for the millstones straight from harvesting. Such kilns seem to have been introduced into the Lake District in the first decade of the eighteenth century and one surviving example, at Hartsop, is dated 1706 (M Davies Shiel, 1976, 66). Consumers were beginning to demand that grain should be 'properly' kilned, that is slowly, so that the grain would be recovered before it was completely dried and deprived of its taste. However, there was a cost since kilning was a labour intensive batch process which meant the miller needed more storage space and an extra hand. There is a record of the thatching of *"Newbrough Mill, house and kilne"* in 1697 (NYCRO ZDV; see J Hatcher, 1978, vol 2, 182) and other records of such kilns at Mandale windmill (1801), Egton Bridge (1822) and Lealholm (last century). There are either relics or stained areas of external walling which indicate their former existence at Thornton-le-Street and Raisdale. Kiln tiles were found at the site of Knowles windmill in West Hartlepool. However, kilns of this type were never common in north east Yorkshire and no example survives.

Barley mills

Barley could be ground to a coarse meal to be mixed with potatoes for pig food, or baked into bannocks for human consumption. As listed in Chief Constables' returns the prices for milling oats and barley were often the same and normally between 30% and 40% cheaper than for milling wheat. Alternatively, the barley might be prepared for the table by simply removing the husk and leaving the berry intact. In other words, it was not ground in the accepted sense. The product, called 'pot barley', or pearl barley, was a traditional dish in Holland and Scotland and was also eaten in England. In Holland it was made in the type of machine described by John Beckman; "... *the millstone is rough-hewn around its circumference; and instead of an understone, has below it a wooden case, within which it revolves and which, in the inside, is lined with a plate of iron pierced like a grater, with holes, the sharp edges of which turn upwards. The barley is thrown upon the stone which, as it runs round draws it in, frees it from the husk and rounds it; after which it is put into sieves and sifted ..."* (Beckman J, 1817, 266). A barley shelling mill of this type was built by James Meikle at Saltoun, East Lothian in 1712 after he had been to Holland to learn the "... *perfect art of sheeling barley"*, and his design quickly became popular in eastern Scotland and Northumberland (Enid Gauldie, 1981, 139). His machine had a horizontal shaft on which a single fluted edge millstone rotated at speed while a perforated sheet casing rotated slowly around it, usually in the same direction. This made for a polishing or pearling action rather than grinding.

In addition to the commercial demand for pot barley there was also a local demand for pearl barley for making into 'frumety'. Frumety takes its name from the Latin word *"frumentum"* and could be made from either barley or less commonly from wheat. To make this dish the shelled and polished pearl barley was soaked overnight in water and skimmed milk to 'cree' or 'creave' it. Then it was heated in a slow oven for about three hours to thicken it to a jelly-like consistency and then served with cinnamon, nutmeg, honey, sugar or raisins (or even with rum, brandy or sherry). In early centuries this dish was seen as a delicacy but in the nineteenth century it was often served in workhouses for example, as part of a weekly routine (Irene Smith, 1966, 2-6). It was also eaten by rural families as a special treat on Christmas eve and New Year's eve, either on its own or served with apple or mince pies (G Young, 1817, 879-80). Many millers gave small bags of pearl barley to their customers just before Christmas and in some Yorkshire villages youngsters from poor families would go 'mumping', ie calling on the better-off farmers to be given a small portion.

Barley mills, developed from Meikle's design, were quite different from grist and flour mills. There is a complete example at Bransdale mill and a second example originally from Caydale mill in the Kirk Collection in York Castle Museum. Records show they were also used at Middleton windmill (1793) and at the water mills at Lealholm (1838), Appleton (1837), Sproxton (1832), Swainby (1842), Costa High (1855) and Raindale (1920). Barley millstones, with their distinctive fluted edges, have been located at Ugthorpe windmill, and at Loftus, Osmotherley, Bilsdale Low, Appleton, Costa High, Farndale High and Raisdale water mills, and also in the water garden at Newburgh Priory.

Millers

In 1623 Thomas Dixon, miller, had been guilty of grinding corn during prayer time on Sundays at the windmill which gave its name to Mill Field (YAS Leeds, R H Scaife m.s. notes for a history of Ainsty, vol v, p36, K J Allison,

FIG 113. BARLEY MILL AT BRANSDALE.

1961, Enclosure by Agreement at Healaugh, W.R., 390). It is not easy to imagine how Dixon thought the turning of the sails could escape notice but remoteness from the 'big house' and village may have been a factor. Nevertheless someone had seen fit to take up the matter. In fact, millers who ignored regulations or long accepted customs were at some risk of accusations by either the authorities or the villagers. Records from the North Riding Quarter Sessions show only two cases of misdemeanors by millers presented between 1657 and 1677, neither directly related to their occupation. On May 8 1661 "… *the milner of Brignall was presented for that he doth usually keep in the back beck a fishlock in the river called Gill Beck, below his mill whereby he taketh and destroyeth much fish at his pleasure and taketh etc divers fish when they are kipper and out of season*" and on January 1672 a Thrintoft miller was presented "… *for setting a leap*", (a wicker work basket for catching fish) in the River Swale (N. R. Rec. Soc., 1888, vol vi, 43). However, there was at least one occasion when unpopularity erupted into direct action, when three Northallerton men were brought before the Quarter Sessions for "… *riotous and unlawful assembly and for throwing down a milldam*" (N R Rec. Soc. 1878, vol vi, 257).

In spite of such lapses millers were, by necessity, very much a vital part of the community. Interestingly, those who had the skills to repair their own mills were valued more than those who could not. In 1636 six jurors attempting to set wages in the North Riding ruled that "*A miller that is skilful in mending of his milne shall not have above fiftie shillings and if he have no skill to mend his mine not above fortie shillings*" (W Grange, 1859, The Vale of Mowbray, 77-78). It is likely that the sons of such skilled millers might well have found work in other mills and, by this means, joining the ranks of those finding a living as millwrights rather than as millers.

Millwrights

On the 8th of January 1621, Richard, the son of Thomas Marshall of Bilsdale, was indentured for apprenticeship with "*John Miller of Hawnbie, millwright*" (J W Wardell, 1956, A history of Yarm, Sunderland, 107). Hawnby is a remote place in Bilsdale but would have been able to serve mills in both Ryedale and the Cod Beck valley. In 1663 "*Jas. Wild of Greeta Bridge … miller and milne wreet by trade …*" petitioned in the North Riding Quarter Sessions for help after "… *he having taken a water corn milne with another partner, was by sudden accident of fire totally burnt down and consumed to the petitioner's damage of £60 and upwards … fire consumed and burnt down a kiln, stable, woolhouse and backe house with two horses standing in the stable, some corn and all his work gear …*" (Quarter Sessions

Records, North Riding Record Society, 1888, vol vi, 69). Greta Bridge is less remote than Bilsdale, standing as it does on the main route across the Pennines from the east to the west into the old county of Westmorland.

Men such as John Miller and James Wild would have been classed as 'common millwrights', working on comparatively humble rural mills. George Foster, millwright of Guisborough, appears in 1752 and Edward Wall of nearby Upsall in 1772 but there is no evidence that either worked in anything but the old tradition.

Emerging at a higher level was a new class of engineer/millwright. When Nathaniel Cholmeley invested in his fine big new mill, on a prime position at Ruswarp near Whitby, a plaque was built into the façade stating that its building was overseen by "PHILIP WILLIAMS, ENGINEER, 1752". Built of quality brickwork, it owes much to similarly large granaries and mills across the North Sea in the ports of Holland and it was exceptional in this region for breaking away completely from the tradition of small stone-built mills. It is notable, also, that Williams was described as an 'engineer', as distinct from a millwright.

Of similar ilk, but not described as other than a millwright, was Andrew Brown (from Scotland) who in 1799 put forward an ambitious proposal for the improvement of Mandale windmill on the bank of the River Tees near Stockton, then only fifteen years old but needing to be demolished because its tower had begun to lean. He had his proposal rejected and a taller tower was built by James Booth, millwright, of Malton (Harewood Papers West Yorkshire Archives, Leeds, WYL 250/1/368). This windmill was almost as exceptional in this area as the water mill at Ruswarp.

During the early and mid-nineteenth century the names of many more millwrights appear on the record; Thomas Weatherall at Danby Howe mill, 1801; John Coulson (of Stokesley), 1801; Chapman & Son, 1803; James Wilson at Howl Beck, Guisborough, 1804; Thomas Garbutt at Danby Howe Mill, 1807; William Booth "*late of Ruswarp and Whitby*" at Rigg Mill, 1822 (perhaps related to James of Malton); Stephen Coulson (of Redcar); Thomas Fairbairn of Whitby, bankrupt in 1825; Isaac Wilkinson, Skelton, bankrupt in 1829, and W E & J Spenceley, Kirkby Moorside windmill.

When Robert Chaloner of Gisborough Hall re-built his mill at Howl Beck in 1804, James Wilson was described by the estate agent as the "*millwright*" and out of a total cost of £652 4s 9d his wages, and costs and profit, were £163 11s 6d. The second largest share (£58 5s 4 1/2d) went to John Aiblewhite, who supplied the ironwork. At Danby Howe mill (1807) the millwright, Thomas Garbutt, was paid £105 4s 8d out of a total of £369 3s 4d 1/4d. At Swainby mill (rebuilt in 1819) the total cost was £431 5s 1d but it is not known what proportion of this went to the millwright (probably John Fairbairn). At Rigg mill William Booth was paid £150 out of a total of £284 for the re-build. John Smith, builder, was employed and paid separately. Local men, working as labourers, were paid by the day by the estate for work done under the direction of James Wilson, estate agent (Burnett coll.).

The trade was sporadic, however. The bankruptcies of William Booth of Ruswarp and others in the 1820s show that millwrighting may have become a precarious business during a period of low investment after the end of the Napoleonic war. Two, at least, turned to other occupations; Andrew Brown to foundrywork and James Wilson to estate management. One miller did the same; William Smith, formerly of the Old Mill at Stockton, started the Stafford Pottery (T Sowler, 358).

The earlier generations of common millwrights worked in wood, mainly oak, for making large pit wheels and spur wheels with wooden felloes and arms, as well as for waterwheels and upright shafts. These timber-built wheels were very bulky and they were unstable in damp conditions. In very dry weather particularly in summer, when mills were less in use, the curved felloes tended to straighten out.

The craft of the millwright changed greatly in the 1840s. The next generation included names listed in directories of the day, such as John Hauxwell of Great Ayton, 1840; Isaac Hartas of Wrelton in the 1840s; the Chapmans of Whitby and Thirsk in the 1840s; James Sleightholme, late of Kirkby Moorside, bankrupt in 1844; Ralph Yates of the Derwent Foundry at Malton; Joseph Carter of Kirkby Moorside; J Crusher of the Market Place in Helmsley; Thomas Butler of Helmsley; Harkers of Driffield and Henry Benson, "*millwright and plough-maker*" of Ruswarp, 1869. They had permanent workshops, most powered by steam to drive lathes and drilling machines, and some with cupola furnaces for melting iron for teeming the castings. In some cases, however, there was spreading of costs. Benson's castings were made at Robert Hutton's Foundry in Whitby and Butler used Joseph Carter's foundry in Kirkby Moorside. Though wood was sometimes still used for the heaviest components, such as waterwheel shafts and upright shafts, it began to be discarded in favour of cast-iron which, though much more brittle, could be made with much finer pitch than cogs on the mortised wooden wheels. Cast-iron combined stability with reduced bulk and it became widely used for the shrouds of waterwheels, pit wheels, spur wheels and crown wheels. New crafts, those of the pattern maker and moulder,

appeared. Marked examples of castings in north east Yorkshire include a bridge post at West Ayton mill "HARKER 1843 DRIFFIELD", the hurst posts at Sinnington mill "WESTWOOD & SON MILLWRIGHTS, 1845, LEEDS", shrouds "CHAPMAN, THIRSK" on the waterwheel at Kepwick (n.d.), the waterwheel by "J CRUSHER HELMSLEY 1857" at Rievaulx, the shroud plates at Bilsdale Low Mill "BUTLER HELMSLEY" and those at Lowna "BUTLER HELMSLEY 1887", the waterwheel at Levisham "H BENSON MAKER RUSWARP" on an arm and "1904" on a shroud plate. However, work on repairs and rebuild for mills did not come on a regular basis and most of these later millwrights undertook other work. At Wrelton Isaac Hartas, for instance, made a wide variety of castings for kitchen ranges and ploughs.

From 1870 John Hauxwell of Yarm took over most of the millwrighting work in local mills in addition to engineering work done for the rapidly expanding iron industry of Middlesbrough and Stockton. He used the Teesdale Foundry in Darlington for his castings. His dated hurst posts include those at Nunnington (1870), Vivers (1870), South Kilvington (1877), Marske (1879), Danby (1880) and Grange Mill, Great Ayton (1901) (Copy letter books of J Hauxwell & Co, 1877 onwards and their Day Book of 1897 onwards).

Millwrights were still listed separately in the directories of the 1890s (eg Bulmer's Directory of North Yorkshire, Cleveland & Richmond Division; Kelly's Directory of the North and East Ridings of Yorkshire, 1893). Notably they were James Hauxwell of Redcar, George Peacock of Northallerton, George Shepherd of Great Ayton, George Hillas of Loftus, John Samuel Ward of Nafferton and Hull, Anthony Fish of Malton, A Maynell of South Otteringham and Francis Barker of Beadlam. However, their work in mills is not well recorded and may have been restricted to repairs and replacements.

While the craft of the millwright may have been to some extent an unreliable form of employment, dressing millstones was a routine requirement. Dressing could be carried out by the miller himself, or by employees working for millwright firms or otherwise by itinerant millstone dressers. In later times, for instance, both George Dowthwaite of Sproxton and Bert Walker of Leeds visited mills in Ryedale, carrying their own tools and walking from mill to mill. It took a matter of three days to lift a top stone, re-dress both top and bottom stones and re-set them, during which time they slept at the mill.

THE LAST CHAPTER

Fig 114. John Hauxwell's workshop, Yarm.

Windmilling died out in this region in the early years of the twentieth century and the last working water mills (Danby, Ingleby Greenhow, Crathorne, Allerston and Hackness) stopped in the 1960s and early 70s. However, the terminal decline of traditional milling had started long before. In fact, flour milling had collapsed in the 1880s, as a result of the import of American and Canadian wheat and the introduction of new milling techniques. The surviving rural mills were kept going by turning to provender milling and by milling their own produce for pig feed but, in the long run, nothing could fend off the day when the millstones would lie still.

In many cases, owners lost interest when their mills reached the stage when they were so badly in need of repair that they could no longer be put right by their millers. Other mills simply got in the way of progress. Water mills had long been a nuisance to agriculture because of the way they backed up water in long leats behind the dams. Sometimes action was taken. For example, the old corn mill at Newsham, on the lower reach of the Rye, was dismantled in 1853 when, along with two others, its dam was removed by the Rye and Derwent Drainage Commission in order to lower the water by six feet to its natural level (J Henderson, 1853). It was pointed out that every wet season did enormous damage to the crops on the banks of the Rye, all for the benefit of one old water mill producing a meagre 10 horse-power. The end came for Commondale mill in 1858 when the North Yorkshire and Cleveland Railway Company bought the site and built a bridge and embankment over part of it. However, most mills simply outlived their day. Faceby mill was also early among the closures. Luke Fenwick was listed as *"corn miller"* in 1851 but in later listings the occupiers of Faceby mill were described as *"cow keeper"*, and Fenwick had become miller at Little Broughton mill in 1853 by which time he would have been 63 years old. In 1879 John Hauxwell made an offer of £45 for all the fast and running machinery in Howl Beck water mill near Guisborough (redundant because of the availability of good flour via the railway), which he was prepared to dismantle and remove without cost to the owner. In other cases the waterwheels were retained for timber sawing (Spite mill, Newburgh mill and Castleton Esk mill) or for bone crushing (Skelton) and later a good number were set to generating electricity (Skelton, Spite, Borrowby, Grange mill at Great Ayton). Alongside these attempts to maintain the viability of the water leats, tenancies were restructured to give the millers more land and subsequent listings in late nineteenth century directories usually list a *"miller and farmer"* or even *"farmer and miller"*. In the end, however, most country mills simply faded away.

Only one mill was substantially developed beyond this date. The mill at Thornton Dale carries a plaque "THIS MILL WAS REBUILT AND ENLARGED BY G F G HILL AD 1919". Hill was the local landowner and owner of the mill. He set up flour milling machinery made by Henry Simons of Manchester and clearly hoped to develop the flour trade.

The letter books of John Hauxwell, millwright of Yarm, provide an insight into the final years of traditional milling from 1876 onwards. The earliest coincided with the opening of the new steam-driven workshop almost under the arches of the railway viaduct. When visited in the 1970s the ground floor was used as a steel fabrication workshop but the upper floors were still full of equipment used in earlier days. Under the roof was the pattern loft with hundreds of wooden patterns for nave plates, shroud plates, gear wheels, mortise wheels and components for hurst frames. There was also a 'brass shelf' with patterns for bearings. From this building John Hauxwell ran a business which employed some 30 skilled craftsmen in its hey-day and served most of the larger mills over a large area of North Yorkshire and further afield. All aspects of millwrighting work were covered except for the teeming of the castings which was carried out at the Teesdale Foundry in Darlington. Hauxwell enjoyed a virtual monopoly in the region. Work on the steam mills of the Tees estuary was the mainstay of the firm but quotations show that they were still involved in small rural water mills and windmills. Up to 1884 there were orders for at least one pair of French burr stones each year and others for silk machines. Several mills were still buying silk for refurbishing silk machines. The penultimate order for a set of French burrs came in 1885 for Conniscliffe mill near Darlington and the last order of all was for a pair of 24 inch diameter burrs for the Governor of HM Prison at Northallerton in 1897.

There were quotations for new waterwheels at Skelton, Marske, Bilsdale Low and Loftus mills, and also for one of W Rymer's mills at either Borrowby or South Kilvington. Of these projected wheels only that for Bilsdale Low mill was not built, the owner settling for a cheaper wooden wheel made by Butlers of Helmsley. At Skelton a new wallower was put in at the same time as the waterwheel; at Marske a new spur wheel and three millstone pinions, and at Loftus a new pit wheel. There was an estimate of £100 for Danby End mill in 1882 for three new pairs of millstones with their cast-iron hurst frames and millstone furniture, and it was agreed that the miller should pay for transport from Leyburn, presumably for millstones which were being dismantled. Another proposed transfer was noted in 1885 when Hauxwell quoted for the removal of a silk machine from Allerston mill to Ebberston mill. Examples of Hauxwell's named and dated cast-iron bosses on hurst frames have been located at Stokesley, Danby, Marske, South Kilvington, Vivers, and Burdon, near Darlington. Hauxwell provided an interesting estimate giving comparative prices for flour and oatmeal millstones for Rudby mill in 1881:

> *"Two pairs of French Bur* (sic) *millstones with irons and two wooden cases, complete for ... £35*
> *One pair of Derbyshire Peak millstones with iron and case, complete for ... £8."*

Almost all of the water mills for which he made estimates, even quite small ones like Jolby, were milling flour while the owners of much larger water mills like Ruswarp, Egton Bridge and Leven Bridge were thinking about installing roller mills. Estimates for Leven Bridge, between 1883 and 1886, amounted to £525 and at Egton Bridge to £380.

Quotations for windmills also suggest declining business. Some ancillary machines were supplied and there was also some structural work. In 1886 Hauxwell prepared an estimate for the removal, repair and re-erection of two sails and repair in-situ of the other two on the windmill at North Ormesby, belonging to N Watson of No 1 Queens Terrace, Middlesbrough. In the same year he estimated for repairs to Greatham windmill:

> *"Sept 30, 1886. Mr N Benson. Estimate for one Mill Sale* (sic) *and framing at Greatham Mill. To make a Mill Sale 29 feet long and five and a half feet wide inside, all of American Red Pine timber throughout, and complete with new sail cloth and leather straps, the whip to be hooped with new hoops, all new cast iron knees slides (?) hooper made and bushed with iron, and to have three coats of No 1 white lead. We to find the labour and tools required to fix the sail on the mill at Greatham for the sum of twenty four pounds and ten shillings, say £24 10 0. Leading machinery and repairing ironwork for striking gear to be over and above this contract. John Hauxwell and Son."*

In 1892 he tendered for repairs to Hornby windmill, situated between Yarm and Richmond. The tender included a new cast-iron brake wheel with path for brakes, iron striking rod *"… with suitable cast iron balance weights to regulate the speed of the mill"*, cast-iron curb on the mill tower, new pitch pine mill framework, *"… cast iron frame and gearing with handle shaft to turn mill top round by hand power when required, mill fly and framework, new roof complete, and to put on four windmill cloth and roller wands … to the total amount of £265"*. In 1894 he tendered to Mr Dobson for two windmill sails, to be delivered and fixed at Ugthorpe mill. These were to be 26 feet long by 5 feet wide, with *"… oak timber framing, each sail to have a weather board striking arrangement"*. The cost was to be £37 10s 0d. It is interesting that common sails were proposed for Greatham mill, roller sails for Hornby and weather board striking for Ugthorpe. Another owner was very realistic about the future of his mill. In 1903 Mr McGee received an estimate for fitting up a 10 or 12 horse-power oil engine at High Hawsker windmill, to be capable of driving two pairs of stones, a wheat scouring machine and a meal dressing machine. Hawsker windmill spent the last years of its working life shorn of its sails and windshaft.

Hauxwell could not have survived on the business from wind and water mills alone and much of his work was concerned with fitting up roller mills for the big mills in Stockton, Darlington and Middlesbrough. Several estimates were for sums approaching £1000 and one, for Blackwell Flour Mill at Darlington, was for £1500. Hauxwell also sold semi-portable machines such as stone mills, cast-iron horse wheels, threshing machines and wind pumps. Then he patented a wheat washing and drying machine, with a perforated sheet drum, called the *"Whizzer"* which he supplied to Henry Simon of Cheadle Heath. In the 1920s these were being sold all over the world, as well as to well known British firms such as Homepride, McDougalls and Joseph Rank, and to local firms such as Sandersons of Stockton.

Steam mills

By the end of the eighteenth century there had been some fifty experiments with Newcomen and Smeaton atmospheric pumping engines for lifting water onto the waterwheels of corn mills, thereby extending their working hours. There were schemes at Hull (pre 1779), Plymouth (1781) and Bootle near Liverpool (pre-1791). There was no other way for harnessing the irregular stroke of the atmospheric beam engine to fast-running millstones, but the system was cumbersome and inelegant and the old coal-hungry engines failed to make a lasting impact on corn milling. They were not tried at all in north east Yorkshire.

The way forward was signposted in 1785 when two of James Watt's rotative beam engines, each rated at 50 horse-power, were set up at the Albion Mills near Blackfriars Bridge in London. This mill was set up to relieve the pressure on milling capacity of the capital city but was also designed to advertise the potential of this new milling technology. John Rennie installed no less than 50 sets of millstones and the project was on quite a different scale from anything tried before. When it was destroyed by fire in March 1796 the loss was estimated at £150,000. Thompson and Baxter built a similar mill in Hull in 1788 (R Gregory, 1992) and there was a corn mill driven by rotative engine in Warrington in 1801. But the engines never became commonly used. In East Yorkshire and Humberside, for instance, the most up-to-date technology was in soaring windmills rather than in steam (R Gregory, 1992).

Steam came to corn mills in the Tees estuary quite late. The first was built by William Jickell, bricklayer, in 1819 at Elysian Place on the east side of Norton Road in Stockton, probably for Colling Cooke, a member of a prosperous Stockton family (T Richmond, 1868, 134). Interestingly, this was before the Stockton and Darlington Railway was built and the coal must therefore have been brought by horse and cart from Trimdon in County Durham. The Elysian mill was quite a modest steam mill but it was important, historically, because it housed the first steam engine in the region. It was short-lived:

> *"The new steam mill for grinding corn, belonging to Colling Cooke, at Stockton was discovered to be on fire a little after 1 am, and the whole of the property except the engine house was destroyed, together with a great quantity of corn and flour. There being a suspicion that the mill was wilfully set on fire a reward of 200 guineas was offered for the discovery and conviction of the incendiaries but without effect"*, 21 March, 1821
>
> (T Richmond, 1868, 137).

The mill was not rebuilt.

By the 1840s, Middlesbrough, Stockton and Hartlepool would develop as railway towns and centres of industry. Their populations were growing, most spectacularly at Middlesbrough where the growth from 1801 to 1841 was from 25 to 5463. This accelerated in the 1850s, with the exploitation of Cleveland ironstone. Locally, the number of mouths to be fed was well beyond the capacity of traditional mills and there was still a big coastwise trade.

An obvious danger in interpreting random references to different steam mills would be to assume that they were all of the same size. In fact, some were no bigger than traditional wind and water mills. The steam mills in Skinner Street, Stockton (1834) and Normanby (1866),

Fig 115. Long Street steam mill, Thirsk.

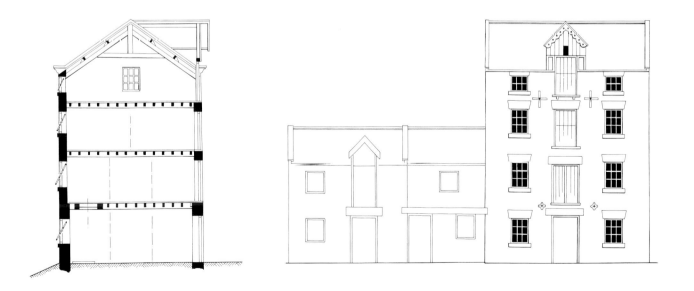

Fig 116. Normanby steam mill.

for instance, each had only three pairs of French stones. The steam engine at Sinnington mill was built to drive the stones when there was a drought and the same thing happened at Thirsk Millgate mill where steam power was added to the mill in 1856 at a cost of £265 11s 6d. (W Grainge, 1858, The Vale of Mowbray). Other small steam mills were built, some by co-operatives, in old market towns like Thirsk, Stokesley and Guisborough, and in expanding villages such as Sleights and Hinderwell. All were constrained by the cost of bringing coal from the Durham coalfield and in every case the railways were an essential component.

However, much bigger mills were built in the 1840s and 1850s when some traditional milling families began to abandon their windmills. Thomas Lisle at Hartlepool, R H Appleton at Stockton, George Winspear at Norton and Stockton were examples of such entrepreneurs. Thomas Wren in the 1840s and R H Appleton in the 1870s appear to have been the clear winners in the race to build big mills.

In 1834 Thomas Wren of Stockton and Yarm fitted steam to an old mill at Lustrum Beck in Stockton. In July 1840 he started work with a larger steam mill called Tees Mill, built alongside an older mill on the quayside at Stockton. He was regarded as a pillar of society in Stockton by 1847, when he was presented with a silver plate inscribed *"To Thomas Wren, Stockton-on-Tees, miller and corn merchant, in public recognition of his high and unimpeachable character for honour and integrity"* (T Richmond, 1868, 203). The presentation may have been made to mark his decision to leave the town, since in 1848 he built an imposing five-storey, seven-bay mill at the Egglescliffe end of Yarm bridge on a site immediately adjacent to an old paper mill. This mill had 17 pairs of stones driven by two steam engines,

each rated at 40 horse-power. Here he achieved an output of 15,000 sacks of flour and in 1850 he handled £50,000 worth of flour by river alone, a scale of milling previously unknown in the region (J W Wardell, 1957, 115). However, Wren's mill was destroyed by fire in 1854 at an estimated loss of £5,000 (T Richmond, 1868, 225) and by 1866 he had moved to (or built?) the Atlas Mill in Mill Wiend at Yarm.

Thomas Lisle finally gave up the unequal struggle at the two windmills at Middleton near Hartlepool about 1850, by which time they were surrounded by iron-works, engine building shops and shipyards, and hopelessly out of period. He moved across the harbour entrance to build a five-storey, five-bay mill on a site not far from Northgate, the main thoroughfare into Old Hartlepool. In 1883 the mill was still using millstones with silk screens but there was a fire in that year. The stack was gone by 1900.

Middlesbrough was served by one windmill, a small steam mill (variously known as the Commercial Street Mill and the Vulcan Street Mill) on Plot 4 in Commercial Street in 1853 and, after 1866, by the Old Packet Wharf Steam Mill (or Packet Wharf Mill) built on the river bank. The latter was a five-storey, eight-bay structure with two wings and it was serviced with a two-bay lucam and landing stage for unloading and loading ships, and with rail track to its ground floor from the Stockton to

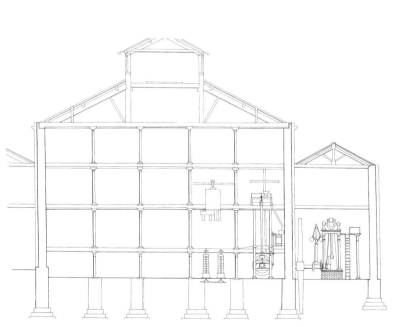
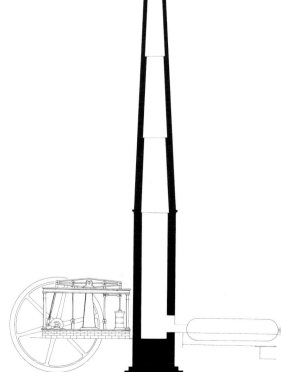

FIG 117. OLD PACKET STEAM MILL, MIDDLESBROUGH.

Middlesbrough railway (TA U/OME 10/91). The five pairs of millstones were set on cast-iron hurst frames and were driven by an entablature type beam engine with a very large flywheel. The name of the first miller is not known but by 1875 the long-established William Rudd and Sons of Yarm took over. By the end of the year they were advertising a range of stock which reflected the needs of the time:

"To Flour Dealers, Bakers, Farmers etc
WILLIAM RUDD AND SONS, millers, Middlesbrough, late of Yarm beg to thank their numerous customers for their hitherto liberal support and having now removed to larger and more commodious premises at Old Packet Wharf Steam Mill, Middlesbrough, ask a continuance of the favours which they have hitherto enjoyed. The above mill has been fitted up with all the latest improvements in milling machinery and every exertion will be used to give satisfaction.
Always in hand
Superfines Bean meal Split beans
Wheat meal Boxings Barley
Barley meal Sharps Oats
Indian meal Bran Hen corn"
(The Dominie, Middlesbrough, 27 Nov, 1875, 46).

Pre-eminent among the next generation of millers was Richard Henry Appleton, son of Richard Appleton of Yarm. R H joined his father in the business in 1835. In 1852 he branched out on his own for a short period of time, taking over the combined wind and steam mill in Dovecote Street in Stockton, after the owner William Gibson had dissolved his partnership with his two sons.

By 1856 R H had moved on and had built a big new steam mill in Dodds Street alongside the Clarence Railway. When this mill was burned in 1869 it was described in the newspapers as a five-storey building, 100 feet long and 60 feet deep, housing 16 pairs of stones and producing 1,500 sacks per week (Middlesbrough Exchange and North Ormesby News, 17 September, 1869). It was said to have been *"... nearly the size of the Middlesbrough Exchange, having been recently enlarged and embellished in such a way as it made quite an ornament to that part of town"*. The cost of the fire was put at between £12,000 and £14,000. In 1866 R H started to build the even more imposing Clarence Flour Mills across the river in South Stockton. Its architect was John Charles Adams, who had moved north in 1864 after winning the Middlesbrough Royal Exchange design competition and who was clearly the leading light in his profession in the region at the time. To begin with the new mill was equipped with millstones. From 1871 the mill ran under the new name of the Cleveland Mill and the proprietors were Appleton, French and Scrafton, thus combining the resources of three well-known local milling families. They were responsible for introducing the gradual reduction process, using chilled cast-iron rolls. Henry McDonnell, the manager, said that *"We are face-to-face with the fact that the venerable millstone is doomed to give place to the chilled iron roller as surely as the wooden walls of old England have already been replaced by armour plated walls of iron and steel"* (H McDonnell, 1884, 93). Appleton claimed to have been the third miller in England to have adopted the Magel and Kaemp system and, a little later, the Seck system and said that, as these proved successful, the old millstones had been phased out (R H Appleton, 1884, discussion to McDonnell's

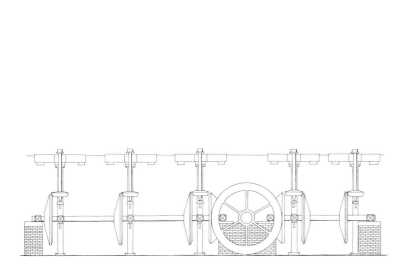

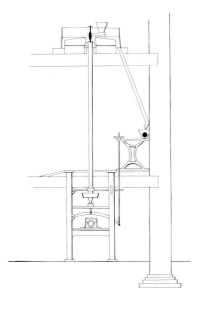

FIG 117. OLD PACKET STEAM MILL, MIDDLESBROUGH.

FIG 118. CLEVELAND STEAM MILL, THORNABY.

paper). Power was supplied by two compound steam engines, developing 500 horse-power between them and driving via pulleys and belts. During a visit of the Institute of Cleveland Engineers to the mill Appleton explained the rationale behind the investment. In 1872, he explained, Britain imported between 1 million and 2 million sacks of flour while in 1883 she imported 12 million sacks. *"This shows that the trade of England in flour has been given into the hands of foreign millers and that if the English miller is to hold his own it must be by adopting all the best and latest improvements and manufacturing on an extensive scale"*. The bulk of the competition came from continental mills using the Hungarian roller mill technique. An exhibition of roller milling was set up in London in 1881, with the intention of stimulating competition. Appleton wanted to compete by buying grain direct from the cornfields and to produce flour every bit as good as that of European millers. He seems to have been very successful. In 1883 Appleton produced approximately $1/4$ million sacks of flour and he claimed that *"... the quality of some flour obtained is worth 8s – 10s per quarter more than could be obtained from the millstone process"*.

The figures speak for themselves. Finally, after eight centuries of recorded history, from 1086 to 1883, the old water- and wind-driven flour mills of north east Yorkshire had become irrelevant. This one giant steam mill could produce more flour than all of the old water mills and windmills together and the tide of progress left them stranded. Some traditional mills struggled on as grist mills to the middle of the twentieth century but they were increasingly seen as relics of a bygone age.

GAZETTEER

INTRODUCTION

Sources used in the Gazetteer

Both primary and secondary sources have been used and I acknowledge, in particular, the work of other researchers:

H E Simmons, collection of summaries of late eighteenth and early nineteenth century insurance policies and other mill references covering the whole of England (Science Museum, South Kensington)

Mitford Abraham, collection of photographs and accompanying notes on mills in north east Yorkshire (John Rylands Library, University of Manchester)

B J D Harrison, transcriptions of medieval records in the Public Record Office which have been published in the Bulletin of the Cleveland and Teesside Local History Society or made available through teaching notes for Leeds University Extra Mural Department courses

P Burnett, collection of copies of legal documents (Whitby Literary and Philosophical Society)

R H Hayes of Hutton-le-Hole, manuscript notes

F Weatherill of Ainthorpe, notes prepared for the SPAB in the 1960s

R Skinner, manuscript on Hartlepool windmills lodged with the Hartlepool Museums Service

The York Excavation Group, records of mills in North Yorkshire.

Many references have been located in:

North Yorkshire County Records Office, Northallerton (NYCRO)

Teesside Archive (TA)

Durham University Library

Borthwick Institute of Historical Research

Letter books of John Hauxwell, millwright, of Yarm (now kept by the Stockton Museums Service).

Useful articles appear in:

The Cleveland Industrial Archaeologist (CIA)

The Ryedale Historian (Rye Hist)

The Bulletin of the Cleveland and Teesside Local History Society (Bull CTLHS)

Yorkshire Archaeological Journal (YAJ)

Surtees Society (Surtees Soc)

Yorkshire Archaeological Society, Record Series (YAS Rec Ser)

Early Yorkshire Charters (ed Farrer) (E Yorks Chart)

North Riding Record Society (ed J C Atkinson) (N Riding Rec Soc).

The most useful North Yorkshire maps are:

Thomas Jefferys, 1771

Henry Cross, 1843, Map of Cleveland divided into Langbaurgh East and West ... published in J W Ord, 1846, History of Cleveland, London

First editions of Ordnance Survey maps (1850s).

The most commonly used local histories are listed under SOURCES. The Victoria County History is invaluable, particularly W Page, ed., A History of Yorkshire, North Riding, University of London, vols 1-3, 1913-1923 (VCH).

The most closely examined newspapers were:

Yorkshire Gazette (Yorks. Gazette)

York Courant

Whitby Gazette

Whitby Times

Malton Messenger

Malton Gazette.

Census Returns (1841, 1851 and 1861) have been used for the names of millers

Nineteenth century directories include:

YORKSHIRE

1822 Edward Baines, History, Directory and Gazetteer of the Co. of York, vol 2

1840 William White, Gazetteer and directory of the East and North Ridings of Yorkshire

1847 Slater

1857 Post Office Directory

1859 T Whellan, History and Topography of the City of York and the North Riding of York, vol 2

1865 Slater

1866-7 White, Directory of the East and North Ridings

1872 Kelly's Directory of the North and East Ridings of York, with the cities of York and Hull

1872 The Post Office Directory of the North and East Ridings of Yorkshire with the City of York

1873 Slater, City, towns and villages in Yorkshire

1889, 1893, 1897, 1901 Kelly

1890 Bulmer, North Yorkshire, Cleveland and Richmond Division

1894 Whellan

1899 W J Cook & Co., Whitby and District.

DURHAM

1827 White (Durham and Northumberland, vol 1)

1828 White (Durham and Northumberland, vol 2)

1834 Mackenzie & Ross

1847 Francis White, General Directory of Newcastle-upon-Tyne

1848 Kelly

1856 Whellan

1858 Kelly

1865 C Whellan, Directory and Topography of the County of Durham, Preston

1868 Mercer and Crocker, Directory and Gazetteer

1873, 1876, 1879, 1890, 1894, 1897, 1902, 1906 Kelly.

REGIONAL

1848 Slater's Royal National Commercial Directory and Topography of the counties of Chester, Cumberland, Durham, Lancaster, Northumberland, Westmorland and York.

The Gazetteer

Where known, grid references are given to six figures. These are adequate for locating standing mills but less so for finding sites with no remains.

The status of each mill is given, ie restored, derelict, demolished, Grade II, etc, except in the case of ancient mills which have left no relics.

Water mills are listed in sequence down the becks, roughly in a clockwise sweep round the region. However, it is common for a single beck to have different names for different stretches. Thus, for instance, Howl Beck at Guisborough becomes Skelton Beck at Skelton. Mills, too, often have more than one name. The same mill might well be named at different periods after its township, its parish or its owner. Osmotherley mill, for instance, was known in an early record as Thimbleby mill, later as Osmotherley mill, then Park's mill and finally as Foxton's mill. Medieval references can be particularly difficult (or even impossible) to disentangle.

Industrial water mills are listed but only in abbreviated form unless they subsequently became corn mills. Windmills are listed by region.

GAZETTEER

WATERMILLS

LEVEN

The Leven flows from the North York Moors in a broad sweep from Kildale, through Great Ayton, Stokesley, Hutton Rudby and Crathorne before entering a narrow gorge leading to the Tees. The tributaries Tame, Ingleby Beck and Broughton Beck also drove mills.

UPSALL, NZ 563160 & NZ 563158 Demolished
The Tame flows south from the flanks of Eston Nab at Upsall (medieval 'Upper Hall') to join the Leven south west of Stokesley.

C13. *"... licence to make a fishpond and to have a mill within his free common pasture of Bernaldby next to Kaldekelde viz in the valley which extends from Kaldekelde up the road leading to Eston on the south side of Micklerigg"*; Grant by Adam de Kirkoswald to Gisborough Priory (Gis Chart, Surtees Soc, vol 86, 201).

1230. A turbary etc lying toward the north "... *from the road when it comes from Lackenby to the mill of Upsale"*; Agreement between the Prior of Gisborough and the freemen of Barnaby and Eston (Gis Chart, Surtees Soc, vol 86, 205-6).

C13. A mill at Upsall with *"soc and molt"* along with a *"croft and toft in Little Upsall"*; Grant by Robert de Tunstall to Gisborough Priory. This grant was later confirmed by Reginald, his son, and Hawyse, his daughter. Hawyse confirmed her grant *"with her corpse"*, that is, on condition that her body would be buried within the Priory precinct (Gis Chart, Surtees Soc, vol 86, 225-228).

1456. A mill in Upsall belonged to John Morley of Normanby (Ft of F, 6 Yorks, 34 Henry VI, no 19; VCH vol 2, 281).

1558. *"... uno mess ... duobus molendinis aquaticis cum pertin in East Upsalle ..."*; Inquisition post mortem for *"Ricus Strangwayes"* (J C Atkinson, 1874, vol 2 pt 2, 4).

1718. Two water corn mills in the lordship of East and West Upsall belonged to William Bradshaw Peirson; Registration of Papists' estates (N R Rec Ser, vol 8, 16-18).

1745. *"... All the messuage, cottages, mills"* in the manor of East Upsall; Abstract of Title, Trustees of Peirson, 1801 (NYCRO ZDZ, mic 1431).

1772. Both mills shown on Jefferys' map.

Trustees of the Peirson family sold the manor to W Ward Jackson of Normanby Hall in 1799 (J W Ord, 1846, 565).

1819. The lower mill only was marked; *"The land of an estate in the Hamlet of Upsall in the parish of Ormesby in the County of York belonging to William Ward Jackson esq, made in the year 1819 by Richard Otley"* (Plan in possession of Mr and Mrs Ryder).

1855. Two *"Corn Mills"* (Ordnance Survey 1st Ed, 6 inch).

Millers; Ralph Breckon (1840, 1841), Oliver Breckon (*"Upsil mill"*, 1865).

One of the mills may have been converted to sawing stone from quarries above the farm. The lower mill was disabled when the Cleveland Railway was built in 1861. The lower masonry of both mills was still visible in 1924. Ironstone mining under Eston Nab, starting in 1850, lowered the water table and today the top mill site is fed by small springs only while the pond of the lower mill is a dry hollow.

NUNTHORPE Demolished
Nunthorpe took its name from the nuns of Hutton (near Guisborough), who settled there for a short time after 1165 on land given by William de Percy of Kildale, Ralph de Neville and Adam de Brus.

nd. *"Ralph de Nevil gave two carucates and one oxgang of land, with a mill in this township"* (J C Atkinson, 1874, vol 2 pt 2, 29).

1231. After the nuns removed again, this time to Baysdale, they kept their lands in Nunthorpe. A dispute between Susannah, the Prioress of Baysdale, and the Abbot of Whitby over lands in *"Gugleflatt and Plumtreflatt"* and the corn mill was settled at a hearing before Serlo, an archdeacon. Whitby Abbey agreed to give up all claims on the lands in Plumtreflatt while the nuns agreed to pay a tithe of one tenth of Gugleflatt and on the mill of Nunthorpe (*"et decimus molendini dictarium monalium in Nunthorpe"*) to the church of Great Ayton (Whitby Chart, Surtees Soc, vol 64, 233; J Graves, 1808, 207; J C Atkinson, 1874, vol 2 pt 2, 29).

There was no reference to the mill at the time of the Dissolution.

There are two possible sites: 1. hollows to the south of the seventeenth century Nunthorpe Hall appear to be the relics of fish/mill ponds; 2. the flat upper section of the Tame valley was dammed by the volcanic Cleveland Dyke so that it had to be drained by cutting 'stells'. Where the two main stells come together and cut through the dyke, near Tree Bridge (*"Plumtreflatt"?*), there is a sufficient gradient to provide a head of water.

KILDALE, NZ 601089 (Leven), Figs 11 & 18 Demolished
This early mill stood on a ledge below Kildale Force, now known as 'Old Meggison' waterfall.

1262-80. William de Percy granted two marks per annum from his mill at Kildale to the Canons of St John the baptist of Healaugh Park along with lands on which a chapel had been built, pasturage for 300 sheep, ten waggon loads of turf from the turbary and a rent charge of two marks per annum and the right to grind at the mill multure free (*"molendium libere et quiete sine multura ad molendinum meum de Kildale"*) (J Graves, 1808, 261).

1321. Assize. *"The jury say that Arnald granted to John 2 marks rent per annum from his mill at Kildale. At Martinmas 1321 one mark rent was in arrears which John son of Arnald was unwilling to pay. At Michaelmas next the mill was totally destroyed by a flood and John son of Arnald, first because he was destroyed by the Scots and then because he was captured and imprisoned by them and then because he paid a ransom to them was a pauper, and could not rebuild the mill for the next two years. Ordered ..."* (Gis Chart, Surtees Soc, vol 68, 582).

1345. Catherine de Meynell received 26s 8d per annum from the mill which she held jointly with John de Percy; Inquisition post mortem for Catherine de Meynill (PRO C 135/76).

1532. The manor of Kildale, including the mill, was rented for £16 13s 0d by Robert Appleby, the bailiff of the Percys for the Kildale estate; Estates of the Earl of Northumberland (PRO SC 6 4366).

1602. *"... Henry Abram als Hebburne for maliciously setting fire in October 1602 to a water mill at Kildale, so*

that it with all the grain etc there was entirely burned ..." (Quart Sess Rec, N R Rec Ser, vol 4).

The estate was sold to John Turner of Upleatham in 1660, then to Robert Bell Livesey of Thirsk in 1810.

1840. *"The low lying lands in the vale are occasionally inundated by floods ... one of the most disastrous on record occurred on the night of July 21 and 22 when the embankments of two artificial lakes or fishponds ... were completely swept away ... An old corn mill was carried away and a bleaching mill destroyed ..."*. Afterwards it was said that the very foundations could not be traced in *"the washen rocks"* (G Dixon, 1891).

A runner millstone (diameter 4 feet 6 inches) and other pieces remain in the Leven below the site. The old mill track from the village is long disused.

KILDALE, fulling/bleach, NZ 595093 (Leven), Fig 11 Demolished
John Boville was described as *"fullo"* in 1635; *"Johannes Boville, fullo"* was buried in 1662. Another John Boville, fuller, died in 1736 (Ingleby Greenhow parish registers).

1806. The *"Fulling Mill and Garth"* and the *"Bleaching Garth"* all in the occupation of Thomas Boville; Survey particulars quoted in a sales notice of 1816 (NYCRO ZK 10523-5).

Peter Willis was *"Bleacher and Manufacturer"* in 1823. Benjamin Claxton was still listed as a bleacher in 1840. But the linen industry was declining and from 1847 to 1860 the site was used as a saw mill and bone mill.

A masonry dam 350m from the mill at the nearest point where solid shale outcrops in the river bed seems to have been replaced by an earthen dam much nearer to the mill. There is a long waterwheel pit running through the foundations of both the early fulling mill and the later bleach mill. The nearby Bleach Mill farmhouse has a window lintel dated "CT 1778".

EASBY, fulling/bleach, NZ 585088 (Leven) Demolished
1790. To sell, a *"fulling mill with barn, stable and dwelling house"* at Easby (York Courant, September).

1840. James Pickering was listed as a bleacher at Easby bleach mill.

Until recently the wheel pit of the demolished mill housed an inward flow water turbine (Gordon Gilkes & Co, Kendal, no 1010) which supplied electricity to Easby Hall. It was driven from a shorter leat than the old mill. Later the turbine drove a stone mill, but this was eventually sold to Joseph Garbutt of Ingleby Greenhow mill.

EASBY, NZ 579091 (Leven), Fig 66 Converted
1790. To sell, a *"corn mill with barn, stable and dwelling house"* at Easby (York Courant, September).

1807. Partnership between William Marr and James Marr,

millers of Easby in the parish of Stokesley, dissolved (London Gazette, 13 October).

1829. *"To be Let. A Capital Water Corn Mill with two pairs of stones, cylinder etc, with an ample and regular supply of water ... William Marr of Easby, Owner"* (Yorks Gazette, 5 December). The advert ran with similar wording in 1832, 1836, 1849 to 1853.

Miller; Christopher Pomitt (1853).

The machinery was removed before 1930 and the building is now converted into an extension to the house. The range consists of a stone-built mill, with a brick extension to the front, and a later in-line and attached mill house. The mill has a dated keystone over the main door, "I M 1799". The overshot waterwheel was about 13 feet in diameter (A Stoyel, pers comm). The hurst posts, surviving in the 1970s, indicated an upright shaft drive with two sets of millstones.

GREAT AYTON (linen, cotton and oil), NZ 564106 (Leven) Demolished

There were three water-powered sites in Great Ayton, the first being at the Little Ayton end of the village.

1788. Nicholas Richardson installed linen spinning machinery in a former brew house and malt kiln. This was later converted to cotton spinning and then in 1803 to an oil mill (NYCRO ZLT).

1795/7. *"James Davison of Great Ayton in the Nth Riding of the Co of York, Cotton Manufacturer. On his clockmaker's Work in his Cotton Mill situated at Great Ayton £600. On his stock in trade in the same £200"* (Royal Exchange Insurance Company).

1808. *"... the inhabitants are chiefly employed in the different manufactories carried on here; there being ... one oil mill, one water corn mill"* (J Graves, 1808, 197).

1817. *"... the oil mill of Mr P Heselton, formerly a cotton mill"* (G Young, 1817, vol 2, 819).

1828. Philip Heselton died. The concern was then rented by Weatherill, Sanderson & Co of Stockton (alternatively, Saunders and Weatheral of Stockton) and was still pressing oil in 1841. The premises were taken over by The North of England Agricultural School and the copper cauldron, lead tank, edge stone and oil machinery taken out. A new waterwheel was then used for threshing and grinding (G Dixon, 1891, 88-9).

Buildings were demolished in 1999.

GREAT AYTON, NZ 558107 (Leven) Demolished

The ancient East mill of Great Ayton stood at the end of Race Terrace.

1282. *"Aton in Cliveland ... a watermill called Westmulne ... worth by the year £5 6s 8d"* and *"... one fourth part of another mill called Estmulne valued at £1 7s 8d"*; Inquisition post mortem for Baldwin Wyke (YAS Rec Ser, vol 12, 237-9).

1353. *"... a water mill and a fulling mill worth 26/8d and not more on account of the lack of tenants and the weakness of the soil"*; Inquisition post mortem of John, Earl of Kent (PRO C135/118).

1570. *"Great Ayton, Earl of Westmorland, Tenants at will ... Wm Wylson ... one water mill for grain situate on the water of the Leven with the water course, suit, and multure ... 26s 8d"*; Confiscated estates of the northern rebels (Humberston Survey; B J D Harrison, CTLHS Bull 44).

1659. *"In this month (October) I purchased of Mr Thoby Humphrey the water Corne Mill and certain Messuages and lands of Greate Ayton, the mill at £38 per annum at 13 years purchase and £8 2s 0d in land at 14 years purchase and a halfe in regard I pay most sessements and repair the millne which cost me in land £583 2s 4d"* (Sir John Lowther's estate book; D O'Sullivan, 1983, A history of the village, pub D O'Sullivan, 47).

1691. The mill at Great Ayton, probably the old East Mill, was in the possession of Ralph Lowther (Exch Dep, Mich 8 Will III, No 3; VCH vol 2, 225).

1771. Marked on Jefferys' map.

1892. Complaint that the Leven *"... is a clear stream from the Hills but it is stopped at the end of the village by a dam 12 ft high and the water is diverted by a sluice feeding a small mill and runs to waste below the village. The sluice is closed and allowed to run through the village only, and not always, on Sundays"*; letter dated September to the local Board of Government on behalf of the residents of Great Ayton (D O'Sullivan, 1983, 91).

"The corn mill, known as Ayton Mill, ... is likely to have been of very ancient foundation. It was formerly a most picturesque set of buildings with red tiled roofs but a disastrous fire destroyed much of it and its buildings were afterwards patched up with brick and covered with corrugated iron sheeting. Mr G A Oxendale tells me that he himself broke up the old mill waterwheel" (Robert Kettlewell, 1938, 86).

Millers; Joseph Ayre (1800), Robert Coulson (1816), John Audus (1840), Francis Audus (1841), John Peacock (1865, 1879), George Metcalfe (1890, 1897, 1913).

The last owner was George Metcalfe and the last miller Jim Huggett. The mill was a two-storey plus loft structure, built of stone. The masonry dam is a feature of Great Ayton and the leat can easily be traced running close to Race Terrace but nothing survives of the mill itself.

GRANGE/WEST, NZ 553103 (Leven) Converted

This was probably the ancient 'Westmulne' of Great Ayton. Later the steading was used for tanning, then oil milling, and finally reverted to corn milling.

1282. *"Aton in Cliveland ... a watermill called Westmulne worth by the year £5 6s 8d ..."*; Inquisition post mortem for

Baldwin Wyke (YAS Rec Ser, vol 12, 237-9).

1741. "... *that water mill Joseph Lawrence called Great Ayton Mill, with all dams, floods, stye and millraces, gutters, soke, grist. Toll, multure to the mill ... at the west end of Great Ayton ...*" (NYCRO Deeds Reg H 261 343).

1765. "*11 July. ... Brother Wilson, Mr James and self saw John Richardson's Oyl Mill near Ayton*"; Ralph Jackson's Diary (TA U/WJ/ 11).

1794. "*On his Water Oil Mill, Storehouse, granaries and dwelling house adjoining brick and tiled with machinery therein situate at or near Great Ayton in the North Riding of the Co of York £140. Utensils and trade £150. Henry Richardson, Stockton in the Co of Durham*" (Royal Exchange Fire Insurance, no 140259).

1817. "... *oil mill of Mr H Richardson at Ayton ...*" (G Young, 1817, 819).

Early C19. "*There were two oil mills one near Ayton Grange, known as the Low Mill, belonged in the early nineteenth century to Henry Richardson, then lord of the manor*" (R Kettlewell, 1838, 85).

1840. "... *both stamper mills were rented by Weatherill, Sanderson & Co of Stockton ...*" (H W Brace, 1960, 99).

c.1843 Bought by John Richardson and converted for crushing rape and linseed (NYCRO ZLT).

1856. Named "*Low Mill*" (Ordnance Survey 1st Ed, 6 inch), but named "*Grange Mill*" in 1895.

Millers; Henry Richardson (1817), Ralph Richardson ("*oil miller*") and Robert Harker ("*oil miller*" 1841), John Dixon (1865, 1879), William Wilkinson (1893, bankrupt in 1895 - London Gazette, 12 February).

The race was dependent on the tailrace of the east mill. A water turbine was brought from the mill site at the Friends School in 1944 and electricity generated until 1957. The Grange mill is now converted into a house. When surveyed in the 1970s it was a shell built of handmade bricks on stone foundations and still retained a raised set of crucks (Eston Grammar School survey). The wheel pit suitable for a wheel 11 feet diameter and 8 feet wide was in the centre of the range.

Carved wooden boards, now at Tocketts mill read "*The bottom grey stone was put in this mill in 1871. The top one in 1901 by J Hauxwell & Son*", "*The French stone was put in this mill by J Hauxwell & Son, 1891*", "*The millwork of the mill was repaired by J Hauxwell & Son, Yarm, 1909*".

STOKESLEY/FIDLER'S, NZ 527088 (Leven), Figs 4 & 49 Demolished

1086. "*Stockeslaye ... one mill of 10s ... land of the King's Thane*"; Domesday Survey (M Faull & M Stinson, 1986).

1259. "... *farm and multure of the mill*" were granted by Hugh de Baliol to his grandsons, John and Robert Eure (J Graves, 1808, 267).

1301. Geoffrey le Melner and Ralph Molendinario contributed to the Lay Subsidy (W Brown, 1896, YAS Record Ser, vol 21).

1664. "*The manor and lordship of Stokesley, with the castle or manor house and 30 oxgangs of land ... a water corn mill with appurtenances, a common bakehouse ...*"; sold by William, Lord Eure to Sir Richard Foster (J Graves, 1808, 225; J C Atkinson, vol 2 pt 2, 62).

1690. "*All that water corn mill situated within the liberties fields of the territories of Stokesley ... all those water corn mills erected and built by the said Sir Richard Foster situate in Stokesley then in the occupation of John Dobson*"; Abstract title deeds of the trustees of Peirson to the Barony and Manor of Stokesley, 1801 (NYCRO ZDZ 1431).

1717. "*On a backwater of the Leven east of the town bridge is a corn mill, probably the mill house which in 1717 contained three water corn milnes and one horse milne all within one house*" (Quart Sess Rec, N R Rec Soc, vol 8, 12; VCH vol 2, 306).

1730. "... *three water corn mills and a horse mill all within one house with the said mill house, two stables ...*", ownership of Bradshaw Peirson; Quarter Sessions at Thirsk (N R Rec Soc, vol 8, 85 & 96; VCH, vol 2, 306).

1790. "*To be let for a term of 14 years. A mill at Stokesley in the North Riding of York. Enquiries to Bradshaw Peirson esq Stokesley*" (Yorks Herald, 13 November). In the same year it was sold to Peter Rorke.

1935. "... *owned by Teesside Farmers Ltd. and is a busy mill. Overshot wheel. Three pairs of stones*" (Mitford Abraham).

Millers; Thomas Fidler (1815, 1822, 1840), William Fidler (1865, 1893), Alfred Moon (1893, 1897, 1913), Annie Moon (1921).

Stokesley mill was a unique relic of a combined horse mill and geared double mill (see Text). The horse wheel shed eventually became a house and remained as such until 1916 when a new house was built. The whole range was demolished in 1983 to make way for a supermarket. One waterwheel, known as the 'big wheel' has been re-erected as a monument near to the bridge.

INGLEBY GREENHOW, NZ 577068 (Ingleby Beck), Fig 68 Converted

Ingleby Beck joins the Leven to the south of Stokesley.

pre 1154. "*Adam de Engleby, for the salvation of his own soul, gave and granted to the church of St Peter and St Hylda at Wyteby, and to the monks serving there, Aengleby mill, free, whole and clear from every service and from any exaction, with all the privileges and liberties which it had enjoyed from his land during all the former part of his life, viz that his homagers should keep in repair the mill dam and house and bring thereto the main timber and millstones as they had till then done*" (L Charlton, 1779, 115; J W Ord, 1846, 431; J C Atkinson vol 2 pt 2, 41).

"Adam de Engleby. Grant to Whitby of Ingleby Mill, also that the men of his land shall repair the dam, bring materials and millstones, (petras molendinas) as in his own time" (Whitby Chart, Surtees Soc, vol 64, 53).

The grant was confirmed by Secily and Wymare, daughters of Adam, and their husbands, Elzy and Ralph, with the condition that the mill be *"... held and possessed by them, with all its liberties and appurtenances in the same manner as Adam de Engleby, by his charter, first gave and confirmed that mill to the said monks"* (L Charlton, 1779, 115).

1205. Guido de Baliol confirmed in front of Geoffrey, Archbishop of York, the grant of the church of Ingleby *"... lest by chance of times or devices of wicked men, the benefactions that had been granted for ecclesiastical uses should be in danger of being weakened or set aside"* (Whitby Chart, Surtees Soc, vol 64, 54; J W Ord, 1846, 431).

1210. Hugh de Baliol confirmed the grant in front of the Prior of Gisborough, including *"Engleby mill, to be held and possessed by them, with all its liberties and appurtenancies in the same mannor as Adam de Engelby by his charter first gave and confirmed that mill to the said monks"* (L Carlton, 1779; J W Ord, 1846).

1211. The Abbot demised the mill to Hugh to be held at a yearly rental of 15s during his lifetime. Then it was to revert to the Abbey (Whitby Chart, Surtees Soc, vol 64, 298; J W Ord, 1846, 431).

1341. *"A Parke and a water mill in ruins"*; Inquisition post mortem for Nicholas de Meynill of Whorlton (PRO C 135/65).

1368. The site of the manor etc and *"the water mill in ruins"* in Greenhow; Inquisition post mortem for Elizabeth de Mauley of Whorlton (PRO C135 201 12; VCH vol 2, 246). This reference is obscure; there is no field evidence of a mill in Greenhow.

After the Dissolution the mill was returned to the lords of the manor of Ingleby, passing from Ralph Lord Eure to Sir David Fowlis in 1609 and later to the de Lisle estate.

Millers; Joseph Coulson (1833); John Coulson (1840), Peter Sturdy (1867, 1873), Joseph Garbutt (1879, 1895, 1905), Jonathan Garbutt (1918), another Joseph Garbutt (1937, 1964).

John Hugill was the last working miller. The machinery was dismantled in 1967 and recovered by the Dorman Museum, Middlesbrough. The mill is now part of a house.

This was a fine example of an early nineteenth century mill. It carries a datestone "1817". Water was brought via a 275m leat from a weir in Ingleby Beck to a long range of buildings with the mill sandwiched between a later wheel house and the mill house. The pitch-back waterwheel was 16 feet in diameter and 4 feet 2 inches wide, on a wooden shaft with cast iron nave and shroud plates and wooden arms. A cast-iron spur wheel drove a cast-iron wallower on the wooden upright shaft with a wooden spur wheel. There had been three sets of millstones and there were three lay shafts from the crown wheel to drive various machines. The upright shaft was extended upwards to drive the sack hoist bevel gear. (Adrian Zealand, Water-powered Corn Mill - Ingleby Greenhow; J K Harrison, Recording the Ingleby Greenhow Mill, 1968, The Industrial Archaeology Society for the North East, Bulletin 7).

LITTLE BROUGHTON, NZ 550086 (Broughton Beck), Fig 119 Demolished

The village of Great Broughton lies alongside Holme Beck but its mill was in Little Broughton to the north of the village.

c.1131. Adam Barn gave a water mill there to Rievaulx Abbey soon after its foundation (Rievaulx Chart, Surtees Soc, 273; VCH vol 2, 255). Broughton Grange is to the south of the village, but if there was ever a mill there the site is now lost.

1286. Little Broughton with a manor house and 200 acres of ploughed land belonged to the Prior of Hexham (Priory of Hexham, Surtees Soc, ii, 67-72).

1472. The 'Black Book' of Hexham Abbey contains references to a mill in *"Parva Broghton"* including *"molendino, cum curse aquae"*, *"dictum molendinum"*, *"Miln-syk"*, *"Miln-gate"*, *"molares molendini"*, *"stagnum molendini"*, *"molendinum aquaticum"* etc (Surtees Soc, vol 46, 65-9).

1477. The Prior of Hexham had a water mill in Kirkby, probably the parish of Kirkby which includes Little Broughton (YAJ vol 38, pt 3, 1954).

1537. Agnes Greenwood had the farm of the mill at 40s per annum at the time of the Dissolution (PRO SC6 4335).

1647. *"... there was a water mill in Little Broughton until 1647"* (Ft of F, Yorks, Mich, 9 Jas I; Ft of F, 20 Jas

FIG 119. LITTLE BROUGHTON MILL (PHOTO, A STOYEL).

I; Chan Inq p m (ser 2), dclxviii; Quart Sess Rec, N R Rec Soc, vol 4, 268; VCH vol 2, 255-6).

Millers; John Grice (1822), Thomas Galloway (1840), George Fenwick (1865), Luke Fenwick (1873), James Coward Skeen (1890, 1895).

The mill was last used in the 1890s. The remains of the dam are immediately to the east of Primrose Hill farm. It was a three-storey brick building set lengthwise with the wheel pit. Its waterwheel was roughly 13 feet diameter by 3 feet 6 inches. Described as gutted and virtually derelict and *"to be demolished in the near future"* (A Stoyel, 1966, pers comm). The mill house had already gone. The ancient track from Broughton village to the mill still exists.

BROUGHTON, linen, NZ 541108 (Broughton Beck) Demolished

This stood on the south bank of Broughton Beck immediately upstream of Broughton Bridge. There were handloom weavers in Broughton in the eighteenth century and the mill was built by the end of the century. George Coverdale, John Davison and Robert Davison were described as *"Linen Manufacturers"* in 1840, when the mill must have been nearing the end of its life.

FACEBY, NZ 501033 (Faceby Beck), Fig 8 Demolished

C16. *"Plaintiff Henry Genkyns ... Manors of Busby, Faceby and Carlton, 40 messuages, 13 cottages, and a mill ..."* (Ft of F, Trinity, 38 Eliz; VCH vol 2, 314).

1771. Marked on Jefferys' Map.

Millers; Josh Helm (1826), Luke Fenwick (1840).

By 1871 Luke Fenwick was at Little Broughton mill and Faceby mill had probably stopped work. It was demolished in 1916. Part of the breast wall of the wheel case, 5 feet 9 inches wide, survives as part of a garden revetment. The most interesting survival is the leat along the foot of a set of medieval crofts running down from the main street of the village to the millpond which is now dry. According to early Ordnance Survey maps the Mere Beck was diverted from a point near Plane Tree Farm into Faceby Beck to supplement the water supply.

SCUGDALE, fulling/flax, NZ 496005, NZ 490004, NZ 489005 (Scugdale Beck) Demolished

There was a *"Wash Mill"* below Sunnyside Farm and a *"Beatling Mill"* near Hollin Farm, both in ruins in 1857; Plan accompanying the proposal for a Head of Scugdale Railway (NYCRO QDP(M) 120 mic 2497/257).

1626. *"There was a walke mill at Huthwaite"* (A T Dingle, 1950, 23-7).

1743. The mill was described as a fulling mill but it was already involved in linen; *"A View of the manor of Whorlton taken by Edward Carter"* (NYCRO ZJX 4/15 mic 911).

1763. A walk mill at Huthwaite was leased to Thomas Boville with a smallholding for £4 per annum (A T Dingle, 1950, 23-7).

1783. Matthew Boville *"... expended in the year 1881 more than £200 in making improvements in the mills and in addition to Bittels according to the Irish method for the more completely finishing the cloth. He is an industrious man"*; Survey of the Whorlton Estate (NYCRO ZJX 4/18 mic 911). The work included a new mill.

1808. *"... bleach grounds of considerable extent carried on with great success by Mr William Boville, a native of the parish"* (J Graves, 1808, 149).

1842. *"Mary Boville held the Bleach grounds at Whorlton"* (A T Dingle, 1950, 23-7).

Leats and retting ponds are still visible below Sunnyside Farm. Part of a sluice gate of the old mill and the dam, leat and foundations of the new mill at Hollin remain.

SWAINBY/WHORLTON, NZ 482015 (Scugdale Beck), Fig 8. Converted

Swainby, at the end of Scugdale, was originally a subsidiary settlement for the lost village of Whorlton.

1341. *"There is a weak castle and manor worth nothing ... and water mill worth £8 per annum"*; Inquisition post mortem for Nicholas de Meynil (PRO C 135/65).

1368. *"A water mill worth £4 per annum, in the hands of the tenants at will (Et est ibid unum molendi' aquat' et reddit per annum 1111 li)"*; Inquisition post mortem for Elizabeth, wife of Peter de Mauley (PRO C 135/201; J Graves, 1808, 143; J C Atkinson, 1874, vol 2 pt 2, 91).

1700. Leased for 21 years to William Wasse, gent (NYCRO ZJX 6/3 Cal).

Early 1800s. *"The buildings consist of an overshot water grist mill, 2 pairs of stones in very bad repair ... This mill must be rebuilt. It is of great use and convenience to the tenantry, but it is very old and inferior construction and quite worn out"*; Estate Book (NYCRO ZJX 4/44 mic 915).

1806. *"The mills are also in a very decayed and delapidated state, and want not only thorough repair but should be taken down and re-built, which would pay good interest for being done if affected on a frugal plan"*; Survey of the Aylesbury Estate by John Claridge of Pall Mall (NYCRO ZJX 4/45 mic 915). The mill was subsequently rebuilt.

1842. *"The buildings consist of a good dwelling house (tiled), a granary and cart house, a 2 stalled and a 3 stalled stable (the latter brick), a cow house for 4 cows, 3 young cattle (very bad), 2 pigsties, and carthouse (all tiled), also a water grist mill with 3 pairs of stones, erected or increased and enlarged about the year 1819 at the expence of the Marquis of Aylesbury ... Lord Aylesbury found one pair of grey stones in 1818, one pair of French stones in 1818 and a pair of French stones in 1835"*; A survey and valuation of the Whorlton Estate 1842/3 (NYCRO ZJX 4/45 mic 915).

1935. *"... ceased to work about twenty years ago and estate sold. Dam (a mile away) sold away from mill so that now there are no water rights. Dismantled by the present owner. One grey stone in mill and one on the gravel at entrance. Water wheel shaft still there."* (Mitford Abraham).

Millers; Stephen Coulson (1789), Jonathan Hugill (1812, 1817), Stephen Coulson (1822, 1842), John Coulson (1841, 1865), Thomas Potts (1892, 1897), John Mason (1901, 1913). (See Coatham and Redcar windmills for more details of the Coulsons).

The mill building survives though converted into a house and with its external appearance modified.

SEAMER, Grid reference not known

1341. Chan Inq p m, 16 Edw III (1st nos), No 47 (VCH vol 2, 292).

1368. *"... a water mill in the hands of the tenants at will is worth 66s 8d"*; Inquisition post mortem for Elizabeth, wife of Peter de Mauley (PRO C 135/201; 42 Edw III, 1st nos, no 44).

1407. *"John Legg accuses William Colynson of withdrawing with his corn to various mills, grinding it outside the demesne and not making the accustomed suit to the lord's mill"* (B J D Harrison, Some Cleveland court rolls of Lord Darcy and Meynill, CTLHS Bull 1, June 1968, 1-6).

1562. In the manors of *"Seamer, Aynderbye* (Ainderby), *Warlayghbye* (Warlaby) *and Boynton"* there were 100 messuages, 40 cattle and a water mill (YAS Rec Ser vol 2, 264; Ft of F, Mich, 4-5 Eliz; VCH vol 2, 292).

1683. Ft of F, Easter, 35 Chas II; VCH vol 2, 292).

1687. Ft of F, Trinity, 3 Jas II; VCH vol 2, 292).

SKUTTERSKELFE, NZ 483069 (Leven)

Skutterskelfe Hall is on the site of a medieval manor house. Though there seems to be no documentation, there is evidence of a weir, leat and tailrace cutting across a loop of the river to the south of the hall (Mrs P Browarska, 1966, pers comm). There are 'Mill Field' names nearby.

HUTTON, paper/flax, NZ 472066 (Leven) Demolished

Hutton Rudby was anciently two settlements facing each other across the Leven. Both were held by the Meynells until Rudby became a separate manor in the thirteenth century. Whereas Rudby declined in post-mediaeval times Hutton prospered and grew into an industrial village. The mill near the bridge in Hutton may have started life as a paper making mill and developed into linen weaving and corn milling.

A new stone bridge was built between Rudby and Hutton in 1755 (P Hastings, 1981, Rudby in Cleveland local government and society, Hutton Rudby and District L H S). If the mill predated this then the leat must have been culverted under the abutment.

1757. A water-driven paper mill alongside the new bridge was insured by John Taylor, paper maker (Sun Fire Insurance no 155644, 7 January). Paper was made from waste from the local linen industry and perhaps from old ropes etc brought from the Tees ports.

1808. *"... paper mill at Hutton ..."* (J Graves, 1808, 177).

1823. Robert Norman was described as a *"coarse paper manufacturer"* (Baines' Directory).

1840. *"... large flax mill with 250 weavers"* ie cottage weavers (White, 1840).

1846. *"The inhabitants of Hutton Rudby are generally employed in the manufacture of linen, which is carried on to a considerable extent by Messrs Robinson and Wilson, who have warehouses in Newcastle upon Tyne"* (J W Ord, 1846, 471).

1859. *"... near to the river is a large building, now a corn mill but once a paper manufactory and afterwards a spinning mill"* (Whellan, 11, 759, quoted in J C Atkinson, 1874, vol 2 pt 2, 120). A steam engine was installed in 1870.

1878. Leven House, The Cleveland Sail-cloth Factory and a *"Water corn mill with iron water wheel, three pairs of mill-stones, hoist, corn screen, flour dressing machine, large granary, cart house, stable, out-buildings, dwelling house, and office and yard"* were advertised in 1878 (Particulars of sale by auction, 20 May).

The railways prolonged the life of the mill but it had closed by 1908 and the building was used as a village hall. The chimney was felled and the mill demolished in 1937.

The corn mill stood at the west end of the sailcloth manufactory but was demolished long before the other buildings.

RUDBY, NZ 469067 (Leven), Fig 120 Shell

References to corn mills in Rudby tend to be obscure. It is not possible to be confident in separating references for the corn mill attached to the paper mill at Hutton from those for the corn mill on the opposite bank in Rudby.

1368. *"A water mill worth £6 13s 4d per annum"*; Inquisition post mortem for Elizabeth de Mauley (PRO C 135/201).

1628. A *"Water Corne Milne ball bancke and laine"* in Rudby; A particular of ye manor and rectorie of Rudbie by William Mason (Leeds City Archives, Ingleby of Lawkland 164).

1800. Thomas Hird was miller at Rudby mill (Chief Constables' Returns, NYCRO QAW).

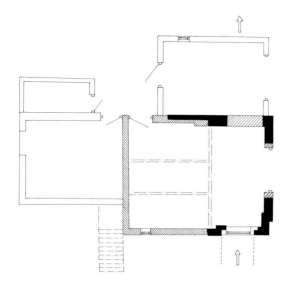

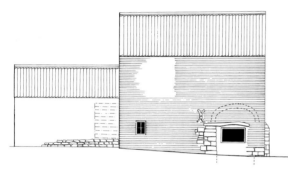

FIG 120. RUDBY MILL.

1808. *"... considerable corn mill at Rudby"* (J Graves, 1808, 177).

1808. Rudby dam and mill and Hutton dam and leat (but not the mill) shown; *A map of the Rudby estate belonging to the Rt Honble Lady Dowager Amherst, situate in Cleveland in the Co of York* (NYCRO).

1817. James Peacock, blacksmith and millwright, overhauled the ironwork of the mill for the miller, Mr Robinson, over a period of four months (Wright and Mawer, 1982, Stokesley Selection, 96).

1832. *"To be let. A capital water corn mill driving three pairs of French stones situated at Rudby on the River Leven, Cleveland"* (Yorks Gazette, 28 July).

1881. John Hauxwell quoted for a new set of Derbyshire grey stones and two sets of French (John Hauxwell's Letter Books).

Millers; Thomas Hird (1800), Robert Robinson (1822), William Burton (1840), Joseph Mease (1862), John Watson (1865), Thomas Stringer (1872, 1879), Thomas Lewis (1879).

Joseph Mease, tenant and occupier, kept a Day Book of corn milling at Rudby mill for the years 1862 to 1864 (entries made near the end of an old Day Book from either Hutton mill or Hutton Bleach Works) but by 1871

Mease was listed as farmer and registrar. By 1894 the building was known as 'Leven Valley'.

The mill is a neat square building with a wide leat running from a dam across the Leven. Neither dam nor leat looks ancient and it may be that there was an earlier leat from further up the Leven to a mill near the moated site, now part of the churchyard.

There is a masonry arch for an internal waterwheel and more masonry in the lower courses but the remainder is built of hand-made bricks. For a time it was used by Joseph Mease's wife, Harriette, as a private school and it seems that all internal timber dates from that time. Harriette was listed as *"school mistress"* in the 1871 Census but Rudby mill was still working at that date and could not have been used as a schoolroom until after 1881. A basalt millstone is used as a lane marker near the mill and a basalt top stone serves as the threshold to the Bay Horse in Hutton.

CRATHORNE, NZ 446075 (Leven), Fig 121 Demolished

The township of Crathorne belonged to the Percys. By 1717 there was both a corn mill and a fulling mill. The references cannot easily be separated.

pre 1260. Grant of a bovate of land by Sir Walter de Percy to Peter Bagod of Crathorne, but reserving the right to the suit of the mill (*"molend' mei de Crathorne"*) (J C Atkinson, vol 2 pt 2, 133).

1328. The mill, along with 12 messuages, 30 tofts etc were quitclaimed by John, son of William de Ryther and Alianora, in favour of William, the Bishop of Norwich, Richard Ayremynne and Master Adam de Ayremynne de Scurth (Ft of F, Yorks, 2 Edw III, no 5; VCH vol 2, 234).

1342. *"... all right and claim I ever had ... to one water*

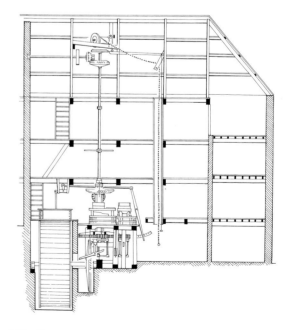

FIG 121. CRATHORNE MILL.

mill with the services of Beatrix Bagot of Crathorne ..."; Quitclaim by William de Ayremynne de Scurth in favour of William de Crathorne (NYCRO ZEA 53 Cal).

1517. *"... two mills ..."* were recorded (Chan Inq p m, ser 2, vol 78, 95; VCH vol 2, 234). Also in 1655.

1672. *"Settlement. Ralph Crathorne ... with Marmaduke Cholmley of Bransby ... etc. in the manor of Crathorne ... to the use of Ralph ... and two water corn mills built under one roof in Crathorne with all soake, suchen, moulture and other profits ..."* (NYCRO ZEA 70 cal).

1717. Ralph Crathorne had a water mill and a fulling mill, leased to George Flounders of Yarm (Quart Sess Record, N R Rec Soc, vol 8, 46; VCH vol 2, 234).

1770. *"This is to give notice that John Flounders of Crathorne ... continues the bleaching of linen cloth to great perfection ..."* (Newcastle Chronicle, 12 May).

1783. John Flounders, bleacher of Crathorne mill *"On his Water Millhouse, Bittering House, Boil House, Sour House and Offices adjoining and communicating, brick and stone built and tiled and slated, and on the mills therein, situated at Crathorne Mill ... known by the name of Bleach Field Mill £200. Utensils and Trade £1000"* (Royal Exchange Fire Insurance, no 867734).

1785. *"John Flounders of Crathorne ... begs to acquaint his friends and the public that he continues the bleaching of linen cloth to great perfection"* (York Courant, 29 March).

1800. *"... extensive bleach yard and a beetling mill where linens are made up similar to Irish"* (J Tuke, 1800, 312).

1801. Joseph Neville, Bleacher and corn miller insured his *"Water Corn Mill and granary £200, on the Water Wheels, standing and going gears, millstones, machines etc therein £200. On the stock in trade and utensils £400".*

1808. *"... extensive bleach ground, with a bleach house ... which consists of two beetling mills and a variety of other machinery, where linens are made up similar to the Irish"* and *"a flour mill at which a considerable quantity of flour is manufactured for the London and other markets"* (J Graves, 1818, 112, 113).

1844. *"To be sold by auction. A Water Corn Mill situated on the bank of the Leven. The mill has an 18 feet fall turning an Overshot Wheel and works with two pairs of stones"* (Midland Counties Herald, 8 August).

1859. *"Crathorne mill flour is acknowledged to be the best flour in Middlesbrough. Sold at the Old Flour Store, Lower East Street"* (Middlesbrough Weekly News and Cleveland Advertiser, 8 January).

Millers; John Neville *"corn miller and bleacher"* (1840), John Watson (1865), Thomas Ketton (1873), Bell and Grange (1873), James Bell (1879), Thomas Dobson (1889), C & J Dobson (1925), Thomas Dobson (1933), Jim Dobson until 1956.

From 1956 John Atkinson used the mill as a farm utility. It was eventually deemed unsafe and was demolished in July 1970. The machinery was recovered but subsequently lost. The mill was a tall brick structure of three storeys standing on top of a stone lower storey. It had a 13 feet 6 inch diameter waterwheel with iron nave and shroud plates and wooden arms and buckets and two sets of millstones, one of them emery. The York Excavation Group (1966) reported that there had been a second waterwheel.

H E Simmons, 1968, Crathorne Mill, NEIAS Bull 5 has details of insurances.

CASTLE LEVINGTON/STONE, NZ 459096 (Leven), Fig 122 Demolished

Kirklevington covers a wide area including Castle Levington, named after a motte castle thrown up on a spur overlooking the river. Castle Levington eventually belonged to the Percys.

Late C13. *"... dua marcatas ... annuatim de molendino de Levington";* grant by William de Percy to Jordanium de Esria (Surtees Soc, vol 117, 46).

1262. *"Manor of Levyngton, mill worth 30s per annum";*

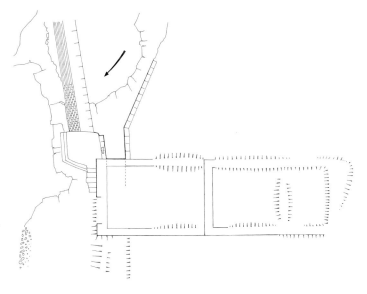

FIG 122. KIRKLEVINGTON MILL (PHOTO, CLEVELAND COUNTY COUNCIL).

Inquisition post mortem (Yorks Inq p m, YAS i, 89; VCH vol 2, 259).

1281. In the manor *"... two water mills are worth by the year five marcs"*; Inquisition post mortem for William de Feugar (YAS Rec Ser, vol 12, 221).

1314. Two water mills; Inquisition post mortem for Henry de Percy. A windmill mentioned in the same inquisition may well have been a replacement for a damaged water mill (Chan Inq p m, 8 Edw II, no 65; VCH vol 2, 259; W Brown, 1886, Yorkshire Lay Subsidy, YAS Rec Ser, vol 21).

1349. *"... one water mill worth nothing"* and one fulling mill worth 8s per annum; Inquisition post mortem for John de Meynill (PRO C 135/104/18).

C17. A water mill and a dovecot were appurtenances to the manor (VCH vol 2, 259).

1861. Named *"Stone Mill"* (Ordnance Survey).

Millers; James Wren (1822), Greenwell Atkinson (1823), Thomas Stamper, *"Stone Mill"* (1840), John Gent (1841), Ralph Hedley, *"master miller"* (1851), Stephen Peacock *"Stone Mill"* (1851), Stevenson Bell (1865), Thomas Elliott *"Stone Mill"* (1873).

The site is downstream from Foxton Bridge in an area called 'Stone Mill Wood'. The dam was founded in a trench cut into a sandstone ledge across the river and still survives in part. The wheel was internal at the end of a very long range of buildings. As one of its names implies, the mill was built of stone. It stood with a thatch-pitch roof until into the twentieth century. The gable wall overlooking the river had a mullioned window very much in the style of those at Thornton-le-Street. The waterwheel was about 16 feet in diameter by 6 feet.

MIDDLETON, NZ 462105 (Leven), Fig 123 Demolished
Though the parish of Middleton straddles an outlier of the Crathorne parish it was always part of the Meynell holdings of Hutton and Rudby. The village had a manor house and a water mill on the Leven.

1808. *"... there was a bleach ground ..."* (J Graves. 1808, 177).

Millers; William Sawyer *"Bleacher and Corn Miller"*

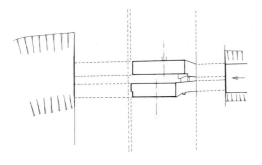

FIG 123. FOUNDATIONS OF MIDDLETON MILL.

(1822), James Coulson (1840), William Wren (1865), Edward Stamper (1873).

The building is demolished to ground level. There are relics of a heavy stone-built dam and a 13 feet wide leat. This was a double mill but probably not all of the same age. There were two wheel pits side-by-side with access for water via twin arches. One waterwheel was roughly 12 feet in diameter and 4 feet 6 inches wide and the other 13 feet 6 inches diameter and 4 feet 9 inches wide.

HILTON, NZ 453108 (Leven), Fig 124 Demolished
The village of Hilton on the opposite bank of the Leven from Kirklevington was a manor in the de Brus fee.

1318. A mill was appurtenant to the manor (Ft of F, Yorks, 2 Edw II, no 40; VCH vol 2, 238).

1618. A mill was recorded (Ft of F, Yorks, Trin, 16 Jas I; VCH, vol 2, 238).

1868. The stoppage of the old road from Leven Bridge to Hilton mill probably damaged milling at Hilton (Middlesbrough Exchange and North Ormesby News, 19 February).

Millers; Robert Wrightson (bankrupt, 1821), James Coulson (1841), Anthony Jackson (1840?, 1865), John Jackson (1872, 1879), William Braithwaite (1889).

The lower courses of this small square building were of masonry and the remainder of hand-made bricks. No machinery survived in 1974. There had been an external waterwheel and a curved slot in the hurst wall showed there had been a spur wheel and upright shaft. The attached mill house was a later addition. The site is now under the embankment of the A19 road.

LEVEN BRIDGE, NZ 445124 (Leven), Fig 125
Converted
1718. *"Corn Mill at Leaven Bridge with all the houses and grounds thereunto belonging, which I bought and purchased of W Thompson, late of Stockton"*, left by William Ward of Guisborough to his son Ralph Ward (Borthwick Institute, Prerogative Court Wills, May 1719).

1767. *"... on his Water Corn Mill adjoining at Leven near Yarm ... in the tenure of Messrs Dowson & Co, Millers, Brick and tiled £500"*; insured by Samuel Howlett of the chapelry of Ugglebarnby (Sun Fire Insurance, no 502552).

1785. *"On their Water Corn Mill and Kiln all adjoining and communicating, in their own tenure, situate as aforesaid, brick and tiles £500"*; insured by William and Robert Taylorson of Leven Bridge (Sun Fire Insurance, no 502552).

1800. *"Thomas Simpson has a Table of Prices for grinding wheat and rye"* (Chief Constables' Returns, NYCRO QAW).

1829. *"To be let and entered upon at May Day next. An*

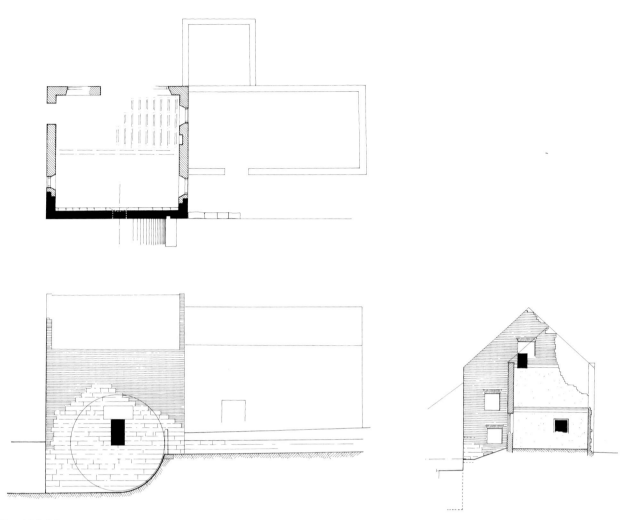

FIG 124. HILTON MILL.

excellent water corn mill with two pairs of stones, cylinder etc situate in a good wheat country and convenient distance from a shipping port ..." (Yorks Gazette, 25 April).

1835. "To be let. All the water corn mill situate on the River Leven, about two miles from Yarm and six from Stockton. The supply of water is very ample and capable of driving two pairs of stones nearly the whole of the year, and extensive business has been carried on by Mr Thomas Wren, the present tenant whose servant will show the premises" (Yorks Gazette, 24 January).

1883. John Hauxwell quoted for Derbyshire greys, silks, elevators, a purifier, and a Eureka.

1901. "... the old mill, gone to decay, is a notable landmark" (M Heavisides, 1901, Rambles in Cleveland and peeps into the dales, Stockton, 2nd ed, 24).

1935. "The mill ... worked until 1925-6 and had two undershot wheels. Dismantled by a man named Lamb ... he kept one wheel and repaired it ... and put in a dynamo" (Mitford Abraham).

Millers; Thomas Simpson (1800, 1805, 1807), William Simpson (1822), Robert Simpson (1830, 1851). In 1840 Bartholemew Gibson, John Jackson and William Simpson were listed as corn millers at Leven Bridge and Ingleby Barwick. William Layfield (1873), William Braithwaite (1890), John Fenwick (1893, 1900), Thomas F Layfield "roller process" (1897, 1905).

There were two mills in the one range; a flour mill to the north of the wide wheel pit and a provender mill to the south. The north building was burned in 1918 and the top storey demolished. The south building continued in use. The site had access by boat to the River Tees a short distance away. It was probably a post-medieval mill since the backwater from the dam seems to interfere with the foundations of the road-bridge and it is not clear which structure is earlier. There is a Georgian mill house immediately below the dam. The mill buildings, now cut down and converted into a dwelling, are built in hand-made bricks and with elliptical arched windows. The drawing records pre-conversion features only.

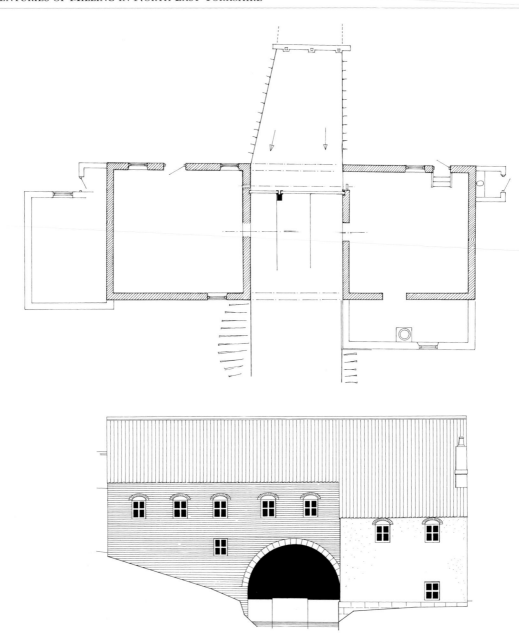

FIG 125. LEVEN BRIDGE MILL.

SOUTH OF THE TEES

There were only three water mills on the flat south bank of the Tees estuary. This was windmill territory.

YARM (Tees)

Yarm commanded the lowest bridging point over the Tees and became the main link between the counties of Yorkshire and Durham. Peter de Brus had a windmill there in 1272. Later there was a water mill.

1538. "… *farm of mill brini newly constructed by Henry Gybson*" and worth 6/8d belonged to the estate of Christopher Conyers; Confiscated estates of rebels (PRO SC 6/4281).

1540. *"I give grant assign and confirm unto my wife … Mill Close and the water belonging to it"*; Will of Thomas Conyers (J Graves, 1818, 79).

1658. A map of enclosures made in 1658, prepared by Wardell, has a water mill on the riverside to the east of the High Street but the mill is not listed in the schedule (J W Wardell, 1957, opp 72).

1830. A mill was shown on Thomas Meynell's Map (J W Wardell, 1957, opp 88).

The term *"brini"* (salt) would normally describe a mill driven, or partly driven, by tidal water. Its use here is obscure.

CALDECOTES, NZ516207 (Tees), Fig 23 Demolished

There was a water mill near the point where the Cargo Fleet flowed into the Tees.

Post 1119. Earnald de Percy gave to Gisborough Priory Caldecotes mill with the lands which Randulph the miller held there *"... molendinum de Kaldecotes cum molta sua, et cum terra quam Radulfus Molendinarius cum praedicto molendino tenebat ... "* (Gis Chart, Surtees Soc, vol 86, 229). Also; *"... et in molendino de Kaldecotes cum molta et secta sua, et cum tofto quod Ranulfus Molendarius cum praedicto molendo quondam tenuit, et cum omnibus aliis pasturis, libertatibus et aismentis at praedictas terras et molendinum infra villan et extra de Ormesby pertinentibus"* (Gis Chart, Surtees Soc, vol 86, 231).

c.1215. William Malbisse gave to the cell of Middlesbrough *"... all his lands and pastures in his freehold of Brackenhoe"* within a boundary where the headland went into *"... Caldecotes Slack, and thence along the middle of the Fleet (Fletum de Caldecotes) to the milldam or mill-race near to Felebridge"* (L Charlton, 1779, 159; J Graves 1808, 455; J W Ord, 1846, 566; J C Atkinson, 1873, vol 2 pt 2, 12).

C13. William de Percy gave land to Gisborough Priory in exchange for the water mill at Caldecotes and a windmill in Ormesby. Part of the agreement was that the tenants of the Priory would continue to pay suit to the sixteenth measure to the mills. Corn from the Canon's house would be ground multure free (Gis Chart, Surtees Soc, vol 89, 590). Also; *"... ex dono Walter de Percy, filii Willelmi, iij bov. et ex dono Willelmi fratris sui, in exchambium pro molendino ventrico de Ormesby et molendino aquatico de Caldecotes"* (Gis Chart, Surtees Soc, vol 68, 278).

1600. Five cottages, a windmill and water mill; bought by James Pennyman from Ralph Rookeby to add to his Ormesby estate (Ft of F, Yorks, Tudors, YAS Rec Ser, vol 8, 151; D W Pattenden, 1990, CTLHS Bull 58, 14).

1791. The name *"Damwell Close"* was recorded, but not the mill; "Plan of the Settled Estates of Sir James Pennyman of Ormesby", 1791 (TA ZDM 77).

WILTON, NZ 582195 Demolished

There was a water mill close to the village and to the south of the castle until the mid-C19.

C13. *"... capital messuage worth nothing and ... a water mill worth £4 per annum"* in Kirkleatham; Inquisition post mortem for William de Thwenge (PRO C 135/63; B J D Harrison, CTLHS Bull 45). Wilton was a chapelry of Kirkleatham in early medieval times and this mill may have been Wilton mill.

1337. *"Farm of two watermills in Wilton in the tenure of John Thorpe £6 13s 4d"*; Inquisition post mortem for John Bulmer (PRO SC 6 4335).

1367. *"... three water mills are worth 33s 4d p a"*; Inquisition post mortem for Ralph Bulmer (PRO C135/137).

1771. A mill at Wilton Castle was marked on Jefferys' Map.

1801. *"One corn mill is capable of grinding 168 bushels per week"* (M Y Ashcroft, 1977, NYCRO, No 15).

1803. The mill had an additional leat from Moordale Beck (Plan in Wilton estate terrier, private possession).

1808. Mill shown as an L-shaped plan immediately below a large dam to the west of the church and to the south of the castle (Wilton estate terrier).

1832. *"Jno. Grierson"* received an allowance of £16 for *"millstone and fitting up"* (Wilton Estate terrier).

1842. *"To be let. From Candlemas 1842. Two water corn mills at Wilton in Cleveland consisting of three pairs of French and Blue stones, drying kiln, corn screen and dressing machine. Mills and machinery are nearly new. Apply to Mrs Rutter of Ormesby ..."* (Yorkshire Gazette, 22 January).

1843. An un-named mill near Court Green was marked on Henry Cross's map (J W Ord, 1846). This may have been an inaccurate representation of Wilton mill.

1894. The site had been cleared (Ordnance Survey 1st Ed, 6 inch).

Millers; Michael Wilkinson (1803), J Grierson (1832, 1839), Robert Wilkinson (1844).

This seems to have been an important mill. Its pond was augmented by water carried in an extremely long leat from Moordale Beck, near Court Green farm, probably at the end of the eighteenth century. The mill was demolished, probably about the mid-nineteenth century, and the pond formalised into an ornamental pond. The name *"Mill Plantation"* survives.

SKELTON AND KILTON BECKS

Skelton Beck flows from Hutton, skirts the town of Guisborough and the castle at Skelton to reach the sea at Saltburn. The tributaries, Waterfall Beck and Saltburn Beck, also drove mills. Much of this area belonged to the de Brus family of Skelton until 1273.

HUTTON/GUISBOROUGH WEST, NZ 600161 (Chapel Beck), Fig 63 Demolished

Ralph de Neville granted a water mill to the nuns of Hutton about 1162. The nuns moved away to Nunthorpe then, after a short time, to Baysdale but retained the mill at Hutton.

1236. *"... one bovate with a house as large as the house in Thorpe adjoining that land and a mill in the same vill"*; Confirmation of grant by Ralph de Neville to the nuns of Baysdale (PRO EYC 1 565 n).

1289. *"... molendinum aquaticum et valet 40s"*; Inquisition post mortem for Hugh de Hotun (YAS Rec Ser, vol 23, 105; J C Atkinson, 1873, vol 2, 52).

1303. Walter, son of John de Thorpe (Pinchinthorpe) to grind his grain *"to the 16th measure"* at the mill of Hugh, son of Richard de Hotun (Gis Chart, Surtees Soc, vol 68, 171-3).

1303. *"... the lepers to grind at my mill to the sixteenth measure"* (Gis Chart, Surtees Soc, vol 68, 172).

John de Hotun gave the manor of Hutton to Gisborough Priory in 1346. The coincidence between the dates of the last reference to Hutton mill and the first reference to the West mill of Guisborough suggests that they were one and the same.

1346. *"The West Mill of Gisborough"*; listing of Gisborough Priory holdings in the Guisborough open fields (Gis Chart, Surtees Soc, vol 86, 143; vol 89, 418).

1539. *"... farm of two water mills for corn and one windmill in Gisburne"*; Robert Trystram, Collector for the Crown (Gis Chart, Surtees Soc, vol 89, Intro, xxxii).

1559. *"... two water mills in Gisburne, with four acres of land pertaining to the said watermills, and all mill-suits, water, water courses, pools and banks belonging to the said watermills ..."*; Grant of Manor etc of Gisborough to Sir Thomas Chaloner (J C Atkinson, 1873, vol 2, 42).

1771. *"West Mill"* marked on Jefferys' Map.

1773. Marked on *"A Rough Map of the Manor of Gisborough ... estate of William Chaloner, by Seagrave"* (NYCRO ZFM mic 1436/209).

1773. January 12 £1 4s 6d was paid *"... by cash for Lonans when Harvey's Mill was on fire"*; Agent's Accounts, Gisborough Estate, 12 January (NYCRO ZFM 75 mic 1415).

There are no further references to the West mill though it was said at mid-century that *"... the mill race may be distinctly traced"* (J W Ord, 1846, 170). The site is under the Guisborough by-pass, formerly a wet field known as 'Mill Holme'.

GUISBOROUGH/NETHER/HOWL BECK, NZ 607168 (Howl Beck), Fig 63 Demolished

This was the earliest mill in Guisborough.

1086. Count Mortain had a church and a mill worth 4s; Domesday Survey (M Faull & M Stinson, 1986).

1119. Robert de Brus gave his mill to Gisborough Priory at its foundation; *"... molendina mea in Gysburne cum soca et molta, sicut ea habin, et ita ut nullus faciat molendina in parochia ejusden villae absqui Cannonicorum licentia et concessa"*, ie *"with soc and molt as I had them so that no one may make a mill in the parish without the license and consent of the Canons"* (Gis Chart, Surtees Soc, vol 86, 4).

1346. *"... et tertium sellionem in parte occidentali molendini de Ravensdale ..."* held by Helyas, son of William Barne of Guisborough (Gis Chart, Surtees Soc, vol 86, 143).

1516. *"Sir John Bulmer was hawkyng in a garth behynd Gisburne and then at the Neder Mylne and could haue no game until he came unto a place callid North Cote."*; Yorkshire Star Chamber Proceedings (YAS Rec Ser, vol 41, 63-72).

1539. *"... two water mills for corn and one windmill"* in Gisborough, £13 12s 2d annually; Robert Trystram, Collector for the Crown (Gis Chart, Surtees Soc, vol 89, Intro xxxii; PRO SC6 4636).

1557. *"... all those our two water mills and one windmill in Gisburne ... and all mill suits, waters, water courses, pools and banks running, belonging or pertaining to the said mills now or late in the tenure or occupation of Allan Richardson and pertaining to the said late monastery ..."*; Sale of the estate to Sir Thomas Chaloner (J W Ord, 1846, App 589-91).

1801. Two mills in Guisborough, together able to mill 300 quarters per week, were listed in the Chief Constables' Returns (M Y Ashcroft, 1977, NYCRO pub no 15).

1804. *"An account of sundry expenses attending the re-building of Howl Beck mill by James Wilson ... total £652 4 s 9d"*; Joseph Hickson's Accounts for the Gisborough estate (NYCRO ZFM 87 mic 1415; see Text).

1826. *"Guisborough Water Mill"*; *"Plan of the estate of Robt Chaloner in the Parish of Guisborough in the North Riding of the County of York ... Thomas Scott, Oulston"* (NYCRO ZFM mic 1436/286).

1879. *"I have calculated the value of the whole loose and fast machinery in Howl Beck Mill, which I will give you ... £45 and clear it all away free of any expence to you"* (John Hauxwell's Letter Book, No 1).

Millers; Jno Wilson (1796), Henry Mills (1799), James Wilson and daughter (1801, 1804), John Askew (1823), Thomas Hansell (1827), Benjamin Pollard (1840, 1848, 1851, 1865), B Pollard & H Jackson (*"Howl Beck and Westgate"*, 1865), Joseph Gibson (1873).

The railway to Guisborough opened to general traffic in 1854, marking the beginning of the end of flour milling in local mills. The machinery was dismantled before the end of the century. The leat, the eighteenth century mill house and some masonry from the mill survive.

TOCKETTS, NZ 626182 (Skelton Beck), Figs 17 & 107 Preserved, Grade II*

The early history of Tocketts mill is obscure. It was possibly the mill of Upleatham, held for a while by Gisborough Priory then by the Tocketts family.

1272. Five water mills with their suit, worth £21 8s 0d; Inquisition post mortem for Peter de Brus (YAS Rec Ser, vol 12, 139-50). In 1408 three were named (Skelton, Saltburn and Skinningrove) leaving two unaccounted for.

nd. Hugh, son of Ralph de Bles, gave the mill at Upleatham and the site thereof to Gisborough Priory (J W Ord, 1846, 185).

Early C13. *"... Hugh Messor paid 6d p.a. to Gisborough Priory for land in Upleatham and ... ttti prec'. sine cibo secturm molend' faciet pro blado cresc' in terra"* (his tenants were to give four boon days for work at the mill) (J C Atkinson, 1873, vol 2, pt 1, 87).

Post-1300. William de Tocottes gave a tithe of his mill in the parish of Marske to Gisborough Priory (Burton's Mon Ebor 349; J G Graves, 1808, 382).

1539. There was a mill at Upleatham (Gis Chart, Surtees Soc, vol 89, 250).

1653-5. *"Mr Tockets frehold. One water mill and one close called Milwood"*; Survey Roll of the manor of Marske, 1653-5 (NYCRO ZQ 1).

After the Tocketts family left Yorkshire the mill was owned by the Lowther family of Wilton but in 1716 the manor, hall, farms, *"water corn mill"* etc were purchased by Edward Chaloner of Guisborough; Abstract of title, Robert Chaloner, 1820 (NYCRO ZNK 1 2/1/705).

1773. Marked on *"Rough Map of the Manor of Gisborough - estate of William Chaloner, surveyed by Seagrave"* (NYCRO ZNK mic 1436/209).

1800. *"John Marr, Guisbro', Wheat 9d, Rye 6d, Beans and Peas 6d, Oats 6d. With proper weights"* (Chief Constables' Returns, NYCRO QAR). The mill was capable of grinding 12 quarters per week (M Y Ashcroft, 1977, NYCRO Pub 15).

1804. Robert Chaloner sold Tocketts mill and valley to Lawrence, Lord Dundas, later the first Earl of Zetland (NYCRO ZNK 1 2/1/706).

1815. Thos Coulson, Tocketts mill had 29 acres in addition to the mill and pasture; *"Plan and particulars of Rt Hon the Lord Dundas's Marske, Redcar and Upleatham estate ... made by Thomas Bradley, land surveyor, Richmond"* (NYCRO ZNK V 3/1/27 mic 629).

1854. George Hesletine came to Tocketts from Skeeby mill near Richmond

Millers; John Smith (1727), Daniel Moor or Moon (1763, 1767), John Wood (1768, 1775, 1779), John Marr (1792, 1804), Robert Toas and Anne Armstrong (1812), Thomas Coulson (1815, 1823), Thomas Pattinson (1822, 1840), Mary Pattinson (mother of Thomas, 1835, 1851), George Heseltine (1854, 1865, 1872), Francis Heseltine (1873), Christopher Nixon (1877), Joseph Rowntree (1887, 1890), William Seaton (1900).

William Seaton moved to the mill in May 1900. There was renewed activity during World War I. After the war meal was sold to local farmers and to pig and poultry keepers in the mining communities of Skelton and Marske, but the machinery ceased work in 1960.

Tocketts mill is the last survivor of the mills on Skelton Beck. Restoration by South Park Sixth Form College started in 1975 and the mill opened to the public in 1983. It is now operated by the Friends of Tocketts Mill and the Cleveland Buildings Preservation Trust (J K Harrison & P W Morgan, 1982, Tocketts Mill, South Park College).

The mill is stone-built, raised to four storeys with Welsh slate roof and regularly spaced windows. The internal structure contains sets of twin memmel beams extending the length of the building and supported on turned wooden columns which may or may not have been between-decks columns from a wooden sailing ship. The 18 feet diameter waterwheel replaced an earlier, smaller diameter and wider wheel. A cast-iron upright shaft drives three sets of millstones, one of them marked "MOUNTAIN & SON, NEWCASTLE UPON TYNE" dating from the early 1870s.

WATERFALL, flax, NZ 641158 (Waterfall Beck)
Demolished
This 'Bleach Mill:' has a recorded history from 1677 to 1817.

1677. William Ward, alum works lessee, was forbidden to *"damnify the new-cut mill race ..."* (NYCRO ZFM Cal).

1757. *"I took a walk with Thos. Presswick ... to his father's mill at Waterfall and saw its operation as beating hemp, washing it etc."*; Journals of Ralph Jackson, ms (TA U/WJ/6).

1773. Marked on *"A Rough Map of the Manor of Gisborough - estate of Wm. Chaloner"* by Seagrave (NYCRO ZFM mic 1436/209).

1817. A canvas manufactury in Guisborough had 16 looms (George Young, 1817, vol 2, 557).

1855. *"Mill Closes"* but no mill (Ordnance Survey 1st Ed, 6 inch).

SWATHEY HEAD, NZ 632171 (Waterfall Beck), Figs 78 & 126 Demolished
This short-lived mill was built in the wooded valley between the Skelton and Gisborough estates, on land sold by Thomas Chaloner in 1588.

1787. Thomas Jackson *"afterwards erected and built a water corn mill on part of the said premises"*; conveyance by Richard Weatherill to Thomas Jackson, miller, Guisborough (NYCRO ZFM 4).

1794. Jackson sold the land and mill to John Appleton who, in turn, sold it to David Dixon of Stockton Bridge. After two years *"... the Messe, Water Corn Mill, Farm, Tithes, Heredits ... the whole 25 acres ... in the occupation of William and Charles Pollard"* were sold to Emma Chaloner on behalf of her son, Robert, who was still in his minority (NYCRO ZFM 4). After 200 years the land again returned to the Chaloner estates.

FIG 126. EXCAVATED REMAINS OF SWATHEY HEAD MILL

1801. Messrs Pollard were grinding wheat at 9d per quarter and barley and rye at 6d per quarter; Chief Constables' Returns (NYCRO QAW mic 1203).

1802. The Pollard's mill rentals ceased in 1802; Joseph Hickson's Accounts Chaloner Estate (NYCRO ZFM 59 mic 3369).

The mill was only 14 feet by 16 feet internal dimensions, with a doorway from a tiny cobbled yard. The water-wheel pit was external and could have held a pitch-back wheel up to 14 feet in diameter. No trace of dam or wooden launder was found. The building was badly founded on steep clay (J K Harrison, 1980, CIA, 12, 11-18).

SKELTON (fulling)

1408. Dower of one third part of a fulling mill was given to Joan, widow of Thomas Fauconberg (YAS Rec Ser, vol 59, 69-74).

By the seventeenth century only the field name "Walkemillbottome" survived. The fulling mill may have been on the same site as the corn mill.

SKELTON, NZ 650197 (Skelton Beck), Fig 17 Part demolished

Skelton mill was sited below the de Brus castle of Skelton.

1272. "... there are five mills with their suit worth £21 8s 0d"; Inquisition post mortem for Peter de Brus (YAS Rec Ser, vol 12, 139-150).

1304. "... four watermills and one wind mill, 7s a week"; Inquisition post mortem for Walter de Fauconberg (YAS Rec Ser, vol 37, 62-3).

1349. "... three watermills of which one is weak and ruinous ... worth £4 before the Death"; Inquisition post mortem for John de Fauconberg (PRO C135/96/4).

1363. "... three water corn mills worth £4 per annum"; Inquisition post mortem for Walter de Fauconberg (PRO C135/170).

1408. The dower of "... one third of three watermills in Skelton and members, called Holbekmyll, Saltbornmyll and Skinnengrefmyll ..." assigned to Joan, the widow of Thomas Fauconberg on his death (YAS Rec Ser, vol 59, 69-74). "Holbekmyll" should not to be confused with Howl Beck mill at Guisborough.

1539. "Farm of a mill called Holbekmylne" worth £5 per annum; Confiscated estates of Christopher Conyers (PRO SC 6, 4281).

1801. One mill was able to grind 6 qrs (54 bushels) per week; Chief Constables' Returns (M Y Ashcroft, 1977, NYCRO pub no 15).

1831. Let for £60 per annum to Nathaniel Stonehouse, who also ran Marske mill for the Zetland estate and had a flour dealing business in Westgate, Guisborough.

1879. "Specification for one water wheel and whaller for Skelton Mill, occupied by Mr W Harrow, £75 10s 0d. You to lead the material from Marske station" (John Hauxwell's Letter Book, No 1).

Millers; Samuel Stonehouse (1801), William Wilson (1823), Nathaniel Stonehouse (1831, 1840, 1865, 1873), William Farrow (1879), J & T Garbutt (1883), Thomas Garbutt (1889, 1893, 1895).

By 1894 the wheel was generating electricity for Skelton Castle. One set of millstones and a bone mill were kept going until the mill was damaged on 15 April 1942 by a bomb dropped from a German bomber. Further demolition took place in 1966 to enable road widening. The fine nineteenth century mill house and part of the mill building has survived. Two millstones from this mill are on display at Tocketts mill. There had been a pitch-back waterwheel driving a cast-iron upright shaft.

Skelton mill had the longest leat in north east Yorkshire, over one mile long. In the late nineteenth century one section of wooden aqueduct was replaced by cast-iron trough sections, 3 feet internal diameter.

MARSKE/NEW/RIFTS WOOD, NZ 663202 (Skelton Beck), Fig 127 Demolished

In medieval times there was a windmill on the coastal fields between Saltburn and Redcar. In the early seventeenth century a water mill was built at the end of Marske Mill Lane in Saltburn.

1640. *"… the tenant to bring great timbers and stones as shall be needed";* Tenancy agreement, James Pennyman (NYCRO ZNK V/3/3/109 mic 1251).

1649. *"Two water mills standing on one parcel of ground called the Oxe Close … for a rent of £46 and a good hen at Christmas";* Lease for 13 years by James Pennyman of Ormesby to Philip Hesseltone, miller (NYCRO ZNK V 3/3/109 mic 1251). In that same year the manor of Marske passed from the Pennymans of Ormesby to the Lowther estate.

1677. *"Two Water Corn Mills and the Rifts, the Mill Bank and Nudill (Newdale) close in Marske for £40 a year for only one year";* Lease by Anthony Lowther of Marske to Robert Corner and Thomas Scott (NYCRO ZNK V 3/3/123 mic 1251).

1679. Anthony Lowther granted a new right of way *"… for horsemen and footmen and for leading horses from the New Mill (a water corn mill) to Upleatham through Mr George Smallwood's land called Pittells and Newdailes where the way has been laid and used",* the way to be *"… only for the use and benefit of the said New Mill and the farmer and occupier thereof and their servants"* (NYCRO ZNK I 2/3/125/6).

FIG 127. MARSKE MILL (PHOTOS, A STOYEL).

1762. Lawrence Dundas bought the Lowther estate, including 5 mills (NYCRO ZNK I 2/1/251 Cal). These mills have not been accounted for.

1801. Chief Constables' Returns, *"Marske, 1 mill, 40 quarters (360 bushels) per week"* (M Y Ashcroft, 1977, NYCRO pub 15).

1815. Marske mill was occupied by Robert Carlisle; *"Plans and Particulars of the Rt Hon the Lord Dundas's Marske, Redcar and Upleatham estates, made by Thomas Bradley, land surveyor, Richmond"* (NYCRO ZNK V 3/1/27 mic 629).

1879. *"Specification for work and machinery required at Marske Mill"* included a new waterwheel, spur wheel and three millstone pinions (John Hauxwell's Letter Book, No 1). An iron hurst post had a cast iron circular plate with "J HAUXWELL MILLWRIGHT YARM".

c.1900. The masonry dam was replaced by a smaller dam and a wooden trough across the face of Jackdaw Crag. Latterly, the supply was augmented by pumping from the Skelton Park ironstone pit, which was said to raise the water level by 1 foot at 2 pm each day.

The romantic name *"Riftswood mill"* was based on the deep gill through which Skelton Beck runs below the mill.

Millers; Philip Hesseltone (1649), William Hindson (1690), William Cockerill (1761), Christopher Cockerill (1783), John Coulson (1783, 1806), Robert Carlile (1815, 1823), Thomas Dove (1835, 1840), Nathaniel Stonehouse (1841, 1851, 1857, 1872), George Stonehouse and Son (1873), Robert Fletcher (1879, 1903), James Marshall (1905), Richard Marshall (1909), Ralph Hood (1905, 1913,1921).

The mill was not used commercially after the Hood family left. It had been a two-storey structure but raised to three-storeys. Some evidence of the double mill of 1649 survives. In the late nineteenth century the hurst pit had been closed up for the much smaller cast-iron wheel. One French millstone was marked "MOUNTAIN & SONS NEWCASTLE TYNE". The machinery survived until demolition of the mill along with outbuildings and old mill house in 1972. The site was excavated by Cleveland County Archaeology Section (S J Sherlock, 1989, Excavation and Survey at Marske Mill, Saltburn, Cleveland County Council).

SALTBURN, NZ 669214 (Saltburn Gill Beck)
Demolished

This medieval steading is at the foot of Saltburn Gill behind Cat Nab, on a tributary joining Skelton Beck a stone's-throw from the sea.

1272. *"... five corn mills worth £21 8s 0d"*; Inquisition post mortem for Peter de Brus (YAS Rec Ser, vol 12, 139-50).

1304. *"... four watermills and one windmill, 7s a week"*; Inquisition post mortem for Walter de Fauconberg (YAS Rec Ser, vol 37, 62-63).

1349. *"... three water mills one of which weak and ruinous, worth £4 before the death"*; Inquisition post mortem for John de Fauconberg (PRO C135/96/4).

1363. *"... three water mills worth £4 per annum"*; Inquisition post mortem for Walter de Fauconberg (PRO C135, 170).

1408. A dower of one third of *"Holbekmyll, Saltbornmyll, and Skinnengrefmyll"* given to Joan, widow of Thomas Fauconberg (YAS Rec Ser, vol 59, 69-74).

1539. The *"farm of Saltbornemylne, 40s"*, reduced to 36s 8d, estates of Christopher Conyers; Confiscated estates of rebels (PRO SC 6 4281).

1840. An engraving by P Brannan shows a stone-built mill with an external waterwheel (Redcar and Cleveland Museums Service LD 460/1975).

1879. John Hauxwell supplied quotations for new waterwheels at both Saltburn and Marske mills (John Hauxwell's Letter Books).

c.1900. Photographs show it to have been a one-and-a-half storey mill, raised in brick by two storeys. It was derelict.

Millers; Robert Wood (1801), Mary Wood, Bryon Wood (1840, 1851, 1865), Robert Wood (1872, 1879, 1888), Thomas Smith (1893, 1895), Robert Stamp (1895).

Saltburn mill was demolished about 1905. Part of the leat is used as a footpath and part of one sluice survives.

MOORSHOLM, NZ 683148 (Dale Beck) Shell

Moorsholm mill stands in a wooded valley between Moorsholm and Stang How. It was served by two leats, one from Dale Beck and the other from Swindale Beck.

1697. *"West of the village is Swindale Beck, at the junction of which with Dale Beck is Moorsholm mill, probably on the site of that mentioned in 1697"* (Ft of F, Yorks, Trin 7, Will III; VCH vol 2, 407).

1828. Robert Watson left the mill to his eldest son, also Robert, with £20 per annum payable to his younger son William; Will of Robert Watson of Skelton, miller (NYCRO ZNK 1 2/1/803 cal).

1840. Will of William Watson of Skelton, miller (NYCRO ZNK 1 2/809 cal).

Millers; Robert Watson (1) (1799, 1800, 1823), Robert Watson (2) (1828, 1840), Mrs Anne Watson (1861,1871), Jonathan Galloway (1871, 1872), Robert Galloway (1881, 1889, 1909), John Sanderson (1913, 1925).

The mill stopped work about 1925 and the waterwheel was taken out in 1939. The range consists of a late eighteenth century two-and-a-half storey mill with an in-line and attached house. The waterwheel was in a lean-to. There was an upright shaft drive to two sets of millstones. The machinery has been dismantled and the floors removed. A 4 feet diameter blue stone survives on site.

HANDALE, NZ 724156, Fig 26 Demolished

Handale Abbey was founded in 1135.

1538. "... *little overshot mylne going with a little water, daubed walles and couered wt thack ... John Coverdale, miller*" (William Brown, 1886, YAJ, vol 9, 221).

1539. "*Site with small orchard and graveyard, worth 3s 4d; a water mill next the priory, 5s; Total value of the lands £4 12s*"; A Survey of the Rental of Handale or Grendale Benedictine Nunnery (YAS Rec Ser, vol 48, 121).

1543. Grant to Ambrose Beckwith, the house and site of the Priory of Handale with lands and a mill (YAS Rec Ser, vol 48, 122).

Little remains of Handale Abbey. The mill leat runs to a small pond and there are the foundations of a long building immediately below the dam with a deep tail-race running into the beck.

HANDALE, cotton

There were two cotton mills in north east east Yorkshire; at Great Ayton and Handale.

1758. "*Roger Beckwith ... sold the same abbey site to Mr Sanderson of Staithes by whose daughter it passed by marriage to Thomas Richardson ...*" (J Graves, 1808, 345).

1808. "*... a cotton manufactury was established a few years ago by Mr Richardson, on the site of the Priory, for the spinning and weaving of dimities, thickits, corduroys etc, but the demand during the war was so reduced as to occasion the discharge of many of the workers and the works are now at a stand ...*" (J Graves, 1808, 346).

1817. "*Some years ago a cotton mill was carried on by Mr Sanderson between Handale and Scaling*" (G Young, 1917, 819n).

The mill was demolished in 1846.

LOFTUS, NZ 719181 (Loftus Beck), Fig 128 Complete, Grade II

Loftus mill was driven from a pond below the confluence of Loftus Beck and Handale Beck.

A mill was left by Tybaud to his daughters Emma and Maude. Ownership was disputed in 1230-1. It passed to Alexander de Butterwicke who left it to daughters Maude and Cecily (VCH vol 2, 387).

nd. "*Peter de Brus granted lands with mill and the suit of the mill to Simon de Brus*" (Gis Chart, Surtees Soc, vol 89, 155, 166-7).

1272. "*Thomas, son of Eudo de Humet, granted to*

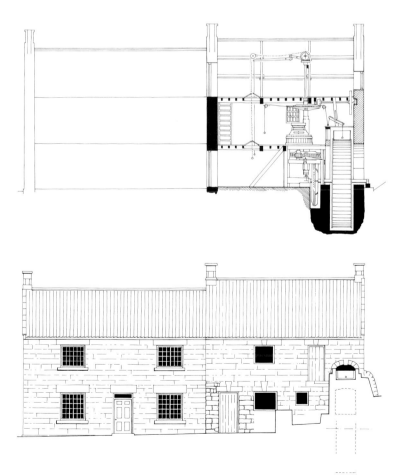

FIG 128. LOFTUS MILL.

179

Gisborough Priory the chief dwelling house and the mill beside the garden with its suit and pool ..." (VCH vol 2, 387). Other sources give Peter de Brus as making the grant.

1539. *"South Loftus ... watermill, Ralph Dale 24s";* Priory Account by Robert Tristram, collector.

1602. The mill *"lately belonging to Gisborough Priory"* was granted to Richard Burrell of London and William Allen (Pat. 44, Eliz, pt XV, m 1; VCH, vol 2, 387).

1638. *"... North Loftus water mill in the occupation of James Wilson with the house to the south side of the mill ... with Soake, Soaken, Tolls, Mulctures, Stones, Wheels, Waters, Water courses, Floodgate, Dam, Cloughs and implements belonging to the mill ..."* conveyance from William Ducke to Zacharius Steward (NYCRO ZNK I 2/2/54-55).

1764. Sir Lawrence Dundas bought the Loftus estate, including the mill.

c.1765. *"... corn mill, Mill, Gambling Potts and Broad Close"* rented for £30 by John Adamson; A particular of South Loftus and Skinningrove as valued by Messrs Robson and Snaith (NYCRO ZNK V 3/1/1/2 mic 629).

The mill was probably rebuilt in the 1790s, possibly to serve the rising population of alum workers.

1818. *"Messuage, water corn mill and 12 acres in North Loftus, now occupied by Jas. Bell";* Lease for 21 years (NYCRO ZNK V 3/3/1-7).

1882. John Hauxwell quoted for a new waterwheel (John Hauxwell's Letter Books).

Millers; John Adamson (c 1763), James Bell (1818, 1822, 1840, 1841), Thomas Hudson (1865, 1871, 1873), Jonathan Hartley (1889, 1895, 1901), Mrs Jonathan Hartley (1893, 1900, 1905), William Hird (1913, 1925), James Hird (1933, 1937).

Loftus mill was last worked by water about 1950. It is a very neat, stone-built, square-plan building. The wooden upright shaft and spur wheel are contemporary. The pit wheel, wallower and the peg gear for the hoist are later. The waterwheel, mainly of iron, is of the late nineteenth century, overshot and 15 feet in diameter. A pulley on a lay shaft from the crown wheel drove an oat crusher. A horizontal shaft from the pit wheel drove a circular saw outside the building. There are two sets of millstones (one French and one grey). A fluted barley millstone and a blue millstone survive at the site.

LIVERTON, NZ 701155 (Mill Beck), Fig 75 Complete, Grade II

The township of Liverton passed from de Brus ownership to the Latimer family of Danby in 1272.

1336. *"... water mill worth 33s 4d per annum";* Inquisition post mortem for William de Latymer (PRO C 135/44).

1753. William Shaw, tenant; *"Field Book of Danby, Sessay*

and Cowick" (NYCRO ZDS IV 1/1/1 mic 1265).

1801. One water mill in Liverton was capable of grinding 37 quarters of corn per week (M Y Ashcroft, 1977, NYCRO Pub 15, App 3).

Millers; William Shaw (1840), T Shaw (1879), Martin R Shaw (1890, 1925), Cecil Shaw (1933, 1937).

The Shaw family bought the mill from the Downe estate in 1928. It last worked for other than domestic use in 1932. The mill is part of a long range with house in the centre, byre at one end and mill at the other. The 14 feet diameter waterwheel is mounted on a wooden shaft and has iron nave and shroud plates, wooden arms and buckets. The wooden clasp-arm pit wheel drove a lay shaft to two sets of millstones, one set of greys and one set of blues marked "W & W 1807". Towards the end of its working life the lay shaft was disconnected from the pit wheel and an oil engine installed. There is a dismantled roasting plate outside the buildings.

KILTON, NZ 711189 (Kilton Beck), Fig 105 Complete, Grade II

Kilton Beck reaches the sea at Skinningrove. There were two adjacent water mills. Skinningrove mill belonged to the de Brus estate, then the Fauconbergs. The slightly later Kilton mill belonged to the de Thweng family who had also inherited part of the de Brus holding after 1272. Kilton mill should be thought of in association with the lost village (now Kilton Thorpe) rather than with Kilton Castle.

1341. *"Et est ibidem unum molendinum aquaticum debile et valet per annum XXXs ... one water mill in disrepair and worth 30s per annum";* Inquisition post mortem of Robert de Thweng (PRO C135/74; J C Atkinson, 1873, vol 1, 336).

1345. *"... unius molendini aquaticas et valebit per annum XXs";* Inquisition post mortem for another Robert de Thweng (J C Atkinson, 1873, vol 1, 336).

1767. Wrongly named *"Wilton Mill"* on a *"Map for John Hall Stephenson of the Kilton Estate"* (P Ryder, 1992, Kilton Mill; an archaeological assessment).

1801. One corn mill was capable of milling 14 quarters per week (M Y Ashcroft, 1977, NYCRO pub 15, App 3).

1843. Wrongly named *"Wilton Mill"* on Henry Cross's map (J W Ord, 1846).

The mill may have been rebuilt in 1847-8 (P Ryder, 1992).

1858-9. John Garbutt advertised *"millstone flour and breadmeal"* and that he was a dealer in a wide range of products including *"maize, barley, beans, peas, oats, linseed and moss litter"* (Loftus Advertiser, nd).

1942. The family business ceased.

Millers; Gilbert Sturdy (1792), Ralph Robson (1800), Thomas Robson (1840), John Child (1865), John Garbutt (1872, 1881, 1895, 1905), James Richardson (1909, 1925), Frederick Richardson (1933), Thomas Hird (1942).

Sections of the medieval mill track from Kilton Thorpe are still used as a road but part was deflected when Kilton Viaduct was built. The leat, over 275m long, started from a timbered dam and now passes under the embanked A174 (altered in 1966). The in-line but detached mill house has Tudor-arched windows. The mill is a 3-bay structure built of coursed sandstone with small windows. There is re-used stonework at the back and a stone dated "1709". The roof was formerly slated. The couples have knee braces designed to provide space for corn bins. The external waterwheel house has been extended upward to a roof ridge which is the same height as that of the mill. The pitch-back waterwheel is on an iron shaft with, unusually, an additional bearing between the wheel and the hurst. The wooden upright shaft and crown wheel are much older. There are two pairs of French stones and one set of grey stones. One French top stone is marked "JAS SAVERY. MAKER. STOCKTON ON TEES 1847". A note pencilled onto the hurst frame states that *"These grey millstones were set in on Sept 10 1909"*. An oat roller and relics of a silk screen remain.

SKINNINGROVE, NZ 713199 (Skinningrove Beck)
Demolished

Skinningrove mill belonged to the de Brus estate and passed to the Fauconbergs, the Conyers, the Athertons, etc.

1272. *"... five corn mills worth £21 8s 0d"*; Inquisition post mortem for Peter de Brus, (YAS Rec Ser, vol 12, 139-150).

1304. *"... four watermills and one wind corn mill"*; Inquisition post mortem for Walter de Fauconberg (YAS Rec Ser, vol 37, 62-3). (See 'Skelton').

1349. *"... three watermills one of which is weak and ruinous ... worth £4 before the Death"*; Inquisition post mortem for John de Fauconberg (PRO C135/96/4).

1363. *"... three water mills worth £4 per annum"*; Inquisition post mortem for Walter de Fauconberg (PRO C 135/170.).

Nd. Batholemew Fanacourt held parts of Skinningrove *"... except a water mill held by Walter de Fauconberg and lands held by Thomas de Thweng"* (PRO C 135/115).

1408. One third of three water mills in Skelton and members, called *"Holbekmyll, Saltbornmyll and Skinnengrefmyll"*; dower assigned to Joan, widow of Thomas de Fauconberg on his death (YAS Rec Ser, vol 59, 69-74).

1539. *"Farm of Skenningrave Mylne 10s"*; Estate of Christopher Conyers, Confiscated estates of Rebels (PRO SC6 4281). This was a much lower value than the mills at Skelton (£5) and Saltburn (£2).

1685. *"A water mill was appurtenant to the manor in 1685, 1687, 1688"* (VCH vol 2, 332).

c.1765. *"Township of Skinningrove. John Adamson, Corn Mill etc £14 yearly rent ... Pennyman Ings, On hand Glaze Mill and two cottages £10. We know not the value of the Glazing Mill, Corn Mill and Lime Kiln ..."*; *"A particular of S. Loftus and Skinningrove as valued by Messrs Robson and Snaith"*, nd (NYCRO ZNK V 3/1/1/2 mic 629). See 'Loftus'.

c 1774. William Readhead had the *"Hall, Garden and Glaz Mill ... Jno Hall has a free rent to the mill"* (NYCRO ZNK V 3/1/1/15 mic 629).

1815. *"Course of old mill dam"* and *"Bleach Garth"* marked; *"Plans and Particulars of the Rt Honble Lord Dundas's Estates of North and South Loftus by Thomas Bradley, landsurveyor, Richmond"* (NYCRO ZNK V 3/1/1/28 mic 629).

1820. Memo *"Pennyman Ings has been sold. The Corn and Glayzing Mill do not exist"* pencilled into *"Valuation of lands of South and North Loftus etc"* (NYCRO ZNK V 3/1/4).

1859. *"Cleveland Rambles, by Chips ... Boulby to Staithes. A small brook runs between two hills and empties itself into the ocean just below the village. It is crossed by a bridge close to Skinningrove Mill, in somewhat romantic and peculiar situation"* (Middlesbrough Weekly News and Cleveland Advertiser, 5 February).

The description 'glazing mill' is associated both with papermaking and with 'glazing' linen cloth but the presence of a Bleach Garth seems to point to the latter. The site was in Skinningrove village, to the west of the manor house and not far from the sea. The leat and steading are lost under the nineteenth century ironstone mining village.

NORTH EAST COAST

A few mills used the short becks running from the moors to the North Sea. The steep-sided valleys are tree-filled but the surrounding high lands were suitable for the plough. Three (or four) of the mills belonged to the Mulgrave estate.

SCALING, NZ 743143 (Waupley Beck), Fig 65
Demolished

Scaling is on the former margin of cultivation beyond which were the moors. The mill served the fields of Grinkle and Waupley. The old trackway from Waupley survives.

1314. The nuns of Handale Priory held much of Waupley. Cecilia de Irton, the Prioress, claimed a moiety of Scaling mill and the claim was upheld at an examination held before the Abbot of Whitby (J W Ord, 1846, 281; J C Atkinson, 1873, vol 1, 250).

1625. *"... all that the water mill of Easington is mentioned in 1625"* (VCH, vol 2, 340).

1792. *"... and all that water corn mill lately erected and built by the said John Wallis upon part of the said close or parcel of ground called the Low Close otherwise Low Bottoms, which said messuage, water corn mill, close and premise are situate lying and between the hamlet township or territories of Scaling ...";* Mortgage for £200 by Gilbert Sturdy, miller, to Daniel Duck, formerly of Osmotherley (NYCRO ZMP 1/4 mic 1643 182).

1817. "*... all that water corn mill with all the machinery and utensils to the same belonging ... a certain building lately commenced by sd John Sturdy ...";* Sale to Robert Wharton Myddleton of Grinkle Park (NYCRO ZMP 1/4 mic 1643 244).

1831. "*To be sold. The Manor of Handall, otherwise Grindall, including a corn mill worked by water. The property is near the sea coast and within two miles of the turn pike road from Whitby to Guisborough*" (Yorks Gazette, April 30). This reference is obscure.

1928. The mill stopped working after the waterwheel jumped out of its bearings and was broken.

1933. "*... overshot wheel, pen trough fallen down ... stones removed to make a wall at Grinkle Park ...*" (Mitford Abraham).

Millers; Gilbert Sturdy (1792), William Wren (1841 census), William Wren (1872), Wren Brothers (1879), Thomas Wren (1893, 1897), William Hugill (1901, 1905). The mill, though derelict, was largely complete in 1967. The mill and old mill house all within the same building were built of rubble stone. Evidence of the 1792 "*lately erected*" status could be seen in the upper courses of the walls with the small vents. A leat led from the top of a waterfall to an external 18 feet diameter by 3 feet overshot waterwheel with cast-iron shroud and nave plates and wooden arms and buckets. The iron shaft had been spliced into the older wooden shaft. The clasp-arm pit wheel and upright shaft with clasp-arm spur wheel were of late eighteenth century date. There were two pairs of stones on the main hurst but mortises in the front of the hurst beam indicated there had been a third set. The reel of a wire machine survived.

The mill and house were demolished in the early 1970s.

ROXBY, NZ 749143 (Roxby Beck), Fig 78 Demolished
This mill has sometimes mistakenly been called Scaling mill. It was situated under a waterfall near a ford on Mill Lane, with the mill house a little way to the north. Nearby is a range of animal houses.

1895. "*Disused*" (Ordnance Survey 1st Ed, 6 inch).

1907-8. Machinery sold for scrap (note from Mr G T Codling, Birch Hill Farm, 1971).

c.1933. "*Ruins of old mill abandoned many years ago ... not a trace of any stones, wheel or machinery ... millstones removed to Grinkle Hall*" (Mitford Abraham).

Millers; Thomas Liversedge (1840), Thomas Roxby (1873).

Mainly demolished in the 1940s. When recorded in 1981 the lower courses of masonry revealed that it was of nineteenth century build. It had been a small square-plan building (17 feet 3 inch by 14 feet 6 inch in internal dimensions) built on a rock ledge with the lower parts of two walls cut into solid rock. The hinge brackets for the tenter beams were of cast-iron. One set of French burr stones remained on site. The waterwheel had been approximately 19 feet 6 inches in diameter and 3 feet wide, fed by a wooden launder from a waterfall approximately 23 feet high. There is a ford above the fall and another immediately below the outfall of the tailrace.

Remaining masonry has now been cleared. The name "LIVERSEED MILL" and a date were inscribed on a stone above an upper doorway.

SEATON/DALEHOUSE, NZ 777181 (Staithes Beck), Fig 46 Demolished
This early medieval Mulgrave estate mill was sited just below the confluence of Easington Beck, Roxby Beck and Newton Beck. It served the lost village of Seaton, the large village of Hinderwell and the later fishing village of Staithes. In the late eighteenth century the old building was incorporated into a much larger building. A handsome mill house was built nearby.

1299. "*... watermill worth 13s 4d per annum at Seaton*" (YAS Rec Ser, vol 31, 99-100).

1314. "*... a water mill worth ...*"; Inquisition post mortem for Edmund de Mauley (PRO C 134 36).

1537. "*Farm of Manor of Seaton, Manor and Watermyll ... £6 16 8d*"; Confiscated estates of Rebels, Francis Bigod (PRO SC 6 4344).

1754. "*... in my way to Boulby went to Dalehouse Mill ...*"; Ms. Ralph Jackson's Journal (TA U/WJ/5).

1801. Hinderwell had one corn mill capable of milling 120 bushels per week. Isaac Moon was the miller; (M Y Ashcroft, 1972, NYCRO Pub 15, app 3).

1919. "*Dalehouse Mill ... in occupation of Mrs Bell. ... The Water Mill is built of stone and contains three storeys; it is large and roomy and includes machinery with the exception of two millstones which belong to the tenant. It was formerly used as a flour mill but is now used for grinding meal, etc*" (Sales Notice, 6 Oct).

1933. "*... very good old country mill going to ruin. Two undershot wheels, one for two French pairs and the other for two grey pairs. ... Owner says that occasionally he uses one wheel for running an oat roller. Mill ceased to work six years ago*" (Mitford Abraham).

Millers; Isaac and Joseph Moon (1840), Ann Moon (1865, 1873), Deull and Sanderson (1879), Henry and John Bell (1889, 1893), John Bell (1897, 1913), Mrs John Bell (1921), George Ward (1925).

The mill was fed with water carried across a wooden aqueduct from Roxby and Newton Becks.

The mill became derelict during World War II and is now demolished. The site is now isolated but in former times the old A174 road ran nearby. Investigation carried out in 1983 (J K Harrison) revealed the footings of two mills, one on either side of the wide wheel pit. That on the east side, clearly the older, had originally contained the old mill house and double mill driven by two waterwheels. The house retains relics of a hearth window and cupboard. An oat roasting plate has been built into the hearth window. The newer mill, on the west side, had been equipped with a single waterwheel and upright shaft drive.

There had been a horse-driven thresher in a nearby barn.

STAITHES, fulling, NZ 779184 (Staithes Beck)
Demolished

1843. *"Fulling Mill"*; Henry Cross's map (J W Ord, 1846).

1852. *"Fulling mill"*; (Ordnance Survey 1st Ed, 6 inch).

It stood with its 'Tenter Hill' in a loop in Staithes Beck. Some old buildings survive but not on the site of the mill itself. The leat has been a very expensive construction cutting through or tunnelling under a 20 feet high shale cliff at the neck of the loop. The site may have been accessible by small boat at high tide.

FLATTY

"Flattymill Dale" was marked on the 1852 Ordnance Survey 1st Ed, 6 inch map at the top of Widgey Top Gill and below Barnby Tofts Farm. The name may indicate the site of a medieval mill. If so it would have served the coastal grain-growing lands of Goldsborough, north Barnby and Ellerby where there are extensive areas of well preserved rigg and furrow. However, there is neither documentary evidence nor human memory of a mill. There is a convergence of old tracks at NZ 817145 but if there was a mill here it has been destroyed by the coastal railway.

FOSS/LYTHE, NZ 831116 (Barnby Beck), Figs 10 & 33
Ruin

The name 'Foss mill' is likely to have derived from the 'force' which provided the power rather than from the 'fosse' or earthwork round the ancient motte overlooking the mill site. Foss mill served Mickleby and the Barnbys

1279. *"... also the same had there 4 mills, which yield yearly £20 ..."*; Inquisition post mortem for Peter de Mauley (YAS Rec Ser, vol 12, 191-194).

1537. *"Farm of mills ... Fosse Mylle, Geo. Bakhouse 26s 8d"*; Confiscated estates of Rebels, Francis Bigod (PRO SC 6 Henry VIII 4344).

1801. Lythe had two corn mills capable of milling 30 quarters per week. George Lynas was the miller (M Y Ashcroft, 1972, NYCRO Pub 15, App 3).

1932. *"... dismantled in 1932. All stones, machinery and overshot wheel gone. Ceased to work about 1900"* (Mitford Abraham).

It was a four-storey mill with an attached and in-line house, the range showing many stages of development. Its foundations were stepped into a number of ledges in the solid rock. The site is below a wath or ford which carried the track from High Lease farm and the Barnbys to Barnby Sleights. Barnby Beck cuts down in a series of falls below the mill into a deep, steep-sided gorge. A blocked tail opening in the lower wall may be medieval. In its later stages it had a waterwheel in an outshot at the gable end and an upright shaft driving three sets of mill-stones. The mullioned windows replacing older plain openings may have been put in to create a picturesque feature at the furthermost point on the walk through Mulgrave Woods which were subject to a Humphrey Repton (1752-1818) landscape scheme in the eighteenth century.

Millers; William Peirson (1890), William and Francis Peirson (1893, 1901, 1905), Francis Peirson (1899, 1905), W Brown (1909). The address in most cases was given as Lythe.

SANDSEND/EAST ROW, NZ 862125 (East Row Beck), Fig 10 Shell, Grade II

The old corn mill was converted for manufacturing Roman cement.

1279. *"... also the same had there 4 mills which yield yearly £20"*; Inquisition post mortem for Peter de Mauley (YAS Rec Ser, vol 12, 191-194).

1537. *"Sands Hende Mylle, Jas. Bakehouse 26s 8d, Est Milne Peter Couper, 13s 4d"*; Confiscated estates of Rebels, Ralph Bigod (PRO SC 6 4344).

1775. *"... one watter mill called Sands End Mill with appurtenancies in Sands End ..."*; property of Constantine Phipps; Abstract of Title (Burnett Coll, 3007).

The old leat on the East Row Beck was used from 1811 to 1932 for driving the Mulgrave Roman Cement mill which made Roman cement from dogger stones from the alum shales.

1932. *"... old flour mill converted into cement (two pairs of stones) and saw mill over sixty years ago and worked until August 1932. One grey stone outside door. Overshot wheel ... owned by the Marquis of Normanby"* (Mitford Abraham).

The Roman Cement mill at Sandsend is an outstanding industrial relic. Dogger stones were brought to the top of a 20 feet high kiln. After calcining the stones were ground under French millstones (one by Corcorans of London). The wheel pit contains the scrape marks of at least three large waterwheels. The main drive was by lay shaft. The leat also drove a saw bench for the estate.

UPPER AND MIDDLE ESK

The Esk flows west-to-east through the heart of the North York Moors, from its head near Westerdale to the North Sea at Whitby. There are several tributaries.

COMMONDALE, NZ 663101 (Sleddale Beck), Figs 32, 39, 59 & 129 Demolished

This was the mill of the Gisborough Priory grange at Skelderskew.

1535. *"Manerium de Skelderskewe cum valle de Colmandale et Molendinum;* Manor of Skelderskewe

A)

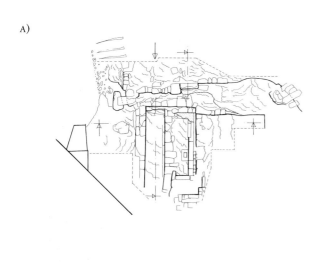

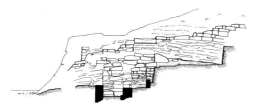

B)

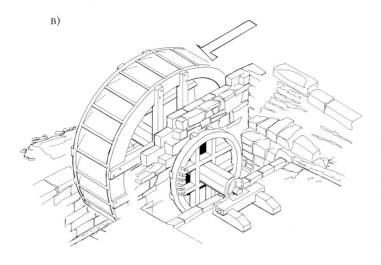

Fig 129. Commondale mill, a) excavated remains and b) conjectured lay out.

with the valley of Colmandale and a water mill there"; Valor Ecclesiasticus (J C Atkinson, 1889, vol 2 pt 2, 22).

1539. *"Colmandale. Capital messuage of Skelderskeugh ... a water and fulling mill ..."*; Minister's Accs, 31-32 Henry VIII, No 181 (Gis Chart, Surtees Soc, vol 89, xxxii).

1539. *"Colmandale, ... 1 cot, 2 small closes and a water mill, William Bennyson 10s 8d"*; Gis Lately Priory Acc, Robert Trystram, Collector (PRO SC 6 4630).

Afterwards the mill was acquired by the speculator, Thomas Legh.

1772. Lease and release, Henry Casson of Skelton gent to Ralph Sanderson of Danby (NYCRO Deeds Reg AZ 413 683).

1812. Lease, John Sanderson to George Moon (NYCRO Deeds Reg DP 168 247).

1816. The mill was bought by Thomas Loy, surgeon, of Stokesley (NYCRO Deeds Reg EB 176 120).

1858. Release, Dorothy Redhead to William Watson, miller, of Roxby (NYCRO Deeds Reg IT 14 20).

1858. Sold to the North Yorkshire and Cleveland Railway Company and subsequently demolished (NYCRO Deeds Reg IT 14 20 mic 386). Bridgework cut across the site. The line was opened 1 April 1861.

Millers; Henry Stonehouse (1812), John Stonehouse (1816), John Shaw (1840), William Watson (1844, 1851).

The site and surrounding area were investigated in 1986 and 1987 (J K Harrison, 1995, CBA Research Report 101) revealing a building founded on solid shale. There was a pit suitable for a 12 feet diameter by 3 feet water-wheel. This mill worked with one set of millstones to the end. Not far away are the mutilated relics of a seventeenth century gable-entry mill house with mullioned windows.

COMMONDALE, fulling/bleach, NZ 664099 (Sleddale Beck), Fig 39 Demolished

1539. *"... a fulling mill rented by Robert Doncaster, Henry Rowe and Robert King, 20s"*; Gis Lately Priory Acc, Michaelmas 31 Henry VIII, Robert Trystram collector (PRO SC 6 4630).

1718. *"... right and interest in a Fuller's Mill at Commondale in the possession of Robert King"* left by William Ward of Guisborough to his son Ralph Ward (Borthwick Institute, Prerogative Court Wills, May 1719).

1753. Thomas King re-built the mill. The dated key stone "T K 1753" is now built into another building near the roadside.

1790. Daniel Duck described how he brought linen to be woven in Lealholm and bleached at Commondale bleach mill (Chronicler of Lealholm, Whitby Gazette, 20 Oct 1967).

By 1844 directories described owners and farmers but no bleachers.

The buildings were dismantled for their stonework about 1910 but some lower courses survived in the 1960s. The leat can be traced where it crosses the Commondale to Westerdale road.

BAYSDALE, NZ 621068 (Black Beck), Fig 28
Demolished
The nuns from Hutton near Guisborough moved first to Nunthorpe and then to Baysdale about 1190.

1539. *"Item the ouershot water mylne hardby the gate xx ffoote long and xiij ffoote brode, stone walles and parte bourdid and couered wt thack and the whole is in decay so that the seid mylne goeth not"* (W Brown, 1886, 327).

After the Dissolution the site of the Priory of Basedale was leased to William Snowhall *"of the household"*.

1564. A *"... moiety of land and watermill in Basedale"*; Fine between Robert Yoward and Ralph Yoward, plaintiffs and Thomas Grey (YAS Rec Ser, vol 48, 94).

1582-3 The mill was mentioned in an agreement between Ralph Yoward and Francis Cholmley (YAS Rec Ser, vol 48, 94).

There is no further reference to the mill. The most likely site is under the modern farm building immediately beyond the medieval arched bridge leading to the Priory site. The line of the leat cutting across a loop in the beck is occasionally revealed by floodwater.

WESTERDALE, NZ 659059 (Esk), Fig 130 Converted
Part of Westerdale, including the mill, was granted to the Knights Templar c.1200.

1307. *"... Molendinum aquaticum & valet per ann. VIII marcas"* (a mill worth 8 marks (£5 6s 8d) per annum) listed among the possessions of the Knights Templar; Exch Anct Extant, no 18 (J C Atkinson, 1874, vol 1, 289-91).

After the suppression of the Templars in 1315 Westerdale was granted to Guy de Beauchamp, Earl of Warwick.

1315. *"... a water mill worth £5 6s 8d per annum"*; Inquisition post mortem of Guy de Beauchamp (PRO C 134/50).

1539. *"Rents of Customary Tenants; Edward Strynger for a water mill 6s 8d"*; Ministers' Account for the estate of

FIG 130. WESTERDALE MILL.

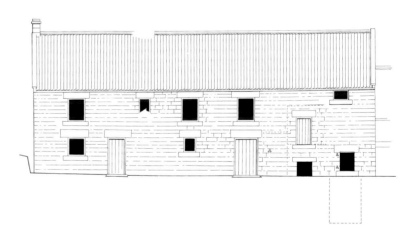

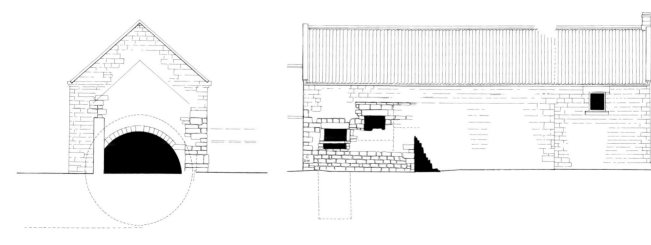

Beverley Minster in Westerdale (PRO SC 6 835/2).

1806. *"Water corn mill"* in the tenancy of John Hugill; Rental of Kildale and Westerdale (NYCRO ZK 10574 mic 1216).

Millers; Andrew Thompson (1840), John Maw (*"Hall Mill"*, 1872), John Benson (1879), Thomas Bowes (1889, 1897), Henry Featherston (1901, 1909), George Dale (1913, 1925), William Dale (1937).

Flour was milled during World War I. In 1937 William Dale, tenant miller, bought the mill from the Feversham estate and converted it into a dwelling. The building has evidence of two early stages of development: 1) an eighteenth century water entry point in the rear wall originally leading to an internal pitch-back wheel approximately 14 feet diameter and 2 feet 9 inches wide, and 2) some walling, doorways and windows of the early nineteenth century.

WESTERDALE (Whyett Beck), Fig 12

Two place names, 'Old Mill Wood' and 'Millers House', now Millinder House, (Ordnance Survey 1st Ed, 6 inch map, 1853) may point to an earlier mill. No relic of this has been found but the relationship between village, 'Christy Gate' and the fine set of medieval field boundaries may indicate an older millstead (see Text).

BROADGATE FARM, threshing, NZ 671049 (Spring Dike) Demolished

A stone mill, straw chopper and thresher were driven by water. Water from Spring Dike was led to a shallow pond behind the barn. The 14 feet diameter by 3 feet waterwheel had cast-iron shrouds and naves and wooden arms and there was a single pair of Derbyshire grey millstones (F Wetherill of Ainthorpe, 1966, Report for SPAB). The use of waterpower ceased in 1942 and a petrol engine was installed. The barn still stands but the wheel shed and machinery have gone.

CASTLETON/ESK, fulling/flax, NZ 683083 (Esk), Figs 12 & 111 Demolished

This old fulling site was converted to flax spinning and then to corn milling.

1432. *"... rent of one fulling mill, 13s 4d"*; Account of John Forster for Lady Maude de Yorke, Countess of Cambridge, Medieval Danby Account Rolls (Sheffield City Library).

1812. *"... that piece or parcel of ground and frontstead whereon a fulling mill formerly stood"*; mortgage for £500 by David Knaggs to the occupier John Watson of Danby, flax dresser (NYCRO Deeds Reg, DP 525 673, mic 316).

1813. *"Water mill lately erected and built by the said Thomas Watson ..."* (NYCRO Deeds Reg, DP 528 674

mic 316). This was a flax spinning mill.

1822. *"The only manufacury in linen thread, for the spinning of which there is a neat and commodious stone building erected a few years ago"* (Baines' Directory).

1840. Owner, Thomas Watson linen thread manufacturer.

1846. *"To be sold by auction. That valuable Flax Mill situate upon the River Esk at Castleton, including an iron water wheel, 14 ft in diameter and 8 ft in breadth. The strong waterpower of the River Esk entirely precludes the necessity of working the mill by steam. The Castleton railway station will be within 250 yards of the premises ..."* (Yorks Gazette, 24 January).

The mill had been converted to corn milling by 1851.

Millers; William Plews (1851), William Coverdale (1871), William Rivis (1873, 1893, 1909), John Rivis (1913, 1921), George Williamson (1925), Arthur Champion (1930).

Corn milling continued until the 1930s. The wheel then drove a saw bench and a generator for charging car batteries. The machinery was scrapped in 1946. The buildings were demolished in 1971 and a new house built on the site.

The building betrayed its origin as a textile mill by the large blocked windows in the gable wall over the waterwheel shed, a feature unknown in local corn mills. There was a wide wheel shed suitable for a waterwheel diameter 14 feet and 8 feet 9 inches wide for using the ample flow of the Esk. The hurst was clearly an inserted framework designed for a spur wheel and upright shaft and three pairs of stones, two of them French burrs.

DANBY HOWE, NZ 691079 (Danby Beck), Figs 12 & 131 Converted

Howe Mill was the medieval mill of Castleton, Ainthorpe and Danby Dale.

1272. *"Danebi. There are ... 2 water mills worth £10 of which Roger de Burton has by charter 100s ... (ii moledina aquatica valent xli. De quibus Rogerus de Barton habet per cartam cs")*; Inquisition post mortem for Peter de Brus (YAS Rec Ser, vol 12, 139-145; J C Atkinson, 1874, vol 1, 272).

1336. *"A water mill worth £6 per annum and a second water mill worth £3"*; Inquisition post mortem for William de Latymer (PRO C 135/44).

1380. *"... a water mill worth 13s 4d per annum"*, the reduction because of the Black Death; Inquisition post mortem for another William Latymer (PRO C 136/15).

1431. *"Rent of 2 corn mills lately in the tenure of Ricc del Howe, 55s, to hold for five years. They maintain the fabric of the mill except great timber which the lady shall find for them. If anyone shall come in the mean time who may be willing to pay more they agree to lease their term"*; Acc of John Forster for Lady Maude de Yorke,

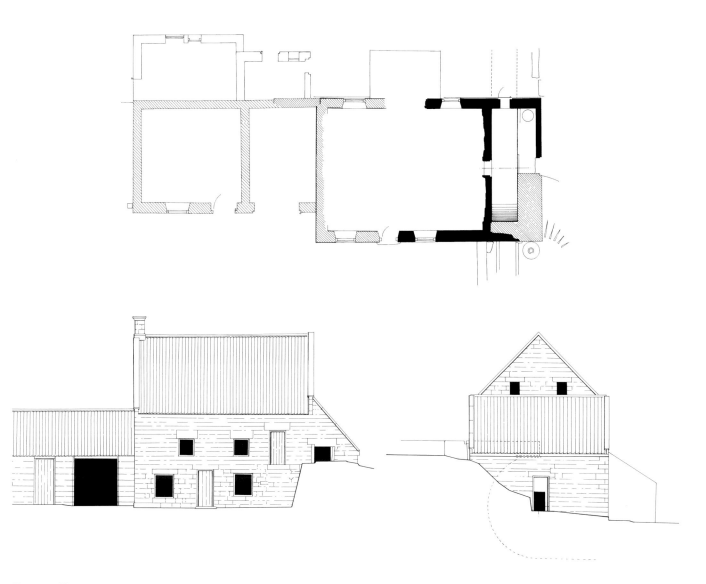

FIG 131. HOWE MILL.

Countess of Cambridge (Medieval Danby Acc Rolls, Sheffield City Library).

1655. A water mill and 23 farms were bought by John Dawney when Sir John Danvers sold the estate.

1807. *"The cost of building a Water Corn Mill by Wm Wilson of Danby"* (NYCRO ZDS IV 14/6 mic 1120 fr 6599). See Text.

For a century the mill was run by members of the Wilson family: William (1753, 1777), William (1800, 1814, 1828 and 1840), George (1851). The Wilsons were important members of the local community and no doubt built the fine mill house.

Later millers; Henry Atkinson (1873), William Milner (1893, 1913).

A stone causeway leads from Danby dale past the mill to Castleton. This mill has a leat over 925m long and had the reputation of having a powerful waterwheel.

Little, if any, of an ancient building survived the 1807 rebuild though the stonework of the doorway in the front facade may have been the original corner of the mill. The 1807 rebuild incorporated a pitch-back waterwheel of 16 feet diameter and 4 feet width inside a well-crafted masonry wheel case. The machinery was removed in 1930 (J C Rutter, 1970) and the building is now used as two dwellings.

DANBY/DANBY END/ESK, NZ 707084 (Esk), Fig 67
Preserved, Grade II

Danby End mill is one of a small minority of post-medieval corn mills.

1803. Council's advice sought following a dispute between the miller, Thomas Thompson and his neighbour, Harrison, on the opposite bank of the Esk

(NYCRO ZEL 2/2/200 mic 1119). The owner Thomas Weatherill had built a mill on the Esk, "... *no mill of any kind being there before*".

Successors of Thomas Thompson were James Thompson (1840, 1851), James and John Thompson (1873), John Thompson (1879, 1893), James G Thompson (1905, 1921), Gatenby Thompson (1922), W W Thompson (1937).

As built the mill was two storeys high with a Smeaton type undershot waterwheel, 14 feet diameter and 5 feet wide, with cast-iron shaft and nave plates and wooden arms, felloes, awes and boards. The finely crafted wooden upright shaft and the compass arm spur wheel are original and the cast-iron pit wheel and wallower may be. An old stone bearing is built into a window lighting the hurst.

Later the mill was raised by two storeys, the original roof timbers being re-used. The mill house was built in 1864 using purchase money when the Esk valley railway line was laid across the land between the mill and the old mill house. Cast-iron hurst frames and an elevator were installed by John Hauxwell of Yarm in 1880. The mill is equipped with French burr stones by "W J & T CHILD, MILLSTONE MAKERS, HULL & LEEDS" but in and around the buildings there are at least two pairs of greys and one set of basalt stones. Latterly there was also a roller mill.

Danby End mill suffered from its close relationship with the Esk. In 1930 the floods were so severe that the waterwheel was completely submerged. Other flood lines are recorded on the doorway masonry.

Danby End mill was worked by E Merrill until 1971 when the waterwheel was damaged. Staff and students of South Park Sixth Form College built and installed a new waterwheel in 1983. The mill itself was restored by Frank Palmer.

FRYUP HALL, NZ 723045 (Low Gill Beck) Demolished
In the small valley below Fryup Hall is the relics of a small rape oil and corn mill which was set up by the Downe estate near the end of the eighteenth century.

1788. Daniel Duck recorded that his elder children went to watch Matthew Agar's rape threshing; J Davison, Diary of Daniel Duck (Whitby Gazette, 21 October 1967).

1840. "*To be sold by Auction. A Water Corn Mill situate at Fryup Hall Estate, lately occupied by Mr Matthew Agar, deceased ...*" (Yorks Gazette, 21 November).

1877. "*Residential freehold estate known as Fryup Hall. ... To sell by auction at the Crown Hotel, Whitby, Wednesday 14th November, ... all the buildings except the small corn mill are in good state of repair*" (Misc Newpaper cuttings, Midd Ref Lib). It is reasonable to think it was out of use by mid-century. The millstones were taken to Castleton Howe mill and today only the foundations remain.

LEALHOLM, Furnace Farm
The name Furnace Farm in Fryupdale at NZ 742068 probably derived from the site of a water-driven forge.

LEALHOLM, threshing, NZ 761076 (Esk) Shell
A secondary leat taken off the main Lealholm corn mill and paper mill leat turned a small waterwheel which drove a threshing machine. It may later have been used in connection with the Lealholm estate workshops. The building survives.

LEALHOLM, NZ 763077 (Esk), Fig 132 Converted
Neither the surviving building nor its major water works appears to be medieval in origin. The existing works may date from the 1760s when a paper mill was being built over the tailrace.

1272. An un-named water mill worth £3 per annum; Inquisition post mortem for Peter de Brus (YAS Rec Ser, vol 12, 139-45).

1336. "*... a water mill worth £3 0s 0d per annum*"; Inquisition post mortem for William de Latymer (PRO C 135/44). This medieval site is not known.

1431. "*Rent of one corn mill called Lelommylne, 16s*" (John Forster's Accounts for the Countess of Cambridge, Medieval Danby Account Rolls, Sheffield City Library).

According to J Davison the mill was demolished about this time and Thomas Watson built a new water mill (Chronicler of Lealholm, Whitby Gazette, 29 Oct 1971).

1763. "*All that water corn mill and stable with the wheels, Cogs, Millstones, Utensils, implements, medure, Races, Dams, Pools and other streams ... in the occupation of Christopher Moon*" (NYCRO Deeds Reg 343, 448).

1780. Christopher Moon, "*corn miller and paper manufacturer*", insured the mill for £200 (Sun Fire Insurance, no 432479).

1838. "*To be sold. A well Accustomed Water Corn Mill situate at Lealholm Bridge, in the parish of Danby, in the County of York, erected on a plentiful stream of water, containing 2 pairs of Blue stones and one pair of Grey Stones, cylinder, Barley Mill, screen etc. The business may be considerable extended, another mill situate near Lealholme Bridge having recently been laid down. Owner Henry Stonehouse.*" William Corner and Roger Yeoman were joint tenants (Yorks Gazette, 14 April).

1860. To be sold "*Lot 2. All that old established and convenient Water Corn Mill situated at Lealhom Bridge in the occupation of Messrs Snaith and Duck ... Lot 3. All that very extensive warehouse and saw mill formerly used as a Paper Mill, Drying Sheds etc by the late Mr William Joy ...*" (Yorkshire Gazette, 28 July). Subsequently sold to Andrew Thompson. Thompson raised the roof of the mill house to the same roofline as the mill (Incised stone "AT 1873" in facade).

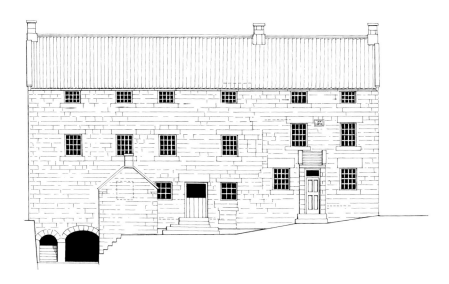

FIG 132. LEALHOLM MILL.

1890. Andrew Thompson Bell took over. Andrew Thompson Bell died in 1947 having been miller for 50 years.

1933. *"Undershot iron wheel. Quite a big mill formerly doing a good flour business. Silks in but not used for 3 to 4 years. Three pairs of stones (two French and one grey) ... grinds for farmers only. Former oats kiln ..."* (Mitford Abraham).

Millers; Christopher Moon (1745, 1763), William Brunton (1800), William Corner and Yeoman Rodgers (1838), Andrew Thompson (1893). The 1851 census lists millers, Ann Winspear, John Brunton, William Corner (*"grocer and miller"*), Yeoman Rogers (*"miller and farmer"*), William Readman (*"inn keeper, miller and farmer"*); not all were at Lealholm mill.

The mill finally stopped work in the winter of the 'big snow' of 1947, when the waterwheel, which was already in a poor state, could not be operated and business was lost.

The mill has been converted first into the 'Nelson Hall' and then into a private residence. The shape of the building is unchanged but the window openings have been changed. Water still flows through the pit suitable for a waterwheel, 14 feet diameter and 6 feet wide, and its adjacent escape race. An outstanding feature of this steading is the scale of the water engineering.

LEALHOLM, fulling/paper, NZ 763076 (Esk)
Demolished

1431. A fulling mill at Lealholm was rented at 13s 4d; John Forster's Accounts (Sheffield City Library).

1762. *"... all necessary conveniences ready fixt"* for *"any person wanting to go into the business of paper making"*
(Newcastle Journal, 17 April).

1763. *"... paper mill erected or now erecting ..."* (NYCRO Deeds Reg AM 343, 448).

1780. *"Elizabeth Gillery of Scarborough in the County of York. On her Paper mill at Lealholm Bridge ... in the tenure of Joseph Longstaffe; Brick and Tile and Stone, Tiled £400"* (Sun Fire Insurance no 432477).

1808. *"... paper mill employs about 20 hands"* (J Graves, 1808, 279).

1815. William Joy was owner and paper maker and Henry Stonehouse was tenant (Chronicler of Lealhom, Whitby Gazette).

1839. *"Change of occupation at Paper, Pasteboard and Millboard Mil ... present occupier Edward Savage"* (General Letter, 10 September).

1860. To sell. Both the corn mill and *"... all that Building theretofore used as a paper mill and then partly occupied as a saw mill and partly as a bacon curing warehouse"* (Yorks Gazette, 28 July). It was turned into a woodturning factory.

Frank Weatherill of Ainthorpe demolished the paper mill and remembered that the stonework of the wheel pit was set in Roman cement. There is a market garden on the site.

LOW WOOD/DELL/WOODLANDS, NZ 762069 (Busco Beck), Fig 133 Demolished

This short-lived corn mill was about a mile south of Lealholm.

Millers; Thomas Stobbart (1822, *"Stobert"* 1823), Sarah Arrowsmith (1839).

The mill (standing at the beginning of this century but

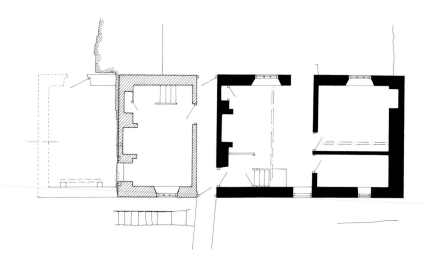

FIG 133. DELL MILL, LOW WOOD, LEALHOLM.

now demolished) was a small building attached to the gable wall of the much older mill house. The house has been raised from a thatch pitch. In past years a right of way ran through the cross passage of the house. The dam is intact.

UNDER PARK, threshing, NZ 772070

A water-driven threshing and stone mill was built onto the west side of the fold yard at Under Park farm in the early nineteenth century. The waterwheel was set so low in the ground it was below ground level. The all-iron waterwheel and the stone mill survived into the 1970s. Later the stone mill was removed and the waterwheel buried.

STONEGATE, NZ 778089 (Stonegate Beck), Fig 134
Converted

To the north of Lealholm is the tributary of Stonegate Beck. The mill served high fields at Ugthorpe as well as lands much closer. There is no early history.

1933. *"... nice little well-built stone mill. Overshot iron wheel. Two pairs of stones, both used. Flour boulter not used for six years ... Miller complains that the tarmacadam roads in this hilly district are so dangerous that farmers object to bringing their corn to be ground at the mill"* (Mitford Abraham).

Millers; George Yeoman (1872, 1913), Thomas Robinson (1925). George *"Yimmin"* was a well-known local personality.

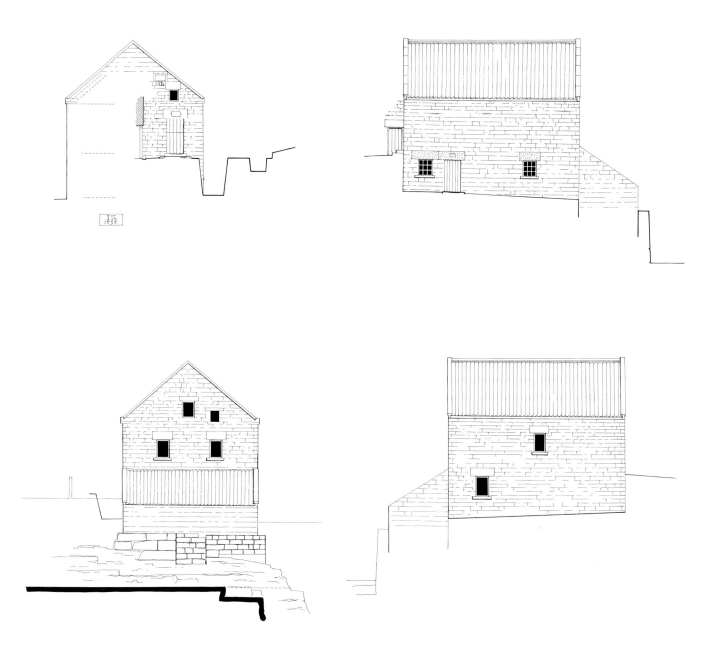

FIG 134. STONEGATE MILL.

The mill stopped work about 1946. It is stone-built with small windows. It had an overshot waterwheel in a lean-to shed and an upright shaft drive to three sets of stones. It is a typical early nineteenth century mill and no earlier masonry has survived. An old datestone "ML 17 GH" is built into a wall near the entrance gate. There were two dams for storing water, both of which survive in good condition. Latterly there was a turbine, Gilbert Gilkes and Gordon, Kendal No 4308. Half of a blue millstone is preserved on site.

GLAISDALE HIGH, NZ 776057 (Esk), Fig 135
Converted
This was a medieval corn mill, then a fulling mill.

Between 1781 and 1791 corn milling was re-established.

1801. Glaisdale listed as having two water corn mills capable of milling 100 bushels per week (M Y Ashcroft, 1977, NYCRO pub. no. 15, App 3). One was probably at Lealholm.

1833. *"To be sold by Auction. A Walk Mill or Fulling Mill situate on the River Esk ... known by the name of Wood Mill, now in the occupation of Rachael Harland"* (Yorks Gazette, 16 February).

1933. *"... ruins of undershot wheel, Stones outside ... one pair French, one pair blue, one grey stone upright and one at entrance of back door"* (Mitford Abraham).

Millers; John Harding (1822), William Harding (1840), Jonathan Harding and William Harding (1851), Richard

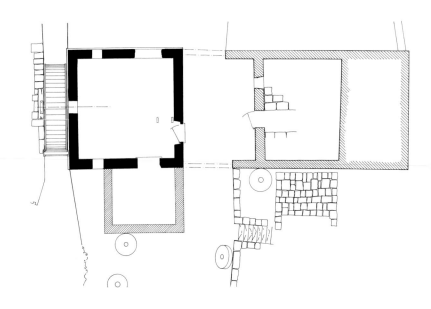

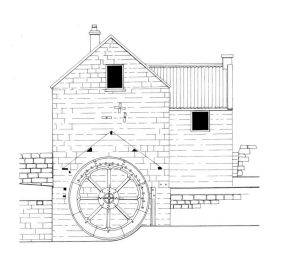

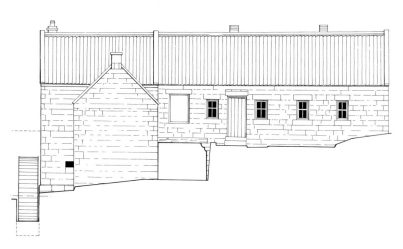

FIG 135. GLAISDALE HIGH MILL.

Andrew (1859, 1861), Robert Andrew (1862), John Maw (1872).

The mill stopped work about 1890. The mill and associated textiles building are now converted into a house. The corn mill is a small square-plan building. The undershot waterwheel is 13 feet 6 inches diameter by 4 feet, with iron shrouds and nave plates, but now no longer on its original shaft. There are five millstones on site, one of them a blue stone. The type of hurst machinery is not known.

Behind the mill there are paving stone footings of a building associated with the fulling process.

GLAISDALE LOW/CORNER, fulling, NZ 779056 (Esk)
Demolished

There has been a second fulling mill not far away. Separating the references is not always possible.

1557. William and Margaret Thompson sold the walk mill to Lawrence Hodgson (George Harland, Whitby Gazette, 24 November, 1969).

1690. One sixth part of *"Corner Walke Mill"* sold to Richard Cass, fuller, Glaisdale (G Harland, 1970, 49).

1743. *"Glaisdale. Thomas Harland of the parish of Danby, fuller, and John Harland of the parish of Egton, fuller, sold for £21 10s 6d to Thomas Wilson one half part, taken to be three days in the week, Monday, Tuesday and Wednesday in every week, of the walke mill known as Low Mill. Also one sixth part taken to be one day in the week, Thursday in every week, of the walke mill called High Mill"* (G Harland, 1970, 49).

1823. John Mackridge was the *"fuller and bleacher"* (Baines Directory).

1830. *"To be Sold. A Fulling Mill and Bleaching ground situate near Glaisdale and now occupied by John Mockridge the owner"* (Yorks Gazette, 24 July).

Glaisdale Low mill collapsed about 1878 (G Harland, 1969). The site was excavated by George Harland in 1961 and a wooden cog wheel on a 1 inch square-section iron shaft recovered (now exhibited at Tocketts mill).

EGTON BRIDGE, NZ 803052 (Esk) Converted

French monks from Grandmont established Grosmont Priory on the banks of the Murk Esk.

1200. Joanna, daughter of William Fossard *"... gave the mill at Egton, with a fishery there"* (J C Atkinson, 1874, vol 1, 201).

n d. Mill at Egton with the pond, water, fisheries, and also out of his forest at Egton, sufficient main timber, both oak and alder, for necessary repairs of the mill; Confirmation of grant by Robert de Turnham, husband of Joanna (J Graves, 1808, 287-8).

1536. *"... water mill in decay 5s ..."*; Suppression of Yorkshire Monasteries (YAS Rec Ser, vol 48).

1539. *"... the house and site of the Priory of the Friars called Bon hommes of the order of St Mary of Grandemont, lately dissolved with certain closes and a mill in Egton, For 21 years at the rent of £6 5s"*; Lease to Edmund Wright (YAS Rec Ser, vol 48, 113).

1544. License to Edmund Wright to alienate the site of the Priory of Grosmont and a water mill (*"unum molend-inum aquaticum cum pertinances apud Egton Bridge"*) to Sir R Cholmeley (YAS Rec Ser, vol 48, 114).

1801. Egton was listed as having two corn mills each capable of milling 60 bushels per week (M Y Ashcroft, 1977, NYCRO pub 15, App 3).

1848. *"... all that freehold messuage or dwelling house together with all that old established water corn mill situate at Egton Bridge, with two pairs of stones, one cylinder, Corn Screen and Blast, together with Drying Kiln, two stables, piggeries and other out buildings ..."*; Sales notice and map, 18 April (Burnett coll, 6471). Richard Garbutt completed the sale to Robert Carey Elwes on the 10th May.

Millers; John Garbutt (1822), John Cornforth (1840), Thomas Winspear (1873), executors of the will of Thomas Meade (1883), John Lee (1889), George Yeoman, (*"and Stonegate"* 1890).

There is a very large stone dam some 46m long, diagonally across the Esk. The handsome, stone-built com-bined mill and house were totally rebuilt in the 1860s. Later, the waterwheel drove the machinery of a wood-working workshop on the opposite side of the leat. The wheel was dismantled in the 1940s. The arch for the axle of the wheel into the mill survives. The corn mill and house have been converted into dwellings.

EGTON BRIDGE, fulling, Grid reference not known (R Esk)

1544. 200 acres plus *"... unum molendinum aquaticum cum pertinances apud Egton Bridge. Ac totum molend(in)um nostrum fullonicum cum pertinances in Egton ... in tenura sen occupatione Roberto Grey. Ac omnia & singula stagna, fossatas, riuous, riuolos & aquarum cursus cum lez slues & mylledammes in Egton ..."*; Conveyance of Priory lands and site to Edmund Wright for £184 13 s 2d" (J C Atkinson, 1874, vol 1 203).

1555. Sir Richard Cholmley bought a fulling mill along with other properties.

GOATHLAND, NZ 836014 (Ellerbeck), Fig 136 Converted

In 1267 the Forest of Pickering, including the plough lands of Goathland, was given by Henry III to his second son, the Earl of Lancaster.

1297. *"Mill worth 5s per annum"*; Inquisition post mortem for the Earl of Lancaster (YAS Rec Ser, vol 31, 73-4).

1301. *"Rogero Molendinario"* paid a small levy to the Lay Subsidy (W Brown, 1896, YAS Rec Ser, vol 21).

1517. *"... tenement with water mill"* rented for 10s per annum by Thomas Vesey; Manor Court Rolls, 1517-21 (A Hollins, nd, 38).

1542. *"All the lands of his Goteland in Pickering Leigh and the mill there called Mylne Place and Waterfeld in the said Duchy of Lancaster"*; grant of lease for 21 years to Sir Richard Cholmley by Henry VIII (A Hollins, nd, 38).

1604. *"... those lands and sheep pasture ... and for grinding Mill Place and Waterfelde in Goteland, alias Gotheland"*, sold by the Crown to Rt Hon Sir Robert Carey and John Barton (F W Peirson, A History of Goathland, 1985, 57)

1821. Engraving *"Goathland Mill and Bridge"*, George Nicholson.

1928. *"Not used since about 1896 ... bought by Mr Burn (the Hydro) ... who turned it into an electric light station worked by a turbine and Arnfield dynamo. Two pairs of stones taken out by Mr Burn"* (Mitford Abraham).

Millers; Frauncis Worfolke (1562), William Worfolke (1572), Richard Boyes (d 1626), Steven Boyes (d 1656), William Boyes (d 1701), James Adamson (d 1732), William Chapman (1826), John Adamson (1836), Robert Hardwicke (1836, 1841), John Garbutt (1845, 1851), James Dowson (1861, 1893, 1901).

The machinery was taken out in 1934 after a fire. The

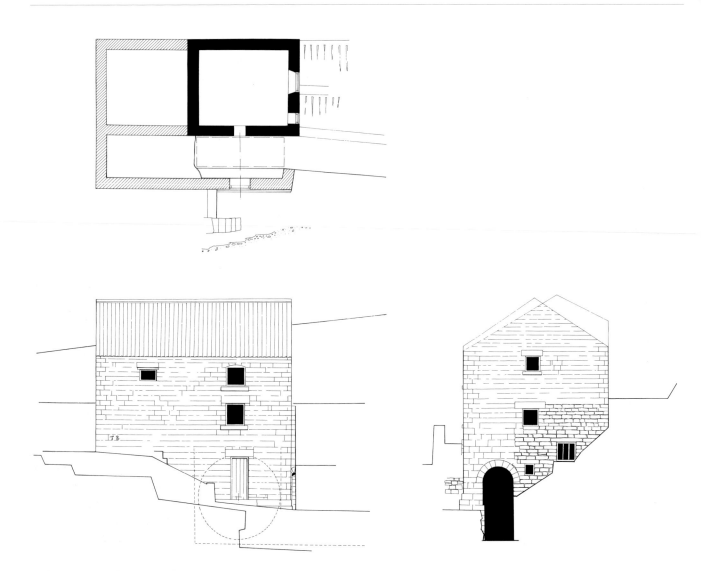

FIG 136. GOATHLAND MILL.

building is now converted to a dwelling but with the turbine preserved. An old building is enclosed within a larger early nineteenth century stone building with arched water outlet. There is a displaced datestone "IW 1716 MR" near the entrance. The roofline was altered in the 1930s. The early leat running directly from the waterfall was replaced by a later leat at a higher level.

BECK HOLE, fulling, NZ 818024 (Murk Esk)
Demolished

A fulling mill in Darnholme was mentioned in 1572 and a fulling mill at Beck Hole in 1650. In the early 1700s Adam Calverton was the fuller.

1787. *"… and all that fulling or walk mill and other messuages"*; mortage indenture, Thomas Carter and William Warner (Burnett coll, 1383).

1815. Described as *"in ruins"* (Sales notice; F Peirson, 1985).

Part of the leat survives on the nineteenth century ironworks site in Walk Mill Close.

GROSMONT, Grid reference not known (R Esk?)

Grosmont Priory was founded on land, near the Murk Esk, granted by Joanna Fossard for the Prior and Brothers of Grandmont near Limoges (1200). A mill at Egton Bridge was given at the time of foundation but the monks also built a precinct mill at Grosmont.

1536. *"The site worth 3s 4d; a water mill in decay, 5s"*; Survey (YAS Rec Ser, vol 48, 113).

1538. *"… the little overshot water mill has not gone for two years but is not yet decayed"* (W Brown, 1886, 213). There is no surviving evidence on the ground.

WHITBY

Most of the mills in this section are on tributaries of the lower Esk but mills on the coast at Newholm and Fylingdales are included because they also belonged to the Percys and to Whitby Abbey.

SLEIGHTS/AISLABY/BRIGGSWATH/GROVES, NZ 866082 (Esk) Demolished

Briggswath took its name from the bridge near an earlier ford across the Esk. There is a flagged causeway to Aislaby.

1190-1211. Reginald de Rosels, Lord of Aislaby granted the ford to Whitby Abbey, with passage through the land near his mill. In return Reginald and his heirs were to have Aislaby mill-pool on the Abbey lands (Whitby Chart, Surtees Soc, 401n; VCH, vol 2, 514). Willelmo Rosell granted *"Molendinorum et piscariae"* at Aislaby (Whitby Chart, Surtees Soc, vol 72, 400).

1724. Indenture *"...all that messuage tenement and farmhold within the Constabulary of Ruswarpe ... called*

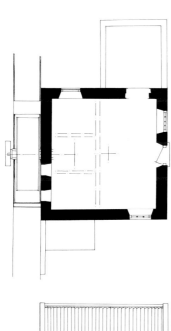

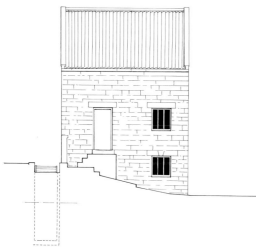

Carr End or Walke Milne Ffarme ..." (Burnett Coll, 1430).

1759. Francis Meade sold the site to John Moss who built *"the leather mill or mill for dressing leather"* on ground called Calf Close Bank; Elgie, Abstract of Title (NYCRO ZRY I, 1/17).

1794. *"... water corn mill with leather mill adjoining in Aislaby Woods"* sold to William Elgie (NYCRO ZRY I, 1/16)

1802. *"William Elgie of Whitby, ... On moveable utensils and trade in his Water Corn Millhouse and warehouse communicating, brick and stone and tiled, situate in ye Township of Whitby ... and called Grove Mill £999. Warranty against steam engine ..."* (Royal Exchange Insurance no 189613).

1817. *"On Monday night a flour mill on the banks of the river Esk, the property of Mr Elgie of Ruswarp was discovered to be in flames, which were not extinguished till the interior of the building was entirely consumed"* (Kentish Gazette, 11 February).

William Elgie then milled at Ruswarp mill. In 1821 Groves Hall and mill were bought by Henry Walker Yeoman. By 1860 the mill had been rebuilt as a steam corn and saw mill and the weir was kept for fishing only. The corn mill was equipped with one pair of French burr stones and one pair of grey stones, corn screen, dressing cylinder and hoist. The saw-mill had 5 circular saws. All were newly built and driven with an engine of 8 HP with a 10 HP boiler (Yorks Gazette, 14 January, 1860).

1879. John Hauxwell of Yarm quoted for a silk machine, elevator, brush machine and bran duster.

Millers; William Jopling; *"master corn miller"* (1881), J Craven (1893).

The dam survives as a fish weir. The mill site is obscured by trees but can be seen from the road bridge, built in 1937.

LITTLEBECK, NZ 979051 (Little Beck), Fig 137
Converted

The early nineteenth century mill has a cosmetic waterwheel built in 1961.

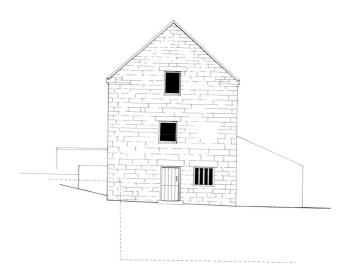

FIG 137. LITTLEBECK MILL.

1928. *"... wheel broken a day before (the visit). ... Three pairs of stones. Flour machinery intact but not worked for many years. Owned and worked by Mr Dobson who lives at Lealholm. ..."* (Mitford Abraham).

Millers; William Hill (1840), William Jopling (1865), Thomas Jopling (1872, 1879, 1889, 1893, 1897), George Jopling (1901), Elizabeth Jopling (1905), John Dugdale (1905, 1913 *"Ugglebarnby"*, 1925), Samuel Dugdale (1909), Henry Pinkney (1905, 1925).

The mill worked until 1942. It is a three-storey square-plan building, all one age, now converted into a dwelling. Except for the main crossbeam under the first floor (scuffed from a sack hoist hatch) almost all of the interior timber has been replaced. The original water-wheel was about 14 feet in diameter and 4 feet wide. There are two blue millstones on site, not necessarily belonging to this mill.

HOBBIN HEAD, rag, NZ 869057 (Iburndale Beck)
Demolished
This was working in the mid-nineteenth century. There are field names *"Hemp Sykes"* and *"Bleach Garth"*.

IBURNDALE/UGGLEBARNBY, NZ 873071 (Little Beck), Fig 138 Converted
1608. Water mill formerly belonging to Whitby Abbey still in the possession of the King in *"Ibwinedale and Eastdaleside"* was worth 10s 0d; Certificate of wind and water mills in the Office of Sir William Spencer (R Bennett & J Elton, 1900, 43).
1777. *"... messuage, water corn mill, stable and plating house in Iburndale"* in tenure of Thomas Donkin (NYCRO Deeds Reg BN 1778 81).
1855. *"... the water corn mill, messuage attached, 3 stall stable, cowhouse, piggeries, outbuildings at Iburndale, Ugglebarnby, occupation of William Hall, tenant ..."* (Yorks Gazette, 1 Sept).
1938. *"Nice old mill, overshot wheel. Two pairs of stones (one grey, one Blue). Both worked. Pair of French burrs in the yard. Flour machinery intact. Weir damaged September 1931 but still working Oct 1933. ... Wheel removed and mill dismantled and building added to cottage about 1938"* (Mitford Abraham).

Millers; William Hill (1851), James Jackson (Ugglebarnby, 1871), William Jackson (1889, 1897), R Stevenson (1899, 1901), John Dugdale (1937).

The stone-built mill building and in-line house have an eighteenth century appearance but much altered. The leat can be traced. The 12 feet diameter by 6 feet wide waterwheel was in an outshot shed on one gable wall. No evidence of the driving gear has survived.

RUSWARP, fulling
References in the Whitby Charter are confusing. There may have been two fulling mills, one at Ruswarp and one at Newholm, or there may have been one only, probably at Ruswarp. The references are included with those for the corn mill, below.

RUSWARP, NZ 888091 (Esk), Figs 54 & 58 Converted, Grade II
Ruswarp mill was built at the upper tidal limit on the

Fig 138. Iburndale mill (photo, Mitford Abraham).

Esk, the word 'warp' describing a bank of mud deposited by a river.

1086. Sometimes seen as the Domesday mill of *"Witebi and Sneton"*.

Pre 1096. It was granted by William de Percy to Whitby Abbey and this was confirmed in 1102 (*"Agge Milne, Cocchemilne, Risewarp Milne, New Milne and Fieling Milne"*) and in 1180.

1396. *"De aqua de Eske cum molend. iijli. vjs"* and *"de molend. fullonic xxxvjs viijd"*; Whitby Abbey Rent Roll (G Young, 1917, 921).

"Risewarp-Stakesby. Villa de Riswarpe et molendino cum bosco qui vacatur Le Kerr" (Whitby Chart, Surtees Soc, vol 72, 398). The editor thought this referred to the Carrs between Briggswath and Ruswarp.

"… stagni molendini de Risewarpe supra ti'ram mean in campo de Snetona"; Affirmation of gift to Whitby Abbey by Alexander de Percy son of William de Percy de Kildale (Whitby Chart, Surtees Soc, vol 72, 420).

"… molendino de Risewerp et aqua de Eske iiii li vi s viii d firm villas de Riswarp molendino fullonico ib xxxxvi s viii d."; Compotis, Brother Stephen de Ormesby and William de Dalton (Whitby Chart, Surtees Soc, vol 72, 558).

"Whitby et cira … aqua de Eske cum molendino iii li vi s viii d

Molendino fullonico xxxvis vii d"; Compotis, Brother Willelmi de Dalton (Whitby Chart, Surtees Soc, vol 72, 572).

"STAKESBY. Molendino et aqua de Eske iiii li vis viii d, novo molendino et molend fullonico xxxvis viiid"; Compotis, Brother Willelmi de Dalton (Whitby Chart, Surtees Soc, vol 72, 581).

1538. *"Risewarp. Johes Pereson tenet unum molm. aquat. Granat. voc. Rysewarp Mylne et r. p. ann. lxs"*; Whitby Abbey Rental (G Young, 1917, 931). Afterwards the Crown sold the mill to Sir Robert Cholmley.

1648. Indenture, *"… Walk Mill situate in Risewarp Carrs in the tenure of George Jackson …"* (Burnett coll, 1439).

1682. *"All those three water corne mills called Riswarpe Mill and all the salmon fishing from the said dam unto the mouth of the River Esk together with the soake and sucken … late in the tenure or occupation of John Longstaffe …"*; quoted in Assignment of Mortgage of Riswarpe Mills, 1700 (Burnett coll, 1424).

Relics of this early mill, which stood upstream from the present Ruswarp Mill, were demolished in the 1980s.

1752. A large 'bolting mill' was built by Nathaniel Cholmley, the event celebrated by a stone plaque " THESE MILLS WERE ERECTED AT THE EXPENCE OF NATHAN[L] CHOLMLEY ESQ[R] BY PHILIP WILLIAMS ENGINEER 1752". The dam may have been raised at the same time (J Graves, 1808, 286).

1765. Nathaniel Cholmley v Samuel Howlett and John Mathews of the Littlebeck Alum Works, York Summer

Assize, concerning the silting up of the Esk (Burnett coll, 1560).

1766. 99 year lease to Messrs Howlett and Mathews (Burnett coll, 1426).

1785. *"Wakefield Simpson, Henry Walker and Abel Chapman of Whitby in the County of York, and William Elgie of Ruswarp near Whitby aforesaid, merchants. On their Water Corn Mill only at Ruswarp aforesaid in their own tenure brick stone and tiled or slated £3000. Utensils and going gears in said mill £2000. Stock therein £1000."* (Sun Fire Insurance, no 5000753).

1800. *"On his Water Corn Millhouse having a kiln therein situate at Ruswarp near Whitby aforesaid in his own occupation, brick and stone built and tiled £1500. On the water wheels, standing and going gears, millstones etc therein £1000. On stock in trade £1000. Warranted no steam engine"*; insured by William Elgie (Royal Exchange Fire Insurance, no 178264).

1802. *"On a Water Corn Millhouse having a kiln therein stone brick and tiled and slated, situated at Ruswarp. … Tenant Richard Tasker, Miller, and known by the name of Ruswarp Mill £1250. Standing and going gears, millstones, etc £500. Stock in trade and utensils £250. Warranted no steam engine. Mill is on the River Esk"*; policy taken by Henry Cholmley of Howsham (Royal Exchange Fire Insurance, no 189748).

1850. The partnership between Elgie and John Corney was dissolved (London Gazette).

1854. *"To be let, the valuable Water Corn Mills known as Ruswarp Mills, containing 3 pairs of French stones, 1 pair of grey stones, and one pair of Shelling Stones etc. The mills are situated at Ruswarp on the River Esk, a mile from the Port of Whitby and close to Ruswarp Railway Station. Apply to the present tenant Mr Corner"* (Yorks Gazette, 4 March).

1907. Inventory of machinery belonging to the landlord and the tenant (Burnett Coll, 200).

1910. Francis Ley of Lealholm bought the mill.

1911. Gutted by fire (Whitby Gazette, 29 Sept). Reconstructed without the cupola and weathercock.

1924. Thomas Hay of Northallerton bought it. The two waterwheels and a gas engine were replaced in 1927 by a 100 HP turbine. Roller mills were installed.

1928. *"One 90 HP turbine replaced two wheels, 1927. Roller mill belonging to T H Hay of Northallerton. Earlier mill … in foreground"* (of photograph). *"On the River Esk and the tide comes up to the weir daily. Lighters from Whitby used to discharge from Hull direct into the mill"* (Mitford Abraham).

1937. *"The edge of the Moorland – a visit to a mill old in tradition and modern in equipment"* (Milling, 26 Nov).

Millers; Francis Burrard (1822), George Grayson (1861), George and Joseph Grayson (1865, 1879), Henry Bell (1885, 1921), Thomas and Henry Hay & Son (1925, 1937). Latterly the mill worked as a provender mill. Work finally stopped in 1962. The six-storey building was converted into flats in 1990. It was a grain store as much as a mill. A board *"Aureum Dei Donum Frumentum Molinus (We grind the corn the golden gift of God)"* is fixed to the façade.

RIGG/AGGE, NZ 911075 (Rigg Mill Beck), Fig 76 Converted

The old name derived from 'hagg' (coppiced woodland). The later name derived from the nearby Rigg Way, an important old route to Whitby.

c.1102. *"... the often named William de Percy and Alan de Percy, his son, gave to our monastery at Witeby in its earliest times ... The town and sea port of Witeby ... Agge Mylne, Cocchemilne, Risewarp Milne, the New Milne, Fieling Milne, the town of Hachanesse and two other milnes. ..."*; Abbot William de Percy's Book (L Charlton, 1779, 70). Given as *"Agge milne, Kocche-milne, molendinum de Risewarp, novum Molendinum, molendinum de Fielinga; villa de Hachenesse et dua molendina"* (Whitby Chart, Surtees Soc, vol 64, 3).

1316. Dispute settled between the Abbot of Whitby and Sir William de Percy in which the Percys were accused of throwing down the mill in order to avoid paying rents to Whitby Abbey and of building a mill, probably a windmill, for their own use in its place. In the agreement the Percys agreed to re-instate the water mill but did not have to make good the eight years of lost rental (L. Charlton, 1779, 241-2; G Young, 1817, 320-1).

1752. *"A water corn mill here was said to be greatly out of repair"* (Priv Act, 26 Geo II, cap 33; J C Atkinson, Memorial of Old Whitby, 240; VCH vol 2, 532).

1822. The owner James Wilson agreed with William Booth for the works including a 20 feet diameter waterwheel (Burnett Coll, see Text).

1933. *"Very old mill with portions of the old (overshot) wheel left on its shaft ... no stones or machinery ... ceased working about 1875"* (Mitford Abraham).

Millers; John Coulson (1803, 1825), Joseph McNeil (1839, 1854, 1865), John Robinson (1841, 1844), William Harrison (1893), John Harrison (1899).

By the early years of this century Rigg mill had become 'picturesque' and its very large waterwheel was much photographed.

The mill stands under a waterfall. It is a tall square-plan mill like several others around the lower Esk. In this case, however, the walls are very thick (some 3 feet 6 inches at ground level). The deep tailrace for the 1822 wheel had to be cut through 10m of solid rock at one point. The waterwheel which eventually replaced the 1822 wheel was 27 feet in diameter, with a ring gear mounted on the arms to drive a lay-shaft. The water trough was raised and lengthened for this wheel. A stone runnel from a tiny spring may have been for domestic use.

COCK, NZ 898088 (Rigg Mill Beck), Fig 77 Converted

The name may derive from the woodcock living in the dale. The mill may have been the mill of Whitby/Sneaton listed in the Domesday Survey.

Pre-1145. The grant of *"Cocchemilne"* (or Kocchmilne) to Whitby Abbey confirmed (Surtees Soc, vol 64, 3).

1396. *"De Cokmylne xxs"*; Whitby Abbey Rent Roll (G Young, 1817, 329).

1539. *"Rent of a water corn mill called Cock Milne demised to Wm Accelon 10s per annum"*; Dissolution Acc of Whitby Abbey (Whitby Chart, Surtees Soc, vol II, 72).

1764. John Sleightholm left the mill to his nephew John Herbert (NYCRO Deeds Reg AK 176 1764).

c.1795. Anne Masefield and John Herbert disposed of the mill to Thomas Willas (NYCRO Deeds Reg CO 114 169).

1836. Described as most picturesquely peeping from amongst *"the umbrageous multitude of leaves"* (Henry Belcher, 1836, 20).

Millers; John Coulson (1803, 1825, 1851), William Cownes (sic) (1866), William Cowens (1872).

The mill stopped work before 1900 and the waterwheel was removed to a new wheel pit alongside the pathway through Cock Mill Woods, a little way from the mill, and used for generating electricity. The mill itself was turned into a dwelling called Waterfall Cottage.

This mill, set under a 20 feet high waterfall, is an example of the tall, square-plan buildings. The external waterwheel had a ring gear on the arms driving a lay shaft.

LARPOOL, NZ 895092 (Stainsacre Beck) Converted

This short-lived mill was probably built at the beginning of the nineteenth century as a coastwise exporting mill with access to a creek in the Esk.

1837. *"... dwelling house, cottage of tenement at Larpool mill"*; agreement for letting, Captain E H Turton to Joseph Coulson (Burnett coll, 3564). Also 1857.

It survives as a house called Glen Esk with little evidence of its former use. The wheel pit has been filled in and machinery taken out. The top bearing frame for the upright shaft remains at first floor level and an iron plate for an oat roaster and a runner millstone survive in the garden.

NEWHOLM, NZ 867116 (Newholm Beck) Demolished

1145. The *"molendinum novum"* listed in early Whitby Abbey charters may have been Newholm mill at Raithwaite Hall (Surtees Soc, vol 64, 3).

1396. *"... de multura ejusd (mill dues) viiijs and the fulling mill at Stakesby"*; Bursars' Accounts but this may have been at Risewarp (G Young, 1817, 921).

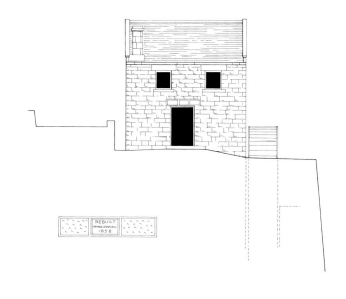

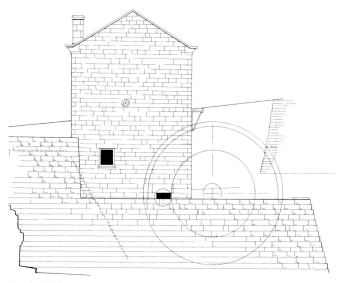

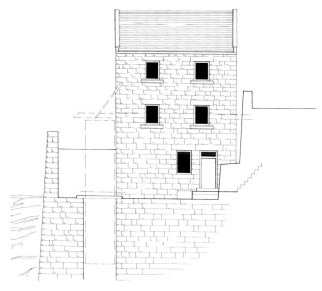

FIG 139. RAMSDALE MILL.

1539. *"... rent of a close called Rathwayte Close and a small watermill called Newholme Milne (ac. unius parvi molendini aquatica voc Newham Milne) in the tenure of John Bukkille"*; Dissolution Account of Whitby Abbey (Whitby Chart, Surtees Soc, vol 72, 735).

The mill was subsequently part of the grounds of Raithwaite Hall. The site is occupied by a garden centre and there has been extensive re-modelling of the old mill pond.

LINGERS, Grid reference not known (Lingers Beck)
"Lingers Mill on Lingers Beck" (W C SS, 740; VCH vol 1, 535). The area was known as *"Ingers Close"* (Whitby Chart, Surtees Soc, 740).

There is no later reference to a mill on Lingers Beck. However, this would have been an obvious site for a mill serving the medieval ploughed fields of the old settlement of Raw.

RAMSDALE, NZ 926035 (Ramsdale Beck), Fig 139
Converted

1102. This mill may have been the *"Fieling mill"* granted by William de Percy to Whitby Abbey along with Ruswarp, Rigg and Cock, New and Hackness mills (Whitby Chart, Surtees Soc, vol 64, 3).

1395. *"In South Fylinge ... mills there £1 0s 0d. Farm of Helwath mill there ... £1 0s 0d"* (Whitby Chart, Surtees Soc, vol 72, 570-81).

1539. *"Farm of Fyling Mylne demised to Wm Jackson"*; Dissolution Account of Whitby Abbey (Whitby Chart, Surtees Soc, vol 72).

1608 *"Whitby Monastery. Water Mill in Branesdale (sic)*

in Parish of ffylinge £0 10s 0d"; Accounts of Sir William Spencer (R Bennett & J Elton, 1900, 43).

1858 A new tall mill with a small ground plan and rusticated masonry was built on the old foundations following a flood of 6 August, 1857.

1931. *"Owned and worked by W J Brown, farmer. Thirty foot overshot wheel. Two pairs of stones. French pair worked. Dam filled in with stones and rock in the great flood of September 6, 1931. A most difficult mill to reach and to photograph"* (Mitford Abraham).

Millers; William and John Thompson (1841), William Ledstone (1840), William Leadstone (1851), John Stainthorpe (1890, 1905), Allen Hoggarth (1909).

After the 1858 rebuild, water was taken from a new dam higher up the beck and culverted under the mill track and then carried on a trough on brackets across the downstream wall of the mill to a large overshot waterwheel in an external wheel case. A ring gear on the arms drove a lay shaft. Today the building is converted into a dwelling. The upstream facade carries a datestone "REBUILT ANNO DOMINI, 1858". A new waterwheel the same diameter as the old was built in 2003.

BAY, NZ 954040 (Mill Beck) Converted

This was a large coastwise trading mill but with evidence of an earlier structure. A 1712 lease refers to *"Bay Mill or Low Mill"*.

1666. *"And all those two water corne mills commonly called or known by the name of the Upper Mill, sometimes called the Middle and Lower Mills with their appurtenances situate in Fileing and all that close of pasture and meadow ground commonly called the Nesse. ..."*; A true copy of Sir Hugh Cholmley's marriage settlement with Lady Anne Crompton (Burnett Coll, 1552).

1771. Not marked on Jefferys' map.

1839. An inscription on the front of the mill records that "THIS MILL WAS REBUILT AND NEW MACHINERY PUT THEREIN AT THE COST OF G J FARSYDE OF FYLINGDALES ESQ, A D 1839. CROSBY BUILDER, SCARBOROUGH".

1849. *"To be let with immediate possession the Robin Hoods Bay water corn mill containing two pairs of French and one pair of Grey stones with new machinery by Westwoods of Leeds"* (Yorks Gazette, 10 February).

1857. Bay mill, along with Ramsdale mill, was damaged in the August 8 flood which was so serious that it resulted in the total destruction of the dam, dwelling house and other outbuildings and the death of Elizabeth Knaggs, the housekeeper (T Whellan, 1858, Hist & Top York & N Riding Yorks, 832-3).

1931. *"Four pairs of stones (two French and two Grey). All gearing and breast wheel in good order. Ceased work in 1925. One pair of French, one pair of Grey and one German (blue) stone outside the mill door. A very good*

business long ago and boats ('billy boys') used to load and unload on shore. Miss Hammond Hutton, daughter of the last miller lives here and is the owner" (Mitford Abraham).

Millers; Thomas Lilley (1822), William Robinson (1841), James and John Hutton (1883, 1921).

The mill was built for the export of flour via sailing boats beached on the sands where the beck reaches the sea. It is a much bigger mill than that at Ramsdale. James Hutton moved to the mill about 1864 and carried on an extensive business. When he died in 1928 the mill stopped work. The buildings were leased by Youth Hostels Association in 1938 and purchased in 1951 to become the Boggle Hole Hostel.

The 1839 rebuild was an expensive project. A natural fall in a shale gorge was used as the foundation of a massive masonry dam. The lower section of this drove an overshot wheel for a two-storey mill. In the 1838 rebuild the mill became a three-storey structure with very tall floors supported on cast-iron columns. Window openings have stone lintels in the outer leaf and brick arches for the inner leaf. There was an internal waterwheel in a well-masoned wheel pit with curved breast wall, arguing that this was a pitch-back wheel. A ring gear on the arms drove a lay shaft with spindles to four sets of stones and, probably, a vertical shaft to a hoist. Infilled slots in the upstream wall show where the bevel gears were. The gearing and shafts must have been of cast-iron since they were scrapped during World War II. It seems there have been two doors in the beck side gable wall and these may have been used for loading carts standing in the bed of the beck for carrying flour to the beach. The mill house stands at right angles to and attached to the mill. After the 1857 flood the water system was made more powerful. The dam was raised and fitted with two escape valves marked "JOHN WESTWOOD, LEEDS, 1858". Water was then carried through a tunnel, lined with masonry.

SCARBOROUGH AND UPPER DERWENT

The Percys held land around Scarborough but the town itself developed as a borough to the west of the castle.

STAINTONDALE, Grid reference not known

1542. *"Robert Hogeson ... for rent of a parcel of land in Staynton called Estbekke upon which a water mill has newly been built 2s"*; Tudor Rent Roll (F C Rimington, 1988, 41-2).

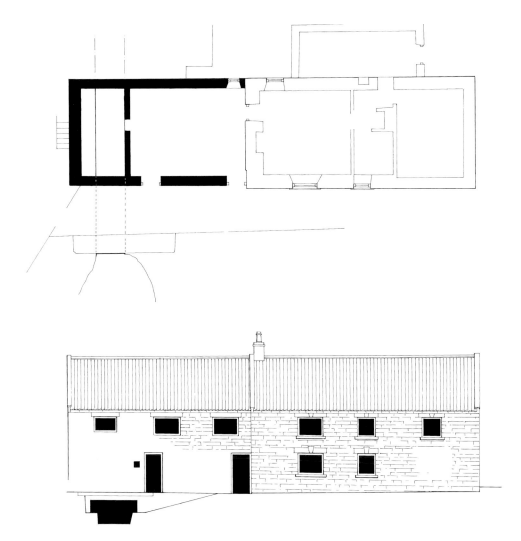

FIG 140. CLOUGHTON MILL.

CLOUGHTON, TA 010936 (Quarry Beck), Fig 140
Converted

This manorial mill stands below the confluence of two becks immediately south of the village.

1609. Cloughton mill, formerly the property of Malton Priory, was disposed of by the Crown to Edmund Ferrers and Francis Philips (Bennett and Elton, 1900, 17).

1928. *"No machinery. Water works turbine for generating electricity"* (Mitford Abraham).

Millers; Thomas Hodgson (1822), Harrison Leadley (1872, 1879), Elizabeth Leadley (1873).

The mill stopped work about 1930. It was converted into two holiday flats in 1960 and is now a single dwelling within a small housing development. It was a small mill with a waterwheel house at one end and an early nineteenth century house at the other. The wheel pit could have accommodated a wheel approximately 10 feet diameter by 6 feet. It was fitted with a Little Giant turbine which generated electricity from 1930 to 1945. The runner of this turbine survives; also four worn millstones and two segments from a cast-iron pit wheel. The building is obscured by extensions and alterations. The drawings record pre-conversion features.

SCALBY HIGH, TA 022906 (Scalby Beck), Fig 141
Shell

1610. Two water mills of Scalby and the water mill at Langdale End on Scalby Beck were disposed of to Edmund Ferrers and Francis Philips; Pat. Jas. 1, pt xxxi-ij, no 1 (R Bennett and J Elton, 1900, 42-3).

1800-10. A 5-mile Sea Cut, made to the designs of Sir George Cayley to deflect flood water from the upper Derwent to the coast, delivered a much enhanced water supply to Scalby and Newby mills. It is reasonable to suppose that the fine new sandstone High Scalby mill was built to exploit this.

1833. *"To be sold by Private Contract. All that Water Corn Mill situate about two miles from the town of Scarborough, called Scalby High Mill, worked by three pairs of stones of different dimensions, with a corn*

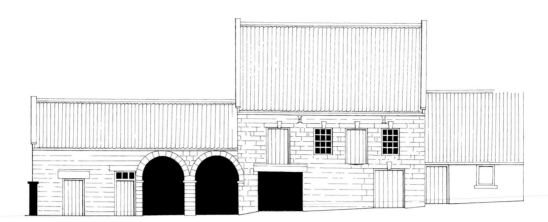

FIG 141. HIGH SCALBY MILL.

screen, fan, Barley Mill etc. Apply to Mr Joseph Robinson at the Mill" (Yorks Gazette, 18 May).

1834. *"To be sold by auction by order of the assignees of Joseph Robinson, all that Water Corn Mill ..."* (Yorks Gazette, 17 May).

Millers; J Pearson (1822), Joseph Robinson (1840), Andrew Wilkinson (1873), Archer Wilkinson (1872, 1893), John Redland and William Wilkinson (1897), B S Wilkinson (1925).

Scalby High mill survives as a shell with the mill house attached. It is a handsome two-storey building, formerly with an internal waterwheel. Evidence of the gearing has not survived.

NEWBY, TA 027907 (Scalby Beck), Fig 142 Demolished

Newby mill stood near the road-bridge on the south side of Scalby Beck alongside the weir forming the sill of the Sea Cut.

1928. *"Flinton's Mill ... Three pairs of stones. One pair in use. Centrifugal silk dresser in ruins. Formerly a very good business and house by the bridge (White House). Ceased to work January 1933. ..."* (Mitford Abraham).

1939. The mill was burned down (Manchester Guardian, 26 April).

Millers; Nicholas Lupton (1822), T Flinton (1855), William Flinton (1879, 1889), Robert Gough (1893).

FIG 142. NEWBY MILL (PHOTO, MITFORD ABRAHAM).

The site is now cleared. The mill was a double-pile, three-storey plus loft structure aligned along the water-course. There was an adjacent mill house.

SCALBY LOW, TA 036908 (Scalby Beck) Converted

This mill used Scalby Beck immediately above the shoreline. Much of its product went by boat to Scarborough.

1164. A mill worth £6 per annum belonged to the Crown and continued in the possession of the Crown; Pipe Rolls, ii Henry II, Pipe Roll Society 46 (VCH vol 2, 477).

1609. The Crown disposed of two mills in Scalby to Edmund Ferrers and Francis Philips; Pat. 7 James I, pt. xxxiii, no 1 (R Bennett and J Elton, 1900, 42-3).

1622. Information was given that corn was being sent from Scarborough to Scalby mills to be ground instead of to the town mills; Scarborough Corporation Records (J B Baker, 1882, 250).

1798. Described in *"Journal and Tour to Scarborough"*, 32 (VCH, vol 2, 479).

The mill was damaged by fire in 1821 and part of the mill house was used as a tea room by 1829. The external waterwheel survived in 1840. The *"... romantic ideas created by the sound of the water mill ..."* were noted in 1845 (Storry, Strangers and visitors guide to Scarborough).

Miller; John Ireland (1840).

SCARBOROUGH, TA 041881 (Falsgrave Beck) Demolished

From 1136 the farm of the town was held by the burgesses. The port was held by the king. Scarborough Low mill was situated on a site now occupied by the Scarborough Valley bridge. It was the lowest of four mills on Falsgrave Beck.

1086. *"Scogerbud ... William de Percy holds this of the Bishop (of Durham) ... a mill"*; Domesday Survey (M

Faull and M Stinson, 1986). The nearest village was Falsgrave. The mill of 'Falls Griff' eventually became known as Scarborough Low mill.

1201. *"The King granted the men of Scarborough, the town of Scarborough and Falsgrave, the mills and other appurtenances at 'the old farm', viz £33 for Scarborough and £10 for Falsgrave"* (Cal Rot Chart 1199-1201, Rec Comm 85b; VCH vol 2, 550).

1235. *"The free flow of water both to and from the mills"* at Scarborough were guaranteed; Chronicle de Melsa, vol ii, 62 (Percy Chart, Surtees Soc, vol 117, 65; K J Allison, 1970, 8).

1275. The burgesses of Scarborough had built *"certain houses and mills"* in order to aid and protect the development of the town and harbour (Cal Pat Rolls, 111; A Rowntree, 1931, 115).

1314. *"When Scarborough was in the King's hands in 1314-15 the burgesses begged for an inquiry as to which of the mills lately built by them at their own expence in the town belonged to themselves and which the King"* (Parl R, i 310a; VCH vol 2, 553).

1320. *"There were four water mills and a windmill belonging to the Crown in 1320"* (Rental Survey, Gen Ser, bdle 17 no 52; VCH vol 2, 553).

1330. *"4 watermills and a windmill"* were worth £16 per annum (A Rowntree, 1931, 553).

1660. *"In 1660-1 the inhabitants knew of only one windmill pulled down in the Civil War and three ancient water corn mills at which before the War all the inhabitants were in theory obliged to grind their corn"* (Exch Dep, Hil 12 & 13 Chas II, no 1; VCH vol 2, 553).

1710. *"A water corn mill, fulling mill and other tenements in Scarborough and Scalby were conveyed by Edward Hinderwell and others to William Hinderwell, sen, and William Hinderwell, jun, in 1710-11"* (Ft of Fines, Hil, 9 Anne; VCH vol 2, 550).

The mill was pulled down in 1820 to enable road widening. Sketches made at the time of demolition show a two-and-a-half storey building with a wooden compass-arm waterwheel (Scarb Reference Library). A 4 feet blue stone is set into the pavement where the mill stood under the bridge spans. The millpond has been landscaped.

HARWOOD, SE 945881 (Jugger Howe Beck), Fig 143
Derelict

This apparently eighteenth century mill stands behind the Mill Inn. Nineteenth century millers had a smithy, wheelwright's shop and a limekiln.

1934. Restored by Robert Upton, one time manager of Buchanan's Mill in Birkenhead (pers comm, Mrs McGreggor).

1936. *"... overshot wheel works one pair of grey stones occasionally ..."* (Mitford Abraham).

Miller; John Stonehouse (1840).

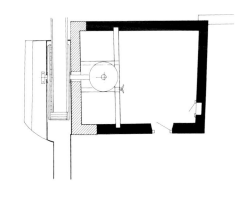
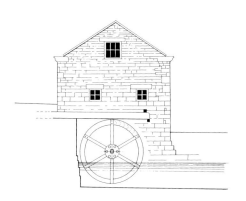
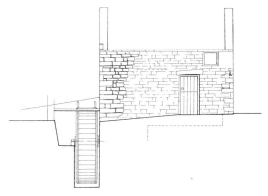

FIG 143. HARWOOD DALE MILL (PHOTO, MITFORD ABRAHAM).

The 11 feet diameter by 3 feet 5 inch overshot water-wheel with cast-iron shaft is in an external shed, now roofless. In the Upton restoration there was a single pair of stones but in an earlier arrangement there were two pairs. The waterwheel gable wall was rebuilt in the nineteenth century. The floor of the mill and the centre of the waterwheel are below ground level. The very humble stone-built, two-storey plus loft building has few windows. The leat is three quarters of a mile long with no pond. After the 1934 restoration it was found to be short of water.

TROUTSDALE, SE 916874 (Troutsdale Beck), Fig 74
Part preserved

This is an attractive millstead with important though incomplete hurst machinery.

1619-21. (Hon Pick ij 46: VCH vol 2, 425n).

C17. It belonged to the families of Ison of Troutsdale, Theakston and Constable (VCH vol 2, 425n).

1845. *"To be sold by auction. Troutsdale Corn Mill near Scarborough, now in the occupation of Mr John Coulson ..."* (Yorks Gazette, 2 August).

1928. *"... delightful little spot ... this mill is owned by Mr Illingworth who has put in a new overshot wheel. Two pairs of stones (blue and grey). The tenant works the grey pair"* (Mitford Abraham).

The mill worked until 1938 and the wooden clasp-arm waterwheel survived until into the 1970s.

Millers; John Coulson (1819, 1841), William Coulson (1851), Robert Barker (1861), Joseph Coulson (1862, 1867, 1879), John Coulson (1873).

The range contains the mill, two mill houses of different ages and farm buildings. The waterwheel had been approximately 13 feet by 2 feet. There is a lay shaft to two sets of millstones in a very cramped hurst.

HACKNESS, SE 968899 (Lowdales Beck), Fig 144
Complete, Grade II

Two mills were granted to Whitby Abbey at the initial grant. Later, one became a fulling mill. The later corn mill was the last working water mill in the region. It survives complete.

Pre 1096. *"... villa de Hachnesse et duos molendina"* granted to Whitby Abbey (Whitby Chart, Surtees Soc, vol 64, 3).

1320. One mill was referred to as the *"upper mill"* (NYCRO ZF 1/1/6).

Nd. *"ii molend aquat ix s nuper in tenure Ric Redhed"* (Whitby Chart, Surtees Soc, vol 72, 747).

1396. *"Farm of mills, £3 6s 8d";* Compotis, William de Dalton (G Young, 1817, 920; Whitby Chart, Surtees Soc, vol 72, 570-80).

1539. *"... two water mills, a cottage and closes in the tenure of William Proctor, 105s 4d. Farm of one fulling mill demised to Wm Porter, 6s 8d";* Dissolution Acc (Whitby Chart, Surtees Soc, vol 72).

1550. *"There is belonging to the said manor 2 water mills and an walke mylle, the said 2 watermills in the occupation of Ingram Proctor for 60s per annum and the walke mylle in the occupation of Henry Braidthwaite and Maulde 6s 8d";* Survey of Hackness Lordship (NYCRO ZF 3/3/1 mic 95).

1807. George Nicholson made a pencil sketch of Hackness mill, quite different to the present structure (York City Art Gallery).

1928. *"... three pairs of stones (two worked). No flour dresser ... oat roller. Overshot wheel (iron)"* (Mitford Abraham).

Millers; Anne Robinson (1851), Thomas Robinson (1861, 1871, 1881, 1891, 1897), G Robinson (1901), David Hayes (1905, 1913), Henry Pateman (1921, 1925).

The mill is on the Derwent estate. The two-and-a-half storey building has been raised at the eaves, probably to accommodate the gearing for the over-driven millstones. The west gable contains masonry of an older building. It was last used in 1973, by the present tenant A Lockey. Water came from a large ornamental pond below Hackness Hall. The 17 feet by 4 feet 6 inch waterwheel, installed between 1900 and 1905, carries the cast inscription "J & L HORSFIELD ENGINEERS LEEDS". It has a combination of cast-iron and tension arms, different on each side, with iron shaft, cast-iron shrouds and sheet iron buckets. It was not designed for Hackness mill, since it has brackets for a ring gear, not needed at Hackness. The pit wheel is cast-iron, packed to fit the waterwheel shaft. The wooden upright shaft is older than the waterwheel. Three sets of millstones (two sets of greys and one set of burrs) were overdriven.

HACKNESS, fulling, Grid reference not known

The fulling mill was on record from 1301 to 1550 (see above). There is no evidence of a separate leat.

AYTON, forge, SE 982874 (Derwent) Demolished

c.1798. *"Ayton Forge"* engraved by J Walker, artist J Hornsey.

1800. *"At Ayton near Scarborough are furnaces and forges for casting and working run and malleable iron"* (J Tuke, 1800, 313).

1817. *"... there was an iron forge, a few years ago, in the Vale of the Derwent, between Hackness and Ayton"* (G Young, 1817, 819).

EAST AYTON/CASTLEGATE, fulling, SE 990852, Fig 41
Demolished

1301. Bartholemew the fuller at Ayton was taxed 6s (W

Brown, 1896, YAS Rec Ser, vol 21).

1768. *"Banks Fulling Mill Garth"* in East Ayton Enclosure Act (F C Rimington, 1964. A note on the fulling industry in the Scarborough District, Trans Scar Arch Soc, vol 1 no 8, 20-21).

The site was excavated in 1964 (F C Rimington, 1965, Trans Scar & Dist Arch Soc, vol 1 no 8, 13-31).

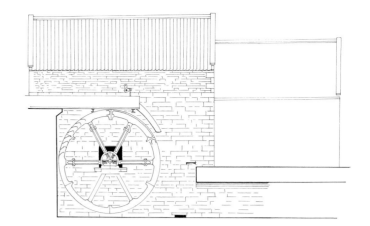

WEST AYTON/DERWENT, SE 988849 (Derwent), Fig 108 Shell, Grade II

The present mill was built in 1843. The medieval mill is thought to have been 50m downstream but on the same watercourse. There may also have been another mill below the bridge.

1086. *"... one mill of 5s ... Aytune"* held by William de Percy; Domesday Survey (M Faull and M Stinson, 1986).

1301. Alan the miller paid 22s and Robert the miller 21s in West Ayton; Lay Subsidy (W Brown, 1896, YAS Rec Ser, 21, 57).

1705. Sarah Hewley granted most of her manor in West Ayton to trustees for the maintenance of dissenting ministers (VCH, vol 2, 443).

1928 *"Undershot wheel and shafting cogged to the wheel rim. Three pairs of stones ... two in use"* (Mitford Abraham).

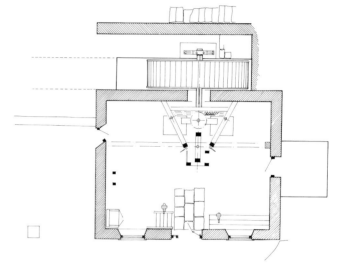

Millers; Richard Robinson (1822), John and Henry Robinson (1840), Francis Prince (1872, 1879), John Britain (1889, 1893, 1909), J Hardy (1913), Thomas Halliday Charter (1921, 1933), Ernest Elsworth (1937). There are references to Alfred Tindell, corn miller, in East Ayton in 1873 and 1893.

The mill was last worked in 1960. The Prince family bought it as sitting tenants in 1980 but the machinery had already gone.

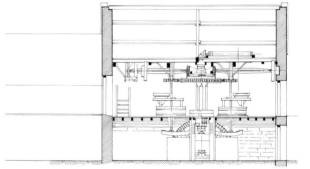

This is a very spacious and handsome building with some machinery. Castings were by "HARKERS, DRIFFIELD". Like many of this vintage it has a fireplace. The floors are supported on cast-iron columns.

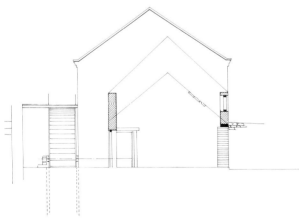

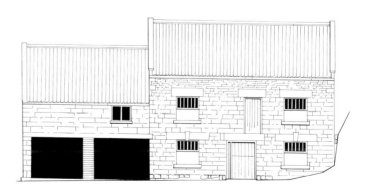

FIG 144. HACKNESS MILL.

The roof couples are similar to those of small textile mills. The waterwheel, formerly in the right hand of the two wings, was 12 feet in diameter and 7 feet wide. The pit wheel ran in a circular recess cut into the pit wheel wall and drove a pinion on a lay shaft to three pairs of stones and a vertical shaft. A wooden pattern for the pit wheel is preserved.

A finely carved stone slab in the central window recess on the top floor carries the Hewley coat of arms but is older than the building. A very similar slab, dated 1700, is set in the Warden's house at Lady Hewley's Hospital in York.

DIP SLOPE VILLAGES AND PICKERING

Most spring line settlements along the foot of the dip slopes of the Tabular Hills from West Ayton to Sinnington had mills in medieval times. In addition, Pickering was an important castle town.

BROMPTON, SE 945820 (Brompton Beck) Converted
A number of small springs from the Corallian limestone feed directly into the mill-pond, pounded behind a 9 feet high dam.

1086. A mill belonged to Berenger de Toni; Domesday Survey (M Faull and M Stinson, 1986).

1235. A mill was *"appurtenant to the manor"* of the Vescys (Ft of F, Yorks 19 Henry III no 17; VCH vol 2, 425n).

1314. *"Manor of Brompton … one water mill £10 per annum (unum molendinum aquaticum de feodo predicto, et valet per annum xli")*; held by William de Vescy from John de Mowbray (Percy Chart, Surtees Soc, vol 117, 220-2).

1569. George Donkyns and George son of Ralph Pollard of Pollard Hall, Bishop Auckland made settlements of tenements and water mill, Brompton (VCH vol 2, 427).

1804. Sir George Cayley observed milling in his mill at Brompton (Hodgson J E, ed, 1933).

1928. *"… worked by turbine which also pumps water to the village"* (Mitford Abraham).

Millers; William Elgie (1822), George Dowsland (1873), George Hoggarth (1893).

The mill stopped work in 1952/3 and was converted into a house. Part of the clasp-arm waterwheel with its square-section wooden shaft is submerged in the pond.

EBBERSTON, SE 897823 (Ebberston Beck) Converted
This mill was driven by Bloody Beck emerging from the southern end of the dry Kirkdale.

C12 & C13. The Hastings family, lords of the manor of Allerston, had rights in the mill (VCH vol 2, 436).

1202. 10s rental from his mill was granted by William, son of Rabell, to Alan Bushell, lord of Hutton Bushell (VCH vol 2, 436).

1272. Two mills in Snainton Ings belonged to the de Boynton family.

1291. Prioress of Wykeham, as guardian to Simon Oghtred's heirs, was called on to warrant a third of *"two mills in Ebberston"* to Philip le Gunneys and his wife (YAS Rec Ser, vol 17, 228; VCH vol 2, 436).

Nd. Thomas Barry gave the mill called Godive to Yedingham Priory (VCH vol 2, 436).

1617. An annuity from the mansion house in Ebberston and *"two water mills and the mylne house"*; grant by Sir Rd Etherington to his son, Thomas (NYCRO ZPK 32 mic 1628).

1885. John Hauxwell quoted for removing a silk machine from Allerston mill to Ebberston mill (John Hauxwell's Letter Books).

1928. *"… worked by turbine. One pair of stones. Makes electric light for own use …"* (Mitford Abraham).

Millers; Christopher Rodgers (1822), John Ward (1873), William Ward (1893).

The mill stopped work in 1939 and was converted into a dwelling by 1949. Part of the ground floor of the mill is preserved as a cellar but with no evidence of the driving machinery. The much altered, stone-built mill was originally of two-and-a-half storeys, of narrow span and probably late eighteenth century in date. The millpond is landscaped. One grey and one burr stone are preserved in the garden.

ALLERSTON, gunpowder, SE 878830 (Allerston Beck)
See J G Rutter, 1962, Trans Scar Arch Soc, no 9, 23-5.

ALLERSTON, fulling, SE 878824 (Allerston Beck)
See J G Rutter, 1962

1436. The Hastings family had both the corn mill and fulling mill at Allerston.

Early C17. *"… two corn mills and a fulling mill"* (YAS Rec Ser, vol 53, 120; VCH vol 2, 423n).

Later it became known as the Bleach mill.

ALLERSTON, SE 878828 (Allerston Beck), Fig 145
Shell, Grade II
This fine mill stands in the main street of Allerston. Water came from springs in Givendale.

1227. Maude, daughter of Cassandra, sued Walter de

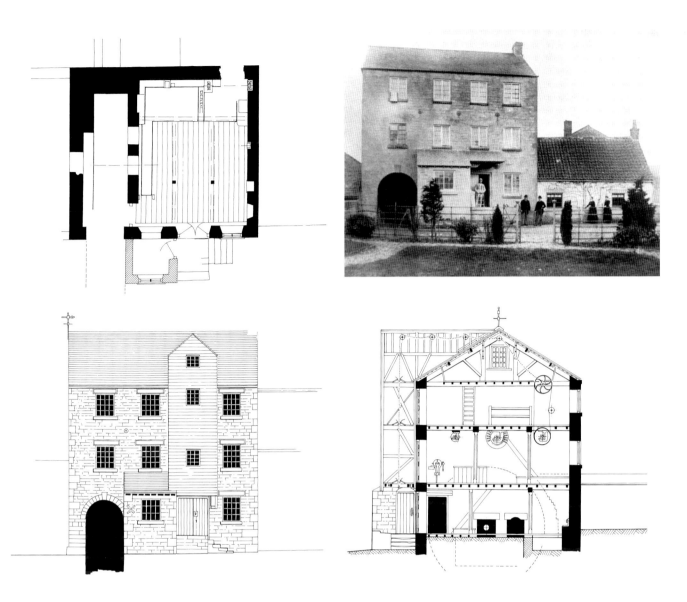

Fig 145. Allerston mill (photo, in possession of Mr Turnbull).

Savage respecting the mill and four oxgangs (VCH vol 2, 422n).

1231. Maude gave the mill to the Knights Templar of Foulbridge (VCH vol 2, 422n).

1322. The mill was listed in the possessions of the Templars when the order was dissolved; Hon of Pickering, IV, 202 (VCH vol 2, 422n).

1436. Water mill and fulling mill followed the descent of the Hastings manor from 1436 (Chan Inq p m, 15 Henry VI, no 58; VCH vol 2, 423n).

1879. John Hauxwell quoted for the removal of the silk machine to Ebberston (John Hauxwell's Letter Books).

1928. *"... worked by turbine. Two pairs of stones. Roller plant not worked since 1922"* (Mitford Abraham).

Millers; Timothy Ruston (1822, 1840), William Ward (1872, 1893 *"and Ebberston"*, 1897, 1901), George Turnbull and Sons (1933).

The waterwheel was supplemented by a gas engine and then replaced by a vertical shaft Gilkes turbine (c.1920, in turn taken out c.1954). Roller mills were installed but flour milling stopped at the end of World War I. Charles Turnbull bought the mill from the Cayley estate in 1920. Provender milling stopped about 1960.

Allerston mill is a handsome stone building, 29 feet by 26 feet internal dimensions, with later lucam. The attached mill house was built about 1890, replacing an old thatched house. Keld water from Givendale fed a long pond with a retaining wall alongside the village street. The mill was probably short of water. The pitchback waterwheel was about 17 feet in diameter, and drove a lay shaft. There are six millstones in the garden.

ELLERBURN HIGH, paper, SE 852844 (Thornton Beck)
1681. Richard Warren son of William Warren of the Paper Mill was baptised on 6 March (Thornton Dale Parish Registers).

207

1773. The Ellerburn High Paper mill was rebuilt by John Hill (J G Rutter, 1969, Trans Scar & Dist Arch Soc, vol 2, no 12).

1786. *"... farm in Thornton called Ellerburn High Paper Mill or Ellerburn Warren"* (York Courant, 5 December). By 1851 three beating engines were still in use and a *"paper maker and farmer"* was listed in the census returns.

The buildings were known as Musdale House in mid-nineteenth century. There is a large pond and a seventeenth or eighteenth century building. The buildings were used as a farm and are now the centre of a fish farm.

ELLERBURN LOW, paper, SE 847842 (Thornton Beck)

1685. *"... newly erected paper mill in Thornton parish"*; Glebe Terrier.

1696. Jane, daughter of William Long of *"ye Waste Paper Mill"* baptised 31 May (Thornton Dale Parish Registers). In 1834 one of the paper mills had a Fourdrinier patent machine. The mill ceased work about 1869. A leat and a single storey building survive. The site is now used as a fish farm.

ELLERBURN, fulling, SE 841841 (Thornton Beck)
Demolished

1335. *"... a water mill worth and paying 53s 4d, a fulling mill (molendinum fulreticum) occupied by ... Robinson worth and paying 20s and a common oven paying 3s"*; Inquisition post mortem for William Latymer of Thornton Dale (N R Rec Ser, new series, S 11, 273-4).

1710. *"... a fulling mill and cottage with a little hemp yard"*; Survey or Terrier of the Manor of Farmanby etc in the possession of the Dean and Canons at Ellerburn (R W Jeffery, 1931, 257).

1741. John Marshall, *"fuller and bleacher"* (R W Jeffery, 1931, 109).

Thomas Boyes was described as the bleacher in 1818 but work ceased soon after 1830. The site is near to the ancient church of Ellerburn. The leat is still in evidence and the house and some outbuildings survive.

THORNTON DALE, SE 836834 (Thornton Beck) Shell
This large mill is a prominent feature of the Thornton townscape.

c.1200. *"... William the miller at Thornton ..."* (Whitby Chart, Surtees Soc, 64, 131; R W Jeffery, 1931, 112).

1275. *"... held of the Lord (Crouchback, Earl of Lancaster) three carucates of land with appurtenances in Kingthorpe, by service of keeping the Forest of Pyckering and it is worth with the mill 12s and three pounds of cummin and one pound of pepper"*;

Inquisition post mortem for Alan, son of Godfrey (R W Jeffery, 1931, 263).

1323. There was a mill of Kingthorpe, probably Thornton (Chan Inq p m, 16 Wdw II no 20; VCH vol 2, 470).

1335. *"... water mill worth 53s 4d per annum, a fulling mill worth 20s and a common oven"*; Inquisition post mortem for William Latymer (Chan inq p m, 9 Edw III; N Riding Rec Soc, new series 2, 273-7).

1506. *"The manors of Farmanby and Esthallgarth ... two mills ..."*; grant by William Hastings to the Dean and Canon of the Royal Free Chapel of St George, Windsor (R W Jeffery, 1931, 250).

1618. Water corn mill *"in heads in Farmanby"*; grant from Sir Richard Cholmley to John Robinson, rector (R W Jeffery, 1931, 238).

The corn mill and the fulling mill passed to the Hill family in 1669.

1685. *"Only there hath been usually paid 5s for one corn mill by Mr John Hill due at Easter each year and 2s for another mill in the occupation of Anthony Champly"*; Glebe Terrier. One of these may have been at Ellerburn.

1889. *"Considerable extensions have recently been made to Mr Boye's flour mill at Thornton Dale. About twelve months ago Mr Henry Simon applied the new roller mill machinery, the system being arranged to work in conjunction with the old millstones, all worked by a water wheel which dates back from the last century. A few months ago, however, the system was applied in its entirety, and the water wheel replaced by a Simon's 'Action' turbine. The first sack of flour was made on the 8th August"* (The Miller, 2 September).

1910. *"To let. Corn Mill situate at Thornton Dale, near Pickering, Yorks, together with water power, suction gas plant, two pairs of millstones and one and a half sack roller milling plant, dwelling houses and thirteen acres of land"* (The Miller, 3 October).

1919 "THIS MILL WAS REBUILT AND ENLARGED BY C F G HILL AD1919" (inscribed stone on facade).

1929. *"Messrs T Burgess & Sons Ltd. ... Top floor and roof built 1920-21. Up-to-date roller plant but one pair of grey stones grinds for farmers (Barley meal etc). Turbine and suction plant"* (Mitford Abraham).

Millers; William Rogers (1733, 1739), Richard Porrit (1777), Joshua Priestman (1822, 1845), John Frank (1857), John, William Gibson (1867, 1872), Mrs E Gibson (1879), John Boyes (1889, 1893), Thomas Mann (1897), John Cussons (1901, 1910), James Cook (1911, 1913, 1919), T Burgess & Sons (1925, 1933).

The Burgess family of Kirkby Fleetham mill had Thornton mill from 1914 and remodelled it from a 2-sack Simon mill to a 4-sack in 1921. The mill was bought from the Hill family in 1947. In 1984 BOCM installed machinery in the building and ran it as a provender mill.

There are three buildings linked together, an older

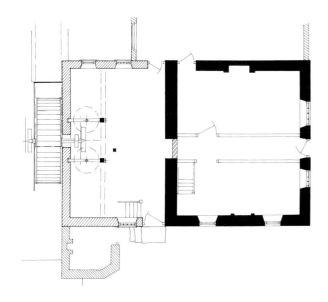

building facing the road but with a similar building behind. In 1919 it was raised in height. There is also a fine mill house. Interestingly, the substantial earth dam post-dates medieval rigg and furrow.

THORNTON LOW, SE 834823 (Thornton Beck)

1594. *"... messuage, mill and cottage"* rented by William Horsley; Farmanby Terrier and Rental (Windsor Church Commissioners, 117122).

1650. *"Water Corn Mill called the Low Mill"*; Parliamentary Survey (Windsor IV A 4).

LEVISHAM, SE 835902 (Levisham Beck), Fig 146
Converted

This mill is in the dale between the villages of Levisham and Lockton.

1246. Ralph gave Thomas half a mark yearly rent from his mill at Levisham in return for Haukesgarth giving up any other claim to the mill. Thomas to have power to distraint in case of default of payment on *"... the iron of the said mill"*; settlement of dispute between Ralph Bolbeck and Thomas de Haukesgarth (Ft of F, 264, 121, 30 Henry III no 121; VCH vol 2, 450).

1252. Mill worth 10 marks per annum; Inquisition post

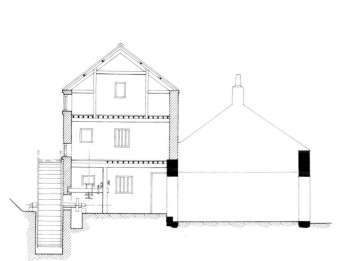

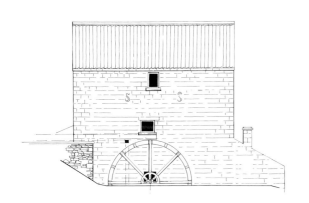

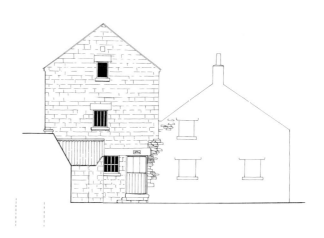

FIG 146. LEVISHAM MILL (PHOTO, MITFORD ABRAHAM).

mortem for Ralph de Bolebeke (YAS vol 21, no 131).

1255/6. 20 acres of land and 16 acres of meadow and a mill to Malton Priory; Grant by Ralph Bolebec (B Mus, Cott MS, Claud D XI fol 116-118d: VCH vol 2, 451).

1276. Peter Toley of Driffield and John, son of William de Marske, claimed the mill and half the manor against Earl Roger but made no progress (VCH vol 2, 450).

1856. Robert Skelton, Lord of the Manor was in financial difficulties and sold out. (Betty Hulse, 2003, Levisham, a case study)

1935. *"Three pairs of stones work regularly …"* (Mitford Abraham).

Millers; Thomas Russell (1872), William Thompson (1840), Joseph Rowntree (1840, and Pickering), George Middleton (1873), Matthew Coultas (1889, 1893), Arthur Duesbury (1897, 1913), Robert Hamond (1921, 1925), T Hawnby (1922, 1937).

The mill last worked in 1963 and the gearing was removed in 1976 (York Excavation Group Report). This is a fine example of a mid-nineteenth century water mill (dated 1846) and backs onto an eighteenth century house. The surviving 15 feet diameter overshot water-wheel with cast iron shrouds, arms and naves is marked "H BENSON. MAKER. RUSWARP" and was installed in 1904. The upright shaft with cast-iron mortise wheels is now missing. There were three sets of stones - one set of burrs and two sets of greys (W Hawnby, 1986, pers comm). Some items are now in the Raindale mill in the Castle Museum in York. A shaft from the crown wheel drove a straw chopper and winnower.

RAINDALE/NEWTON, SE 813923 (Raindale Beck), Fig 147 Demolished

This was the medieval mill of Newton-on-Rawcliffe, a planned village on the edge of the Tabular Hills. It may have ceased working for some centuries since one account says there was a house on the site of the mill until the mid-nineteenth century.

1836. Illustrated as a one-and-a-half storey thatched

FIG 147. RAINDALE MILL BEFORE REMOVAL TO YORK (PHOTO, MITFORD ABRAHAM).

building (Henry Belcher, 1836, opp 59).

1848. *"To be sold by Auction. All that water corn mill with appurtenances situated at Newton near Pickering and now occupied by William Bulmer, tenant. Apply Mr Thomas Hill, Newton, the owner"* (Yorks Gazette, 17 June).

1925. *"New wheel made and put in by Boulton of Pickering who owns this mill. Last worked by Henry Boulton (son of James) in 1921. Two pairs of stones, iron pit wheel. Roof put over the wheel (overshot and all of wood) 1909. Saw bench at back of mill worked by Henry Boulton. Very ancient mill and numerous pack horse tracks to it from moorland farms (Stape, Saltergate etc also very steep track from Newton and Levisham …"* (Mitford Abraham).

Millers; Thomas Hill (1840), John Smith (1872, 1873), William Sawdon (1890s), Henry Boulton (1900).

The mill stopped work in 1921. It was given to the Kirk Collection and removed to The Castle Museum, York in 1953. It opened to the public in 1966. The stone-built, two-storey plus loft mill is probably of the early nineteenth century. It has a 14 feet diameter hexagonally arranged clasp-arm waterwheel, wooden upright shaft and clasp-arm spur wheel.

PICKERING HIGH/NORTH, SE 797845 (Pickering Beck), Figs 6 & 44 Shell

Pickering was an important defensive site and market town, which passed from the Crown to Simon de Montfort, to the Duchy of Lancaster (1262) and back to the Crown (1326). It had three water mills. The north mill under the Mill Tower and castle walls was almost certainly the earliest.

1201. The vill, with the market, mill and stock; grant by King John to the *"men at farm"*; Cal Rot Chart 1199-1266, Rec Comm, 85; Yorks Inq p m (YAS 111 72-5; VCH vol 2, 468).

1298. Edmund, the Earl of Lancaster had two water mills in Pickering as well as a water mill at Goathland (YAS Rec Ser, vol 31, 73-4).

1611. *"North Water Mill and South Water Mill, Pickering, £13 per annum"*; Minor Speculative Purchases; James I to John Wilson and Robert Morgan (R Bennett and J Elton, 1900, 26).

1702. The lease of both mills at Pickering was held by Anthony Collcott at £13 per annum. Colcott tried to revive the ancient Crown monopoly on milling and to force the local inhabitants to have their corn ground at his mills. However, there was strong opposition, led by prominent townspeople, Sam Harding and John Jackson, and the case before the York Assizes was dismissed in 1702 (John Rushton, Points of View, Pickering Gazette and Herald, Sept 9, 1976). Subsequently Colcott sold the mills to Harding and Jackson.

1810. *"Mill at Pickering"*, engraving by George Nicholson of Malton showed the mill as having two waterwheels and sluices supported on a wooden frame.

1832. *"To be sold or let. A well accustomed and old established Water Corn Mill situate at Pickering, known by the name of High Mill, with two water wheels, a plentiful supply of water and all Machinery for driving three pairs of stones, viz, one pair of French stones 4 ft 4 in, one pair of gray 4 ft 8 in and one pair of blue stones 4 ft together with cylinder, corn screen, barley mill etc. The present tenant, Mr Christopher Lyon (who has had a lease for the last seven years and is declining business) will show the premises. Further particulars from Mr Robert Pierson of Middleton, the owner"* (Yorkshire Gazette, March).

1834. Advertised with similar wording except that the tenant was then William Strickland and *"The property is near the termination of the Railway from Whitby to Pickering, which passes within a few yards of the mill"* (Yorkshire Gazette, January). The mill was advertised again in 1845, 1847 and 1856.

1885. John Hauxwell of Yarm provided a quotation for new machinery to Mr Windle the occupier (J Hauxwell's Letter Books).

1928. *"Two pairs of stones worked by one wheel. Two pairs of French stones formerly worked by ruinous wheel on side nearest mill. Sam Baker ceased to work the mill in 1931 and in 1932 W Lumley (corn merchant) of York took it over and started grinding again"* (Mitford Abraham).

1953. *"Today the mill is a branch of the Yorkshire Farmers Ltd and Mr W Lumley is the master ... there are two pairs of stones, one pair of French and one pair of greys. ..."* (William R Mitchell, A day I spent in Pickering, Dalesman, vol 15, 231).

Millers; John Richardson (1789), Richard Simpson (1793), Pearson & Pennock (1822), John Pearson (1840), Matthew Metcalfe (1866, 1873), J & E Windle (1872), J A Cowley (1889), Thomas Peirson (Manager for the High Mill Co Ltd, 1893), Samuel Baker (1897, 1925).

The mill last worked in 1958 and today it is empty. It is a tall three-storey building which has been raised to provide storage. Its monumental facade has prominent string coursing, rusticated stonework and three loading doors. The wheelhouse behind the mill used to contain two waterwheels. Relics of older brick buildings survive in the northern gable wall. The dwelling house is attached to the rear of the wheelhouse.

PICKERING SOUTH/LOW/VIVERS, SE 796833
(Pickering Beck), Figs 6 & 148 Converted, Grade II

To the south of the town Pickering Beck flows across flat ground. It drove a second mill variously known as *"nether mill"* c.1562, *"South Mill"* by 1611, *"Lower Mill"* in 1745 and *"Beavers Mill"* 1841. The site was variously

FIG 148. VIVERS MILL, PICKERING (PHOTO, MITFORD ABRAHAM).

used for corn milling, fulling, paper-making and then corn milling again.

1298. Edmund, Earl of Lancaster, had two water mills worth together £20 in Pickering (YAS Rec Ser, vol 31, 73-4).

1321. 3s 4d rent of two mills in Pickering (PRO SC 6/1085/12).

c.1562. William Methau *"... felled and caryed awaye in Dauby (Dalby) sixe Timber trees of oak, but this was for repairing of the Queen's nether mylne of Pykeringe and by warrant of John Bradde, Surveyor of the Queen's woodde there"* (R W Jeffery, 1931, 289).

1619/21. John Norden, Deputy Surveyor General to the Crown surveyed the Crown estates in Pickering and inquired after the present condition of any mills, including a *"ffullinge mill of xiiis iiid rente"*, at Pickering but the local people denied any knowledge of it (N R Rec Ser, new series, 1, 38).

1758. *"... water corn mill now to be used for working leather and for fulling, with the condition that no corn be ground there"*; lease Isaac Harding and others to James Boddy (S McGeown and J Rushton, 1989, Mills on the Costa, 22).

1777. Pickering Low mill *"now a paper mill"*; agreement between James Boddy and John Hood, bleacher, and William Wharton, gent over a half share (S McGeown and J Rushton, 1989, 23).

1797. *"House and Water Corn Mill adjoining lately erected on land in Pickering purchased by Thomas Hind and Wm Piper, gent"* mortgaged by Thomas Hind of Hutton Rudby, miller, to John Taylor of Foxton, yeoman (NYCRO Deeds Reg, CN 1796-7).

1800. *"Near Pickering is a mill for making coarse paper"* (J Tuke, 1800, 313).

By 1801 the new miller was the Quaker, Joseph Rowntree.

1834. *"To be let. ... The well accustomed Water Corn Mill, in extensive business, situated near Pickering. Apply to Joseph Rowntree, Pavement, York or to John Rowntree, Low Mill, Pickering"* (Yorks Gazette, 12 April).

1842. Mill *"... lately occupied by Joseph Wardell and Joseph Rowntree, now by Thomas Sowerby"*; mortgage by Thomas Sowerby to Thomas Mitchelson of Pickering, Esq (NYCRO Deeds Reg HC 1842-44).

1857. *"Sale at the Black Swan Inn, Pickering, Low Mill, Water corn mill, house, garden, stabling, piggery, corn screens, cylinder etc ... occ. of Thos Sowerby"* (Malton Messenger, 7 Feb).

1929. *"Owned and worked by A Boddy & Sons of Kirkby Mills. Three pairs of stones (one French and two Grey). Two other pairs in the bottom floor not worked. Centrifugal dresser (silk) used for stone ground flour. Iron undershot wheel"* (Mitford Abraham).

Millers; Windle & Co (*"steam Roller Mills & Beavers"*, 1893), J C Rivis (1901, 1925), G A Boddy & Sons (1933). Vivers mill is a fine four-storey plus loft building of four different stages of stonework with attached mill house, standing in Paper Mill Lane. There is a datestone, 1844, in the back wall. Last worked by Ryedale Farmers in 1967

it was converted into a dwelling over a number of years starting in 1975, but retains some machinery including the large undershot waterwheel with 32 wrought iron buckets, cast-iron shrouds, arms and nave plates set on an iron shaft. The iron pit wheel, designed for fitting to a wooden shaft, drove a wooden upright shaft, square-section below and turned above. The cast-iron hurst frames are marked "HAUXWELL MILLWRIGHTS YARM 1870". There is one set of Derbyshire greys.

PICKERING LOW, SE 793826 (Pickering Beck), Figs 6 & 149 Converted, Grade II

A third mill was built on a new site at Pickering by the Duchy of Lancaster. It took over the name *"Low Mill"*. In legal documents the distinction between the old Low mill or South mill and the new Low mill is not always clear.

1801. Joseph Rowntree owned the old South mill and was also tenant to the Duchy of Lancaster at the new Low mill (J Rushton, 1977, pers comm to Tom Cooper).

1928. *"New waterwheel put in 1927. Only one pair of stones worked ..."* (Mitford Abraham).

Millers; Ann Rowntree (1822), John Rowntree (1834), Joseph Rowntree (1840), William Harris (1851), John Parnaby (1872), Ann Sellars (1893), Sellars Bros (1901, 1913), George Sellars (1921, 1925). The Rowntree family lived here in 1920 when one brother, Joseph, went to York and started the Rowntree chocolate empire.

Pickering Low mill is a tall three-storey plus loft structure originally housing both mill and house, of early nineteenth century date. It had a 17 feet 6 inches diameter wooden waterwheel along one of the long walls and a 10 feet diameter clasp-arm spur wheel, now preserved in the Ryedale Folk Museum. The mill was built on a relatively poor site with a low head of water and it was built

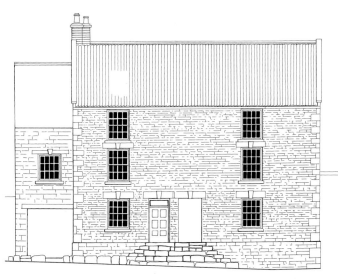

FIG 149. PICKERING LOW MILL.

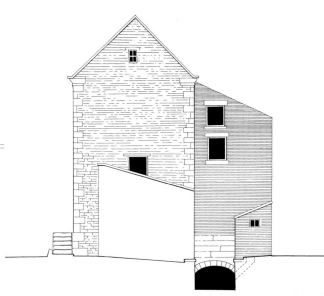

with its ground floor 4 feet above ground level to clear floods. Floorboards on the 1st and 2nd floors are over 2 inches thick with few joists beneath.

COSTA HIGH/AISLABY, SE 777839 (Oxfold Beck), Figs 15, 42 & 69 Preserved, Grade II

Two mills were built on Costa Beck, a medieval water-course replacing the winding Oxfolds Beck flowing from Keld Heads. Both mills belonged in early times to Middleton, Cawthorne and Wrelton. Later, Costa High mill was the corn mill of the township of Aislaby.

1260. A *"… closed piece of land land called Miln Holme"* in Aislaby; grant by Hugh le Bigod to the church of St Mary in Malton in return for lands in Levisham (Cal Charter Rolls, vol 2, 1275-1300).

1628. Aislaby corn mill left by widow Lady Marshall to her son Arthur Marshall (S McGeown & J Rushton, 1989, 17).

1671. *"… one cloth mill"* and *"my corn mill called Costay Mill in the parish of Middleton, in fee"*; bequest by Samuel Marshall to his son and daughter (S McGeown and J Rushton, 1989, 17).

1758. *"… a water corn mill now to be used for leather and fulling. … It is only to grind corn with the consent of the occupier of Costa Mill"*; leased by Isaac Harding to James Boddy (Doc 31,7,1758, Beck Isle Museum; S McGeown & J Rushton, 1989, 23).

1793. *"Water Mill commonly called or known by the name of Costa Mill … formerly used as a corn mill and afterwards converted into and now occupied as a fulling mill. …"*; one tenth share conveyed by Richard Simpson to Batty Tuke of Beverley on condition that no corn would be ground there (NYCRO ZRM 16; S McGeown and J Rushton 1989, 24).

1797. *"Messuage, mill adjoining called Upper Costa Mill upon the River Costa, ground of four acres called the Bleaching Ground"*; sale of shares by James Pennock *"tanner of Pickering"* to John Campion *"of Lower Costa Mill, Middleton, bleacher"* (Deeds formerly in the possession of Yorkshire Water Authority).

The mill was then rebuilt as a corn mill.

1928. *"Hood's Mill and a busy little business. Undershot wheel. Three pairs of stones. Flour dresser not used since 1912"* (Mitford Abraham).

Millers; John Hood (1822, 1841, died 1846), John Hood (1855-1913).

The mill was sold to the Ouse Valley Water Authority in 1941 but the Hoods remained as tenants until 1961. The mill stopped work in 1960.

The well-preserved mill has a datestone "I S 1819" over the main entrance. The ground plan masonry indicates its former use as a combined corn and fulling mill eg. evidence for an earlier waterwheel outside the south east gable and a blocked, arched exit similar to that for the surviving wheel. A pair of blue stones survives in the ground floor.

The early eighteenth century house in-line with the mill contains a set of crucks and was still thatched in 1885. Ground floor windows retain window seats. The upper floor was a partitioned chamber.

As built in 1819 the mill had two sets of millstones but the hurst was later extended. The sluice gate is raised by a roller and chains and the mill retains its wooden under-shot clasp-arm waterwheel and wooden upright shaft. The National Rivers Authority (now the Environment Agency) built a new wooden pit wheel, designed to fit with the very coarse gearing of the 1819 cast-iron wallower. Some machinery survives in York Castle Museum.

COSTA LOW/MIDDLETON, SE 776837 (Oxfold Beck), Figs 15, 42 & 150 Converted

This was the ancient township corn mill of Middleton. It became a flax mill, then reverted to corn milling.

1266. Hugh Bigod the holder died and his successor Eustace de Pert brought an action against Hugh de Hagwortheham, Adam de Bulmer and Bernard de Bergh and others of the Wrelton estate to force them to use the mill at Middleton (YAS Rec Ser, vol 82, 163). He brought a similar action against William de Pickering and the Prior of Malton to force them to do suit at the mill *"as they ought"* (YAS Rec Ser, vol 81, 24).

1617. The manor of Middleton and water mill; conveyance, Thomas Middleton and his son Thomas to Thomas Danby, Michael Metcalfe and Thomas Danby (YAS Rec Ser, vol 58, 92).

1743. Thomas Robinson of Cropton stated in a letter to J Hill of Thornton Dale that he was resolved to build *"a mill for fulling cloth upon a branch of the Costa"* (S McGeown and J Rushton, 1989, 25).

1797. *"Sale … modern built messuage, barn, stable and outbuildings, water mill used as a bleaching mill upon River Costa, three parcels inclosed land upon part of which buildings are erected … estate of George Grayson, bankrupt"* (Yorks Gazette, 5 December).

1849. To let *"All that Water Corn Mill known as Costa Mill … with a never failing supply of water. It contains two pairs of French Stones, one pair of Grey stones, Barley Mill, cylinder and screen"* (Yorks Gazette, 27 January).

1855. *"To be let. All that Water Corn Mill known as Costa Mill upon the River Costa. It contains two pairs of French stones, one pair of grey stones, barley mill, Cylinder, and Screen. Apply to Mr John Pearson at the mill"* (Yorks Gazette, 10 February).

1860. *"To let. Costa Mill … containing 3 pr of stones and all requisite machinery for the same, with a never-failing spring of water for the use thereof. Apply John Pearson, Costa, Pickering"* (Yorks Gazette, 10 November).

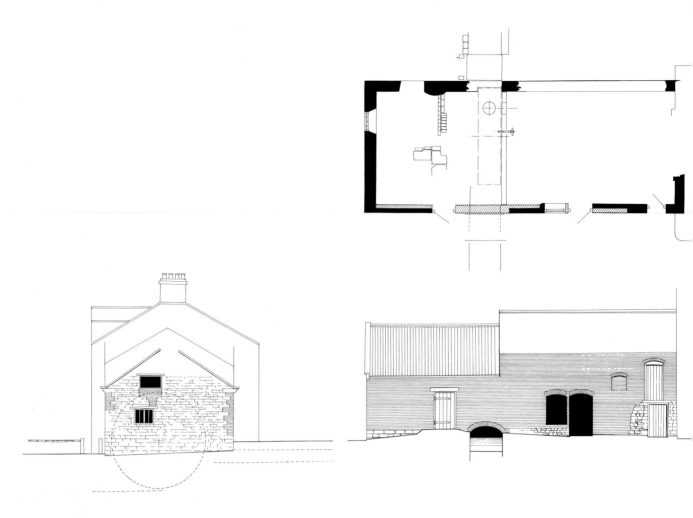

FIG 150. COSTA LOW MILL.

1928. *"... worked by turbine, but only does a little grinding for the owner who lives alongside ..."* (Mitford Abraham).

Millers; Robert Tate (1851), George Allanson (1857), William Meggeson (1863), Alexander Robertson (1871), Thomas Stephenson (1872, 1889), Robertson and Stephenson (1890).

Latterly, the 16 feet diameter waterwheel inside the building drove a water pump which continued in use after the wheel was replaced by a vertical axis Francis turbine. Milling ceased by 1937. Costa Low mill could not be run if Costa High mill dammed back the upper race.

The original two-storey mill straddling the watercourse was partly raised to four storeys. There is an in-line two-storey house. The top two storeys were removed in 1944 and the remaining two storeys converted into a dwelling in 1994. The lower courses of both buildings are of limestone with the upper courses of hand-made bricks. The plan of the mill with the very large wheelhouse is similar to that of Costa High.

KIRKBY MISPERTON, Grid reference not known (Costa Beck or Derwent?) Demolished

1086. A mill worth 5s 6d belonged to Berenger de Todeni; Domesday Survey (M Faull & M Stinson, 1986).

1145-55. *"... mill of Kirkby Misperton for 20s yearly. No reduction in rent in case it be broken down or burnt, but timber will be provided from the Forest of Spaunton for its repair";* demise by Abbot Savary to Peter and Hugh, clerks: Chartulary of St Peter's, York (Farrar ed, Early Yorks Charters, vol 1, 476-7).

1324. Granted by Richard de Kirkby Misperton to John de Dalton of Pickering (Ft of F, Yorks, 17 Edw II no 63; VCH vol 2, 444).

1594. Thomas Phelippe had a water mill in Kirkby Misperton (Yorkshire Fines).

SEVEN

The Seven flows from the head of Rosedale through the Tabular Hills to Sinnington and then out into the open land of the Derwent valley.

THORGILL, SE 709965 Demolished
This post-medieval mill was built in a dale-side gill. It survived into the ironstone mining era but finally gave way to competition from Rosedale mill.
1773. Two water mills in Rosedale; purchase by William Garbutt of Lastingham. The vendor of Thorgill mill was John Dawson, miller (NYCRO ZEL 2/15 mic 1526, frames 564-5). Garbutt then sold to John Peirson.
1820. *"Township Mill"* (R H Hayes, 1971, 31).
1838. *"Mill"* (Tithe Map).
1853. *"Old Mill"* (Ordnance Survey 1st Ed, 6 inch).
It was sold to the Guardians of the Pickering Union in 1872 and taken over by the Rosedale and Pickering Co-op Independent and Prudential Society in 1875. It was given up in 1882.
1894. *"Old Mill now Two Cottages"* (map in possession of Janet Dring, Hartoft).
According to one source the building was commenced in 1850 but was never finished. Latterly, it was known as the *"Co-op Mill"*.
The surviving dam provides a head sufficient for an overshot wheel. The *"mill now two cottages"* survived as ruins in the 1970s. A building of herringbone dressed masonry 28 feet long and 14 feet wide appeared to have a waterwheel shaft hole in one gable. On the other hand, R H Hayes thought that a smaller and older building immediately downstream had been the mill (Trans Scar Arch Soc, No 12, 40).

ROSEDALE, SE 725958 (Seven), Figs 26, 27 & 106 Shell, Grade II
The mill is the on the site of the Rosedale nunnery mill.
1330. First mention (Ft of F, Yorks, 52 Henry III, no 121; VCH vol 2, 453).
1570-1. *"... manor of Rosedale, late in the possession of the late Earl of Westmorland ... the site of the late priory of Rosedale with all buildings ... with a water corn mill, four crofts called Kilnegarth, Mylnegarth, Barkerhousegarth and Kirkegarth"*; grant to Ambrose, Earl of Warwick (NYCRO ZBA 5/1/13 cal).
1576. *"The Queen, plaintiff and Ambrose, Earl of Warwick ... Manor of Rosedale, 40 messuages, 6 mills with lands ..."* (YAS Rec Ser, vol 48, 152).
1609. *"Tenants at Lease, Thomas Watson; site of late Priory ... capital messuage called the Manor House of Rosedale and the water corn mill, £4 per annum"*; Survey of Rosedale (PRO E 315 vol 22 ff 80-91).

C 17. The Victoria County History gives the following references; Ft of F, Yorks, 52 Henry III; Mich 15 Jas I; Hil 11 Chas I; Yorks Fines, Tudors, YAS ii 88, Mich 20 Chas II; Chan Inq p m 25 Edw I w 25a, Trin 1 Anne; 23 Edw III 1st nos, no 75 (VCH vol 2, 453).
1773. Two water mills in Rosedale purchased by Wm Garbutt of Lastingham, miller (NYCRO ZEL 2/15).
1796. *"Watercorn Mill and Messuage or Dwelling House"* occupied by John Peirson; William Hardwick of East Side, Rosedale, sold to John Wilson, miller, Guisborough.
nd. Single storey, thatched mill with external water-wheel; engraving by William Richardson, published by R Sunter, York.
1853. The old mill was rebuilt (inscribed stone "GEORGE WILSON 1853" over doorway). Some elements of the old mill, including a stone bearing, were presented to the Gatehouse Museum in Newcastle upon Tyne (R H Hayes, 1985, 31).
1928. *"Old mill house on right ... lowered four years ago. Turbine replaced overshot wheel thirteen years ago. Three pairs of stones (two French and one grey). Dresser not used since 1912. Saw bench in front of mill. Dynamo put in nine years ago ..."* (Mitford Abraham).
Millers; George Wilson (1840, 1872), Joseph Acconley (1890, 1893, 1897, 1908), W Milner (1909, 1937).
This is a finely built mid nineteenth century mill. It incorporates a dated stone "FC 1667" in the front wall. The old leat from Northdale Beck was probably augmented by a bigger leat from the Seven near Waterhouse Well at the time of the rebuild. The final part of the race was by cast-iron pipes, flanges of some of which can be seen protruding above ground in front of the nearby nineteenth century terrace. The tailrace is culverted under the yard. The 14 feet 6 inches diameter pitch-back wheel was replaced by a Gilkes turbine (No 2620) which drove belts to an adjacent barn for generating electricity until 1956. Formerly the three sets of millstones were driven by an upright shaft with a crown wheel driving three overhead lay shafts on the first floor. There was probably an oat roasting plate. The mill house to the right of the mill pre-dates the mill.

ROSEDALE, fulling, SE 738944 (Seven) Demolished
There are foundations and a leat cutting across a loop in the Seven below Mill Farm. Richard Medd of Hartoft was described as *"weaver and fuller"* in 1712.
1844. On August 23 a young man was killed in *"... a fulling mill at Rosedale. ... He was perching a blocking or woolen warp, when by some means the piece caught him, taking him along with it on the flywheel, wrapping his whole body within its fold, except his legs, which were left sticking out one side, and which were consequently entangled in the machinery and both broken. ..."*

(Stamford Mercury, 23 August).

1858. *"Old Mill"* on map; On the deposit of magnetic ironstone in Rosedale, Nicholas Wood (North of England Institute of Mining Engineers, 1858-9, vol III, opp. 89).

SPIERS BANK, HARTOFT END, blast furnace, SE 753931 (Hartoft Beck) Demolished

Slag heaps, earthworks, dam and pond indicate an early blast furnace.

LOW ASKEW, SE 744897 (Ings Beck) Shell

A spur of land within the Spaunton boundaries running to this site may indicate a medieval steading belonging to the 'dry' village. A barn mill was built in the nineteenth century by Mr Gill of Sutheron Lodge (pers comm, W Featherston, Lastingham, 1976).

The tenants of Spaunton had to repair the mill of Spaunton (St Mary's Charter, York Dean and Chapter Ms 16 A, f 179).

1837. *"To be sold by auction. A Water Corn Mill with one pair of Blue Stones, one pair of Grey ditto, Barley Mill and Dressing Mill, situate at Lastingham in the county of York. The mill is almost entirely new, and is built of the best stone and cemented. It is well watered and the dams are new"* (Yorks Gazette, 29 July).

1928. *"... threshing machine worked by the wheel, also one pair of grey stones. Pair of old German blue stones against wall of wheel house"* (Mitford Abraham).

There was a wood and iron waterwheel roughly 14 feet in diameter by 3 feet in an outshot to the barn. It drove one set of stones, a thresher and a straw chopper via a ring gear and a hexagonal section upright shaft (W Featherston, 1976, pers comm). Later the wheel drove a generator. Work ceased about 1948 and the machinery was taken out in 1962

LASTINGHAM, SE 729905 (Hole Beck), Fig 57
Preserved, Grade II

This was probably the mill of Lastingham monastery. After the monks moved to St Mary's Abbey in York they retained possession of the Lastingham lands.

1538. *"Rents and farms in Lastingham, Richard Eston 30s 0d, Watermill"*; Dissolution Survey of St Mary's Abbey, York, 1538-40 (PRO SC6 4595).

1599. *"... cottage, garth and lime pit; cottage and meadow close; mess and three closes, 2 garths and close called Ryding; water corn mill with soken and grist belonging to it; all in Lastingham ..."*; mortgage for £400 (NYCRO ZDA DDDA 2 cal).

1759. *"Water corn mill with dwelling house belonging and adjacent to the mill called the Mill Stable"*; and again in 1773, 1776, 1796.

1775. *"All that Water Corn Mill with a Dwelling House,*

Outhouses and a parcel of ground being at Lastingham ... now occupied by Peter Pratt, the owner"; Sale Notice (pers comm, 1998, Isabel McLean).

1776. *"John Cook of Lastingham in the parish of Appleton, miller, mortgager, and John Sigsworth of Haram, mortgagee. ... On their water corn mill at Lastingham aforesaid and in the tenure of the said John Cook, thatched, £100"* (Sun Life no. 367432).

1929. *"Not worked for about twenty years. Machinery (including flour) and overshot wheel intact. Shed on right was formerly the kiln for drying oats. One pair of stones removed to Kirby Mills (Boddy)"* (Mitford Abraham).

Millers; John and Barker Potter (1872), John Watson (1890), Jackson Cook (1893).

The original water leat from Hole/Eller Beck is now filled in. In the eighteenth century watercourses were cut from Loskey Beck to serve Bain Wood Farm and from Hole Beck to serve Camomile Farm. Both were deflected below both farms to supply water via the 'Mill Race' to supplement the old leat at Lastingham.

This is a small 2-storey mill with a ground plan 20 feet by 15 feet. There is an attached mill house, probably of late eighteenth century date, and a stable, part used as a dwelling, on the other side of the wheel-house. Steps to the hurst platform are of masonry. The outer leaf of the wall between the waterwheel and the hurst has been rebuilt. The roof has been raised from the thatch pitch at the front but not at the back. The iron pit wheel was disposed of during World War II. Apart from this the mill is a well-preserved example of early eighteenth century lay-out. The all-wood, clasp-arm waterwheel, 14 feet diameter by 2 feet 6 inches, drove a short wooden lying shaft via a cast-iron wallower to two sets of millstones. The sack hoist was driven by rope from the waterwheel shaft. One set of 4 feet diameter blue millstones remained on site in the early 1990s.

CROPTON, SE 747889 (Cropton Beck/Seven), Fig 151
Complete, Grade II

This mill was driven by leats from Cropton Beck (Little Beck) and the Seven.

1349. *"In demesne ... a water mill, £4 13s 4d"*; Inquisition post mortem for Thomas Wyke of Lindell (PRO C 135/97).

1884. Mill renovated, possibly by Wards of Hull. Iron waterwheel replaced wooden wheel of 1820 (Matthew Clarke, 1976, pers comm).

1887. House rebuilt on the site of a cruck-built house (R H Hayes, 1974, pers comm).

1928 *"Formerly a good business, but its position at the bottom of Cropton Bank and the bad road makes it very difficult for motors to reach it. Large iron overshot wheel ... In great flood of September 1927 water rose to 16 ft*

FIG 151. CROPTON MILL (PHOTO, W HAYES, C1930).

and came through the mill and house at 3.30 am. Set wheel in motion but luckily it got blocked by a piece of timber" (Mitford Abraham).

Millers; George Morley (1822), William Bearcroft (1872), Robert Page (1873), James Thorpe (1893, 1897, 1905), James Rymer (1909, 1913), John Hebden (1921, 1925). Mill worked until 1938-9. Damaged by floods in 1945. The three-storey mill has a hipped roof and three doorways set above each other in a gable wall. The 16 feet diameter waterwheel drove three pairs of stones and a vertical shaft via a lay shaft.

APPLETON, SE 746878 (Seven), Fig 62 Shell

This mill may have been a combined corn mill and fulling mill.

1236. *"Demise by William, son of Savari de Apelton to Thomas de Lin ... of his myll at Apelton, with multure and suit for 3 years ... at a rent of 5 marks of silver ... and 12 hens yearly to the Lord of Cropton. The lessor will keep up the mill and pond"* (Yorks Deeds, YAS Rec. Series, vol xii, 97).

1538. *"Rents and farms in Appleton, Lionel Endson 40s. Farm of water corn mill with 4s 0d to King's bailiff of Cropton. Farm of fulling mill 10s 0d, Thomas Burton"*; Dissolution Survey of St Mary's Abbey, York, 1538-40 (PRO SC6 4595).

1566. *"1 water mill commonly called Appulton Myll with a close commonly called the Myll Home (2 a) in the tenure of John Bonnell"*; Alienation (PRO C66/1024).

1728. *"Water corn mill upon River Seven, belonging to Appleton, with the soak, millstones, pick axes ..."*. The owner was Thomas Grindwell (NYCRO ZPF 1).

1742. *"Water corn mill, malt kiln, messuage ..."*; Thomas Ross to Jane Brotton and Mary Brotton (Appleton deeds, in possession of J & M Allison).

1775. *"John Thompson of Appleton Mill will show premises"*; Sale Notice for estate in Cropton (York Courant, 16 May).

1780. *"... that newly erected messuage and corn mill in ownership and occupation of John Thompson ..."*; mort-gage confirmed (Appleton deeds).

1790. *"Sale, water corn mill called Appleton Mill ... John Tate, tenant, John Thompson, owner"* (York Courant, 2 Feb).

1794. *"New erected messuage, barn, stable and out-buildings, water corn mill adjoining ... occ. of John Tate. ..."*; mortgage redeemed by John Thompson and John Harding (NYCRO Deeds Reg, CL 1794-96).

1810. *"Newly erected house, barns, stables and out-buildings, water corn mill adjoining in Hamley, late occupation of John Tate"* (NYCRO Deeds Reg, DM 1810-11).

1814. *"Appleton Mill. Sale at the White Swan, Pickering. Dwelling house, stable for six and buildings adjoining, also water corn mill attached to the house, drying kiln adjoining, new erected building adjoining mill capable of being converted into a good stable, chamber above. Mill latterly put into repair at considerable expense ..."* (York Herald, 14 Feb).

1856. *"Appleton. Tenders for Mill Dam to be erected over Seven at Appleton Mill near Pickering."* (Malton Messenger, 2 Aug).

1900. The mill started grinding pig meal and eventually became a pig farm (R H Hayes & J Hurst, n d, 54).

1929. *"One pair of stones, but two pairs on ground floor (one dated 1771). Circular saw formerly in use. Threshing machine also in mill ... very old mill. New shaft put into wheel October 1929"* (Mitford Abraham).

Millers; John Tate (1797), Robert Sigsworth (1806), Thomas Dowson (1840), Thomas Rounter (1851), William Milestone (1887), Frank Todd (1888), Charles Dowthwaite (1890).

The mill stopped work in the mid 1940s. The corn mill is on one side of the wide water leat and a barn (possibly the early fulling mill) formerly containing a threshing machine on the other. The wooden waterwheel was rebuilt to the old design by Charles Marwood in 1929. All mill machinery is dismantled but the sack hoist drum is preserved in the barn. Five millstones, including two basalt and two French stones, and a barley millstone remain on site. The attached house dates from the time of J Thompson (c.1770).

APPLETON, fulling (Seven)

1538. *"Farm of fulling mill 10s 0d, Thomas Burton"*; Dissolution Survey, (PRO SC6 4595).

The fulling mill may have been on the corn mill site. There is a 'Tenter Garth' in the valley below Hamley Farm.

SINNINGTON, Grid reference uncertain (Seven)
Demolished

1180. A right of way for wains and for pack horses *"... from the ford on the road from Appleton to Sinnington down the valley to another ford near my mill, and so by the river bank through the middle of the town of Sinnington"*; Grant by Roger de Clere to St Mary's Abbey (Early Yorks Charters, ed Farrar, 1, 457).

1335. *"... ruined water mill"* was appurtenant to the manor; Chan Inq pm, 9 Edw III, 1st nos, no 51 (VCH vol 2, 489-92).

The medieval Sinnington mill appears to have been near an area called *"the Buttes"* (situated at SE 741868); St Mary's Charter.

There are remains of a leat and building under Hob Hill Bank (SE 744869) (Madge Allison, 1987 and 2007). On the other hand, the St Mary's Charter, 1180, describes a ford on the road from Appleton to Sinnington (probably at SE 737865) and a second ford *"near my mill"* (probably SE 740867). Again, it has been suggested that the partly buried late eighteenth century bridge on Sinnington village green may have been built over an early mill leat, later maintained as a flood channel (J G McDonnell, 1966, Ryedale Historian, No 2, 50-53).

SINNINGTON GRANGE, SE 739841 (Seven), Fig 109
Complete, Grade II

1844. A fine mill (five-bay, four-storey plus undercroft and roof loft) was built on an entirely new site by Mr Hartas of Wrelton, with a beam engine built slighty later to supplement a wide undershot wheel and machinery *by "W WESTWOOD & SONS MILLWRIGHTS 1845 LEEDS"*. The façade carries a plaque "SINNINGTON GRANGE MILL MDCCCXLIV".

1929. *"The Grange Mill owned and worked by George Turnbull & Sons. Mr Dan Turnbull lives here and his brother Charles at Allerston Mill. Fine mill. Five pairs of stones, including two French pairs. No flour made since before the War. Most flour machinery taken out. Breast wheel. Steam engine was formerly housed in a small building on right, which is now the office. Engine done away with when they discontinued making flour"* (Mitford Abraham).

Millers; Thomas Hartas (1840), John Hartas (Bankrupt 1850), J & T Hartas (1868), John Hartas (1872), George Turnbull & Son (1893, 1937).

From 1951 the mill was used as a dryer for locally grown grain destined for Thornton mill. The steam engine has gone but the cast-iron waterwheel, 16 feet diameter by 9 feet, remains. The drive was via an intermediate shaft and a horizontal lay shaft to six vertical spindles driving millstones and ancillary machinery. The floors are of two-and-a-half inch thick boards supported on cast-iron columns.

SINNINGTON, Grid reference not known (Seven)
This site may have been that of a grange mill of Yedingham Priory.

1826. The *"Water corn mill and threshing machine and water race in the Seven river at Sinnington Grange ... in the occupation of John and Thomas Hartas"*; conveyance to Thomas Hartas of Sinnington Grange, gent (NYCRO Deeds Reg FC 1825, 6).

1929. *"The old mill was worked by a member of the old Quaker Hartas family. The old building is still there but wheel and machinery gone. It was burnt out a few years ago. ..."* (Mitford Abraham).

This mill was in a range of buildings down-stream from the new mill, its leat running between the new mill and the mill house. Two sets of stones were driven by an undershot wheel. It was burned on 4 November, 1921.

MARTON, SE 732829 (Seven)
This mill was built about 1840 as a water mill but the water was found to be deficient and it was never equipped with machinery (Arthur Champion, 1976, pers comm). According to another source it was a steam mill (J G Rutter, 1970, Industrial Archaeology in north east Yorkshire, Area II, Trans Scar & Dist Arch Soc, vol 2 no 13). Now it is part of a garage business.

HUTTON-LE-HOLE, SE 705899 (Hutton Beck)
Demolished

A leat can be traced on the east side of Hutton Beck from the waterfall at the north end of the village green to a house dated 1793 near the stepping stone crossing.

1782. *"William Robinson of Hotton-le-Hole, miller"* was buried at Lastingham (R H Hayes & J Hurst, n d, 16).

DOVE AND HODGE

The Dove and Hodge Beck run south out of the North York Moors through the two broadly similar dales, Farndale and Bransdale. The market town of Kirkby Moorside serves the two dales and part of Ryedale.

FARNDALE HIGH/OVER, SE 668971 (Fish Beck), Figs 14 & 152 Converted, Grade II

This is the highest mill on the Dove.

1276. Nicholas Devias granted an annual rent of 11 marks from his two water mills in Farndale to his wife Alice (Yorkshire Deeds, YAJ Part 61, vol 16, part 1 1900, 92).

1301. Simon the Miller paid 7s 9d, the largest contribution in the dale; Lay Subsidy (William Brown, 1896, YAS Rec Ser, vol 21).

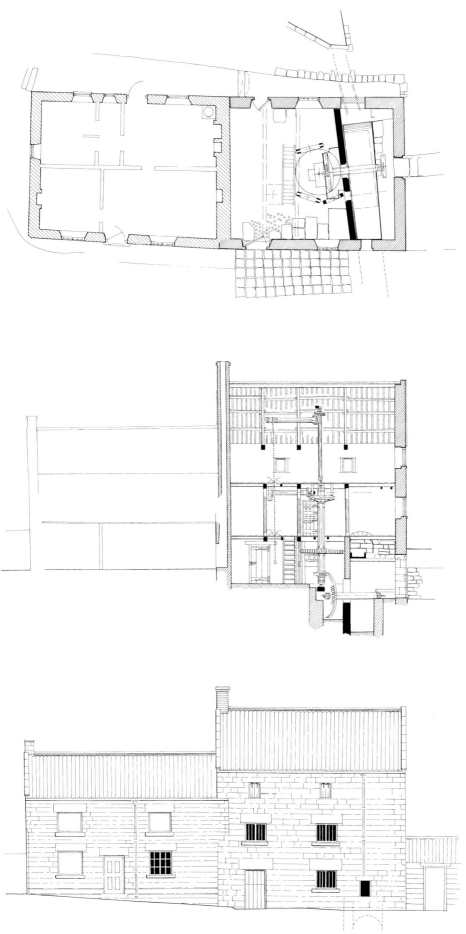

Fig 152. Farndale High mill

1353. *"In Farndale there are two water mills worth 60s 0d per annum and not more because of the deficiency of tenants and workers (operas) on account of the mortality"*; Inquisition post mortem for John, Earl of Kent (PRO C135/118).

1569. *"... a water mill for grain 13s 4d situated on the banks of the Dove with course of water, suit and soke"* held by Francis Burton; Humberstone's Survey, Confiscated estates of the northern Earls.

1610. *"... a capital tenement called Hall House ... water corn mill called Over Mille ... etc ... 110s 1d"* held by

Francis Burton; Survey of Kirkby Moorside (PRO LR 2/186).

1663. *"... one water corn mill situate and being upon the water of the Dove in Farndale commmonly called Farndale Over Mill"*; conveyance, Mary Burton, widow of John Hartas, yeoman, Farndale (NYCRO ZEW I 1/20).

1687. Conveyance, John Hartas and Rodger Bell to Robert Thomson, mariner, of Danby for £95 (NYCRO ZEW I 1/20).

1699. *"... water corne mill on River Dove in Farndale West Side or Farndale Over Mill"*; Release, Robert Thompson to Thomas Gowland, yeoman of Farndale (NYCRO ZEW I 1/20).

1719. Sarah and Thomas Knaggs sold the mill to Thomas Duncombe of Helmsley.

1811. William Strickland left Farndale High mill to take over Bransdale mill and a relative, John Strickland, may have run Farndale High mill after this time. The initials "IG WR JS 1826" are carved on a nearby gate post.

1933. *"Three pairs of stones and flour dresser still used occasionally. Undershot wheel ..."* (Mitford Abraham).

Millers; John Garbutt (1872), Ann Garbutt (1879, 1893), Joseph Potter (1897, 1905).

The mill worked until about 1927. It was sold in 1992 and converted into a house but with part of the machinery retained.

Fig 152. Farndale High mill (photos, JKH & R H Hayes).

This mill was driven by two leats, the older one from Fish Beck (Blakey Gill), 200m long, and a later one from the Dove, 550m long. Both fed into a pond separated from the mill by an abutment wall. The waterwheel pit is skewed inside the main building, indicating that an older arrangement was incorporated into the nineteenth century building. The new three-storeys plus loft mill is of fine quality dressed sandstone. There was a wooden clasp-arm waterwheel of 11 feet diameter by 4 feet on a square-section wooden shaft, driving a cast-iron pit wheel and wallower on a wooden upright shaft. There are three sets of millstones and a peg gear driven sack hoist. All, except the waterwheel, appears to be of mid-nineteenth century date.

FARNDALE WEST, SE 673952 (West Gill Beck) Demolished

Relics of an ancient mill can be seen on West Gill Beck. This mill was the origin of the village name Low Mill.

1276. Nicholas Devias granted an annual rent of 11 marks from his two water mills in Farndale to his wife Alice (Yorkshire Deeds, YAJ Pt 61, vol 16, pt 1, 1900, 92).

1353. In Farndale *"... two water mills worth 60s per annum and not more because of the deficiency of tenants on account of the mortality"*; Inquisition post mortem for John, Earl of Kent (PRO C135/118).

1610. *"Anthony Abilson, 16s 6d ... messuage, water corn mill called Lowe Mill, house, 7 closes ..."* (PRO LR 2/186).

1771. Marked on Jefferys' map.

This medieval corn mill was served by a dam at SE 670972. Parts of the leat and the abutment wall of the pond survive. The back wall of the mill is incorporated into the present house built by W & M Barker in 1752. The site may also have been used as a fulling mill at the time of the Dissolution. There is a 'Tenter Hill Farm' on the opposite side of the Dove.

FARNDALE LOW/NEW, SE 673953 (Dove), Figs 14 & 104 Converted, Grade II

1817. *"... water corn mill on the Dove river in Farndale called Farndale Low Mill, house erected in yard near the mill by Emmanuel Strickland ..."*; mortgage by Charles Duncombe of Duncombe Park (NYCRO Deeds Reg, EG 1818-1819). This may be the first reference to the new mill served by a dam across the Dove.

1933. *"Worked by turbine. Three pairs of stones and flour dresser (disused). Works a saw bench. ..."* (Mitford Abraham).

Millers; Leonard Hardwick (1840), Wm Hugill (*"miller and farmer"* 1851), George Johnson (1872, 1879), Mabel Johnson (1890, 1893), Clarke Thompson (1901, 1905), John Maw (1909, 1913), George Ernest Dobson (1921, 1935), son-in-law of Maw.

The mill had a saw bench using a vertical axis turbine (brought from Sproxton mill) from before 1910. Corn milling continued with one set of stones and the turbine also drove a generator from 1938. Work stopped about 1960. The building has been converted into a dwelling. The masonry dam across the Dove deflected water into a wooden launder, then through a culverted leat to the mill. The mill is a striking, well-built square-plan building of three storeys, with an external door into each storey. The masonry details of the windows and chimney are of high quality. The internal waterwheel drove an upright shaft drive and two sets of stones.

LOWNA, SE 688911 (Dove), Figs 42 & 73 Partially preserved, Grade II

A water-driven corn mill is enclosed within the tannery buildings.

1564. Fulling mill and water course on the River Dove at Gillamoor; lease to William Collyer (PRO, E 164/37 1569-70).

1801. Dinah Moor sold *"... all that fulling mill ... sock, socken, multure ..."* to Thomas Baxter who already occupied the mill. However, Baxter did not operate the mill for fulling (John T Capron, 1967, 42-43).

1803. *"Two messuages, barn, stables, and outbuildings, fulling mill adjoining and one messuage, on River Dove, shop, press and water course ... occ by Thomas Baxter"* (NYCRO Deeds Reg, CZ 1803-5).

1813. A map shows the mill (NYCRO ZEW mic 1599/84).

1840. Baxter set up a tannery (J T Capron, 1967).

1887. New waterwheel with cast-iron shrouds marked "BUTLERS, HELMSLEY, 1887".

1929. *"... undershot wheel and one pair of stones, hay chopper, dynamo and saw bench"* (Mitford Abraham).

Millers; John Baxter (I) (1801, 1857), John Baxter (II) (1857, 1906), John Baxter (III) (1906, 1966).

This early fulling mill site developed into a corn mill. The site was then developed for tanning. The 1801 description leaves no doubt there was a corn mill on the site at that time. This survives reasonably intact. The spacious wheelhouse is similar to those at the Costa mills and may be an indication of an early arrangement with corn mill on one side of the race and fulling mill on the other. The 15 feet diameter undershot waterwheel mounted on a wooden shaft drove a lay-shaft for three sets of millstones and an ancillary vertical shaft.

The tannery was covered with a roof supported on cast-iron columns by Carters of Kirkby Moorside. The waterwheel was finally set to work pumping water around the tannery and for crushing bark. There was also a belt-driven bone crusher in the attached barn. The tannery closed about 1914 (J T Capron, 1967, 42-4).

GILLAMOOR, SE 687904 (Dove), Fig 153
Demolished

Little remains of this tiny medieval steading.

1154-83. *"Also I give them my arable land by Gedlingasmore Mill, formerly occupied by Godfrey their servant"*; grant by Robert de Stuteville to St Mary's church; Curia Reg Rolls, Yorks Fines (R H Hayes & J Hurst, n d, Hutton-le-Hole, 57).

1205. *"Nicholas de Stuteville gave 4 marks per annum from his mill at Gillamoor to Keldholme Priory"* (Burton Mon Ebor; VCH vol 1, 514).

1276. *"... five water mills valued at £23 8s 8d"* in the Kirkby Moorside area, including two in Farndale, one at Gillamoor and one in Bransdale; Inquisition post mortem for Baldwin Wyke, heir to the Stutevilles.

1353. *"In Gillingmore there is one water mill worth 20s 0d and not more because of the deficiency of tenants on account of the mortality"*; Inquisition post mortem for John, Earl of Kent (PRO C 135/118).

1610. The mill was in the tenure of William Stainhouse, James Marsigill and John Wood; Survey of Kirkby Moorside (PRO LR 2/186).

1791. *"Newly erected water corn mill on water Dove in Douthwaite Dale, Kirkby Moorside, newly erected messuage adjoining with Holme of 1 acre, lane called Mill Lane adjoining house, lately purchased by Jos Shepherd of Robt Wood of Gillamoor"*; mortgage by Jos Shepherd, miller, to Geo Hoggas of Bilsdale, yeoman (NYCRO Deeds Reg, CG 1790-92).

Millers; John Baldwin (1882, 1890), Bryan Tyerman (1893).

It stopped work in 1895. The undershot wooden waterwheel fitted with paddles was pulled out in 1912 and the mill became ruinous (R H Hayes, 1969, Rye Hist, No 4). The weir, the very short leat and the lower walls of the small two-storey mill remained in 1990. The waterwheel, a small and primitive single-arm construction, was housed in an external, gabled shed. The attached and in-line house, carrying a datestone "I E S 1779", is still lived in. There were doors between house and mill at both ground and first floors, indicating that the upper floor of the house was probably used as a granary. A large set of greys and remains of a set of French burr stones are on site.

DOUTHWAITE, saw mill, SE 698895 (Dove)
Demolished

"Douthwaite (Duthwthwayt xiii cent) mill is near Hutton-le-Hole" (VCH vol 1, 525).

1856. Marked on the Ordnance Survey 1st Ed, 6 inch map, due west of Hutton-le-Hole.

The mill is remembered locally as 'Johnny's Mill'. A stone clew post survives on site (Douglas Smith, 1981, pers comm).

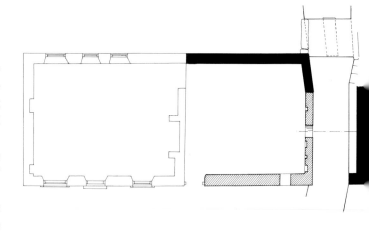

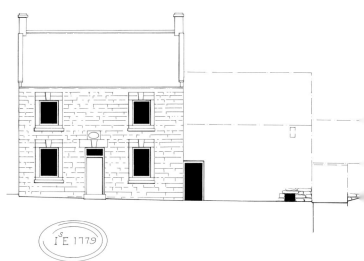

I͏ᔆE 1779

FIG 153. GILLAMOOR MILL.

YOAD WATH, SE 707877 (Dove) Shell

The empty buildings of a corn mill, later converted into a woodworking factory, stand in an isolated hamlet to the north of Kirkby Moorside.

1801. Thomas Rivis took land on which the mill would be built.

The Rivis family had long been the millers of Sherburn mill in the East Riding (G R Rivis & Mrs M Rivis, 1990, pers comm).

1839. *"To be let on lease. That old established water corn mill situate on the west side of the River Dove or Yoad Wath Bonny Bank in the vale of Yoad Wath and about one mile from Kirkby Moorside in the North Riding of Yorkshire. The mill is in excellent working condition, having recently been put into thorough repair. Apply Mr Franks, farmer, Hutton-le-Hole"* (Yorks Gazette, 7 Sept).

1867. The Ryedale Saw Mill and Steam Joinery Works was set up partly at Kirkby Moorside and partly at Yoad Wath. It produced window frames, summer houses, green houses and pigeon lofts. The concern was run by Walter Porritt (J Rushton, 1972, Shopping in Old Ryedale, Rye Hist No 6).

1909. George Rivis gave up the mill to Mr Porritt after some years of not working.

1928. *"Last worked about 1910 by Boddys of Kirkby Mills after being idle for some years. Dismantled and used for making electricity for Mr Hill's house (Ravenswyke) who has put in a turbine. No millstones"* (Mitford Abraham).

Millers; Thomas Rivis (after 1801), William Rivis (1819, 1822), Mrs Rivis (1831, 1840), William and John Rivis (1864), George Rivis (1866), John Maude (1873), George Rivis (*"and Sproxton"* 1890, 1909), Boddys (1928).

There is a large dam. The mill is a large three-storey, L-plan building of rubble stone with hipped roofs, and appears to be all of one age.

KELDHOLME, Grid reference not known (Dove) Demolished

There was probably a mill immediately to the north of the nunnery precinct, ie near the keld from which the Dove emerges. This became a fulling mill and developed into an industrial mill after the Dissolution.

1151. *"... the place of Keldholm with all the cultivated land to the North, by the footpath leading from the mill by Haverberg by the wood which falls into Rumesdale and Wymbelthwayte and Arkelcroft and the park and the mill with suit and multure of Kirkby ..."*; Grant by Robert de Stuteville, lord of Kirkby Moorside to the nuns of Keldholme (Early Yorks Charters, vol 9, 92-3). Rumsdale Plantation is to the north of Kirkby Moorside, on the west side of Dowthwaite dale. This note appears to refer to a mill at Keldholme.

1349. A fulling mill was worth 8s p a; Inquisition post mortem for Thomas Wyke of Liddel (PRO C 135/97).

1535. *"Cistercian nunnery founded by Robert de Stuteville. For the half year ending at Whitsuntide, 20s received by Dame Elizabeth Lyon the Prioress there from Anthony Aisson farmer of the corn mill there"*; Account of the Receiver, Leonard Beckwith (YAS Rec Ser, vol 48, 126).

1569. Ralph Bowes had the water mill worth £4 6s 8d (PRO E 164/137).

Caleb Fletcher built a house on the site of the nunnery.

1795. James Masterman of Richmond and Caleb Fletcher of Kirkby Moorside (grocers) insured a *"Water Oil Mill, stone built and tiled situate at Keldholm ... £150. On Machinery and going geers, Presses and Rollers therein £150. On Cisterns, Coppers and utensils in the same £50. On the millstones £30. On the stock in trade £600. On the Water Wheel of their Mill £20"* (Royal Exchange Fire Insurance, no 143301).

1797. The same partners insured a *"Water Oil Mill, stone and tiles situate at Keldholm ... £400. On the Water and Pit Wheel, machinery and going geers therein £250. On Cisterns and other utensils £150. On stock in trade £1000. Warranted to have no steam engine"* (Royal Exchange Fire Insurance, no 156189).

1800 *"... an oil mill lately erected at Kirkby Moorside"* (J Tuke, 1800, 140).

1822. *"A flax spinning manufactury carried on by Caleb Fletcher"* (Baines).

1827. *"To be sold at the Flax Spinning Mill situated at Keldholme, near Kirkby Moorside in the North Riding of Yorkshire. Capital water wheel, three shafts and three cast metal pillars, etc"* (Yorks Gazette, 6 October). This seems to indicate dismantling.

KIRKBY, SE 704860 (Dove), Fig 154 Converted

The manorial mill of Kirkby Moorside was on the site later known as Kirkby Mills.

1086. *"Hugh, son of Baldrick has ... one mill of 4s"*; Domesday Survey (M Faull & M Stinson, 1986).

1276. *"Manor of Kirby Moresheved ... a water mill worth £18 per annum"*; Inquisition post mortem for John de Stuteville (YAS Rec Ser, vol 12, 167-8).

1282. *"... five water mills valued at £23 8s 8d"* in the Kirkby Moorside area; Inquisition post mortem for Baldwin Wyke (YAS Rec Ser, vol 12, 246-51). The five would include two mills in Farndale, one in Gillamoor, one in Bransdale.

1719. Thomas Duncombe took council's opinion on his right to erect mills at Rievaulx and Kirkby and was advised that there was no customary soke which would exclude the building of a new mill (NYCRO ZEW VI 20/2 mic 1307).

1772 Rental, *"Joseph Foord for Kirby Mills 3. 1. 3"*. (NYCRO ZEW IV 5/8); see McLean, I M, 2005, 18).

1781. *"... building a New Mill"* at Kirkby Mills, including

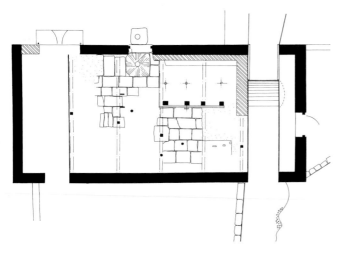

FIG 154. KIRKBY MILL (PHOTO, R H HAYES).

prices for the masons' work, getting stones *"on the moors"*, roofing etc Duncombe memorandum signed by Joseph Foord (NYCRO XEW X mic 1427 001867).

1845. *"Water Corn Mill. apparatus nearly new"*; to let by Richard Hugill, draper, Helmsley and T Dobson, grocer, Kirkby Moorside (Yorks Gazette, 22 February).

1896. *"… stone built mill, corn, undershot waterwheel, 14 ft x 5 ft fall, full head of water, 3 pairs of stones"*; Sale particulars (NYCRO ZEW IV 13/1).

1928. *"A Boddy & Sons. Roller Mill plant and two pairs of stones (one French and one Grey). Makes stone-ground whole meal and flour. Turbine. Also oil engine"* (Mitford Abraham).

Millers; John Dunning, *"Kirkby Moorside Mill"* (pre 1724), Thomas Snowden, *"Kirkby Mill"* (1736), Nicholas Medd (1745), William Robinson *"Kirkby Mills"* (up to 1823), Edward Coverdale (1840, 1866, 1872, 1890, 1893, 1905), George Boddy (1909, 1913), G A Boddy & Sons (1921, *1933 "also at Newburgh Easingwold and Vivers Mills"* (1937).

George Boddy installed a turbine in 1916 and removed two pairs of stones. The mill last worked in 1950 and the family sold the mill in 1957. The surviving building is a long structure, 58 feet external dimension. It appears to have had a waterwheel at each end. After 1845 there was one waterwheel with a lay shaft to three pairs of stones. The south facade is of two builds, the upper two floors with wooden window lintels.

KIRKBY LOW/WATH, Grid reference not known

1823. A pencil drawing of 'Wath Mill' was made by George Nicholson (York City Art Gallery).

1928. *"Roof etc fell in about 1915. Nothing left of the wheel or machinery. Pair of French stones … broken grey stone"* (Mitford Abraham).

Millers; John Parnaby (1872), John Maud (1879), W Garbutt (1897).

SALTON, Grid reference not known (Dove)

1086. There was a mill at Salton; Domesday Survey (M Faul & M Stinson, 1986).

The mill was granted to Hexham Priory by Archbishop Thurston of York.

1430. *"The services of the tenants included the buying of a palfrey for each new prior and carrying provisions for him and his suite when they travelled in Yorkshire. They were also bound to convey all timber and other materials necessary for the repair of the manor houses and the prior's mill, at which they grind their corn"*; Priory of Hexham (Surtees Soc ii, 76-7; VCH vol 1, 552).

1577. Robert Scarth was miller (NYCRO ZRI).

Depopulated in seventeenth century. Ponds survive near Wellfield House. This was the lowest mill on the Dove.

BRANSDALE, SE 621979 (Hodge Beck), Figs 14, 102 & 113 Preserved, Grade II

Bransdale mill is the highest mill on the Hodge Beck.

1276. Bransdale mill was worth two and a half marks (YAJ, 1900, Part 61, vol 16, part 1, 92).

1353. *"In Brannesdale there is a water mill worth … and not more because of deficiency of tenants on account of the mortality"*; Inquisition post mortem for John, Earl of Kent (PRO C135/118).

1569. Mill worth 10s per annum belonging to the Earl of Rutland and tenanted by George Cowder; Humberston Survey of confiscated lands of the Northern Earls (Martin Watts, 1984, The mill at the World's end; Bransdale mill, Kirkby Moorside).

1610. Henry Petch paid 10s per annum for it; Survey of Kirkby Moorside (PRO LR 2/186).

1781. *"New erected water corn mill"* (NYCRO Deeds Reg, BT 1781-3).

1811. William Strickland of Farndale High mill purchased Bransdale mill (NYCRO Deeds Reg, DL 1810-11). He started rebuilding the outbuildings in 1816, and always dated his work. An example is "Know thy end, 1817" on the mill house. The same date is on the west gable of the old mill.

1820. One and a half storey mill with a two storey house; *"Plan of Mr William Strickland's estate lying in Bransdale near Kirbymoorside, Yorkshire, surveyed and drawn by J Moon, April 1820"* (NYCRO ZEW M31 mic 1599 159).

1837. "PER ME EML STRICKLAND, COLL REC CANTAB, SACERDOTEM VICARIUM INGEBY GREENHOW, 1837", graffiti on mill house. Emmanuel was the son of William.

1842. It was raised, re-faced and re-equipped by William Strickland and carries a date stone "W S 1842".

1923. The Strickland family sold to the Feversham estate.

1928. *"A most interesting old mill ... French stones by Marris, Hull, 1842. Very fine pair of 5 ft 6 in diameter grey stones in use. Old grindstone at back geared to pit wheel. Overshot iron wheel. Dresser and cleaner still in mill, but not used for 20 years. Old abandoned oat meal mill. ... A very fine example of an old country mill which should certainly never be allowed to disappear."* (Mitford Abraham).

Millers; William Strickland (1840), John and Noah Strickland (1854), Hugill Strickland (1872, 1913), Peckitt (1911?).

The mill ceased work in 1917. The house was abandoned in 1950 and acquired by the National Trust in 1968. It is now preserved.

Water was taken from two small becks to a range of buildings consisting of part of the old mill, the mill of 1842 and the old mill house. Other buildings include a new mill house, set at right angles to the main range, barn, byre, cart shed, smithy etc. A cast-iron waterwheel with some tension spokes was probably second-hand. It drove an all-iron upright shaft driving gear to three sets of stones, one a French set by "GEORGE MARIS. MAKER. HULL. 1842" and another, a set of greys, inscribed "1870 N J S" (Noah John Strickland) and "H.S." (Hugill Strickland). The mill also contains a grain cleaner and a flour dresser. It is thought that the cast-iron driving gear was made at the foundry of George Russell

in Kirkby Moorside. On the other side of the waterwheel from the 1842 mill is part of the old mill building equipped with an oat kibbling mill, pearl barley mill and oat roasting plate. The kibbling mill and barley mill were driven from the new waterwheel via a pinion.

The Department of Architectural Studies at Leeds Polytechnic carried out a survey in 1973.

ELM HOUSES, SE 618956, Fig 155 Demolished

This small farm mill was built between 1828 and 1854.

1828. Not marked; Survey of Lord Feversham's Estate in Bransdale (NYCRO ZEW IV 1/13/10 mic 694).

1854. Shown on Ordnance Survey 1st Ed, 6 inch map.

1867. *"A Water Corn Mill was formerly in full operation on the premises, and might well be restored"* (Yorks Gazette, 5 Jan).

This was probably wishful thinking. The dam remains but the building is demolished and the site overbuilt. Part of the wooden clasp-arm waterwheel with a single set of arms was uncovered in 1996. There are three mill-stones on site, a set for oat shelling and one French stone. The clasp-arm waterwheel was curiously old fashioned but, nevertheless, there are no pre-nineteenth century references.

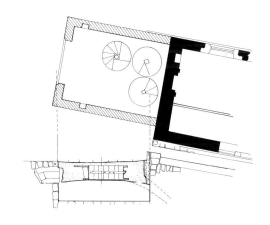

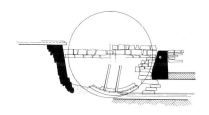

Fig 155. Excavated foundations and waterwheel at Elm Houses.

SPOUT BANK, woollen, SE 663884 (Hodge Beck) Demolished

1720. *"... the ruins of the woollen and bleaching establishment settled here by Ralph Richardson of Heathercote which occurred in 1720"* (Thomas Parker, Notes on Welburn, Rye Hist, no 10, Spring 1980).

1741. *"Skiplam township, George Richardson for a fulling mill £3"*; Duncombe estate rental (NYCRO ZEW IV 5/6). Also 1772.

1781. The mill was drawn; *"A Plan of the Township of Skiplam situate in the parish of Kirkdale in the Co of York, the property of Charles Slingsby Duncombe Esq taken by J Foord, 1781"* (NYCRO ZEW M1 mic 1599/13). The site was visible in the mid-nineteenth century but no traces of the building remained when Hayes looked for it in the late 1970s. Part of the leat is visible.

See Isabel McLean, 1996/7, The lost Watermill of Kirkdale; the Spout Bank Fulling mill in Cogg Hole, Ryedale Historian, no 18, 12-16.

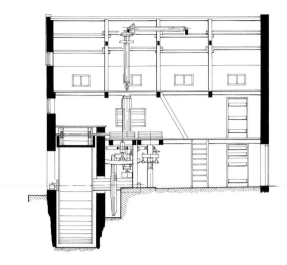

HOLD CAULDRON/FADMOOR/SKIPLAM, SE 668869 (Hodge Beck), Fig 156 Complete

The name derives from the 'Howle Cauldron' or deep swirling hole in the beck immediately below the mill.

1704. After its rebuilding by Matthew Foord the mill was burned down by a mill servant from Howkeld mill (Thomas Parker, 1856, ms, Ryedale Museum).

1726. *"Howle Caldron Mill"*; lease by Thomas Duncombe to John Mason (NYCRO ZEW IV 7/4 mic 6973).

1734. An inscribed stone "M FOORD LAT 54. 19, 1734" is built into the front of the building.

1781. Mill shown on a different alignment to the present structure; *"A Plan of the township of Skiplam situate in the township of Kirkdale in the county of York, the property of Charles Slingsby Duncombe Esq, taken by J Foord, 1781"* (NYCRO ZEW M1).

1784. A datestone "PETER PEAT 1784 HOLD CAUDRON" was transferred to a garden in Kirkby Moorside (R H Hayes, 1969, The story of Gillamoor and Fadmoor, Rye Hist No 4, 16). Isabel McLean believes this should have read *"Pratt"*.

1881. John Hauxwell carried out an evaluation of machinery belonging to the tenant (John Hauxwell's Letter Books).

1928. *"In bad condition ... three pairs of stones. Centrifugual silk dresser. Two water troughs (one high, one low) to the wheel. ..."* (Mitford Abraham).

Millers; Richard Walkington (1724), John Pattinson (1759), Peter Pratt (up to 1770), John Potter (pre 1779), William White (died here 1810), William White Junior (until 1827), Henry Stonehouse, William Wood (1840), William Baldwin (1840, 1872, 1879), Thomas Bowes (1889, 1921).

FIG 156. HOLD CAULDRON MILL (PHOTO, R H HAYES).

This mill is served by a 'Millgate' leading from Fadmoor and Gillamoor and a pannierway through Brockhill Haggs to Sleightholmedale. An early water system from a dam adjacent to the mill was replaced by a new leat alongside a loop in the Hodge on the opposite bank to the mill and then crossing it via an aqueduct.

According to one source the mill stopped working in

1920. The two-storey plus loft building is of coursed rubble. Originally the house was free-standing. The 15 feet diameter waterwheel on its wooden shaft is of wooden clasp-arm construction with a hexagonal geometry for the arms. There is a cast-iron pit wheel and cast-iron wallower driving an oak upright shaft with cast-iron spur wheel driving three sets of stones, one inscribed "W J & T CHILD MAKERS HULL & LEEDS".

WELBURN/HOWKELD, SE 686852 (Howkeld Beck), Fig 157 Converted, Grade II

The Hodge goes underground near St Gregory's Minster at Kirkdale and re-emerges as a keld feeding Howkeld Beck. The water was ponded to drive a mill.

1539. The farm of a water mill, tenement and closes demised to Rowland Blythe was worth £2 13s 4d in 1538; Dissolution Account of Rievaulx Abbey (Surtees Soc, vol 83, 311-34).

1545. The mill was granted to William Ramsden of Longley and Edward Hoppey of Halifax; L & P, Henry VIII, xx(i), g, 1081 (28) (VCH vol 1, 520).

1649. "… two Water Mills standinge both under a Roof called Hawkell Milnes …" (York Minster Archives, Hailstone Coll., Welburn).

1825. Sketch by George Nicholson shows lower walls as they stand today.

1825. *"John Potter from Hold Cauldron bought Howkeld Mill from Thomas Hill of Thornton Dale, then proprietor of part of the Welburn Estate but could not get on for want of corn to grind. He was obliged to sell it to the Duncombes, who had bidden their tenants not to give a single bushel to multure. …"* (Thomas Parker, 1858).

1833. The old wood framed mill with *"… high pitched roof covered with thatch, having a water wheel at each end of it"* was burned down and the present building set up (Thomas Parker, 1858; Rye Hist, no 10, 1980, 43).

1841. *"Joseph Potter, 20, Miller"* (Census Returns)

1860. The mill was further improved by Richard Potter (Thomas Parker, 1858).

1898. John Hauxwell quoted for putting in a Tattershall turbine (J Hauxwell's Letter Books).

1928. *"Very old mill worked by turbine. Roller mill … two pairs of stones (one French, one Grey) makes stone ground flour and wheat meal. Good business."* (Mitford Abraham).

Millers; Matthew Ford (1702), John Potter (1777-1825),

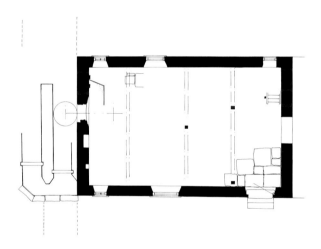

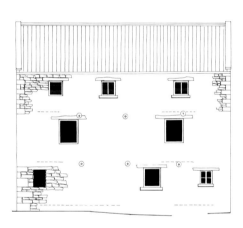

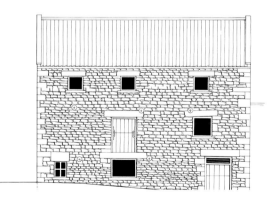

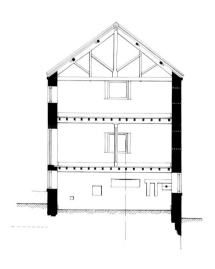

FIG 157. HOWKELD MILL.

227

FIG 158. HAROME MILL.

Richard Potter (1840, 1850), John Potter (up to 1869), Richard Cusson (1872, 1913), Richard Cusson & Son (1921, 1925), Ernest Cusson (1933, 1937)

The mill worked until the 1960s producing flour for biscuit making. It is a three-storey structure with small windows, those on the south facade with wooden lintels. It is built in coursed limestone rubble. A horizontal slot cut into the hurst wall was made for a spur wheel. All machinery, including the later turbine and Tattershall Break Machine has gone and the building is converted into a house. See McLean I A, 2005, The millers of Howkeld corn mill, 7-12).

HAROME, SE 647816 (Riccal), Fig 158 Shell, Grade II

The early corn mill at Harome was driven from the Riccal. The later mill was driven from a strong 'keld'. Harome Fulling mill was on the Rye and is described in the next section of the Gazetteer.

1216-72. Land *"... in the town and territory of Harom, except the toft called Holm behind the Milne"*; grant by John Tincto to Dominus Peter (HMC Rutland, Belvoir Charters, 4163-4166; R H Hayes and M Allison, 1988, Rye Hist, no 14).

1285. *"... two water mills were listed in the Inquisition post mortem of Robert de Ros (1285) and William de Ros (1345)"* (YAS vol ii; Cal Inq p m vol 8, 333, York Library; VCH vol 1, 493n).

1430. There was a corn mill and a fulling mill (Chan Inq p m, 9 Henry VI no 48; VCH vol 1, 487n).

1584. Thomas Bared left his title in *"Harome mylne"* to his wife, and *"... to my son Christopher all my working towilles, cogges, trundle heads, spindels and two chests, one with a lock and one other that do want a lock but there is a lock in Robert Scott's chest which I give to Chris"* (Borthwick Wills vols 13, 15, 22; R H Hayes & M Allison, 1988, 35).

1928. *"A very nice small mill, owned and worked by Mr Knowlson ... formerly worked by water from the River Rye, but owing to a dispute some years ago the weir was removed. Water from spring now feeds the dam. One pair of grey stones and oats roller worked. Turbine put in 1923 and also makes electric light"* (Mitford Abraham).

Millers; Thomas Wood (1642), William Simpson (1739), John Boyes (1830), John Sadler (1872,1879), John Sigsworth (1890,1905), Mrs E Sigsworth (1909, 1913), Christopher Knowlson (1921, 1937).

The waterwheel was taken out in 1923 and a Gilkes turbine installed. In 1944 oat milling stopped and the millstones and gearing were taken out. Then, a Bentall plate mill and a roller mill were driven from the turbine. The earlier drive was by upright shaft.

The mill is a two-storey limestone rubble building dating from before 1780.

BILSDALE AND RYEDALE

The Seph and the Rye both flow south through the northern moors and the Tabular Hills and the Rye becomes the major flow across Ryedale

RAISDALE, NZ 538006 (Raisdale Beck), Fig 103 Converted

This apparently isolated steading was the mill of a lost settlement sited near Hall Garth Farm and of assarts around the dale edge.

1539. *"… mill in the tenancy of William Est … (de firma unius molendini ibidem sic in tenura Wilelmi Est …)* in *Billesdale cum Baysdale"*; Rievaulx Dissolution Acc (Rievaulx Chart, Surtees Soc, vol 83, 315).

1637. *"… tenement, Raisdale Mill House with the water corn mill there … £2 2s 0d"* leased by John Saunderson; *"The rentall and survey of divers manners, lands and tenements of the Right Hon George Earl of Rutland … by Henry Pelham, Francis Harker and John Wells"* (NYCRO ZEW IV 1/4, mic 1158; M Y Ashcroft and A M Hill, 1980, Bilsdale Surveys 1637-1851, 18).

1642. *"Raysedale Myll"*, John Saunderson, tenant; *"The survey of the honour of Bilsdale … surveyed by Thomas Bankes"* (NYCRO ZEW IV 1/5 mic 1158; M Y Ashcroft and A Hill, 1989, 49).

1781. *"Raisdale Mill Farm. William Garbut …"*; *"A correct survey of Bilsdale … by William Calvert of Sutton on Trent"* (ZEW IV 1/7 mic 1023; M Y Ashcroft and A Hill, 1980, 78).

1814. *"Raisdale Mill, William Garbutt …"*; Survey of Bilsdale (NYCRO ZEW IV 1/12/5, ZEW IV 1/12/11 mic 1024; M Y Ashcroft and A Hill, 1980, 97).

1826. *"Raysdale Mill, Henry Garbutt …"*; *"A survey of several farms situate in Bilsdale … by Tukes and Ayer"* (NYCRO ZEW IV 1/17/6&7 mic 694; M Y Ashcroft and A Hill, 1980, 136).

1848. Rebuilt by John Garbutt.

1930. *"Ceased work 1910. Two pairs of stones. Dismantled pearling stone now at Swarthmoor Hall, Ulverston. Flour dresser in fair order. Overshot wheel in ruins …"* (Mitford Abraham).

Millers; William Garbutt (1781, 1814), Henry Garbutt (1826), John Garbutt (1849, *"farmer and miller"* 1851), R Garbutt (1890), James Cobb (1893), J Garbutt (1897, 1913).

The group of buildings is made up of a free-standing mill with a dated lintel "W GARBUT 1849", mill house ("W GARBUTT 1810" on door lintel), farm buildings and a smithy dated 1773. The mill (disused) was sold to Lord Ingleby in 1939.

There is a short leat from a stone dam, now missing. The pitch-back waterwheel had cast-iron nave plates on a wooden shaft. The cast-iron pit wheel drove a cast-iron wallower on an octagonal-section wooden upright shaft. The cast-iron tenter beam brackets were bolted to very large masonry slabs set in the wall between the water-wheel and pit wheel. There were two sets of stones, one a set of greys with top stone inscribed "I G 1877" and bed stone inscribed "W H A 1849". Two old stones and a pearl barley stone remained outside the building in 1973. The crown wheel drove two overhead lay shafts. An old shed behind the mill, now demolished, was formerly known as the 'drying shed' and a small fire opening under the stairs in the mill may have provided the heat. A re-used lintel inscribed "I I G G 1775" is set upside down in the wall above the waterwheel.

BILSDALE/SEAVE GREEN, NZ 562003 (Seph), Figs 13 & 159 Converted

This mill was built for a settlement called Bilsdale and also served assarts around the northern end of the dale.

1538. *"… one tenement with mill in tenure of William Webster, 12s 0d"*; Rievaulx Dissolution Acc (Rievaulx Chart, Surtees Soc, vol 83, 311-334).

1637. *"William Webster holds by lease one corne mill, and paies at the said feastes yearlie 14s 4d"* in the Manor of Kirkham from George Earl of Rutland; Pelham, Harker and Wells (NYCRO ZEW IV 1/4; M Y Ashcroft and A Hill, 1980, 7).

1642. *"The mill having noe ground to it"* worth £3 per annum; Thomas Bankes, (NYCRO ZEW IV 1/5; M Y Ashcroft and A Hill, 1980, 39).

1781. Mill Farm, leased by Richard Garbutt (NYCRO ZEW IV 1/7; M Y Ashcroft and A Hill, 1980, 76). *"A correct survey of Bilsdale … William Calvert"* shows a waterwheel on the up-slope gable wall and not on the back wall as in the late nineteenth century (NYCRO ZEW IV 1/7; Bilsdale Maps, NYCRO pub No 32, 1983).

1814. *"Mill, Richard Garbutt …"* (NYCRO ZEW IV/1/12/5; M Y Ashcroft and A Hill, 1980, 92).

1826. Richard Garbutt of Stocking had the house and mill etc; Tuke and Ayre's survey (NYCRO ZEW IV 1/13/6 & 7; M Y Ashcroft and A Hill, 1980, 130).

1928. *"Two pairs of stones, 1 French, 1 Grey, Eureka wheat dresser and wire flour dresser not used for 20 years. Wood breast wheel (iron buckets) … stone bearings"* (Mitford Abraham).

Millers; Jonathan Garbutt (*"Town Green, farmer and miller"* 1851), John Garbutt (1890), John Garbutt & Sons (*"and Ingelby"* 1893).

The mill stopped work in 1939. It was sold from the Feversham estate in 1944, along with most Bilsdale farms. The waterwheel and gearing were removed in 1960 and the building was converted into a dwelling in 1973.

There is a long leat. The mill had an external waterwheel on one of the long walls. There is a dovecot in the apex of a gable wall. The mill was originally free-standing but

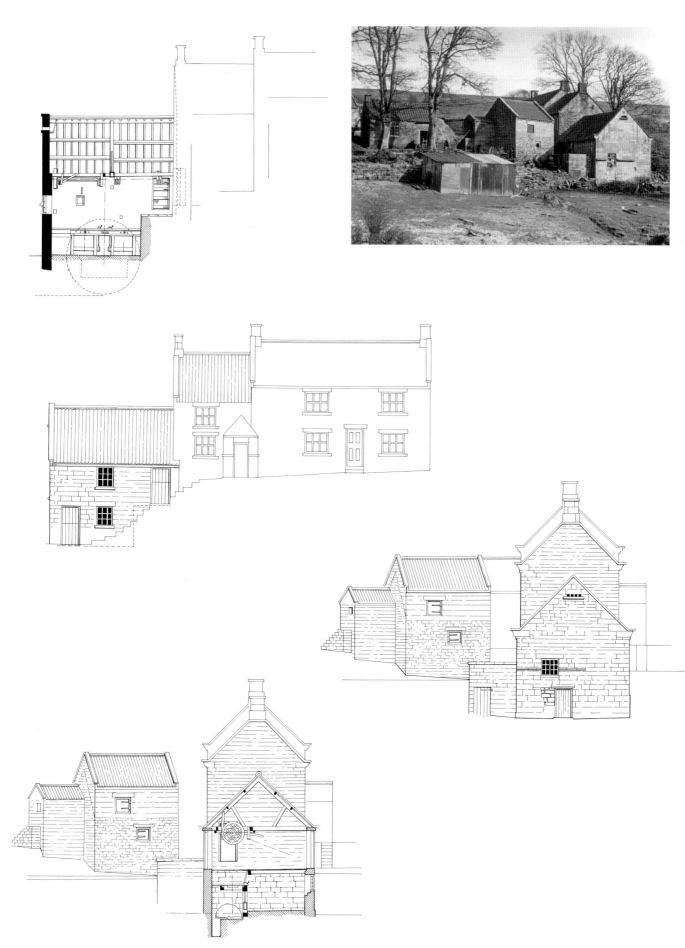

FIG 159. SEAVE GREEN MILL, BILSDALE (PHOTO, A STOYEL).

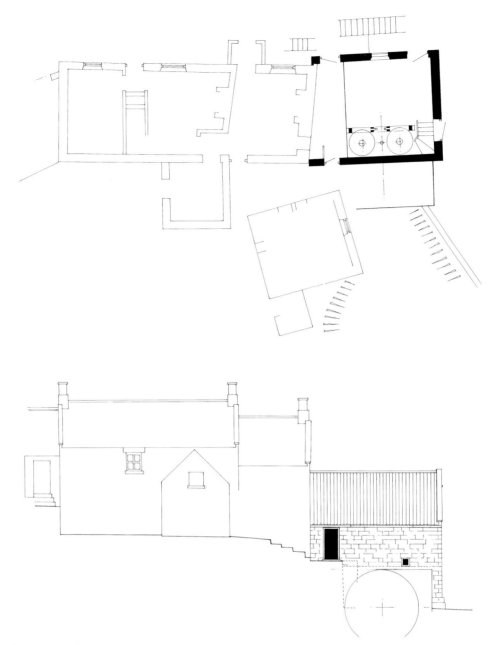

FIG 159. SEAVE GREEN MILL, BILSDALE

is now integrated into a long range of buildings running up the hillside. The attached house appears to cut through the end of the original mill. The overshot water-wheel was 12 feet diameter by 4 feet wide (A Stoyel) and there were two sets of stones. The hurst beam was dated 1803.

BILSDALE LOW/NETHER, SE 572953 (Seph), Fig 64
Preserved, Grade II
This was probably the mill for a medieval settlement called Stainton situated near Grange.

1637. *"William Coulson holds one tenement called Nether Mill House, one backhouse, one barne, one water corne*

mill ..." etc altogether worth £2 6s 6d from George the Earl of Rutland; Pelham, Harker and Wells (NYCRO ZEW IV 1/4; M Y Ashcroft and A Hill, 1980, 19).

1642. *"The Mill Farme, William Cowlson tennant per annum £10"* but *"The mill itself is not worth aboue 40s per annum by reason it is much out of repaire. About £40 would repaire it and then it would bee worth £10 per annum"*; Thomas Bankes (NYCRO ZEW IV 1/5; M Y Ashcroft and A Hill, 1980, 46).

The mill was acquired by Charles Duncombe along with the Helmsley estate in 1688.

1771. Named *"Low Mill"* on Jefferys' map.

1781. John Coulson had *"Low Mill"*; William Calvert (NYCRO ZEW IV 1/7; M Y Ashcroft and A Hill, 1980, 84).

1785. *"Coulson's mill rebuilt"*, *"dam repaired"*, mill fitted with *"… spur wheel and other articles un-necessary for a mill so situated"* for Charles Slingsby Duncombe (NYCRO ZEW X mic 1427 001868).

1814. David Helm was miller and farmer at *"Low Mill"* and paid £8 per annum for the mill out of a total rental of £51 19s 5d (NYCRO ZEW IV 1/7; M Y Ashcroft and A Hill, 1980, 103).

1826. *"Bilsdale Mill"*; Tuke and Ayre's survey. William Helm was miller (NYCRO XEW IV 1/13/6 7 7; M Y Ashcroft and A Hill, 1980, 103, 125).

1880. John Hauxwell quoted for a new iron waterwheel but this work was not carried out (John Hauxwell's Letter Books).

1928. *"Two pairs of stones (1 French, 1 grey). Undershot wheel. Very old mill. Flour dresser and wheat cleaner on top floor. Not used for a long time"* (Mitford Abraham).

Millers; William Coulson (1603, 1637), Thomas Coulson (1754), John Coulson (1781), David Helm (1814), William Helm (1826, 1851), John Garbutt (1872, 1889), William Wood (1890).

Edward and Hazell Garbutt bought Low mill from the Feversham estate in 1944 and restored it with the help of Tom Harrison of Gilling in the 1970s (*"Ted's Old Mill by the Stream"*, Evening Gazette, 18 August 1979).

There is a dam and a short leat. The 11 feet diameter wooden clasp-arm waterwheel (with cast-iron shrouds by "BUTLER HELMSLEY", c.1890) is in a separate wheel shed on a gable wall. It has a cast-iron pit wheel and wallower and a wooden upright shaft. There are two sets of millstones, one a set of French stones with a cast-iron ring round the eye marked "JAS SAVERY MAKER STOCKTON-ON-TEES, 1849". The crown wheel drives two wooden lay shafts. Gear segments were cast by Carters of Kirkby Moorside. There was a segment from a barley millstone. Half a basalt stone is cemented into the dam and another dated 1669 is used as a hearth stone in the house. There was probably a roasting plate, now replaced by a peat hearth taken from the mill house.

This mill is not all of the same age and may at one stage have had a countershaft drive.

FANGDALE BECK, smithy, SE 568946 (Seph) Shell

1840. William Wood moved from Hold Cauldron mill to Fangdale Beck to work as a blacksmith (M Hartley & J Ingleby, 1972, 32).

By 1909 John Wood had added a foundry to the smithy. It was equipped with a cupola which used pig iron from Middlesbrough. Its best known product was the Wood's plough. A 10 feet diameter waterwheel of non-mill-wrighting design was served by an open channel some 140m long to drive a drilling machine, lathe, grindstone and blower for the cupola. Ploughmaking stopped in 1925. Smithy hearths survive.

LASKILL, fulling, Grid reference not known (Seph)

1709. The Duncombe estate built a new fulling mill in Bilsdale; Agent's Accs (NYCRO ZEW IV 6/3/1; Isabel McLean, Ryedale Historian, No 18).

1781. *"Tenter Close"* and *"Tenter Garth"* in Laskill; William Calvert (NYCRO ZEW IV 1/7; Bilsdale Maps, 1781-1857, NYCRO Pub 32).

LASKILL, bloom smithy, SE 564903 (Seph)

1539. A *"fabrica"* valued at 26s 8d was contracted to Richard Rawlinson; Ministers' Accounts (Rievaulx Chart, Surtees Soc, vol 83; J G McDonnell, 1972, An account of the iron industry in Upper Ryedale and Bilsdale c 1150-1650, Rye Hist, no 6, 23-50).

The site is below Timberholme Farm. A leat is visible from the Laskill to Hawnby road.

ARDEN, SE 521907 (Arden Beck), Figs 26 & 52
Complete, Grade II*

The Benedictine nunnery of Arden was founded in Thorodale in 1150.

1189. *"… the monks condoned the nuns in regard to all dams, inclosures for the animals, the rough words of their men and other irregularities"*; settlement to a dispute between the monks of Rievaulx and the nuns (VCH vol 3, 113).

1536. *"The site of the late Priory … one water mill with one acre of meadow to the same adjacent. …"* leased to Thomas Welles for *"good and faithful service"* for £8 9s 8d (YAS Rec Ser, vol 48, 88).

1541. *"The site of Priory at Arden with land pertaining and also one water mill with appurtenances"* granted to Thomas Culpepper, a gentleman of the King's Chamber (YAS Rec Ser, vol 48, 89).

Conveyed to Sir Arthur Darcy (1540) and then to Ralph Tancred (1574).

1846. William Megginson, the miller, carried out repairs to sluices and pen trough (Lucy Beckett, 1976, Rye Hist, No 8, 10-18).

1929. *"Two pairs of stones. Pair of grey stones … Pair of blue (german) stones … worked by trundle gearing (very rare). Old fashioned oat kiln … metal base where oats were spread and metal handle revolves to spread oats. Overshot wheel. … Mill ceased work in 1912"* (Mitford Abraham).

Millers; William Megginson (1846, one top millstone is inscribed "W M"), William Megginson (1872, 1879), Mary Megginson (1883, 1893), John Bowes (1909, 1925).

Arden mill is the most important surviving mill in North Yorkshire; now a grade II* Listed Building.

The 14 feet diameter by 2 feet clasp-arm waterwheel is mounted on a square-section wooden shaft. The pit wheel is of clasp-arm construction but with cast-iron face gear segments. One pair of stones (5 feet in diameter) was centre-driven via a lantern gear and the second pair (blue stones 3 feet 6 inches diameter) was driven by a lantern gear and there was a second lying shaft on the opposite side of the pit wheel. Tentering was by lighter lever. The mill has an oat roasting plate set into the front wall. A set of raised crucks survives.

A description of the mill was included in David Jones, 1969, Water powered corn mills of England, Wales and the Isle of Man, TIMS, 324-344.

HAWNBY, fulling, SE 542894 (Rye) Demolished

This fulling mill existed for just over one hundred years.

1658. *"… that tenement or cottage with a little garth and ffulling mill … late in the tenure or occupation of Robert Grime. …"* (NYCRO, ZPI).

1762. *"Fulling mill formerly belonging to the Howgill family"* (NYCRO Deeds Reg, AK 1760-4).

HAWNBY, SE 542894 (Rye) Demolished

1301. *"Radulpho molendario"* contributed to the Lay Subsidy (W Brown, 1896, YAS, Rec Ser, vol 21).

1658. *"… that watercourse and Grist Mill and a House and Garth thereunto belonging … in the tenure or occupation of Charles Harrison and John Masterman or one of them … also water courses stream races Mill pools, Soak, Sucken Toll Mulctures. …"*; Indenture (NYCRO, ZPI).

1771. Marked but not named on Jefferys' map.

Millers; John Dowson (1822), William Garbutt (1840), Francis Garbutt (1872, 1879), Thomas Lightfoot (*"Shopkeeper and Miller"* 1889, 1895).

According to local sources the mill had stopped work by 1870 and was demolished before 1917. The nearby mill house is dated 1781.

CAYDALE/OLD BYLAND, SE 545867 (Caydale Beck), Fig 53 Converted

This may have been the grange mill for Old Byland.

1598. *"Caerdale Mill"*; Christopher Saxton's *"Plan of Old Byland"* (Rye Hist, 1974, No 7, 62).

1771. Marked but not named on Jefferys' map.

1762. *"As they being two of the head springs the Millner is afraid of wanting Water to the Milln, to prevent which he is going to make another Dam"*; letter from Richard Chapman to Lord Fauconberg owner of the Newburgh estate referring to work by Joseph Foord in making the Old Byland water course which was going to affect the water supply to the mill (NYCRO ZDV, mic 1271).

1929. *"Originally owned by the Wombwell estate of Newburgh Hall. Tenanted by Aaron Robinson (uncle of Tom Robinson of Rievaulx mill) until Tom Ellis came in 1881 … two pairs of stones, wire and brush boulter and pearling machine which dealt with barley and smutted wheat and was also used for preparing wheat for frumerting at Christmas time. He made flour but his trade declined when Rievaulx mill put in a silk dresser. About 1910 Tom Ellis gave over the mill and handed over to a son-in-law, Thomas Medd. The mill ceased work in 1917"* (Mitford Abraham).

Millers; Thomas Bradley (1840), Aaron Robinson (1873, 1879), Thomas Ellis (1889, 1905), Thomas Medd (1909).

Mitford Abraham bought the mill after World War I and dismantled it in 1928. The pearl barley machine went to the Kirk Collection at the York Castle Museum. The waterwheel was rebuilt in 1929 to generate electricity.

The beck was diverted along a leat to a pond and escape race (now known as the 'waterfall') and today the original bed of the beck is dry. The buildings consist of an L-shaped range, the mill/house wing being 65 feet long and the other wing, originally farm buildings, 45 feet long. The whole is now incorporated into the house. The wheel pit was inside a spacious wheelhouse open to the roof. The hurst wall has been re-built in good quality masonry. The 14 feet diameter by 3 feet waterwheel had a single set of clasped arms and drove a centre set of stones and a countershaft to a second set. The hurst beam (now re-located) has three carved meal spout boards inscribed "S B FECIT ANO 1729", "T F" and "I K + R H FECIT 1750 1841". Formerly there were two blue stones on site.

The mill house retains its fireplace beam and fire hood incorporating a bread kiln.

CAYDALE, fulling/paper, SE 565870 (Caydale Beck) Demolished

1539. A walk mill at 'Tilehouse' was valued at under £2 (Dugdale Monasticum, v, 354; J McDonnell, 1974, Limestone and water, Rye Hist, no 7, 50-67).

1597. John Blanchard, silk weaver, of York bought a new-built house in the manor of Old Byland. *"By 1610 he had a paper mill, a house for drying paper and tubs and troughs for working the paper"* (RCHM, 1987, 1888).

1598. *"Walkemill"* and *"Tenterbanke"*; Christopher Saxton's Plan of Old Byland (Rye Hist, 1974, no 7, 62).

1635. Used as a fulling mill (NYCRO ZD VI/1/18).

RIEVAULX, SE 576852 (Rye), Figs 16, 25 & 55 Converted, Grade II

The Cistercian Abbey was founded by Walter Espec in 1131. No medieval documentation for the precinct mill has survived but there are buried foundations.

1538. *"Farm of a corn mill … 6s 8d per annum"* (Rievaulx Chart, Surtees Soc, vol 83, 311-334). The property was acquired by the Duke of Rutland.

1706. George Tayler was paid £43 for rebuilding Rievaulx

mill; Thomas Stent's Accounts (NYCRO ZEW IV 6/3/1 mic 2957/803).

1928. *"Owned by Lord Feversham and tenanted by Thomas Robinson. Raised fifty years ago. Two pairs of stones (one French and one Grey). One pair of French stones at back of mill. ... Grey stones used. Centrifugal silk dresser dismantled and stored away at top of mill, not used since 1916. ... Thomas Robinson brings his flour from Burgess's mill, Thornton le Dale and retails it to farmers all over this district. His uncle Aaron Robinson had Caydale mill ..."* (Mitford Abraham).

Millers; Thomas Robinson, previously of Thornton Dale, (1810, 1839), John Robinson (1873, 1887, 1913), Mrs Bessie Robinson (1921), Thomas Robinson, Arthur Robinson (1928).

The mill became disused in 1961 and is now converted into a house but retains its waterwheel (cast-iron shrouds marked "J CRUSHER, HELMSLEY, 1857"), pit wheel, two lying shafts and sack hoist. See Text.

There are three buildings in an L-shape. The mill has two lower storeys of sandstone and the upper, added about 1875, of rubble limestone. Attached is a two-storey building with some re-used carved tracery. In front of this is a cart shed with an old waterwheel shaft separating the two cart bays.

There were three ponds in the hillside behind the site. Water from the lower dam was controlled by a hinged-lever non-return valve. A Blackstone paraffin engine was added about 1900. Hauxwells of Yarm did a refit in 1904 and rebuilt the waterwheel in 1919.

RIEVAULX, blast furnace (SE 575851) Demolished

The French immigrant, Lambert Seimar, set up a water-driven hammer at the ironworks at Newbridge in Sussex in 1496. He came to Rievaulx immediately before the Dissolution as the tenant of two forges, one at Laskill and the other at Rievaulx.

1538. *"Le iron smithie within the same site in the tenure of Lambert Semer 26s 8d per annum. ..."* (Rievaulx Chart, Surtees Soc, vol 83, 311-334).

1540. *"Lambert Semer holdyth at will of the lord the iron smythes (unus molendini vacati le yron smithies) adjoining unto the site of the late monastery"*; Ministers' Acc (Rievaulx Chart, Surtees Soc, vol 83, 311-341).

1576-8. A blast furnace was built near the disused abbey buildings. Documentary evidence covers 1586 (new hearth), 1616 (partially rebuilt), 1641 and 1647 (closed down) (H R Schubert, 1957, Appendix X).

The waterwheel for the furnace bellows was served by the long leat (sometimes known as a canal) which ran from the Rye and in front of the corn mill. The furnace site is now occupied (probably) by the 'Mill House' which is dated 1729. The calcining ground is above the house and the slag heap below.

RIEVAULX, fulling, SE 576845 (Rye) Demolished

1538. *"Farm of le Walk Milne within same site lately in tenure of Lambert Seimar, 60s 0d per annum"* (Rievaulx Chart, Surtees Soc, vol 83, 311 - 341).

1540. *"On the southest there of a peace of grond belongyng to the walk myll cont. di rod and at the southest therof standyth the walke myle with a garth adioining. ..."* (Survey of Abbey Lands, Belvoir Castle, Misc. MS 106, 154).

SCAWTON

1598. *"Scawton Milne"* near Holleheade Wells on Scawton Beck; Christopher Saxton's Plan of Old Byland (Rye Hist, 1974, No 7, 62).

1610-35. A paper mill at Stocking/Scawton was converted into a *"Mall Mill"*.

1635. *"A messuage, house, land and fulling mill in Stocking"* (NYCRO ZDU).

1771. Three waterwheels were marked on Thomas Jefferys' map. This is obscure.

FORGE FARM, finery, SE 576843 (Rye)

When the blast furnace was built a finery was established at the site now known as Forge Farm. There are earthworks and slag remains.

SPROXTON/OLD HELMSLEY, SE 605825 (Rye), Fig 160 Demolished

1145. Land bounded on the west by *"... the road from Griff to Sproxton Mill"*; part of his second grant to Rievaulx Abbey by Walter Espec (Rievaulx Chart, Surtees Soc, vol 83, 16-21).

Nd. *"... molendinum de Sproxton"*; grant of land in Helmsley to Rievaulx Abbey by Edward de Ros (Rievaulx Chart, Surtees Soc, vol 83, 23).

1226. *"Richard de Sproxton by view and delivery of the Abbot's foresters may have timber in that wood for building and repairing the mill dam of Sproxton, as much and as often as necessary, within these boundaries. ... Richard may not take oaks, holly, sycamore or ash trees in any part of the said wood"* (YAS Rec Soc, Yorks Fines, 1218-31, 82).

1235. Agnes de Norton was to grind her corn to the twentieth measure at Sproxton mill (YAS Rec Ser, vol 67, 1237-46, 31).

1298. Water mill worth 26s 8d per annum; Inquisition post mortem for Robert de Sproxton (YAS Rec Ser, vol 81, 100-2).

1333. Agnes de Norham had to grind at Sproxton mill to the twentieth measure; confirmation by Edward III of gifts to Rievaulx Abbey (Rievaulx Chart, Surtees Soc, vol 83, 291-3).

1349. Water mill worth 40s 0d per annum; Inquisition

FIG 160. SPROXTON MILL (PHOTO, MITFORD ABRAHAM).

post mortem for William de Sproxton (PRO C135/104/7). Sproxton became part of the Honour of Helmsley in 1557.

1637. *"Jane Crosland, widow, holds at will one other house with a water corn mill, with one close called the Mill Holme 2s and pays £8";* Survey of Sproxton (NYCRO ZEW IV 4/4).

1644. Jane Crosland had *"three water corne mills ... at racke rent"* (Borthwick, Archbishop's Visitation R1/VIA/10f, 151V; J McDonnell ed, 1963, 159).

1705. *"Paid Edw. Sadler and others repairing Helmsley and Sproxton mills £19 0s 4d",* and in 1706 *"Paid Edward Sadler for work done to Sproxton Mill and for the Blue stones £50 0s 0d";* Thomas Stent's Accounts (NYCRO ZEW IV 6/3/1).

1832. *"To be let and entered upon the 25th day of March next. An excellent Water Corn Mill situate at Sproxton in the parish of Helmsley in the North Riding of the county of York. The mill is capable of doing a great deal of business, having two powerful waterwheels, and has four pairs of stones and a Barley Mill. Rent and further particulars from Mr Thomas Phillips of Beadlam Grange, near Helmsley. ..."* (Yorks Gazette, 11 February).

1884. *"Helmsley Mill, Yorkshire, on the banks of the Rye. ... The waterwheel after 50 years service, was replaced during the summer of 1884 by a turbine by Mr Rivis, the present occupier. The wheel had decayed. Turbine is a 32 in Trent manufactured by Mr C L Hett of the Anchor Foundry, Brigg"* (The Miller, December).

1887. Advertised as *"Old Helmsley Corn Mill"* (J McDonnell, ed 1963, 167).

1928. *"Ruins of old mill (owned by Lord Feversham) on the Rye. Ceased work 1916. Rollers and turbine formerly here. Three pairs of stones"* (Mitford Abraham).

1934. *"The passing of Mr R Rivis, miller, of Helmsley (Yorkshire) removes another old standard from the ranks of country millers. A few years ago Mr Rivis' father installed a roller flour plant of two sacks per hour capac-*

ity in the Ryedale mill, which is situated in beautiful woodland country close to Duncombe Park. ... This mill was one of the first in Yorkshire to be driven by a water turbine ..." (Miller, 5 February).

Millers; John Fenwick (1822), George Rivis (1873, 1897), R Rivis (1905, 1913).

In its final form Sproxton mill was a part stone-built and part brick-built two-storey plus loft, square-plan building with a hipped roof and the main entrance at first floor level. There was no living accommodation, the miller living in Helmsley. It was dismantled soon after it stopped work, the turbine going to Farndale Low mill.

HELMSLEY HIGH, SE 610841 (Borough Beck)
Demolished

The history of the Helmsley mills is obscure. The mill at the north end of Helmsley was probably the medieval Helmsley High mill or *'Over mill'.* There may have been a low or *"neyther"* mill near the late nineteenth century bobbin mill (J McDonnell, ed, 1963, 166-8). On the other hand, one of these mills may have been Sproxton mill.

1285. *"... two water mills worth £12 per annum ..."* and in *"Peole ... likewise a member of the same manor ... a water mill worth 60 shillings per annum";* Inquisition post mortem for Robert de Ros de Hanlake (YAS Rec Ser, vol 23). The location of Peole is not known.

1343. *"... two water mills worth £21 per annum"* and an oven; Inquisition post mortem for William de Ros (PRO C135/71/16).

1528. *"... two water mills and a common bake house";* Lease to George Sandwith, bailiff to the Earl of Rutland (Belvoir Charters, no 1918; J McDonnell ed, 1963, 166).

1555. *"... water mill called Over Mylne in Helmsley with a cottage in Castell Rowe, of the yearly rent of 13s 4d, and another mill called Neyther Mylle at £4 for 21 years at £12 13s 4d per annum";* Lease to John Richardson (Belvoir Charters, no 1917; J McDonnell ed, 1963, 166).

1637. *"... one house and garth in Helmsley, 10s ... and certain grounds thereto belonginge and three water corn mills ... held at racke rent";* lease to Mrs Jane Crosland (Belvoir Charters, no 1920; YAS Rec Ser, vol 15, 94; J McDonnell ed, 1963, 166).

1697. *"A pair of millstones for Helmsley Mill, £15"* and in 1705 *"Paid Edw. Sadler and others repairing Helmsley Mill and Sproxton Mill, £19 0s 4d";* Thomas Stent's Accounts (NYCRO ZEW IV 6/3/1).

1771. The High mill was marked but not named on Jefferys' Map.

1784. *"... the Old Mill";* rental of £70 per annum paid by Richard Dinsley (J McDonnell ed, 1963, 167).

1823. The mill was marked on *"Survey of several farms situate in Bilsdale ... Tuke and Ayers"* (NYCRO IV 1/13/6 & 7).

This mill probably ceased work soon after, with the trade

transferred to Sproxton mill. Today the leat can be found but a bungalow stands on the site. The name 'Millscut' survives.

HELMSLEY, bobbin, SE 615836 (Rye) Demolished
This may have been a second mill within Helmsley.
1637. Jane Crosland held the lease of three mills. This may be a reference to another mill in Helmsley (J McDonnell ed, 1963. 166). It may have stood to the south of the town at the end of Saw Mill Lane, but no evidence survives.
1870. The saw mill or Bobbin Mill was built by the Feversham estate to take advantage of the railway (NYCRO ZEW IV 7/28).

HAROME, RYE HOUSE, fulling, SE 633822 (Rye) Demolished
Whereas Harome corn mill was driven by the Riccal the fulling mill was driven by the Rye.
1301. *"William Full"* contributed 5d to the Lay Subsidy (W Brown, 1896, YAS Rec Ser, vol 21).
1430. *"A water mill for grain and a fulling mill here ..."* (Chan Inq p m, 9 Henry VI no 48; VCH vol 1, 487).
1557. *"... to my son Robert one pair of walker sheares ... my walke mylne is in decay ..."*; left by Robert Billingham (Borthwick Wills, vols 13, 15, 22; R H Hayes and M Allinson, 1988, 35).
1637. *"... the said Walk Mill"* described in a perambulation near Rye House; Survey of Harome (HMC Rutland, Belvoir Charters, 4163; R H Hayes and M Allinson, 1988).
1859. *"The Rye, after sinking at the cascades near Helmsley resurges at a place called Walk Mill"*, implying that the mill itself had gone (Whellan, History and Topography of York, vol 11, 858-9).
Some evidence of the leat survives on the east bank of the Rye.

NUNNINGTON, SE 675794 (Rye), Fig 110 Complete, Grade II
This is a very fine four-storey mill a quarter of a mile east of the village.
1086. Ralph Pagenel had a mill worth 3s per annum in *"Merlesveinn"*; Domesday Survey (M Faull and M Stinson, 1986).
n.d. *"A mill worth 8 marks of John Pagnal ..."* (YAS Rec Ser, vol 31, 9-10).
The mill then descended with the manor (Yorks Inq YAS iii, 9; Cal Inq p m, 10-20 Edw II 345; Pat Jas I pt xiv; VCH vol 1, 545).
1301. A miller paid tax in the Lay Subsidy (W Brown, 1896, YAS Rec Ser, vol 21).

1874. Rebuilt (J G Rutter, 1970, Trans Scar & Dist Arch Soc, vol 2, no 13, 1970). The new waterwheel was built by a Manchester firm, the components being brought by rail. The railway to Helmsley opened in 1870.
1928. *"... undershot wheel with 2 ft drop ... three pairs of stones (two French and one grey). Two pairs in use. Centrifugal dresser good order but not used for 25 years. Makes some wheatmeal. Mill rebuilt and raised by two floors in 1875. Makes electric light for Nunnington Hall"* (Mitford Abraham).
Millers; Christopher Foxton (1872, 1901), Hodgson Foxton (1905, 1913), Christopher Foxton (1921, 1937, 1950).
Flour milling stopped in 1903 but the mill continued to grind oats, some imported from Russia, which were sold to racehorse trainers. The brothers, Christopher and Arthington Foxton, gave up the tenancy in 1952 and the mill finally stopped about 1956 (Susan Clive, n d, A short history of Nunnington, private). It is now used as a farm store but the waterwheel and the machinery survive. The feasibility of restoration is being explored.
Nunnington mill is a four-storey stone building with regularly spaced windows. Some of the masonry is rusticated. A very large leat provided water from the Rye for the wooden-armed 16 feet diameter by 5 feet 2 inch iron waterwheel on an iron shaft. The 7 feet diameter pit wheel drives a cast-iron wallower. The 8 feet 10 inches diameter spur wheel is of wooden clasp-arm construction. There is a wooden upright shaft and three pairs of stones (one burr by "W J & T CHILD, MAKER, HULL & LEEDS" with a silent feed system, and two greys). Each is set on cast-iron hurst frames by J Hauxwell of Yarm, dated 1871. The second floor is a garner floor with no machinery. The third floor contains the hoist.
The old hurst posts are used as inner leaf window lintels in the building, proving that the rebuild and the refit are contemporary. The new downstream wall is set about 4 feet outside the old. Main beams are of memmel. The thick floor boards require no joists. There is a fireplace on the first floor.

GILLING, Grid reference not known (Holbeck)
1218. *"Geoffrey de Etton ... granted the mill of Gilling to Simon, son of William de Cliffard and his heirs to hold by service of a lb of pepper"* (Ft of F, 3 Henry III no 39; VCH vol 1, 480).
1374. The de Ettons had a mill (J Rushton, nd, 75).
1720. *"... overfall water corn milne with horse gate and cow gate"* (Quart Sessions Rec, N R Rec Soc, vol 8, 81; VCH vol 1, 480).
South of Gilling East at SE 619766 there is a 'Mill Wood'.

COULTON, SE 643736 (Marrs Beck), Fig 56 Complete, Grade II
This isolated mill between Coulton and Scackleton may have belonged to Byland Abbey.

nd. *"... in an undated charter Richard (Wyvill) granted to his nephew Lawrence his mill of Slinsgby"* (Harl Chart, 112, E56; Yorks Inq YAS iii, 151; VCH vol 1, 559).

1218. There was a Slingsby mill in the manor of Coulton (YAS Rec Ser, vol 67, Fines 1218-31; VCH vol 1).

pre 1721. *"The Fairfaxes gained the manor in the sixteenth century, installing an overfall wheel at their corn mill before 1721"* (J Rushton, nd, 74).

1823. Two pencil sketches by George Nicholson show the mill as it survives today (York City Art Gallery).

1932. *"Overshot wheel. One pair of French, one pair of Grey Stones. Blue stone on floor near door. Framework of silk screen and smutter still in mill. Pulley outside works saw bench and oat roller"* (Mitford Abraham).

Millers; W Dennison (1642), John Peirson (1803, 1811), Thomas Harrison (1893).

The mill was last used about 1950. There is a wooden clasp-arm waterwheel with hexagonal geometry for the arms. The drive was by two lying shafts, one of which survives. The old hurst frame survives behind a later frame. One set of segmented burrs marked "W T & J CHILD MILLSTONE MAKER HULL & LEEDS" is used as a road marker in Coulton village. A blue stone is used as the threshold to the mill.

SCACKLETON SE 646739 (Marr Beck) Demolished
An old leat runs from near the outfall from Coulton mill through Soulby Wood to a hollow under a steep slope. It represents the remains of a mill recorded in the thirteenth century (NYCRO ZQG (F) Mic. 2814 fr.1283). There is anomaly in the parish boundary to accommodate this leat.

HOVINGHAM, SE 666757 (Marrs Beck) Demolished
1823. The mill was the subject of two pencil sketches by George Nicholson (York City Art Gallery).

1928. *"... now the estate saw mill for Hovingham Park. Formerly a corn mill and grey stones on floor at back entrance. Mill dam being cleaned out. Turbine put in ten years ago"* (Mitford Abraham).

NEWSHAM/HABTON, SE 746762 (Rye) Demolished
Newsham mill was the lowest mill on the Rye, below the confluence with the other main flows in Ryedale.

1364. *"A mill was attached to the manor of Great Habton ..."* (Ft of F, 39 Edw III, no 2; VCH vol 2, 444).

1599. Mill in Little Habton (Yorks Fines, Tudors, YAS IV, 135; VCH vol 1, 444).

1652. (Ft of F, Yorks; VCH vol 1, 444)

1710. *"To devoted and virtuous wife Lettice for life one third of ... mills ... etc in Little Habton, Newshome and Bangthorpe, Yorks"*; will of John Bower of Malton (NYCRO ZFY 8 mic 1564).

1777. *"... a tenement and water corn mill called Newsham mill and a windmill in Little Habton etc to John Rushton of Newsham Mill"*; conveyance by John Bower of Scorton (NYCRO ZFY 10 mic 1564).

1846. Following The Rye and Derwent Drainage Act, Newsham mill valued at £1147 2s 8d for *"the site, buildings, wheels, gearing, stones, machinery, ashlar work etc"*, was taken over and the mill dam removed (John Henderson, 1853, 129-51).

WATH, SE 677749 (Wath Beck) Demolished
1343. *"At Wath, about half a mile south of Hovingham, on the road to Malton, standing by the stream, is the Mill House, an old stone building. The capital messuage here is mentioned in 1343"* (Chan Inq p m 17 Edward III, 1st nos, no 143; VCH vol 1, 64)

HAMBLETON HILLS

The Coxwold Gap, between the Hambleton and Howardian Hills, is drained by the Holbeck to the east, the Long Beck/Elphin Beck system to the south and the Sutton/Balk/Thirkleby Beck which flows from the western scarp of the Hambleton Hills.

AMPLEFORTH, SE 582782 (Holbeck), Fig 161 Shell
The mill was driven by a tributary of the Holbeck, rising on Ampleforth Moor near Studford Ring. The tailrace fed back to 'Water Gate'. It has been suggested that there was an earlier mill further up the beck (J McDonnell, 1970, Gazetteer of local place names in the vicinity of Byland Abbey and Newburgh Priory, Rye Hist no 5, 41-63).

1295. *"... in the vill of Ampleforth a water mill worth 23s per annum"*; held by Robert de Sproxton (YAS Rec Ser, vol 94, 21-4).

1361. *"A mill belonging to Adam de London ... was afterwards in the possession of Moxby Priory"*; Dugdale Monasticum, iv 567 (VCH vol 1, 463).

1611. James I granted the mill to Felix Wilson and Robert Morgan (Pat Jas I, pt v, 1; VCH vol 1, 463).

1835. *"To be let. A water corn mill at Ampleforth. The mill contains one pair of blue stones and one pair of greys. The premises now occupied by John Sigsworth"* (Yorks Gazette, 14 March).

1853. *"To be sold. All that capital water corn mill running two pairs of stones with the dressing machine and*

237

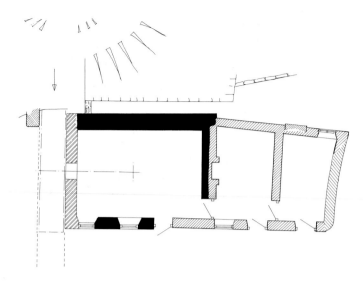

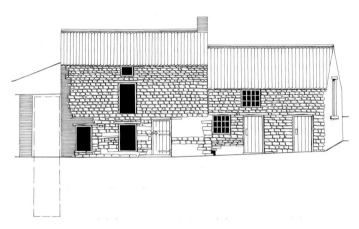

FIG 161. AMPLEFORTH MILL.

other machinery. The mill is about one mile distant from Ampleforth railway station and steam power could be added at small expence" (Yorks Gazette, 12 November).

1930. *"No wheel, gearing or machinery. Formerly worked by overshot wheel. Disused for a long time"* (Mitford Abraham).

Millers; George Sigsworth (1835, 1853), Simeon Hutchinson (1840), John Stanhope (1873), James Dennis (1890), James Rymer (1893).

The mill had two embanked ponds. The late eighteenth century/early nineteenth century mill is built of rubble stone with an old house attached and a newer house nearby. Scrape marks on the rebuilt gable wall suggest a waterwheel about 18 feet in diameter. At an earlier stage there may have been an internal waterwheel. Evidence suggests that this was an upright shaft mill with two lay shafts from the crown wheel. The old house was linked to the mill at both ground and first floor levels for use as a granary.

OLDSTEAD, SE 533803 (Long Beck), Fig 162 Converted Oldstead mill, at the foot of Cockerdale and close to Oldstead Hall, was probably the mill of Stocking Grange. The monastic buildings stood on the flat ground immediately to the west of Oldstead Hall. There is little good ploughing land at Oldstead and the village probably only grew to its present size as a result of the flax industry at the end of the eighteenth century.

1929. *"... very old mill. Ceased to work about 1909. Two pairs of stones (one French and one Grey) ... flour boulter still in ... spur wheel has new hornbeam cogs ... overshot wheel ... pentrough broken"* (Mitford Abraham).

Millers; John Hardy (1840), Thomas Weatherill (1873, 1893).

The mill is a late eighteenth century/ early nineteenth century two-storey with loft, stone-built structure with attached mill house. The mill house post-dates the mill. According to local sources it worked until immediately after World War I. Afterwards local farmers used Newburgh mill. It was converted into a house in 1979. However, it retains its 15 feet diameter overshot water-wheel with cast-iron shrouds by "BUTLER, HELMSLEY", a clasp-arm pit wheel with very early cast-iron gear segments, cast-iron wallower, wooden upright shaft and 9 feet 6 inch diameter clasp-arm spur wheel which formerly drove three sets of stones. The spur wheel is one of a group in this locality which were of very large diameter. There is a French millstone by "GEORGE MARIS HULL MAKER 1838". Stone nuts were engaged by means of forked levers. Interestingly there is no crown wheel and no evidence for the type of drive used from the top of the upright shaft. There are two parallel contouring leats, the original being supplanted by a leat at a higher level for driving a turbine.

OLDSTEAD, fulling, SE 533801 (Long Beck) Demolished

c.1840. Named as *"Walk Mill"* on the Tithe map.

A leat runs from the site of the corn mill, terminating in disturbed ground about 185m from the mill. Stonework has been cleared from the mill site and the wheel pit filled with cinder etc. Upstream, and on the opposite side of the beck, is a short ditch thought to have been used as a retting pond.

There is evidence from various sources of eighteenth century flax working at both Oldstead and Kilburn.

BYLAND, SE 548788 (Long Beck), Fig 22 Demolished Savignac monks from Furness finally settled in 1177 at 'Bella Landa' (Byland), formerly part of the waste land of Roger de Mowbray's manor of Coxwold.

1538. At the Dissolution there were two water-driven mills, a corn mill within the Abbey precinct and a fulling mill.

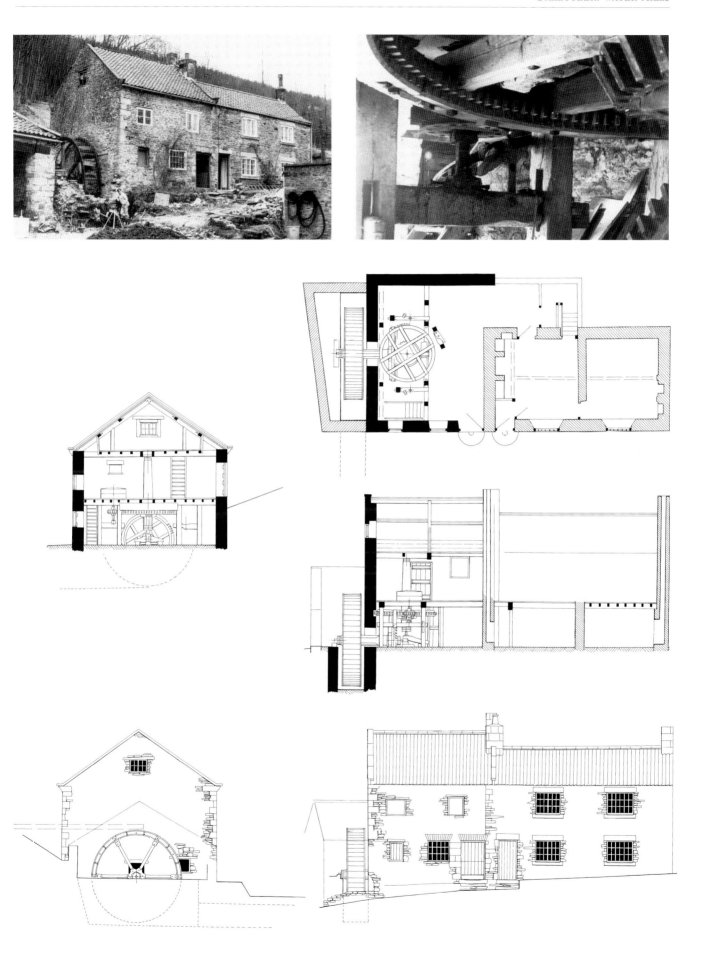

Fig 162. Oldstead mill.

1540. The demesne lands of Byland, the site of the Abbey, the church and steeple, water mill and closes were granted to Sir William Pickering (L & P, Henry VIII, xvi, g, 107, 28; VCH vol 2, 18).

The precinct corn mill probably dated from 1234 when a large earthwork dam was created to hold water from Oldstead (J McDonnell & M R Everest, 1965, The waterworks of Byland Abbey, Rye Hist, no 1; J McDonnell, Inland fisheries in medieval Yorkshire, 1066-1300, Borthwick Papers no 60; S A Harrison, 1986, The stonework of Byland Abbey, Rye Hist, no 13). The Long Beck was ponded in the valley to the north of the precinct. The sunken ground between the surviving gatehouse and the Abbey ruin is the dried out remains of a millpond, which may be that dating from 1234. A 5 feet diameter millstone serves as a threshold of the house on the site of the mill.

LOW PASTURE, SE 552783 (Long Beck), Fig 22
Demolished

This may have been a pre-monastery mill, which may have become the first corn mill of the Abbey. By 1540 it was a fulling mill (J McDonnell, 1965).

There is a leat from *"Pond Bay"* (Ordnance Survey maps) along a distinct terrace to high ground immediately behind the present Low Pasture House. There is a second dam immediately behind Low Pasture with a drainage conduit under the buildings. The scale of the water engineering works indicates that this site was developed for more than fulling.

NEWBURGH/COXWOLD, SE 538766 (Long Beck), Figs 22 & 48 Derelict, Grade II

This mill on Long Beck is part of the Wombwell estate.

1154-7. *"... all that land of the east side of Coxwold beyond the fishpond ..."*; Boundary Description (Husthwaite L H Soc, Aspects of Coxwoldshire, 1992, 24). After the Dissolution Newburgh Priory, along with *"Coxwold mills"*, was acquired by Anthony Bellas.

1605. The mill and the *"Stanke"* were marked on an estate map (NYCRO ZDV VI mic 1504).

1685-6. *"To Ja Nightingale for Buckett boards and bucketting and new cogging the 2 mills at Newburgh, £4 3s 4d"*; Faucenberg Estate Account Books, (NYCRO ZDV V), summarised by J Hatcher, 1978, vol 2, 176-182.

1689. *"To Mich Barehead for making two new water wheeles for Newburgh mills, £7 9s 9d"*. *"To Robert Athey for 8 days thatching the mill, 8s 0d"*. *"To Robert Waters for 24 days cutting, sawing, felling and making a new Cogg Wheele for Newburgh Mill, £2 4s 0d"* (NYCRO ZDV V).

1697. Thatching of *"Newbrough Mill, house and kilne"* (NYCRO ZDV)

1722. The 'Stanke' had been drained; *"An accurate survey of Newbrough, the estate of ye Right Honble Thomas,* *Lord Fauconberg, by William Palmer and William Jones"* (NYCRO ZDV).

1813. *"If used as a mere grist mill, rent is sufficient, but if a tenant can make flour for the bakers of Thirsk it will be cheap at the price ... overshot wheel and three sets of stones"*; Survey and Valuation (NYCRO ZDV V mic 1285/317).

1854. Fish pond re-created and saw mill established; *"Plan of the Township of Newburgh belonging to Sir George Wombwell, bart, revised and corrected by Henry Scott"* (NYCRO ZDV V).

1929. *"... wooden building is the Wombwell estate saw mill worked by overshot wheel. Corn Mill (worked by Messrs Boddy of Kirkby Moorside) has two pairs of stones (one French and one grey). Rollers put in many years ago but not worked since 1920. Overshot wheel worked machinery by cogs on the outside rim"* (Mitford Abraham).

Millers; Francis Asqwith (1822), Francis Ashworth? (1840), George Muncaster (1872, 1879), George Boddy (1889, 1905), George Boddy & Son (also Kirkby Moorside & Easingwold, 1909, 1913), G A Boddy (1921, 1925).

This mill, though now derelict with roof and floors all down, is a most interesting relic. It was driven from an elevated watercourse from the outfall from the Low Pasture site across the low-lying lands to the fish/mill pond near Newburgh Priory called the 'Stanke'. This pond survives (now enlarged) and a road runs across the dam. The mill is stone-built to the first floor and handmade brick to the roof, dating from the seventeenth century. The later top floor has four fireplaces and was used as a dwelling. A 12 feet 4 inches diameter overshot waterwheel with a ring gear driving a lay shaft to three pairs of stones, all of mid-nineteenth century date, survives. The wooden trough across the outside of the south facade carried water to a saw bench.

KILBURN/WILDON GRANGE, SE 517791 Demolished

A Beck runs through the village of Kilburn, under the famous white horse on the south west scarp of the Hambleton Hills, but there is no sign of a millstead.

1275. *"... mill worth £1"*; Inquisition post mortem for John de Eyville (YAS Rec Ser, vol 12, 91).

1530. *"... milnestede to build a mill upon in the manor of Wyldon and a mill race through the whole lordship of Kilburn to the said mylnestede, to be made from the town or banks of Kylburne to the said milnestede, with the soken of the townships of Overkylburne and Netherkylburne"*; demise by John, Abbot of Byland, to Richard Lascelles (30 Henry VIII, PRO C 344, 419; VCH vol 2, 21).

This refers to a mill near the farmhouse at Wildon Grange. The lane to this farm is still called 'Mill Field Lane'. The lower section of the leat to this site is a diversion of the old beck and the old course is now almost invisible. Where the leat swings west, immediately behind the farmhouse, there is a hollow, a relic of the tailrace.

BAXBY, SE 513753 (Elphin Beck), Fig 163 Shell

This former Wombwell estate mill is on an isolated steading with no proper road access. There were two manors at Baxby in the time of the Domesday Survey, one of which later became Husthwaite. The other became part of the manor of Thornton-on-the-Hill. *"The*

mill with another which has disappeared, formed for centuries a part of the manor of Thornton-on-the-Hill" (Ft of F, Yorks, 5 Edward III no 11; VCH vol 2, 14).

1169. Suit of the mill at Thornton was granted to Peter Daiville of Kilburn (E Smith, 1992, in Coxwoldshire, Husthwaite L H Soc, 69).

1230. Matilda Percy (wife of John Daiville) paid suit to the mill. Henry II granted one load of timber yearly from the Forest of Galtres for the repair of this mill (Chan Inq p m, Edw III, 2nd nos, no 96).

1275. *"Manor of Thornton-on-the-Hill and the mill"*;

FIG 163. BAXBY MILL.

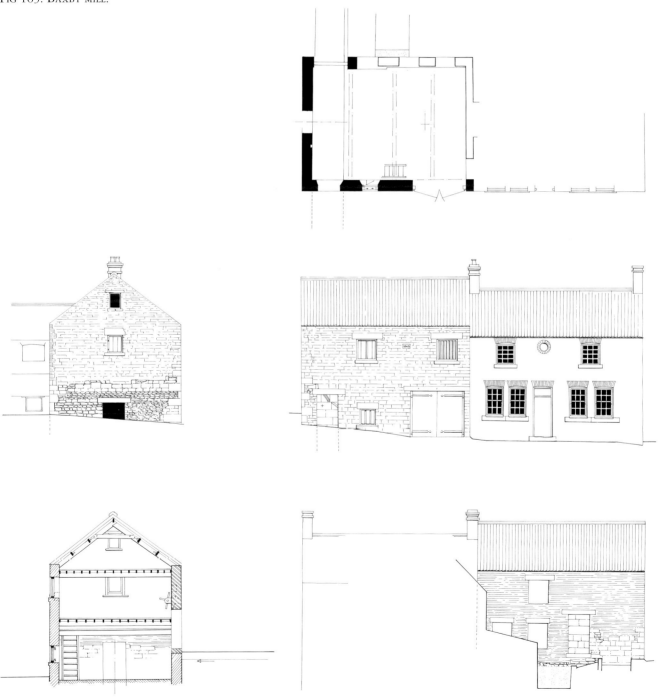

Inquisition post mortem for John Davyll (Yorks Inq p m; YAS i, 160; VCH vol 2).

1301. John Daiville conveyed Thornton manor and two mills to John de Ellerker (E Smith, 1992, 69).

1391. William Daiville got permission from Byland Abbey to remove and rebuild the mill of Baxby (E Smith, 1992, 69).

1609. Angram Grange, Baxby mills and land in Coxwold; Newburgh Title Deeds (NYCRO ZDV I 5 mic 1352).

1658. Christopher Goulton was charged with converting one of the mills into a cottage (E Smith, 1992, 71).

1761. John Chapman formerly of Baxby Mill House in the parish of Coxwold a prisoner for debt in the castle of York (London Gazette, 4 April).

1929. *"No wheel or gearing. Ceased to work 50 years ago. Dam dry. Millstone at back door. Millstone built into mill where wheel walls show marks of revolving wheel touching wall. Dated 1849"* (Mitford Abraham).

Millers; John Asquith (1787), Thomas Asquith (1816), William Reid, (*"Baxby Mill" 1872*), (1879).

The mill is now empty and most of the leat filled in.

This early steading was upgraded in the early 19th century. A datestone of 1849 is inserted into the front facade of the mill but this refers to the last rebuild including a brick wall to the rear. The front wall and lower courses of the end and rear walls are of ashlar quality masonry,

probably from Byland Abbey. Masonry from the wheel pit has been used to block the doorway to the waterwheel. There was an internal, low breast waterwheel 4 feet 9 inches wide and a jack roll used for lifting a water-trap or gate has survived. The attached mill house dates from 1909 but the walls of an older thatched house survive in the end gable and rear walls. Two old sandstone millstones and one blue bedstone have survived.

RAVENSTHORPE/BOLTBY, SE 494849 (Gurtoft Beck), Figs 20 & 164 Converted

This mill was served by water from an embanked pond fed by the moat of the now vanished Ravensthorpe Hall.

1142. *"... and by the same water to the place where the water is withdrawn from its own course and then beyond the water up to the top of the brow of the hill ..."*; boundary description for land granted by Odo de Boltebia to Rievaulx Abbey (EYC vol 9, 89).

1272. *"One water mill in Ravensthorpe worth 8 marks per annum";* Inquisition for Nicholas de Bolteby (YAS Rec Ser, vol 12, 72).

1301. Michaele Molendinario contributed 4s to the Lay Subsidy (W Brown, YAS Rec Ser, vol 21, 83).

1308. The mill was worth £5 per annum; Inquisition post mortem for Willelmo Cantilupo (YAS Rec Ser, vol 21, 83).

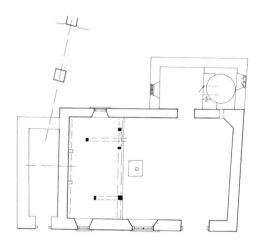

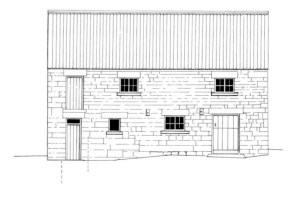

FIG 164. RAVENSTHORPE MILL.

1642. The mill and house and pasture about it rented by John How; Duncombe Park Surveys (NYCRO IV 1/5, mic 1158).

1930. *"Worked by turbine for fifteen years, formerly by overshot wheel. Three pairs of stones ... German blue (dismantled), French not used and English greys in use. Ruinous old boulter and dresser ..."* (Mitford Abraham).

Millers; Hornby (Boltby, 1822), James Coulson (1851), William Weatherill (1873, 1893).

The mill is now a shell and used as a garage. It had an internal waterwheel with a hurst big enough for an upright shaft drive. There is a roasting plate in an outshot behind the mill. Part of a grey bed stone stands in front of the house.

SUTTON-UNDER-WHITESTONECLIFFE, SE 482826
(Sutton Beck), Fig 4 Demolished

1086. *"Land of Hugh, son of Baldrick. Gerard, Hugh's man has ... one mill"*; Domesday Survey (M Faull & M Stinson, 1986).

1684. Sutton Mill was leased by Archbishop Dalden of York to Thomas Craven on behalf of the trustees of Roger Baine deceased (NYCRO Z 68 cal).

1824. *"To be sold. All that capital new-erected Water Corn Mill, supplied with a never failing stream of water and held by lease for three lives under his Grace the Archbishop of York, late in the possession of John Davies. Situate at Sutton-u-Whitestonecliffe ..."* (Yorks Gazette, 15 May).

1828. *"To be sold. All that new-erected Water Corn Mill etc situate at Sutton-u-Whitestonecliffe, now in the occupation of Mr Jonathan Bellwood, the tenant"* (Yorks Gazette, 13 September).

1930. *"Turbine put in 20-30 years ago and replaced overshot wheel. One pair of grey stones used"* (Mitford Abraham).

Millers; Jonathan Bellwood (1828), Christopher Kendrew (1840), Robert Rennison (1872), George Milner (1879), Thomas Humphrey (1893, 1901), Mark Kilvington (1905, 1925).

The mill stood to the west of Sutton Hall on the edge of the village. It was built of stone with a central doorway and four Yorkshire sliding sash windows in the facade. A German blue millstone used as a road marker is inscribed "I B 1768 +". The mill survived until into this century and the in-line mill house is still standing. The leat flowed behind Sutton Hall but has been filled in.

BALK/BAGBY, SE 475808 (Balk/Thirkleby Beck), Fig 112 Converted

This site would be the logical place for the corn mill of the village of Bagby but there is no trace of a medieval structure.

c 1790. The present Balk mill was built as a flax spinning mill, probably to utilise machinery patented by John Kendrew and Thomas Porthouse of Skerne mill, Darlington, in 1787 and improved by John Marshall of Leeds in 1790. The village is an industrial hamlet, with several brick-built houses including a three-storey tenement. Balk Beck was dammed some 275m from the mill to produce a very large pond. The leat from this led to a smaller pond on the opposite side of the road from the mill. These ponds are now dried out.

1930. *"In very poor and neglected condition. Mill gave up grinding for farmers about 1910. Owner still grinds for his own use. Undershot breast wheel ..."* (Mitford Abraham).

Millers; Thomas Hare (1873), Joseph Hare (1893).

This mill was built of small hand-made bricks to a plan of 30 by 40 feet internal dimension. The floors were supported on cast-iron columns and the glazing bars for the windows were also of cast-iron. As reconstructed as a corn mill, in the middle of the nineteenth century, it had a lay shaft to three sets of millstones and an ancillary upright shaft. The waterwheel was on the north eastern gable wall.

The machinery was removed during World War II. The water rights were signed away and the humped bridge carrying the road over the leat was demolished. The building is now used as a furniture workshop and show room.

THIRKLEBY, SE 478796 (Thirkleby Beck), Fig 165 Shell

This mill served the villages of both Great and Little Thirkleby and there were tracks to both villages, that to Great Thirkleby still forming the road and that to Little Thirkleby now preserved as a footpath only.

"A mill was mentioned in the sixteenth century" (VCH vol 2, 55).

1930. *"Built of stone and very old. Mill house built of brick. Overshot wheel. Good business but only one pair of stones. Turbine put in and makes own electric light"* (Mitford Abraham).

Millers; John Smith (1822), William Moyser (1873), Joseph Burton (1889, 1897), T Pollard (1901, 1921), J T Pollard (1925), Wilfred Burton Pollard (1937).

The late eighteenth century mill belonged to the Thirkleby estate until 1923. It worked with turbine and one set of stones until 1966. The two-storey plus loft building is of very good quality dressed stone, with three-bay brick-built mill house attached to and destroying the original gable wall of the mill. The waterwheel was external to the mill building. It had an upright shaft and there has been a roasting kiln. The hoist survives.

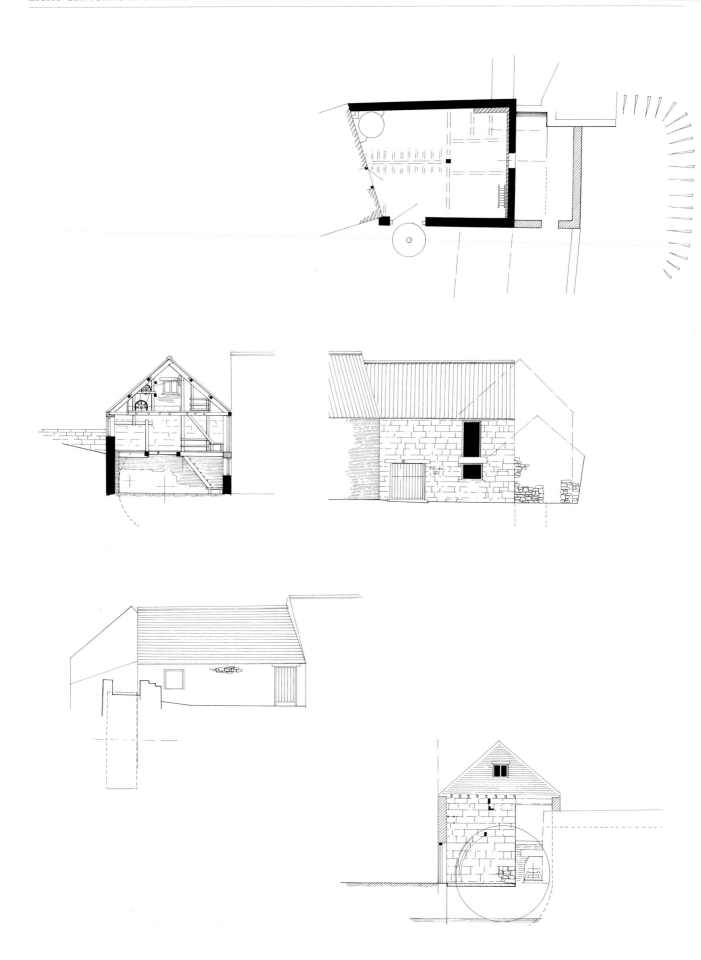

Fig 165. Thirkleby mill.

COD BECK AND THIRSK

Cod Beck runs south under the western scarp of the North York Moors. There were big mills on Cod Beck and smaller mills on the tributaries from the scarp of the Moors.

INGLEBY ARNCLIFFE, NZ 451006 (Carr Beck)
Demolished
A lengthy leat takes water from Scarth Nick and Scarth Wood across the Carrs to the mill site.
1280. *"… one toft in Erneclyve between the mill pond and the cemetery"* and also *"the tithe of the mill"* worth 21d; parts of the gift of William Yngram to Gisborough Priory (Gis Chart, Surtees Soc, vol 89, 431-2; J C Atkinson, vol 2 pt 2, 104). By 1434 a windmill had been built but the water mill survived.
1640 The diary of Timothy Mauleverer, starting in 1640, recorded his personal view of the problems of running a water mill (NYCRO TD 38).
1843. Not marked on Henry Cross' map (J W Ord, 1846). Poor water supply may have been the reason for its early demise. The mill site is under a modern agricultural building.

BORDELBY/MOUNT GRACE, SE 446986, Figs 21 & 166
Shell
The manorial mill of the village of Bordelby became the mill of the Carthusian Mount Grace Priory in 1396.
Pre-1396. *"… rent of one mark per annum from his mill of Syvehill (unas marcae de molendino mea de Syvehill)"* in Bordelby; grant by Robert de Lascelles, lord of Bordelby, to Rievaulx Abbey at some date before the Carthusians arrived (Rievaulx Chart, Surtees Soc, vol 83, 206).
The estate and mill were bought by Sir James Strangways after the Dissolution.
At some time in the nineteenth century a new estate mill was built.
1880. John Hauxwell carried out repairs to the water-wheel and the millstones (John Hauxwell's Letter Books).
1933. *"Twenty foot diameter breast wheel working threshing machine and winnowing machine … worked also two pairs of stones (one French and one grey). French pair not worked since 1907. Mill not worked for several years"* (Mitford Abraham).
The ornamental pond below the Priory buildings may have been created from a former millpond. The water from this pond feeds an embanked millpond used in the nineteenth century to drive two pairs of millstones in a barn. The large external wheel case formerly held a 24 feet diameter pitch-back waterwheel with cast-iron

FIG 166. MOUNT GRACE (PHOTO, MITFORD ABRAHAM).

shrouds and naves and with ring gear on the arms – almost certainly of mid-nineteenth century date. Two pairs of millstones, one marked "SAVERY-MAKER-STOCKTON AND LEEDS", were probably driven by lay shaft. The wheel may have been used for driving a saw bench after corn milling ceased.

COTE GILL/HIGH MILL, SE 461981 (Crabdale Beck)
Demolished
This mill was built in one of the lots enclosed under the Parliamentary Enclosure Act of 1755.
1786. A half part of the allotment, including *"a corn mill and other buildings"*; surrender by Appleton Bennison, stone mason of Thimbleby (NYCRO Deeds Reg BY 543 722).
A flax mill was established on the site by Mr Poynter and William Yeoman of Pateley Bridge at the end of the century.
1809. Partnership between John Chippendale, William Poynter and William Yeoman of Osmotherley … flax spinners, dissolved by mutual consent (London Gazette, 23 January)
1840. Shares in land called *"Coat Gill upon which a water corn mill and other buildings were erected"*; surrender by Thomas Yeoman to George Poynter (NYCRO Deeds Reg GS 78 103). The use of *"corn mill"* continued until 1850.
A map (c 1830) shows a spinning mill with a separate *"Bleach Mill"* 185m to the west. Two mills were listed in 1838 but one was unoccupied. The other had two waterwheels representing 6 HP and employed 23 persons. In 1852 John Dobby, late of Osmotherley, York, flax dresser, was an insolvent debtor in York goal. The mill seems to have closed for a while in 1896 and finally in 1915.
Today the early corn mill/spinning mill complex is gone, apart from one wall incorporated into a later building. The massive dam and its stone apron survive.

LOW, bleach, SE 460979 (Crabdale Beck) Demolished

This mill has been totally demolished but the dam survives. It was marked as an L-shaped building on an 1847 map.

SPITE/OSMOTHERLEY, SE 461968 (Cod Beck), Fig 72 Converted

This mill was built on Lot 23 in the 1755 Enclosure Act. In October 1765 Anthony Reed and William Robinson sold the lot to Thomas Paul, miller, and Thomas Alderson, both yeomen, of Ellerbeck. The mill was probably built by Robert Paul of Ellerbeck. The name 'Spite' appeared in the nineteenth century, derived from a supposed conflict with Osmotherley mill.

1771. Nothing marked on the site of Spite mill on Jefferys' map.

1782. Death of Richard Paul of the 'New Mill' (Osmotherley Parish Reg.).

1791. *"... cottage, garth, toft and croft and allotment no 23 on which a house and mill had been built"*; mortgage by Robert and Nathaniel Paul to Thomas Flintoft for £350; Minutes of commissioners appointed to execute the Enclosure Act.

1792. *"To be sold. A newly erected over fall Water Corn Mill, situated at Osmotherley ... seven miles from Northallerton, with a water wheel 18 feet in diameter. Further details from Mr John Weighell of Osmotherley, the owner"* (Yorks Herald, 7 February).

1840 Sold to Robert Haynes of Thimbleby Hall.

1929. *"Ceased working about twenty years ago. One pair of stones at back. Formerly worked by overshot wheel. Turbine now works for electric light at Thimbley Hall and saws timber for the estate. The mill was the one where the north end of Snilesworth farmers took their grain and Arden for the south end"* (Mitford Abraham).

Millers; John Cundale (1822), George Cowens (1826, 1832, 1840, 1850), Nathaniel Wetherill (1851), George Maclean (1854, 1862), Stephenson Bell (1864, 1874) Thomas Walker (1891, 1893), Joseph Peirson (1897, 1901).

Spite mill was a lay-shaft mill. On the gable wall at the opposite end to the waterwheel there has been an external flue, possibly indicating a demolished drying kiln. There were three pairs of French stones.

The dam was strengthened and raised in 1943 (date on concrete pen-stock) possibly to drive a saw bench under a wooden lean-to across the front of the mill. The driving gear and millstones were missing by the 1960s but hurst posts remained. The building was converted into a dwelling in the early 1990s.

THIMBLEBY/OSMOTHERLEY/FOXTON'S, SE 452965 (Cod Beck), Figs 45 & 167 Converted

This mill was the demesne corn mill of Thimbleby and Osmotherley, in the manor of Northallerton. From before 1284 the manor was in the patrimony of the Bishop of Durham. Later it was transferred to the Bishop of Ripon and then to the Ecclesiastical Commission.

1359. Mill in *"Thymbleby"*; release by John, son of Roger Mauduyt, to John de Crumelbothum (Yorks Fines, 1327-47, 70).

1589-1595. Leased to Thomas Todd for £2 6s 8d p a (Durham Univ Lib, ASC CCB Box 92, 10 220822).

1602. *"These are to require and authorise you to deliver unto Thomas Todde, bearer hereof, out of my woods of Osmotherley, two trees such as shall meet for his use reserving the trees lately marked there and also one crooked tree growing in the loning there meet to be a pair of siles"*; Instruction by Tobias Matthew, Bishop of Durham, to his woodman (Durham Univ Lib, ASC CCB Box 92, 220830 8).

1803. Leased, Oswald Thompson, miller, Osmotherley and Thos Fisher, miller, to Richard Park (NYCRO Deeds Reg, CZ 24 35).

1826. *"To be sold. A valuable Water Corn Mill, well supplied with water, with three pairs of stones, two cylinders etc, in complete repair ... now in the occupation of Richard Park, the owner"* (Yorks Gazette, 19 August).

1836. *"To be sold by auction by order of the assignees of Benjamin John Weatherell, a bankrupt. A capital modern and well-built water corn mill ... called Parks Mill, with three pairs of French stones etc"* (Yorks Gazette, 24 September).

1843. The leasehold was bought by Christopher Foxton, the miller of Nunnington mill, on behalf of Hannah Foxton (his mother?). Hannah Foxton died in 1845 and left the mill to her two sons, Christopher (miller at Nunnington) and John (biscuit maker of West Hartlepool).

1913. The mill, by this time known as Foxton's mill, was sold to Allan and Leonard Boville, bleachers of Osmotherley (Deeds of Osmotherley mill, Mrs D V Arnold).

1929. *"Three pairs of stones and flour machinery intact. One pair used for grinding. Overshot wheel"* (Mitford Abraham).

Millers; Benjamin John Wetherell (1815), Richard Park (1822), William Hornsey and Francis Carver (1840) John Stephenson (1861), George Moon, *"Old Mill"* (1873, 1889), William Boville (1893, 1901), L & A Boville (1910, 1913).

Latterly it was used as a meal mill only and the flour milling stones and silk screens were taken out. The large diameter cast-iron spur wheel was put in to replace a wooden wheel in 1941. The mill made electricity up to 1962. The mill was kept in preserved condition by Mr

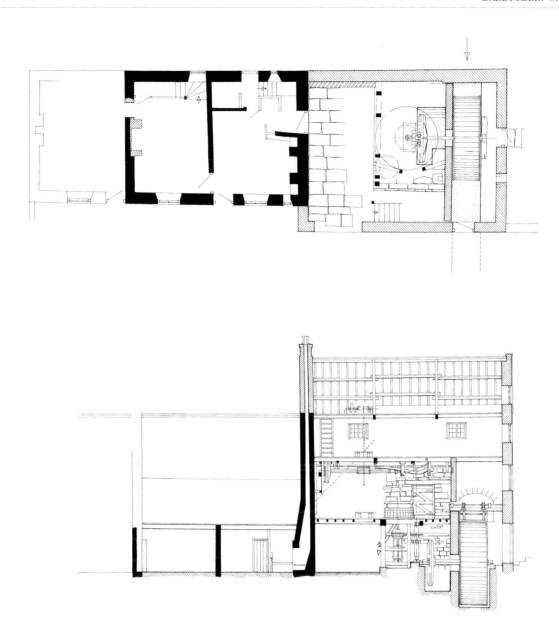

FIG 167. OSMOTHERLEY MILL.

and Mrs D V Arnold but sold in 1981. It was dismantled in 1982 and the machinery taken to Temple Newsham Hall, Leeds.

The range of buildings bears traces of many rebuilds. There is an old steep-pitched gable wall, probably seventeenth century, built into the upstream wall of the mill. The in-line house has a fireplace beam and screened entrance from the mill. The leat brought water to a sliding hatch pen-stock, operated by a quadrant gear and rack, over a 14 feet diameter, pitch-back waterwheel on an iron shaft, also fitted with an 8 feet diameter cast-iron pit wheel. There was a mid-nineteenth century cast-iron upright shaft with a very large diameter cast-iron spur wheel driving three sets of stones via cast-iron stone nuts.

CLACK LANE, fulling, SE 447965 (Cod Beck)

Formerly a fulling mill belonging to the Bishop of Durham.

1589. Fulling mill worth £1 13s 3d per annum; lease to Anthony *"Perese"* (Durham Univ Lib, ASC CCB Box 92, 1). It continued with the Pearson family until the middle of the seventeenth century and then with the Wetherell family until Benjamin John Wetherell became bankrupt in 1841.

1809. *"Osmotherley fulling mill ... consists only of a shed or room on each side of the waterwheel, wherein the fulling machinery works. The dam at the head of the watercourse takes a great deal of labour to keep it up, and I think the whole premises may be worth nine pound per annum. ... Viewed 19 Oct, D Turner";* Notitia Plan

(Durham Univ Lib, ASC CCB 1981 321798 35).

1842. *"Mary Boville & Son took over the Walk Mill and bleaching ground at Osmotherley which had been started by Milner & Co in 1823"* (A T Dingle, 1950, 23-7).

1904. Described as *"Walk Mill (Bleaching)"* (Ordnance Survey).

The property became known as Boville Park. The complex had three waterwheels, one of which survives.

ELLERBECK, SE 433966 (Cod Beck), Fig 168 Complete
This is clearly an old mill.

Late C12. Philip de Colvill granted to the Hospital of St James at Northallerton 2 acres of land near his holding in Ellerbeck, making a condition that he should be allowed to make supports for the mill dam there (YAJ vol 16, 159-60; VCH vol 1, 435).

1539. Listed in Valor Ecclesiasticus (Rec Comm v 85; VCH vol 1, 434).

1652. *"... two water grist mills here under one roof"* (Close pt XIVI, m 24; VCH vol 1, 434).

1838. *"To be sold. One third part of the manor of Ellerbeck"* including the *"valuable Water Corn Mill"* (Yorks Gazette, 22 September). It was re-advertised in 1839.

1847. Notice of auction sale at Ellerbeck mill (NYCRO Z 250 mic 1519).

1850. *"To be sold by order of the High Court of Chancery at the Golden Lion Inn, Northallerton ... a leasehold estate being one third part of the manor of Ellerbeck ... including a Water Corn Mill"* (London Gazette, 29 January).

1860. *"Sale of manor and estate of Ellerbeck at present held under two year leases from the Dean and Chapter of Christ Church, Oxford. Christopher Smith is the tenant of the mill"* (Yorks Gazette, 25 August).

1933. *"Breast (top) wheel (iron with wood buckets). Two pairs of French and one pair of grey stones. Two pairs worked. Silk dresser ceased to work 50 years ago"* (Mitford Abraham).

Millers; A Norman (1840), Christopher Smith (1860, *"corn dealer, Northallerton & Ellerbeck"* 1873), Joseph Pratt (1890, 1905), Hannah Barker (1909, 1933).

According to one source the mill stopped work in 1939. The hipped-roof building is spacious inside and may have contained a mill house at an earlier period. There have been many alterations to the stonework of the facade. It has been raised by three courses and the original windows blocked. It seems that the ground floor has been lowered. The 15 feet diameter, pitch-back waterwheel drove a wooden upright shaft with a large diameter spur wheel. One pair of grey stones remains.

FOXTON, SE 421962 (Cod Beck) Demolished
The manor house of the lost village of Foxton survives as a row of cottages with one seventeenth century doorway. The mill belonged to the Kirkby Sigston estate.

1240. *"Now"* Robert grants to *"the aforesaid William all the aforesaid mill at Foxton with appurtenances to have and to hold to the said William and his heirs ... forever, rendering therefrom by the year 10 marks"*; confirmation of grant to William de Colville by Robert de Clairvaux (NYCRO XFL 7).

1842. *"Henry Lee, late of Foxton Mill near Northallerton ... formerly corn miller and farmer but late out of business, bankrupt ..."* (London Gazette, 4 October).

1929. *"Foxton Mill (Osmotherley) has one pair of stones still at work grinding the farmer's meal"* (Mitford Abraham in Yorks Herald, 7 October).

Millers; Robert Lee (1822), Henry Lee (1840), Robert Lee (1872), John Oliver (1890).

One set of stones was still working in 1929 but the mill was demolished before 1939, after a horse had fallen through the first floor. It was a three-storey structure built of sandstone, with ground floor entrance at the front and first floor entrance at the rear. The lower part of one gable wall survives.

KEPWICK/COWESBY, SE 452905 (Sorrow Beck), Fig 169 Converted, Grade II
Kepwick mill is a very neat, early nineteenth century three-storey building, formerly belonging to the Newburgh estate.

C13. *"... terram et molendinum cum tota sequela et pratum quod monasti predicti habent in villa de Sylton ex dono Simonis Blundi de Leeke"*; Grant by William Malebys son of Hugh Malebys to Byland Abbey (NYCRO ZDV I mic 3167, 225).

1379. *"The manorial mill of Over Silton was first mentioned"* (Chan Inq p m, 3 Ric II, no 89; VCH vol 2, 52). After the Dissolution the mill went to the Newburgh estate.

1771. It was marked on Jefferys' map.

1845. *"To be let, a small water corn mill situate at Kepwick"* (Yorks Gazette, 22 March).

1857. *"To be let, the Old Established Water Corn Mill called Cowesby Mill, situate 5 miles from the market town of Thirsk and 6 miles from Northallerton, in the occ of Mr John Hill, now turning 3 pairs of stones"* (Yorks Gazette, 17 November).

1935. *"... Breast wheel. Three pairs of stones. Makes wheat meal. Kept in excellent order"* (Mitford Abraham).

Millers; Richard Hoggart (1822), Jonathan Hill (1840), John Hill (1857), J C Sowerby (1872), John C & George B Sowerby (1879), James Chapman (1889, 1893), R Fawcett (1897, 1905).

The leat passes through the embankment of the old Kepwick waggonway. The mill still has its 14 feet diameter cast-iron waterwheel by "CHAPMANS, THIRSK" on

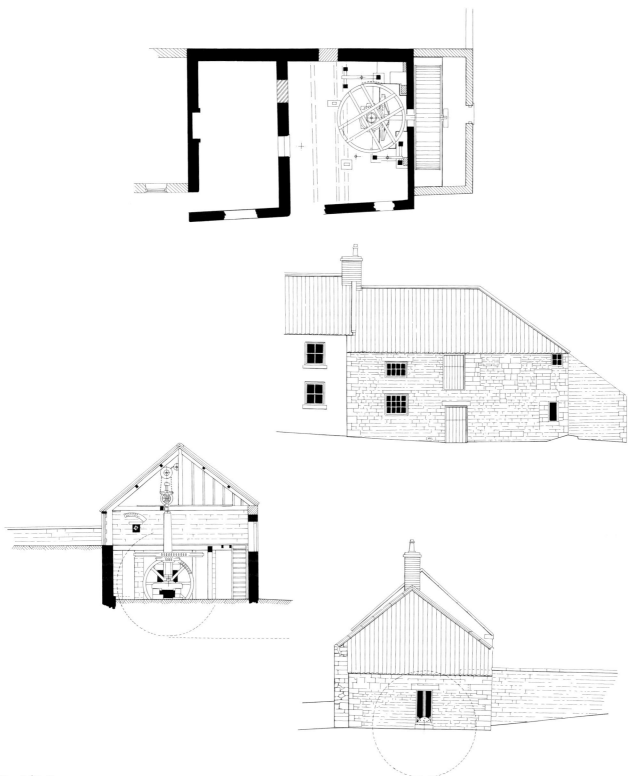

Fig 168. Ellerbeck mill.

a hexagonal shaft. A cast-iron pit wheel drove a lathe-turned wooden upright shaft with a clasp-arm spur wheel driving three pairs of stones.

The building has very fine detailing in the doorway, kneelers, buttresses etc. It was converted in 1999, retaining the machinery. The old mill house was burned down in the 1890s and a brick house built on the foundations.

BORROWBY/GUELDABLE, SE 431887 (Broad Beck), Fig 170 Converted, Grade II

1698. Water corn mill was held in fourth shares (NYCRO ZBA 1/34/39).

1749. "Rental. Farm of Borrowby Mill. 21s 4d" (W Grainge, 1858, The Vale of Mowbray, 257).

c.1817. *"Main spindle turned and hardened"* for Mr Hamack by James Peacock of Stokesley (Mawer and

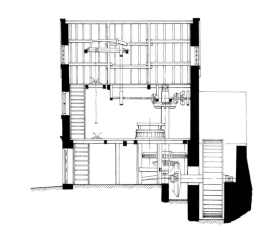

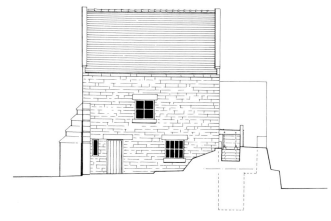

FIG 169. KEPWICK MILL.

Wright, Stokesley Selecton, 96).

1851. *"To be let or sold. All that Water Corn Mill situate in the township of Borrowby in the North Riding of the Co of Yorks. The mill contains two pairs of French stones, one pair of Grey stones, 2 dressing machines, corn screen, Iron Water Wheel nearly new. Apply to George Moon, the owner upon the place"* (Yorks Gazette, 18 October).

1852. *"Capital Water Mill, near Thirsk, lately occupied by George Moon, a bankrupt ... the mill has been recently erected"* (Yorks Gazette, 28 February).

1884. John Hauxwell quoted for a new waterwheel and this was probably the wheel which survived until 1980 (John Hauxwell's Letter Books).

1935. *"Well appointed mill. One of Rymers' three water-mills. Overshot wheel works three pairs of stones"* (Mitford Abraham).

Millers; George and John Moon (1822), George Moon (1840, 1852), Robert Chisman (1873, 1890), William Cottam (1893), Dick Meggison (from Arden mill, 1906). Rymers of Thirsk had the mill until about 1940. They eventually consolidated their business at Thirsk and

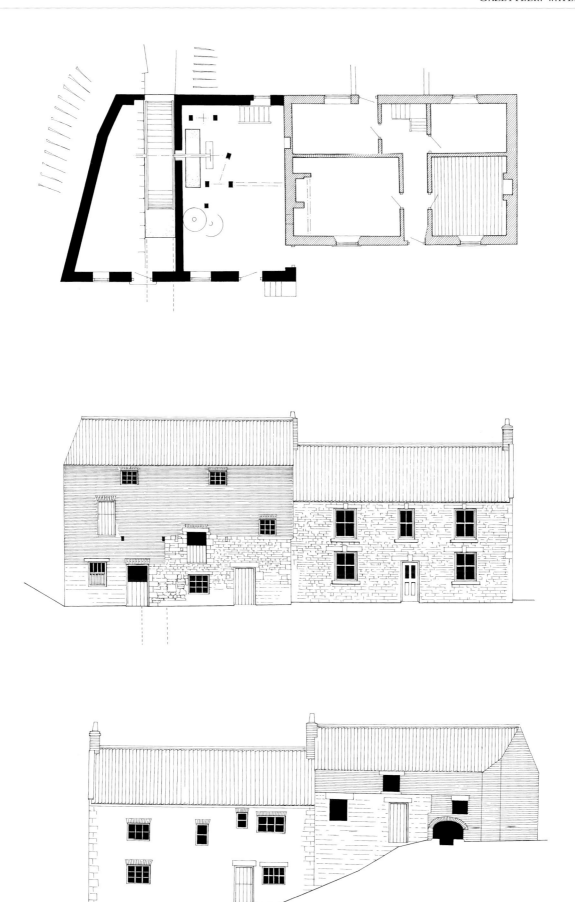

FIG 170. BORROWBY MILL.

FIG 170. BORROWBY MILL.

South Kilvington and dismantled their mill at Borrowby. The 16 feet diameter by 4 feet waterwheel generated electricity in its later working days and survived until the 1970s. The mill was converted into a dwelling in 1980. The irregular plan building has a stone-built lower storey and brick above. The in-line and attached mill house is stone-built. The loft of the house was connected with the mill.

BRAWITH, Grid reference not known (Cod Beck?)
Brawith is the site of a deserted medieval village.
C17-18. A water mill was attached to the manor of Brawith in addition to that at Thornton-le-Street.
1771. A mill was marked on Jefferys' map.

THORNTON-LE-STREET, SE 413865 (Cod Beck), Fig 47
Complete, Grade II
This is a fine example of a seventeenth century double mill. A description appears in VCH vol 1, 455.
1349. Dower in the manor and mill of Thornton-le-Street; claim by Alixe widow of Sir John de Wassard from Robert de Wadesley (VCH vol 1, 455).
1572. The miller William Smythe was not to be *"hurt"* (presumably by eviction or raised rentals) *"so long as he doth pay his Rents and doth keppe the milne in Reparation"*; Will of John Talbot of Thornton-le-Street (NYCRO ZQM IV 1/26 cal).
1670s. James Ella was the miller (Mr R E O Ella, 1994, Norfolk, pers comm)

1734. *"Water corn mill called Thornton Mill with house, kiln, stables and outbuildings and soake, soaken, mulchine and scite belonging and closes belonging to the mill … in the occupation of Stephenson at a yearly rent of £40"* leased to William Stephenson (NYCRO ZQM IV 1/4 cal).
1793. The estate including *"corn mill called Thornton Mill"* bought by Samuel Crompton (NYCRO ZQM 1/7 cal).
1935. *"A semi ruinous place owned by Lord Derby. Two pairs of stones inside and several outside. About twice a year the mill is worked and tenant's barley is ground. Big breast wheel. … Sun dial dated 1666 on corner stone of mill"* (Mitford Abraham).
Millers; William Smythe (1572), James Ella (1670s), T Metcalfe (1822), Thomas Wilkinson (1840, 1872), James Hodgson Blenkin (1893), J Barker (1897, 1901).
This mill has mullioned windows and moulded string-courses. There is a small four-centred arched doorway to the wheel chamber and a large opening to the mill chamber. Above the string-course it is brick-built, later raised at the eaves but with original verge copings and finials re-instated. It has a very large wheel pit. When built it had two waterwheels. Today it has a single large undershot waterwheel, clasp-arm pit wheel, cast-iron wallower and a wooden upright shaft with a large diameter spur wheel, formerly driving four pairs of millstones. A section of wall between the wheel pit and the mill is timber-framed. At an unknown date a drying kiln has been built over part of the wheel pit.

KIRBY KNOWLE, SE 468872, Fig 19 Demolished

The leat skirting a breached dam and dry pond behind the church yard are all that survive of this ancient mill.

1291. *"... mill worth 40s 0d"*; Inquisition post mortem for Anketin Salveyn (YAS Rec Ser, vol 23, 98).

N.d. *"To thys manor belonges one water mille in the tenure or occutyen o' one Michael Yorke painge at Penthicoste and Scainte Martyn & by even portions thairfor xls"* (W Grainge, 1858, 367).

1590. The mill was still standing.

It *"was at length burned down by accident and never rebuilt"* (W Grainge, 1858, 367).

SOUTH KILVINGTON, SE 424842 (Cod Beck), Fig 171 Complete, Grade II

This is one of few workable mills in the region.

1315. *"Galfred de Upsall was lord of Upsall, and he sold to the Abbey of Byland an annuity of five marks out of his water mill at Kilvington, which Hugh his son and*

Pope Gregory confirmed' (Burton's Mon Ebor, 333; W Grainge, 1859, 263).

1624. *"There was a mill in South Kilvington in the 17th and 18th centuries"* (Ft of F, Yorks, Hil, 20 James I; East 23 Charles II; Recovery R Trin. 35 Geo III rot 223; VCH vol 2, 41).

1932. *"Rymer Bros. (Thirsk) have this mill. Iron undershot wheel. Three pairs of stones in use. Two French pairs make wheat meal for bread. Dresses big bran (13 lbs per ton). Dynamo for own electric light and for house. At the back of the mill there is a wash house where there is a combined dolley and rinsing machine formerly worked from the wheel by means of shafts and pulleys"* (Mitford Abraham).

Millers; William Wright (1840), William Rymer (1866, 1872, 1879), James & William Rymer (1893), James Rymer (1897, 1921), Rymer Bros (1925, 1933).

The tall, narrow brick-built mill, aligned along the leat, stands partly on older masonry walls of a mill which may have straddled the leat. The lucam on the down-

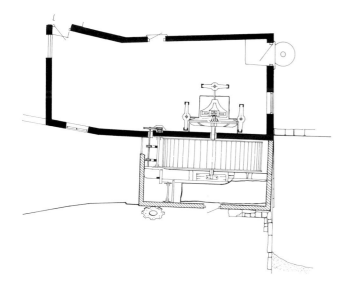

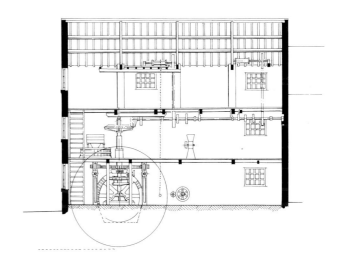

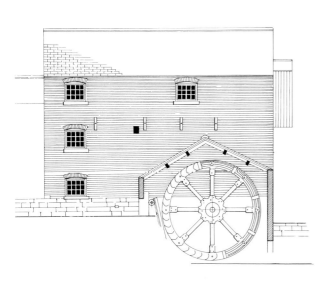

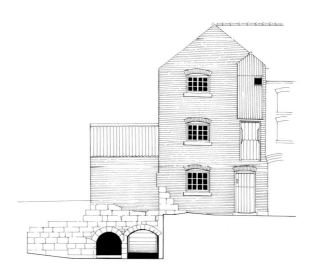

FIG 171. SOUTH KILVINGTON MILL.

Fig 172. Thirsk mill (photo, Mitford Abraham).

stream gable wall is a later addition. The attached and in-line mill house was built in the 1880s.

The dam was restored by the late Pamela Preston and the mill by John Fauvet in the 1980s.

After 1930, the water level could be raised at the dam by placing planks in slots in piers on top of the dam wall. The mill has a wood and iron waterwheel, with cast-iron running gear, an iron upright shaft driving three sets of millstones and a lay shaft from the crown wheel at first floor level for ancillary machines. The hurst frames are marked "J HAUXWELL MILLWRIGHT YARM 1877".

THIRSK, SE 429982 (Cod Beck), Fig 172 Demolished

Thirsk is the market town of the Vale of Mowbray. There was a large mill near the bridge over Cod Beck until the 1970s.

1086. *"Sorebi ... a mill which renders 20s"*; Domesday Survey (M Faull & M Stinson, 1986).

1147. *"... 5s per annum from Thirsk mill"*; grant by Roger de Mowbray to Newburgh Priory in return for Newburgh giving up certain assarts; also 12d from the same mill for acquisition of further assarts (Folio 81, Byland Chart, Egerton MS, 2823; Janet Burton, The settlement of disputes between Byland Abbey and Newburgh YAJ vol 55, 1983, 67-72).

1627. *"Lord Strange's Milnes in Thirske"* mentioned in connection with tenants' duties (NYCRO Z 122/35 cal).

Late C19. Part of the mill (in Millgate) was used as a tobacco manufactury.

1856. Steam power was added.

1859. *"The mill is the property of Frederick Bell Esq, now leased to a joint stock company called The Thirsk Provident Corn Milling Society. The capital consists of two thousand shares of one pound each. The holders of which have the privilege of purchasing their flour twopence per stone under the regular market price. The concern is in a prosperous condition and the shares a considerable premium"* (W Grainge, 1859, 118). The company held the mill until 1879.

1890. William Rymer was the owner.

1932. *"Rymer Bros Mill. Three pairs of French stones worked formerly by one undershot wheel and another undershot wheel works three pairs of grey stones. Busy mill. Flour plant all gone ... Engine at rear dismantled but chimney remains. The wheel which formerly worked the French burrs now works the oats roller etc"* (Mitford Abraham).

Miller; James Armstrong (1822).

This was a large three-storey plus loft building some 120 feet long, part of which had circular vents to the loft. The 50 feet chimney was dated 1855. Several courses of old stonework were incorporated into the east wall. The race was formerly half a mile long. There were two inside waterwheels, one 16 feet diameter by 12 feet and the other with a shaft 12 feet long (Jennifer Tann, 1967, A survey of Thirsk, Yorkshire, Industrial Archaeology, vol 4, No 3, 232-245).

The mill is now demolished and the site is laid out as a garden.

GAZETTEER

WINDMILLS

NORTH OF THE TEES

These windmills are strictly outside the boundary of the area covered by this survey but they are included because they were part of a larger group round the Tees estuary. This section of gazetteer is somewhat abbreviated.

EGGLESCLIFFE GRANGE/ELLIF'S, NZ 412139
Demolished

Grange mill was built in the nineteenth century

1857. *"There are two windmills in the township"* (W Fordyce, 1857, 220).

1897. *"A flour mill, in the occupation of Messrs Ellif and Hodgson, known as the Grange Flour Mill … was totally destroyed by fire in the early hours of Saturday, March 13. The mill is described as a six storied building, which was formerly driven by both wind and steam power. On the mill being recently re-modelled, the wands were taken off, and the plant operated by steam alone"* (The Miller, 5 April).

Millers; Robert Emmitt, *"Grange"* (1828), Emmitt and Wastell (1828), James Emmitt, *"Egglescliffe Grange"* (1856), John Dunning (1879), William Ellif, *"Bentley Mill"* (1889 and *"Grange Mill"* (1894), Edward William Ellif, (1890) Ellif and Hodgson, *"recently re-modelled"* (1894, 1897).

The brick-built tower with gallery at fourth floor, an ogee cap roof and a fantail with a tall finial stood at the corner between the A67 (Yarm to Darlington) and Valley Gardens. 'Ellif's Gardens' are nearby.

EGGLESCLIFFE, NZ 417137 Demolished
The much older Egglescliffe windmill stood on the bluff across the river from Yarm.

1644. Three mills including the windmill in the West Field north of Tanners Bank were let to Thomas Stott for 6s per annum (Royalist Compositions, Surtees Soc, vol III, 27; B J D Harrison, 1978, Society and land in a south Durham township - Egglescliffe, 1560 - 1700, Bull CTLHS no 35).

1750. *"Windmill Bank in Mr Consett's Ground"*; *"A Plann of the River Tees from Peirsburgh to Yarm by Richard Richardson of Darlington, 1750"* (NYCRO ZGD (A) XIV (M)).

1852. Accident to A Dermond who had been repairing the wand of a windmill occupied by Mr William Fidler (Yorks Gazette, 28 August).

1932. *"… formerly a stage mount mill which has evidently been raised. Ceased to work before 1920"* (Mitford Abraham).

Millers; William Fidler and John Fidler (1822/3), John Fidler (1828), William and John Fidler (1848), John Fidler (1856), Mrs Eleanor Burton (1894).

The brick-built tower had five floors of which the top two were vertically walled ie raised. Latterly it had an ogee cap roof.

STOCKTON OLD MILL, NZ436195 Demolished
1786. Samuel Smith and William Smith, miller*, "… dug and wrought large quantities of clay within his copyhold"*; Halmote Rolls (T Sowler, 1972, 483).

1790. *"To be sold by Private Contract, and entered upon at pleasure. A windmill adapted for flour and oil trade, with a dwelling house and out-offices. The mill stands well for the wind and has a cast metal axle tree, three pairs of stones, and stands within half a mile of Stockton. Apply to William Smith at the mill"*, (Yorks Herald, 9 October). A further advertisement had the additional information that it had *"… other conveniences for dressing flour, and all proper utensils for crushing rape and linseed ..."* (Yorks Herald).

1791. "On utensils and trade in his windmill and in the granary and warehouse under the same, brick and timber built, situate in Stockton £100"; Isaac Stephenson, miller, Stockton (Royal Exchange Fire Insurance, no 124935).

1794. *"On a corn mill with going gears and machinery therein and warehouse under, brick with a cone of timber, situate in the parish of Stockton ... and known by Stockton Windmill, £400";* Henry Richardson of Stockton (Royal Exchange Fire Insurance, no 140259).

1830. *"To be let and entered upon immediately. A capital Wind Corn Mill situate within half a mile of Stockton-upon-Tees and within a short distance of the Clarence Rail Road, late in the occupation of James Catchesides, containing three pairs of stones, dressing machinery etc ... Apply Thomas Hall"* (Yorks Gazette, 21 August).

1831. *"To be sold by auction. All that capital freehold Wind Corn Mill ... at present unoccupied"* (Yorks Gazette, 11 June). Purchased by Thomas Wren.

c.1834. A painting shows the mill as a smock mill, one of only two recorded in the Tees valley (William Wheldon, Stockton Museum Service). It had a four-storey steam mill and granary alongside (E Radcliffe, 2004, 4-29).

1854. Destroyed by fire.

Millers; Henry Richardson (1787), William Smith (1790), John Stephenson (1790), Isaac Stephenson (1791, 1803), James Catchesides (1827, 1828, 1830).

STOCKTON NEW/DOVECOT, NZ 441191 Demolished
This was the second windmill to be built in Stockton. It stood on an extension to Dovecot Street, afterwards known as Windmill Lane.

1814. *"The new corn mill at Stockton (built by ... Twedell) was opened, 10 January"* (T Richmond, 1868, 121).

1826. Shown along with two buildings (possibly a house and granary) and marked as being in the possession of *"Mr Hugill"*, W Murphy, *"Plan of the Town of Stockton from actual Survey engraved by W Murphy, Edinburgh"* (History of Stockton and Thornaby in Maps, CTLHS; NYCRO mic 1882).

1829. Brewster's map (by J Chipchase) labels Mill Lane.

1850. Damaged by fire. The partnership between Robert Gibson and Thomas Gibson *"carrying on business as millers"* was dissolved on 20 September (London Gazette, 27 September).

1852. R H Appleton of Yarm took over the wind and steam mills of Thomas Gibson on *"the west side of Stockton"*.

1857. *"... a Windmill, containing three pairs of stones (French) and one pair of Grey stones, flour machine, bolting mill, corn screen, two blasts, and wheat elevators and other requisites ... late the property of Ralph Gibson deceased"* (London Gazette, 12 May).

Millers; Robert Hugill (1827, *"Stockton New Mill"* (1834), Bartholemew Gibson, *"Dovecote Street"* (1835), R Gibson, *"111 High Street and New Mill"* (1847), Robert Gibson and Thomas Gibson (1850), William Gibson, *"executors of"* (1856).

MOUNT PLEASANT, NZ 448206, Fig 86 Demolished
Built between 1814 and 1824 on the highest ground within the town boundary, near the turnpike road north and convenient for Portrack Lane leading to the wharf at Portrack.

In the late nineteenth century the sails provided power for puddling clay for the Clarence Pottery. The mill was photographed by Heavisides by which time it had lost either one or two of its sails (M Heavisides, 1906, In and around picturesque Norton, Stockton). It was a seven-storey tower with ogee cap roof, reefing gallery with iron rails, patent sails and fantail.

Millers; Robert Hugill (1827), John Lax (1873, 1894), Frederick Watson (living at Mount Pleasant in 1897 and 1906).

NORTON (medieval)
1307. Robert de Teviedale was described as *"... plying his craft in the moving shadows";* Roll of Bishop Bec of Durham (Surtees Soc, vol 25, 25-28, 37).

1310. de Teviedale was paid 20s from the Bishop's purse for cutting wood for *"... making a mill to go by wind";* Roll of Bishop Bec.

NORTON/SUMMERHOUSE, NZ 445219 Demolished
Summerhouse windmill was built in a backyard on the west side of the village green of Norton, now part of the Summerhouse School playing field, c.1850.

1857. *"Windmill corn"*, with warehouses (Ordnance Survey 1st Ed, 6 inch).

1863. *"A flour mill, in the occupation of Mr Winspear on the west side of Norton was totally destroyed by fire. The building belonged to Mr Colpitts, and the damage done was estimated at £1500, 8 April"* (T Richmond, 1868, 260).

NORTON/PORTRACK LANE/ALBION, NZ 449213
Demolished
Portrack Lane windmill stood on Albany Road south of Norton. Later known as Albany Steam Mill

1818. *"... good windmill."* (Robert Surtees, 1828, History and Antiquities of County Durham, vol 3).

1836. *"Albion mill in Albany Road, Norton, now a store used by John Farrer"* (R Harbron, A village story, no 1, Norton Heritage Group).

1857. *"Portrack Lane Windmill"* standing in open fields (Ordnance Survey 1ˢᵗ Ed, 6 inch map).

1873. *"Wind and Steam Corn Mill for Sale at Norton, near Stockton on Tees. Apply T James Thomson, Millfield Ironworks, Stockton on Tees"* (Guisborough Exchange and Skelton, Loftus and Brotton News, 13 June). This notice appeared seven more times, the last on 3 October.

Millers; Robert Moor (1851), Frederick Watson, *"Portrack Lane"* (1856, 1865), Michael Arrowsmith, *"Portrack Lane"* (1865).

ELWICK, NZ 449315, Figs 36 & 101 Converted

Relics of a post mill stood into the twentieth century. Early C13. There was a mill at Burntoft (Surtees Soc, vol III, 386; VCH vol 3, 237).

1536. Stephen Booth of the Close died seized of a messuage and mill in Elwick held of the Earl of Westmorland (VCH vol 3, 239).

1938. 'Stob mill' was painted by Karl Wood (Usher Gallery, Lincoln, no 1949).

The old 'stob mill' is said to have carried the date 1555 (F Linton, 1973, pers comm). The tower mill was built some 185m to the north of the 'stob'. According to parish registers John Hutchinson was miller at *"Elwick Mill"* in 1856 and 1860 but miller at *"Elwick New Mill"* in 1860.

1853. The tower mill was not shown on 1st ed OS.

1864. *"A WIND CORN MILL containing three pair of stones, and about nine acres of land attached, situated near Elwick … now occupied by Mr William Jobson"*, to let (Stockton and Hartlepool Mercury, 9 January).

Millers; Thomas Pickering (1828), John Hutchinson, *"Elwick Mill"* (1856), *"Elwick New Mill"* (1860), William Raw (1865, 1873, 1879, 1890), John Wilson, a millwright from near Doncaster, (1894, 1902).

In 1916 a storm took off one of the wands. John Wilson stripped two sails and fitted them to the older mill at Hart. By the 1980s it was a handsome but derelict eight-storey tower containing most of its machinery, though it had lost its gallery and cap roof. Gearing and shafts are all in cast-iron. The mill had three pairs of French burrs, over-driven by cast-iron quants and each equipped with a centrifugal governor. The brake wheel had been badly broken. It was converted into a dwelling in the 1990s but retains some machinery.

HART, NZ 473345, Fig 85 Partly restored

1314. The farm of *"the mill of Hart"*; let by Bishop Kelloe of Durham to one of his bailiffs, Richard le Mason, for one year (Reg Palat Dunelm, Rolls Series II; VCH vol 3, 255; Cuthbert Sharp, 1816, 36).

1361. *"… one third part of the manor of Hart including*

a windmill there"; Inquisition post mortem for Isobel Clifford (Chan Inq p m, pt 1, no 52; VCH vol 3, 255). The mill was also referred to in 1390 and 1437 (VCH, vol 3, 255).

1762. Shown as a post mill; *"A draught of the entrance of the River Tees … by Joseph Dobson"*.

1770. Shown as a post mill; Plan of lands, parcel of the manor of Hart, late of the estate of Hon James Lumley (Hartlepool Museums).

1814. A *"tremendous gale of wind … at Hart the windmill was blown down, with three men in it, December 16"* (T Richmond, 1868, 309).

The magnesian limestone tower mill was built by the Newburn estate as a replacement.

Millers; Thomas Lisle (1828), William Lisle (1834), Henry Brown (1851), Thomas Lisle (1856), Thomas Stephenson (1856, 1858), Paul Bastow (1865, 1879), John Bastow (1890, 1894, 1902), William Raw (1906, 1914).

By 1890 the mill had four roller-reefing sails. One wand was blown off in 1893 and the Bastow family moved away. Repairs were carried out and in 1900 the mill was rented to the Darling family. Two patent sails were removed from Elwick mill and installed at Hart in 1916. The mill worked during World War I, when reputedly a soldier rode one of the wands through a complete turn (R Darling, 1986, pers comm).

In 1988 a partial restoration was carried out by the Cleveland Buildings Preservation Trust (project supervised by Chris Naisbitt).

Lugs on the arms of the cast-iron spur wheel suggest it had been designed for bolted iron gear segments, and therefore not specifically designed for Hart. Timbers of the first floor suggest it was designed for two sets of stones and was subsequently modified to take three.

HARTLEPOOL (medieval), Fig 35

A windmill stood on the headland of Hartlepool but outside the town walls near the site of a medieval friary.

1300. *"… herring house, common oven, windmill and tolls within the borough"*; possessions of the Friars of Hartlepool held by the Bishop of Durham. (Hatfield Survey, Surtees Soc, 177-8).

1558. *"… the Freers (Friary) and mill and lands in Hartlepool for life to his two sons, Matthew and Cuthbert"*; will of Cuthbert Conyers (Durham Wills and Inventories, Surtees Soc, vol 1, 184; VCH vol 3, 264).

c.1558. The mill was illustrated on the *"Plan of the Town and Harbour of Hartlepool"* by the Dutch cartographer Roberto Dromeslawer (British Mus, maps 186 h 1, 4).

1666. The townsfolk of Hartlepool were forbidden to cross the wall to go to the *"North Sandes Wind Mill"* under penalty *"... he or she shall pay for every tyme soe doinge to the use of this town xiid or he be punished at the discretion of the Maior"* (W Boagey, Historical Notes on Stranton, Hartlepool Museums).

By the nineteenth century the mill was remembered only by the place names 'Mill Point' and 'Milbank'.

MIDDLETON (old), NZ 521338, Figs 35 & 81
Demolished

c.1558. Shown as a post mill on the sandy spit; Dromeslawer's *"Plan of Hartlepool"*.

MIDDLETON (new), NZ 520337, Fig 87 Demolished
A second and bigger windmill was built nearby.

c.1760. John Middleton, a millwright, moved from Guisborough and rebuilt the windmill at Middleton (Milburn G E, 1983 Proc. Wesley History Society, vol 4, pt 3, 81)

1771. *"Saturday the Seventh (September). I rode with Mr Wilson round Seatin Snuke before dinner and after dinner we looked through Jn Middleton's Wind Mill"* (Ralph Jackson's Journal, TA U/WJ 13).

1792. *"3 March 1792. John Middleton of Hartlepool in the Co of Durham, miller, on his dwelling house called Middleton House situated as aforesaid £200. Wind Corn Mill near, separate, Stone and timber £100. Utensils and stock and standing and going gears and machinery therein £200. Shelling mill and granary under one roof, a communication between the two mills by a wooden axle tree £100. Utensils and stock therein £300"* (Sun Fire Insurance, no 597382).

1793. *"To be sold by private contract. A capital windmill situated near Hartlepool in the Co of Durham for the manufacture of flour; she works four pairs of stones, a barley mill and two flour machines. Apply to Mr Middleton who is declining business"* (Yorks Herald, 24 August).

1798. To sell or to let. The mill was capable of *"... manufacturing 6000 sack annually ..."* and that *"... its situation is particularly well adapted for the shipping of grain and flour, being in the immediate vicinity of the Town and Port of Hartlepool, and the tide flowing nearly up to the granaries. There is also a kiln for drying grain, a coach house, cart house, workshop and stabling for six horses"* (Newcastle Advertiser, July).

1800. *"On a corn windmill house near ... £350. On the wooden movable top, standing and going gears thereon £850. On the shelling mill, communicating by an axis with the above £100. On the machinery and going gears therein £100. All brick tiled and slated except for the wooden top of the windmill"*; insured by John Middleton and Richard Johnson, grocer, mortgagees (Royal Exchange Fire Insurance, no 174785).

1800. *"On stock in trade including bolting cloth etc in his wind and shelling mill at Middleton £250, Brick and tiled excepting top of windmill"*, insured by the miller, William Walker (Royal Exchange, no 174786).

1837. Two tower windmills, one considerably bigger than the other, close together in Middleton; engraving by W Finden published in *"Views of the Ports, Harbours and Watering Places of Great Britain"*.

1841. Both mills shown; J T W Bell's *"Plan of the Port and Town of Hartlepool in the Co of Durham"* (W W Tomlinson, History of the North Eastern Railway, opp 347).

1851. Two windmills, one of them incorrectly as a post mill, were drawn by W O Mossman, *"Plan of Hartlepool Harbours, Docks and Bay"* (Cuthbert Sharp, 1851, opp 3).

1857. *"There is a windmill, three houses and a beer shop in the village"* (W Fordyce, vol II, London, 293).

1859. The larger of the two windmills only appears in Carmichael's painting, (Hartlepool Museums).

1895. The tall eight-storey tower with a round cap, patent sails and a fantail had disappeared (NER Plan of the Harbours, Docks, Timber Ponds etc in the Port of Hartlepool).

Millers; William Walker (1800, 1828, 1834), William Lisle (1844, 1851, 1856).

STRANTON/NEW/KNOWLE'S/WHITE, NZ 518329, Fig 82 Demolished

1576. The miller, Edward Johnson fell out with his neighbours and in the ensuing row one of them claimed on oath that Johnson was *"... generally suspected to lyve in whoredom with the said Janet Slaiter, and that he hath kept hir and doeth kepe hir still ... for that she cometh every week once or twise to him to the milne at least. And that this examinant further syth that he hard the said Johnson confesse and say that he had comitted adultery with the said Jane Slaiter, and that he would never refuse hir as long as breth was in him ..."* (W Fordyce, 1857, 283).

1802. Post mill named as *"Stranton Mill"*; R Dodds' *"Chart of Hartlepool Bay"* (Durham University Library).

1816. Three-storey mill on a stone-walled reefing mound, with common sails stayed back to a sprit extending from the wind shaft (Cuthbert Sharp, 1816, History of Hartlepool, Frontispiece).

1822. Robert May's engraving shows the tail pole etc. At this time it was still known as the 'New Mill'.

1844. The mill, dwelling house and granaries were valued for the West Harbour & Coal Dock Railway Company by Bryan Stratton, a Stockton millwright, at £280 as *"old materials"*.

1848. The stub only; Thomas Thorpe, lithograph, *"West Harbour and Dock"* (Robert Wood, 1967, plate 1).

1849. But *"Stranton Mill"* was named on *"Chart of the River Tees from Stockton to the Sea, from a recent Survey by James Johnson, made by order of the Tees Navigation Company, 3 Feb"*.

NEW STRANTON/NEWBURN RAWE, NZ 517324, Fig 90
Demolished

Pre-1480. A small settlement called Rawe was established by the Bishops of Durham on the shoreline south of Hartlepool. Later there was a post windmill.

1762. Rawe mill was shown as a post mill (though incorrectly named); *"A draught of the entrance of the River Tees carefully surveyed in January, 1762. Most humbly dedicated and presented to the Right Honerable the Master, Wardens and Assistants and Elder Brethrren of the Corporation Trinity House … by Joseph Dobson, Pilot".*

Access to the sandy shore where sailing ships could be berthed was reduced to a tunnel in 1841 when the Stockton and Hartlepool Railway was built.

1848. Shown as a tall tower mill with ogee cap roof and large granaries round its base; Thomas Thorpe's lithograph *"West Harbour and Dock"* (Robert Wood, 1967, Plate 1).

1858. Captured in Carmichael's panoramic *"West Hartlepool from the Tower of Christchurch"* (Hartlepool Museums).

1860. Shown as a tall tower mill; *"West Hartlepool from near Cliff House"* (Robert Wood, 1967, plate 3).

1884. Named on *"England - East Coast. Tees Bay surveyed by Staff Commander W F Maxwell RN", 1891"* but based on T H Tizard's survey of 1884.

Millers; James Sheraton, *"Stranton"* (1827, 1834, 1858), James Davison, *"Newburn Mill"* (1851), Thomas Sedgewick, *"miller, Newburn Mill"* (1865).

STRANTON CHURCH, NZ 509320 Demolished

This mill may have been built using the machinery taken from Knowle's mill. It had no fantail.

1845. *"… a windmill which hath lately been erected thereon by the said James Sheraton …"*; Conveyance of a plot of land near Stranton church, George and John Thompson to James Sheraton of Newburn Rawe mill (R Skinner, m s, Hartlepool Museums Service).

1857. The painting of Navvy Nan and her donkey used the church, the windmill and the Blacksmiths Arms as a backdrop (Hartlepool Museums Service).

1857. *"June 21 - Early this morning the windmill of Mr Wm Sheraton of Stranton was discovered to be on fire, and in about four hours the building and all its contents were entirely consumed. A neighbouring house was much damaged by the wands of the mill falling upon it"* (T Richmond, 1868, 232).

N.d. In a later fire insurance policy it was described as an eight-storey mill. The first floor had a warehouse and gas engine; the second was used for storage, an oat crusher, two disused millstones and joiner's bench; the third had a disused Eureka dressing machine; the fourth was a warehouse; the fifth had a millroom containing four sets of stones; the sixth and seventh floors a warehouse and the eighth an office. It seems clear the mill was not being driven by wind (R Skinner, m s, Hartlepool Museums Service).

1889. The cast-iron windshaft was dragged off the top of the tower using a very long rope and a host of schoolboys (Northern Mail).

Millers; Stephen Lee (1873,1879), George Foster (1890), Foster and Armstrong (1894, 1897).

The tower was sold to George Foster of Greatham windmill in 1889 and used for making bread meal and feedstuffs. It was taken over by Camerons Brewery in 1912 and demolished.

DOCK, NZ 506329 Demolished

The Dock windmill stood at the end of a short track to the west of Swainson's Dock.

1848. Shown on Thomas Thorpe's lithograph *"West Harbour and Dock"* (Robert Wood, 1967, plate 1).

1857. Marked on Ordnance Survey 1st Ed, 6 inch map.

1884. Shown as *"Dock Windmill"*; *"England – East Coast. Tees Bay surveyed by Staff Commander W F Maxwell RN, 1891"*, but based on T H Tizard's survey of 1884.

1887. Shown on E E Denyer's engraving *"West Hartlepool from Haswell House, Foggy Furze"* (Robert Wood, 1967, plate 8).

Miller; Henry Brown (1851, 1856 *"Dock Mill"*).

WEST HARTLEPOOL/LEE'S, NZ 507323 Demolished

The windmill stood near Sedgewick Hall and was sometimes called after Stephenson Lee, lately home from Australia. The flour was sold in sacks carrying a kangaroo as a trademark.

1848. Shown on Thomas Thorpe's lithograph *"West Harbour and Dock"* (Robert Wood, 1967, plate 1).

1857. *"Lee's Mill"*; *"Stranton in 1857"*, reproduced in C J Watson, typescript notes, *"West Hartlepool 1847-67"*. Also shown as *"West Hartlepool Mills (Corn)"* on Ordnance Survey 1st Ed, 6 inch map.

1865. Two boys were killed by being caught in a rotating shaft at *"Mr Sedgewick's Mill at West Hartlepool"* (Sussex Advertiser, 28 November).

1887. Shown in E E Denyer's engraving of *"West Hartlepool from Haswell House, Foggy Furze"* (Hartlepool Museums).

OWTON, NZ 493293

A medieval post windmill at Owton has disappeared without trace.

1543. *"Robert … Lambert … lands here, including a windmill … a manor house of stone roofed with slate were forfeited to the Crown"* (C Sharp, 44n; Cal S P Dom, 1566-79,

280; Exch K R Misc Bks xxxviii, fol 234; VCH vol 3, 367). *"John Jackson holds one windmill in Owton with suit, soke and multure for a term of years, for 53s 4d per annum"*; Rents of tenants (PRO E 164/37-38; B J D Harrison, 1969, Some evidence of Tudor enclosure and depopulation in Cleveland, CTLHS Bull 5, 6-8).

GREATHAM, NZ 493279, Fig 89 Demolished

A six-storey tower mill was built at the beginning of the nineteenth century, near the centre of the village. It replaced an earlier windmill situated near Greatham Villa at NZ 492281 (OS 1st Ed).

1857. *"The village of Greatham ... contains a corn-mill, seven public houses and several shops"* (W Fordyce, 1857, vol II, 299).

1886. Estimate for a new sail, John Hauxwell.

Millers; William Howd (1828), George Albion Tate (1848, 1850), J Wilson (1858), W Robinson (1873), Richard Stonehouse (1879), George Foster (1890, 1902), Maxwell Foster (1906, 1939).

The brick tower had a very tall ogee cap roof with a finial, four anticlockwise common sails and a fantail. It had three pairs of stones. It was worked by auxilliary oil engine until 1942 and was demolished in March 1948.

NEWTON BEWLEY, NZ 466266, Fig 173 Converted

The township of Newton Bewley belonged to the Prior of Durham. References in the Halmote Rolls for 1365 – 1370 (Halmote Rolls, 1296 – 1394; Surtees Soc, vol 32; L Still and J Southeran, 1966) are contained in the Text.

Post-1341. Mill at *"Oventon Belu"*, List of works carried out during the time of John Fossor, Prior of Durham (L F Salzman, 1952, 392-3).

1464. *"Newton. Villa ibendenam molendino reddit dare per annum 39 li 17s 4d ..."*; Inventory of the Prior of Durham (Surtees Soc, vol 58, 1872).

1793. *"To be sold by auction. A windmill situate at Newton Bewley in the County of Durham, lately belonging to and in the occupation of William Wood, a bank-*

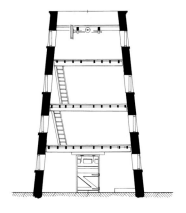

FIG 173. NEWTON BEWLEY MILL.

rupt, and held by lease for 21 years under the Dean and Chapter of Durham ..." (Yorks Herald, 18 May).

1801. *"... on his Windmill House for grinding corn timber built situated at Newton Bewley between Wooliston (Wolviston) and Greatham in the County of Durham £100. On the standing and going gears millstones etc £200. Warranted no steam engine"*; insured by Joseph Laing (Lacey?) of Portrack near Stockton (Royal Exchange Fire Insurance Company, 19 June 1801). The *"timber built"* description is obscure.

1857. The *"... village contains several cottages ... a public house and a corn mill"*; W Fordyce, 1857, 315).

Millers; William Heslop (1813, 1818), Matthew Grieveson (1820, 1822), Luke Short (1824), Thomas Pickering (1827), Joseph Agar (1828), John Whitlock (1851, 1858), John Wilson (1873, 1890), Edward Wilson (1894, 1914).

The surviving relic is a neat, very small (16 feet internal diameter at ground level), brick-built tower with no reefing stage. It was converted into part of a dwelling in the 1980s.

SOUTH OF THE TEES

The following completes the windmill cluster which existed around the Tees estuary both in medieval times and during the nineteenth century.

YARM, NZ 417126 Demolished

Yarm was one of the two ports in Cleveland in early medieval times. There was a post windmill from medieval times, then a tower windmill.

c.1145. The multure of a mill; grant by Peter de Brus to the Hospital of St Nicholas in Yarm (YAS vol 92, 222; J C Atkinson, 1874, vol 2 pt 2, 168).

1272. *"... a windmill in Yarm, worth 30s per annum"*; Inquisition post mortem for Peter de Brus (YAS Rec Ser, vol 12, 139-45).

1369. *"... a mill in the hands of the tenants at will"*; Inquisition post mortem for John, Lord D'Arcy (J C Atkinson vol 2 pt 2, 166).

1539. *"Yarm. Farm of windmill there, Henry Gibson, 26s 8d. He makes all repairs except timber, millstones and iron"*; Confiscated estates of rebels (PRO SC6 4281).

1658. *"Manorial mill"* standing on rising ground at the south end of West Street; Enclosure Map (J W Wardell, 1957, opp 72).

At the beginning of the nineteenth century a 12-storey tower mill *"the loftiest in England"* was built by Richard Appleton (The Miller, 2 July, 1883).

1815. The *"corn mill at Yarm"* caught fire on 8 March (T Richmond, 1868).

1827. Following the arrival of the Stockton and Darlington Railway to Yarm Richard Appleton added steam power to his windmill (The Miller, 2 July, 1883).

1830. A windmill was marked near the Old Market on Thomas Meynell's Map (J W Wardell, 1957, opp 88).

1832. *"To be sold by auction. A wind corn mill containing one pair of French and one pair of blue stones, situate at Yarm ... now in the occupation of Mr George Grieveson. Apply to Mr John Sherwood of Ingleby Greenhow near Stokesley, the owner"* (Yorks Gazette, 28 January).

1837. *"Stob Mill Field"* in the occupation of William Kilvington and Robert Southeran and the *"Mill Scite"* in the occupation of Thomas Wastell; A Schedule of Tithable Lands in the Parish of Yarm (J W Wardell, 1957, opp 88 & 176).

1848. 11 May *"Richard Appleton's mill was destroyed by fire"* (T Richmond, 1868, 204).

Millers; Richard Appleton, *"corn factor and corn miller"* (1822), *"corn miller"* (1828), George Grieveson (1832), Richard Appleton *"miller and merchant"* (1840, 1847), *"corn miller & factor"* (1848).

In 1849 the Leeds Northern Railway viaduct was built very close to the windmill site in the old market green at the south end of West Street but the tower stood in 1894 (Ordnance Survey 1st Ed, 6 inch map). It was demolished before 1915.

KIRKLEVINGTON/GROVES, NZ 423098 Demolished

1314. A windmill worth 26s 8d; Inquisition post mortem for Henry de Percy (Inquisition post mortem, 8 Edw II no 65 m 16; VCH vol 2, 259).

1352. *"One windmill destroyed, worth nothing"*; Inquisition post mortem for Henry de Percy (PRO E 152/89).

1843. Mill marked at Saltersgill Grove, Kirklevington; Henry Cross's map (J W Ord, 1846).

1857. *"The Groves Mill (Corn)"* (Ordnance Survey 1st Ed, 6 inch).

HIGH LEVEN, NZ 448125 Demolished

1843. Marked but not named on Henry Cross's map (J W Ord, 1846).

1856. *"Corn Mill"* (Ordnance Survey 1st Ed, 6 inch).

1935. *"High Leven Mill ... not worked for over 40 years. Two pairs of French burrs still in ..."* (Mitford Abraham).

Millers; Bartholemew Gibson, *"Leven Bridge and Ingleby Barwick"* (1840), Thomas Kilton (1848).

This seven-storey, brick-built windmill had a reefing stage at second floor. The cap had been removed by the early 1900s. The tower was demolished and rebuilt as a dwelling in 1964.

SOBER HALL/BLACK, NZ 447129, Fig 98 Shell

1843. Marked but not named on Henry Cross's map (J W Ord, 1846).

1847. *"Great Church Field and Little Church Field"* south east of the windmill (Ingleby Barwick Tithe Award).

1856. *"Corn mill"* (Ordnance Survey 1st Ed, 6 inch).

1935. *"Black Mill. Said to have been dismantled a hundred years. Older than High Leven and much better built"* (Mitford Abraham).

This is an interesting group of buildings consisting of a big granary, windmill and horse wheel shed. The tower is said to have stood at its full seven or eight storeys in 1914 but had been cut down to four storeys by 1930. It was of very similar design to the tower at High Leven. It was probably built to serve the town of South Stockton and its railway. The horse wheel shed was not marked on the 1856 Ordnance Survey 1st Ed, 6 inch map. An offset doorway at first floor in the windmill tower was designed to accommodate a bridge and a shaft leading to a pre-existing window in the granary.

THORNABY, NZ 451165 Mound

There was a post windmill in the township of Thornaby. Early C13. *"Thornaby, Also Ryvall xiid ad sanct Martin term' pro decima molend"*; Rent Roll formerly in the possession of Admiral Chaloner (J C Atkinson, 1874, vol 2 pt 2, 183).

1275. William de Boyville, then lord of Thornaby, imprisoned Robert the Miller of *"Thormanby"* until he was released on the bail of two salmon (Hundred Rec Comm 1 129; VCH vol 2, 293).

1538. *"... a water mill and a windmill were appurtenant to the manor of Stainton"* formerly held by Gisborough Priory; Valor Ecclesiasticus, (Rec Comm, vol 95, Pat 22 Eliz. pt xi m; Yorks Fines, Tudors, iii, no 163; VCH vol 2, 294).

1539. The *"... farm of manor or grange with closes and 16 bovates of land and meadow and a windmill"*; demise to Thomas Gower, knight (of Sexhow) for £15 (Priory Acc for Michaelmas, 31 Henry VIII; VCH vol 2, 294).

1641. The townsfolk of Thornaby complained that the King's garrison defending Stockton Castle against the marauding Scots crossed the river, grazed the meadows in Thornaby and *"... have broken a windmill nighe the towne and doe assault and draw their swords upon your peticons"* (Conway Papers, SP 16-497-112; T Sowler, 1972, 72-3).

1684. The windmill was mentioned (Ft of F, Hil 24 & 25 Chas II; VCH vol 2, 298).

The 45 feet diameter platform can be seen on Thornaby Green about 65m north of the church.

MANDALE, NZ 460176 Demolished

1800. *"Mandale Mill was built this year"* (Thomas Richmond, 1868, 99). It belonged to Lord Harewood of Harewood House near Wetherby who owned land on the Yorkshire bank of the River Tees.

1800. Thomas Langdale of *"Mandell"* was miller; Chief Constables' Returns (NYCRO QAW).

1801. *"MANDALE near Stockton-upon-Tees.*

To be Let and entered upon immediately, a new erected wind corn mill, situated at Mandale in Cleveland in the County of York, with Three Dwelling Houses, the Granaries, a Kiln and other suitable conveniences and about Four Acres and an Half of Land occupied and employed therewith, the property of Lord Harewood.

MANDALE is situate on the banks of a Navigable part of the River Tees in an excellent Corn Country and is a short distance from the several market towns of Stockton, Darlington, Stokesley, Guisbro' and Yarm. The Mill is built upon a new and much improved construction, will contain about 600 sacks of flour, and is calculated to grind 150 quarters of Corn in a week in its present state, but at an inconsiderable expense may be made to grind double that quantity, and the granaries adjoin the river and will contain 2000 quarters of corn. For further particulars apply to Mr Raisbeck, at his Office, Stockton. September 22, 1801." (Notice in possession of G B Burton).

1804. Partnership between John Bennington and George Goundry of Mandale, Co York, millers, to be dissolved by mutual consent *"... Business is to be carried on by George Goundry"* (London Gazette, 28 August).

1804. *"George Goundry of Mandale Mill in the parish of Stainton and township of Thornaby in Cleveland, Co of York. On the building of Mandale Corn Mill and granary adjoining thereto, situate in the parish of Stainton aforesaid £1000, standing and going gear etc £1000. Warranted no steam engine"* (Royal Exchange Fire Insurance, no 213525).

1805. *"George Goundry of Mandale Mill ... stock in trade including boulting cloths, sacks and all moveable utensils in his corn mill house and granary adjoining £55 ..."* (Royal Exchange Fire Insurance, no 219984).

1806. Estimate for repairs at Mandale, £327 (letter to Lord Harewood, WYL 250/1/368).

1810. The windmill granaries were cut off from the River by the Mandale Cut across the Mandale Loop on which the windmill had been built. Lord Harewood received £2000 and some land in compensation.

N.d. *"TO MERCHANTS, MILLERS, AND CORN MILLERS. MANDALE MILL. To be let and entered upon immediately.*

A CAPITAL and COMPLETE MODERN WINDMILL, upon an improved construction, built with brick, and covered with lead. Five floors, Fifty one feet long by twenty feet wide; sash windows, with dressing mills and machinery, surpassing most other mills in the kingdom.

Also, a neat messuage, brick and tile, of two storeys, with stable, cow house, swine styes, kitchen garden and upwards of four acres of exceedingly rich pasture land. A good accompting house.

A public house with stabling and convenient sheds for the accommodation of travellers and teams.

A granary seventy eight feet long by thirty feet, three stories (sic), capable of containing upwards of eight hundred lasts of corn, adjoining the River Tees, with a crane, a weighing house and a salting house and a large storehouse fifty four feet by eighteen feet, for coals and timber.

These premises are situate in one of the finest corn districts in the North Riding of the County of York, on the great road from Stokesley, and one mile from the market and port of Stockton, adjoining the River Tees, and at all times accessible for shipping. The whole has been recently and substantially built at very great expence, is in complete repair, and suitable for carrying on a most extensive coasting and foreign trade. Every reasonable encouragement will be given to any person or company of persons disposed to engage the premises for the purpose of carrying on an extensive trade, or manufactury, provided satisfactory assurances are given.

(Press cutting in Stockton Ref Lib; The date 1862 is given in T Sowler, 1972, 349).

1815. The mill built in 1800 was demolished and rebuilt by James Booth, Millwright of Malton, because its tower had tilted and become unsafe (Harewood papers, West Yorkshire Archives, Leeds, WYL 250/1/368). The new tower was eight storeys high, with a reefing stage at mid height and a round cap roof.

1890. It was destroyed by fire.

Millers; Thomas Langdale (1800), George Goundry (1804), Sampson Langdale (1808, 1840), Samuel Kitching, *"The Windmill, Mandale Road"* (1868), Mark Robinson (1890), Thomas Burton (1893).

TOLLESBY

1804. *"Mill Hill"* adjacent to and N E of Tollesby Hall *"Marton and Tolsby Estate belonging to Bartholemew Rudd Esq lying in the North Riding of York"* (TA U/5/89).

MARTON

c.1300. *"De Staytona ... de esta farama recipit int' de Martona vis ... de decimi Molendini ventrici, and the same touching Staynsby, Berewyck at Hemlington ..."*; Admiral Chaloner's Rent Roll (J C Atkinson, vol 2 pt 2, 183; Gis Chart, Surtees Soc, vol 84, 430, 34).

1303. A windmill worth 13s 4d; Inquisition post mortem for John de Blaby (YAS Inquisition post mortem iii 148; VCH vol 2, 266).

1675. Shown on Ogilby's strip map of Whitby to Durham.

1764. *"Mill Field"* and *"Low Mill Field"* south of *"Marton Town"*; A Plan of the Marton Estate in Cleveland, belonging to Sir John Ramsden Bart, by Thomas Forster (TA U 5/90).

1804. *"Great Mill Hill"* named, to the S E of Marton village; *"Marton and Tolsby Estate belonging to Bartholemew Rudd Esq"* (TA U/5/89).

1815. Marked near Marton Hall *"... where Captain Cook was born"*; Palliser Thompson, Map of the Tees (British Library, maps 1202.29).

1842. *"Fatal accident. On Friday last, as Mr Ralph Hedley, miller, of Marton, was adjusting the wands of his mill, a gust of wind arising, and the brake of the mill not being on, the wands were set a-going and he was struck by them so violently that he died on the Sunday following"* (York Herald, 4 June).

Millers; Simpson and Wetherall (1801), Samuel Stephenson, *"flour miller and corn dealer"* (1822), Ralph Hedley, *"New Lane, Newham"* (1840).

STAINTON, NZ 483140 Demolished

1591. *"... a water mill and a windmill were appurtenant to the manor of Stainton"* (Yorks Fines, Tudors, YAS iii 165; VCH vol 2, 294).

1854. A windmill marked at east end of the village (Ordnance Survey 1st Ed, 6 inch).

HEMLINGTON/COULBY

1353. *"... weak windmill worth 3s per annum"*; Inquisition post mortem for John, Earl of Kent (PRO C135/118; VCH vol 2, 295).

1843. Marked at Viewley Hill to the north of the village; Henry Cross's Map (J W Ord, 1846).

NEWHAM, NZ 504154 Demolished

1771. A windmill at mid-point between Hemlington and Marton; Jefferys' Map.

1843. Marked on Henry Cross's map (J W Ord, 1846).

ACKLAM, NZ 487177

1300. *"In Ackelom ... we have a toft and a croft ... We also receive there 2s for tithe of the windmill"*; Gisborough Priory Rent Roll (R C Kirby, Ancient Middlesbrough, Gleanings of Local History, 1900, 72).

1581. A mill belonged to the manor (Chan Inq p m, Series 2 CXCVIII, 42), *"... probably the windmill reckoned amongst its appurtenances ... in the next century"* (Ft of F, Yorks, Mich 13 Chas I; VCH vol 2, 222).

There is a Mill Hill near Acklam Hall. Mill Farm was immediately to the north of Acklam Hall (Map 9, CTLHS, Middlesbrough's History in Maps, Plan of Middlesbrough, 1874 by E D Latham; TA CB/M/E (1) 1/30).

AYRESOME, NZ 490192, Fig 35

1618. A drawing of a post windmill at Belwether Cross near Middlesbrough; John Gibbon's *"Plan of the Scite, Cell and Towne of Middlesbrough"* (PRO MPE 524; CTLHS, 1980, Middlesbrough Maps, no 1).

MIDDLESBROUGH/STONEHOUSE'S, NZ 494208, Fig 97 Demolished

1832. No windmill was marked on the plots on *"Plan of Middlesbrough showing land ownership"*, by Richard Otley (TA U/OME 8/6).

1840. Windmill and granaries marked; *"Middlesbrough 1840, Town Plan"* (TA OME 8/7).

The Roman Catholic church was built on the adjacent plot to the south in 1847, and by 1853 the windmill was completely surrounded by buildings.

1869. *"A singular transformation has been affected in Middlesbrough within the past few days. All our readers will know the old mill standing off Sussex Street and which, but a few years ago, waved its arms in the centre of green pastures. The population has largely increased and the mill has for some years past stood in the very heart of the town. Nevertheless its trade has gone to decay and it has, like many another thing in these changing times, been compelled to change its work and its fortunes. Some time ago the mill was bought by the Rev A Burns for the purpose of church extension. In persuance of the objects contemplated the mill has for the past few weeks been converted into a school and in future it will supply not as was its custom food for the body but food for the mind. And another transformation yet. The old begrimed chimney is to be lowered, 'architecturally treated' and converted into a campanile or bell tower. Lie quiet shade of Pugin! I have not done yet. The mill itself is to be improved upon and made beautiful as ever, by being lowered and covered with an ornamental roof, and it will answer the purposes of a large bell tower for the church. The mill house affords accommodation for 100 infants, and the school room is, of course, in the basement storey, and with the alterations which have been carried out, has been made to look very cheery and comfortable."* (The Middlesbrough Exchange and North Ormesby News, Friday, 8 January).

Millers; John Foster (1840, 1841), Robert Foster (1841).

The windmill was on the intersection between Wellington Street and Brougham Street (formerly Cross Street) in the old town of Middlesbrough. Part of the tower was still standing in 1895 but it had gone before 1908.

NORTH ORMESBY, NZ 510196 Demolished

This windmill stood immediately to the west of the junction of Westbourne Grove and Kings Road near the former Whitehouse Farm.

1875. Shown on John Dunning's map (TA U/OME 8/24).

1886. John Hauxwell provided an estimate, *"Jan 20. Mr N Watson, no 1 Queens Terrace, Middlesbrough. Estimate to repair 4 windmill wands and put them in working order and giving them two coats of white paint. Cost £43"* (John Hauxwell's Letter Books). At the time it was occupied by John Dunning. Hauxwell supplied another estimate in 1888.

1895. *"Windmill, disused"* (Ordnance Survey 1st Ed, 6 inch).

Millers; William Fidler (1865), William Smith (1872, 1873), W Snaith (sic) (1879).

The mill was gone before the end of the century. The mill house is still standing but indistinguishable from its later neighbours.

CARGO FLEET/CLEVELAND PORT, NZ 515205, Fig 88
Demolished

A large windmill was built at Cleveland Port near Cargo Fleet at the beginning of the nineteenth century.

1803. A three-fold increase in Philip Heselton's rent to £300 at Cleveland Port may have marked the completion of a large windmill (D W Pattenden, Cargo Fleet and Cleveland Port, CTLHS, Bull 48, 5).

1815. Drawn as a six-sailer on Palliser Thompson, Map of the Tees (British Library, maps, 1202.29).

1832. Marked at *"Cleveland Port"* on R Otley's *"Plan of Middlesbrough showing land ownership"* (TA U/OME 8/6).

1840. Joseph Heseltine paid £169 per annum for house, mill, granaries and land at Cleveland Port (TA PR/OR/6/2 & 3).

1840. *"Since the improvement of the navigation to Stockton and the recent extension of the Stockton and Darlington Railway to Middlesbrough ... it has greatly declined in its commerce"* (William White, Directory).

c.1840. The windmill is shown in a vignette on an undated *"Map of Middlesbrough"* (TA U/OME 8/7).

1857. *"Corn mill"* (Ordnance Survey 1st Ed, 6 inch).

Millers; William Tindall (1822), *"a master corn miller and two journeymen millers"* (1851).

The port declined in importance as navigation to the upper reaches of the river improved. Soon after 1853 the windmill was demolished to make way for Ormesby Ironworks.

ORMESBY/NORMANBY

These references may have been to one windmill, to two or even three. There are no relics on the ground.

William de Percy granted a water mill in Caldecotes and a windmill in Ormesby to Gisborough Priory, the Priory undertaking that their tenants would do suit at the mills (Gis Chart, Surtees Soc, vol 68, 279).

The windmill lay *"... between Caldecotes and the grange of Rievaulx which is in the field of Normanby"*; confirmation of grant (Gis Chart, Surtees Soc, vol 89, ch 481; D W Pattenden, 1990, CTLHS, Bull 58, 1-15).

1324. William de Worsall acquired half the windmill from Walter de Stokesley and Mary his wife (Ft of F, 17 Edw III no 92; VCH vol 2, 280).

1331. *"A moiety of one windmill in Normanby"*; possession of the Wyrkesal family (Ft of F, Yorks, Edw III No 44; Yorks Fines 1327-1347, 45; VCH vol 2, 280).

1600. James Pennyman bought the manor of Ormesby with 10 messuages, 5 cottages, a windmill and a water mill with land in Ormesby, Caldecotes etc (Ft of F, Yorks Tudor; YAS vol VII, 69).

1606. Manor of Ormesby with 10 messuages, 14 cottages, a windmill and lands in Ormesby and Caldecotes; James Pennyman, senior, and James Pennyman, junior, defendants, James Tothill (Ft of F, Yorks, Easter, James I vol 53, 48, 49).

1653. Part of the Ormesby estate including *"... a cottage in Normanby and a close of pasture adjoining called Milne Lease ... and Windmill Close together with the windmill standing on it"* was sold to William Tooms (TA U/PEN 1/50).

1717. Lease and Release, Viscount Cheyne, Sir Edward Northey, Alexander Duncombe one quarter part to each John Rudd, John Jackson, John Jackson, Christopher Malcolm etc *"1 watermill, 1 windmill, 1 dovecote etc ... in Normanby and the windmill and horse mill, the close in which the windmill stands ..."* (TA U/PEN 1/169).

1723. Field names *"Mill Garth, Mill Field, Mill Leazes"* only (TA U/PEN 179/80).

ESTON

1368. A windmill; Inquisition post mortem for Hugh de Eston (Chan Inq p m, 42 Edw III 1st nos, 44; VCH vol 2, 279).

nd. Matilda daughter of Hugh de Eston had 1 toft *"next the mill of Eston, as my father gave it"* (Gis Chart, Surtees Soc, 717).

WEST COATHAM

1340. *"... windmill in ruins."* at West Coatham; Inquisiton post mortem for Ralph Bulmer (PRO 135/192).

1367. *"Ruinous windmill"*; Inquisition post mortem for Ralph Bulmer (PRO 135/192).

COATHAM (medieval)

Coatham and Yarm were the two early ports on the south bank of the Tees. Both were part of the de Brus holding. The earliest documentary evidence of a windmill in the Tees estuary refers to that at Coatham.

"Roger son of William de Thocotes gave a saltwork in

Cotum near the windmill" (Gis Chart, Surtees Soc, vol 89, 114).

Hugo son of Radulphi Delblel de Lyum gave the *"... situm molendini suide Cotum et ipsum molendinum cum omnibus pert. suis in aquis, stagnis, et omnibus alii aysiamenti suis et ab ipso molendino decem et novem pedes versus occidentem, et vide sient divisae se extendient usque et Miles et duas salinas cum omnibus pert. suis unam seil ex aquiloni parte ipsuis molendin ..."* (Gis Chart, Surtees Soc, vol 89, 116). A later document referred to the *"molendini Prioratus"*.

C12. *"Roger de Toccotes gave a fourth salt work near the mill in the same place"* (Coatham) (J W Ord, 1846, 185).

1340. A windmill in Kirkleatham was valued at £4 per annum (PRO 135/63).

1535. The Priory was receiving a rental from *"Cottome with windmill there £20 14s 0d"* (Valor Ecclesiasticus, Record Commission, vol 5, 1825).

1613. A windmill at *"Cottome alias Cottam"* worth £2 per annum, ex monastic lands; grant to Francis Morrice and Edward Sawyer (J C Atkinson, 1874, vol 2, 110).

1619. *"... one broad flatt near the windmill"*; *"John Meaburn of Kirkleatham to John Turner of Gisbroughe ..."* (NYCRO ZK 459).

COATHAM/MARSH HOUSE, NZ 579251 Demolished

A tower windmill was built near Whim Farm, later Marsh House, before 1774.

1771. Arthur Young commented on the granaries etc at East Coatham.

1774. Windmill close to Whim Farm; Thomas Atkinson *"A Plan of the Parish and Manor of Kirkleatham belonging to Charles Turner Esq"* (NYCRO ZMI DN88).

1779. Windmill near 'Whim' and Todd Point, with an obviously man-made 'cut' leading from the water's edge; *"A Plan of the Boundary between the manors of Kirkleatham and Wilton and the land from Cargo Fleet to Green Spring, by John Mowbray"* (NYCRO ZK 9501 mic 1982 2604).

1801. Kirkleatham, *"... one windmill which can grind 240 bushels of corn per week"*; Chief Constables' Returns (NYCRO QAW mic 1203; M Y Ashcroft, 1977, NYCRO Pub 15, App 3). William Wilson (miller) was listed as having proper weights and a table of prices for milling wheat, barley and oats.

1804. Andrew Irvine Esq tenant of Whim Farm, East Coatham, including mill and granary; John Mowbray's Farm Evaluation (NYCRO ZK 6963 mic 2200).

1815. Windmill at Coatham burned down in February (T Richmond, 1868, 124).

1815. Shown with neither sails nor cap near to Marsh Farm; Palliser Thompson, Map of the Tees (British Library, maps 1202.29).

1869. *"On a site not far from Marsh House stood a wind-mill accidentally destroyed by fire upwards of 40 years ago. The remains of it may perhaps account for the stone and earth mounds"* which had puzzled some visitors to the resort; Letter from a *"Resident of Coatham"* (Redcar and Saltburn Gazette, 10 September).

COATHAM, NZ 603252 Demolished

The second tower windmill in Coatham was built on a different site, near to the present-day railway station in Redcar.

1832. A tower windmill was shown in L Haghe's stone engravings made to illustrate W A Brook's paper *"Observations on Port William at Redcar ... projected by W A Brooks, CE, Stockton"*.

1838. Robert Coulson was the occupier of Coatham windmill and in the 1841 census he was listed as *"Agent to Lloyds"* (D Phillipson, 1994, All her glories past; the story of the Zetland Lifeboat, Smith Settle, 36-41).

1841. Shown on Henry Cross's map (J W Ord, 1846).

1849. Shown on *"Chart of the Tees, from Stockton to the Sea, from a recent Survey by James Johnston, made by order of the Tees Navigation Co, 3 Feb, 1849"*.

Millers; Robert Coulson, *"Redcar"* (1822), *"b Nottinghamshire"* (1861), James Coulson (1865), Robert Dowson (1873).

Coatham windmill was a tall tower with four sails, domed cap and fantail (P Sotheran, Redcar in Retrospect, 1975, pl 17). The tower was used as an observatory at the time of World War I. Demolished in 1934.

REDCAR, NZ 609250 Demolished

1833. Shown in L Haghe's stone engraving made to illustrate W A Brook's paper *"Observations on Port William at Redcar ..."*

1838. *"A newly erected and excellent corn mill of seven floors advertised to be sold by auction at the Cock Inn, Guisborough"*. There was also a newly erected granary and drying kiln, a large house and *"... from its contiguity to the fashionable bathing place of Redcar, commands respectable lodgers during the season ..."* (York Herald, 16 June).

1841. Census returns listed Coulson as an engineer. In 1848 he was listed as a lodging house keeper (D Phillipson, 1994, 36-41).

1849. Shown by James Johnston, *"A chart of the Tees from Stockton to the Sea, from a recent survey by James Johnston, made by the order of the Tees Navigation Co, 3 Feb 1849"*.

Millers; Stephen Coulson, *"millwright"* (1822, 1840), *"engineer"* (1841), Robert Coulson (1851, 1861), George Cooper (1865, 1873), Henry Holmes (1872).

Redcar mill was a fine six-sail tower mill. The last vestiges were cleared away in 1964.

MARSKE

A post windmill stood in the West Field of Marske. The site may have been near Rye Hills Farm from which Green Lane runs down to *"Mill Howl"* and *"Mill Close Howl"* on the coast.

1304. Four water mills and one windmill worth 7s per week (£8 2s per annum); Inquisition post mortem for Walter de Fauconberg (YAS Rec Ser, vol 37, 62-3).

1319. Windmill was listed; Inquisition post mortem for Walter de Fauconberg (PRO C 134/63).

1349. Windmill *"worth 13s 6d before the Mortality"*; Inquisition post mortem for John de Fauconberg (PRO C 135/96).

1363. Windmill worth 13s 4d per annum; Inquisition post mortem for Walter de Fauconberg (PRO C 135/170).

1408. *"The profits of a windmill called Rydekermyll, otherwise Leymilne ..."*; Assignment of dower to Joan, widow of Thomas Fauconberg (YAS Rec Ser, vol 59, 69-74).

1538. *"... windmill in the West Field of Marske ..."*, in other words between Marske and Redcar, was held by Gisborough Priory at the time of the Dissolution.

1539. Farm of a windmill reduced from 40s to 26s 8d (ie by 1 mark); Confiscated estates of rebels, Estates of Christopher Conyers (PRO SC 6/4281).

1608. *"Gisborough Monastery Windmill in the East Field of Marske in tenancy of Robt Rookbie, £0 6s 8d"*; Certificate of Windmills and Watermills in the possession of James I (R Bennett and J Elton, 1900, 43). The *"East Field"* is actually situated to the west of Marske. Marked on 1857 O.S. map as *"Marske, Detached"*.

1609. Windmill in Marske West Field, *"recently erected"* (Pat 7 Jas I pt xvi m 10-11; VCH vol 2, 403).

1649. *"... one wind corn mill called Redcar Mill in Marske and Redcar, formerly the property of Katherine Atherton, daughter and co-heiress of John, late Lord Conyers, deceased ..."*; James Pennyman of Ormesby Hall to Dame Ellinor Lowther (NYCRO ZNK I 2/3-14).

1762. *"Near to Mathew Ingledew's farm ... belongs a mill, now out of repair, for which he is allowed £24 0s 0d"* ; ; *"A Particular of the estate of the late William Lowther"* (NYCRO ZNK V 3/8/46).

YEARBY, NZ 605212

There is evidence of a post windmill to the east of the village.

c.1700. Shown on *"Charles Turner, Esq., His Seat att Kirkleatham in Cleveland"*, Knyff and Kip.

1774. *"Mill Flatt"*, *"Little Mill Flatt"* and *"Great Mill Flatt"* marked on Plan of the Parish and Manor of Kirkleatham (NYCRO ZMI 71).

GUISBOROUGH, NZ 610159 Demolished

Gisborough Priory had a windmill in Guisborough.

1346. Philippus de Gartona had lands in the town and field of Guisborough, viz one toft and croft and three roods near the *"molendinum ventriticum"* (Gis Chart, Surtees Soc, vol 86, 75).

1539. *"... two water mills for corn and one windmill ... in Gisburne ... £13 12s 2d"*; Robert Trystram, Collector for the Crown (Gis Chart, Surtees Soc, vol 89, xxxii).

1557. *"... all those our two water mills and one windmill in Gisburne aforesaid ... now or late in the tenure or occupation of Allan Richardson and pertaining to the said late monastery ..."*; grant to Thomas Chaloner (J W Ord, 1846, 589-91).

1843. Marked on Henry Cross's Map (J W Ord, 1846).

1853. Marked (Ordnance Survey 1st Ed, 6 inch).

1858. J Metcalfe, the last miller, became a committee member of a new steam mill belonging to the Guisborough Co-operative Corn Milling Society.

The windmill stood beside an old trackway (later Cleveland Street) which led from Westgate to the old water mill at Howl Beck.

NORTH COAST

LOFTUS, NZ 720183, Fig 174 Demolished

In 1764 Sir Lawrence Dundas bought the Loftus estate and subsequently carried out many improvements. The tower mill was built to serve the increasing population working in the alum industry.

1843. Marked as a post windmill but not named; Henry Cross's map (J W Ord, 1846).

1858. *"Windmill (corn)"* (Ordnance Survey 1st Ed, 6 inch).

Miller; Thomas Hudson (1872, 1879).

The mill house still stands to the north west of the town centre near the lane running north from the point where Zetland Terrace becomes the High Street.

EASINGTON, NZ 749176, Fig 30 Demolished

Field names to the south east of the manor house and village provide evidence of a medieval mill.

1865. *"Mill Field"*, *"High Mill Field"*, *"South Mill Field"*, *"Long Mill Field"* and *"Mill Pasture"*; *"The Manor and Estates of Easington and Bowlby and also Grinkle Park in the Parish of Easington in the North Riding in the County of York"*; map (NYCRO ZMP 1/12 1712, 346).

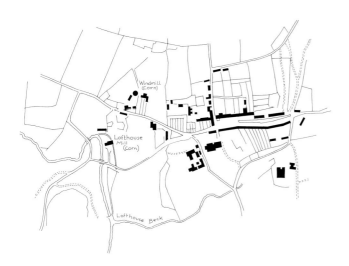

FIG 174. LOFTUS WINDMILL (PREPARED FROM ORDNANCE SURVEY 1ST ED, 6 INCH MAP 1853).

HINDERWELL, NZ 792166, Fig 96 Demolished

A stone-built tower mill was built in Hinderwell village in 1828.

1830. *"To be sold by auction. A recently erected wind corn mill, 7 storeys high and in complete working order, with two pairs of French stones, cylinders etc. situated on a parcel of land fronting the town street of Hinderwell on the road leading from Whitby to Guisborough. The beautiful and substantial stone built tower has only been erected about two years and the machinery was executed by a first class workman without regard to expense"* (Yorks Gazette, 22 May).

1868. *"It having been considered by many persons desirable to convert the above property into a union mill in £5 shares, a meeting will be held at the Shoulder of Mutton Inn, Hinderwell, on Tuesday, the 3rd of November ..."* (Whitby Gazette, 31 October). This project seems to have failed.

1872. *"Sale of Hinderwell Steam and Windmill. Steam Mill of recent erection with 3 pairs of French stones, superior 15 HP engine by Bolckow and Vaughan, with Cornish boiler by Butler and Sharp ... the windmill contains 3 pairs of French stones. The Whitby and Middlesbrough Railway (now constructing) passes close to the Mill premises ... to be sold as a result of the dissolution of Messrs Corner & Co"* (Whitby Gazette, 8 June).

1933. *"Steam mill added, 1848. Both plants ceased to work before 1900 ... All machinery removed September, 1915 ... very good building"* (Mitford Abraham).

Millers; J Corner and W Webster (1865), William Bishop (1879).

The mill was a slender, seven-storey tower with reefing stage at fourth floor. It had four sails on an iron cross and a fantail.

UGTHORPE, NZ 791115, Fig 83 Converted

A small tower windmill was built at the end of the eighteenth century, probably on the site of a post mill.

Post 1245. Lands in Ugthorpe were acquired by Gisborough Priory, partly by agreements with Handale Priory (Gis Chart, Surtees Soc, vols 86 and 89, 668, 943 7, 988-9). A miller was mentioned but not a mill.

1649. *"... one intack on the north side of Ugthorpe Windmylne"*; demise, John Stangley to William Stangley (Burnett Coll, no 1273).

1727-1746. Owner/millers were George Cook, Matthew Cook, Matthew Cook and George Cook; Egton Parish Registers (Margaret Denham, 1979, pers comm).

1776. *"7 December. My Dwelling House wherein I dwell with all the stabling outhousing Garth and lands which I have ... and all that my Corn Windmill situate at Ugthorpe"*; will of Matthew Cook of Ugthorpe in the parish of Lythe in the County of York Miller, left to George Cook his son (Borthwick Institute: Exchequer Court Wills, February 1777).

1801. *"Samuel Simpson, miller, Ugthorpe"* (M Y Ashcroft, 1977, NYCRO, Pub No 15, App 3).

1853. *"... wind corn mill"* released by William Hogarth of Ugthorpe, miller ... to Robert and John Wilson, Ugthorpe, millers (Burnett Coll, no 1327).

1860. *"Mr John Linton will offer by auction ... all that capital Freehold Corn Windmill, Dwellinghouse, and garden, with the small garth near the same, called 'Hunt House Garth' containing about one acre situated at Ugthorpe aforesaid, now occupied by Messrs John and Robert Wilson, the owners. The Mill contains Two Pairs of Stones - one French and the other Grey - a Cylinder, and all other conveniences for carrying on to the greatest advantage the Business of a prosperous Agricultural Mill to the rising population of the district. The high elevation of the Mill gives it an advantage over the mills in the neighbourhood, and is the only one in the extensive parish of Lythe. 23 July"* (Whitby Gazette, September 1935).

1928. *"Mr Dobson (owner) refuses to spend any more money on its upkeep. Ruins of fantail on ground. Three pairs of stones, flour dresser in basement. The last 4-armed mill on the Yorkshire coast"* (Mitford Abraham).

Millers; George Cook etc (1727, 1746), Matthew Cook (1776), Samuel Simpson (1801), Matthew Linton (1840), William Hogarth (1853), James Wilkinson (1872), C Walker, *"Miller and Corn Manufactor"* (1872), Peter Watson (1889). Robert Dobson bought the mill in 1889 and worked it until 1906, when it was taken over by his son, another Robert.

It is said locally that the date 1796 was carved on a timber under the first floor. An early photograph shows the three-storey tower with ridged cap roof, winding wheel and roller reefing sails with flat boards on the leading edges. Later it acquired a fantail in addition to the old winding wheel. It stopped work temporarily during World War I but was restored to work in 1920. It was restored cosmetically in 1935, with new cap roof and wands (Oliver Stonehouse, pers comm). According to some sources it had a cast-iron mortise brake-wheel and cast-iron stone nuts. A pair of grey millstones and a barley millstone remain on site.

WHITBY

This group of windmills served the town and port. The windmill at Fylingdales is included in this section, in line with the geographical grouping used in the gazetteer of water mills.

NEWHOLM/DUNSLEY/SKELDER/SELLY HILL, NZ 862096, Fig 95 Demolished

Selly Hill is the name of the slope on which the mill stood. Skelder was the general area. Newholm and Dunsley are local townships.

1822. *"William Appleton's Mill was totally destroyed by fire ... nothing but bare wall left standing."* (Stamford Mercury, 19 April).

1831. *"Appleton's mill"*; Robert Cooper's Map of Whitby (Whitby Museum).

1888. *"To be sold by private treaty. The wind and steam corn mill near Newholm, near Whitby. The mill has three pairs of stones. Attached is a good dwelling house, with 12 hp engine and boiler"* (The Miller, 2 April).

1907. *"For sale. Windmill in good position, with good house and outbuildings ... leaving through ill health. Apply to W Appleton, miller, Newholme"* (The Miller, 4 March).

Millers; John Appleton (1831, William Appleton (1840), William Appleton, *"Newholme and Stainsacre"* (1873), John Appleton (1889), William Appleton (1897, 1907, 1913).

A photograph by F M Sutcliffe shows a six-storey, stone-built tower with ogee cap roof, fantail and four roller reefing sails. There was also a steam engine chimney stack. The mill house survives.

UNION, NZ 894111, Fig 94 Demolished

This was an exceptionally fine five-sailed tower mill set within a granary range.

1800. The first meeting for the proposed windmill took place at the White Horse and Griffin on 10 March. The stated objective was *"... to relieve the suffering of the poor ... considering the very high price of wheat and the frequent practice of grinding inferior grain (so) that good bread is difficult to procure"*. J Watson was among those who were authorised by this meeting to hold further meetings and to set up Articles and Rules; *"Rules for*

the government of the Union Mill, printed by Thomas Webster" (Whitby Museum).

The foundation stone was laid on 16 June by T Fishburn and T Broddick. A commemorative mug carried the message:

> "From stormy blasts
> And dangers ill
> May God protect
> The Union Mill".

1803. *"19 March 1803. Thomas Fishburn Jnr, Esquire, and the Trustees of the Union Windmill in the parish of Whitby in the County of York. On a Corn Wind Mill called the Union Mill, with granaries, dwelling house, and drying kiln all (in) communication, brick and stone built and tiles, situated in the township of Ruswarp in the parish of Whitby aforesaid, £500. On the standing and going geers, millstones, wire machines, dressing mills etc therein, £499. Warranted no steam engine ..."* (Royal Exchange Fire Insurance, no 198785).

1814. *"For 14 years the business was conducted by Mr John Watson, president ... all the heavy debts contracted at the erection of the mill were paid off, and the institution, freed of all encumbrances, was brought to yield a substantial benefit to members"* (G Young, 1817, 628).

1815. John Watson and the original trustees quit responsibility. They were criticised for *"... greatest carelessness and wrecklessnesss imaginable"* in giving up the mill *"to the assumed and illegally elected President and his illiterate committee"*; Pamphlet written by Jno Hugill, auctioneer (Whitby Museum). The new president was called Cunningham.

1852. Mill had lost one wand. *"No distribution of flour that year."* (Yorks Gazette, 6 March).

1888. Union Mill Society was wound up on 11 July, following storm damage to mill.

1909. *"Quite recently pulled down ..."* (R T Gaskin, 1909, The Old Seaport of Whitby, 228).

The windmill was built in the middle of a three-storey granary, 11 bays long with a pedimented central feature and chimney stack at each end. The tower was nine storeys high with a reefing gallery at the sixth floor and a tall ogee cap roof. At the end of its life it had five patent sails set on an iron cross and an eight-sail fantail on a tall frame.

STAKESBY/ANDERSON'S/ARUNDELL, NZ 892108, Fig 84 Demolished

Stakesby mill was sometimes known by the names of its owners.

1778. *"Wind Corn Mill in the several ownerships of Elizabeth Knaggs and James Lewis"*; Indenture between Mark Noble, Whitby, gent, and Robert Clarke, Ruswarp, gent (Burnett Coll, 4572).

1796. *"... Brickyard, Rope Ground, also 2 houses, Warehouse, Corn Mill built in same close"*; Lease and release, Thomas Scarth, owner, to Robert Moorsom of Stokesley (Burnett Coll, 4601-2).

1806. *"Arundell Closes ... also messuages built thereon with the common gardens of Rope Ground and house near to and occupied with the rope ground, also that other then lately erected house with warehouse, corn mill and buildings then standing ..."*; Release quoted in indenture of 1825 (Burnett Coll, 4629).

1817. *"... the corn mill now occupied by Mr T Anderson at Low Stakesby was once an oil mill"* (G Young, 1817, 819).

1843. Marked but not named on Henry Cross's map (J W Ord, 1846).

1862. *"... and all that my wind corn mill with the dwelling house, granaries ... situate at or near Lower Stakesby, now in the occupation of George Fletcher"*; Will of Wakefield Simpson Chapman (Burnett Coll, 4629).

1869. *"For let ... the windmill at Stakesby near Whitby, together with the house and granaries ... apply to William Ruff, Stakesby ..."* (Whitby Gazette, 27 March).

The tower, with no gallery and with an endless chain winding wheel on the cap, was shown in an engraving in R T Gaskin, The Old Seaport of Whitby, 1909, Forth & Hudson, 228.

Millers; T Anderson (1817), Thomas Anderson and Son (1822), George Fletcher, *"Low Stakesby"* (1838), Cornelius Walker (1873).

Later it was fitted with a fantail and patent sails and survived in this form until 1877 when it was demolished as part of improvements to the gardens of Arundell House.

BAGDALE/WREN'S, NZ 891109 Demolished

Bagdale mill (built before 1796) was also known by the names of its owners.

1800. William Nicholls was the miller; Chief Constables' Returns (NYCRO, QAW).

1842. Painting by George Weatherill (Whitby Museum).

1843. Marked but not named on Henry Cross's map (J W Ord, 1846).

1857. *"... all that wind corn mill and messuage cottage or dwelling house situated in or near Bagdale, called Bagdale Mill Field ... now in the occupation of George Burnett"*; Conveyance, 17 April (A Whitworth, 1991, 35). Bagdale mill was demolished in 1862 (R T Gaskin, 1909, 228).

ABBEY

1316. Agreement between the Abbot of Whitby and Sir Alexander Percy (L Charlton, 1779, 241-2).

1540. *"One close of arable land called Wynd Mylne Flatt containing by estimate 20 acres, also one windmill on*

the hill near the said monastery at Whitby (unum molm ventric scit super montem juxta dem nup Monasti'cium de Whitby, xxs)" (G Young, 1817, 931).

1557. *"In the grant of John York to Richard Cholmeley two water mills and two windmills were conveyed"* (Yorks Fines, Tudors, YAS I, 205; VCH vol 2, 512).

1666. *"... and all that messuage with the appurtenances late in the tenure or occupation of Lambert Russell reputed to be part of the Windmill Flatts, the Windmill, Spittle Bridge, closes ..."*; A true copy of Sir Hugh Cholmeley's marriage settlement with my lady Anne Crompton (Burnett coll, 1552).

1817. *"The windmill was on a small eminence, still remaining, a little to the east of the abbey"* (G Young, 1817, 500n).

Ordnance Survey 1st Ed, 6 inch map has the name *"Windmill Hill"* to the south east of the abbey.

STAINSACRE, NZ 914084 Demolished

There was a stone-built tower mill on the hill to the south of the inn.

1816. William Henderson built the mill and became its first miller (NYCRO Deeds Reg, EA 1816-17).

1844. *"To be sold. A fine stone built Wind Corn Mill with patent sails, 2 pairs of French millstones and flour cylinder, corn screen, Barley Mill etc ... occ. by Mr Henderson, the owner, who intends to decline business"* (Yorks Gazette, 2 November).

1888. *"To be sold by private treaty ... Also the Windmill of Stainsacre. This mill has two pairs of stones, a house adjoining with granary and stable. Apply to J Appleton, Newholme Mill, Whitby, Yorks"* (The Miller, 2 April).

Millers; William Henderson (1851, 1861, died 1869), William Appleton, *"Stainsacre and Newholme"* (1872, 1909).

The mill, a stone-built five-storey tower mill with ogee cap roof, four sails and fantail, was demolished about 1920.

HIGH HAWSKER, NZ 925076, Fig 100 Shell

Hawsker windmill was built by George Burnett, said to have been former manager of the Union Mill in Whitby but also associated with Bagdale mill.

1862. *"... 2 cottages, yard attached with newly erected messuage and windmill, corn outhouse and premises lately erected by George Burnett upon some part of garden in Green Gate ..."*; Mortgage by Burnett to Richard Parkinson, Thorpe, Fylingdale, gent (NYCRO Deeds Reg, IY 1862-3).

1868. The mill, *"... a solid structure, built of brick only a few years ago, carried on by George Burnett, the owner"* was destroyed by fire and *"... the mill wands fell and were broken to pieces"* (Whitby Gazette, 4

September and Yorks Gazette, 19 September). It was refitted with double shuttered sails, an ogee cap and tall fantail stage.

1903. John Hauxwell quoted for fitting an oil engine and two sets of French burr stones with cases and driving gear (John Hauxwell's Letter Books).

1904. *"I beg to announce that Hawsker Mill is now open for the sale of Flour, Breadmeals, Offals of all kinds, Corn, Cattle Cakes, and Foods, Artificial Manures etc. I am prepared to execute any quantity of farmers' grinding ... Jas Maxwell McGee"* (Whitby Gazette, 8 January).

Millers; George Burnett (1872, 1889), John Wilson (1899), James McGee (1904), William Appleton, *"and at Newholme"* (1909).

It was built 64 feet tall with 14 inch thick brick walls, ogee cap roof, four sails and a tall fantail frame. There was a house to one side and a granary to the other. It had three pairs of stones at the second floor. The sails were still working in 1915 but it had an auxiliary engine from 1903. It was gutted before 1928 and three floors were removed in 1960. The stub is used as a grain store.

FYLINGDALES

There may have been a short-lived windmill at Fylingdales but the references are obscure. The field name *"Yaddow Mills"* near to Farsyde House survived to be recorded on early Ordnance Survey maps.

1789. *"William Lynas of Fylingdales in the County of York, miller. On a corn windmill situate in a field called Thoricks, Fylingdales aforesaid, in his own tenure, timber £300"* (Sun Fire Insurance, no 561422).

1801. *"... Wind Corn Mill not occupied"* at Robin Hoods Bay; Chief Constables' Returns (NYCRO QAW).

SCARBOROUGH

With the exception of medieval mills at Burniston and Scarborough the windmills in this group are of late eighteenth or early nineteenth century date, reflecting population growth.

RAVENSCAR/BEACON/BLUE ROBBIN/PEAK, NZ 976006, Fig 99 Shell

The heavily built masonry tower is a distinctive landmark.

1857. William Hammond, owner of the Raven Hill estate, advertised for a windmill builder in August 1857 (Malton Messenger, 8 August).

1858. *"On Thursday week, Peak was the scene of great rejoicing in consequence of the marriage of Mr W H*

Hammond's second daughter to Rev Johnson Barker of Leicester. ... Tenants and children had a repast provided at Raven Hall Inn and the workmen of the estate had a collation at a mill now in the course of erection near the moors" (Scarborough Mercury, 25 September).

1928. *"Ravenscar Windmill ... an exceptionally well constructed stone building with floors of magnificent oak and pitch pine beams. It continued to work (with a slight break about 1900) until 1902, when in November of that year and with only two arms left it lost them both in a gale during the night. The miller had set them before retiring for the night to the west, but the gale wind changed to the east and set the arms revolving in the reverse direction. The miller got out of bed, having been awakened by the noise, and climbed to the top of the mill and tried to stop the arms, but was unable to do so, and had no sooner reached his home less than 100 yards distant when they were both blown off the mill. A portion of one arm was actually blown right across the road into the quarry from which the stones came to build the tower ..."* (Scarborough Evening News, 24 March).

The machinery was taken for scrap to help with the war effort, and was presumably, therefore, of cast-iron. It had an ogee cap roof and four arms on a cast-iron cross. Holes in each stone for lifting tongs are a prominent feature. There was no reefing stage, which means it must have had patent sails.

BURNISTON

C12. *"The mill at Burniston was granted with two carucates of land ... by Uchtred son of Thorkill de Cleveland to Whitby Abbey"* (Whitby Chart, Surtees Soc, 4 22; VCH vol 2, 478).

SCARBOROUGH COMMON/VICTORIA/HARRISON'S, TA 036883 Converted, Grade II

A post mill stood between Gallows Close, Bracken Hill and the Common near the site of the gallows, formerly near the main gates on the York Road. Later, a tower mill was built off Victoria Road.

1320. *"There were four watermills and a windmill belonging to the Crown ..."* (Rentals & Survey (Gen Ser) 64 bdle 17, no 52; VCH vol 2, 553).

1330. *"... four watermills and a windmill, £16 per annum"* belonged to the town and burgesses of the town (A Rowntree, 1931, 410).

1661 *"... the inhabitants knew of only one windmill pulled down in the Civil War ..."* (Exch Dep Hil 12 & 13, Charles II no 1; VCH vol 2, 553).

1723. A post windmill was illustrated immediately outside the *"Olde Mote"* near to Newborough Bar on *"A New and Exact Plan of the Town of Scarborough, Anno 1723"* (M Edwards ed, 1966, Scar & Dist Arch Soc, opp p 58).

1784. 10 May. Thomas Robinson petitioned Scarborough Common Hall for permission to build a windmill on Windmill Hill (NYCRO DC/SCB C43).

1787. *"… until the late building and establishment of that ample windmill, which now supplies and dominates the town"* (Sotheran's Scarborough Guide).

1787. *"… a noble windmill"* (James Schofield, 1787, Guide to Scarborough, 12).

1793. *"16 April. Cant Candler & Co of Scarborough in the County of York. On a windmill situate in a field near Scarborough aforesaid in the tenure of … £800. Mealhouse near £50. Granary near £200. House adjoining £250"* (Sun Fire Insurance, no 614014).

1793. *"Eleazor Sherwood … on utensils and stock in a windmill situate in a field near Scarborough aforesaid £250"* (Sun Fire Insurance, no 614015).

1829. *"To be let, a good wind corn mill 5 storeys high situated on the common between Falsgrave and Scarborough in the Co of Yorkshire, now in the occupation of Mr Stubbs, who will show the premises"* (Doncaster Gazette, 24 April).

1844. *"To be let. A modern built Windmill situate on the South Cliff, Scarborough. The mill has recently been put into complete repair. App. Messrs Gibson and Penrose, Scarborough"* (Yorks Gazette, 9 November).

1850. *"To be sold by auction. All that valuable Wind Corn Mill situate and being near the Common at Scarborough … formerly in the occupation of Mr Samuel Newton, but now unoccupied …"* (Yorks Gazette, 6 April). It was bought by Moses Harrison, formerly a farmer at Cloughton.

1910. The sails were blown down in a heavy storm (A Rowntree, 1931, 227-8).

Millers; Newton (pre 1850), Moses Harrison (1872, 1879, 1889, 1893).

The seven-storey tower formerly had four double-sided patent sails, an eight-sail fan and an ogee cap roof. There had been a wooden upright shaft. The sails were removed in 1898. Afterwards the mill operated by engine. There was a fire during World War I but the gas engine installation did not stop work until 1927. *"… once a week the whole assembly had to be lifted up on two huge bottle jacks so that the phosphor bronze cup in which the central shaft rested could be oiled."* (Scarborough Evening News, 31 August, 1984).

This mill was partially restored as a prominent townscape feature by Stephen Beecroft in the late 1980s and now incorporates an iron wind shaft from a Lincolnshire windmill (Alan Coombes, The Windmill of their Minds, The Guardian, 16 August, 1990).

ALBION, TA 042892 Demolished

This mill stood on North Cliff, Scarborough, where Osborne House now stands.

1819. *"To be let or sold. A substantial Tower Wind Corn Mill nearly new, with patent sails and flier, containing six floors, two pairs of French stones, 4ft 6inches, two cylinders and corn screens. The premises are situated near to the entrance on the north side of the town and on the west side of the road leading towards Whitby … Messrs English and Wilson are present owners"* (Yorks Gazette, 6 November).

1839. Along with many other windmills it was damaged in the severe storms of 1839. It was repaired as a four-sailer.

1864. Engraving; Rock & Co, 2050.

1866. Marked on the *"Plan of Scarborough"* (M Edwards ed, 1966, 69).

GREENGATE, TA 041891 Demolished

This tower mill stood at the foot of Mill Street on North Marine Road, formerly called Greengate. It was quite close to Albion Mill.

1828. *"To be sold by private contract. All that freehold brick Wind Corn Mill with sails, utensils etc situate in Greengate, immediately adjoining the town of Scarborough, in excellent repair and lately occupied by Mr William Gibson"* (Yorks Gazette, 31 May).

1828. *"To be sold by the order of the Assignees of Mr William Gibson a bankrupt … All that excellent freehold brick Wind Mill now used as a Bone Mill, with such of the sails, utensils etc as were the property of the said William Gibson, situate in Greengate, near Scarborough, and now in the occupation of Mr John Southwell for a term of 14 years from June 21, 1825"* (Yorks Gazette, 11 Oct).

1866. Marked on the *"Plan of Scarborough"* (M Edwards ed, 1966, 69).

Miller; John Weldon (1840, and Scalby water mill).

SOUTH CLIFF

"The sails of four windmills stood out against the skys; Greengate … Albion Mill … the Common Mill … and one on the South Cliff where St Martin's church stands" (A Rowntree, 1930, 272).

1844. *"To be let. A modern built windmill situate on the South Cliff, Scarborough. The mill has recently been put into complete repair. Apply to Messrs Gibson and Pennock, Scarborough"* (Yorks Gazette, 9 November).

PICKERING AND RYEDALE

There was a scatter of windmills along the southern boundary of the North Yorks Moors, some in medieval times and four at the beginning of the nineteenth century.

OLD MALTON, SE 793740 Converted

Old Malton tower windmill stands to the west of the road from Pickering to Malton at Windmill Farm. It lost its sails on 26 October 1906 and is now a dwelling.

SLINGSBY

1215-35. *"In an undated charter Richard"* (Wyvill) *"granted to his nephew Lawrence his mill of Slingsby"* (Harl Chart, 112, E 56; VCH vol 1 559).

Mid-C13. A messuage and half a carucate of land with a windmill in the vill of *"Lengesby"*; grant by Nicholas de Stapilton to the Augustinian canons of Malton; Old Malton Chart (British Library, Cotton Claud D XI f 101 u).

1301. Windmill and *"two watermills under one roof"* (Yorks Inq, YAS vol 31, 151-2).

SWINTON

The canons of Malton had a grange at Swinton.

1539. *"... one windmill ... demised to Edmund Rasyn"*; Dissolution Acc of Old Malton Priory (PRO SC 6 Hen VIII 4618).

AMOTHERBY

The Priory had a grange at Amotherby, again with a windmill on it.

C13. *"... farm of windmill 20s"*; Old Malton Chart (British Library, Cotton Claud DXI f 283).

FOULBRIDGE/SNAINTON

There was a post windmill on the carrs alongside the Derwent to the south of Snainton Ings where reclaimed land was distant from Ebberston mill.

1272. *"A mill at Snainton"* belonged to Ingram de Boynton (Bovington) (Ft of F, Yorks, 56 Henry III, no 4; VCH vol 2, 425). It was not stated whether this was a wind or a water mill.

1273. The manor of Snainton and the *"empty windmill"* of Foulbridge belonged to the order of the Knights Templar (Add ms 6165, fol 316; VCH vol 2, 428).

1307. The windmill belonged to the Templars (Anct Ext, Exch K R, no 16; VCH vol 2, 428).

1326. There was a water mill at Foulbridge (Chan Inq p m, 1 Edward III 1st nos no 88; VCH vol 2, 425).

The order of Templars was suppressed in 1311.

MIDDLETON, nr Pickering.

1316 the Hospital of St Leonard's in York granted a messuage and croft in Middleton (near Pickering) with a windmill for 5s per annum to Richard son of Thomas de Boynton (YAS, Rec Ser, vol. 65 Deeds 4, 107).

PICKERING Demolished

1827. *"To be sold by auction under a Commission of Bankrupt, awarded against William Hodgson ... corn factor now or late of Pickering. A Wind Corn Mill situate at Pickering, with steam engine of nine horses power attached ... all lately erected. The Mill is unusually large and powerful, having 13 floors and contains four pairs of stones and one pair of shelling stones, and all the necessary machinery and gear for the production of flour. Late the property of William Hodgson, bankrupt"* (Yorks Gazette, 27 March).

1828. *"To be sold by auction under a Commission of Bankruptcy warranted agent ... William Hodgson, now or late of Pickering. A dwelling house with a brewery adjoining occ by sd bankrupt, also the Wind Corn Mill"* (London Gazette, 27 March).

1837. *"To be sold by auction by order of the executors of the late Mr Josh Wardell, deceased. A remarkable well built Wind Corn Mill with five new pressure sails, a steam engine of 9 horse power. The mill is unusually capacious and powerful, having 13 floors, contains four pairs of flour stones and one pair of shelling stones etc. Situate within 200 yards of the termination of the Pickering and Whitby Railway"* (Yorks Gazette, 4 November).

1839. *"Gale damage on Monday last ... the owner of the windmill will be a great sufferer; the sails which were put up by the late Mr Wardell a short time ago at considerable expense are partially destroyed, the wind carrying the fragments a great distance ..."* (Yorks Gazette, 12 January).

1839. *"To be sold. To be taken down. An excellent modern brick-built Tower Windmill ... having five new pressure sails 36 feet long and 8 feet 6 inches wide"*. (The machinery list included the three pairs of flour stones, one pair of grey stones, a shelling mill, a barley mill, corn screen, dressing machine etc). *"But little used and will be disposed of at a considerable sacrifice"* (Yorks Gazette, 2 February).

1841. The advertisement containing the words *"... to be taken down"* was repeated (Yorks Gazette, 17 April 1841; Norfolk Chronicle, April 1842).

The mill does not appear on Ordnance Survey 1st Ed, 6 inch maps.

APPLETON-LE-MOORS/SPAUNTON

1266. *"A windmill at Appleton"*; claim made by Mabila, the widow of Philip de Fauconberg, against St Mary's Abbey, York.

1675/6. *"Manor, capital messuage of Spaunton with ... East Winde Milne Field"*; Bargain and Sale, William Medd to John Booker, York (NYCRO DDDA/5 cal).

Where the road leading from Appleton-le-Moors to Lastingham cuts through the scarp a *"Great Windmill Field"* and a *"Little Windmill Field"* were marked on the Tithe Map (R H Hayes, 1986, Excavations at Spaunton Manor, North Yorkshire, Rye Hist no 13, 4-25). Lastingham belonged to St Mary's.

KIRKBY MOORSIDE, SE 696864, Fig 175 Converted

1839. This tower windmill was built for the Rivis family of Yoad Wath mill (according to local lore, by the Rickabys who also built the Rosedale Chimney). A stone plaque in the tower reads "G RIVIS 1839 W & J SPENCELEY".

1845. *"To be let. A capital wind corn mill with two pairs of stones, corn screen, dressing machines etc and all machinery and necessary appliances in excellent repair being all nearly new. Situated in the market town of Kirkby Moorside. Apply to Mr Rowland Hugill, draper etc, Helmsley, or to Mr F Dobson, grocer, Kirkby Moorside, who will show the same"* (Yorks Gazette, 22 February).

1861. *"Sale at the White Horse Inn, Kirkby Moorside. Wind corn mill and house, workshops, stable, coach house, yard, garden adjoining at the West end of Kirkby Moorside. Mill erected about 20 years ago, cost £1000. Six storeys and three pairs of stones. George Rivis in the*

premises, Richard Hugill of Helmsley, owners" (Malton Messenger, 2 March).

According to local sources the arms were removed to Hawsker mill about 1875. This brick-built tower was six storeys high with cast-iron window frames and ventilators. It has been converted into a dwelling with the curb and top courses of brickwork removed.

GILLING

Nd. *"... Deodand paid for death in Gilling due to spindles and blades of windmill 18d"* (YAJ vol 15, 210).

AMPLEFORTH, SE 592794 Demolished

1823. *"To be sold. A newly erected wind corn mill situated at Ampleforth near Easingwold. Apply to Mr C T Bainbridge, Easingwold"* (Yorks Gazette, 8 March).

1852. *"On the heights above Ampleforth ... a mile from the town ... the ruins of the building may yet be traced."* 'Windmill House' and 'Windmill Hill' straddle the main road between the village and Ampleforth College.

EASINGWOLD Demolished

n.d. In a memorandum of agreement between the Rt. Honourable Thomas Raynes and William Salvin Esqr both of Easingwold the said William Salvin is required *"... to keep in good repair the mill, millstones, sails and cloths."* Vallis Eboracensis (Thomas Gill, 1852, History of Easingwold).

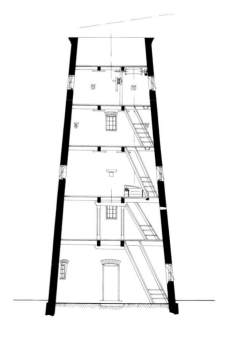

FIG 175. KIRKBY MOORSIDE WINDMILL.

COD BECK

BROMPTON

The stump of a large, brick-built tower mill survives at Brompton near Northallerton. It was built to serve a growing population of linen workers.

1806. *"William Elgie of Brompton in the parish of Northallerton, County of York, miller. On stock in trade including bolting cloths and all movable utensils in his windmill house and chamber all in the one building, brick and timber built, situated at the East End of Brompton aforesaid £800. Warranted no steam engine"* (Royal Exchange Insurance, no 227394, 3 December).

1831. *"To be sold … pursuant to a decree of the High Court of Chancery … an establishment situate at Brompton … comprising a dwelling house, capital windmill … held under the Bishop of Durham"* (London Gazette, 28 June).

1832. *"To be sold. A capital windmill, situated at Brompton …"* (Yorks Gazette, 22 September).

1856. *"To be let. A capital wind corn mill in excellent repair situate at Brompton, near Northallerton, within a short distance of the Brompton Railway Station. Apply to Mr Hamilton, Northallerton"* (Yorks Gazette, 12 January).

1872. Owned by the Northallerton Provident Corn Milling Society.

Millers; John Scaife (1863), Stephen Clarke (1866).

INGLEBY ARNCLIFFE

1434. *"A windmill valued at 19s 6d …"*; Rental (NYCRO ZFL 134 mic 1291).

1694. *"If Coz. Pierse will pay me £31 and let me have his windmill for £30 interrest which is due I am willing to receive it so that Coz. Pierse will be pleased to bring me the sd mill to Arncliffe and the millstones, all intirely whatever belongs to the sd mill. Mr Ward valued the sd mill and stones for £20"* (Timothy Mauleverer's Diary, NYCRO TD 38). There is no evidence that this mill was in fact moved to Ingleby.

A field name is now the only evidence of this mill.

DROMONBY

"South East of Dromonby House is Mill Hill, perhaps the Windmill Hill of 1479 and the site of the mill of 1311" (Exch K R Misc Bks, xxxviii fol 241d; VCH vol 2, 253). The mill of 1311, belonging to the Prior of Hexham, may have been a windmill at Dromonby or alternatively may have been the water mill at Little Broughton.

1479. *"Windmill Hill"* (Gis Chart, Surtees Soc, vol 96, 389-90).

C17 and C18. *"There was a windmill …"* (Ft of F, Yorks, Mich 17, Jas I; Ft of F, Yorks, Easter, 21 Jas I; Recovery R Trin, 6 Anne, m 20; VCH vol 2, 253).

APPENDICES

APPENDIX 1. Domesday mills in the North Riding

(derived from M Faull and M Stinson, 1986).

Land of the King
"SOREBI" (Sowerby near Thirsk) *"3 carucates and 2 others belonging to the hall, with a mill which renders 20s …"*
"MALTUNE" (Old Malton) *"… late held by Siward and Torchil … a church there and site of one mill"*

Land of Archbishop of York
"SALETUN" (Salton, SE 716800) *"… late held by Ulf … a mill rendering 5s"* *"STIVEINGTON"* (Stillington) *"… late held by St Peter … one mill of 3s"*

Land of William, Bishop of Durham
"SCOGERBUD" (Scarborough) *"… William de Perci holds this of the Bishop … a mill"*

Land of Earl Hugh d'Avranches
"WITEBI and SNETUN" (Whitby and Sneaton) *"… Earl Siward held this … Earl Hugh has it and William de Perci of him … It is a manner all waste, only in Prestebi and Sourebi which the Abbott of York has of William … there are 2 ploughs in lordship; and … one mill of 10s …"*

Land of Robert, Count Mortain (half brother of William the Conqueror and Earl of Cornwall from 1088)
"GHISBURG and MIDDLETON and HOTON" (Guisborough) *"… Uchtred had three manors there. Now the Count has … a church and a mill of 4s"*
"BOLEMERE and STIDNUN" (Bulmer and Stittenham) *"… late held by Ligulf and Norman … one mill of 2s"*

Land of Count Alan (founder of Richmond Castle)
"ALDEBURNE" (Aldborough) *"… a mill"*
"BRUNTON" (Brompton-on-Swale) *"… one mill of 5s 4d"*
"ALRETUN" (Ellerton-on-Swale) *"… one mill of 6s"*
"SCORETUN" (Scorton) *"… Bodin now has there three ploughs and one mill of 3s"*

"BEDALE" Bodin now has there two ploughs and 17 villanes and 5 bordars and a mill of 5s"
"BRUNTUNE" (Patrick Brompton) *"… three knights of Earl Alan have it now … and a mill of 5s"*
"CRACHELE" (Crakehall) *"… Now two knights of Earl Alan have it … one mill of 4s"*

Land of Berenger de Todeni (Tosny) (held lands in Lincolnshire, Oxfordshire and Nottinghamshire)
"CHIRCHEBI" (Kirkby Misperton) *"… Berenger Todeni now has it and the Bishop of York of him. In the demesne three ploughs and twelve villanes and half the church with the priest, and one mill payes 5s 4d"*
"DALBI" (Dalby, SE 991712) *"… one mill of 5s"*
"BRUNTUN" (Brompton in Pickering Lythe) *"… one mill of 5s"*

Land of William de Percy (accompanied William on the Scottish expedition of 1072)
"AYTUNE" (East Ayton) *"… one mill of 5s"*
"TOPCLIVE" (Topcliffe) *"… one mill of 5s"*

Land of Ralph Pagenal (Paynel)
"MERLESVEINN" (Nunnington) (The entry includes sokeland at WICHU (Wykeham) near Malton, Stonegrave, East Ness and South Holme). *"… one mill of 3s"*

Land of Hugh, son of Baldrick (Sheriff of York after 1069)
"SUDTUNE" (Sutton-under-Whitestonecliffe) *"Gerard, Hugh's man, has there 1 plough and 8 villagers with 2 ploughs … one mill"*
"CHIRCHEBI" (Kirkby Moorside, SE 697866) *"… Hugh, son of Baldrick has 2 ploughs there, and 10 villanes with 3 ploughs. A priest is there and a church and one mill of 4s"*

Land of the King's Thanes
"STOCKESLAYE" (Stokesley) *"… a priest is there and a church and one mill of 10s and 8 acres of meadow".*

APPENDIX 2. First records for water-driven corn mills (other than those listed in the Domesday Survey)

1096   Hackness (2 mills); grant to Whitby Abbey

1102   Ruswarp, Rigg, Cock, New Mill, Fylingdales; grant to Whitby Abbey

1141   Gillamoor; grant to St Mary's Abbey

1142   Ravensthorpe; water course mentioned in boundary description

1145   Sproxton; mill mentioned in boundary description

1151   Ingleby Greenhow; confirmation of grant to Whitby Abbey

1154   Newburgh; grant of land 'beyond the fishpond'

1162   Hutton, near Guisborough; grant to nuns by Ralph de Neville

1164   Scalby; Crown possessed a mill worth £6

1169   Baxby; Peter Daiville; grant of suit of mill at Thornton

1180   Sinnington; mill mentioned in description of right of way

1189   Welburn; *"Miln Holm"* mentioned in title agreement

1190   Sleights; grant of ford with passage through land in Aislaby

1200   Thornton Dale; William was the miller

1201   Pickering High; mill farmed out by King John

1202   Ebberston; grant of 10s from the mill

1215   Caldecotes; boundary description

c.1216 Harome; grant of land *"behind the mill"*

1218   Gilling; grant

1218   Coulton; *"Slingsby mill in manor of Coulton"*

1227   Allerston; dispute

1231   Nunthorpe; dispute

1236. Appleton

1240   Foxton; grant to Robert de Clairvaux

1246   Levisham; dispute

1260   Costa High, Aislaby; *"Miln Holm"* in grant by Hugh le Bigod

1260   Crathorne; grant by Walter de Percy to Peter Bagod

1262   Kildale; grant of rental to Healaugh Park

1262   Castle Levington; mill worth 30s per annum

1267   Costa Low, Middleton; dispute with tenants of Wrelton

1272   Danby; *"two watermills worth £10"*

1272   Farndale; grant of rent from two mills

1272   Loftus; grant to Gisborough Priory

1272   Skinningrove, Skelton and Saltburn mills plus two others; Inquisition Peter de Brus

1272   Lealholm; *"watermill worth £3"*

1275   Kilburn; Inquisition

1276   Bransdale, Farndale (two mills), Kirkby Moorside

1279   Foss, Sandsend, Egton; *"four mills yielding £20"*

1280   Upsall; two mills held by Gisborough Priory

1280   Ingleby Arncliffe; boundary description

1282   Great Ayton; *"Westmulne worth 106s 8d and one quarter of Estmulne worth 27s 8d"*

1285   Helmsley; two mills worth £12 per annum

1291   Kirby Knowle; Inquisition

1295   Ampleforth; mill worth 23s per annum

1297   Goathland; mill worth 5s per annum

1298   Pickering; two mills in Pickering

1299   Seaton; water mill worth 3s 4d

1307   Westerdale; Knights Templar had a mill worth £5 6s 8d per annum

1314   Scaling; Prioress of Handale claimed moiety of mill

1315   South Kilvington; annuity out of a mill

1318   Hilton; mill appurtenant to manor

1323   Kirkleatham, rent of mill 110s

1327   Glaisdale High; water mill appurtenant to manor

1330   Rosedale

1336   Liverton; *"a watermill worth 33s 4d"*

1337   Gilling; *"mill pond"*

1344   Kilton, *"watermill worth 30s"*

BLACK DEATH

1346   Barnaby; grant of right to build a mill to Gisborough Priory

1349   Cropton; a mill worth £4 13s 4d per annum

1359   Osmotherley; lease of mill at Thymbleby

1367   Wilton; *"three watermills worth 53s 4d"*

1368   Seamer; *"watermill in hands of tenants at will, 66s 8d"*

1368   Hutton Rudby; *"watermill worth £6 13s 4d"*

1368   Whorlton; *"... a watermill"*.

APPENDIX 3. Millers recorded by name suffixed by *"molendinario"* in the 1301 Lay Subsidy

LANGBAURGH		
Yarm (wind)	Giliot	1s 8d
Seamer	Nicholao	2s 11d
East Rounton	Willelmo	5s
Stokesley	Radulpho	6d
Wilton/W Coatham (wind?)	Willilmo	
Mickleby	Willelmo	2s 7d
Kirkleatham/E Coatham (wind)	Johanne	1s 6d
	Stephano	1s 11d
Castle Leavington (wind)	Ricardo	3s 10d
Roxby nr Hinderwell	Willelmo	1s 7d
Nunthorpe	Roberto	2s 3d
Marton	Rogero	1s 4d
Lythe	Roberto	9d
Borrowby nr Lythe	Thoma	5d

RYEDALE		
Hovingham	Willelmo	1s 4d
Slingsby	Willelmo	2s 8d
	Galfrido	2s 1d
Stonegrave	Waltero	7d
Kirkby Moorside	Radulpho	7d
Bransdale	Alano	3d
Farndale	Simone	7s 9d
Pockley	Rogero	1s
Wombleton	Willelmo	1s 3d
Rycolf	Radulpho	9d
	Johanne	4s 6d
Scawton	Willelmo	4s 1d
	Waltero	2s 8d
New Malton	Willelmo del Wyndmillen	1s 6d
	Johannne	4d
Swinton	Johanne	5d
Helmsley	Rogero	11d

PICKERING		
Ayton (Scarborough)	Alano	1s 10d
	Roberto	1s 9d
Goathland	Rogero	1d
Thornton Dale	Simone	2s 3d
	Hugo	10d
Wykeham	Waltero	1s

ALLERTON		
Knayton	Roberto	1s 7d

BIRDFORTH		
Boltby	Michaele	4s

Thirlby	Roberto	2s 9d
Hawnby	Radulpho	2s 3d
Kilburn	Ricardo	11d
Kilvington	Ada	3s 6d
	Stepheno	1s

WHITBY		
Hackness	Rogero	4d
	Martino	4d
	Ada	2d
Newham/Ruswarp	Radulpho	2s 5d
Stainsacre	Nicholao	10d

APPENDIX 4. Monastic mills

WHITBY ABBEY (Benedictine, 1077)
Grants: Rigg, Cock, Ruswarp, Newholm, Fylingdales and Hackness (2 mills) (William de Percy), Ingleby Greenhow (Adam de Ingleby)

GISBOROUGH PRIORY (Augustinian, 1119)
Grants: Guisborough (Robert de Brus), Caldecotes (Arnald de Percy), Barnaby (Adam de Kirkoswald), Upsall (Robert de Tunstall), Loftus (Thomas de Humet), Guisborough West, Commondale
Guisborough, East Coatham, Acklam, Thornaby windmills

RIEVAULX ABBEY (Cistercian, 1131)
Precinct mill
Grange mills: Bilsdale Low, Raisdale
Grants: Sproxton, Newsham-on-Tees, Gilling, Nunnington, Stonegrave, Broughton, Welburn (Howkeld), Faceby, Silton, Bordelby, Cowesby, Borrowby
Normanby windmill

BYLAND ABBEY (Savignac/Cistercian, 1177)
Precinct mill
Grange mills: Tylas, Oldstead, Caydale
Grants: Low Pasture, Kilburn/Wildon, Hovingham, Coulton

ARDEN PRIORY (Benedictine, 1147)
Precinct mill

HANDALE (Cistercian, 1153)
Precinct mill
Grant: Moiety of Scaling mill, William de Percy

KELDHOLME (Cistercian, 1154)
Grants: Kirkby Moorside (Robert de Stuteville), Gillamoor (Nicholas Stuteville), Edstone

ROSEDALE ABBEY (Cistercian, 1160)
Precinct mill

HUTTON/NUNTHORPE/BAYSDALE (Cistercian, 1162)
Precinct: Basedale

GROSMONT (Grandismont)
Precinct
Grant: Egton Bridge (Joanne Fossard)

MOUNT GRACE (Carthusian, 1398)
Grant: Bordelby

FOUNTAINS ABBEY (Cistercian, 1132)
Grant: Dromonby windmill

BEVERLEY MINSTER
Grant: Westerdale

HEALAUGH
Grant: Kildale

KIRKHAM ABBEY (Augustinian, 1125)
Grant: Bilsdale (L'Espec)

MALTON PRIORY (Gilbertian)
Grants: Goathland, Ebberston, Kingthorpe Slingsby, Amotherby and Swinton windmills.

BRIDLINGTON PRIORY
Grant: Cloughton

YEDINGHAM PRIORY
Grant: Ebberston (Hawise de Clere)

WYKEHAM (Cistercian, 1153)

NEWBURGH PRIORY (Augustinian)
Grant: Coxwold

ST MARY'S, YORK (Benedictine)
Precinct: Lastingham
Grants: Appleton-le-Moors
Spaunton windmill

APPENDIX 5. Earliest recorded dates of fulling mills

1301 Hackness; Matthew the fuller, was taxed at 8s in the Lay Subsidy

1301 East Ayton; Bartholemew the fuller, taxed at 6s in the Lay Subsidy

1335 Ellerburn; *"molendinum fulreticum"* worth 20s; Inquisition post mortem for William de Latymer

1349 Kirkby Moorside; fulling mill worth 8s; Inquisition post mortem of Thomas Wake

1349 Castle Leavington; fulling mill *"demised anew for 8s per annum"*; Inquisition post mortem for John, Earl of Kent

1350 Farndale; fulling mills *"worth nothing on account of the deficiency of tenants and workers"*; Inquisition post mortem for Earl of Kent

1353 Great Ayton; one fulling mill and one water mill worth 26s 8d; Inquisition post mortem for Earl of Kent

1396 Ruswarp; *"fulling mill worth £1 16s 8d"*; Whitby Abbey Bursar's Accounts

1396 Newholm/Stakesby?; *"... molend fullonic, xxxvjs viid"*; Whitby Abbey Bursar's Accounts

1408 Skelton; *"one third of a fulling mill"*; Inquisition post mortem for Thomas Fauconberg

1432 Castleton; *"rent of one fulling mill 13s 4d"*; Danby Account Rolls

1436 Allerston; Ralph de Hastings had a fulling mill

1538 Commondale; *"One fulling mill ... 20s per annum"*

1538 Rievaulx; *"... ye Walke Milne ... 60s per annum"*

1539 Tylas/Caydale

1538 Appleton; *"... 10s farm of fulling mill formerly St Mary's"*

1540 Byland/Low Pasture

1544 Egton Bridge; *"molendinum fullonicum"* granted to Edmund Wright

1557 Glaisdale Low; sold to Lawrence Hodgson, fuller

1557 Harome; *"walke mill in decay"*

1564 Lowna; William Collyer granted a lease on fulling mill

1558 Osmotherley

1608 Keldholme; former corn mill

1619 Pickering

1628 Swainby; leased to John Stainthorpe, fuller

1635 Stocking; former paper mill converted into 'mall mill'

1635 Kildale; John Boville, fuller, married Alice Rudd

1650 Beck Hole

1658 Hawnby; *"... fulling mill ... late in tenure of Robert Grime"*

1675 Skinningrove; *"glazing mill"*

1691 Crathorne; *"Water corn mill and a fulling mill"*

1709 Laskill

1710 Easby; occupied by James Todd

1712 Rosedale; *"Richard Medd, weaver and fuller, Hartoft"*

1720 Spout Bank; *"woollen bleach mill"*

1724 Sleights; Carr End Farm formerly called Walke Mill Farm

1743 Glaisdale High; *"Wood Walk Mill"*

1743 Costa Low; *"Mr Robinson, Cropton, resolved to build a fulling mill"*

1755 Costa High

1840 Oldstead; Tithe map

1843 Staithes; Henry Cross n.d. Bransdale; Name *"Tenter Field"* survives.

APPENDIX 6. Earliest recorded dates of tower windmills

Date of building where known	*First record*	
	1769	Bagdale
	1773	Coatham
	1778	Stakesby
	1784	Scarborough Common
c.1790		Stockton Old Mill
	1792	Middleton
1796		Ugthorpe; (dated timber)
1800		Union, Whitby
1800		Mandale
	c.1800	Greatham
	1801	Marton
1802		Whitby Union
	1803	Cleveland Port
	1806	Brompton; (*"newly erected"*)
1814		New Mill, Stockton; (Richmond)
	1814	Hart; (old mill blown down)
	1815	Stranton; ('Knowles')
	1815	Yarm
	1816	Stainsacre
	1816	Redcar
	1818	Albion, Norton
	1819	Albion, Scarborough; (*"nearly new"*)
	1821	Newburn
	1822	Newholm, Whitby; (burned)
	1822	Egglescliffe; millers John and William Fidler
1823		Ampleforth; (*"newly erected"*)
	1824	Mount Pleasant, Stockton
	1825	Greengate, Scarborough; (lease)
	1827	Pickering; (*"lately erected"*)
1828		Hinderwell
	1828	Newton Bewley
	1835	Middleton; (second windmill)
1839		Kirkby Moorside; (date-stone)
1840		Middlesbrough
	1843	Sober Hall
	1843	High Leven
	1843	Loftus
	1843	Coulby Newham
	1845	Church mill, Stranton; (*"lately erected"*)
	1845	Middleton St George; Thomas Calvert, miller
	1848	Dock
	1848	West Hartlepool
	1857	Grange, Egglescliffe
	1857	Summerhouse, Norton
1858		Ravenscar; (*"in course of erection"*)
	1860	Elwick; (Parish Registers)
	1860	Hawsker; (*"lately erected"*)
	1864	North Ormesby; William Fidler, miller.

APPENDIX 7. German blue stones

Liverton; dated 17...

Moorsholm; one stone diameter 4 feet used as threshold

Loftus; one runner stone standing against front wall

Marske; quadrant fragment recovered in 1987 excavation

Wilton; referred to in 1842

Glaisdale High; one 4 feet diameter stone in garden

Lealholm; *"two sets of blue and one of grey"*, Mitford Abraham

Ruswarp Country; described as *"thribble stones"* in 1765

Iburndale; Mitford Abraham

Bay; Mitford Abraham

Ravensthorpe; Mitford Abraham

Bilsdale Low; one dated 1666? in house, one in dam

Arden; two stones diameter 3 feet 6 inches set in mill floor

Caydale; one stone diameter 4 feet in fireplace hearth

Rievaulx; one stone diameter 3 feet 6 inch now at Ashberry Farm

Ampleforth; *"1 pair of grey and one pair of blue"* in 1835

Sproxton; set installed by Edward Stent in 1706

Lastingham; one stone diameter 4 feet formerly outside the mill, now removed

Coulton; two stones diameter 3 feet 7 inch, one used as threshold, one in rear wall

Gillamoor; one stone used as road sign to Fadmoor village

Low Askew; Mitford Abraham

Appleton; one stone diameter 3 feet 10 inches (*"one pair"* in 1837)

Costa High; one stone on site

Pickering High; *"one pair"* in 1832

Levisham; one stone used as road sign for Lockton village

Troutsdale; one set diameter 3 feet 7 inches in situ

Stonegate; part of one stone diameter 3 feet 10 inches

Danby End; two stones in an outbuilding

Howe; one set put in, 1807

Thirkleby; Stone 4 feet 6 inches, dated "May 12 1774", used as a road sign at Little Thirkleby

Rudby; one used as threshold in Bay Horse, one as a sign near mill

Baxby; bed stone diameter 3 feet 10 inches used as threshold to house extension

Hart windmill; one stone diameter 4 feet used as threshold

Yarm windmill; *"one pair of French and one of blues"* in 1832

Common (Scarborough); *"one pair"* in 1843

Kirkby Moorside windmill; one stone set in mill floor.

APPENDIX 8. Barley mills

Ugthorpe windmill; one stone with milled edge near house

Loftus; one stone with milled edge stone outside house

Lealholm; barley mill for making frumerty for Ruswarp mill in 1838

Swainby; barley *"frenched"* for Christmas frumerty in 1842

Osmotherley; one stone with milled edge

Caydale; used by Aaron Robinson until 1875, now in Castle Museum.

Raindale; *"decayed"* in 1920s.

Bransdale; complete mill plus stone with milled edge from a second

Bilsdale Low; stone with milled edge outside mill

Appleton; 22 inch barley stone near house (recorded in 1837)

Costa High; stone with milled edge (recorded in 1855)

Farndale High; stone with milled edge on top floor

Sproxton; recorded in 1832

Raisdale; stone with milled edge near mill

Newburgh; in Priory water garden

Middleton windmill; recorded in 1793.

APPENDIX 9. Roasting plates and drying kilns

PLATES

Liverton; kiln plate leaning against garden wall

Ravensthorpe; kiln plate in situ

Bransdale; kiln plate in situ

Bilsdale Low; foundations in situ

Loftus; chimney in gable wall

Dalehouse; 4 feet 9 inches diameter plate in situ

Arden; complete kiln in situ

Ruswarp; *"Four plates for drying oats"* in 1756

Thirkleby; foundations in situ

KILNS

Lealholm; extension to rear of mill, now demolished

Egton Bridge; drying kiln recorded in 1848

Rigg; *"small drying house"* recorded in 1822

Spite; possible site against gable wall

Thornton-le-Street; built over waterwheel pit

Hold Cauldron

Raisdale; possible site at rear of mill

Chop Gate; possibly in detached building at rear of mill, now demolished.

Mandale windmill; recorded in 1801.

APPENDIX 10. Preservation

1. Tocketts Mill. Grade II* Listed Building. The most complete preserved mill in the region with three pairs of millstones, grain cleaner, silk machine, two elevators, sack hoist. Mid-nineteenth century building and machinery on a medieval steading. Restored by South Park Sixth Form College. Run by the Friends of Tocketts Mill and the Cleveland Buildings Preservation Trust. Open on Sunday afternoons during the summer season.

2. Danby Mill. Very attractive mill on the banks of the Esk with three pairs of millstones. Built in 1800 but heightened later. Restoration by Frank Palmer. New waterwheel by South Park Sixth Form College.

3. Low Mill, Bilsdale. Attractive small dales mill. Wooden clasp-arm waterwheel and two pairs of millstones. Evidence of an eighteenth century mill but 'improved' at the turn of the century. Restored by Edward Garbutt. Not open to the public.

4. South Kilvington. Handsome brick-built mill with waterwheel, cast-iron driving machinery and one pair of millstones. Used regularly. Probably of early nineteenth century date on an ancient steading but late nineteenth century machinery by John Hauxwell. Dam restored by late Miss P Preston. Mill restored to working order by John Fauvet. Not open to the public.

5. Costa High. Property of the Environment Agency. Very handsome mill built in 1819 and containing much of its original machinery. Waterwheel and pit wheel restored by National Rivers Authority. Original upright shaft and spur wheel. Millstones missing. Not open to the public.

6. Bransdale. Attractive and remote dales milling hamlet, owned by the National Trust. Mill built in 1842 on an old steading. Suspension waterwheel on cruciform shaft, cast-iron running gear, three pairs of millstones, grain cleaner and flour dresser. Buildings restored and secure. Machinery not running. A public footpath runs through the hamlet. Mill not open to the public.

7. Arden. Very important mill dating from the beginning of the eighteenth century. Mill kept in good repair by the Mexborough estate. Waterwheel and gearing of wood. Adjoining house destroyed by flood in June 2005.

8. Lastingham. Very interesting eighteenth century remains partly preserved. Kept in good repair. Not open to the public.

9. Marske Mill. The site of Marske Mill was excavated by Cleveland County Archaeology Service and left open for public inspection. No machinery. Foundations well-presented and interpretative boards on site.

10. Drummer Hill horse wheel (Ingleby Greenhow). Set up in 1850 this wheel was restored by South Park Sixth Form College. Not open to the public.

11. Urra Farm horse wheel and shed (Bilsdale). Now exhibited at the Ryedale Folk Museum, Hutton-le-Hole.

12. Hart windmill. Windmill tower of 1814 with upright shaft and wind shaft assembly restored along with cap roof and fantail by the Cleveland Buildings Preservation Trust as a landscape feature. Not open to the public.

13. Scarborough windmill. Empty tower restored as main feature of an hotel, and now a striking feature of the Scarborough townscape. Windshaft assembly from an East Riding mill.

GLOSSARY

The majority of technical terms are explained in four diagrams, two showing early mills and two showing early nineteenth century mills.

The following general terms also appear in the text:

assart, a medieval enclosure normally, in north east Yorkshire, under the moor edge

bere, a type of barley (Scottish)

bolter, a sieve for dressing flour

carvel, a boat-building term applied to flush rather than overlapping planking

chartulary, a collection of charters

garner floor, a floor for storing grain

garth, a small enclosure, normally close to a dwelling

glazing mill, a term associated both with flax finishing and paper making

glebe, church land

grange, an outlying monastic farm

hurst, the framework supporting the millstones and containing the primary gearing of a water mill

maslin, a mixed crop of wheat and rye

messuage, a dwelling, normally of relatively high status

multure, the portion of grain taken by the medieval miller as his share

tenter garth, a field which contained frames for stretching fulled cloth

tuck mill, a fulling mill (Welsh).

TERMINOLOGY

It may now never be possible to unravel terminology specific to north east Yorkshire. Much of the pioneering recording work on old mills was carried out in south east England and later writers tended to use the terminology used by earlier authors. In any case millwrighting terminology was always a curious mixture of words borrowed from other trades, along with local dialect words and terms used specifically by millwrights. The last millers at Levisham and Osmotherley mills were unaware of names such as pit wheel, wallower and spur wheel and simply referred to them all as 'gearing', and in general millers learned what millwrighting terminology they had from the millwrights themselves during their visits to make repairs. For instance, Noel Wright of Osmotherley mill knew about 're-soling' a waterwheel because he helped Daniel Adamson of Hauxwells of Yarm to carry out this task. Nevertheless it was possible to record a few terms used by local people and which may have been distinctive to the region. For instance, the term 'ringing' seems to have been used locally for the cases of millstones rather than 'tun' or 'vat' and the term 'agitator' was used instead of the foreign sounding 'damsel'. Throughout north east England the arms of windmills were called 'wands'.

The following terms, some of which may have been specific to the North East, have been collected in conversation and documents:

'Dog leg', a short bent piece of wood used as a toggle across the eye of a top millstone for attaching a lifting rope (J Hird)

'Ligger', bottom or 'lying' millstone

'Pick and haft', bill and thrift, (J Hird)

'Doddle stick', damsel, (Henry Smith, farmer, Ugthorpe)

'Ringing', tuns (A Bradley of Hauxwells)

Additionally, the following (some no more than spelling variations) have been collected from documentary sources:

'Battlements', top stones of a wall (Rigg mill, 1822)

'Bye clough', escape race (John Hauxwell's Letter Books)

'Cheakes for clowes', iron cheeks for sluice gate posts (Swainby mill)

'Flags', paving stones (Rigg mill)

'Gavelicks', iron crow bar for lifting a top stone (Swainby mill)

'Parpin wall', a single thickness partition wall (Rigg mill)

'Skillboards', shroud plates (Hauxwell)

'Stock wall' (Rigg mill)

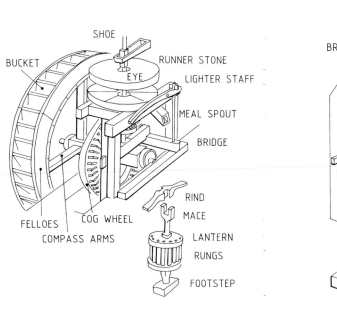

Fig 176. Medieval water mill machinery.

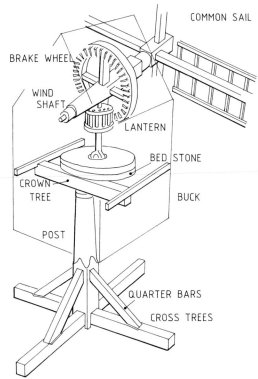

Fig 177. Medieval windmill machinery.

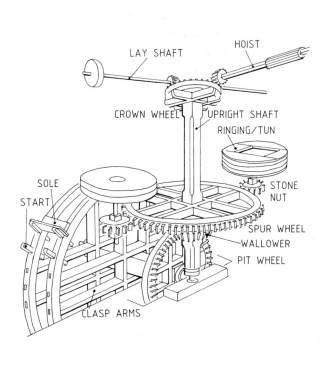

Fig 178. Early Nineteenth century water mill machinery.

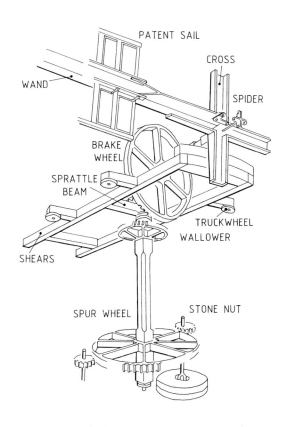

Fig 179. Nineteenth century windmill machinery.

SOURCES

Agricola G, 1556, De re Metallica, translated by H C Hoover, New York, 1950

Alexander W, 1877, Northern rural life, Aberdeen

Allison J K, 1970, East Riding water mills, E Yorks Local History Society

Apling H, 1984, Norfolk Corn windmills, vol 1, Norfolk Windmills Trust

Appleton R H, 1884, Visit to the Cleveland Flour mills, South Stockton, Proc Cleveland Inst Eng, 119-131

Ashcroft M Y, 1977, To escape the monster's clutches, NYCRO pub 15

Ashcroft M Y & Hill A, 1980, Bilsdale Surveys 1637–1851, NYCRO pub 32

Aston M, 1985, Interpreting the landscape, Batsford

Atkinson J C, 1868, A glossary of the Cleveland dialect

Atkinson J C, 1874, History of Cleveland, ancient and modern, Barrow, vol 1, vol 2 pt 1, vol 2 pt 2

Austin D ed, 1982, Boldon Book, Phillimore

Baines E, 1822, Directory and Gazetteer, vol 2

Baker J B, 1882, The history of Scarborough from the earliest date, Longmans Green

Barker R, 1990, Prisoners of the Tsar, Annual Report of the Whitby Lit & Phil Society, 14-21

Beckmann J, 1817, A history of inventions and discoveries, vol 1, London

Belcher H, 1836, Illustrations of the scenery on the line of the Whitby and Pickering Railway, Longmans

Bennet R and Elton J, 1898 & 1900, History of corn milling, vols 1, 2 (1898) & 3 (1900), London

Bennett J and Vyner B E, 1979, The watermill at Norton-on-Tees, Cleveland County Council

Benson G, 1919 & 1929, An account of the city and county of the City of York, vols 1 & 2, York

Beyern, 1735, Theatrum machinarum molarium oder schwau platz der muhlen bau kunst, Leipzig

Bockler G A, 1661, Theatrum Machinarium Novum, Nurembourg

Brace H W, 1960, History of seed crushing in Great Britain, London

Brewster J, 1829, The parochial history and antiquities of Stockton-upon-Tees, Stockton

Brown W, 1886, Description of the buildings of twelve small Yorkshire priories at the Reformation, YAJ vol 9, 197-215 and 321-333

Brown W, 1896, Yorkshire lay subsidy, 1301, YAS Record Series, vol 21

Brown W, 1894, Lay Subsidy, 1297, YAS Record Series, vol 16

Buckland S, 1987, Lee's patent windmill, Mills Section SPAB

Burnett P, 1945, Glaisdale Head, Notes of the Whitby Naturalists, 29-31

Capron J T, 1967, Lowna mill, Gillamoor, Ryedale Historian, No 3, 42-4

Carus-Wilson E M, 1941, An economic revolution of the thirteenth century, Economic History Review, 39-60

Charlton L, 1779, History of Whitby and Whitby Abbey, York

Collingwood-Bruce J, 1863, Hand-book to Newcastle-upon-Tyne, Longmans Green

Darby H C, 1977, Domesday England, Cambridge

Daniels R, 1995, The church, the manor, and the settlement; the evidence from Cleveland, CBA Research Report 101, 78-89

Davies Shiel M, 1978, Watermills in Cumbria, Dalesman

David E, 1977, English bread and yeast, Penguin

Desagulier J T, 1744, A course in experimental philosophy, London, vol 2

Diderot D, 1763, Pictorial Encyclopedia of trades and industry

Dingle A T, 1950, History of Osmotherley, private

Dixon G, 1891, History of the Friends' School, Andrew Reid.

Drummond J C & Wilbraham A, 1958, The Englishman's food, Jonathan Cape

Earnshaw J R, 1973, The site of a medieval post mill and prehistoric site at Bridlington, YAJ vol 45, 19 – 41

Edwards M ed, 1966, Scarborough 966-1966, Scarborough and District Archaological Society

Faull M L and Stinson M, Domesday Book; 1986, Yorkshire, Phillimore, Parts 1 & 2

Fordyce W, 1857, History and Antiquities of the County Palatinate of Durham, vol 2, Newcastle

Gaskin R T, 1909, The Old Seaport of Whitby

Gauldie E, 1981, The Scottish country miller, John Donald

Gimpel J, 1976, The medieval machine, Victor Gollancz

Grainge W, 1859, Vale of Mowbray: a historical and topographical account of Thirsk and its neighbourhood, London

Grainger J, 1794, A general view of the agriculture of County Durham

Graves J, 1808, The history and antiquities of Cleveland in the North Riding of the County of York

Gregory R, 1985, East Yorkshire Windmills, Skilton

Gregory R, 1992, The use of power in the early development of Hull, Industrial Archaeology Review, vol XV, No 1, 7-20

Gribbon H D, 1969, The history of water power in Ulster, David and Charles

Harland G, 1970, Queen of the dales, Horne, Whitby

Harrison A and J K, 1973, The horse wheel in North Yorkshire, Industrial Archaeology Review, Vol 10, No. 3, 247-265

Harrison B J D, 1978, Society and land in a South Durham Township; Egglescliffe 1560-1700, CTLHS Bull 35, 1-11

Harrison B J D & Hutton B, 1984, Vernacular houses in North Yorkshire & Cleveland, John Donald

Harrison B J D, 1983-4, Fourteenth century inquisitions post mortem for the Cleveland area, CTLHS, no 44, 22-26, no 45, 45-51, no 46, 27-29

Harrison J K, 1974, Stokesley mill, CIA no 1, 1-8

Harrison J K, 1980, An eighteenth century corn milling venture in Guisborough, CIA no 12, 11-18

Harrison J K, 1995, Investigations at Commondale Mill, Moorland Monuments, CBA Research Report 101, 197 - 210

Harrison S A, 1986, Stonework of Byland Abbey, Ryedale Historian, no 13, 26-47

Hartley D, 1973, Food in England, MacDonald

Hartley M & Ingleby J, 1972, Life and tradition in the moorlands of north east Yorkshire, Dent

Hastings R P, 1980, Rudby-in-Cleveland: The medieval landscape, Hutton Rudby and District Local History Society

Hatcher J, 1978, The architectural evolution of corn watermills in north and east

Yorkshire, unpublished dissertation, Leeds Polytechnic

Hayes R H and Allison M, 1988-9, Harome: the history of a village, Ryedale Historian, No 14, 1988-9

Hayes R H & Hurst J, nd, The history of Hutton-le-Hole, Helmsley

Hayes R H, 1969, The story of Gillamoor and Fadmoor, Ryedale Historian. No 4, 7-14

Hayes R H, 1st ed 1971, 3rd ed 1985, Rosedale, the story of Yorkshire's most beautiful dale, North York Moors National Park.

Hayes R H, 1986, Excavation of Spaunton manor, North Yorkshire, Ryedale Historian, no 13, 4-25

Hayes R H, 1988, Old roads and pannier ways in north east Yorkshire, North York Moors National Park

Heavisides M, 1906, In and around picturesque Norton

Hellen J A, 1970, Some provisional notes on wheelhouses and their distribution in Northumberland, Journal of the Geographical Society, University of Newcastle upon Tyne, 18, 19-29

Hellen J A, 1972, Agricultural innovation and detectable landscape margins: the case of wheelhouses in Northumberland, Agricultural History Review, vol 20, part 2

Henderson J, 1853, Report on the Rye and Derwent drainage, Royal Agricultural Society of England, vol 14, 129-51

Hey D, 1986, Yorkshire since AD 1000, Longmans

Hills R, 1988, Papermaking in Britain, 1488-1988, Athlone

Hobsbawm E J and Rude G, 1969, Captain Swing, Lawrence and Wishart

Hodgen M, 1939, Domesday watermills, Antiquity, vol 136

Hollins A, nd, Goathland, Whitby, re-print North York Moors National Park

Holt R, 1988, The mills of medieval England, Blackwell

Hughes A E, 1965, North country life in the eighteenth century, Durham, vol 2

Hutton K, 1976, The distribution of wheel houses in the British Isles, Agricultural History Review, vol 24, Part 1

Jackson R, Journal, manuscript in Teesside Archives

Jeffery R W, 1931, Thornton-le-Dale, Wakefield

Jeffery P S, 1952, Whitby lore and legend, Whitby

Jones D, 1968, Water powered corn mills of England, Wales, and the Isle of Man, Transactions of the Second Symposium of the International Molinological Society, Denmark, ch 27

Kealey E J, 1987, Harvesting the air, Boydell

Kettlewell R, 1938, Cleveland Village, Great Ayton

Kirby R L, 1900, Ancient Middlesbrough, Andrew Reid

Latham R E, 1965, Revised medieval Latin word list

Lees B A, 1935, Records of the Templars in England in the twelfth century – the inquest of 1185, OUP

Lennard R, 1959, Rural England 1086-1135, Oxford

Longstaffe W H D, 1854, The history and antiquities of the parish of Darlington

Luckhurst D, nd., Monastic watermills; a study of mills within English monastic precincts, SPAB

Major J K, 1978, Animal powered engines, Batsford

Major J K, 1982, Eifel millstone production, TIMS no 5, 343-6

Marshall W, 1788, The rural economy of Yorkshire, vol 1, London

McDonnell H, 1884, The gradual reduction system of manufacturing flour by chilled iron rollers, Proceedings of the Cleveland Institution of Engineers, 91-131

McDonnell J and Everest M R, 1965, The waterworks of Byland Abbey, Ryedale Historian, no 1, 32-41

McDonnell J, ed., 1963, A history of Helmsley, Rievaulx and District, York

McDonnell J, Inland fisheries of medieval Yorkshire 1066-1300, Borthwick publication no 60

McGeown S & Rushton J, 1989, Mills on the Costa, unpublished report for owners of Low Costa mill

McLean I, 1996/7, The lost watermill of Kirkdale; the Spout Bank fulling mill in Cogg Hall, Ryedale Historian, no 18, 12-16

Minchinton W E, 1979, Early tide mills: some problems, Technology and Culture

Ord J W, 1846, History and antiquities of Cleveland, Simpkin & Marshall

Owen J S, 1975, Early days at the Rosedale mines, CTLHS Bulletin No 28, 1-11

Page W ed., Victoria County Histories, A history of Yorkshire North Riding, University of London, vols 1, 2 and 3

Page W ed, Victoria County Histories, County of Durham, vol 3

Parker T, 1858, manuscript, Ryedale Folk Museum; see History of Kirkdale with the townships adjacent, 1980, Ryedale Historian, no. 10, 5-46

Pattenden D W, 1985, Cargo Fleet or Cleveland Port, CTLHS, vol 48, 1-16

Pattenden D W, 1990, Ormesby 1066-1601, CTLHS, Bull. 58, 5-15

Pattenden D W, 1991, The township and parish of Ormesby, 1601–1801, CTLHS, Bull 61, 12-18

Pattenden D W, 1994, Early water supplies in Ormesby, CIA, no 22, 13-19

Pelham R A, nd., Fulling mills; a study in the application of water power to the woollen industry, SPAB occasional publication, no. 5

Ramelli Augustino, 1588, Le diverse et artificiose machine, Paris

Reynolds T S, 1983, Stronger than a hundred men, John Hopkins University Press

Richardson J, 1812, Reports of the late John Smeaton FRS made on various occasions in the course of his employment as a Civil Engineeer, London

Richmond T, 1868, The local records of Stockton and the neighbourhood, Stockton

Rimington F C, 1988, The history of Ravenscar and Staintondale, Scarborough Archaeological and Historical Society.

Rimington F, 1965, The East Ayton fulling mill, Transactions of the Scarborough & District Archaeological Society, vol 1, No 8, 23-31

Roberts B, in Spratt and Harrison eds, 1989, The North York Moors Landscape Heritage, David and Charles

Rowntree A, ed, 1931, History of Scarborough, Dent

Royal Commission for Ancient Monuments in England, 1987, Houses of the North York Moors, HMSO

Royal Commission for Ancient Monument in England, 1989, Inventory of houses in the North York Moors, HMSO

Rushton J, nd, Ryedale Story, Ryedale District Council

Rutter J G, 1969-71, Industrial archaeology in north west Yorkshire, Trans Scar Dist Arch Soc, 3 vols

Ryder P J, 1992, Kilton mill, Cleveland: an archaeological assessment, Napper Collerton Partnership

Salzman L F, 1952, Building in England down to 1540, Oxford

Schubert H R, 1957, History of the British Iron and steel industry from c 450 BC to AD 1775, Routledge and Kegan Paul, 148, App VII

Sharp C, 1816, History of Hartlepool, first edition; second edition with supplementary history, 1851

Smeaton J, 1759, An experimental enquiry concerning the natural powers of water and wind to turn mills....

Smeaton J, 1766, Reports 1 & 2.

Smiles S, 1862, Lives of the engineers, vol 2

Smith I, Frumety, 1966, Durham Local History Society Bulletin, no 7

Sowler T, 1972, A History of the Town and Borough of Stockton-on-Tees, Teesside Museums and Art Galleries

Spratt D & Harrison B J D, 1989, The North York Moors landscape heritage, David and Charles

Still L & Southeran J, 1966, The origins of medieval Billingham, Billingham U D C

Stoyel A, 1992, Medieval millstones - the clockwise theory and its applications, SPAB Wind and Water mills Section Newsletter, no 50, 18-24

Stoyel A, 1995, Perfect pitch, the millwrights' goal, SPAB Wind and Water mills Section.

Strada Jan de, c.1617, Kunstliche abrisse aller hand, wasser, wind, ross und handt muhlen

Surtees R, 1828, History & antiquities of the County of Durham, vol 3

Tucker D G, 1977, Millstone quarries and millstone makers, Post medieval Archaeology, 1-12, plates I-XIV

Tucker D G, Millstone making in the Peak District of Derbyshire, Industrial Archaeology Review, vol VIII no 1, 42-58

Tucker D G, 1987, Millstone making in England, I A Review, vol. IX no 2, 167-188

Tuke J, 1800, A general view of the agriculture of the North Riding of Yorkshire, London

Tweddell G M, 1875, The people's history of Cleveland, Stokesley

Vyner B E, 1995, Moorland monuments, CBA Research Report 101

Waites B, 1997, Monasteries and landscape in north east England, Multum in Parvo Press

Ward O F, 1982, Millstones from La Ferte-sous-Jouarre, France, Industrial Archaeology Review, Vol VI, No. 3, 205-10

Wardell J W, 1957, A history of Yarm, Yarm

Watts M, 1991, The use of millwrighting techniques as a guide to dating wind and water mills, SPAB, Wind and Water mills Section

Watts M, 2000, Water and wind power, Shire Publications

White L, 1962, Medieval technology and social change, Oxford

Whitworth A, 1991, Yorkshire windmills, M T D Rigg

Young A, 1771, A six months tour through the north of England, vol 2

Young G, 1817, A history of Whitby and Streoneshalh Abbey, Whitby, vols 1 & 2

Zealand A & Harrison J K, 1968, Water powered corn mill at Ingleby Greenhow, N E Industrial Archaeology Society, Bull 7

(2nd edition)

Angerstein R R, Illustrated travel diary, 1753-55 (trans T & P Berg, London, Science Museum, 2001)

Bellamy J M, 1979, Trade and Shipping of Hull, E Yorkshire, LHS, 9.

Duncombe P, 2001, Great goldsmith, Australia, Leonard Communications.

Grainge W, 1858, The Vale of Mowbray.

Harrison J K, 2005, The 'rise' of the white loaf; evidence from the north of England concerning the development of milling technique in the eighteenth century, SPAB Mills Section (Rex Wailes Memorial Lecture).

Hodgson J E, ed, 1933, Aeronautical and miscellaneous note book of Sir George Cayley, Newcomen Society, Extra publication, no 3.

Lawson-Tancred T, 1937, Records of a Yorkshire Manor, Arnold.

McLean I A, 2005, Water from the Moors, NYMNP.

McLean I A, 2005, The millers of Howkeld water corn mill, 1632-1850, Ryedale Historian, No 27, 7-14.

Milburn G E, 1983, Proc. Wesley History Society, vol. 44, pt 3.

Radcliffe E, 2004, Stockton biographies; Thomas Wren & Sons, millers and corn merchants, Stockton-on-Tees Local History Journal, No 7, 4-29 .

Svedenstierna E T, Tour of Great Britain 1802-3, David and Charles, reprinted 1973.

Townson R, 1799, A brief tract on various types of stone suitable for millstones, in Tracts and observations in Natural History and Physiology.

Wardell N, 2007, The Coulson Family – Millers of North Yorkshire, Sigma Books.

INDEX OF MILLS

Main references and figures in **bold**

WINDMILLS

TEXTILE, PAPER, OIL AND OTHER INDUSTRIAL MILLS

STEAM